Burglary

International Library of Criminology, Criminal Justice and Penology – Second Series
Series Editors: Gerald Mars and David Nelken

Titles in the Series:

Burglary

Edited by

R.I. Mawby

The University of Plymouth, UK

ASHGATE

Wherever possible, these reprints are made from a copy of the original printing, but these can themselves be of very variable quality. Whilst the publisher has made every effort to ensure the quality of the reprint, some variability may inevitably remain.

Published by
Ashgate Publishing Limited
Gower House
Croft Road
Aldershot
Hampshire GU11 3HR
England

Ashgate Publishing Company
Suite 420
101 Cherry Street
Burlington, VT 05401-4405
USA

Ashgate website: http://www.ashgate.com

British Library Cataloguing in Publication Data
Burglary. – (International library of criminology, criminal
  justice and penology. Second series)
  1. Burglary 2. Victims of crimes 3. Burglary protection
  I. Mawby, Robert
  364. 1' 62

Library of Congress Control Number: 2007929016

ISBN: 978-0-7546-2596-4

Printed in Great Britain by TJ International Ltd, Padstow, Cornwall

Contents

PART II   POLICY RESPONSE

Acknowledgements

The editor and publishers wish to thank the following for permission to use copyright material.

AB Academic Publishers for the essay: Alan Trickett, Denise R. Osborn and Dan Ellingworth (1995), 'Property Crime Victimisation: The Roles of Individual and Area Influences', *International Review of Victimology*, **3**, pp. 273–95. Copyright © 1995 AB Academic Publishers; R.I. Mawby and S. Walklate (1997), 'The Impact of Burglary: A Tale of Two Cities', *International Review of Victimology*, **44**, pp. 267–95. Copyright © 1997 AB Academic Publishers.

American Society of Criminology for the essay: Laura Dugan (1999), 'The Effect of Criminal Victimization on a Household's Moving Decision', *Criminology*, **37**, pp. 903–30.

Australian Academic Press Limited for the essay: Michael Townsley, Ross Homel and Janet Chaseling (2000), 'Repeat Burglary Victimisation: Spatial and Temporal Patterns', *Australian and New Zealand Journal of Criminology*, **33**, pp. 37–63.

Blackwell Publishing Limited for the essays: C. Nee and M. Taylor (1988), 'Residential Burglary in the Republic of Ireland: A Situational Perspective', *Howard Journal*, **27**, pp. 105–16; Richard Wright and Robert H. Logie (1988), 'How Young House Burglars Choose Targets', *Howard Journal*, **27**, pp. 92–104.

Copyright Clearance Center for the essay: Martyn J. Gay, Christopher Holton and M.S. Thomas (1975), 'Helping the Victims', *International Journal of Offender Therapy and Comparative Criminology*, **19**, pp. 263–9. Copyright © 1975 Sage Publications, Inc.

Oxford University Press for the essays: Mike Maguire (1980), 'The Impact of Burglary upon Victims', *British Journal of Criminology*, **20**, pp. 261–75; Matthew B. Robinson (1998), 'Burglary Revictimization: The Time Period of Heightened Risk', *British Journal of Criminology*, **38**, pp. 78–87; Natalie Polvi, Terah Looman, Charlie Humphries and Ken Pease (1991), 'The Time Course of Repeat Burglary Victimization', *British Journal of Criminology*, **31**, pp. 411–14; Kate J. Bowers, Shane D. Johnson and Ken Pease (2004), 'Prospective Hot-Spotting: The Future of Crime Mapping?', *British Journal of Criminology*, **44**, pp. 641–58. Copyright © 2004 Center for Crime and Justice Studies;

Palgrave Macmillan for the essays: Ken Pease (1991), 'The Kirkholt Project: Preventing Burglary on a British Public Housing Estate', *Security Journal*, **2**, pp. 73–77. Copyright © 1991 Butterworth-Heinemann; Kate J. Bowers (2001), 'Small Business Crime: The Evaluation of a Crime Prevention Initiative', *Crime Prevention and Community Safety: An International Journal*, **3**, pp. 23–42. Copyright © 2001 Perpetuity Press Ltd; P.M. Cozens, T. Pascoe and D. Hillier (2004) 'Critically Reviewing the Theory and Practice of Secured-by-Design for

Preface to the Second Series

The first series of the International Library of Criminology, Criminal Justice and Penology has established itself as a major research resource by bringing together the most significant journal essays in contemporary criminology, criminal justice and penology. The series made available to researchers, teachers and students an extensive range of essays which are indispensable for obtaining an overview of the latest theories and findings in this fast-changing subject. Indeed the rapid growth of interesting scholarly work in the field has created a demand for a second series which, like the first, consists of volumes dealing with criminological schools and theories as well as with approaches to particular areas of crime criminal justice and penology. Each volume is edited by a recognized authority who has selected twenty or so of the best journal essays in the field of their special competence and provided an informative introduction giving a summary of the field and the relevance of the essays chosen. The original pagination is retained for ease of reference.

The difficulties of keeping on top of the steadily growing literature in criminology are complicated by the many disciplines from which its theories and findings are drawn (sociology, law, sociology of law, psychology, psychiatry, philosophy and economics are the most obvious). The development of new specialisms with their own journals (policing, victimology, mediation) as well as the debates between rival schools of thought (feminist criminology, left realism, critical criminology, abolitionism and so on) make it necessary to provide overviews that offer syntheses of the state of the art.

GERALD MARS
Honorary Professor of Anthropology, University College, London, UK

DAVID NELKEN
Distinguished Professor of Sociology, University of Macerata, Italy
Distinguished Research Professor of Law, University of Cardiff, Wales
Honorary Visiting Professor of Law, LSE, London, UK

Introduction

Burglary is a common crime in most industrial societies – one that evokes anxiety among the public and, particularly, its victims (van Kesteren, Mayhew and Nieuwbeerta, 2001; Nicholas, Kershaw and Walker, 2007). The case of Tony Martin, a Norfolk eccentric who in 2000 was found guilty of the murder and wounding of two young burglars, graphically illustrates concern over burglary in Britain. While few burglars commit violence against their victims, and – unlike in the USA (Zimring and Hawkins, 1997) – homicide in the course of a burglary is extremely rare, public sentiment at the time indicated that many people saw burglary as both common and very serious, yet perceived it as being given little priority by government, police or courts.

As with much popular debate, the facts suggest otherwise. At the time, burglary rates were in the midst of a steady decline, both in Britain and in other Western societies, and in Britain a range of government policies addressed burglary reduction, improving detection rates and harm minimization. Yet there is an element of truth in the Tony Martin narrative. Burglary is, next to vehicle crime, the most common property crime; victims are in many cases severely affected; and police detection rates remain low. This selection of essays aims to address the nature of burglary and policy initiatives over the past 30 years, to help us appreciate why burglary continues to evoke this concern.

It is, however, important to acknowledge that the term 'burglary' encompasses a variety of offences that may mean very different things to its victims and may require very different measures (Mawby, 2001). Burglary is generally understood to refer to a situation where someone enters property without permission in order to steal something, and this is the definition adopted by the International Crime Victims Survey (ICVS) (del Frate *et al.*, 1993). However, burglary is defined (in law) and categorized (by the police) differently in different countries: it is not, for example, always necessary for theft to take place, or even to be intended. In many countries it refers only to situations involving forced entry, excluding incidents where offenders gain access through an open door or window, as well as cases of 'distraction burglary', that have recently received considerable attention from the police and policy-makers in Britain (Distraction Burglary Task Force, 2002; Home Office, 2002; Lister, and Wall, 2006; Thornton *et al.*, 2003).

The complexity of defining and comparing burglary rates is compounded by questions relating to the nature of the property 'broken into'. This includes residential property, outbuildings and garages, caravans and park homes, hotels, and other commercial premises and public buildings.[1]

Given the extent of variation, what burglary 'means' to the public in general and victims in particular may, not surprisingly, be very different. Nevertheless, it is clear that by the early 1990s the British public saw burglary as one of the most common, and serious, crimes. This

---

[1]   For current Home Office definitions of burglary in England and Wales, see www.homeoffice.gov.uk/rds/pdfs06/countburglary06.pdf.

paralleled a dramatic increase in burglary, with the British Crime Survey (BCS) identifying 6.4 per cent of households as victims in 1995 (Nicholas, Kershaw and Walker, 2007), with risk higher than in most countries covered by the ICVS (van Kesteren, Mayhew and Nieuwbeerta, 2001), including the US (Langan and Farrington, 1998). Public concern was often so extreme that, as Lesley Noaks illustrates in Chapter 26, in some neighbourhoods residents employed private security patrols.

At the same time, many victims of burglary were greatly affected. The act of unlawful entry to the home is seen as an invasion of privacy, even in former communist societies (Mawby *et al.*, 1999), and concern that the householder may be confronted by the burglar often evokes fear and sleeplessness. The extent to which victims experience anxiety and concern is well illustrated in Mike Maguire's early research (Chapter 7), and reiterated more recently by R.I. Mawby and S. Walklate (Chapter 8) who note the wider implications for children in the home. In the US, Laura Dugan (Chapter 5) even found that a significant minority of victims subsequently chose to move home.

Moreover, while it was originally standard policy for the police and victim assistance programmes to reassure victims that 'lightning rarely strikes twice', identification of repeat victimization showed very clearly that it did, and that victims of burglary, along with victims of violence and vehicle crime, were at increased risk of future victimization (Anderson, Chenery and Pease, 1995; Farrell, 1992). As Julie Ashton *et al.* (Chapter 1) discovered, burglars themselves can rationalize their decisions to return to the same properties. While Ken Pease can be credited with much of this early research, later studies (Farrell and Pease, 2001; Polvi *et al.*, Chapter 11; Robinson, Chapter 12; Townsley, Homel and Chaseling, Chapter 14) confirm that this is a worldwide phenomenon.

In the light of this bleak prognosis, evidence from the last decade suggests that burglary reduction strategies might constitute a success story. For example, following a number of government-led programmes, public concern over burglary in England and Wales has declined, the incidence rate has fallen to 2.5 per cent in 2006/07, and repeat burglaries are less common (Nicholas, Kershaw and Walker, 2007). Although rates of burglary are still relatively high compared with other Western industrial societies, it seems that burglary is less of a problem than it was 10–15 years ago. But is this due to the programmes put into place by New Labour, or is it as Solomon *et al.* (2007) suggest the result of wider influences? The remainder of this Introduction addresses the nature and extent of burglary and policy responses. The next section attempts to explain burglary patterns by reviewing crime data and burglars' accounts of their motivations and strategies. The following sections then address policy concerns, first in terms of burglary reduction strategies, then in terms of the ways in which victims and their burglars are dealt with.

Explaining Burglary

Much of the earliest research on describing and explaining burglary patterns, and the strategies deployed by burglars' took place in North America, although this has been supplemented by research in other industrial societies, including Britain, Australia, the Irish Republic and the Netherlands.

This research reveals clearly that burglary is rarely a random event. Most researchers have suggested that burglaries tend to involve at least some rudimentary planning, and few are opportunist (Butler, 1994; Maguire, 1982; Nee and Taylor, Chapter 9; Wiersma, Chapter 16). Why particular properties/victims are targeted is thus a key question for researchers. One approach to answering it involves comparing levels of risk. Alternatively, some researchers have interviewed known burglars about their choice of targets, even though, as Richard Wright *et al.* demonstrates in Chapter 17, these 'failed burglars' may be atypical of burglars in general.

A consistent finding among researchers is that burglary of commercial and other corporate premises is far more common than residential burglary (Clarke, 2003; Mawby, 2006). Overwhelmingly, research has found that businesses experience more crime than do individuals, and the evidence for burglary parallels this. The 1994 International Crimes against Businesses Survey (ICBS) (van Dijk and Terlouw, 1996) clearly demonstrates this, while in England and Wales, the second Commercial Victimization Survey (CVS) found that as many as 25 per cent of retailers and 22 per cent of manufacturers had experienced at least one burglary in the preceding year and repeat victimization was particularly common (Taylor, 2004). It appears, then, that potential burglars prefer to target commercial and other corporate premises, rather than private dwellings.

Despite that, most research has addressed household burglary. Here again, though, there is considerable evidence that there is no such person as the 'average victim', with risk varying markedly according to location of property, design and planning features, household characteristics, and other aspects of lifestyle.

One approach to explaining such variations is routine activity theory (Felson and Cohen, 1980) which attempts to explain the incidence and distribution of crime in terms of three sets of actors: potential victims, potential offenders, and law-enforcement agencies and other 'capable guardians'. In the case of victims and their homes, four factors have been linked to risk of burglary (Cohen, Kluegel and Land, 1981; Lynch and Cantor, Chapter 6), namely:

- target exposure – the visibility and accessibility of the home
- guardianship – the extent to which the home is protected
- target attractiveness – value of property that might be stolen
- proximity – distance of target from potential offenders

Similarly, Paul Cromwell, James Olson and D'Aunn Avary (Chapter 4) identified three types of clue used by burglars in assessing risk:

- surveillability: the extent to which the premises are overseen by passers-by and neighbours
- occupancy: as suggested by the presence of a car, noise, lights and so on
- accessibility: including the presence or absence of window locks, an alarm, open windows and so on

If we combine these approaches, four dimensions appear to be crucial to explaining variations in risk of burglary to domestic and corporate property: location, target attractiveness, social protection and technological protection.

In terms of location, given the relatively short distances travelled by most burglars (Wiles and Costello, 2000), property distanced away from where potential offenders live, or pass through during their routine activities, will tend to have relatively low levels of burglary.

As a result, rural areas tend almost universally to experience least burglary, while within urban areas burglaries are most common in inner-city and commercial/leisure centres and more impoverished areas of public or privately rented housing (Bottoms and Wiles, 2002; Cohen and Cantor, Chapter 3; Lynch and Cantor, 1992; Rountree and Land, Chapter 13). The BCS adds to this analysis. Thus, half of recorded burglaries occur in just 20 per cent of districts, and both recorded data and victim survey findings identify burglary as prevalent in the most deprived areas (Walker, Kershaw and Nicholas, 2006). Moreover, buildings located on the periphery of residential areas are more at risk, partly because they are more likely to be on the everyday travel routes of offenders and partly because strangers will be less obvious (Brantingham and Brantingham, 1995). Identification of such burglary hot-spots has led to sophisticated crime mapping (see Bowers, Johnson and Pease, Chapter 2).

To a certain extent, target attractiveness (Maguire, 1982; Wright and Logie, Chapter 18) as a priority seems to conflict with this. It may be that the concept receives more weight than it warrants and relies too much on the accounts of known burglars, who may exaggerate their professionalism (Cromwell, Olson and Avary; Wiersma, Chapter 16). Certainly, it is likely to feature in the strategies of the (minority) of professional burglars who identify their targets well in advance. On the other hand, as Alan Trickett, Denise Osborn and Dan Ellingworth demonstrate in Chapter 15, although homes in more deprived areas experience most burglary, more prosperous targets within these areas, or at least those that look more prosperous, are at the greatest risk. Moreover, in England and Wales, ACORN areas categorized under 'urban prosperity' also have high rates (Nicholas, Kershaw and Walker, 2007), suggesting that burglars will target affluent housing in areas adjacent to where they live. In Philadelphia, Hakim and Gaffney (1994) also found commercial burglary *more common* in affluent suburbs, suggesting that offenders associated such locations with more valuable items available to steal. Target attractiveness may also help to explain higher rates for commercial than for residential property, as well as variations between commercial properties stocking different goods. Similarly, it partly explains a concentration of repeat burglary some four months after the original offence, when insurance claims have been met and stolen goods replaced (Anderson, Chenery and Pease, 1995; Polvi *et al*.; Robinson, Chapter 11).

Social protection is used here to refer to variations in the extent to which police Chapter 12 and other 'capable guardians', like neighbours or occupants/employees, provide a policing function that deters would-be burglars. Although there is little evidence that police patrols – including the private patrols described by Noaks (Chapter 26) – or neighbourhood watch (Bennett, 1990; Rosenbaum, Chapter 28) reduce levels of burglary, research that focuses on burgled premises or the perceptions of burglars themselves suggests that visibility of access points is an important consideration in choosing which property to target (Jackson and Winchester, 1982). For example, restricted access to the rear of commercial property may leave burglars with the option of forced entry in 'public view' or finding a property with a less visible point of access. With regard to commercial burglary, isolated property and buildings that are away from main roads, secluded, remote or near woods, parks and so on experience more break-ins (Hakim and Gaffney, 1994; Mawby, 2003).[2] In the US, Bichler-Robertson and Potchak (2002) also found that businesses with low-visibility alley access to the rear were at highest risk. Of even more relevance is evidence of 'self-policing': burglars tend to

---

[2]   See also www.scotland.gov.uk/cru/kd01/crime/crime-01.htm.

avoid occupied property. Thus premises tend to be burgled when they are empty (Bennett and Wright, 1984; Cromwell, Olson and Avary, Chapter 4; Maguire, 1982; Phillips and Walker, Chapter 10): commercial premises at night and residential property during the day. Among the public, those who leave their homes empty for longer, especially after dark, experience higher than average levels of burglary (Hoare and Cotton, 2006; Jackson and Winchester, 1982; Lynch and Cantor, Chapter 6). Even where premises are empty, signs of occupancy, such as lights left on or on timer switches and televisions left on, may deter burglars. Another aspect of 'surrogate occupancy', leaving a car in the drive, was commonly cited as a deterrent. However, the recent growth of burglary in order to access car keys (Donkin and Wellsmith, 2006; Levesley *et al.*, 2004) seems to be limiting the importance of this, suggesting that target (that is, car) attractiveness may exert a stronger influence.

Technology provides alternatives to social protection. While the views of burglars on how much target hardening acts as a deterrent are mixed, other research suggests that improved locks and bolts (on windows and doors), CCTV, outside lighting, alleygating, and burglar alarms may, in certain circumstances, act as a deterrent. For example, the 2006/7 BCS concluded that 'households with no home security measures were almost ten times more likely to have been victims of burglary than households where there were simple security measures such as deadlocks on doors and window locks' (Nicholas, Kershaw and Walker, 2007, 76), and homes with more security experienced a higher ratio of 'attempted' (that is, failed) burglaries than successful ones.

Reducing Burglary

However, research also demonstrates that those who are at most risk, as well as other socially disadvantaged groups, such as the elderly, are least likely to invest in target hardening. As a result, numerous crime reduction initiatives in disadvantaged areas of the UK, especially in areas of predominantly public housing, have involved government investment. Many of these have been the subject of programme evaluation, resulting in a plethora of publications on 'what works' (Sherman *et al.*, 1997) in burglary reduction, distinguishing Britain from other countries (Eck, 2002). These include the Kirkholt burglary reduction project, developed in the late 1980s as a partnership in crime prevention between the police and probation service in Greater Manchester (Forrester, Chatterton and Pease, 1988; Pease, Chapter 27; Tilley, 1993), and other initiatives within the Safer Cities programme (Ekblom, Law and Sutton, Chapter 22, 1996), the Secured by Design (SBD) initiative (Armitage, 2000; Cozens, Pascoe and Hillier, Chapter 20; Pascoe and Topping, 1997), the Burglary Reduction Initiative[3] launched in 1998 as part of the government's Crime Reduction Programme (Maguire, 2004; Tilley, 2004; Tilley *et al.*, 1999), and projects targeting older people such as Locks for Pensioners (Mawby and Jones, 2006) and the Distraction Burglary initiative (Lister, Wall and Bryan, 2004). While most have concentrated on domestic burglary, some have provided incentives for businesses to improve their security (Bowers, Chapter 19; Mawby and Jones, 2007). Many, including the Kirkholt project, have prioritized recent victims of burglary in recognition of the fact that reducing repeats may be the most effective way of cutting overall burglary rates (Farrell and Pease, 1993; National Board for Crime Prevention, 1994).

---

[3]   Subsequently renamed the Reducing Burglary initiative.

Much of the emphasis in these initiatives has been on technological innovations – locks and bolts, lighting and alleygating – although some have incorporated social prevention, especially neighbourhood watch-based schemes, and others – for example, the Distraction Burglary initiative – have prioritized educating vulnerable groups. However, despite the close association between target hardening and reduced risk, evaluations of these initiatives have not always been positive. This is epitomized by the Locks for Pensioners initiative, which found that respondents with more security were less at risk than those with less security, but that those served by the initiative were at just as high risk as were other households excluded from the scheme (Mawby and Jones, 2006). While the Home Office has arguably put considerable positive spin on the success of such initiatives, some academics, including Hope (2004), have argued that the Crime Reduction Programme has been a failure.

This raises the question of why some initiatives succeed while others fail. Essentially, we may draw a distinction between design and implementation failure. Design failure implies that a project was designed in such a way that it failed to address burglary reduction measures adequately. Implementation failure implies that, although the initiative targeted appropriate measures, its implementation failed to meet proposed outputs. In the first case, evaluation of phase 1 of Safer Cities demonstrated that initiatives that were designed around a suite of crime reduction measures were more successful than those that depended on a single strategy (Ekblom, Law and Sutton, Chapter 22, 1996), while evaluation of the Burglary Reduction initiative suggested that educating householders to use security measures is crucial (Johnson and Bowers, 2003). In the second case, the importance of clear leadership and effective partnership work has been stressed; other evaluations point to poor take-up as a reason for disappointing outcomes (Bowers, Chapter 19; Maguire, 2004; Mawby and Jones, 2007).

One of the key issues here, however, concerns official response to these evaluations. Evaluation of successful burglary reduction initiatives is valuable, because policy-makers can learn from success and replicate projects that are proven to reduce burglary. But policy-makers can also learn from failure. This implies not just that they should avoid further investment in failed strategies, but that they should also learn what it is about the strategy that failed and consequently what needs to be adjusted. For example, if the deterrent impact of target hardening is reduced by limited publicity for a scheme, future initiatives should prioritize publicity as a means of getting the message across to potential burglars and be designed in ways that enable publicity to be maximized. The problem with a government response that, according to Hope (2004), denies failure is that any potential lessons to be learnt from that failure are ignored.

Responding to Burglary

A rather different policy agenda addresses harm minimization: that is, ensuring that when crime occurs victims receive adequate and appropriate support. As we have seen, burglary has a big impact on many of its victims, and the first task of support agencies is to address victims' needs. However, a wealth of evidence indicates that secondary victimization is common: victims' treatment by agencies such as the police and courts often exacerbates the harm they experience.

The police are generally the first and most common public-sector agency with which burglary victims have contact. It is therefore important that the police provide them with a satisfactory service. However, victims, including burglary victims, have traditionally been critical of the service they receive from the police (Mawby, 2007). Criticisms cover lack of interpersonal skills, poor response times, failure to take the incident seriously, not keeping the victim informed of further developments, and failure to apprehend the offenders or recover stolen property. This is particularly evident in post-communist societies (Mawby, Ostrihanska and Wojcik, Chapter 24; Zvekic, 1998), but is also found across the world. As a result, a number of measures have been adopted to improve the 'victim-mindedness' of the police, including victim awareness training (Rosenbaum, 1987; Winkel, 1989), callback programmes (Skogan and Wycoff, 1987), performance monitoring (Bunt and Mawby, 1994) and the introduction of guidelines and codes of practice (Home Office, 2005; Wemmers and Zeilstra, 1991). The latter have also been introduced to the courts, although the low clear-up rate for burglary means that relatively few burglary cases proceed that far (Langan and Farrington, 1998).

Detection rates for burglary have traditionally been relatively low (Burrows, 1986). In England and Wales in 2003–2004, 18 per cent of household and 11 per cent of other burglaries were cleared up, compared with a detection rate of 28 per cent for all indictable crimes (Thomas and Feist, 2005). This is largely due to the nature of the offence. Burglaries are usually committed when the home is empty and in the absence of witnesses. Unlike violent offences, then, there is rarely an available witness to name or describe the perpetrator, and unlike drug offences the identification of an offence does not almost inevitably bring with it the identification of a suspect. This has a number of implications. First, there has been a policy shift towards crime reduction rather than detection. Second, there has been a concern to distinguish between primary and secondary detection methods, and highlight the former as indicators of police success. Third, there has been a recent renewed optimism towards detection, with a variety of focused initiatives being piloted. In England and Wales, many of these either stemmed from, or were evaluated as part of, the Home Office's 'Police Operations against Crime' in the early 1990s. The research by Timothy Coupe and Max Griffiths (Chapter 21) was one such evaluation. Having identified the importance of the ways in which the police initially responded to burglary complaints, they suggested that an improvement in police response would increase the detection rate (see also Blake and Coupe, 2001). Equally, they advocated a more planned approach to house-to-house enquiries, and a more systematic monitoring of cases so that the CID and SOCO's could concentrate their efforts (and resources) on those cases where there was some prospect of detection. However, as closer examination of the much vaunted Operation Bumblebee initiative by the Metropolitan Police (Stockdale and Gresham, 1995) demonstrates, there is little evidence of any significant and long-term improvement.

Ideally, police response to crime victims should encompass a service approach alongside a concern to do everything possible to clear up the crime. The public expects the police to investigate crimes and make some effort to clear them up: indeed, not to do so is to undermine the notion that the police take victims' complaints seriously. But victims also expect the police to respond sympathetically, to treat them as people rather than crime numbers, to provide help or advice where necessary, to keep them informed of any progress regarding 'their' crime, and to refer them to other support services when appropriate.

In response to criticisms of the way in which victims were treated by public-sector agencies, specialist victim services emerged in a number of Western societies in the 1970s and 1980s. Two of the first countries to adopt support services were the US and England and Wales, although the nature of the services offered contrasted markedly. In the US, more emphasis was placed on victims of violent and sexual crimes, services tended to prioritize personal counselling, and court-based programmes were common. This led some to identify a mismatch between victims' needs and service provision (Davis, Lurigio and Skogan, 1999). In England and Wales, as Martin Gay, Christopher Holton and M.S. Thomas outline in (Chapter 23) burglary was initially seen as the 'ideal' crime for Victim Support, services were more practically based, and support at the time of the offence was accorded greater priority than court-based services. Elsewhere in the world, services have tended to adopt varying elements of each model (Mawby, 2001). However, the ICVS (van Kesteren, Mayhew and Nieuwbeerta, 2001) illustrates that the UK remains one of only a few areas of the world where many burglary victims receive support. Recent changes to Victim Support in England and Wales mean that the original emphasis on providing a personal, practical service to burglary victims has been diluted: services have been centralized and direct personal contact is becoming a rarity. The essay by Gay, Holton and Thomas can thus be read as a description of a key phase in the emergence of victim services, to be compared with new managerialist alternatives that appear to have been introduced without critical appraisal.

Policy responses to burglary can also, finally, be considered in the context of sentencing the persistent burglar. While efforts at social crime reduction are inevitably limited by low clear-up rates, this has not prevented policy-makers advocating imprisonment as the appropriate sentence for burglars. Traditionally, those convicted of burglary in England and Wales were considerably less likely to be incarcerated that their US equivalents (Langan and Farrington, 1998; Lynch *et al.*, 1991), although the recent increased use of imprisonment in England and Wales might have narrowed the gap. On the other hand, the 'accredited programmes' offered by the probation service provide an extension of the offence-directed aspects of intensive probation, while restorative justice offers a constructive alternative that addresses risk management by incorporating the needs of both offenders and victims. In the light of such developments, it is worth revisiting the now defunct Victim/Burglar Group operated in Plymouth by the probation service in the late 1980s and early 1990s (see Nation and Arnott, Chapter 25. This provided a structured programme for convicted burglars subject to a probation order, part of which involved them in group discussions with burglary victims, thereby offering victims the opportunity to express their anger and fears, albeit towards someone other than 'their' burglar. Evaluation demonstrated that most felt they benefited from the experience. Additionally, being confronted by victims proved beneficial to offenders, who were forced to confront and re-evaluate their actions. Following Sykes and Matza (1957), one of the advantages of this was that it enabled probation officers to challenge 'techniques of neutralization'. In other words, burglars were less able to hide behind excuses that 'victims can afford it' or 'it didn't really affect the victim', and instead were left with the clear message that their actions had impacted on their victims.

Nevertheless, low clear-up rates mean that burglary reduction initiatives remain a more promising policy option. These in turn depend on clearly identifying homes and areas at greatest risk. The identification of burglary hot-spots and repeat burglary is thus of practical, as well as theoretical, importance. Reducing burglary, and hence reducing the stress it causes, depends on a clear understanding of which properties are most at risk and why this is the case. Only then can one move towards designing and implementing effective policies.

References

Anderson, D., Chenery, S. and Pease, K. (1995), *Biting Back: Tackling Repeat Burglary and Car Crime*, Crime Detection and Prevention Series, no. 58, London: Home Office.

Armitage, R. (2000), *An Evaluation of Secured by Design Housing within West Yorkshire*, Home Office Briefing Note 7/00. London: Home Office.

Bennett, T. (1990), *Evaluating Neighbourhood Watch*, Aldershot: Gower.

Bennett, T. and Wright, T. (1984), *Burglars on Burglary*, Aldershot: Gower.

Bichler-Robertson, G. and Potchak, M.C. (2002), 'Testing the Importance of Target Selection Factors Associated with Commercial Burglary Using the Blended Approach', *Security Journal*, **15**(4), pp. 41–61.

Blake, L. and Coupe, R.T. (2001), 'The Impact of Single and Two-officer Patrols on Catching Burglars in the Act', *British Journal of Criminology*, **41**(2), pp. 381–96.

Bottoms, A.E. and Wiles, P. (2002), 'Environmental Criminology', in M. Maguire, R. Morgan and R. Reiner (eds), *The Oxford Handbook of Criminology: Third Edition*. Oxford: Oxford University Press, pp. 620–56.

Brantingham, P.J. and Brantingham, P.L. (1995), 'Criminality of Place: Crime Generators and Crime Attractors', *European Journal of Criminal Policy and Research*, **3**(3), pp. 5–26.

Bunt, P. and Mawby, R.I. (1994), 'Quality of Policing: The Consumer's Perspective', *Public Policy Review*, **2**(3), pp. 58–60.

Burrows, J. (1986), *Investigating Burglary: The Measurement of Police Performance*, Home Office Research Study no. 88, London: HMSO.

Butler, G. (1994), 'Commercial Burglary: What Offenders Say', in M. Gill (ed.), *Crime at Work*, Leicester: Perpetuity Press, pp. 29–41

Cohen, L., Kluegel, J.R. and Land, K. (1981), 'Social Inequality and Predatory Criminal Victimization: An Exposition and Test of a Formal Theory', *American Sociological Review*, **46**, pp. 505–24.

Clarke, R.V. (2003), *Burglary of Retail Establishments*, US Department of Justice, Community Oriented Policing Series, no. 15 available at: www.cops.usdoj.gov.

Davis, R.C., Lurigio, A.J. and Skogan, W.G. (1999), 'Services for Victims: A Market Research Study', *International Review of Victimology*, **6**, pp. 101–15.

Frate, A.A. del (1998), *Victims of Crime in the Developing World*, Rome: UNICRI.

Frate, A.A. del, Zvekic, U. and van Dijk, J.J.M. (1993), *Understanding Crime: Experiences of Crime and Crime Control*, Rome: UNICRI.

Distraction Burglary Task Force (2002), *Tackling Distraction Burglary*, at www.crimereduction.gov.uk/boguscaller8.htm.

Donkin, S. and Wellsmith, M. (2006), 'Cars Stolen in Burglaries: The Sandwell Experience', *Security Journal*, **19**(1), pp. 22–32.

Eck, J.E. (2002), 'Preventing Crime at Places', in L.W. Sherman *et al.* (eds), *Evidence-based Crime Prevention*, London: Routledge, pp. 241–94.

Ekblom, P., Law, H. and Sutton, M. (1996b), *Domestic Burglary Schemes in the Safer Cities Programme*, Research Findings no. 42 at www.homeoffice.gove.uk/rds/pdfs/r42.pdf.

Farrell, G. (1992), 'Multiple Victimisation: Its Extent and Significance', *International Review of Victimology*, **2**, pp. 85–102.

Farrell, G. and Pease, K. (2001), *Repeat Victimization*, New York: Criminal Justice Press.

Farrell, G. and Pease, K. (1993), *Once Bitten, Twice Bitten: Repeat Victimisation and its Implications for Crime Prevention*, Home Office Crime Prevention Unit Paper 46, London: HMSO.

Felson, M. and Cohen, L.E. (1980), 'Human Ecology and Crime: A Routine Activity Approach', *Human Ecology*, **8**(4), pp. 389–405.

Forrester, D., Chatterton, M. and Pease, K. (1988), *The Kirkholt Burglary Prevention Project, Rochdale*, Crime Prevention Unit Paper no.13, London: HMSO.

Hakim, S. and Gaffney, M.A. (1994), 'Substantiating Effective Security', *Security Dealer*, August, pp. 148–57.

Hoare, J. and Cotton, J. (2006), 'Property Crime', pp. 85–108 in Walker, A., Kershaw, C. and Nicholas, S. (eds), *Crime in England and Wales 2005/2006*, Research Development Statistics 11/05, London: Home Office. Also available at www.homeoffice.gov.uk/rds/pdfs06/hosb1206.pdf.

Home Office (2002), *Distraction Burglary Good Practice Guide*, (www.crimereduction.gov.uk/burglary48.htm).

Home Office (2005), *Code of Practice for Victims of Crime*, London: Home Office at: www.homeoffice.gov.uk/213275/victims-code-of-practice?view=Binary.

Hope, T. (2004), 'Pretend it Works: Evidence and Governance in the Evaluation of the Reducing Burglary Initiative', *Criminal Justice*, **4**(3), pp. 287–308.

Jackson, H.M. and Winchester, S.W.C. (1982). *Residential Burglary*, Home Office Research Study No. 74, London: HMSO.

Johnson, S.D. and Bowers, K.J. (2003), *Reducing Burglary Initiative: The Role of Publicity in Crime Prevention*, Home Office Research, Development and Statistics Directorate Findings 213, London: Home Office.

Langan, P.A. and Farrington, D.P. (1998), *Crime and Justice in the United States and in England and Wales, 1981–96*, Washington, DC: US Department of Justice, Bureau of Justice Statistics. See also at :www.ojp.usdoj.gov/bjs/abstract/cjusew96.htm.

Levesley, T., Braun, G., Wilkinson, M. and Powell, C. (2004), *Emerging Methods of Car Theft – Theft of Keys*, Home Office Research, Development and Statistics Directorate Findings 239, London: Home Office.

Lister, S. and Wall, D. (2006), 'Deconstructing Distraction Burglary: An Ageist Offence?', in M. Cain and A. Wahidin (eds), *Ageing, Crime and Society*, Cullompton; Willan Publishing, pp. 101–23.

Lister, S., Wall, D. and Bryan, J. (2004), *Evaluation of the Leeds Distraction Burglary Initiative*, Home Office Online Report 44/04, at: www.homeoffice.gov.uk/rds/pdfs04/rdsolr4404.pdf.

Lynch, J. *et al.* (1991), *Profiles of Inmates in the US and England and Wales, 1991*, US Department of Justice, Bureau of Justice Statistics Special Report.

Maguire, M. (1982), *Burglary in a Dwelling*, Heinemann: London.

Maguire, M. (2004), 'The Crime Reduction Programme in England and Wales: Reflections on the Vision and the Reality', *Criminal Justice*, **4**(3), pp. 213–37.

Mawby, R.I. (2001), *Burglary*, Cullompton: Willan Press. Mawby,

Mawby, R.I. (2003), 'Crime and the Business Community: Experiences of Businesses in Cornwall, England', *Security Journal*, **16**(4), pp. 45–61.

Mawby, R.I. (2006), 'Commercial Burglary', in M. Gill (ed.), *The Handbook of Security*. Basingstoke: Palgrave Macmillan, pp. 281–301.

R.I. (2007), 'Public Sector Services and the Victim of Crime', in S. Walklate (ed.), *Handbook of Victimology*, Cullompton: Willan Press, pp. 209–39.

Mawby, R.I. and Jones, C. (2007), 'Attempting to Reduce Hotel Burglary: Implementation Failure in a Multi-agency Context', *Crime Prevention and Community Safety: An International Journal*, **9** (3), pp. 145–66.

Mawby, R.I. and Jones, C. (2006), 'Evaluation of a National Burglary Reduction Initiative Targeting Older People', *Crime Prevention and Community Safety: An International Journal*, **8** (4), pp. 209–27.

Mawby, R.I., Gorgenyi, I., Ostrihanska, Z., Walklate, S. and Wojcik, D. (1999), 'Victims' Needs and the Availability of Services: A Comparison of Burglary Victims in Poland, Hungary and England', *International Criminal Justice Review*, **9**, pp. 18–38.

National Board for Crime Prevention (1994), *Wise After the Event: Tackling Repeat Victimisation*, London: Home Office.

Nicholas, S., Kershaw, C. and Walker, A. (2007), *Crime in England and Wales 2006/07*, HOSB II/07, London: Home Office, at: www.homeoffice.gov.uk/rds/pdfs07/hosb1107.pdf.

Pascoe. T. and Topping, P. (1997), 'Secured by Design: Assessing the Basis of the Scheme', *International Journal of Risk, Security and Crime Prevention*, 2(3), pp. 161–73.

Rosenbaum, D.P. (1987), 'Coping with Victimization: The Effects of Police Intervention on Victims' Psychological Readjustment', *Crime and Delinquency*, 33, pp. 502–19.

Sherman, L., Gottfredson, D., Mackenzie, D., Eck, J., Reuter P. and Bushway S. (1997), *Preventing Crime: What Works, What's Promising and What Doesn't*, Washington, DC: US Department of Justice.

Skogan, W.G. and Wycoff, M.A. (1987), 'Some Unexpected Effects of a Police Service for Victims', *Crime and Delinquency*, 33, pp. 490–501.

Solomon, E., Eades, C., Garside, R. and Rutherford, M. (2007), *Ten Years of Criminal Justice under Labour: An Independent Audit*, London: Centre for Criminal Justice Studies.

Stockdale, J.E. and Gresham, P.J. (1995), *Combatting Burglary: An Evaluation of Three Strategies*, Home Office Crime Detection and Prevention Series, Paper no. 59, London: Home Office.

Sykes, G. and Matza, D. (1957), 'Techniques of Neutralisation', *American Sociological Review*, 22, pp. 664–73.

Taylor, J. (2004), *Crime against Retail and Manufacturing Premises: Findings from the 2002 Commercial Victimisation Survey*, Home Office Findings no. 259 at: www.homeoffice.gov.uk./rds/pdfs04/r259.pdf.

Thomas, N. and Feist, A. (2005), *Detection of Crime*, in S. Nicholas, D. Povey, A. Walker and C. Kershaw, (eds), *Crime in England and Wales 2004/2005*, Research Development Statistics 11/05, London: Home Office, pp. 115–36. Also available at www.homeoffice.gov.uk/rds/pdfs05/hosb1105.pdf.

Thornton, A., Hatton, C., Malone, C., Fryer, T., Walker, D., Cunningham, J. and Durrani, N. (2003), *Distraction Burglary amongst Older Adults and Ethnic Minority Communities*, Home Office Research Study no. 269, London: Home Office, at: www.homeoffice.gov.uk/rds/pdfs2/hors269.pdf).

Tilley, N. (2004), 'Applying Theory-driven Evaluation to the British Crime Reduction Programme: The Theories of the Programme and of its Evaluations', *Criminal Justice*, 4(3), pp. 255–76.

Tilley, N. (1993), *After Kirkholt – Theory, Method and Results of Replication Evaluations*, Home Office Crime Prevention Unit Paper no. 47, London: Home Office.

Tilley, N., Pease, K., Hough, M. and Brown, R. (1999), *Burglary Prevention: Early Lessons from the Crime Reduction Programme*. Home Office Crime Reduction Reseach Series Paper no. 1, London: Home Office.

van Dijk, J.J.M. and Terlouw, G.J. (1996), 'An International Perspective of the Business Community As Victims of Fraud and Crime', *Security Journal*, 7, pp. 157–67.

van Kesteren, J., Mayhew, P. and Nieuwbeerta, P. (2001), 'Criminal Victimisation in Seventeen Industrialised Countries: Key Findings from the 2000 International Crime Victims Survey' at: www.minjust.nl:8080/b_organ/wodc/reports/ob187i.htm.

Walker, A., Kershaw, C. and Nicholas, S. (2006) (eds), *Crime in England and Wales 2005/2006*, Home Office Research Development Statistics 11/05, London: Home Office. Also available at: www.homeoffice.gov.uk/rds/ pdfs06/hosb1206.pdf.

Wemmers, J.M. and Zeilstra, M.I. (1991), 'Victims Services in the Netherlands', *Dutch Penal Law and Policy*, 3, The Hague: Ministry of Justice.

Winkel. F.W. (1989), 'Responses to Criminal Victimization: Evaluating the Impact of a Police Assistance Programme and Some Social Psychological Characteristics, *Police Studies*, 12(2), pp. 59–72.

Wiles, P. and Costello, A. (2000), *The 'Road to Nowhere': The Evidence For Travelling Criminals*, Home Office Research Study no. 207, London: Home Office.

Zimring, F.E. and Hawkins, G. (1997), *Crime is Not the Problem: Lethal Violence in America*, New York: Oxford University Press.

Zvekic, U. (1998), *Criminal Victimisation in Countries in Transition*, Rome: UNICRI.

Part I
Burglary: Risk and Impact

[1]

Repeat Victimisation:
Offender Accounts

Julie Ashton, Imogen Brown, Barbara Senior and Ken Pease[1]

The repeated victimisation of the same people and places has recently assumed prominence in our analysis and understanding of crime, although its full implications for crime and criminal justice practice have yet to be acknowledged. A sample of officially processed burglars were interviewed. It was found that repeated offending against the same target was common, and characteristic of those most confirmed in a criminal career. It shows that an offender's tendency to commit repeated offences against the same target tends to cross crime types, and that the reasons are typically rational, even viewable as common sense. It suggests that change or presumed change in a target is the primary factor which reduces repetition.

Key Words: Repeat victimisation; offenders' perspectives; crime victims

Introduction

In recent years, the concentration of victimisation on the same people and places has come to be recognised as a fundamental fact about crime and as a major opportunity for its prevention. This recognition has been described as the most important criminological insight of the decade.[2] Alongside the build-up of data about crime concentration has come a series of demonstration projects which show that crime, particularly property crime, can be reduced by preventing repeats.[3] Prioritising the prevention of repeats may prove a good way of reducing both the volume of crime and (incidentally) the inequality of its distribution. Why might this be so? The prevention of repeat victimisation directs resources to the places and people where victimisation is most likely in the

near future.[4] It also deploys them in areas of highest crime, since areas suffer a high volume of crime because of differences in the rates at which people and places are chronically victimised.[5] The prevention of repeats provides a focus and a pace for implementing crime prevention that are in general difficult to achieve (the drip-feeding effect).

The place of repeat victimisation as a tactic in crime prevention now seems secure, with the establishment of a Home Office Task Force to advance its recognition, its incorporation as a police Key Performance Indicator, and growing interest and research in the USA, Sweden and Australia. It has other fundamental implications, for instance in changing the way

International Journal of Risk, Security and Crime Prevention

in which crime statistics are collected and presented. Crime concentration (the number of victimisations per victim) must in future be considered alongside prevalence (the number of victims per head of population) and incidence (the number of victimisations per head of population). Neglect of this has led to the failure to recognise how unequally the burden of crime is borne, and has obscured the self-evident priorities for prevention which flow from that.

Repeat victimisation and criminal and victim processing

Repeat victimisation has implications for criminal justice and for victim support. It is to implications for offender processing that the next wave of repeat victimisation research will be directed. Generally, repeat victimisation shifts the perception of an offence away from that of a random occurrence to that of the manifestation of a relationship, however perverse and undesired by at least one of the parties that relationship is.

The last 20 years has seen a movement towards recognising abusive relationships as criminal. Domestic violence and child abuse by intimates demanded an alternative way of considering crime victimisation. By contrast, other crime types still tend to be seen as one-off events. If much crime involves the same victim and same offender, there are many implications. Detection is facilitated, since the police will concentrate on those who previously offended against a victim. The role of victim support changes to incorporate crime prevention (see below).[6] The role of mediation and reparation is enlarged. Offence-focused work in probation may properly be directed at the relationships with victims which facilitate offence repetition. To the extent to which these relationships are concentrated in particular communities, the role of communitarian responses to crime may be focused more precisely.

In exploratory work,[7] advantage was taken of a question in the British Crime Survey which addresses the question of whether the offence was of the same type, done in the same way and 'probably' by the same perpetrators. Put

Table 1. Series crime as a proportion of repeated crime and all crime

Crime type	No. of crimes	Series/repeats (%)	Series/total (%)
Vehicle theft	341	57	9
Theft from vehicle	1649	70	31
Damage to vehicle	1783	76	39
Bicycle theft	358	66	19
Burglary with loss	842	74	26
Break-in with damage	195	96	41
Attempted burglary	433	78	29
Theft from dwelling	69	70	28
Theft from outside dwelling	923	90	47
Damage to outside dwelling	860	93	63
Theft from person	364	74	16
Attempted theft from person	117	33	5
Other theft	1187	76	30
Damage to personal property	91	100	55
Assault	1824	84	59
Threats	1616	93	72

Source: *The 1992 British Crime Survey.*

Julie Ashton, Imogen Brown, Barbara Senior and Ken Pease

simply, how much crime involves repeated similar events 'probably' by the same person? Table 1 summarises the results. It will be seen that most repetitions are series events. That is to say, when a person is victimised by the same type of crime more than once, those events tend to be very similar, and attributed to the same perpetrator. For crimes of violence in particular, series events account not just for most of the repeats, but most of all crime suffered. Looking at assault, the reader will see that 59 per cent of all violent crime is not a one-off event, but forms part of a series. The qualifier 'probably' by the same person is least necessary for assaults, which are the crimes where the victim is most likely to see the perpetrator, so we can say with confidence that most assaultive crime consists of series of similar events involving the same assailant(s) and the same victim.

Offender targetting

So far unpublished research by Inspector Steve Everson of West Yorkshire Police suggests that the people committing crime against the same target are primarily the same offenders, ie a second offence against the same target is overwhelmingly committed by the same person or group which committed the first. Further, these tend to be the more prolific offenders. Thus, even if the proportion of crimes detected remains constant, detecting those who commit repeat crimes will prevent more crime by deterrence, incapacitation and possibly offender change than would a more conventional approach.

What is clearly necessary is a raft of research in which offenders are asked about repetition. Such research is just beginning to appear.[8] Research of this kind will clarify the role which repeat victimisation might play in offender targetting.

One contentious issue is whether repeat victimisation flags risk or increases risk. Even now, it seems possible to confirm that victimisation *increases* risk of further victimisation, rather than merely flagging high-risk places and people.[9] This is a point which can be confirmed by research with offenders.

If it is their experience during a first offence against a given target which makes its repetition likely, then clearly victimisation increases risk. By this account, the day after a crime, a crime is more likely than before its occurrence. The importance of this for preventive strategy is difficult to overstate.

Victim support

Repeat victimisation has enormous implications for the practice of victim support. A long-standing criticism of police responses to repeat victims is the lack of communication between officers. Ideally, each officer attending knows the history of events at a particular address. In practice, this is far from true. This is no less true of victim support volunteers. One could argue that the victim support database should ensure that each volunteer knows the full extent of what has been experienced, across visits. If it is possible for the same volunteer to attend repeated incidents against the same person, this would at least provide organisational recognition of the reality of chronic victimisation. These organisational changes seem necessary to optimise the service to troubled victims. The extent of the victim support role in helping *prevent* repeat victimisation is more contentious and remains to be fully debated.

Probation

Why should probation officers be interested in repeat victimisation? It's clear that some officers involved in the exercise reported below regarded it as something of an indulgence by West Yorkshire Probation Service to become involved in this work, so the case needs to be made.

- *Offence-focused work.* Such work is now central in probation practice. It is difficult to see how this approach can be well-founded without some attention to the linkages between offences. Offence-focused work which regards suitable victims as interchangeable (which in our view comprises the bulk of such work, with the exception of offences like domestic violence

International Journal of Risk, Security and Crime Prevention

and incest, where the relationship is unavoidably central) misses the point insofar as particular victims are repeatedly targetted. The officer practising such work could be charged with naivety.

- *Mediation-reparation.* Repeated victimisation of the same target suggests either malice against or callous indifference to the suffering of the same people. Arguably, the shame which should attend repetition should be greater than would be the case for one-off victimisation. Exploration of previous victimisation involving the same parties is a necessary condition of the process being honest from the offender's point of view. Reintegrative shaming is (a priori) more powerful when the true extent of repetition is acknowledged.

- *Practical arrangements.* If offending is concentrated on the same victim (or even small area) this should arguably be taken into account in the solicitation of victim impact statements, location of Community Service placements, the question of who should be notified or patrolled when tagged offenders break their curfew, who should be notified of offender release, and the like. The presumption of equal risk should not underpin the ways in which punishment is dispensed and communicated.

The project in hand

In the research reported here, offenders officially processed for at least one burglary and in statutory contact with the West Yorkshire Probation Service during October-November 1996 were invited to complete a questionnaire in which they were asked whether they had ever repeated crimes against the same target (person or place). The questionnaire had been piloted on all those coming onto orders for a two-week period earlier that summer. This pilot survey had led to modifications of the questionnaire and measures to ensure that officers did invite those whom they supervised and who were eligible to complete the questionnaire. Offenders eligible were those meeting the

burglary criterion under supervision at the Huddersfield and Dewsbury offices, including those attending a Day Centre as a condition of Probation, or on a Community Service Order from the same offices, or on a Combination Order administered from those offices, or on remand or under sentence at Armley Prison, Leeds, with a home address such as would lead them to be supervised by those offices. The questionnaire sample comprised 173 men and 13 women, with a mean age of 25.9, and standard deviation of 7.8 years.

In the event, officers are believed, from conversation and office differences in number of questionnaires completed, to have varied in their rates of return. In the light of this, we cannot claim that the sample was representative of those for whom the Probation Service had responsibility during the period in question. Even if officer collaboration had been complete, there are other reasons why the questionnaire would not represent the actions of the population of recently active offenders with burglary in their records. Notably:

- Those who failed to fulfil their appointments would be excluded.

- Those sentenced to short prison sentences or on remand and subsequently acquitted would be under-represented, because of their release before interview.

- Participants may be inclined to understate their involvement in undetected crime to a probation officer, who is after all an officer of the court.

Thus, the sample is biased through variation in officer participation and in the exigencies of the situation. The net effect of the last-named bias is almost certainly to understate the criminal activity of the participants. A final point which must be made concerns the consequences of not asking respondents the total number of offences of each type they had committed. The questionnaire successfully identified many repeat offenders, but it did not distinguish between those who could have been (they had committed more than one offence in

International Journal of Risk, Security and Crime Prevention

a category) and those who could not. It was important that questions be as little intrusive as possible, but the consequence was that it remained impossible to distinguish those who had committed two or more offences of a type (and hence were potential repeaters against the same target) from those who had not, and were therefore not potential repeaters. For instance, those who said they had not stolen the same car more than once are non-repeaters. However, some of them will only admit to ever stealing one car, and hence could not be a repeater in this category. The proportion of those admitting to repeats will therefore be a *minimum* number. Another reason for believing the level of repetition to be a minimum is that some interviewees (see below) disclosed repetitions that they had not divulged as questionnaire respondents. This would be picked up if any kind of repetition had been acknowledged in the questionnaire, but would not in cases where the questionnaire revealed none, since the interview would not have taken place.

Respondents who acknowledged repeated offences against the same target were invited to interview by one of the writers (BS), to explore the reasons for and circumstances of the repeats. Eighty-six acknowledged 'repeaters' against the same target were scheduled for interview. In the event, 70 interviews were successfully completed. Of these, 57 admitted repeat burglary against the same target, and 29 admitted other kinds of

repetition. The reasons for not seeing the remaining 16 were that their order had been completed before they could be seen, warrants were out for their arrest, orders had been breached, and intended interviewees had been moved from Armley to other prisons.

The results will be presented in two parts. First is the extent of repetition, gleaned from the questionnaires. The second incorporates more discursive accounts of the reasons for repetition, gleaned from the interviews.

Sample prevalence of repeats

Examining the prevalence of repeats has two fundamental purposes:

1. It may demonstrate that offending against the same victim is sufficiently common for it to be routinely addressed in dealing with offenders.

2. It may demonstrate a general tendency to repeat, evident across crime types. If such a tendency exists, it may assist the police in offender targetting, offender profiling and charging practice.

Table 2 summarises the number of respondents who admitted to repeated offending of different types. Note that these are minimum estimates, given that we do not know how many respondents committed one (or no) offence of

Table 2. Proportion admitting repeats by offence type (n=186)

Repeat type	% of sample
Burglary	31
Theft of motor vehicle	8
Theft from motor vehicle	5
Repeated criminal damage of same household	13
Repeated criminal damage of same business	8
Repeated violence against same person	16
Repeats of different crime against same person/household	8
Repeats of different crime against same business	8
Use of force against different people but in the same place	18
Taking or taking from different cars in the same place	18

International Journal of Risk, Security and Crime Prevention

a particular kind, and hence could not have committed a repeat. Note too that repeats here do not distinguish two from more than two events, so that the Table does not approximate the number of events attributable to those who repeat.

To restate, one third of a sample of people defined as having at least one official processing for burglary admitted repeated burglary against the same target. Smaller proportions admitted repetition of other offence types against the same target, but since the sample was not defined in terms of other offence types, these smaller proportions are bound to be underestimates. Looked at another way, what proportion of the sample admitted any repetition against the same target? Table 3 presents the numbers. Excluding repetitions defined only by place, a respondent can score between 0 and 8 repetition types. A respondent scoring 0 admits no repetitions against the same target. A respondent scoring eight repetition types asserts repeat victimisation of all eight types set out in the first eight rows of Table 2. Table 3 shows that 54% of respondents admitted no repetitions, 23% one repetition type only, 8% two repetition types, with up to 2% admitting six repetition types.

Table 3. Frequency of repetition type admissions (n=186)

Number of repetition types	% of respondents admitting
0	54
1	23
2	8
3	8
4	4
5	2
6	2

Thus, roughly one quarter of the respondents admitting repeatedly offending against the same target in respect of at least two offence types. Put another way, a probation officer facing someone as defined by our sampling approach will know that half the time the

person concerned has committed more than one offence against the same target. Half of those who have repeated crime in this way will have done so by way of two or more crime types.

What are the characteristics of people who repeat in different ways? Correlating the number of different repetition types admitted (as in Table 3) with age at first offence and number of previous convictions yields correlations which suggest that the repeaters are those most established in criminal careers. The correlation between age at first conviction and number of repetition types is significant beyond the .001 level of probability. It shows that repeaters typically came to official notice earlier than non-repeaters. The relationship between number of prior convictions and repetition is in the predicted direction, but is not statistically reliable, perhaps because of some missing data in this field.

It will be recalled from an earlier section that Steve Everson found that more frequent offenders were also more often repeaters, and the present finding is consistent with Everson's.

The next point concerns whether any particular kind of repeat better distinguishes respondents in terms of their conviction history. Analyses of variance were conducted, with age at first conviction and number of previous convictions as the dependent variable, and repetition/non-repetition of each type separately as the independent variable. The results can be readily summarised. The separation of those who repeated from those who did not, in respect of each offence type (except repeated criminal damage of businesses), did reliably differentiate respondents according to age at first official process. The differentiation according to number of previous convictions was also consistent, but not statistically reliable. Thus for *each* offence type, those who repeated began their offending career significantly earlier than those who did not. Repeaters also had more prior convictions, but not to a statistically reliable extent.

The emerging impression is that the tendency to repeat crime against the same target is a

International Journal of Risk, Security and Crime Prevention

general attribute, and is expressed across crime types. This impression is strengthened by looking at 2 x 2 contingency tables separating those who repeat from those who do not within each offence type. For instance, is the tendency to repeat violence statistically independent of the tendency to repeat burglary? The answer is that it is not. Given that eight types of repetition were examined here, there were twenty-eight bivariate comparisons possible. Twenty-six of these departed significantly from statistical independence. Thus the tendency to repeat one crime type against the same victim is generally associated with the tendency to repeat another crime type against the same victim. Some offenders tend to concentrate their offending repeatedly against the same target. They tend to be those most established in a criminal career.

The conclusion of an attribute of 'repetition compulsion' (to borrow a phrase from psychoanalysis) is only tentative here. The inability in the present study to distinguish repeat-eligibles (those who had committed two or more of an offence type but had not committed repeats against the same target) and repeat-ineligibles (those who had committed one or no offence of a particular type) limits the strength of reachable inferences. The bias of the sample towards burglars also limits generality. Both these limitations were integral to the design of the study, and were seen as the price of limiting the scale of the study and asking questions which would be answered without undue suspicion about how the results could be used. Integration of further work in this tradition with work of the type being done by Steve Everson promises a clear and applicable account of the tendency to retrace one's steps to crime.

The reasons for repeats

The prevalence of repeats gives no clue about why they happen. This study was deliberately set up to be exploratory, and to investigate reasons in particular. With rich qualitative data of this kind, the choice for analysis lies between, on the one hand, developing complex coding schemes and laborious classification of

responses, and on the other a more user-friendly general summary of burglar accounts of why they repeat. The second approach was preferred. This is defensible only if the original data on which the conclusions are reached are made available to those who wish to test the inferences made. The original interview data are available on request to interested readers.

• Burglary

The reasons for repeats against the same target are easily summarised. Most are sub-types of the general observation by one burglar, 'Why change a successful plan?'. Another point which became clear in a variety of different ways was the relationship between repeats and the market in stolen goods. Off-licences will predictably yield drink, schools and electrical stores will predictably yield computers, and homes will predictably yield 'whatever you didn't take away last time you burgled them'. In short, stealing to order or to supply a known market is more readily done by repeat offences than one-off offences. Each of the reasons for repetition offered bears the hallmark of rationality of approach.

Each common reason for repeating burglaries will be set out with three quotations from the interviews in support.

Because the first time was easy

> The house would be targetted again 'a few weeks later' when the stuff had been replaced and because the first time had been easy...

> X and friends targetted this school again. They did so because of how easy it had been the first time...

> X would target the same house four or five times because of how easy and successful it had been the first time.

Because the first time was profitable and goods of value remained

> X had also stolen mountain bikes and tools from the garages and sheds of houses...There were sometimes two or three bikes in a garage but he

International Journal of Risk, Security and Crime Prevention

could only steal one at once. Knowing the bikes were there for the taking, X said he waited until the owners would have forgotten about it and returned to steal another bike.

Clubs 'always have money in the Bandits'. X had information that the Bandits were well used and usually contained over £100....The second occasion .... they used the same method as before and stole around £500 from the machines.

It was a chance to get things which you had seen the first time and now had a buyer for.

Because once the lie of the land was known, it became easy

Once you have been into a place it is easier to burgle because you are then familiar with the layout, and you can get out much quicker.

Being familiar with the inside of a property made it easier a second time.

Keys to the door were usually hanging round, either on a shelf or the top of furniture near to the door in empty houses, so they used the keys to unlock the doors to get out and to use for the next time they broke in.

Because new goods would be available after replacement

The reason for targetting the house again was the quality of goods and that the insurance would have been paid out so the things would have been replaced.

X would wait about three months before burgling a house again. The same house was targetted for the quality of goods, the easy access, and the hope that the goods had been replaced.

X targetted this factory again six months later, when he knew the tools would have been replaced.

Because of a grudge against the victim (primarily schools)

X burgled his father's business three nights in a row. X had left home because he could not put up with the rules his father set... X also burgled his parents' home. He bore a grudge against his parents... X said he had burgled his parents' home four times.

X had targetted the schools they had attended because they knew their way around the school and also the classrooms which housed the computers. They enjoyed doing these schools as they hated school and had a grudge against some of the teachers.

X targetted the small engineering firm where he used to work. He did this to get his own back on his former employer who had dismissed him from the firm.

Grudge attacks were particularly often manifest in criminal damage of homes and schools.

The reasons for stopping repetition are simply summarised as change or the presumption of change:

Change

If a complex alarm had been installed or other security such as bars had been placed at the windows or dogs, then (we) left it alone.

X would return two or three times to the same factory or until they noticed security had been installed, or if they received inside information .... that security patrols, dogs or silent alarms were being installed.

X planned to target this house again but the reason they didn't was because the occupants had installed security lighting around the house and the side door had been replaced with another.

Presumption/suspicion of change

X said that they never went back more than twice to the same house for fear of being 'trapped' next time.

X said he did not return to this school because he thought he had been lucky. Also he wondered if a silent alarm had been installed since the alarm had not activated this time. Greed gets caught... don't go back if you sense something different.

X said he would only go back to the same house twice.... X said that if a house is persistently burgled then the police put cameras in the house. A pressure pad activates a camera in the house, and then they have got you.

- Vehicle crime

Reasons for repeated vehicle crime involving the same vehicle concentrated on ease, desirability of the vehicle, greater value of replacement accessories, grudge and fun. Grudge offences tended to involve criminal damage rather than theft. A few examples will suffice.

> X frequented golf course car parks. He waited until the owners had finished a game and watched them put the clubs into the boot of the car. When the owners left the car X said he broke into the boot with a screwdriver and stole the clubs. X said he targetted the same cars again a few weeks later. He waited until he thought the clubs would have been replaced and the car theft forgotten.

> X had stolen the stereo from the same car more than once. He would return to the same street and if he spotted the same car parked on the street he would take the stereo again if it had been replaced. ... You get more money for brand new things.

> X bought a car from a family he knew. X found out later that the car had been used by a friend of the family to kill himself... When X found out he was livid. He went back...and hit the male member of the family. On his way from the house he scraped the side of their car parked in the drive with a stone. ... X went back to the family who had sold him the car one night and smashed the car again with a brick, causing considerable damage to the car.

> X stole his Grandma's car on three occasions... on each occasion he used the car to run his girlfriend home late at night. On the first occasion his Grandma reported him to the police. He stole the car again for convenience and to take his girlfriend home. The third occasion was for his convenience also. It was easy to steal. This time he was chased by the police and crashed it into the wall. ... He bore no grudge (sic).

> X had been told by a buyer that any key for one of the new Ford cars would also fit one in five of any other car of that make. X and friend were given a key and they walked around a long-stay car park trying the key. They eventually found a car that the key fitted. They deactivated the alarm by opening the bonnet and ripping out the wires, then drove off. On their way to deliver the car to the buyer, they were stopped by the police and arrested. About a month later the same car was parked in the same car park. X and friend stole the same car again and successfully delivered it to the buyer.

> X said he had stolen one particular Cosworth more than once from the drive of a house, and another which was always parked on the same street... The buzz was the reason for taking the car and having the experience of 'what some folk have every day'. Usually it appeared on the drive again after a while so they would take it again. It was easy.

> X had stolen the same car 15 times from the same driveway. He did it for fun and to see how many times he could get away with it. He was caught and charged but he did it again. It was not a fast car. He just did it for a buzz.

> X said they would return two or three times some days to the same car park and had taken stereos out of the same cars when they had been replaced. New ones get more cash.

- Violence

Repeated violence, as would be inferred from the analysis of the British Crime Survey detailed earlier, surrounded troubled relationships.

> X had assaulted a person who had previously gone out with X's girlfriend... He had punched this person in a pub and later in the town centre where he 'gave him a beating'.

> X had used violence on the same person because he owed him money for drugs... X said he punched this person whenever he saw him.

> X had used violence against a former friend.... This friend had got 'stroppy' and tried to show X up in front of other people. 'It was the way he talked to me'. On two occasions he beat the person up and once he threatened him with a sword to scare him.

> The violence occurred when X's ex-girlfriend got her father and brothers to threaten X when X had broken down the door of his ex-girlfriend's house. X said they came round and he hit them with a cricket bat. Other times he ended up fighting one of her brothers whenever

International Journal of Risk, Security and Crime Prevention

they met. He said he had punched his ex-girlfriend's father when the father had threatened him after trying to see his son.

X said he used violence against another lad he knew because he owed him money. He beat him up in the street and in his home until he got his money back.

Repeats in this category are a depressing litany of fights over drug debts, fights with the family of ex-partners, and fights because friends or partners have become 'stroppy' or 'mouthy'. Chronic offending in these circumstances, as noted at the beginning of this report, is now well recognised.

The nature of repetition

As noted, many of the advantages of repetition concern ease of action and predictability of outcome. There are some circumstances in which a second or subsequent action may be taken against a person who or object which is functionally equivalent to the first. We would like to refer to this as isomorphic repetition. Thoughts along these lines began when the research preparatory to the Huddersfield 'Biting Back' project showed that, after a burglary, houses two doors away were more likely to be victimised than houses next door. It was conjectured that this was because semi-detached houses two doors away were more similar than the next door (mirror-image) house. Similar thoughts occurred here. One respondent noted:

Having done one Petrol Station, then burglars are familiar with the layout of the other stations in that chain. This makes it easy to move around when the burglar has knowledge of where the stock and safe is kept.

In a somewhat different way, all Ford Mondeos have similar layouts. In a still different way, all brothers of an ex-partner with whom one is disenchanted share the essential attributes which may make for violent victimisation. To simplify, different places or people may be functionally equivalent, so that victimisation of them may be no more problematic than victimisation of precisely the same person or object. This kind of repetition demands theoretical development. Tracing the patterns of functional equivalence and similarity is beyond the scope of this paper, but seems like one of the next steps in clarifying the issue. We should perhaps distinguish between repeat victimisation, isomorphic victimisation, and independent victimisation. Establishing the lines on which isomorphism runs is as important as it seems daunting.

Conclusions

What does the research contribute to our awareness of repeat victimisation and its crime control implications?

- It confirms that repetition of crime against the same victim or target is a practice common amongst those offenders who included at least one burglary in their records.

- It suggests that repetition against the same target is a characteristic of those most confirmed in a criminal career.

- It reveals that repetition tends to be a characteristic which crosses crime types, so that those repeating one crime type against the same target will also tend to repeat other crime types against the same target.

- It establishes that the reasons for repeating acquisitive crime against the same target are quite rational. Factors like the predictability of the market for goods make repeats rational.

- It shows that change or supposed change in the target is the primary factor which prevents repetition.

- It suggests a principle of isomorphism which extends the notion of what constitutes a repetition.

- It concludes that the awareness of repeated victimisation of the same or similar targets is essential for offence-focused probation work.

• It speculates on the existence of functionally equivalent (isomorphic) offences, as well as direct repeats. For instance, one interviewee noted that the layout of all petrol stations in a chain had safes and stock similarly located, so to have burgled one makes the subsequent burglary of any much easier.

Notes

1   Julie Ashton is a Senior Probation Officer, West Yorkshire Probation Service, Imogen Brown is a Research Officer, West Yorkshire Probation Service, Barbara Senior is an Administrative Assistant, West Yorkshire Probation Service, and Ken Pease is Professor of Criminology, University of Huddersfield.

Thanks are due to Les Moss, Assistant Chief Probation Officer, West Yorkshire Probation Service, for his support and encouragement.

2   See Skogan, W. (1996) In Brady, T.V. *Measuring What Matters*. Washington: NIJ.

3   For examples of this, see the following: Anderson, D., Chenery, S. and Pease, K. (1995) *Preventing Repeat Victimization: A Report on Progress in Huddersfield*. Police Research Group Briefing Note 4/95. London: Home Office; Forrester D., Chatterton, M. and Pease, K. (1988) *The Kirkholt Burglary Prevention Project, Rochdale*. Crime Prevention Unit Paper 13. London: Home Office; Lloyd S., Farrell, G. and Pease, K. (1994) *Preventing Repeated Domestic Violence: A Demonstration Project on Merseyside*. Crime Prevention Unit Paper 49. London: Home Office; Webb, J. (1996) *Direct Line Homesafe: An Evaluation of the First Year*. Nottingham: Janice Webb Associates.

4   See Polvi, N., Looman, T., Humphries, C. and Pease, K. (1990) Repeat Break and Enter Victimisation: Time Course and Crime Prevention Opportunity. *Journal of Police Science and Administration*. Vol. 17: pp 8-11.

5   See Trickett, A., Osborn, D., Seymour, J. and Pease, K. (1992) What is Different about High Crime Areas? *British Journal of Criminology*. Vol. 32: pp 81-89.

6   Farrell, G. and Pease, K. (1997) Repeat Victim Support. *British Journal of Social Work*. Vol. 27, pp101-113.

7   Chenery, S., Ellingworth, D., Tseloni, A. and Pease, K. (1996) Crimes which Repeat. *International Journal of Risk, Security and Crime Prevention*. Vol. 1, pp 207-215.

8   See Bennett, T. (1995) Identifying, Explaining and Targetting Burglary Hot Spots. *European Journal of Criminal Policy and Research*. Vol. 3: pp 113-123; Ericsson, U. (1995) Straight From the Horse's Mouth. *Forensic Update*. Vol. 43: pp 23-25.

9   Lauritsen, J.L. and Davis Quinet, K.F. (1995) Repeat Victimization among Adolescents and Young Adults. *Journal of Quantitative Criminology*. Vol. 11: pp 43-166; Osborn, D.R., Ellingworth, D., Hope, T. and Trickett, A. (1996) Are Repeatedly Victimised Households Different? *Journal of Quantitative Criminology*. Vol. 12: pp 223-245.

[2]

PROSPECTIVE HOT-SPOTTING

The Future of Crime Mapping?

Kate J. Bowers, Shane D. Johnson and Ken Pease*

Existing methods of predicting and mapping the future locations of crime are intrinsically retrospective. This paper explores the development of a mapping procedure that seeks to produce 'prospective' hot-spot maps. Recent research conducted by the authors demonstrates that the risk of burglary is communicable, with properties within 400 metres of a burgled household being at a significantly elevated risk of victimization for up to two months after an initial event. We discuss how, using this knowledge, recorded crime data can be analysed to generate an ever-changing prospective risk surface. One of the central elements of this paper examines the issue of how such a risk surface could be evaluated to determine its effectiveness and utility in comparison to existing methods. New methods of map evaluation are proposed, such as the production of search efficiency rates and area-to-perimeter ratios; standardized metrics that can be derived for maps produced using different techniques, thereby allowing meaningful comparisons to be made and techniques contrasted. The results suggest that the predictive mapping technique proposed here has considerable advantages over more traditional methods and might prove particularly useful in the shift-by-shift deployment of police personnel.

Introduction

The proliferation of Geographical Information System (GIS) has increased interest in crime mapping through the identification of locations historically suffering high rates of crime or disorder. While the past is the only basis on which to anticipate the future, the way in which facts about the past are chosen and weighted will determine the predictive power achievable. Crime patterns anticipated using data from even the recent past may be erroneous (Townsley and Pease 2002; Johnson and Bowers 2004a)—or may not be. Some areas have enduring high crime rates, where the allocation of resources represents an efficient resource targeting strategy.

It is almost a truism to note that while the information we have is about the past, it is the future that we need to know about. However, this truism has permeated the content of the literature less than one might suppose. Two recent publications (Gorr and Olligschlaeger 2002; Groff and LaVigne 2002) compare and discuss prediction methods. Their review of previous work and recommendations to practitioners and researchers are evidence-based and extremely helpful. These include abandonment of forecast methods using the same month from a previous year, explore leading indicators (using past values of independent variables that are associated with crime to predict the current value of the dependent variable) and specify minimum crime numbers to constitute a unit for prediction purposes. There is much in common between the recommendations of Gorr and Olligschlaeger and our conclusions. However, our approach derives from

*Jill Dando Institute of Crime Science, University College London, Third Floor, 1 Old Street, London, EC1V 9HL.

different research origins, and (we hope) that merits a separate account of its origins and development, even though some of the conclusions are similar to the leading indicator views of the authors cited here. Attention in this paper is exclusively upon residential burglary.

In their review, Groff and LaVigne (2002) note the distinctiveness of an approach based upon repeat victimization. They write:

> The research on repeat victimization suggests that much more could be learned from further examination of the composition of hot spots and the extent to which repeat victimizations could be used to predict not just future victimizations, but future hot-spot areas. Such studies should explore the question across different sized hot spots as well as different types of crime problems, and should explore the 'near repeat' concept in further detail. Depending on future research findings in this area, repeat victimization has the potential to provide a simple method that could be employed by users of all skill levels. . . . (Groff and LaVigne 2002: 36–7)

At around the time at which those words were written, two of the present authors were submitting for publication three papers which sought to explore the liberalized notion of repeats along the lines suggested (Johnson and Bowers 2004a; Bowers and Johnson 2004; Johnson and Bowers 2004b). The key findings of the research were that the risk of victimization is communicable, with properties within 400 metres and, particularly, on the same side of the street as a burgled home being at an elevated risk for up to two months after an initial event.

As will be explained more fully below, the notion of predictive mapping taken here is event-based rather than area-based. Given what we now know about sequences of burglary events, every such event should revise the predicted probability of burglary for the burgled home itself and for homes on the same side of the street, within 400 metres and of the same design as the burgled home. The essential difference between this approach and those reviewed and researched by Groff and LaVigne (2002) and by Gorr and Olligschlaeger (2002) is that previous work is based upon area incidence and characteristics. The present work, by contrast, is based upon inferences about area patterns yielded by individual events, summed and weighted as their predictive power wanes. For this approach, the crime event is focal and feeds into an ever-changing predictive map.

Making the crime event, rather than an area crime rate, focal has interesting ramifications. For policing purposes, identification of an ellipse defining a hot spot is, of itself, useless. What does a police officer do next, once she finds herself standing in the middle of a designated hot spot? Groff and LaVigne (2002) stress that until one knows what is heating the hot spot, action can be aimless. Operating from the level of individual households, as with the approach reported here, the pattern of risk within the hot spot is clarified by prior research on repeat victimization and near repeats. Because of this, where the police officer goes and what she does is much more evident to her.

While we believe our approach to mapping has both transparency for police practitioners and a more focused immediate application to policing within high-crime areas, it is clear that the predictive power of this approach at the area level must be at least comparable to that yielded by alternative approaches, and the present paper addresses that issue. It uses only a crude approximation of what we know about the communicability of risk from a burgled home. There is, we believe, latent predictive power in the approach which remains to be explored.

642

PROSPECTIVE HOT-SPOTTING

Even if the approach taken here proves inferior at the area level, it would remain useful for deployment decisions within hot spots designated by other means. If it proves at least comparable in predictive power to other approaches, it may be that the approach has a case for being regarded as, provisionally, the method of preference in predictive mapping, and research effort directed accordingly.

As a final point, we anticipate the possibility that, aesthetically, the maps based upon this approach will be less pleasing than more conventional maps, on first sight looking more fragmented and incoherent. However, predictive mapping should not be a beauty contest, and the type of map we propose here may just be the ugly ducking of the fairy story.

To restate the central point, our recent work has demonstrated that the risk of victimization can be regarded as communicable (e.g. Johnson and Bowers 2004a), with the risk of victimization increasing for houses within 400 metres of a burgled household for a period of around one to two months, and especially on the same side of the street as a burgled home. Added to evidence about repeat victimization (for reviews, see Pease 1998; Farrell and Pease 2001), this has important implications for predicting where crimes are most likely to occur and opens up the possibility of undertaking prospective mapping. Here, we mean the production of maps which show future risk—not just of previous victims, but of the local neighbourhood. In what follows, we discuss some of the technical issues involved in generating prospective hot spots, how their efficiency may be measured and preliminary results regarding the comparison of the predictive accuracy of prospective and retrospective hot spots. In this process, we use only two related facts about communicated risk, namely its distribution in time and space relative to burglary events. It thus represents about the most basic prospective map possible.

Prospective Mapping Approach

To generate a prospective risk surface, we used a modification of the moving window technique used in hot-spot detection (Bailey and Gatrell 1995). To do this, a two-dimensional grid (with *n* equally sized cells) is generated and overlaid on the study area. An estimation of the likelihood of crime occurring within each cell—an index of *risk intensity*—is generated using a recursive algorithm. For each cell, every crime event that occurred within 400 metres of the centre of the cell is identified. In traditional hot-spot research, this 400-metre radius would be referred to as the bandwidth of the model. The critical conceptual difference between hot-spotting and the technique developed here is that, for hot-spotting, the bandwidth is relatively arbitrary, or is selected on the basis of the statistical properties of the distribution of the data[1] (see Brunsden 1995), whereas we use this specific distance of 400 metres here, as this is the distance over which we have shown that the risk of burglary is communicable.

A weighting is then given to each crime event. This is derived using information both on the distance of the point to the centre of the cell and the time that has elapsed since the event occurred. For instance, crimes that occurred closest to the centre of the cell

---

[1] With such approaches, the challenge is seen as producing a map that identifies an optimum number of areas where the density of crime *was* highest. What the optimum number is will vary. Thus, for this approach, the selection of a bandwidth is not informed directly by criminological research.

that occurred most recently are given the greatest weighting. The weightings of each crime event that occurs within the 400-metre bandwidth are then summed to produce the risk-intensity measure. A variety of different equations may be used in the derivation of the weightings, an inverse function being illustrated below.

$$Y(i) = \Sigma 1/\text{distance from cell centre} \times 1/\text{time since event occurred}$$

However, as the resulting risk surface[2] is essentially a series of cells, there is a problem with using a distance weighting that is derived using the coordinates of the centre of the cell. The reason is that risk-intensity values are not generated for individual points (such as the mid-point of the cell) but for the entire cell. For this reason, we present analyses here that use an algorithm that computes a risk intensity for the entire cell rather than the cell mid-point. Thus, a crime event that occurred *within* a cell would have the same weighting, irrespective of where it was positioned within that cell.

Estimating the accuracy of the predictions

An important element of the work involves the evaluation of the accuracy of the predictions made. Nice-looking maps do not equate to an efficient model. One problem with previous crime mapping has been the lack of evaluation of how effective maps are at predicting the location of future crimes (but see Gorr and Olligschlaeger 2002). On first consideration, it appears quite straightforward to do this; you simply use, say, two-years'-worth of data, the first of which is used to define the hot spots and the second of which is plotted on top of the resulting hot spots, to see the extent to which the crimes that 'happened next' have been captured. However, there are several problems with this simple idea—some more severe than others.

First, such exercises are often visual in nature. In other words, the investigator looks to see whether the hot spots capture the new crime incidents or not. This practice is particularly prolific with 'grid'-style coverages, which are raster images (which are, essentially, pictures and hence do not record information about the spatial location of each square) and not vector in format (where the *x* and *y* coordinates of the shapes are known, so they can be spatially located). It is therefore not possible to command the GIS to count the number of new incidents in each grid square, as it cannot spatially intersect the two data sets. This precludes the systematic evaluation of the technique.

Secondly, crime mappers have tended to concentrate on one style of hot-spot mapping at a time (but see Jefferis and Mamalian 1998). Consequently, there is little documentation on comparisons between the effectiveness of different mapping techniques. In order to prove that one has an effective map, you need a method of comparing current methods to others extant. Moreover, as a starting point, the predictive accuracy of a map (or any technique) should also be compared with a random distribution of some kind.

Thirdly, there are a number of different components that should be considered when evaluating map 'effectiveness'. The number of hits that a particular hot-spotting technique makes in terms of new incidents captured is only one of them, and, indeed,

[2] A risk surface is a graphical representation of the estimated probabilities of an event, or series of events, occurring at each of the various locations within a geographical area of interest.

might not be the most important. Some important factors in determining map effectiveness are 1) the 'hit' rate; and 2) the area covered by the hot spot(s). This is crucial—a hot spot that covers the whole area of interest would have a 100-per-cent hit rate, since it would capture all the new crimes—but it wouldn't be any use operationally. Thus, an alternative way of conceptualizing the measurement issue is to consider how efficient the procedure would be in operational terms. For instance, how many crimes could be prevented for every 10 metres-squared patrolled, searched or swiftly targeted with crime-prevention measures. A more sensitive approach then would be to measure the effectiveness of the procedure as a rate of events identified per metre-squared considered—a measure that we will subsequently refer to as the *search efficiency rate*; 3) the number of hot spots identified within a particular area. It is unlikely that, with offence-location data, a hot-spotting procedure will only come up with a single hot spot. However, there will be substantial operational gain to keeping the number of hot spots manageable for operational purposes. It is difficult to say what the optimal number is; too many will create logistical problems, as it will be difficult to deploy resources to all of the areas; too few might perhaps cause too many resources to be concentrated into a limited number of areas; and, 4) the travelling distances between hot spots might be important factors in some cases. Even if the procedure was shown to have a relatively high search-efficiency rate, the effectiveness of the technique in operational policing might be limited if the areas that had high values were randomly distributed across the area considered. Officers would not only have to patrol the areas of high risk, but they would also have to travel between a large number of these, consequently increasing the effort involved and the resources required. For this reason, it may be the case that the shorter the distance between the locations, the better.

We see it as particularly important that a map's utility is evaluated before it is used in an operational setting. We have therefore endeavoured to design a system for map evaluation that allows comparisons to be made between different hot-spot maps. There are a number of different evaluation criteria that may be produced for each map, and which go a fair way towards quantifying the different measures of effectiveness outlined above. These are:

Hit rate—the number of new crimes that are captured by the defined hot-spot area.

Area—the extent of the hot-spot areas. It is expressed both in terms of total area across all hot spots and average size of hot-spot area.

Search efficiency rate—the number of crimes successfully predicted per kilometre-squared. Using a standardized index allows different procedures and different hot spots to be meaningfully compared.

Number of hot spots—a count of the number of different hot-spot areas produced by the technique.

Area-to-perimeter ratios—the overall and/or the average area-to-perimeter ratio. These are calculated by simply dividing the area of the hot spot by its perimeter. The larger this is, the more 'compact' the area is; in other words, the more area is covered in the shape per length of perimeter. This could be seen as a measure of efficiency of the hot spot in terms of how practical it is to cover the area.

Using measures such as the search efficiency rate has distinct advantages. A police officer can make two mistakes: not be somewhere/do something at a place where a crime happens, or be somewhere/do something at a place where a crime does not happen.

BOWERS ET AL.

A simple hit (or miss) rate calculation will not capture this, as it assumes that the police are omnipresent within potentially very large hot-spot areas. In reality, they cannot be at every location at every time, which is why it is useful to know the average hit rate per metre-squared across a number of different maps or scenarios. A second advantage is that this approach allows graduated effort on an obviously discernable basis. This allows users to patrol or target harden whatever number of households adds up to the greatest risk within the confines of their operational availability.

Lessons from geographic profiling

Similar issues to those discussed above have been raised in relation to geographic pro-filing. In this endeavour, the aim is to identify the residence of an offender based on the spatial location of a series of presumably related offences. To do this, a risk sur-face—sometimes referred to in the literature as a jeopardy surface—is generated. Superimposing this surface onto a cartographic map of the area produces a geoprofile, which represents an optimal search area (Rossmo 1999). The implication for opera-tional policing in respect of offender identification is that the search for the offender's residence should begin where the probability density of the geoprofile is highest (the centre). The aim of the technique is to generate a search strategy that will be more effi-cient than a random approach. The effectiveness of the approach may be assessed by measuring the total proportion of the target area that must be covered before the offender's residence is discovered. This percentage is referred to as the hit-score per-centage. Lower hit scores are associated with optimized search strategies, although these are influenced by the size of the target area identified by the jeopardy surface. Thus, for a single offender, it is possible to generate two different jeopardy surfaces with different-sized target areas. The different surfaces may have different hit-score per-centages associated with them. In its simplest form, interpretation of the hit-score per-centage should be treated with caution, as it does not take the size of the target area into account—only the proportion which must be searched. Thus, a jeopardy surface may have a 1-per-cent hit-score percentage, which translates into a search area of 28 kilometres-squared, whereas a second may have a hit rate percentage of 10 per cent but a search area of only 2 kilometres-squared. Clearly, then, unless jeopardy surfaces of the same size are to be compared, the hit-rate percentage measure may be misleading. For this reason, to test the effectiveness of a jeopardy surface, the hit-score percentage must be compared with some form of distribution, to determine whether it offers pre-dictivity that exceeds chance. To do this, a series of hit-score percentages are compared with the chance distribution. For a random search strategy, the probability of locating an offender residence at any point is simply the reciprocal of the number of points that can be searched. Thus, for 100 points or locations, the probability would be $1/100$. To examine the effectiveness of the jeopardy surface, the number of points that have a risk-intensity score that is equal to or greater than the hit score for the point which identifies the offender's home residence are compared to the total number of points within the target area. The results are then compared with a random distribution using an index of dissimilarity, such as the Gini coefficient (Goodall 1987).

The search for offender locations affords interesting parallels with some of the tech-nical issues confronted here. In particular, it shows that area or scope of search should be accounted for in measures of map efficiency. It also demonstrates that it is difficult to make judgments on efficiency in the absence of any comparison (here, a random distribution). However, the fundamental difference between the two enterprises should be stressed. Here, we are concerned with the proportion of future crime events which can be addressed on the basis of routine prediction based upon past events. This is very different from the search for a single location (an offender residence). In essence, the hot-spot map searches for many high-risk locations simultaneously and the most efficient way of safeguarding these. Therefore, it is not possible to apply geographic-profiling methods directly in the evaluation of offence-based maps.

The issue of calibration

It should be stressed here that the accuracy of any procedure used to generate hot spots or jeopardy surfaces is directly related to the estimation model and any parameters used. To accommodate this, a number of different models have been produced. For some, an inverse distance and time weighting was used (see the equation above), whereas, for others, an inverse exponential function was used. It is, of course, possible to use a constant in any equation. A constant may also be added for some ranges of distances (both in space and time) but not others.

One particular challenge relates to the size of the cells used to generate the two-dimensional grid. The implications of this issue here are similar to those elsewhere, particularly in relation to the ecological fallacy (e.g. Brown 1991). This problem occurs where data of any kind are aggregated up to some areal unit that is larger than the smallest resolution at which it can be measured (e.g. area crime rates vs individuals' experience of victimization). One problem that arises is that an invalid assumption may be made that the average experience for the entire area is common to all. For instance, in areas of high crime, it may incorrectly be assumed that all people are victimized or are at the same level of risk. To avoid this problem, it is important to select the appropriate size of grid. Clearly, this issue is particularly important in the current endeavour.

The advantage with the approach taken here is that, unlike in traditional hot-spotting, where both bandwidth and grid size are unknowns and often determined by guesswork, or atheoretical statistical criteria, we have a theoretical reason for using a 400-metre bandwidth (this being the distance over which research suggests burglary risk to be communicable). However, the size of the grid squares is still open to debate. To distinguish between the bandwidth and the grid size, consider the illustration below.

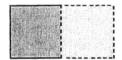

On the left of this illustration,[3] the bandwidth and grid size for the two cells are the same. The area which is displayed on the map (the grey shading) is the same size as the area used in the derivation of the grid (the solid and dotted-line boxes). There is no

---

[3] As noted above, the risk-intensity value is generated by counting how many crimes occur within a specific radius (the bandwidth) of the mid-point of the cell. However, in the illustration presented, the search area for each cell is shown as a square rather than a circle to emphasize the point discussed.

BOWERS ET AL.

overlap in the data used to derive the grids in these cases. On the right, the bandwidth remains the same. However, in this case, the grid size is a lot smaller and, hence, there is a large amount of overlap in the data used to derive the risk-intensity values for two adjacent cells. The second of these approaches has some significant advantages; first, it predicts crime risk at a more localized level; the smaller the grid size, the more localized the predictions. Secondly, it requires fewer data to produce a sensible picture of risk, because it uses much of the same data in more than one grid. As we explain later, these grids can later be aggregated to defined hot-spot areas. Therefore, we recommend that the smallest grid size be used that is practical within the constraints of computing power and GIS software.

Prospective Hot-Spot Mapping: An Empirical Example

A number of prospective maps have been generated for data available for the county of Merseyside. To generate the maps, we used historic data for the year 1997 (for no particular reason other than its availability to us at the analysis stage). Burglary data were acquired for the 22,704,000-metres-squared grid in South Liverpool, shown as Figure 1. Two levels of resolution have been used to generate the maps. Figures 2 and 3 show maps that use 10,816 cells and grids that are 50 × 50 metres. Other maps have been generated using 10 × 10-metre cells.

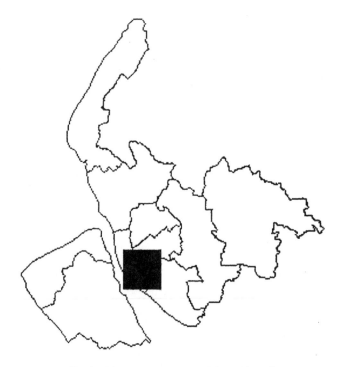

FIG. 1   Map of Merseyside and the grid used

PROSPECTIVE HOT-SPOTTING

For the maps shown here, we used two months' data (1 August to 30 September 1997) to generate the maps, and two (1 October to 30 November 1997) to test their accuracy. In addition to using data for the grid, we used data for a 400-metre buffer zone to minimize edge effects.

As discussed above in relation to calibration, grids of different sizes could, of course, be used to present the data. However, computing power limits the size of the grid and resolution used. For instance, for the same-sized grid, it was only just possible to gene-rate a risk surface for cells that measured 10 × 10 metres. For Figure 2, the risk-intensity values for each cell were generated by taking the product of the inverse of both time and distance weightings. The distance weighting was derived using the following equation:

Distance weight = 1 + number of complete 1/2 grid widths between event and cell centroid[4]

As indicated earlier, the advantage of using this approach is that it does not artificially inflate the importance of events that happen to be close to the mid-point of the cell, which, after all, is an arbitrary point within the limits of the cell. Events which occurred within 8 cells of a particular cell were considered; those further away were not.[5] The time weighting was computed by simply counting the number of weeks since the event occurred. In this case, this was the number of weeks which had lapsed between the event and 1 October 1997, the date for which the prospective map was generated.

Thus, if a burglary occurred within a cell, one week before the date of the map, it would have a weighting of $1/1 \times 1/1 = 1$; if a burglary occurred two weeks ago and in the neighbouring cell, $1/2 \times 1/2 = 1/4$; and so on. In each map, the cells are shaded to reflect the risk-intensity value. The darker the cell, the greater the risk-intensity value. To allow easy comparisons to be made between the different maps, each cell was assigned to a quantile, depending on the risk-intensity value. Thus, the 20 per cent of cells with the highest risk-intensity values were shaded in black, and the 20 per cent of cells with the lowest values are shaded in the lightest grey colour. Figure 2 also shows burglaries occurring within the next two days (symbolized as stars) and between three days and one week (symbolized as circles) following 1 October 1997. Visual inspection of the risk surface and the location of the burglaries that follow indicates a consider-able amount of overlap between the predicted areas of high risk and the burglaries. However, as emphasized earlier, it is important to evaluate this in further detail.

In addition to generating prospective hot spots, we also generated some more tradi-tional hot spots (which do not use temporal weightings), to enable comparisons to be made. Figure 3 shows a hot spot generated using the moving window technique and a quatric kernel algorithm used by Ratcliffe (2000). As suggested by Ratcliffe, we used a bandwidth of 200 metres. When compared, the maps shown in Figures 2 and 3 share a number of features. This is hardly surprising, as crime clusters in space. However, there also exist a number of differences between the two maps. For instance, all of the burgla-ries occurring within the following week, located within the white dashed grid in the upper left quadrant of each map, are captured in the hottest part of the prospective map but not in the hot-spot map.

---

[4] The cell centroid is the point at, or *x* and *y* coordinates of, the exact centre of the grid square **for which a risk value is being derived.**
[5] This meant that only events within approximately 400 metres of each cell were considered here.

BOWERS ET AL.

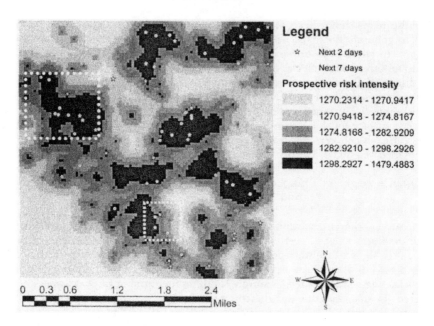

FIG. 2   Prospective hot-spot map using 50-metre grid squares (and the burglaries which
occurred within the next week)

Figure 4 shows another commonly used hot-spotting technique. The map has been
generated using police beats—an approach commonly employed by the police (see
Townsley and Pease 2002). Figure 4 uses the same data that were used to produce
Figures 2 and 3. In this case, however, the six police beats with the highest number of
burglaries occurring within them have been selected as hot spots. This technique does
not incorporate any temporal weighting of incidents; and uses pure counts of incidents
to determine high-risk areas. Consideration of Figure 4 suggests that there is some
overlap between the designated hot-spot areas and the location of consequent burglaries, but, on first sight, this map does not appear to be as accurate as the maps in
Figures 2 and 3.

So far, to compare the accuracy of these maps, we have simply plotted where subsequent burglaries occurred. As the procedure is only intended to be accurate for the
immediate future, we chose to plot data for the next two days and the next week. However, to evaluate the map using the procedures suggested above, further processing is
required. It is worth noting at this point that GIS packages usually only give the option
of producing raster or picture grid coverages, which merely allow the user to visually
inspect the relationship between other types of data and the grid. For the current
research, it was important to generate a vector grid that would allow the data sets to be
spatially related using the GIS. Thus, a FORTAN program was written to generate a vector grid. This was subsequently imported into the GIS.

Hence, using the spatial join command in the GIS, we were able to count how many
burglaries occurred within the 20 per cent of cells with the highest risk-intensity values.

PROSPECTIVE HOT-SPOTTING

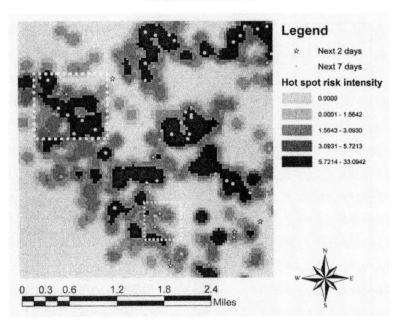

Fig. 3   Hot-spot map using 50-metre grid squares (and the burglaries which occurred within the next week)

Table 1 shows the results. Here, the percentage of incidents captured by the hot spots (or the simple hit rate) is given for each of the three maps shown in Figures 2, 3 and 4 above, along with the total area of hot-spot coverage (in metres-squared). It is clear from Table 1 that the prospective method (Figure 2) is more accurate than both the retrospective hot-spotting technique (Figure 3), particularly for predictions for the next two days. Specifically, the prospective map captured 62 per cent of the burglaries occurring in the next two days, whereas the retrospective map captured 46 per cent of these incidents. Here, compared to the retrospective model, the prospective model correctly predicted an additional 19 per cent of incidents. Expressed in a slightly different way, the prospective model was 35 per cent (= $16/46 \times 100$) more accurate. It is important to emphasize that the difference in the level of predictive accuracy for the prospective and retrospective techniques is greatest for predictions regarding the more immediate future (two days). The theory that underlies the prospective approach leads us to anticipate precisely this pattern, and, hence, the rationale for the technique is validated.

Table 1 also shows a calculation of the search-efficiency rate, which, as mentioned above, measures the number of crimes successfully predicted per square kilometre. The advantage of this measure is that it is standardized by area, and, hence, allows easy comparison between maps. The table shows the search efficiency rate for burglaries occurring in the two days following the map production. As with the simple hit rate, this measure shows that the prospective map is the most effective of the three using this criterion. It also emphasizes the inefficiency of the beat model compared to the other two hot-spotting procedures.

BOWERS ET AL.

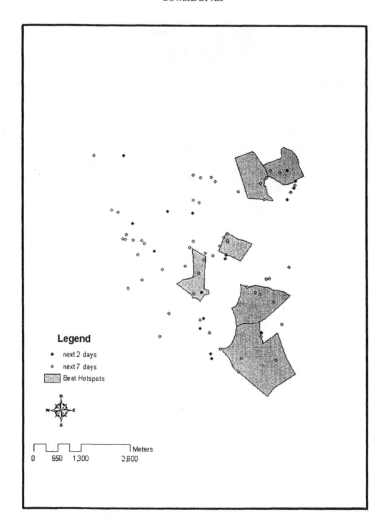

FIG. 4   Hot-spot map using police beats (and the burglaries which occurred within the next week)

TABLE 1   *Relative predictive accuracy of the different techniques*

	2 days (26)	1 week (70)	Area covered	Search efficiency (2 day per km²)*
Prospective	62%	64%	5,405,000	2.96
Retrospective	46%	56%	5,405,000	2.22
Beat	12%	24%	5,083,886	0.59

* Scaled by a factor of 1,000,000 to ease interpretation.

PROSPECTIVE HOT-SPOTTING

One point which requires further discussion is the specific procedure used to generate the retrospective hot spots. To standardize the comparisons between the prospective and retrospective methods, the same historic data were used for each technique. Thus, we used two months' historic data for every method. Since our past research has shown that victimization has an impact over 400 metres and for around two months, the algorithm used to generate the prospective maps weights each burglary event by the amount of time that elapsed since the event occurred and the date on which the map was produced. Retrospective hot-spot maps do not do this. However, because we only used two months' historic data here, this may increase the accuracy of the hot-spot maps, as events that occurred close in time (within two months) were effectively weighted in the analysis, as these were the only data points used. A second point is that, to generate the retrospective hot spot using the moving window technique, we used a bandwidth of 200 metres and an equation that weighted events on the basis of propinquity. The reason for using a bandwidth in retrospective hot-spotting is essentially to produce a smooth risk surface. As far as we are aware, there exists no (theoretical) reason for selecting this bandwidth other than the fact that it produces nice-looking maps. Thus, under the conditions in which we tested the retrospective hot-spotting techniques here, burglary events were essentially weighted both spatially and temporally. The reason for this, however, was entirely atheoretical. One way of testing the accuracy of the various methods more systematically would be to use longer periods of historic data, e.g. one year. Additionally, it will be necessary to repeat the current exercise using different geographical areas and different periods of time.

Area-to-perimeter ratios

As discussed above, an alternative and complementary index that may be used to evaluate hot-spot efficiency involves the comparison of the area and perimeter of the hot spots produced. Using the following method to calculate these ratios also results in the production of another simple measure that can be used in determining map efficiency, namely the number of hot spots produced by different hot-spot measures. To explain the area-to-perimeter ratio measure in more depth, let us take two examples:
1. In this case, the shape is long and thin; the area is 9 square units; the perimeter is 20 lengths:

☐ ☐ ☐ ☐ ☐ ☐ ☐ ☐ ☐

area/perimeter = 9/20 = 0.45.

2. Here, the shape is more compact; the area is still 9 square units but the perimeter is only 12 lengths:

☐ ☐ ☐
☐ ☐ ☐
☐ ☐ ☐

area/perimeter = 9/12 = 0.75.

The second of these shapes has a higher area-to-perimeter ratio and therefore may be seen as more efficient in operational policing terms, in that a patrolling journey of any given length will traverse a greater number of vulnerable places.

BOWERS ET AL.

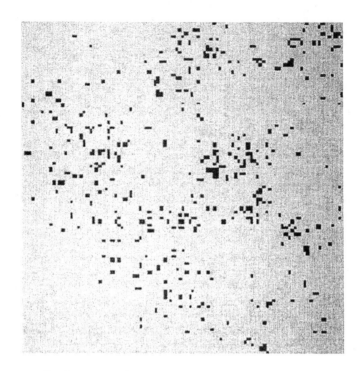

Fɪɢ. 5   Hot-spots from aggregating burglaries to grid squares

For the purposes of illustrating the area-to-perimeter ratio technique, a further form of hot-spot mapping is introduced here. Figure 5 shows the results of a simple grid aggregation using the same data as have been used in the production of the maps shown above. In this case, hot areas are identified by simply adding up the number of burglary offences that fall into each of the 50-metre grid squares. Every square that contains a burglary offence has been defined as a hot area in this case.

The two maps in Figures 2 and 5 look dramatically different. There are many more coloured grids in Figure 2 than in Figure 5 and the 'hot' grids are far less dispersed in Figure 2 than in Figure 5. It is useful to examine a refined version of Figure 2, which becomes more easily comparable with Figure 5 by selecting a subset of the 'hottest' squares—specifically, the top 447 of the 10,816 grid squares displayed. The reasons for selecting these cells are twofold: first, this displays an equal number of squares to those defined as hot from simply aggregating the burglary data (Figure 5), which enables easier visual comparison. Figure 6 is, therefore, directly comparable to Figure 5 in terms of the number of squares that it defines as hot. Secondly, this produces defined 'hot-spot' areas from the prospective map in Figure 2, which is necessary for the production of area-to-perimeter ratio calculations.

The next step is to identify the number and boundaries of distinct shapes or 'hot spots' shown in Figures 5 and 6. The figures themselves make this procedure look deceptively straightforward—to the beholder, the 'blobs' already look as if they are

PROSPECTIVE HOT-SPOTTING

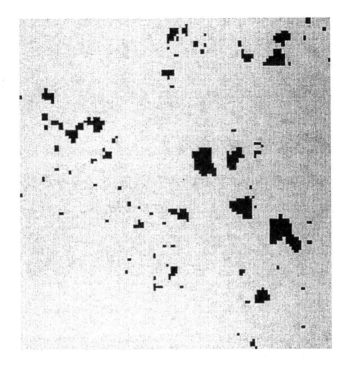

Fig. 6 Top 447 'hot grids' from prospective mapping function

distinct shapes. In reality, in the GIS, these are still a series of coloured grids that are sometimes located next to, but independent of, each other. We have not yet found a GIS function that enables us to define these as distinct shapes easily (it is possible to do this by manually digitizing the areas, but this is time-consuming and impractical for operational policing purposes). The only procedure we have found to date involves converting the information from the likes of Figures 5 and 6 to raster grids and then converting them back into shape (or vector) files! The disadvantage of this fairly clumsy procedure is that the resulting shapes are approximations (and not exact replications) of the hot spots in Figures 5 and 6 above. The advantage of the new representations is that they represent distinct shapes, and hence their areas and perimeters are known. Summary data for these are displayed as Table 2.

TABLE 2   *Summary area–perimeter (AP) statistics*

Map evaluation criteria	Prospective mapping function	Aggregate grid squares	Hot-spot function
Mean area	12,778 m^2	2,400 m^2	56,502 m^2
Mean perimeter	377 m	219 m	925 m
Number of hot spots	79	330	19
Mean AP ratio	19	10	51

A number of patterns are evident from Table 2. First, the prospective mapping technique identifies 79 discernible areas of high risk—considerably less than the number identified using the aggregate-grid-squares approach (330). However, the traditional hot-spotting method yielded a lower number of discernible areas than the prospective function (19). For operational policing, a smaller number of defined areas may offer an advantage, as these will be more manageable to visit and police. It is a certainty more practicable to distribute resources across 19 (or even 79) areas, rather than 330. Secondly, the mean area-to-perimeter ratio is almost twice as high for the prospective technique than it is for the aggregate grid squares, thereby indicating an operational advantage of this technique. However, the hot-spot function has a higher area-to-perimeter ratio than either of the other techniques. This indicates that the traditional hot-spot shapes, followed by the prospective shapes, are more 'efficient' in terms of the length that would need to be patrolled to cover the same area. The aggregate squares are not as efficient as the other two methods in these terms.

With the current models, therefore, the prospective model outperforms the other two by having a high search-efficiency rate. At present, the hot-spotting technique offers some advantage in terms of hot-spot shape efficiency. Interestingly, other prospective models, generated as part of the research but not reported here, yield different search-efficiency and shape-efficiency levels. Early indications suggest a reciprocal function linking the two indices of efficiency. In other words, increasing shape efficiency might decrease search efficiency and vice versa. More research is required to determine the nature of this relationship. However, in the meantime, it will suffice to say that it is likely that there will be a trade-off between the accuracy and the functionality of prospective maps, which will require the careful balancing of needs.

What Next?

This paper seeks to present a method of hot-spot designation which is distinctive in being event-derived, i.e. in being generated from individual crimes, rather than from areal crime rates. The closest it comes to previously suggested methods is with leading indicators. In one sense, the method uses each crime event as a leading indicator, modifying area predictions on the basis of individual risk—both the direct risk of repetition and referred risk to nearby places and imminent times. The results are very promising, in that the prospective method, crude as it is in not incorporating some known patterns of repetition, outperforms a traditional, more sophisticated method. Of particular interest is the fact that the superiority of the prospective approach is greatest in the two days following a crime event, which is the time horizon for which police briefings apply. The research needs now to develop by making comparisons with a wider range of conventional hot-spotting procedures, and by refinement to incorporate more dimensions of communicated crime risk.

On this last point, we know, for example, that the extent to which space–time clustering is evident varies across different types of area. For instance, space–time clustering is greatest in more affluent areas (Bowers and Johnson 2004a). Thus, it is likely that the manipulation of the parameters used in the modelling process will increase the predictive accuracy of the risk surface across different areas, available for refinement to release latent predictive power. The refinement of the algorithm for areas with different characteristics represents one of the next steps in this research.

PROSPECTIVE HOT-SPOTTING

There is further work to be done on assessing the optimum time periods and prospective algorithms in the production of the predictive-risk surfaces. For instance, maps could be produced using a year's historic data rather than two months', or inverse exponential weightings rather than reciprocal ones. Furthermore, there are important judgments to be made concerning the geographical area used to define the maps, as the use of different areas. And, the size of the grid squares that contribute to the definition of the prospective hot spots requires consideration.

We also aim to refine the technique further to increase its utility in operational policing. For instance, it would be useful to explore the advantages of generating a series of maps on a daily basis—one for each police shift. For each shift, this could be done by adding the previous shift's burglary incidents to the historic data and removing the data for the most historic shift and analysing the consequent data-set. Assuming a daily pattern of three shifts (daytime, evening and nighttime), doing this for, say, six shifts would allow a comparison of the maps generated for the equivalent shifts over two consecutive days. This would allow us to see whether the maps for different shifts showed similar trends or whether they differed. In the case of the former, this may mean that a single daily map would suffice for policing purposes. In the case of the latter, this would suggest that it would be wise to generate one map for each shift, in the way described.

A final comment on the prospective approach taken here is that it assesses risk at the direct neighbourhood level. This is distinct from concentrating solely at the level of the individual or of the community. There are direct advantages of this. For instance, it may help to realize the goal of neighbourhood-level crime prevention, which has largely eluded practitioners to date. It also balances the aims of identifying those most at risk and the need to minimize the geography that requires special attention. In relation to this point, traditionally, hot spots have been defined as larger areas. Part of the appeal of the prospective approach is that it offers the potential for within-hot-spot differentiation. In other words, it informs the allocation of police resources in terms of where to go within more traditional hot spots. Take two scenarios: in an undifferentiated hot spot, an officer might be able to visit n households at random; they might also to be able to visit the same number of households within prospective hot spots. However, it is likely that the ratio of visits/burglaries (for both historic burglaries and for future locations) will differ for the two approaches, as the latter areas will be defined by local levels of risk.

Notwithstanding the considerable research agenda which remains, we believe that a trial of the present system in police briefings is not premature. Indeed, in so far as operational experience will shape the research agenda, it seems urgent.

REFERENCES

BAILEY, T. C. and GATRELL, A. C. (1995), *Interactive Spatial Data Analysis*. Harlow: Longman.
BOWERS, K. J. and JOHNSON, S. D. (2004), 'Domestic Burglary Repeats and Space–Time Clusters: The Dimensions of Risk', *The European Journal of Criminology*, in press.
BROWN, P. J. B. (1991), 'Exploring Geodemographics', in I. Masser and M. Blakemore, eds, *Geographic Information Management: Methodology and Applications*, 221–58. London: Longman.
BRUNSDEN, C. (1995), 'Estimating Probability Surfaces for Geographical Points Data: An Adaptive Kernel Algorithm', *Computers and Geosciences*, 21: 877–94.
FARRELL, G. and PEASE, K. (2001), *Repeat Victimisation*. Monsey, NY: Criminal Justice Press.

GOODALL, B. (1987). *The Penguin Dictionary of Human Geography*. Harmondsworth, Middlesex: Penguin.

GORR, W. and OLLIGSCHLAEGER, A. (2002), *Crime Hot Spot Forecasting: Modelling and Comparative Evaluation*. Final Report to the National Criminal Justice Reference Service (NCJRS).

GROFF, E. R. and LAVIGNE, N. G. (2002), 'Forecasting the Future of Predictive Crime Mapping', in N. Tilley, ed., *Analysis for Crime Prevention (Crime Prevention Studies Vol. 13)*. Monsey, NY: Criminal Justice Press.

JEFFERIS, E. S. and MAMALIAN, C. A. (1998), *Crime Mapping Research Center's Hot Spot Project*. The Second Annual Crime Mapping Research Conference, December, Arlington, VA, USA.

JOHNSON, S. D. and BOWERS, K. J. (2004a), 'The Burglary as a Clue to the Future: The Beginnings of Prospective Hot-Spotting', *The European Journal of Criminology*, 1: 237–255.

JOHNSON, S. D. and BOWERS, K. J. (2004b), 'The Stability of Space–Time Clusters of Burglary', *British Journal of Criminology*, 44: 55–65.

PEASE, K. (1998), *Repeat Victimisation: Taking Stock*. Crime Detection and Prevention Series, Paper 90. Home Office: London.

RATCLIFFE, J. (2000), 'Aoristic Analysis: The Spatial Interpretation of Unspecific Temporal Events', *International Journal of Geographical Information Science*, 14(7): 669–79.

ROSSMO, D. K. (1999), *Geographic Profiling*. Washington, DC: CRC Press LLC.

TOWNSLEY, M. and PEASE, K. (2002), 'Hot Spots and Cold Comfort: The Importance of Having a Working Thermometer', in N. Tilley, ed., *Analysis for Crime Prevention (Crime Prevention Studies Vol. 13)*. Monsey, NY: Criminal Justice Press. Table 1: Percentage of burglaries correctly predicted using the three different hotspotting techniques (actual number of burglaries in parentheses).

[3]

RESIDENTIAL BURGLARY IN THE UNITED STATES: LIFE-STYLE AND DEMOGRAPHIC FACTORS ASSOCIATED WITH THE PROBABILITY OF VICTIMIZATION

LAWRENCE E. COHEN
DAVID CANTOR

This study both ascertains the characteristics of individuals and their life styles that are differentially related to risk of residential burglary and tests a hypothesis that accounts for certain discrepant findings reported in previous studies of burglary victimization. Using Goodman's log-linear technique to analyze (1975–76) National Crime Survey data, we find that 2,133 of 54,343 households in the sample were burglarized in a twelve-month reference period. The following types of persons headed households with greater than average odds of burglary victimization: (1) central city residents, (2) the young, (3) persons with incomes higher or lower than average, (4) nonwhites, and (5) persons whose homes are unoccupied relatively often. The types of persons heading households least likely to be burglarized were the following: (1) older citizens, (2) persons residing outside the central city, (3) citizens in middle-income categories, and (4) persons whose homes are occupied relatively often. In general, the data support Hindelang's hypothesis that differences in the findings of previous burglary studies on variations in the burglary rate for whites across income categories may be due to different sampling procedures.

A body of descriptive and quantitative data accumulating within the last decade describes the nature and distribution of burglary offenses, burglary offenders' social and psychological attributes, and the characteristics of census tracts and households most often selected as targets by burglars (Clinard and Quinney, 1973; Clarke, 1972; Chimbos, 1973; Conklin and Bittner, 1973; Scarr, 1973; Dunn, 1974; Reppetto, 1974; Pope, 1975). Although such information has proved useful for understanding the patterning of burglary incidents and for identifying characteristics common among burglary offenders and targets, survey data consistently indicate that some

---

LAWRENCE E. COHEN: Associate Professor, Sociology Department, University of Texas at Austin. **DAVID CANTOR**: Doctoral Candidate, University of Illinois at Urbana-Champaign.

This paper benefited considerably from the comments of James Kluegel and Kenneth Land. Funding for this study was provided by the following United States government grants: National Institute for Mental Health 1-R01-MH31117-01, and National Science Foundation, SOC-77-13261.

114   L. E. COHEN, D. CANTOR

of the most crucial determinants of burglary victimization rates relate closely to the characteristics and life styles of citizens (Ennis, 1967; Reppetto,
1974; Hindelang, 1976). Analyses of victimization data suggest that such
socioeconomic and demographic factors as income, race, and age are related
to role-structured behaviors, which, in turn, are differentially associated
with criminal victimization. Hence, the circumstances under which many
crimes (e.g., burglary) occur appear to be neither random nor trivial, but
are structurally significant phenomena that depend heavily on the spatio-
temporal organization of human activities (see Hindelang, Gottfredson, and
Garofalo, 1978; Cohen and Felson, 1979; Cohen, Felson, and Land, 1980).

Although the surveys that examine the offense of burglary consistently
report that variations in the likelihood of victimization are significantly related to citizens' socioeconomic and demographic characteristics, the directions of the relationships are not always in accord. This study will identify
the social and demographic characteristics of citizens that enhance or reduce burglary victimization risk. In addition, in an attempt to account for
some discrepant findings reported in previous studies of burglary victimization, we test the hypothesis that variations in findings are due to different
sampling frames.

PRIOR BURGLARY VICTIMIZATION RESEARCH

The number of systematic empirical studies of burglary victimization
is quite small. One of the most extensive investigations is Michael
Hindelang's (1976) analysis of data on common theft and assault victimizations in eight large American cities.[1] Thirty percent of the total household
victimization rate in this study was accounted for by burglary offenses.[2]
Among the victim characteristics substantially related to risk of burglary
for the eight-city aggregate, households headed by nonwhites had burglary
rates greater than the rates of households headed by whites, and this difference remained when income was controlled. In addition, the risk of burglary victimization increased with family income, but decreased markedly as
the age of the head of the household increased (Hindelang, 1976:291–292).
These findings with respect to the race, age, and income of burglary victims
are consistent with Reppetto's (1974:57–60) earlier but smaller victim survey conducted in the greater metropolitan Boston area.

A third victimization study that included burglary in its assessment of
offense patterns is the National Opinion Research Center survey reported

1. The eight cities are Atlanta, Baltimore, Cleveland, Dallas, Denver, Newark, Portland,
and St. Louis.
2. Hindelang's definition of burglary is identical to that used in this study. A household
burglary is defined here as a forcible entry into a residence, or an attempt to enter forcibly, or
an unlawful entry into such a premise without force. This crime is not necessarily attended by
theft.

RESIDENTIAL BURGLARY IN THE UNITED STATES 115

by Ennis (1967). Like Hindelang and Reppetto, Ennis (1967: Tab. 14) reported that burglary rates were higher for nonwhites than for whites. However, contrary to the findings reported in the other two studies, the NORC survey found burglary rates for whites to be inversely, rather than directly, related to income. Interestingly, Ennis reported that among the nonwhites in the sample, the rate of burglary for the highest-income category ($6,000 or more per year) was substantially greater than that recorded for two lower-income categories.

In brief, findings from these three studies are inconsistent with respect to the relationships among income, race, and risk of burglary victimization. Ennis's data suggest that among whites, the lowest-income groups are the most likely victims of burglary, while among nonwhites, the upper-income groups face the greatest risk of victimization. Hindelang and Reppetto do not report this interaction between race and income. Rather, they each observe the risk of burglary victimization to be directly related to income across racial categories. Hindelang (1976:294) explains the discrepancy among these findings by pointing out that the NORC survey is a national sample, while his and Reppetto's studies sample large urban areas:

> Given the correlation between extent of urbanization and rates of crime, it would be expected that high income whites in the suburbs are relatively isolated from burglary, while high income whites in the city are prime targets for burglary.

Studies of offenders' place of residence generally find that a disproportionate number of these persons reside in urban areas; and empirical evidence suggests that burglaries are most often committed by people who live near the scene of the burglary (Hindelang, 1976:294). Thus, suburban residents (typically white and wealthier than urban residents) are relatively isolated from offenders, while urban residences are well within striking distance of urban offenders. Hindelang also cites data for burglary showing that persons arrested for burglary are typically much younger than are persons arrested for other index offenses. If those engaging in burglary are disproportionately young persons, their mobility may be limited because of restricted access to automobiles. Since many of the items frequently taken from households during burglaries are bulky, youths engaging in this offense may concentrate their efforts on targets in or near their own neighborhoods (Hindelang, 1976:294).

In sum, Hindelang argues plausibly that high-income urban residents make good burglary targets because they live relatively close to areas in which a disproportionate number of burglary offenders are concentrated and because their homes are perceived by potential burglars to contain valuable property. Hindelang notes as well that proximity may also explain why, in his and Reppetto's studies, nonwhites with the lowest family incomes were found to have higher rates of burglary than whites (except for the highest-income category). Apparent affluence, Hindelang suggests, may

116   L. E. COHEN, D. CANTOR

play a role in the selection of targets secondary to ease of access (proximity).
Nonwhites with low family incomes are selected more often as targets for
burglary (in lieu of more affluent white households) because they are more
accessible to burglars, who appear to be disproportionately nonwhites (Hindelang, 1976:295).

Hindelang's explanation for this discrepancy is based on the assumption that both proximity and affluence have independent effects on the risk
of burglary victimization, and that proximity may have a stronger influence
on burglary risk than does affluence. Thus, his findings (and Reppetto's)
and Ennis's can be reconciled as follows: Lower-income whites in the national sample analyzed by Ennis have higher rates of burglary than higher-
income whites simply because they are much more likely to be near likely
offender populations than are high-income whites. Since blacks of all income levels are likely to be proximal to offender populations, proximity for
this group is in effect controlled, leaving affluence the sole effect to be
shown.

Interestingly, Hindelang's discussion also at least intimates that there
may be an interaction between proximity and affluence, such that affluence
has a stronger effect among the affluent who live closer to offender populations; that is, "high income whites in the city are prime targets for burglary" (p. 294). Clearly, then, prior research underscores the need to examine
the risk of burglary victimization within a multivariate framework, with
proximity as one variable.

Hindelang's hypothesis to account for the discrepant findings of burglary victimization studies has yet to be tested. An adequate test requires a
national probability sample of households, large enough to permit the simultaneous control of the factors substantially related to the risk of burglary victimization. The statistical technique needed to analyze these data
should allow for the determination of both the magnitude and direction of
relationships among variables, as well as the estimation of specific para-
metric effects for various population subgroups.

National Crime Survey (NCS) data are well suited to a test of
Hindelang's hypothesis, and log-linear models provide the multivariate
technique appropriate for uncovering systematic patterns among data in
cases where the analysis calls for the use of categorized dependent variables. Here we will use Goodman's (1972a, 1972b) procedure for log-linear
analysis to ascertain the risk of burglary victimization, simultaneously examining the effects of relevant life-style and demographic factors. If
Hindelang's hypothesis to account for the aforementioned discrepant findings in previous studies of burglary victimization is correct, then we should
expect to find that (1) high-income groups in general have a higher risk of
burglary victimization than lower-income groups; (2) central city residents
have a higher risk of burglary victimization than non–central city residents;
and (3) area type is a stronger predictor of burglary victimization than is
income.

RESIDENTIAL BURGLARY IN THE UNITED STATES 117

DATA AND METHODS

This study uses *NCS* data, collected by the Census Bureau for the Department of Justice, for 1975–76. The *NCS* samples the entire non-institutionalized population of the United States[3]; thus, our sample is more representative of the country than are most burglary victimization studies. Because of the relative rarity of burglary victimizations among certain subgroups of the population, most of the previous studies of burglary victimization have been limited in their attempts at multivariate analyses. The *NCS* sample size of approximately 60,000 households, in contrast, allows us to examine relationships among variables that cannot be studied with smaller surveys.

The *NCS* design and interviewing procedures, discussed at length elsewhere (see Penick and Owens, 1976), call for a panel study. For every person age twelve and over in selected households, social, demographic, and victimization data are obtained through six personal interviews. Each household is interviewed once every six months after an initial interview. This ensures that all individuals are reporting for periods completed between January and June of 1976. Approximately one-sixth of the sample were interviewed each month and asked about victimizations occurring during the six-month period before the month of the interview. Hence, this procedure produced reports of victimizations pertaining to July 1975 through June 1976.

Our review of prior burglary victimization studies indicates that age, race, income, and area type are the social and demographic risk factors that are strongly associated with the probability of burglary victimization. We will assess how these factors independently and jointly increase or reduce susceptibility to burglary victimization. We include a measure of household occupancy in our analysis because interviews with apprehended burglars indicate that they prefer to burglarize unoccupied places (Walsh, 1974:404; Reppetto, 1974:17); hence, assuming all other things to be equal, the greater the proportion of time a residence is occupied, the lower the risk of burglary.

Age of the household head is categorized as sixteen to twenty-nine, thirty to forty-nine, and fifty and older. Income, defined as total yearly family income, consists of four categories: less than $7,500, $7,500 to $14,999, $15,000 to $24,999, and $25,000 or more. Race, as a dichotomous variable, consists of whites and nonwhites.[4] Area type is classified as central

---

3. The structure of the *National Crime Survey* is a stratified multistage cluster sample of approximately 60,000 households selected from the entire nation. Its design closely resembles that of the *Current Population Survey,* which is also conducted by the Census Bureau.

4. The category of nonwhites consists of blacks and persons of other races who are not white, such as Asians. Persons of Spanish heritage are counted as white. Persons of racially mixed parentage are classified in their father's racial category. The race of the respondent is determined by observation for members of the same family and by inquiry for households with persons unrelated to the household head.

118   L. E. COHEN, D. CANTOR

city or "other,"[5] with households in areas not defined by the Census Bureau as central cities all included in the non–central city residual category labeled "other."[6] Finally, household occupancy is a dichotomous variable, indicating for each household in the sample whether there was at least one household member who did not go to school or engage in work at least fifteen hours per week (the United States Department of Labor's definition of part-time employment).[7] Households in which all persons were in the labor force (employed or looking for work), were going to school, or reported they were working (not necessarily for pay) away from the household for at least fifteen hours per week were classified in the "less occupied" household category. Households in which at least one person was unable to work, retired, keeping house, or participating in activities away from home for less than fifteen hours a week were classified in the "more occupied" category. Thus, if it were possible for at least one person to be home during the day for a total of fifteen hours per week, the household was classified as "more occupied." If not, it was classified as "less occupied."

ANALYSIS

Among our sample of 60,350 households, complete data were available for 54,343 homes, of which 2,133 were victimized by residential burglary during the period under analysis.[8] Table 1 presents the likelihood ratio chi-square statistics for the relationships among race, age, income, area type, household occupancy, and whether or not those sampled reported being the victim of a burglary during the twelve-month reference period.

The following analysis uses both a model-fitting and selection procedure to estimate effect parameters. The former procedure is used to select the most parsimonious model of the influence of these five factors on the

---

5. Central city is defined as an incorporated city (or cities) that is central to an urbanized area and/or a standard metropolitan statistical area. It is bounded by city limits. A central city or combined central cities must have a population of 50,000 or more. The difference between an urbanized area and SMSA is that the former excludes those places that are separated by rural territory and the densely populated fringe. An SMSA includes the entire county (or counties) in which it is located.

6. Two other city-type classifications were also tested here: (1) central cities of over 250,000, central cities of under 250,000, and other non-central cities, and (2) central cities and those non-central cities that did not include areas that were not defined by the Census Bureau as "a place." The results did not differ from those reported below. Since the former classification increased the size of our table substantially and created a large number of empty cells, we conducted this analysis without the household occupancy variable.

7. The interviewer did not ask the major activity of those persons twelve to fifteen years of age. For our analysis, we assumed that these persons were in school. Those persons who were unable to work were classified as not being away from home for at least fifteen hours a week.

8. Those households that did not have complete data on the variables used in this study were excluded from our analysis.

RESIDENTIAL BURGLARY IN THE UNITED STATES 119

risk of burglary victimization. The latter procedure estimates individual effects of each factor.

The large number of cases for which data were obtained make it possible to take a very general approach to answering the question of how the five factors affect the risk of burglary victimization. Specifically, we are able to consider both the simple additive (main) effects of each factor and the unique way in which these variables might interact to influence the risk of burglary victimization.

To begin, we constructed a six-way contingency table of race, by income, by age, by area type, by household occupancy, by whether or not a particular household was the target of a burglary in the twelve-month reference period. Data from this table were then used to estimate what is commonly termed the *saturated model* (Goodman, 1972a), so called because it is the most general: It includes terms for all main effects and interaction effects for the influence of the five independent factors and the risk of burglary victimization. We employ the conventional .05 level of significance when selecting the most parsimonious model for this crime.

Model H_1 in Table 1 indicates that when we test for the significance of the six-way interaction in the saturated model, we find it is not significant. This model, which eliminates the six-way interaction, yields a chi-

TABLE 1. Models and Likelihood Ratio Chi-Squares for Income (I), Race (R), Age (A), Household Occupancy (O), Area Type, (C) and Burglary (B)

Marginals[a]	χ^2	*df*	α
H_1 [IRAOB] [IRACB] [IROCB] [IAOCB] [RAOCB]	3.70	6	>.5
H_2 [IRB] [IAB] [IOB] [ICB] [RAB] [ROB] [RCB] [AOB] [ACB] [OCB]	51.44	63	>.5
H_3 [IAB] [RB] [OB] [CB]	71.87	81	>.5
H_4 [IB] [RB] [AB] [OB] [CB]	91.24	87	<.4
H_5 H_3 –[RB]	76.27	82	>.5
H_6 H_3 – [OB]	80.89	82	>.5
H_7 H_3 – [CB]	122.15	82	.003
H_8 H_4 – [IB]	137.24	90	<.002
H_9 H_4 – [RB]	96.41	88	<.3
H_{10} H_4 - [AB]	237.07	89	.000
H_{11} H_4 – [OB]	102.94	88	<.15
H_{12} H_4 – [CB]	142.98	88	.000

[a]All models fit the [IRAOC] marginal.

Note: .1 was added to every cell before computing every model.

120   L. E. COHEN, D. CANTOR

TABLE 2.   Coefficients of Partial Determinants for Two-Factor Interactions for Income (I), Race (R), Age (A), Household Occupancy (O), Area Type (C) with Burglary Victimization (B)

Model		Effect	χ^2	df	α	Coefficient of Partial Determination
H_{13}	$H_8 - H_4$	[IB]	46	3	.000	.31
H_{14}	$H_9 - H_4$	[RB]	5.17	1	<.02	.04
H_{15}	$H_{10} - H_4$	[AB]	145.83	2	<.01	.61
H_{16}	$H_{11} - H_4$	[OB]	11.76	1	<.01	.10
H_{17}	$H_{12} - H_4$	[CB]	51.74	1	<.01	.35

Note: .1 was added to every cell before computing every model.

square value of 3.70 with 6 degrees of freedom, which is not significant at the .05 level. Consequently, we may conclude that eliminating the six-way interaction from our model does not cause us to lose a great amount of power when describing the observed data. We next fit the model with all three-way interactions involving the dependent variable. Subtracting H_1 from H_2 yields a chi-square value of 47.74 with 57 degrees of freedom, which is not significant at the .05 level. This implies that all four- and five-way interactions that include the dependent variable are not statistically significant (see Table 1).

Model H_3 eliminates all three-way interactions except those that are significant (i.e., except the interaction involving income, age, and the dependent variable). This model implies a null hypothesis that the relationships involving the risk of burglary victimization and the variables of income-race, income-household occupancy, income-area type, race-age, race-household occupancy, race-area type, age-household occupancy, age-area type, household occupancy-area type are all nonsignificant at the .05 level. Subtracting Model H_2 from Model H_3 produces a chi-square value of 20.43 with 18 degrees of freedom, which allows us to accept this null hypothesis at the .05 level.

Table 1 indicates that, among all the models, Model H_3 is the most parsimonious. When we subtract Model H_3 from H_4, we obtain a chi-square value of 19.37 with 6 degrees of freedom, which is significant at our predesignated confidence level. Thus, the income-age interaction with the dependent variable is statistically significant at the .05 level. Similar interpretations can be made for the two-way interactions involving the variables of race, occupancy, area type, and the risk of burglary victimization when we compare Model H_3 with models H_5 through H_7.

Using Model H_4 as a baseline, we computed the coefficient of partial

RESIDENTIAL BURGLARY IN THE UNITED STATES 121

determination (CPD) (adjusted for degrees of freedom) in order to determine the overall (main) effects of the two-way interactions (Goodman, 1972a:1056–58) when all other independent variables are held constant. The larger the CPD, the greater the main effect of the independent variable on the risk of burglary victimization. Table 2 displays the CPD for each two-way interaction (H_{13} – H_{17}). This table indicates that the strongest predictor of burglary victimization among the independent variables is the age of the head of the household (.61), followed in turn by area type (.35), income (.31), household occupancy (.10), and race (.04).

To assess the direction of the effects of the variables contained in Model H_3, we estimated the standardized beta effect parameters. These coefficients represent the additive effects of each category of each independent variable on the odds of burglary victimization.[9] A positive coefficient indicates that, controlling for all other independent variables, there is a greater than average chance that the home of an individual falling in a designated category of an independent variable will be burglarized. A negative coefficient indicates a lower than average chance of having one's home burglarized. A coefficient of zero indicates no difference from the average risk. In Goodman's (1972a, 1972b) framework, a standardized coefficient is equal to the effect parameter divided by its standard error. For large samples, this coefficient is approximately normally distributed and can be used as a test statistic for determining the statistical significance of effect parameters.

Inspection of Table 3 indicates income to have a parabolic effect on the risk of burglary victimization. That is, the lowest- and highest-income categories among our sample appear to face the greatest risk of burglary victimization. The effect parameters in Table 3 show that those with family incomes of less than $7,000 (.84) and $25,000 or more (.68) per year have the highest risks of burglary victimization. Table 3 also demonstrates that as the age of the household head increases, the risk of burglary victimization decreases. Those age sixteen to twenty-nine (1.25) have the greatest chance of being burglarized, while those ages thirty to forty-nine (.19) have a slightly greater than average chance of being victimized by this crime. Finally, heads of households who are fifty or older (−2.29) have a much lower than average chance of being victimized by burglary, when all other independent variables are held constant.

The directions of the effects of race, household occupancy, and area type are each consistent with the findings of previous research on burglary victimization. Nonwhites (.59), less occupied households (.59), and residents of central cities (1.40) all have a greater than average chance of vic-

9. Technically speaking, when the beta effect parameters are being used, the dependent variable is actually the natural log of the odds ratio. However, since the former is a monotonic transformation of the latter, an increase in one implies an increase in the other.

122   L. E. COHEN, D. CANTOR

TABLE 3.   **Standardized Beta Effect Parameters for Model H₃, Age (A),
Race (R), Occupancy (O), Area Type (C), Income (I) with Burglary
Victimization (B)**

Independent Variables	Main Effects	3-Way Interactions		
Income		*16–29*	*30–49*	*50+*
$0–$7,500	.84	.43	.89	−1.53
$7,500–$14,999	−1.33	.01	−.17	.15
$15,000–$24,999	−1.07	−.18	−.36	.58
$25,000+	.68	−.08	−.10	.24
Age				
16–29	1.25			
30–49	.19			
50+	−2.29			
Race				
Nonwhite	.59			
White	−.59			
Major activity				
Less occupied	.59			
More occupied	−.59			
Area type				
Central city	1.40			
Other	−1.40			

Note: .1 was added to every cell before computing every model.

timization, compared with, respectively, whites, more occupied households,
and residents of other area types, when all independent variables are simultaneously controlled.

Inspection of the significant three-way interaction effect among income, age, and the risk of burglary victimization reveals that, in order of
relative magnitude, those aged thirty to forty-nine with incomes of less than
$7,500 per year (.89) face higher than average odds of burglary victimiza-
tion, as do (1) those fifty or older with incomes of $15,000 to $24,999 (.58),
(2) sixteen to twenty-nine year olds with incomes of less than $7,500 per
year (.43), (3) those who are fifty or older with incomes of $25,000 or more
per year (.24), and heads of households fifty or older whose family income
is between $7,500 and $14,999 (.15).

The following three-way interaction characteristics were found to be
related to lower than average odds of burglary victimization: (1) age fifty or

RESIDENTIAL BURGLARY IN THE UNITED STATES   123

older with a family income of less than $7,500 per year (−1.53), (2) age thirty to forty-nine with a family income of $15,000 to $24,999 (−.36), (3) age sixteen to twenty-nine with a family income of $15,000 to $24,999 (−.18), (4) age thirty to forty-nine with a family income of $7,500 to $14,999 (−.17), (5) age thirty to forty-nine with an income of $25,000 or more per year (−.10), and (6) age sixteen to twenty-nine with an income of $25,000 or more per year (−.08). Finally, households headed by a person between the ages of sixteen and twenty-nine with a family income of $7,500 to $14,999 (.01) face an approximately average risk of burglary victimization. We will discuss these significant three-way interaction effect findings more systematically in the following section.

SUMMARY AND CONCLUSIONS

As we have previously indicated, if Hindelang's hypothesis is correct and does indeed account for the discordant research findings, than we should expect to find the following: (1) high-income groups in general to have a higher risk of burglary victimization than lower-income groups, (2) central city residents to have a higher risk of burglary victimization than non–central city residents, and (3) area type to be a stronger predictor of burglary victimization than is income.

Our analysis, for the most part, supports Hindelang's hypothesis. Specifically, central city residents have rates of burglary victimization considerably higher than those of non–central city residents, and area type (CPD = .35) is a stronger predictor of burglary victimization than is income (CPD = .31). However, although it is true that our highest-income group had a greater than average risk of burglary victimization, our lowest-income category had the highest risk of all income groups. The data indicate that the relationship between income and risk of burglary victimization is parabolic for both central city and other areas. The poorest and wealthiest citizens in both the central cities and the outlying areas have the greatest risk of burglary victimization among the four income categories employed in this study. Except for this deviation in the findings, Hindelang's hypothesis does appear to clear up the discrepant findings of previous burglary victimization studies.

Although there are many possible post hoc interpretations of the finding that income has a parabolic effect on the risk of burglary victimization for both the central cities and other areas, perhaps the most plausible is that there are at least two different types of burglars operating in the United States. For one group, proximity may be the most important factor in the selection of burglary targets. A disproportionate number of these burglars could reside in the low-income areas of central cities and outlying areas, and capitalize on situational opportunities to burglarize the very poor, who reside close to or within the same neighborhoods. On the other hand, there

124   L. E. COHEN, D. CANTOR

may also be a group of more professional burglars for whom affluence is the most important criterion in the selection of burglary targets. These burglars may prey upon the very rich in both the central city and other areas.

This interpretation could also account for the significant three-way interaction among age of head of household, income, and risk of burglary victimization. For example, young, poor burglars who reside in disproportionate numbers in low-income areas may capitalize on opportunities to burglarize the poor, relatively young residents who live in or near their neighborhoods, and who often possess items either coveted by the young or easily convertible into cash. The finding that those fifty or over in higher-income groups have substantially higher odds of victimization than do those of this age category who are in the lowest-income category may, in turn, indicate that these persons are more likely to be victimized by professional burglars for whom affluence is the most important criterion in target selection.

The findings obtained from our national sample (with respect to the parabolic relationship between income and burglary victimization) differ from those reported in the NORC survey. This difference most likely results from our use of more controls than were employed by Ennis in the NORC study. Presumably, had Ennis used the same controls, he would have uncovered a similar relationship.

We indicated previously that the descriptive literature on burglary offenders consistently reports that finding an empty dwelling is of considerable importance to burglars when selecting victims. The importance of occupancy in the selection of burglary targets is illustrated among our sample in several ways. First, our analysis has determined that what we defined as less occupied households were more likely to be burglarized than were households we defined as more occupied. Second, although household occupancy patterns are difficult to estimate with these data, we believe that the relationship between the age of the head of the household and the risk of burglary victimization provides additional support for the importance of the occupancy factor.

For example, on the basis of offender interviews cited earlier, it is logical to assume that, all other things being equal, the greater the proportion of time a household is unoccupied, the greater the probability that it will be burglarized. The reader will recall that the CPD values obtained from our analysis demonstrate that, with all other factors equal, the age of the household head is the strongest determinant of the risk of burglary victimization. The standardized beta effect parameters further indicate that our youngest age cohort (sixteen to twenty-nine) has the highest risk of burglary victimization, while our oldest category (fifty or older) contains the least likely targets, and those in the middle age category (thirty to forty-nine) have odds of being victimized that are just slightly above average.

The fact that burglary decreases as the age of the head of the household increases was also reported by both Reppetto and Hindelang. In our

RESIDENTIAL BURGLARY IN THE UNITED STATES 125

judgment, this finding could be interpreted as illustrating the importance of occupancy patterns as a determinant of the selection of burglary targets by potential offenders. Indeed, age may be a better indicator of household occupancy than is the occupancy variable employed in our analysis. For example, it is well established that younger people spend considerably more time outside the household than do older citizens (Census Bureau, 1973). The reader will also recall that the age category of fifty or over had the lowest standardized beta effect parameter (-2.29) of all the categories of the variables employed in this study, indicating that persons in this group had a lower risk of victimization than any other category of individuals used in this analysis. Hence, it is quite plausible that, because older citizens spend more time at home than do others, they deter burglars from selecting them as targets.

Our analysis reveals the following profile of the person most likely to be burglarized: a central city resident who is young, poor or wealthy, nonwhite, and frequently away from home. On the other hand, the person least likely to be burglarized is an older citizen, who resides outside the central city, who is in a middle-income category, and whose home is relatively likely to be occupied. Even though direct policy implications are not easily derivable from this analysis, these data suggest that the key to a reduction in burglary rates may be tighter social organization of neighborhoods, whereby residents pool their resources to increase guardianship of their own property and that of their neighbors. Reppetto (1974:86–87) found those neighborhoods with the lowest burglary rates to (1) manifest strong territorial concern, as in tightly knit ethnic neighborhoods, (2) have residences with limited access available to nonresidents, in which physical impediments (e.g., gates, guards, closed-circuit television) prevent outsiders from easy entry until they pass a security check, and (3) be removed from the urban core areas (unless those core areas are comparatively affluent). Although the latter two characteristics are not feasible means of preventing burglary in high-crime areas, the first is a remote possibility. Reppetto (1974:87), for example, believes that it may be possible to cut burglary rates by modifying environmental characteristics to heighten surveillance capabilities and also by encouraging a sense of neighborhood concern among residents. If citizens were educated to feel a sense of commitment and a responsibility to alert police to suspicious activities, this might deter the prospective burglar. According to Reppetto, this program would not require much change in "the existing scheme of things," but it might form the basis for an effective model of crime control (Reppetto, 1974:87).

Although such a program may or may not be effective, knowledge about who is most likely to be victimized by burglars, and where and when these crimes most often occur, can have important implications for public education, police patrol strategies, and environmental engineering (Hindelang, 1976:417). Dissemination of such information may, at a minimum, educate citizens so that they may take protective measures in order to deter

126   L. E. COHEN, D. CANTOR

burglars more effectively. Indeed, as more complete and specific data become available, the understanding of burglars' behavior may ultimately lead to a program that effectively curtails this crime.

REFERENCES

CHIMBOS, P. D.
   1973   "A Study of Breaking and Entering Offenses in 'Northern City,' Ontario."
          Canadian Journal of Criminology and Corrections 15: 316–325.

CLARKE, S. H.
   1972   *Burglary and Larceny in Charlotte-Mecklenburg: A Description Based on
          Police Data.* The Mecklenburg Criminal Justice Planning Council.
          Chapel Hill: University of North Carolina, Institute of Government.

CLINARD, M. B., and R. QUINNEY
   1973   *Criminal Behavior Systems: A Typology,* 2d ed. New York: Holt, Rinehart
          and Winston.

COHEN, L. E., and M. FELSON
   1979   "Social Change and Crime Rate Trends: A Routine Activity Approach."
          American Sociological Review 44 (4): 588–608.

COHEN, L. E., M. FELSON, and K. C. LAND
   1980   "Property Crime Rates in the United States: A Macrodynamic Analysis,
          1947–77, with *ex ante* Forecasts for the Mid-1980's." *American Journal of
          Sociology* 86 (1): 90–118.

CONKLIN, J. E., and E. BITTNER
   1973   "Burglary in a Suburb." *Criminology* 11 (2): 206–232.

DUNN, C. S.
   1974   "The Analysis of Environmental Attribute/Crime Incident Characteristic
          Interrelationships." Ph.D. diss., School of Criminal Justice, State University of New York at Albany.

ENNIS, P. H.
   1967   *Criminal Victimization in the United States: A Report of a National Survey,* Field Surveys II. Washington, D.C.: Govt. Printing Office.

GOODMAN, L. A.
   1972a "A General Model for the Analysis of Surveys." *American Journal of Sociology* 77 (6): 1035–1086.

   1972b "A Modified Multiple Regression Approach to the Analysis of
          Dichotomous Variables." *American Sociological Review* 37 (1): 28–46.

HINDELANG, M. J.
   1976   *Criminal Victimization in Eight American Cities: A Descriptive Analysis
          of Common Theft and Assault.* Cambridge, Mass.: Ballinger.

HINDELANG, M. J., M. GOTTFREDSON, and J. GAROFALO
   1978   *Victims of Personal Crime.* Cambridge, Mass.: Ballinger.

PENICK, B. K. E., and M. E. B. OWENS, III, eds.
   1976   *Surveying Crime.* Washington, D.C.: National Academy of Sciences.

RESIDENTIAL BURGLARY IN THE UNITED STATES 127

POPE, C. E.
1975 "Dimensions of Burglary: An Empirical Examination of Offense and Offender Characteristics." Ph.D. diss., School of Criminal Justice, State University of New York at Albany.

REPPETTO, T. A.
1974 *Residential Crime.* Cambridge, Mass.: Ballinger.

SCARR, H.
1973 *Patterns of Burglary,* 2d ed. Washington, D.C.: Govt. Printing Office.

UNITED STATES BUREAU OF THE CENSUS
1973 *Who's Home When?* Washington, D.C.: Govt. Printing Office.

1976 *National Crime Survey—National Sample Survey Documentation.* Washington, D.C.: Govt. Printing Office.

WALSH, M.
1974 "A Study of the Fence and How He Operates." Ph.D. diss., School of Criminal Justice, State University of New York at Albany.

[4]

The Rational and the Opportunistic Burglar

Paul. F. Cromwell, James N. Olson and D'Aunn Wester Avary

There were substantial differences between our findings and those of previous research efforts in several critical areas. Unlike in previous research, our informants were "free world" active burglars. We interviewed them in their own social and physical environment and we went with them to reconstruct their past crimes. We found important variations between what they initially told us (in the relatively structured interview setting of Session 1) about the process of selecting a target and committing a burglary, and what they actually did when presented with a field simulation. For instance, during Session 1 many informants specified the attributes of a desirable burglary target and discussed the manner in which they would case, probe, and ultimately commit a hypothetical burglary. However, when subsequently visiting sites of burglaries they had previously committed, the characteristics of the target sites and the techniques used to burglarize those targets were seldom congruent with the completely rational approach they had reconstructed during the earlier interview. The sites, more often than not, were targets of opportunity rather than purposeful selections. There were three common patterns: (a) The burglar happened by the potential burglary site at an opportune moment when the occupants were clearly absent and the target was perceived as vulnerable (open garage door, windows, etc.); (b) the site was one that had been previously visited by the burglar for a legitimate purpose (as a guest, delivery person, maintenance worker, or other such activity); (c) the site was chosen after "cruising" neighborhoods searching for a criminal opportunity and detecting some overt or subtle cue as to vulnerability or potential for material gain.

RATIONAL RECONSTRUCTION

Most of our burglar informants could design a textbook burglary. During Session 1 they often described their past burglaries as though they were rationally conceived and executed. Yet upon closer inspection, when their previous burglaries were reconstructed, textbook procedures frequently gave way to opportunity and situational factors. This phenomenon might be termed *rational reconstruction.*

We suggest that research reporting that a high percentage of burglars make carefully planned, highly rational decisions based upon a detailed evaluation of environmental cues may be in error. Our findings indicate that burglars interviewed in prison or those recalling crimes from the past, either consciously or unconsciously, may engage in rational reconstruction—a reinterpretation of past behavior through which the actor recasts activities in a manner consistent with "what should have been" rather than "what was." This phenomenon is no different than what might be observed after asking a police officer how he or she conducts an interrogation. Most will respond in a manner consistent with departmental policy and procedures. However, in a real-life situation, the officer may have developed procedures of his or her own and may utilize techniques gained on the streets or learned from fellow officers rather than those learned in the police academy. If a researcher wishes to know how police officers conduct interrogations, real-life observations will provide more valid data than interviews. The same is true for understanding burglars and how they function.

We found substantial differences between the information obtained during the office interview during Session 1 and what the informants actually did before, during, and after their real burglaries. Few burglars would initially admit to being opportunistic. Professionalism, creativity, and inventiveness are valued attributes among burglars, and simple opportunism is not consistent with the self-image of most burglars. Past criminal events tend to be remembered as though committed in a manner consistent with their self-image.

This is not a matter of lack of knowledge about the techniques of burglary or the ability to discriminate between vulnerable and risky targets. Most burglars, even novices, appear to know how to discriminate a vulnerable residence from one that is less vulnerable. As seen in Table 4.1, the informants successfully discriminated target sites that had been previously burglarized by other burglars from those that were designated as high risks by other burglars.

Table 4.1 High Risk Versus Previously Hit Burglary Ratings

Site	At present (now)	Assuming no one is home	Assuming no one is home and $250 cash is inside
		Hypothetical Circumstances	
High risk	2.12 (135)	4.31 (117)	5.36 (109)
Previously hit	3.72 (136)	5.93 (114)	7.01 (106)
	$F(1,249) = 17.09$	$F(1,213) = 10.41$	$F(1,199) = 12.08$
	$p < .05$	$p < .05$	$p < .05$

The individual burglary attractiveness ratings (means) of burglars alone under the circumstances that actually prevailed at the time of the site inspection (now) and hypothetical circumstances for high risk and previously hit sites. The number of individual ratings from which each mean was obtained is given in parentheses. The results of two-sample tests comparing high risk and previously hit means are given below.

Control subjects ($n = 20$) also rated the previously burglarized and high risk sites. Table 4.2 reveals that they, too, could discriminate between more vulnerable and less vulnerable targets. They did, however, generally rate the sites higher (more vulnerable) than did the actual burglars. This is most likely attributable to the burglars' experience in discriminating risk cues relating to occupancy; in the hypothetical situations (assuming no one is at home) the ratings of control subjects generally did not consistently discriminate high risk from previously hit targets.

Although data from the control subjects indicate that novices can discriminate between vulnerable and less vulnerable targets about as well as burglars, it is doubtful that they know how a "proper" burglary should be conducted. On the other hand, our informants, including the least experienced, were capable of describing how a rationally conceived burglary would be planned and conducted. This is probably the result of information shared on the streets and in jails and reformatories.

ROUTINE ACTIVITIES

Our study concludes that a completely rational model of decision making in residential burglary cannot be supported. Rather, the study

Table 4.2 High Risk Versus Previously Hit Burglary Ratings for Controls

Site	At present (now)	Hypothetical Circumstances	
		Assuming no one is home	Assuming no one is home and $250 cash is inside
High risk	3.20 (359)	5.13 (358)	6.12 (359)
Previously hit	4.77 (251)	5.78 (270)	6.38 (263)
	$t(608) = 7.05$ $p < .05$	$t(626) = 2.80$ $p < .05$	$t(620) = 0.87$ $-p > .05$

The individual burglary attractiveness ratings (means) of control subjects under the circumstances that actually prevailed at the time of the site inspection (now) and hypothetical circumstances for high risk and previously hit sites. The number of individual ratings from which mean was obtained is given in parentheses. The results of two-sample tests comparing high risk and previously hit means are given below.

tends to support a *limited rationality* model; specifically Cohen and Felson's (1979) concept of "routine activities." *Routine activities* is an opportunity theory that holds that normal movement and activities of both potential victims and potential offenders play a role in the occurrence of the criminal event. Cohen and Felson link criminal events to the interaction of three variables:

(1) the presence of motivated offenders,
(2) the availability of suitable targets, and
(3) the absence of capable guardians.

When these variables converge, there is a greater likelihood that a crime will occur.

Routine activities theory has been used to explain the rise in crime rates over the past 30 years. The authors conclude that the number of caretakers (guardians) at home during the day has decreased because more women are participating in the work force, leaving a greater percentage of homes unguarded during the day. With the decline of the traditional neighborhood, other guardians (friends, neighbors) have dwindled. Furthermore, the supply of marketable, easily transportable goods (jewelry, TVs, VCRs) has increased, making the volume of available targets much greater. With the coming of age of the baby boomers between 1960 and 1980, there was an increase of the number of motivated offenders and thus an increase in the predatory crime rate (Siegel, 1989).

Routine activities theory focuses on the life-styles of both offenders and victims. Cohen and Felson (1979) found that time spent away from home was significantly related to the level of crime. Activities away from home increase the level of interaction between victim and criminal and thereby the probability that a criminal event will occur (Lab, 1988). Time spent in activities away from home also leaves the home unguarded, increasing the probability that the home will be burglarized.

The normal activities of criminals also affect crime rates. Offenders are more likely to commit crimes if their daily activities bring them into contact with potential victims. When questioned as to how a particular residence was selected as a burglary target, the responses given by informants were frequently consistent with routine activities theory.

Jesse, a professional burglar, stated:

When I was younger I used to ride my bicycle over to the skating rink. If I saw a house that I liked while I was coming to the rink, I'd do it [burglarize] on the way home.

Ramon, Jesse's co-offender, explained his approach to target selection:

When I'm going to work or over to a friend's house or someplace, I keep my eyes out for a good place to hit. I've been watching this one house on my way to work for a couple of weeks.

Debbie explained her reason for choosing a particular neighborhood to commit a large number of burglaries:

These people out here [lower middle-class neighborhood] don't have much money. You know the wives got to work and there aren't hardly any of them home during the day. I come out here about 9:00 [a.m.] and have the whole neighborhood to myself.

Stefan, an experienced burglar, described another neighborhood:

This neighborhood is full of families with kids in elementary school. I don't do this part of town in the summer. Too many kids playing around. But now [February] the best time to do crime out here is between 8:00 and 9:00 [a.m.].

All the mothers are taking the kids to school. I wait until I see the car leave. By the time she gets back, I've come and gone.

Quantitative Support for Routine Activities Theory

To partially validate the ethnographic data supporting routine activities, we compared 300 previously burglarized residences to 300 residences with no official record of having been burglarized. Each residence was evaluated in terms of its attributes on variables relevant to routine activities theory: distance from the residence to the nearest corner, and distance from the residence to the nearest stop sign, traffic light, school, commercial business establishment, park, church, and four-lane street. Other variables included the number of lanes of traffic in front of the residence, the average speed of traffic in front of the residence, and the presence or absence of a garage or carport.

Table 4.3 displays the results of the stepwise discriminant analysis performed to determine which variables best discriminated between the burglarized and nonburglarized sites. The resulting discriminant function accounted for over 50% of the variability between burglarized and nonburglarized residences and correctly classified 90.5% of the burglarized residences and 80% of the nonburglarized targets. Separate Pearson correlations indicated that the slower the traffic in front of the residence and the closer the residence was located to a school, church, corner, stop sign/light, or four lane street (other than a four lane business street), the greater the likelihood the residence would be burglarized. The presence or absence of a garage was also a discriminating variable. Residences with no garage or those with open carports were more likely to be burglarized than those with a garage. Our informants explained that it was easier to discern whether someone was at home when they could easily observe if there was a car parked at the site, indicating that the resident was home.

These results tend to suggest that as burglars go about their everyday activities, traveling to and from activity hubs such as school, work, and recreational facilities, they come into contact with residential sites near those facilities. Residences on or near their transportation routes (four lane streets) are also potential burglary targets. When burglars stop at a traffic light or stop sign they have a brief opportunity to view the sites nearby and may choose a potential target during those moments. It is possible that this (rather than the surveillance explanation) accounts for the disproportionate selection of corner houses as burglary targets.

Table 4.3 Burglarized Versus Nonburglarized Residences

Stepwise discriminant analysis among physical attributes related to whether a residence was burglarized. The .05 criterion level was used for inclusion in the analysis.

Attributes	Correlation within the stepwise discriminant function	Separate Pearson correlations with burglarization	Significance of separate Pearson correlations
Distance to school[a]	.66	.57	$p < .05$
Driving speed[a]	.47	.27	$p < .05$
Distance to four lane[a]	.41	.41	$p < .05$
Garage absent[a]	.33	.37	$p < .05$
Distance to business[a]	−.18	−.03	$p > .05$
Assessed value	—	.25	$p < .05$
Carport absent	—	.18	$p < .05$
Distance to corner	—	.14	$p < .05$
Distance to stop sign	—	.14	$p < .05$
Distance to church	—	.08	$p < .05$
Distance to park	—	.01	$p > .05$
Number of street lanes in front	—	−.13	$p < .05$

a. These five variables entered the discriminant function that accounted for over 50% of the variation between burglarized and nonburglarized sites with a Wilks' lambda of .49 (X^2 (5) = 429.83, $p < .01$) and correctly classified 90.5% of the burglarized sites and 80% of the nonburglarized sites.

Thirty-nine percent of the burglarized houses were located on a corner. Approximately 25% of the houses studied were corner houses.

OPPORTUNITY AND BURGLARY

Although the professional burglars among our informants tended to select targets in a purposive manner, analyzing the physical and social characteristics of the environment and choosing targets congruent with the template developed from experience, by far the greater proportion of the informants were opportunistic. The targets they chose appeared particularly vulnerable—at the time. Thus most burglaries in the jurisdiction studied appeared to result from the propitious juxtaposition of target, offender, and situation.

An opportunistic burglar is not necessarily an amateur. Selecting targets by completely rational processes does not alone differentiate the

skilled (professional or journeyman burglar) from the novice or amateur. As stated earlier, opportunism does not necessarily imply lack of
rationality. A burglar may make a completely rational decision to take
advantage of certain criminal opportunities when they arise or to seek
out or even create opportunities in a systematic manner.

TYPOLOGIES OF BURGLARS

Bennett and Wright (1984) found three categories of burglars: planners, searchers, and opportunists. The *planner* selects a target well in
advance of the offense; the *searcher* reconnoiters an area seeking out a
suitable target; and the *opportunist* responds "there and then" to an
attractive set of environmental cues—for example, an open garage door
at a site that is apparently unoccupied at the precise time the potential
burglar arrives on the scene. Bennett and Wright concluded that only
7% of their sample of 117 burglars were opportunists. They found it
"surprising that so few offenders mentioned committing opportunistic
crimes" (p. 44), and suggested that their limited definition of "opportunistic" and the age and experience level of their sample might account
for the small number of opportunistic burglars.

We chose a broader definition of *opportunist,* one that incorporated
two of Bennett and Wright's categories: searcher and opportunist. The
searcher takes advantage of sought out opportunities and the opportunist responds to presented opportunities. We considered burglars in both
categories to be opportunists. The opportunist may commit the burglary
immediately after searching the target or may wait until the situation is
more advantageous for the commission of a criminal act. Bennett and
Wright (1984) delineated between the searcher and opportunist categories on the basis of the elapsed time between perception of the criminal
opportunity and commission of the crime. The searcher allowed time to
pass between locating a target and committing the burglary (presumably
for planning purposes); the opportunist committed the burglary there
and then. With the exception of very inexperienced juveniles, few
burglars (and none in our sample) fit the Bennett and Wright (1984)
definition of opportunistic. Whether or not a burglar waits and plans
after site selection appears to be determined more by the immediate
situation than by his or her orientation as opportunistic or planner (or
irrational versus rational).

Opportunism, by our definition, turns on the target selection process, not on the time between selection and commission of the burglary. A rational process might well necessitate taking advantage there and then of a particular juxtaposition of situational factors. For example, while reconstructing a past burglary, Ramon stated:

I saw this place one day when I was cruising looking for a place to hit. It looked perfect, but it was too big to do alone. I needed a posse [gang of burglars]. I got me three other dudes and went back about a week later and did it.

He explained that the house appealed to him because of the apparent affluence of the residents, the secluded location of the house on the lot, and an unlocked garage door. However, the house was very large and could be approached from several directions. He feared that without lookouts and extra persons to search once inside, the risk would be too great. His decision to burglarize the site was an opportunistic one, although his process was that of a planner. Several other prior burglaries reconstructed by the same individual were purely opportunistic. In one instance, he "happened by" a vulnerable target while on his way home from a party. The site was vulnerable right then. He committed the burglary with no further planning than to probe briefly to determine whether the house was occupied. Although unquestionably opportunistic, the burglary was nonetheless rational: The site was unoccupied, a window was open, and the neighborhood appeared to be deserted. He could not have expected to find a more advantageous set of circumstances than those that were presented there and then.

Exploiting opportunity characterized the target selection processes in over 75% of the burglaries reconstructed during our research. Even professional burglars among our informants often took advantage of presented opportunities when they arose. Chance opportunities occasionally presented themselves while the professional was casing and probing potential burglary targets chosen by more rational means. When these opportunities arose, the professional burglar was as likely as other burglars to take advantage of the situation.

Our subjects can be placed along a continuum, with the novice burglar at one pole, the professional at the other, and the journeyman near the center.

The novice is at the beginning of his or her career as a burglar or a juvenile who commits one or more burglaries and then desists. The novice frequently learns from older, more experienced burglars in the same neighborhood. These older burglars are often relatives, frequently older siblings. The novice is usually initially allowed to go along with the older burglars, acting as the "lookout" for the older youth. As the novice learns the techniques of burglary, he or she may become a permanent member of the older group of burglars or may take the knowledge gained from the older group back to his or her own peer group and begin committing burglaries with the younger group without continued supervision from the older burglars.

A major determinant of whether the novice stays with the older group or returns to his or her own age cohort is whether he or she can locate and develop a market for the property obtained from burglaries (see Chapter 5, "Developmental Processes of Drug Use and Burglary" for a more detailed discussion). Older mentors, who teach novices the techniques of burglary, often conceal the identity of their fences. Until younger burglars can find a regular market for their stolen property, they have to depend on the older burglar. Even when they go out on their own they must rely on their mentors to sell the property for them (and pay a fee or a percentage of the gains). Once the market is established, however, the novice may advance along the continuum toward the journeyman level. Four of the informants in the present study were novice burglars.

Once an individual has mastered the technical and organizational skills, made the requisite contacts for marketing stolen property, and developed what Sutherland (1937) called a "larceny sense," he or she may be considered a *journeyman* burglar. The journeyman category corresponds roughly to Shover's (1971) "serious thief." Journeymen are experienced, reliable burglars. The burglary style of the journeyman burglar is marked by a preference for searching out or creating opportunities, much like the searcher category identified by Bennett and Wright (1984) and the suburban burglar studied by Rengert and Wasilchick (1985). Rather than waiting for criminal opportunities to present themselves during ordinary daily activities, the journeyman searches out or creates opportunities. Selecting a community or neighborhood in which he or she feels comfortable, the burglar cruises around looking for a target site that looks vulnerable. The burglar may plan the act by casing the site for a period of a few hours to several days to assess the ease or difficulty of access and egress. Assistance in the form of additional persons may be necessary and the burglar may require time to put a team together. He or she may also determine that the situation and circumstances make a there-and-then hit advantageous and commit the crime immediately after target selection. In our study, 21 of the informants were classified as journeymen.

Professional burglars constitute the elite of the burglary world. They are differentiated from the other categories by the level of their technical skill, their organizational abilities, and the status accorded them by peers and generally by law enforcement authorities. Professionals do no usually commit crimes of opportunity. They plan and execute their crimes with deliberation. They have excellent contacts for disposing of stolen merchandise. They may or may not be drug addicts. Drug addiction does not preclude the designation *professional*. The primary difference between the professional and the journeyman burglar is the status accorded to each. Their status is recognized and accepted by others (other thieves, law enforcement, fences, etc.), and they are accorded "respect" befitting that status. Five of the informants in our study were considered professional burglars.

SUMMARY

We found considerable disparity between what burglars divulged in interviews during Sessions 1 and 2, and what they actually did while committing their crimes. We suggest that prior research, which involved interviewing burglars in prisons, jails, or in probation and parole settings, may have arrived at erroneous conclusions based upon misleading information supplied by the informants. We use the term *rational reconstruction* to describe the tendency of burglars (and other persons) to describe past events as though they were performed in the ideal or proper fashion. Our research technique, staged activity analysis, was devised to overcome this problem. The data we obtained through the use of this design should be more reliable and valid than data obtained from interviews alone. We concluded that burglars are less rational (and more opportunistic) than indicated by most previous research.

51a

References

Bennett, T., and Wright, R. (1984), 'Burglars on Burglary: Prevention and the Offender', Aldershot: Gower Publishing..

Cohen, L.E., and Felson, M. (1979), 'Social change in Crime Rates Trends: a Routine Activity Approach', *American Sociological Review*, **44**, pp. 588-608.

Lab, S.P. (1988), 'Crime Prevention: Approaches, Practices and Evaluations', Cincinnati, OH: Anderson.

Rengert, G., and Wasilchick, J. (1985), 'Suburban Burglary: a Time and Place for Everything', Springfield, IL: Charles C. Thomas.

Shover, N. (1971), 'Burglary as an Occupation. Doctoral

Dissertation, 'University of Illinois. Ann Arbor, MI: University Microfilms.

Siegel, L. (1989), 'Criminology', (3rd Ed.) St Paul, MN: West.

Sutherland, E.H. (1937), 'The Professional Thief', Chicago: University of Chicago Press.

[5]

THE EFFECT OF CRIMINAL VICTIMIZATION ON A HOUSEHOLD'S MOVING DECISION*

LAURA DUGAN
Georgia State University
National Consortium on Violence Research

Only a small body of research addresses the impact of criminal victimization on moving (Skogan, 1990; Taub et al. 1984). Knowledge of this under-researched relationship is important for three reasons. First, moving is costly to the victim both in monetary and psychological terms. Second, if a victimization-mobility relationship exists, then it may partially explain why people migrate to suburban areas from cities. Third, because residential mobility reduces social control that, in turn, potentially results in more crime, evidence that criminal victimization leads to more mobility may help explain a cycle that perpetuates disorder and neighborhood decline (Bursik and Grasmick, 1993; Horwitz, 1990; Miethe and Meier, 1994; Skogan, 1990; Skogan and Maxfield, 1981). This study uses a longitudinal version of the National Crime Survey that includes 22,375 households to test the hypothesis that criminal victimization is associated with an increased probability that a household moves.

The cost to victims of crime is substantial, ranging from damaged or stolen property to personal injury and mental anguish. Researchers have attempted to estimate property and production losses, as well as expenses incurred during medical, mental health, and emergency response services (Miller et al., 1993; Perkins et al., 1996). Researchers have also estimated the costs of pain, suffering, fear, and lost quality of life (Cohen, 1988; Miller et al., 1993). However, until now, these estimates have omitted the costs incurred by victims to protect themselves from repeat victimization. One of the most costly prevention methods of this sort is moving.

Victims may face substantial monetary costs if they decide to move in response to victimization, including lease-breaking penalties, or realty, mortgage, and transfer tax costs. Additionally, moving can stress victims, both emotionally and socially, if they become isolated from neighborhood

---

* I would like to thank Daniel Nagin, Stephen E. Fienberg, John Engberg, James Lynch, Marshall DeBerry, Lisa Broidy, and Anne Garvin for their valuable comments and assistance. Furthermore, without the support of the staffs from the 1997 ICPSR Summer Workshop and the Bureau of Justice Statistics, this work may not have been possible. I also have much appreciation for remarks received from Mark Warr and the anonymous reviewers.

904   DUGAN

activities. Such isolation disrupts local support systems, potentially resulting in lost relationships, anxiety, stress, and even serious mental disorder
(Faris, 1934; Faris and Dunham, 1939; Jaco, 1954; Kposowa et al., 1994;
Thoits, 1983). Therefore, in addition to averting the costs imposed on victims from outside sources, crime prevention may also avert the costs that
victims impose on themselves by moving.

If victims are more likely to move after a crime, broader concerns are
raised regarding the social costs to the community. Given the financial
burdens of moving, it is likely that victims who leave a neighborhood to
avoid repeat victimization are more financially secure than those who
choose to stay, suggesting an out-migration of wealth from crime-ridden
communities. In fact, Cullen and Levitt (1997) find that high-income
households are five times more likely to move in response to increases in
their local crime rate than low-income households. Additionally, Liska
and Bellair (1995) show that the association between nonwhite urban communities and high robbery rates is partially because of white flight from
crime-ridden neighborhoods. Not surprising, evidence shows that affluent
households also avoid moving into neighborhoods with high crime rates
(Katzman, 1980; see also Skogan and Maxfield, 1981).[1] Therefore, as more
households leave an area, the neighborhood is left with higher concentrations of poverty, increasing the demand for limited public services.
Because population mobility, concentrations of poverty, and limited
resources are all associated with increased criminal activity, a crime/mov-
ing/crime cycle develops (Hirschi, 1969; Miethe and Meier, 1994; Sutherland, 1955; Tittle and Paternoster, 1988).

THE EFFECTS OF CRIME VICTIMIZATION
ON MOVING

As mentioned above, moving after a victimization may be precautionary
behavior to avert future victimization. Indeed, substantial evidence exists
of people taking precautionary measures in response to victimization.
Using survey data from Seattle, Rountree and Land (1996a) show that
members of burglarized households are more likely to behave cautiously
by remaining home more often, locking doors, purchasing a weapon,
installing extra locks, window bars, or an alarm system—all are changes to
make the environment safer. Similarly, Ferraro found that people victimized within the past year were more likely to have also changed their daily
activities during that period (see also Keene, 1998; Skogan and Maxfield,
1981; Warr, 1994). What has not been established in this literature is that

---

1. Hellman and Naroff (1979) find a decline in crime would indeed increase a
neighborhood's property value.

HOUSEHOLD MOVING DECISIONS 905

victimization results in moving. As described above, this is a particularly costly form of precautionary behavior.

A household may decide to move after it evaluates its perceived risk and fear of a repeat victimization balanced against its benefits from remaining at that location (see Taub et al., 1984 for an outline of such a decision-making process). Although many personal and contextual attributes contribute to individual fear levels and perceptions of crime risk, evidence suggests that personal crime victimization is directly related to perceived risk. Using data from a nationally representative survey, Ferraro (1995) directly tests the effect of having been victimized within the past year on both fear and perceived risk and finds that victimization is positively associated with perceived risk, especially risk of property crime. However, when controlling for risk perception, individual victimization is independent of reported fear level (see Warr, 1994, for a discussion on the relationship between victimization and fear). Ferraro (1995) also shows that precautionary behavioral changes and fear are two distinct—but not independent—outcomes of a high perception of crime risk. Although perceived risk and fear are clearly relevant when exploring responses to victimization, measures of fear and risk perception are absent from the survey data used in this study. Regardless, the above evidence suggests that victimization positively affects the probability that a household moves.

This study uses longitudinal data from the National Crime Survey (NCS)[2] that follows 22,375 addresses over a three-year period to test the hypothesis that criminal victimization increases the probability that a household moves. Also tested is whether this probability is conditioned by the nature of the crime. Specifically, I hypothesize that the probability of moving will be higher in response to violent as opposed to nonviolent crime, and for crimes committed near the victim's home.

The analysis advances previous research on crime and mobility in two important ways. One segment of earlier research using aggregated data produced mixed results. Earlier studies found little or no relationship between crime and mobility rates. For instance, in his investigation of white urban flight, Frey (1979) found that a city's crime rate is independent of the rate at which its white residents move away (see also Guterbock, 1976). Later investigations that use more sophisticated analysis to study neighborhood-level aggregations of population and crime figures have uncovered a significant relationship between crime and mobility. Using a panel of 137 cities from 1976 to 1993, Cullen and Levitt (1997) show that as urban crime increases, more people leave the city. Liska and Bellair

---

2. More recent versions of this survey are entitled the National Crime Victimization Survey (NCVS).

906   DUGAN

(1995) revisit the white urban flight issue raised by Frey and, indeed, find that white mobility is related to robbery rates when allowing for an appropriate lag period. Furthermore, in another investigation with Logan, they find that robbery rates also lead to decreases in the white population of suburbs (Liska et al., 1998). One important problem with studies based on aggregate data is that these works can only show an association between overall crime and migration rates. Instead of measuring the movement of victims, they may be measuring the judgments about crime as a problem, which is the focus of the second method of studying crime and mobility.

Individual-level studies use survey instruments to investigate the effect of judgments about crime on moving or intentions to move.[3] An early study uses the supplemental attitude questionnaire for the 1973 Central City Sample of the NCS to retrospectively ask the reasons people have moved from their prior neighborhood. This work influenced an earlier consensus among researchers that moving decisions are unrelated to an individual's concern about crime, because it found that less than 3% of movers left for that reason (Hindelang et al., 1978; see also Rifai, 1976). Similarly, Skogan and Maxfield (1981) compared the concern about city crime for whites who left Chicago for the suburbs with those who remained, and found no significant difference. They did, however, find a difference when conditioning on income level. Of the households with incomes higher than $20,000, those who left the city were significantly more concerned about crime.

Using surveys that ask respondents to evaluate safety, several researchers find that a household's judgment about neighborhood crime problems and its actual mobility decision are independent (Droettboom, et al., 1971; Katzman, 1980; Newman and Duncan, 1979; South and Deane, 1993). For instance, using two waves of interviews (1966 and 1969) with 1,476 households in 43 metropolitan areas, Droettboom et al. (1971) found that decisions to move outside of the neighborhood were not related to earlier judgment about the seriousness of neighborhood crime and violence as a problem.

It is, however, unclear whether a response indicating a household's judgment about the seriousness of local crime as a neighborhood problem captures its concern for its own safety. Research in this area attempts to unpack perception into two types—judgments related to the broader community and individual concern about personal risk (Rountree and Land, 1996b; Tyler and Cook, 1984). Although one might anticipate that these judgments are highly correlated, evidence suggests that they are distinct.

---

3. Research of this type is often part of the larger literature studying a wide range of factors associated with moving decisions. Therefore, crime is merely one piece of a larger model predicting residential mobility.

For instance, Tyler and Cook (1984) found that some survey respondents believe that irresponsible firearm usage and drunk driving are widespread social problems, yet they feel that their own risk of victimization is low. Not surprising, previous victimization has been shown to be a strong predictor of both the judgment of an unsafe neighborhood and a concern about personal risk (Rountree and Land, 1996b). To date, there has never been a study that examines the relationship between actual victimization and moving.

Although fear of crime and perceived victimization risk have been shown to have important effects on adaptive behavior, the findings pertaining to the effects of actual victimization on moving are not as clearly delineated. By using prospective, tangible measures, crime incidents and moves, with a nationally representative sample, this study explores a new question: Does criminal victimization lead to mobility? This question is important from a policy perspective because if victimization is related to a household's moving decision, then these costs need to be incorporated into cost/benefit analyses for proposed crime prevention policies and programs.

CRIME TYPE AND LOCATION

As a secondary hypothesis, this research postulates that the probability of moving will be greater for violent as opposed to nonviolent crimes because violent crimes often impose additional burdens on the victim that include medical or mental health services, productivity losses, pain, and suffering (Miller et al., 1993). Therefore, consequences of violent crimes may intensify the victim's fear of a repeated violation, thus making it more urgent to avoid crime. Indeed, Skogan and Maxfield (1981) found, using victimization survey data from three cities, that fear levels between victims and nonvictims are greatest in cases in which the victim suffered a violent offense and needed medical attention. However, Warr and Stafford (1983) show that both the seriousness and perceived risk of a specific crime are multiplicative factors that determine the degree of fear a person feels toward that type of crime. For instance, although survey respondents in Seattle rank some violent crimes as more serious, they fear burglary more because the likelihood of a burglary outweighs the likelihood that the respondents will be victimized by the investigated violent crimes. It may be, however, that after each type of crime, victims perceive themselves at equal risk regardless of whether they were victims of a violent or property crime. Because violent crimes are the more serious crime type, victims of violent crimes may then be more fearful and, therefore, more likely to move as a precaution.

This analysis also tests the hypothesis that victimization will only increase the probability of moving if the crime was committed within the

908   DUGAN

immediate neighborhood. Moving as a crime prevention strategy makes sense only if the household is trying to avoid another incident near the home. Incidents outside of the victim's immediate neighborhood should have less influence on the perceived risk of not moving. Indeed, such victimization would possibly increase the perceived safety of the neighborhood, therefore decreasing the probability that a household moves.

The remainder of this article is organized as follows. First, the contents and sampling technique used by the NCS are summarized. Because the focus of this research is household moves, the method used to measure moves is then described in detail. Next, an event history model using a household's victimization experience and other relevant factors is estimated to test the hypotheses concerning the relationship between victimization and residential mobility. The study ends with a summary of the results and concluding remarks.

DATA AND METHODS

DATA

This analysis uses longitudinal data from the NCS for the years 1986 to 1990 (U.S. Department of Justice, 1993). NCS data are a collection of individual interviews conducted with the residents of a population sample of 59,000 addresses every six months for three years.[4] This file includes 33,272 addresses of the 59,000 people in the sample. The contents of the data include detailed information that is relevant to any study of residential mobility, such as age, income, housing tenure, and length of residence.

The NCS also offers detailed information on all criminal victimizations reported by each household member over the age of 12 that occurred within the six months prior to the interview. Because the NCS provides details of each victimization, it is possible to categorize an incident by crime type, violent or property, and by the location of each incident according to its proximity to the victim's address. This analysis distinguishes criminal incidents that took place within one mile of the victim's home from those that occurred farther away.

Often, victims report several similar criminal incidents that are difficult to distinguish from one another. For example, a household member may notice several items missing from the property, but is unable to recall the dates of each theft, or a household member may repeatedly be threatened by someone, again with little recollection of the dates and details of each incident. When more than three such events are reported, the interviewer

---

4. The sample size differs for different samples of the NCS.

HOUSEHOLD MOVING DECISIONS 909

labels it as one series incident and records the details of the most recent.[5] Series incidents introduce ambiguity when enumerating a household's victimization history. The lack of distinguishing detail for each event raises concern that crime rate estimates could be artificially inflated if each series incident is counted as the reported number of events.[6] Similarly, if each series incident is merged into only one event, crime rates will likely be underestimated, because, by definition, a series incident represents at least three events. To balance potential inflation of the estimates with the risk of undercounting, this analysis equates each series incident to three events.[7]

MEASURING MOVES

The NCS uses a rotating panel sampling design, in which the sampling unit is the residential address (for a detailed description of the sampling design, see Fienberg, 1980; Saphire, 1984). Interviewers attempt to contact all household members that reside in the selected address every six months for three years. After the interview cycle is complete, the address is replaced and a new cycle begins. When the interviewer finds that the current residents at an address are different from the previous residents, they are assigned a new household identifier, thus implying that the prior household has moved. This feature of the sampling design makes it possible to measure moves and, consequently, to examine the relationship between criminal victimization and household mobility.[8]

Distinguishing between the current household and the prior household at an address is complicated because it is sometimes not possible to interview any household member. When interviewers are precluded from interviewing the household, they mark the address with the same household number and record the reason for failing to obtain an interview. Potential reasons for noninterviews could be a refusal, no one home, vacancy, or new construction. Clearly some reasons, such as vacancy or new construction, indicate that the previous household members have moved. These households are treated as "movers" in the current analysis.

---

5. The latest version of the NCVS only labels an incident as a series if six or more similar victimization events occur.

6. For example, in this data, one person reported 365 incidents of violent crime victimization during the previous six-month period. Because of concerns of possible exaggeration leading to artificial inflation, the national crime estimates calculated by the Bureau of Justice Statistics exclude all series incidents.

7. Two weights were considered here: three and the reported number up to the 95th percentile. Preliminary results were not sensitive to either weight.

8. This method assumes cases in which all household members (or the sole member) passed away—therefore, not moving—are so small in number they will not affect the results.

910   DUGAN

Other explanations do not provide such clarity. Unless the next actual interview confirms that the household is the same or has been replaced, the ambiguous noninterviews are treated as missing. Of the 125,985 potential interviews, 7,264 are ambiguous, and, therefore, treated as missing cases.

Although the NCS is constructed with repeated observations of the same address, its purpose is to annually estimate cross-sectional crime rates (Perkins et al., 1996). The Bureau of Justice Statistics (BJS) did not choose a rotating panel sample design to facilitate multivariate longitudinal analysis, and because of confidentiality precautions, linking household information over time by address is challenging (Fienberg, 1980). Among others who have been successful in this task is Marshall DeBerry of the BJS who carefully constructed links across all measures that correspond to the same address in one sample throughout all seven enumeration periods (U.S. Department of Justice, 1993). In addition, DeBerry created new variables that summarize the occupancy status of the housing unit throughout all periods. His efforts make the identification of movers feasible.

DATA STRUCTURE

The unit of analysis for this research is the household.[9] Households were only included in the final data set if any of its members were interviewed in both the first and second reporting periods,[10] creating an important feature of the data that simplifies the model. The final data set includes only initial households so that once a household moves, its address is removed from the analysis. Figure 1 illustrates this data structure. The numbers in the boxes at the end of each row show the number of households in the sample during that interview period. The 858 decrease in the number of households (or addresses) between periods two and three indicates that 858 households moved within six months of their third interview.

About 23% of the households moved during the three years that they participated in the NCS, an average of nearly 8% of households moving each year. The percentage of the U.S. population that changed residence around this time period is close to 17% annually (Long, 1988:51). It is not surprising that this sample underrepresents the movers because it consists

---

9. The underlying assumption is that if an individual moves, the entire household moves, as well. This assumption ignores roommate situations in which a person is easily replaced by someone new. By ignoring individual replacements, the coefficients are biased toward zero, because such a replacement after a victimization will appear as a nonmove.

10. Because of this selection criteria, all households within the final data set had a bounding interview.

HOUSEHOLD MOVING DECISIONS   911

Figure 1. File Structure that Identifies Movers

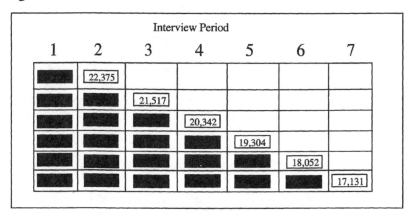

only of those households that did not move within their first year in the
survey. Also, household mobility rates are lower than individual rates (see
footnote 9). Although the households that moved are removed from the
data without replacement, and the proportion of "stayers" increases with
each time period, a decrease in the moving (or hazard) rates in each subsequent time period does not occur, as we would expect. The hazard rate of
this sample seems to follow no trend—0.038, 0.055, 0.051, 0.065, and 0.054,
for periods 2 through 6. For these reasons, the results of this study are
generalizable only to households that have remained in their home for at
least one year.

In addition to the overall hazard rate, each household has its own hazard rate for each period—interpreted as that household's probability of
moving by period $t+1$, conditioned on being in the sample in period t. The
estimate of interest for this analysis is the proportion of an individual
household's hazard rate, or probability of moving, associated with the victimization of its members.

MODEL

The object of this research is to measure the impact of victimization on a
household's moving probability, which could be modeled as either a con-
tinuous- or a discrete-time process. Although households can be victimized or move at any point in continuous time, measurements are only
taken at discrete periods (once every six months). Furthermore, dates of
each victimization are available, creating potential for continuous-time
modeling, but moving dates and dates of other relevant household changes
are not. Therefore, the more appropriate modeling choice is a discrete-
time event history model in which spell length is measured by the time

912   DUGAN

that the household lives at the address.[11]

This model allows us to estimate the hazard rate, or conditional probability that a household moves by time $t+1$, given that it is in the sample in time t. The log-likelihood of the discrete-time event history model that accounts for censored data (households that fail to move during their participation in the NCS) is equivalent in form to the likelihood of a logistic regression model that pools all of the households for each period (see Allison, 1982 for details). Therefore, this analysis will use the logistic regression shown by equation 1 to estimate the probability of moving after a criminal victimization.

$$Move_{t+1} = \beta_0 + \beta_1 Vic_t + \beta_2 Ability_t + \beta_3 Inertia_t + \beta_4 Adaptation_t + \beta_5 Urban_t + \beta_6 Time_t: \quad (1)$$

Use of the stacked logistic model does not violate the assumption of independent error terms if the data follow an underlying Markov process with successive conditioning. For this model to meet that condition, moving status in time $t+1$ must only be dependent on the moving status and explanatory variables in time t. Because all measures of earlier victimizations are included as an explanatory variable in time t (*Previous Crime*), it is reasonable to assume a Markov process.[12]

The response variable of Equation 1 is an indicator of whether the household has moved by the following interview period (*Move*). The explanatory variables are categorized as either victimization variables (*Vic*), or control variables, which are categorized as either *Ability*, *Inertia*, or *Adaptation*, depending on the underlying process relating each to moving. In addition, indicator variables for urban setting (*Urban*) and time periods (*Time*) are included in the model. The explanatory variables and their predicted impact on the probability of moving are listed in Table 1. A negative sign means an increase in the variable is predicted to decrease the probability that the household moves. Conversely, a positive sign means an increase in the variable will subsequently increase this probability. When the effect of a variable on the probability of moving is unclear, it is marked as "no prediction."

---

11. Had the intervals been much smaller than every six months, a proportional hazard model may have been more appropriate.

12. More formally, the Markov property states the state of Y in time $t+1$ is only dependent on the state of Y and X in time t. Therefore, $f_{Y_{t+1}|Y_t, X_t}(y_{t+1} | y_t, x_t)$ is independent of $f_{Y_{t-1}|Y_{t-2}, X_{t-2}(y_{t-1}|y_{t-3},x_{t-3})}$. In addition, the parameters of the likelihood equation of the binomial conditional distribution, $f_{Y|X,\beta}(y | x,\beta)$, can be estimated with the joint likelihood equation of $f_{Y,X,\Psi}(y,x,\Psi)$, which can be written as $f_{Y_7} | Y_6, X_6 \Psi f_{Y_7} f_{Y_6} | Y_5, X_5, \Psi f_{Y_6} f_{Y_5} | Y_4, X_4, \Psi f_{Y_5} f_{Y_4} | Y_3, X_3, \Psi f_{Y_4} f_{Y_3} | Y_2, X_2, \Psi f_{Y_3} f_X, \Psi$, where $f_{Y_7} | Y_6, X_6, \Psi$ is the conditional distribution of the response variable at time 7, given the response variable at time 6 and the explanatory variables at time 6 (for more details, see Whittaker, 1990).

HOUSEHOLD MOVING DECISIONS 913

Table 1. Explanatory Variables and their Predicted Impact on Residential Mobility

Variable	Predicted Sign
Victimization	
Recent Nearby Property Crime	+
Recent Away Property Crime	0
Recent Nearby Violent Crime	+
Recent Away Violent Crime	0
Previous Nearby Crime	+
Previous Away Crime	0
Ability to Move	
Black	−
White	no prediction
Female-Headed Household	−
Low Income	−
High School Dropout	−
Presence of Children	−
Number of Members	−
High Income	+
College Educated	+
One Member	+
Inertia	
Age	−
Length at Residence	−
Missing Length Measure	no prediction
Own Home	−
Adaptation	
Recent Broken Marriage	+
Change in Number of Members	+
Urban Setting and Time	
Urban	+
Time 2–5	no prediction (all four)

VICTIMIZATION VARIABLES

Victimizations are distinguished by type, location, and reporting period—current or previous. However, crime-type distinctions are only made for victimizations reported during the current interview period.[13] *Property Crimes* are crimes the NCS codes as personal larceny or household crimes. Examples include burglaries, purse snatching, and car thefts.

---

13. Crime types for previous victimizations are grouped together under the assumption that they jointly contribute to the cumulative effect of victimization on a household's moving decision.

914   DUGAN

Examples of *Violent Crimes* include rape, robbery, and assault.[14] The crime-type hypothesis predicts that the coefficient of *Violent Crime* will have a larger magnitude than that of *Property Crime*.

To test the location hypothesis, all victimization incidents are categorized in terms of their proximity to the household reporting the incident. *Nearby* refers to crimes that occurred within one mile of the victim's home, and *Away* refers to all crimes outside of that radius. The predicted signs of the coefficients of all *Nearby Crimes* are positive, and it is expected that victimizations away from the victim's home will have no effect on the probability of moving.

Because the timing of a move after a crime may differ across households, the model includes two measures of victimization to specify when each incident was reported. Figure 2 describes the construction of *Recent* and *Previous Crimes* when a household is victimized (denoted by V) between periods t-1 and t. Event V, and other incidents during the same period, are recorded as *Recent Crime* in period t. Therefore, if the household moved during interval A, it would appear in the data that the household moved after a recent victimization. By including *Recent Crime* in the model, it is possible to estimate the association of a victimization with the probability that the household moves between the following two interview periods (i.e., during interval A).

If the household remains in the data beyond period t+1 (denoted by interval B), event V will contribute to *Previous Crime*, the variable describing the household's history of victimization. *Previous Crime* is measured by the mean number of victimizations reported by a household during all periods earlier than the current, a metric that essentially summarizes its victimization history by averaging over all earlier periods. For example, the value of *Previous Crime* in period four represents the average number of crimes that were reported in periods one through three. This measure combines both property and violent crime because it is assumed that both jointly contribute to the cumulative effect of crime on a victim.

Recent and *Previous Crimes* were designed to capture different reactions to a criminal victimization. A move after a recent crime assumes that the household is reacting immediately to the event, whereas a move in response to a previous crime assumes the household was either unable to move immediately, or it is reacting to the cumulative number of crimes over time.

---

14. Violent crimes committed by the spouse are not included in this analysis because spousal violence has less to do with a victim's perception of danger within the neighborhood than violent crimes by other perpetrators. It is not clear whether a household would move to avert future incidents of spousal violence.

HOUSEHOLD MOVING DECISIONS 915

Figure 2. Timing of Victimization Classification

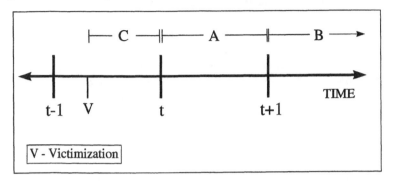

One potential source of measurement error could result from households that move after a victimization but before the next period (shown in Figure 2 as interval C), because those households are not interviewed. If such a household reported no victimizations in period *t*-1, then it would mistakenly be recorded as an unvictimized household that moved. Missing information between a household's most recent interview and its moving date will inflate estimates of non-victims' likelihood of moving, biasing the coefficient estimate towards 0, thus making any estimate of the effect of *Recent Crime* on moving conservative.

ABILITY TO MOVE

Twelve variables are included as controls in the model because they implicitly measure the household's ability to move, and because they have been found to be related to residential mobility in previous research. Six of these variables represent conditions that limit a household's moving ability. Without money or viable housing options, a household cannot move (see Landale and Guest, 1985 for further discussion). *Black*, *Female-Headed Household*, *Low Income* (defined by a family income of less than $12,500), *High School Dropout*, *Presence of Children*, and *Number of Members* are included to account for these conditions (see Deane, 1990; Frey, 1979; Landale and Guest, 1985; Long, 1988; Newman and Duncan, 1979; South and Deane, 1993; and Speare et al., 1975 for further explanations of the effect of these factors on mobility).[15,16,17]

15. *White* is also included in the model with no predicted sign. Therefore the omitted race variable includes nonblacks and nonwhites.

16. Measurements used in this model include both individual and household characteristics. The individual characteristics are *High School Dropout, Age, Length at Residence, Recent Broken Marriage, Black, White*, and *College Educated*, and they describe the "reference person" at the sampled address. The reference person is the person

916   DUGAN

Because these conditions reduce the probability that a household moves, the signs of all six coefficients are expected to be negative.

The remaining ability variables represent conditions that facilitate moves, thus increasing a household's probability of moving. These conditions are *High Income* (defined by a family income of $75,000 or more), *College Educated*, and *One Member* (see Cullen and Levitt, 1996; Deane, 1990; Landale and Guest, 1985; Long, 1988; Newman and Duncan, 1979 for further explanations of the effect of these factors on mobility). The signs of the coefficients for all three variables are expected to be positive.[18]

INERTIA

This category of control variables represents characteristics that make a household more resistant to move. For instance, as the household head gets older (*Age*), lives at the residence for a long time (*Length at Residence*), or owns the home (*Own Home*), the household is less likely to move because of a reduced incentive for change. Prior research has associated these types of measures with increased residential satisfaction, which thereby decreases a household's likelihood of moving (Speare, 1974; Speare et al., 1975; see also Bach and Smith, 1977; Cadwallader, 1992; Deane, 1990; Long, 1988; Newman and Duncan, 1979; Rossi, 1955; and South and Deane, 1993 for further explanations of the effect of these factors on mobility).[19]

ADAPTATION

The third category of control variables represents household changes that may prompt a moving decision. For instance, after a marriage dissolves (*Recent Broken Marriage*), the residence is either too large for the remaining ex-spouse, or is sold as part of a settlement between the former partners. Similarly, as the household membership grows (*Change in the Number of Members*), the home may be too small to accommodate its

---

identified as owning or renting the living quarters and can be thought of as the "head of household."

17. Long (1988) found that the general mobility rates are contrary to the theory presented here. The highest mobility rates are among the least educated.

18. Long (1988) found that mobility rates among the wealthy were lower than other income groups because they have location-specific capital.

19. Some households did not report the number of months that they lived at their current address. To avoid missing data, these cases were set to 0 in the first interview period and then allowed to increase with each subsequent period under the assumption that these households resided at the address for less than one month. An indicator variable was then used to see if these households had a different probability of moving than the other households that did report their length at residence. The results show that they do not.

HOUSEHOLD MOVING DECISIONS   917

members needs, thus creating a need to move. This is consistent with Speare's model of residential satisfaction which claims that dissatisfaction arises when the household changes, and the living quarters no longer meet residential needs (Speare, 1974; see also Cadwallader, 1992; Deane, 1990; Long, 1988; and Speare et al., 1975 for further explanations of the effect of these factors on mobility).

URBAN SETTING AND TIME

Evidence of a recent urban decline drives the prediction that the coefficient of *Urban* will be positive (Cadwallader, 1992; Cullen and Levitt, 1996; Frey, 1979; Guterbock, 1976; Katzman, 1980; Long, 1988; Skogan and Maxfield, 1981; South and Deane, 1993).[20] Also, because the sample changes after each batch of households moves, indicator variables for each time period are also included in the model, allowing the hazard rate to change. However, if the victimization trends are correlated with the trend of the overall hazard rate, potential for error exists in the pooled estimates.[21] To better understand how pooling may affect the results, the analysis is conducted separately on all five periods and compared with the pooled results.

RESULTS

SUMMARY STATISTICS

Table 2 describes the metric, mean, standard deviation, and range of all of the variables in the model. These statistics were calculated using the appropriate weights for each year.[22] The means of the indicator variables (with a 0–1 range)—such as *Move by Next Period*, *White*, and *Urban*— measures the proportion of the pooled sample that meet the condition described by the variable's name. For instance, 87% of the observations (which include repeated households) have a white reference person and 5.2% moved.

The recent crime measures have means ranging from 0.013 per household, for *Recent Nearby Violent Crime*, to 0.091 per household, for *Recent Nearby Property Crime*. All four measures have standard deviations

---

20. Long (1988) finds that the mobility rates of urban residents depend on whether they own their home. Renters who live in the city have lower rates of mobility than suburban renters.

21. For example, if after controlling for other factors, the victimization and the mobility rates decrease similarly over time, the assumption of homogeneity may be violated.

22. Each household was weighted with the basic cross-sectional weight increased by a factor of six to account for repeated observations (U.S. Department of Justice, 1993). This weight is then adjusted by a parameter specified by the BJS according to year.

Table 2. Summary Statistics

Variable	Metric	Mean	S.D.	Range
Move by Next Period	1 if true, 0 if not	0.052	0.407	0–1
Victimization				
Recent Nearby Property Crime	number of crimes	0.091	0.671	0–8
Recent Away Property Crime	number of crimes	0.051	0.468	0–6
Recent Nearby Violent Crime	number of crimes	0.013	0.282	0–11
Recent Away Violent Crime	number of crimes	0.017	0.310	0–9
Previous Nearby Crime	average number of previous crimes	0.135	0.691	0–10
Previous Away Crime	average number of previous crimes	0.089	0.528	0–8
Ability				
Black	1 if true, 0 if not	0.107	0.565	0–1
White	1 if true, 0 if not	0.871	0.613	0–1
Female-Headed Household	1 if true, 0 if not	0.201	0.732	0–1
Low Income[a]	1 if true, 0 if not	0.376	0.886	0–1
High School Dropout[b]	1 if true, 0 if not	0.237	0.778	0–1
Presence of Children	1 if true, 0 if not	0.215	0.750	0–1
Number of Members	number of residents	2.597	2.582	1–16
High Income[c]	1 if true, 0 if not	0.034	0.332	0–1
College Educated[d]	1 if true, 0 if not	0.218	0.755	0–1
One Member	1 if true, 0 if not	0.211	0.745	0–1
Inertia				
Age	age of ref. person	48.336	31.854	14–96
Length at Residence	in months	147.584	270.685	6–1182
Missing Length Measure	1 if true, 0 if not	0.031	0.32	0–1
Own Home	1 if true, 0 if not	0.695	0.842	0–1
Adaptation				
Recent Broken Marriage[e]	1 if true, 0 if not	0.005	0.125	0–1
Change in Number of Members	change in number	−0.017	1.165	−9–9
Urban Setting and Time				
Urban	1 if true, 0 if not	0.739	0.802	0–1
Time 2	1 if true, 0 if not	0.221	0.770	0–1
Time 3	1 if true, 0 if not	0.201	0.758	0–1
Time 4	1 if true, 0 if not	0.184	0.733	0–1
Time 5	1 if true, 0 if not	0.104	0.709	0–1

[a]Households with an annual family income of less than $12,500.
[b]The reference person had less than 12 years of schooling and is over the age of 18.
[c]Households with an annual family income of $75,000 or more.
[d]The reference person had four or more years of post high-school education.
[e]The reference person was divorced or separated since the previous interview period.

larger than 0.28, suggesting much variation exists in this data set. Although many households report no recent criminal victimizations, the summary statistics show that there is enough variation within the data to pick up the effects of a recent victimization on moving. Similarly, the mean number of average previous crimes reported is 0.135 per interview period with a standard deviation of 0.691.

MODEL RESULTS

The predicted signs, coefficients, t-statistics, and odds ratios for the logistic regression predicting the probability that a household moves by the next interview period are reported in Table 3. The odds ratios are included to compare magnitude across explanatory variables and for interpretation. The regression was run with normalized weights for each year the household was in the sample. The weighting procedure is the same as that described in footnote 22, but normalized so that summation of the weights does not exceed the total number of observations. Because of the concern that there is little theoretical justification to use weighted data in likelihood-based multivariate analysis (Fienberg, 1980, 1989; Hoem, 1989; Saphire, 1984), the analysis was run with and without weights. The results show little difference in the magnitude and no difference in the significance of the weighted and unweighted results, therefore this table reports the results of the weighted analysis (see also Lohr and Liu, 1994).

Of the 15 control variables with predicted signs, 9 match their expectation and are significant beyond the 0.05 level ($t = 1.645$), 4 are not significantly different from 0, and 2 are significant but have signs opposite of the expectation.[23] To illustrate one method of interpreting these results, we can take a closer look at the estimated parameters for *Own Home*—the result with the largest magnitude. The negative coefficient indicates that owning a home, on average, is associated with a decrease in the probability that the household moves. The odds ratio tells us that about 47 home owners have moved within in the previous six months to every 100 that did not move.

A closer look at the ability variables shows that, as expected, households with more members, including children, have a lower probability of

---

23. With the large number of explanatory variables in this model, there is potential for loss of efficiency because of multicollinearity. However, among the victimization variables intercorrelations are surprisingly small, with the largest correlation—between *Recent Nearby Property Crime* and *Previous Nearby Crime*—is only 0.18. Omission of either does not change the result of the remaining correlate. Also, the magnitude of correlation between the victimization variables and the other control variables is minimal. However, correlation among the control variables are sometimes as high as –0.89 for race indicators. Since the focus of this research is on the effects of victimization on moving, any loss of efficiency in the control variables is of far less concern.

920   DUGAN

Table 3.   Model 1 Logistic Results with Moving by Next
           Interview Period as Response Variable

Variable	Pred. Sign	Coefficient	T-Statistic	Odds Ratio
Victimization				
Recent Nearby Property Crime	+	0.1111	3.23	1.118
Recent Away Property Crime	0	−0.1117	−1.77	0.894
Recent Nearby Violent Crime	+	0.0258	0.30	1.026
Recent Away Violent Crime	0	−0.0730	−0.82	0.930
Previous Nearby Crime	+	0.0900	2.50	1.094
Previous Away Crime	0	−0.0884	−1.55	0.915
Ability				
Black	−	0.0364	0.36	1.037
White	.	0.0020	0.02	1.002
Female-Headed Household	−	−0.0206	−0.50	0.980
Low Income	−	0.1392	4.32	1.149
High School Dropout	−	0.0149	0.39	1.015
Presence of Children	−	−0.1233	−2.82	0.884
Number of Members	−	−0.0378	−2.70	0.963
High Income	+	0.1852	2.10	1.203
College Educated	+	−0.0452	−1.19	0.956
One Member	+	0.1101	2.45	1.116
Inertia				
Age	−	−0.0093	−8.73	0.991
Length at Residence (in months)	−	−0.0006	−3.96	0.999
Missing Length Measure	.	−0.0419	−0.51	0.959
Own Home	−	−0.7460	−21.37	0.474
Adaptation				
Recent Broken Marriage	+	0.5500	3.38	1.733
Change in Number of Members	+	0.0519	2.33	1.053
Urban Setting and Time				
Urban	+	−0.1241	−3.58	0.883
Time 2	.	−0.3718	−7.54	0.689
Time 3	.	0.0270	0.59	1.027
Time 4	.	−0.0275	−0.58	0.973
Time 5	.	0.2365	5.12	1.267

moving than other households. Also, the significant and positive *High
Income* coefficient suggests that those households with a greater family
income have a higher probability of moving than middle-income households. Furthermore, as expected, households with only one member are
more mobile than other households.

All five of the control variables that fall under inertia or adaptation classification have coefficients in the expected direction with a significance
beyond the 0.01 level. As the reference person gets older or lives at the

residence longer, the probability of moving decreases. Residents who own their homes are less likely to move than if they rent. Also, as the number of household members increases or if a marriage dissolves, the probability of moving increases.

Four of the remaining eight explanatory variables do not have enough significance to draw any conclusion about their influence on a household's moving decision.[24] The remaining two variables—*Low Income* and *Urban*—have coefficients with signs opposite of the prediction. The results show that *Urban* households are less likely to move than nonurban households, and *Low Income* households are more likely to move than households with higher income. This last result is not entirely surprising because data compiled by the Current Population Survey show that persons of lower status have higher mobility rates (Long, 1988; Speare et al., 1975). This dynamic may be explained by the reduced tendency for this group to form strong community bonds.

Turning now to the results for the victimization variables, the primary hypothesis of this research predicts that a household's victimization experience increases the probability that it moves. Consistent with this prediction, the coefficients of all three nearby crime variables are positive. Two of the three coefficients, those of *Recent Nearby Property Crime* and *Previous Nearby Crime*, are significant at a 0.01 level or greater. In addition, the three variables that measure victimizations outside of the neighborhood have the expected null effect, a result that further supports the main hypothesis.[25]

A secondary hypothesis predicts that the impact of violent crimes on a household's moving decision is greater than the impact of property crimes. The small coefficient and lacking significance associated with *Recent Nearby Violent Crime* provides no support for this hypothesis.[26]

The odds ratio of *Recent Nearby Property Crime* implies that, on average, about 112 households move immediately after a recent property crime for every 100 that stay. Similarly, as the average number of earlier victimizations increases by one, on average, about 109 households move to every 100 that remain. Another statistic used to interpret the relationship between victimization and moving is the marginal impact of a *Nearby*

---

24. The insignificant control variables with prior predictions are *Black, Female-Headed Household, High School Dropout*, and *College Educated*.

25. Interactions were initially included to see if recent and previous victimization jointly affect the probability that a household moves, and to see if previous victimization experience interacts with the reporting period. All interactions had a null effect, and were, therefore, not included in the final model.

26. The reduced significance of the coefficient for violent crimes may be a consequence of low power caused by fewer incidents of violent crimes in the sample a rate of 13 per 1000 compared to 88 per 1000.

922   DUGAN

Crime on the probability that the household moves. This statistic is commonly calculated by specifying characteristics for a typical household and then calculating the probability that it moves with each additional victimization. The marginal probabilities of moving after *Recent Nearby Property* and *Previous Nearby Crimes* are shown in Figures 3a and 3b using the median characteristics of the sample to represent a "typical" household.[27],[28] Without being victimized, the typical household has a low probability of moving (0.045). After the first property crime victimization, the probability of moving within the next year increases by 0.0056—a 12% increase. Similarly, as the average number of previous victimizations moves from zero to one, the probability of moving increases from 0.045 to 0.050—an increase of about 10%.

The analysis was also conducted separately on all five time periods and compared to the pooled results. Although the model controls for time trends, it is still possible that the victimization trends are correlated with the moving rates over time, causing a bias in the estimated victimization coefficients. If the pooled estimates are valid, we would expect to see similar results repeated in the separate time periods. The estimated odds ratios are reported in Figure 4 for both *Recent Property* and *Previous Crimes* near and away from home. The first pair of bars in each graph are the repeated odds ratios for the pooled observations and the remaining bars represent the ratios for each separate time period. A single asterisk indicates that the odds ratio is significantly different from 1 at a level of 0.10 or better.[29]

The graphs show that even when the analysis is done separately, the main hypothesis of this research is supported. Nearly all of the odds ratios associated with the two nearby victimization variables are greater than 1, and one-half have ratios with significant magnitudes. Further, criminal victimizations that occur outside of the victim's neighborhood clearly do not increase the probability that a household moves.

DISCUSSION

This research was designed to test a main hypothesis predicting that a household's probability of moving increases after any of its members are

27. Coefficient estimates were only used in the probability equation if the t-statistic was 2 or greater.

28. The typical household has two members without children, who have been living together in the city since at least the last interview period. The reference person is 48 years old, white, and owns the home in which he or she has occupied for 96 months, or eight years. Although the reference person has a high school degree, he or she did not complete four years of college. The family income is neither low nor high.

29. The level, 0.10, was used instead of 0.05, as with the pooled results because fewer observations are included in each time period.

HOUSEHOLD MOVING DECISIONS   923

Figure 3a   The Probability that a Household with Median
            Characteristics Moves within a year for Each
            Recent Property Victimization

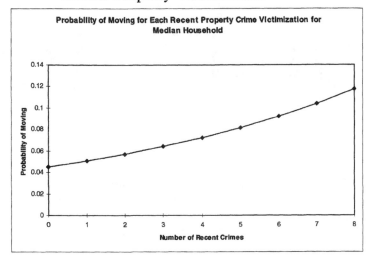

Figure 3b. The Probability that a Household with Median
            Characteristics Moves for Each Previous
            Victimization

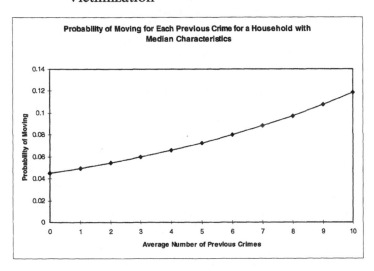

924   DUGAN

Figure 4.   Victimization Odds Ratios Over Time

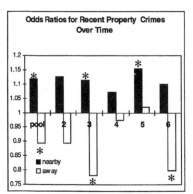
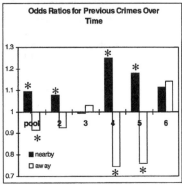

victimized. I find strong support for the hypothesis. The conclusion is reinforced by the finding that crimes committed away from the victims' homes do not influence their moving probabilities. Moving as a crime prevention strategy makes sense only if the victim is trying to avoid another incident near the home.

One secondary hypothesis predicting that violent crime more strongly affects the probability of moving is unsupported by this research. This lack of support has at least three possible explanations. First, perhaps households really do respond more to violent crimes than property crimes, but the small number of reported violent incidents reduces the power needed to statistically isolate this effect. Or, similarly, those households that were victimized by a violent crime may have moved before the next reporting period (during interval C in Figure 2); therefore they appear to be nonvictimized households that moved.

Alternatively, this hypothesis may be false; property crime victimization may influence a household's moving decision more than a violent victimization. Consistent with Warr and Stafford's (1983) explanation, perhaps even after experiencing a violent crime, victims still perceive themselves at too low a risk to warrant a move, or it may be the case that less extreme prevention strategies are more easily identified to protect against a violent crime because the victim is always present during the offense. For example, a person robbed on the way to work may simply choose a different route, thus making a move unnecessary. In contrast, with property crimes like burglary, the anonymity of the offender makes it more likely that the victim blames the entire neighborhood. Perhaps, once the neighborhood is a focus for blame, a move is deemed the most effective prevention. A closer look at the circumstances of each crime may provide better insight as to whether a prevention strategy other than a move is apparent. For

HOUSEHOLD MOVING DECISIONS 925

instance, an assault by an acquaintance may have less influence on a moving decision than one committed by a stranger, because the acquaintance can be more directly deterred than a stranger. In fact, fear of victimization may be more related to fear of strangers than fear of crime (Ferraro, 1995; Warr, 1994). Further investigation of this type should consider other classifications of criminal circumstances based on the anonymity of the offender.

Regardless of crime type, the results do show a consistent, positive association between criminal victimization near the home and moving. However, limitations in the data suggest avenues for further research. For instance, because measures of risk, perception, or fear are absent from the data, this analysis cannot establish the processes that drive the victim to move. Additionally, because the data contain only information on the household—not the community—the model omits relevant contextual information important to any study of mobility or crime. Since other crime-related factors, such as neighborhood crime rate, are missing, this analysis provides no information on how crime influences nonvictims' moving probabilities (see Warr, 1994 for a discussion on indirect victimization). Also, other unmeasured neighborhood factors could be driving the household's probability of both victimization and moving, therefore inflating coefficient estimates. Future investigations should include measures with both neighborhood characteristics and household crime experiences to further isolate the effect of victimization on moving.[30]

This result has several implications in criminology, ranging from researchers systematically underestimating victim costs to communities developing and perpetuating a crime/moving/crime cycle. The persistence of the victimization/moving result suggests a caution to researchers who estimate crime costs to victims, because it implies that victims are willing to incur substantial costs for self-protection. Since moving is an expensive prevention method, it is likely that victims will first try alternative prevention strategies. In fact, the strong effect of *Previous Crimes* suggests that many households do not choose to move immediately after a crime, a delay that may indicate that households first try alternative and less costly prevention methods before investing in a move (see Rountree and Land, 1996a). Therefore, a meaningful and comprehensive estimate of crime costs will include the self-imposed costs of prevention ranging from increasing security in the home to moving out of the neighborhood.

Furthermore, these results support the broader concern that increases in

---

30. Because movers are not interviewed, it is not possible to address evidence claiming that "pulls," such as better jobs, influence a move greater than "pushes," such as victimization (Frey, 1980; Skogan and Maxfield, 1981). However, omission of such "pulls" are unlikely to bias the results of this study because they are probably uncorrelated with a household's victimization experience.

926   DUGAN

crime lead to increases in residential mobility, which, in turn, can lead to more crime (Cullen and Levitt, 1997; Katzman, 1980; Liska and Bellair, 1995; Skogan and Maxfield, 1981). Further investigation of these data using interactions of *Low Income* and the *Nearby Crime* variables supports the claim that low-income households have a lower probability of moving after suffering from a recent property crime than other victimized households ($t = -1.97$).[31] However, this relationship does not hold when examining the more general interaction between *Low Income* and *Previous Nearby Crime* ($t = 0.27$). Moreover, preliminary analysis of an earlier version of these data lacks evidence that the victimized households are replaced by those with significantly less wealth.[32] Furthermore, exploration of victim moving patterns contributes little to the debate that crime leads to white flight (Frey, 1979; Liska and Bellair, 1995; Liska et al., 1998). Of the 392 households that were victimized, moved, and then replaced by another household, most (82.9%) were replaced by a household of the same race.[33] Only 9.4% of the households were white and replaced by a black household, and 7.7% were black and replaced by a white household.[34]

Finally, the results of this research have implications of potential biases in the annual crime estimates calculated from NCVS data. If households are more likely to move after a victimization, there is reason to be concerned that national crime statistics are underestimated. However, without following the households after they move to compare their experiences with those of their replacements, we cannot validly isolate the magnitude of this bias. In fact, if victimization is more a function of the neighborhood than the individual, the replacement household will have the same risk of victimization as its predecessor, thus decreasing the chance of this type of bias. Clearly, more research is needed in this area to further understand the implications of mobile victims on estimates of victimization rates.

---

31. This investigation is considered preliminary because the measure of low income here is crude (1 if household income is less than $12,500, 0 otherwise), because its value is the same regardless of household size and it does not account for inflation over time.

32. The data used to test the differences in wealth are crude. In an earlier version of this data, only 308 of the victimized households reported their family income range, moved, and were replaced by households that also reported their range. The middle values of the reported ranges were set to their 1984 values for comparison. Although, on average, the replacement household reported a higher income, the difference was negligible ($t = 0.85$).

33. These statistics are based on an earlier version of this data.

34. A white or black household refers to the race of the household head only.

HOUSEHOLD MOVING DECISIONS 927

REFERENCES

Allison, Paul D.
1982 Discrete-time methods for the analysis of event histories. In Samuel Leinhardt (ed.), Sociological Methodology. San Francisco: Jossey-Bass.

Bursik, Robert J., Jr. and Harold G. Grasmick
1993 Neighborhoods and Crime: The Dimensions of Effective Community Control. New York: Lexington Books.

Bach, Robert L. and Joel Smith
1977 Community satisfaction, expectation of moving, and migration. Demography 14:147–167.

Cadwallader, Martin
1992 Migration and Residential Mobility Macro and Micro Approaches. Madison, Wisc.: The University of Wisconsin Press.

Cohen, Mark A.
1988 Pain, suffering, and jury awards: A study of the cost of crime to victims. Law & Society Review 22:537–555.

Cullen, Julie Berry and Steven D. Levitt
1997 Crime, urban flight, and the consequences for cities. National Bureau of Economic Research, Inc. Working Paper No. 5737.

Deane, Glenn D.
1990 Mobility and adjustments: Paths to the resolution of residential stress. Demography 27:65–79.

Droettboom, Thedore, Jr., Ronald J. McAllister, Edward J. Kaiser, and Edgar W. Butler
1971 Urban violence and residential mobility. American Institute of Planning 37:319–325.

Faris, Robert E.L.
1934 Cultural isolation and the schizophrenic personality. American Journal of Sociology 40:155–169.

Faris, Robert E.L. and H. Warren Dunham
1939 Mental Disorders in Urban Areas: An Ecological Study of Schizophrenia and other Psychoses. Chicago: University of Chicago Press.

Ferraro, Kenneth F.
1995 Fear of crime interpreting victimization risk. Albany, N.Y.: State University of New York Press.

Fienberg, Stephen E.
1980 The measurement of crime victimization: Prospects for panel analysis of a panel survey. The Statistician 29:313–350.
1989 Modeling considerations: Discussion from a modeling perspective. In Daniel Kasprzyk, Greg J. Duncan, Graham Kalton, and M. P. Singh (eds.), Panel Surveys. New York: John Wiley and Sons, Inc.

Frey, William H.
1979 Central city white flight: Racial and nonracial causes. American Sociological Review 44: 425–448.

928   DUGAN

Guterbock, Thomas M.
    1976   The push hypothesis: Minority presence, crime, and urban deconcentra-
            tion. In Barry Schwartz (ed.), The Changing Face of the Suburbs.
            Chicago: The University of Chicago Press.

Hellman, Daryl A. and Joel L. Naroff
    1978   The impact of crime on urban residential property values. Urban Studies
            16:105–112.

Hindelang, Michael J. , Michael R. Gottfredson, and James Garofalo
    1978   Victims of Personal Crime: An Empirical Foundation for a Theory of
            Personal Victimization. Cambridge, Mass.: Ballinger Publishing Company.

Hirschi, Travis
    1969   Causes of Delinquency. Berkeley, Calif.: University of California Press.

Hoem, Jan M.
    1989   The issue of weights in panel surveys of individual behavior. In Daniel
            Kasprzyk, Greg J. Duncan, Graham Kalton, and M. P. Singh (eds.), Panel
            Surveys. New York: John Wiley and Sons, Inc.

Horwitz, Allan V.
    1990   The Logic of Social Control. New York: Plenum Press.

Jaco, E. Gartly
    1954   The social isolation hypothesis and schizophrenia. American Sociological
            Review 19:567–577.

Katzman, Martin T.
    1980   The contribution of crime to urban decline. Urban Studies 17:277–286.

Keane, Carl
    1998   Evaluating the influence of fear of crime as an environmental mobility
            restrictor on women's routine activities. Environment and Behavior
            30:60–74.

Kposowa, Augustine J., Gopal K. Singh, and K.D. Breault
    1994   The effects of marital status and social isolation on adult male homicides
            in the United States: Evidence from the National Longitudinal Mortality
            Study. Journal of Quantitative Criminology 10:277–289.

Landale, Nancy S. and Avery Guest
    1985   Constraints, satisfaction and residential mobility: Speare's model reconsid-
            ered. Demography 22:199–222.

Liska, Allen E. and Paul E. Bellair
    1995   Violent-crime rates and racial composition: Convergence over time.
            American Journal of Sociology 101:578–610.

Liska, Allen E., John R. Logan, and Paul E. Bellair
    1998   Race and violent crime in the suburbs. American Sociological Review
            63:27–38.

Lohr, Sharon L. And Joanna Liu
    1994   A comparison of weighted and unweighted analyses in the National
            Crime Victimization Survey. Journal of Quantitative Criminology
            10:343–360.

HOUSEHOLD MOVING DECISIONS 929

Long, Larry
  1988   Migration and Residential Mobility in the United States. New York:
          Russell Sage Foundation.

Miethe, Terance D. and Robert F. Meier
  1994   Crime and its Social Context: Toward an Integrated Theory of Offenders,
          Victims, and Situations. Albany, N.Y.: State University of New York
          Press.

Miller, Ted R., Mark A. Cohen, and Shelli B. Rossman
  1993   Victim costs of violent crime and resulting injuries. Health Affairs
          12:186–197.

Newman, Sandra J. and Greg J. Duncan
  1979   Residential problems, dissatisfaction and mobility. Journal of the Ameri-
          can Planning Association 45:154–166.

Perkins, Craig A., Patsy A. Klaus, Lisa D. Bastian, and Robyn L. Cohen
  1996   Criminal Victimization in the United States, 1993. A National Crime
          Victimization Survey Report. Washington, D.C.: Department of Justice.

Rossi, Peter H.
  1955   Why Families Move. Glencoe, Ill.: Free Press.

Rountree, Pamela Wilcox and Kenneth C. Land
  1996a   Burglary victimization, perceptions of crime risk, and routine activities: A
          multilevel analysis across Seattle neighborhoods and census tracts.
          Journal of Research in Crime and Delinquency 33:147–180.
  1996b   Perceived risk versus fear of crime: Empirical evidence of conceptually
          distinct reactions in survey data. Social Forces 74:1353–1376.

Saphire, Diane Griffin
  1984   Estimation of Victimization Prevalence Using Data from the National
          Crime Survey. Lecture Notes in Statistics. Vol. 23. New York: Springer-
          Verlag.

Skogan, Wesley G.
  1990   Disorder and Decline: Crime and the Spiral of Decay in American
          Neighborhoods. New York: Free Press.

Skogan, Wesley G. and Michael G. Maxfield
  1981   Coping with Crime: Individual and Neighborhood Reactions. Beverley
          Hills, Calif.: Sage.

South, Scott J. and Glenn D. Deane
  1993   Race and residential mobility: Individual determinants and structural
          constraints. Social Forces 72:147–167.

Speare, Alden, Jr.
  1974   Residential satisfaction as an intervening variable in residential mobility.
          Demography 11:173–188.

Speare, Alden, Jr., Sidney Goldstein, and William H. Frey
  1975   Residential Mobility, Migration, and Metropolitan Change. Cambridge,
          Mass.: Ballinger Publishing Co.

Sutherland, Edwin H.
  1955   Principles of Criminology. Chicago: J. B. Lippincott Company.

930   DUGAN

Taub, Richard P., D. Garth Taylor, and Jan D. Dunham
    1984   Paths of Neighborhood Change: Race and Crime in Urban America.
            Chicago: The University of Chicago Press.

Thoits, Peggy A.
    1983   Multiple identities and psychological well-being: A reformulation and test
            of the social isolation hypothesis. American Sociological Review
            48:174–187.

Tittle, Charles R. and Raymond Paternoster
    1988   Geographic mobility and criminal behavior. Journal of Research in Crime
            and Delinquency 25:301–343.

Tyler, Tom R. and Fay Lomax Cook
    1984   The mass media and judgments of risk: Distinguishing impact on
            personal and societal level judgments. Journal of Personality and Social
            Psychology 47:693–708.

U.S. Department of Justice, Bureau of Justice Statistics
    1993   National Crime Surveys: National Sample, 1986–1991 [Near-Term Data
            Through Calendar Year 1991] (ICPSR 8864) Part 40: Longitudinal File,
            1986–1990. Ann Arbor, Mich.: The University of Michigan.

Warr, Mark
    1994   Public perceptions and reactions to violent offending and victimization.
            In Albert J. Reiss, Jr. and Jeffrey A. Roth (eds.), Understanding and
            Preventing Violence. Vol. 4. Consequences and Control. Washington,
            D.C.: National Academy Press.

Warr, Mark and Mark Stafford
    1983   Fear of victimization: A look at the proximate causes. Social Forces
            61:1033–1043.

Whittaker, J.
    1990   Graphical Models in Applied Multivariate Statistics. New York: Wiley.

Laura Dugan is Assistant Professor in the Department of Criminal Justice at Georgia
State University and a member of the National Consortium on Violence Research. Her
research interests include the consequences of criminal victimization and the efficacy of
victimization prevention policy.

[6]

ECOLOGICAL AND BEHAVIORAL INFLUENCES ON PROPERTY VICTIMIZATION AT HOME: IMPLICATIONS FOR OPPORTUNITY THEORY

JAMES P. LYNCH
DAVID CANTOR

The purpose of this article is to test criminal opportunity theories of victimization for the crimes of burglary and household larceny. Using the National Crime Survey and the Victim Risk Supplement, this test includes direct behavioral and ecological measures of concepts central to the theory. Ecological concepts are measured at several different levels of aggregation. Of particular importance is the introduction of a control for the dangerousness of the block in which the housing unit is located. Other ecological variables include (a) the environmental design of the housing unit (location, protective practices, single family versus other), (b) the degree of social disorganization in the neighborhood, (c) the location of commercial establishments in the neighborhood, and (d) the perceived dangerousness of the neighborhood. Measures of key behavioral concepts include (a) time spent in the house during the day, and (b) time spent in the house during the evening. None of the environmental design variables have a significant effect on victimization. The significance of the other ecological and behavioral measures differ by type of crime. These results are discussed in light of the importance of refining opportunity concepts, especially with respect to how they apply to different types of crime.

For decades, the study of crime has focused almost exclusively on explaining criminal motivation. More recently, criminologists have shifted their focus to understanding why criminal events occur. This approach to the

This was truly a joint effort. The order in which the authors' names appear in this article was determined by the flip of a coin. This article was written under Grant 86-IJ-CX-0085 from the National Institute of Justice. The opinions expressed in this article are solely those of the authors and do not reflect the policy of NIJ. The data used in this article were made available by the Inter-university Consortium for Political and Social Research. The NCS and VRS data were collected by

336   JOURNAL OF RESEARCH IN CRIME AND DELINQUENCY

study of crime has emphasized the identification of factors that afford the *opportunity* for criminal acts (Cohen and Felson 1979; Hindelang, Gottfredson, and Garafalo 1978; Clarke 1983; Cornish and Clarke 1986).

One of the principal attractions of opportunity theory is its potential to provide more practical guidance for crime control strategies than theories of offender motivation do. The former suggests that crime can be prevented by changing the victim or the target rather than by changing the behavior of the offender. On its face, opportunity seems more amenable to change than motivation.

Despite this practical and intuitive appeal, the theory remains too general and ill-defined to link particular behaviors with opportunity concepts. This lack of specificity is due largely to the limitations of empirical tests of the theory. Specifically, most empirical tests of opportunity theory have focused on the social structural correlates of victimization without taking into account the ecological contexts[1] in which these crimes occur and the behavior of the victim. More recently, work has been done that incorporates ecological context and specific behaviors into opportunity models (Sampson 1986; Hough 1987). The limitations of these models, however, still leave open the question of whether observed relationships between the sociodemographic characteristics of victims and victimization could be due to the behavior of the victim or to the ecological contexts in which they occur. Specifically, these models have often included only one ecological unit when several different levels may be required. This unit is often large and internally heterogeneous with respect to crime and opportunity. Moreover, the measures used to characterize areal units and persons with respect to opportunity are often only indirectly related to the concept. All of these limitations can result in misspecifying opportunity models.

In addition, empirical tests of opportunity theory have been used to predict the incidence of broad crime classes such as "violent crime" or "property crime" that include very heterogeneous events. It is unlikely that a single opportunity model can explain or predict these internally heterogeneous classes of crime. Variables that correlate with one component of the crime class may be negatively related to another. This will result in quantitative

the Census Bureau under the sponsorship of the Bureau of Justice Statistics (BJS). The sponsor, the collector, and the Consortium bear no responsibility for the analyses or the interpretations presented here. The authors would like to thank Richard Titus for his useful comments on earlier drafts of this article, Vicki Schneider for her help with the ICPSR data, David Naden for his assistance in preparing the segment-level files, and Norma Chapman for her general assistance throughout. Three anonymous reviewers provided very detailed and helpful comments.

models that are misspecified and have low explanatory power (Lynch 1987; Lynch and Biderman 1984). Constructing crime-specific models for explaining more narrowly defined classes of crime could improve our ability to predict and to understand victimization risk (Cornish and Clarke 1987).

This article attempts to refine opportunity theory further by building on previous models that included both measures of ecological context and behavioral measures of opportunity concepts. Specifically, several different levels of ecological context are included in the models tested here. Moreover, a new and particularly stringent control for the "dangerousness" of the ecological context is used in this model in order to provide a more conservative test of the effects of behavioral variables net of ecological context. Finally, separate analyses are done for burglary and household larceny to see if different opportunity models predict the occurrence of different subclasses of property crime. This approach to multilevel analysis is not necessarily superior to those that have been taken heretofore, it complements them. If our findings differ substantially from those of previous work in the area, then we will know that the limitations of previous multilevel models affect substantive results. If our findings do not differ from those of earlier multilevel models, then the appropriateness of these models will be confirmed.

THE OPPORTUNITY MODEL

Opportunity theories are rooted in the work of urban geographers (Jacobs 1961; Newman 1972) who contend that environmental-design factors may deter or prevent offenders from choosing particular targets for crime. This tradition later developed into what is now known as "environmental criminology" (Brantingham and Brantingham 1981; Jeffery 1977). The opportunity perspective was not integrated into a comprehensive theory of crime causation, however, until the late 1970s, when several different groups of researchers began analyzing victimization data in the United States and other countries (Hindelang et al. 1978; Cohen and Felson 1979; Cohen, Kluegel, and Land 1981; Sparks, Genn, and Dodd 1977; Van Dijk and Steinmetz 1983).

Cohen and Felson (1979) presented a formal version of this theory to explain the occurrence of criminal events. The basic assumption of their model was that these events depend on the coincidence of: (a) a motivated offender, (b) a suitable crime target, and (c) absence of a capable guardian. Cohen et al. (1981) went a bit further in refining the concept of target suitability by dividing it into four dimensions:

338   JOURNAL OF RESEARCH IN CRIME AND DELINQUENCY

1. Target exposure—The visibility and physical accessibility of the target.
2. Guardianship—The ability of persons or objects to prevent crime from occurring.
3. Target attractiveness—The material or symbolic value of persons or property.
4. Proximity—The physical distance between potential targets and populations of potential offenders.

The first generation of empirical tests of opportunity theory were designed to test the plausibility of the general approach to understanding the occurrence of crime. Sociodemographic characteristics of respondents and gross activity measures such as labor force participation, were used to measure opportunity concepts (Cohen and Cantor 1981; Cohen et al. 1981; Hindelang et al. 1978). The second generation of empirical tests used more direct behavioral measures of opportunity concepts (Lynch 1987; Hough 1987; Gottfredson 1984). Questions were asked about respondents' behaviors that placed them in situations rather than inferring behavior and situations from social status. Although both of these traditions seemed to support the general utility of the opportunity approach, they did not include extensive measures of ecological context.[2]

Some question was raised about the relative importance of behavioral determinants of opportunity and ecological contexts by comparative case studies of communities and neighborhoods. In these studies, behavioral measures of opportunity concepts such as time out of the home had little or no effect on victimization when area was held constant (Greenberg et al. 1982). However, the small number of people interviewed in each community and the atypical areas chosen raised some doubts about the accuracy and generalizability of these results.

More recently, tests of opportunity theory that include both behavioral measures of opportunity concepts and ecological context have been done with large, nationally representative samples of persons (Cantor and Lynch 1988; Sampson and Wooldredge 1987; Hough 1987; McDowell, Loftin, and Wersima 1989).[3] They suggest that both ecological context and behavioral variables affect risk of victimization.

Although these multilevel opportunity models are useful, only a very few studies have employed such models. The problems inherent in obtaining both ecological- and individual-level data inhibit the broad-based use of this approach. Moreover, the particular strengths and weaknesses of the available data on individuals and areas raise some questions about the utility of these models for assessing the relative affect of opportunity variables on risk. The specific problems with previous models incorporating ecological context are discussed in the following section.

ESTIMATING MODELS OF VICTIMIZATION WITH ECOLOGICAL CONTEXT

Models of victimization risk that have included ecological variables have two major problems that limit their utility in refining opportunity theory. The first involves the quality of the data on ecological units. Most models use only one areal unit when there is good reason to suspect that opportunity dimensions, including proximity, may be affected by factors operating at different levels of aggregation, for example, block, neighborhood, and community (Taylor and Gottfredson 1986). Moreover, the ecological units used have been large and often internally heterogeneous with respect to opportunity dimensions. This lessens the accuracy of the data as a descriptor of the particular area. The second problem involves the quality of the measures of opportunity dimensions at the household or individual level. The information used to measure concepts such as exposure or guardianship is often not directly related to the behavior or conditions included under that concept. To the extent that inadequate measurement has affected empirical tests of opportunity theory, the influence of opportunity variables may not be properly identified.

Choosing One Ecological Unit

There is considerable debate over the appropriate ecological unit for the study of crime. Ecological studies of offender residences have used communities, "natural areas," census tracts, and blocks (Shannon with McKim, Curry, and Haffner 1988; Bursik and Webb 1982; Schuerman and Kobrin 1983). It is not surprising that such debates rage given that many of the factors known to be related to crime can be expected to vary across different ecological units. Physical design features such as access to the residence, amount of through traffic, building structure, proximity to commercial areas, and population density vary by block and subblock areas. Some aspects of the social organization of areas vary at the neighborhood level. The level of economic resources tends to vary by neighborhood units as does the level of political organization (Hunter 1974) and neighborhood image (Taub, Taylor, and Dunham 1984; Stark 1987). Given this variation then, no one level of ecology should be entirely adequate for use in models predicting victimization risk.

Size and Heterogeneity of the Areal Unit Chosen

A number of studies have included two levels of aggregation in analyzing household victimization risk—neighborhood and household. One important problem in prior research has been the size and variable operational
definition of neighborhood. In analyses using the National Crime Survey
(NCS) data, neighborhoods were defined as four contiguous enumeration
districts (Sampson, Castellano, and Laub 1981; Cohen et al. 1981). In some
cases this could be an area consistent with the concept of neighborhood,
whereas in others it could be much larger and more heterogeneous. Because
crimes vary substantially across small areas, the size (and variability) of the
census's definition of "neighborhood" could be a real impediment to the use
of these data in multilevel models. Aggregating data into a unit consisting of
four contiguous enumeration districts may mask areal differences at the
neighborhood level and lead to a misspecification of neighborhood effects.
Analyses done with the British Crime Survey (BCS) clustered observations
within "electoral wards" of approximately 5,000 people, including about 50
respondents within each ward (Sampson and Wooldredge 1987). Although
this definition of an ecological unit does not vary, as in the NCS, it may be
too large to characterize neighborhoods adequately.

Smith and Janjoura (1989) conducted an analysis of burglary victimization using 57 neighborhoods in three different SMSAs. Their definition of a
neighborhood comes the closest to capturing ecological variation that is
specifically linked to a theoretically meaningful unit.[4] As with the two studies
cited above, however, the unit chosen may be too heterogeneous to capture
variation at lower levels of aggregation. The average size of a neighborhood
was 1.5 square miles. This is extremely large in light of the substantial
variation in crime rates at the block or block group level.

Using Structural Attributes to Measure
Opportunity Concepts at the Areal Level

The ecological units used in empirical models are often characterized by
aggregated social structural characteristics of their residents (Hough 1987;
Sampson and Wooldredge 1987; Smith and Janjoura 1989). The density of
motivated offenders in an area, for example, may be measured by the
proportion of the adult population that is unemployed. Although this indicator
of the density of motivated offenders makes sense, it does not completely
measure the concept. Generally, social structural attributes of persons are not
highly correlated with offending. Aggregating these attributes of persons to

characterize areas will not produce good ecological measures of proximity. The same general argument can be made for other opportunity concepts such as attractiveness or guardianship.

Using aggregated sociodemographic characteristics of residents to describe the level and type of criminal opportunity in areas can be more or less damaging depending on the purpose of the analysis. If the intent is to determine which attributes of areas affect the opportunity for victimization, then the incompleteness of these measures may not be a problem. If the errors in measurement are reasonably random then the relative effects of areal characteristics on victimization risk may not be affected. If, however, the intent is to test the effects of individual-level factors after all of the effects of ecological factors are held constant, then the incompleteness of the measures can be a more substantial problem. To the extent that the effects of ecological factors are understated due to measurement error, the effects of individual level variables can be overstated.

Limited Range of Opportunity Variables
at the Household and Individual Level

The number and variety of behavioral measures of opportunity concepts have also inhibited the testing of opportunity theory. The social roles or statuses of respondents are often used to measure key opportunity concepts. Exposure, for example, is measured by a person's major activity. Persons working are considered higher on exposure than persons who keep house (Cohen et al. 1981). This distinction does not completely differentiate the exposed from the unexposed. We know that there is considerable variation in exposure within the work force, such that persons with certain jobs are more exposed than those with others (Block, Felson, and Block 1984; Lynch 1987; Collins, Cox, and Langan 1986). Moreover, the use of social roles and statuses as measures of opportunity concepts is also unsatisfying because these indicators lack the specificity necessary to interpret the relationships observed. Although major activity has been interpreted as an indicator of time outside of the home on the job, it could as easily be interpreted as a measure of the vitality of a person's social life and therefore the exposure of a person or a measure of the volume of goods that a person has and therefore the attractiveness of a person as a crime target.

More recent tests of opportunity theory, including some multilevel models, have used more direct and specific measures of opportunity concepts (Maxfield 1987; Sampson and Wooldredge 1987; Miethe, Stafford, and Long 1987; Gottfredson 1984). While this movement to greater directness and specificity in measuring opportunity concepts is a step in the right direction, it has been quite modest. At most, four or five survey questions have been used to measure several major opportunity concepts. Given the complexity and variety of routine activities and social contexts that can affect opportunity, much more information would be required to claim that we have adequately measured this variety. Moreover, some factors affecting opportunity such as the physical design of structures and areas have been routinely excluded from models altogether.[5] To the extent that opportunity concepts are poorly or incompletely measured at the individual level, the resulting multilevel models may overestimate the effect of ecological factors on the risk of victimization.

Predicting Broad Crime Classes

Empirical tests of opportunity theories have been complicated by the need to balance precision in measurement with considerations of sampling error and sample size. Defining very narrow classes of crime will increase the internal homogeneity of crime categories and thereby reduce measurement error. This, in turn, will improve the predictive power of empirical models. Empirical tests of opportunity models, however, have often used broad crime classes such as "property" or "violent" crime. This has been done to increase the number of crime incidents available for analysis. Crime is a rare event and even large-scale victimization surveys like the NCS and the BCS identify a relatively small number. To further reduce this number by defining narrow, but more internally homogeneous, classes of crime severely limits our ability to conduct multivariate analyses.

Some compromise must be reached between the requirements of good measurement and of multivariate analysis. One approach would involve testing crime-specific opportunity models using crime classifications somewhat narrower than property crime and violent crime. If these tests are conducted using the same data, then comparisons of the result would indicate whether the same opportunity models predict specific crime classes equally well. If that is the case, there is no need to distinguish these crime classes in subsequent analyses.

Summary

The foregoing should not be interpreted as an indictment of previous empirical tests of opportunity theory that involve multilevel models. However, the issues noted raise legitimate doubts about the findings of previous research. Many of these doubts may be unfounded or unresolvable, but the only way to remove these doubts is to conduct analyses that examine previous results using somewhat different approaches to the problems outlined above. This is the intent of this analysis.

DATA AND METHOD

The following analysis takes a different approach to including ecological context in opportunity models than those used heretofore. Specifically, this analysis incorporates a number of different levels of geography into the model, including municipality, neighborhood, block, and housing unit levels. As part of this strategy, the model includes measures of opportunity concepts and "dangerousness" at a very small level of geography. This is done by taking advantage of the cluster design of the NCS to generate indicators at the block or "segment level." Segments are clusters of four housing units that serve as the ultimate sampling unit in the NCS sample. In addition, the models estimated here draw on the Victim Risk Supplement (VRS) to provide many more specific measures of opportunity dimensions than previous multilevel models. These innovations should provide useful tests of (a) the affects of attributes of areas of different sizes on opportunity and (b) the relative affects of ecological context and individual behavioral measures of opportunity concepts on victimization risk. Finally, opportunity models are used to predict two subclasses of property crime—burglary and household larceny. The results are compared and similarities and differences are highlighted.

Data Base and Logic of Analysis

The analysis is based on data from a supplement to the NCS.[6] The VRS was a special supplement to the NCS conducted in February of 1984. As part of this supplement, approximately 10,000 housing units were interviewed. The purpose of the supplement was to collect detailed information on factors commonly thought to influence the probability of victimization.

Logistic regression was used to test the hypotheses that are supported in previous research (see Table 1). This statistical method was used because of the skewed distribution of household victimization in the sample. Even though the VRS contains approximately 10,000 responding households, the infrequent nature of household victimization does not yield a large number of incidents to analyze.

Given the small number of victimizations available for analysis, the multilevel models were estimated with several restrictions in order to pre-

344   JOURNAL OF RESEARCH IN CRIME AND DELINQUENCY

TABLE 1:   Summary of Hypotheses Supported in Previous Empirical Tests

1. The greater the distance from the central city, the lower the risk of household victimization.
2. Risk of household victimization is directly related to the disorderly appearance of the neighborhood that the unit is in.
3. The greater the amount of commercial activity in the area, the higher the probability of household victimization.
4. The greater the frequency that neighbors watch each other's housing units, the lower the risk of household victimization.
5. The closer the unit is to the residences of potential offenders, the higher the risk of household victimization.
6. The number of units in a structure should be inversely related to risk of household victimization, especially household larceny.
7. The greater the visibility of the unit, the greater the risk of household victimization.
8. The more security measures taken in a housing unit, the less the risk of household victimization.
9. The amount of time the unit is occupied is inversely related to risk of household victimization.

serve statistical power. First, all higher-order interactions were assumed to be zero. Second, equations were estimated in three different stages. The first equation was a bivariate model that included the opportunity variable that is hypothesized to affect the dependent variable. The second equation introduced household-level sociodemographic controls (i.e., age, race, and marital status of head of household). By comparing the results of this to the bivariate model, the importance of opportunity variables could be assessed after individual characteristics are taken into account. The third equation added the control for dangerousness of the block as described in the following section.

Measuring Variables in the Model

DANGEROUSNESS OF THE AREA

To create the measure of dangerousness, we formed a five-category typology using crime rates from the VRS segments. This typology included five categories of area types:

1. urban areas with high violence and property crime rates
2. urban areas with high property crime rates

3. urban areas with low crime rates
4. rural areas
5. other areas

The distinctions between urban (categories 1-3), rural (category 4), and other (category 5) areas reflect procedural differences in the construction of segments in the NCS. Urban segments are formed on the basis of grouping four contiguous housing units in an urban area. Units within a rural segment may be adjacent but not proximate to each other. Other segments represent a residual category that includes units that have been built since the 1970 census and "special places" (rooming houses, group quarters). The units within this last category are not likely to be proximate or adjacent.

These differences in the structure of segments are important for two reasons. First, they make necessary substantive distinctions between urban and rural segments. In rural areas the meaning of neighborhood or "block" is not as clear as it is for urban areas. In addition, the rural segments are not designed to necessarily include households that are in the same small area. Rather, they are structured to include all housing units that are on the same large area of land. Second, the "other" segments represent a mix of units that does not constitute a homogeneous category. For both of these reasons, it was important to treat both rural and "other" segments as different from urban segments in the typology.[7]

The three categories of urban segments were formed using the following procedure:

1. NCS data from 1979 through 1983 were used to aggregate victimization reports for the entire 3.5 years that each segment was in sample.
2. The aggregated victimization rates were used to construct four different crime rates for the segment: serious violent crime, personal theft away from home, burglary, and household larceny.[8]
3. The rates computed in step 2 above were dichotomized at the median. These variables were entered in to a latent class analysis (McCutcheon 1987) that produced three "types" of urban segments.[9]
4. Victimization rates were computed using the VRS segments by aggregating all data for the entire time period that the segment was in sample (excluding the month when the VRS was actually conducted).
5. Using the typology from the latent class analysis computed with the 1979-1983 data, the VRS segments[10] were classified into the three types computed in step 3.[11]

The three urban classes created from the latent class analysis are viewed as representing three distinct area types. The first are areas with extremely high crime rates, including serious violent crime. Individuals living in this area are those who are most proximate to offenders. This is based on the assumption that violent crimes tend to be clustered within a relatively short distance from the offender's home. The second type represents an area with extremely high property crime rates. This is interpreted as an area with either property that was attractive to steal or where there was high exposure and/or low guardianship of property. The third (and most prevalent) type is composed of the segments with relatively low crime rates.

MEASURES OF CRIMINAL OPPORTUNITY

The measures of criminal opportunity were divided into four different levels of analysis: (a) municipal, (b) neighborhood, (c) segment, and (d) unit.

Municipality. Municipality was used to supplement the segment typology by indicating whether or not the unit is located in a central city (hypothesis 1). Because the typology has an urban-rural break, the introduction of municipality further distinguishes between the suburbs and central city.

Neighborhood characteristics. The neighborhood indicators are based on a series of items from the VRS that pertain to the 2-3 block area around the respondent's home. Three measures were created for the analysis at this level. The first is a measure of residential proximity of offenders to the housing unit (hypothesis 5). It is based on a VRS item that asked each respondent, age 16 years or older, whether crime in the area was committed largely by persons within or outside the area (VRS-3, question 24). Those claiming that there was no crime in the neighborhood or that crime in the area was committed by outsiders received a score of 1, those claiming that half of the crimes were committed by residents received a score of 2, and those claiming all the crime was committed by residents were given a score of 3. A mean of this score was taken across all respondents in the segment. This mean was used in the analysis.

The second variable provides an indicator of the amount of commercial activity in the area (hypothesis 3). This was measured by using the item that asked whether there were any convenience stores, grocery stores, bars, fast food restaurants or liquor stores in the neighborhood (VRS-3, question 20a). The total number of such places was computed for each respondent answering the question. A mean of this sum was then computed for all persons interviewed in the segment.

The third neighborhood variable is an indicator of the degree of "disorderly appearance" (hypothesis 2). It was measured by interviewer observation of the presence of litter or trash. Because it was measured by observation, it is available only for housing units where a personal interview was administered. This constitutes about half of the sample.[12]

Segment level. In addition to the primary control at the segment level, that is, the segment typology, a second indicator was created that measures the amount of guardianship exerted by immediate neighbors (hypothesis 4). The VRS contained an item that asked one respondent in each household whether "neighbors watch one another's place when no-one is at home" (VRS-3, item 23). This variable was scored a 2 if the answer to this question was "yes," a 1 if it was "sometimes," and 0 if it was "no." The mean of this variable across all units in the segment was then used to represent guardianship by neighbors within the block.

Housing-unit characteristics. The third level of aggregation is for characteristics of the housing unit. The model included two characteristics of the housing unit—the physical structure of the unit and the activities of the members of the household. Three different measures of the physical structure were used. The first is whether the structure is a single-family residence or not (hypotheses 6 and 7).

The second measure was a combination of several VRS items that examined the exposure of the structure from the street (hypothesis 7). Interviewers were asked to report on: (a) the distance from the road to the unit, (b) whether the unit was visible from the road and (c) the speed limit of the nearest road (VRS-4, items 9, 10, and 12). These variables were all measured on ordinal scales. The distance and speed-limit scales ranged from 1 to 4. The visibility scale ranged from 1 to 3. To form the variable used in the analysis, the mean of these three scales was taken for each housing unit.[13]

The third measure was whether the household had taken any security measures to protect the unit or valuables (hypothesis 9). These included whether there was a burglar alarm, guard dog, guns/firearms, or valuables that had been marked (VRS-3, items 21a, 21b, 21c, and 21d). The mean number of measures in each housing unit was used in the analysis.[14]

Two different activity variables were constructed (hypothesis 10). The first represented the amount of time household members spent outside of the home during the day. This was measured using VRS items that separately asked about work, school, and shopping activities for all persons that were at least 16 years old (VRS-1, item 32c; VRS-3, items 16a, 16c, and 18a). Each of these employed a scale that ranged from 1 to 5.[15] The mean of each of these variables was taken across all persons in the household. The sum of these means for each activity measure was then computed for each household and used in the analysis. A second scale measured occupancy during the evening. This was constructed in a similar way using the number of times each household member 16 years of age or older worked at night, went to school at night, or engaged in leisure activities at night (VRS-3 15d, 16g, 17a).[16] The variable used in the analysis was the mean of these variables over all persons in the household.

DEMOGRAPHICS OF HOUSEHOLD

The demographic characteristics include: (a) age of the head of the household, (b) whether the head of the household is married, and (c) whether the head of the household is White.[17] All three of these variables have been used in previous analyses as proxies for different types of opportunity structures (Cohen et al. 1981; Cohen and Cantor 1981; Hindelang et al. 1978). Households with heads who are young, unmarried, and non-White should have a higher probability of being victimized.

DEPENDENT VARIABLES

Burglary and household larceny are the two dependent variables. Larceny involves theft from both around and inside the home. Burglary requires that the theft be from the home (or a building on the property) and involve unlawful entry. These types of crime were chosen because they are prevalent and because they occur at or near the home where the NCS provides useful measures of the social context of victimization. For purposes of the analysis, these two variables were dichotomized into two categories: (a) no crime reported for the 6-month reference period and (b) at least one crime reported for the 6-month reference period.

RESULTS

The means, standard deviations, and sample sizes for all variables in the models are displayed in Table 2. The results of the logistic regressions for burglary and home larceny are displayed in Tables 3 and 4, respectively. In Tables 3 and 4, each column represents one of the three equations estimated for each of the opportunity variables included in the model. Column 1 provides estimates for the bivariate equation that only includes the opportunity variable listed in the table. Column 2 is for the equation that includes the opportunity variable and the sociodemographic controls. Column 3 provides the full model with the opportunity variable, the sociodemographics and the segment-level typology.

TABLE 2: Descriptive Statistics for Variables Included in Logistic Regression Equations

	N	Percentage in Category	Minimum	Maximum	Mean	Standard Deviation
Controls						
Age of head of household	9,553[a]	—	15	99[a]	47.7	17.7
Marital status of head of household						
Married	5,541[a]	58	—	—	—	—
Not married	4,012	42	—	—	—	—
Residential location						
Urban, high violent crime rate	478[a]	5	—	—	—	—
Urban, high property crime rate	1,337	14	—	—	—	—
Urban, low crime rate	3,248	34	—	—	—	—
Rural	2,484	26	—	—	—	—
Other	2,006	21	—	—	—	—
Opportunity						
City type						
Central city	2,768	29	—	—	—	—
Not central city	6,778	71	—	—	—	—
Trash and litter	7,493	—	0	1	0.28	0.40
Commercial establishment	9,553	—	1	5	2.02	1.44
Offender within neighborhood	9,341	—	0	3	1.32	0.61

(continued)

349

TABLE 2 Continued

	N	Percentage in Category	Minimum	Maximum	Mean	Standard Deviation
Neighbors watch house	9,552	—	0	3	2.39	0.63
Unit type						
Multiple-unit structure	3,243	34	—	—	—	—
Single-family structure	6,294	66	—	—	—	—
Visibility from street	5,657	—	3	11	6.11	1.60
Internal security	9,471	—	0	36	2.84	7.65
Occupancy during day	9,233	—	-5.81	7.68	0.03	1.87
Occupancy during night	9,242	—	-3.46	10.25	0.05	1.98
Dependent						
Burglary victimization						
Not victim	9,259[a]	97	—	—	—	—
Victim	294	3	—	—	—	—
Household larceny victimization						
Not victim	9,101	95	—	—	—	—
Victim	452[a]	5	—	—	—	—

a. Sample size computed using the maximum number of cases available for analysis (*N* = 9,553). The number used to estimate equations depends on the opportunity variable included in the model.

TABLE 3: Unstandardized Logistic Effect Parameters for Selected Opportunity
Variables on Burglary by Whether Demographic and Residential
Controls Are in the Model

	Controls Introduced			
	None	Demographics[a]	Segment Danger[b]	N[c]
Municipal				
Central city	.45*	.37*	.11	9,546
Neighborhood				
Trash and litter	.66*	.53*	.30*	7,493
Commercial establishments	.17*	.11*	.05	9,553
Offender within neighborhood	.36*	.26*	.16***	9,341
Segment (immediate neighbors)				
Neighbors watch houses	−.24*	−.15***	−.10	9,552
Housing unit				
Single-family structure	−.32*	.04	.09	9,537
Visibility from street	−.04	−.13	−.03	5,657
Internal security	.0	.0	.0	9,471
Occupancy during day	.07**	−.01	.01	9,233
Occupancy during night	.14*	.07**	.08*	9,242

a. Includes age of head and marital status of head.
b. Also includes age and marital status.
c. Represents sample size with opportunity, demographics, and residential location
variables in the equation.
*$p < .01$; **$p < .05$; ***$p < .10$.

The results for each of the opportunity variables is discussed by level of
aggregation. Only the coefficients for the opportunity variables are discussed. Unless specifically mentioned, the effects of the sociodemographic
controls and the segment typology remained significant and in the expected
direction for all of the equations displayed in Tables 3 and 4.

Municipal and Neighborhood Level

The results for central city are similar for both burglary and household
larceny. The effect of central city is significant and positive in both the
bivariate model and when the sociodemographics are included. It drops to
insignificance, however, once the segment typology is introduced.

The effects of neighborhood disorganization (trash and litter) differ
slightly for burglary and household larceny. In both cases, this variable is
positively related to risk in the bivariate model and after sociodemographic
variables are controlled. This relationship is substantially reduced, however,

352   JOURNAL OF RESEARCH IN CRIME AND DELINQUENCY

TABLE 4:   Unstandardized Logistic Effect Parameters for Selected Opportunity
Variables on Household Larceny by Whether Demographic and
Residential Controls Are in the Model

	Controls Introduced			
	None	Demographics[a]	Segment Danger[b]	N[c]
Municipal				
Central city	.36*	.31*	.01	9,546
Neighborhood				
Trash and litter	.47*	.39*	.17	7,493
Commercial establishments	.18*	.15*	.07**	9,553
Offender within neighborhood	.38*	.30*	.20*	9,341
Segment (immediate neighbors)				
Neighbors watch houses	−.03	.05	.09	9,552
Housing unit				
Single-family structure	−.25*	−.01	.00	9,537
Visibility from street	−.06***	−.05	−.02	5,657
Internal security	−.01	−.01	−.01	9,471
Occupancy during day	.13*	.05***	.06	9,233
Occupancy during night	.09*	0	−.01	9,242

a. Includes age of head and marital status of head.
b. Also includes age and marital status.
c. Represents sample size with opportunity, demographics, and residential location
variables in the equation.
*$p < .01$; **$p < .05$; ***$p < .10$.

once the segment typology is introduced. For burglary, neighborhood disorganization remains significant across all three equations estimated. For household larceny, however, this variable drops to insignificance after the segment typology is introduced.

The effect of commercial activity in the neighborhood also differs across each type of crime. For both crimes, this variable is significantly positive in the bivariate case and when the demographics are introduced into the equation. For burglary, the effect drops to insignificance once the typology is introduced. For household larceny, it remains significant after the typology is introduced.

The final neighborhood-level variable, the source of offenders, is significant for both types of crimes. This result provides evidence that segments or blocks may be too small as units to measure the proximity to potential offenders. Larger areas, at least as large as a 2- to 3-block area, may be necessary to measure the influence of living proximate to residences of motivated offenders.[18]

Segment Level

The extent to which neighbors watch each other's homes does have a significant effect on burglary, but not household larceny. For burglary, this variable is significant after controlling for the demographic characteristics of household. Not surprisingly, it completely drops out of the model when the segment typology is introduced. This suggests that guardianship at the block level is related to risk of burglary. This variable has no effect on household larceny, however. The bivariate relationship is not significant and this does not change after introducing the other controls.

It is difficult to interpret the effects of introducing the segment typology on the relationship between neighbors watching houses and burglary victimization because the temporal order of the variables is ambiguous. If we assume that the dangerousness of the area (as indicated by the segment typology) occurs in time prior to current watching practices, then the fact that the relationship between watching and victimization decreases when the segment typology is introduced suggests that the effect of watching is spurious. The level of watching has no effect on victimization risk. High levels of watching occur in safe areas, but watching itself has no effect on risk. If, however, we assume that the current level of watching in a block is a function of longer term patterns of surveillance, then we cannot say that persistent patterns of risk in a block occur before current surveillance practices. If this is the case, then we cannot say that the level of watching does not affect burglary risk. Rather, it would be more plausible to interpret these findings as indicating that high levels of surveillance are one of the attributes of low crime areas that keeps crime low.

Housing-Unit Characteristics

The variables at the housing-unit level provide mixed support for several basic-opportunity hypotheses. None of the environmental-design variables seem to be significant after introducing the demographic controls. This is the case for both burglary and household larceny. The number of units in the structure has a significant bivariate relationship indicating that multiunit dwellings have higher rates of victimization than single unit dwellings. After controlling for demographic variables, however, this drops to insignificance. It stays insignificant when the segment typology is introduced. Similarly, the accessibility of the unit to the street drops to insignificance when the typology is introduced into the model. The relationships found prior to controlling for the typology seem to be due to the fact that housing units with these characteristics are generally located in dangerous areas. After controlling for this fact with the residential typology, the effects disappear.

The effects of internal security measures are insignificant in the bivariate as well as in the multivariate models. Taking one or more of the security measures tested here does not have statistically significant effects on victimization risk.

The opportunity variables that measure the amount of activity out of the home by unit residents indicate different effects for each type of crime. For burglary, occupancy during the day has a significant bivariate relationship with victimization. This drops to insignificance, however, after introducing the demographic controls. The extent that the unit is occupied during the evening does have a significant effect on risk even after the segment typology is introduced. The opposite pattern occurs for household larceny. Daytime occupancy has a significant effect on risk, while that of nighttime occupancy has no effect at all.

DISCUSSION

This analysis has a number of implications for refining opportunity theories of victimization. First, it suggests that ecological factors that affect the risk of household property crime operate at different levels of aggregation. Some elements of opportunity are a function of neighborhood, for example, whereas others are functions of blocks. Second, a number of the hypothesized relationships between victimization and opportunity variables measured at the unit level persist even after strict controls are employed for the dangerousness of the social context at the segment level. Perhaps just as importantly, several of the hypotheses were not significant. Third, different opportunity models predict burglary and household larceny.

The Need for Multiple Levels of Geography

Because the foregoing analyses included several levels of geography, it was possible to assess the effect of factors at one level while holding constant the characteristics of larger or smaller areas. The fact that the effect of central city residence (hypothesis 1) becomes insignificant when the dangerousness of the block is held constant supports the belief that victimization risk varies substantially within central cities. This calls into question the utility of using units as large as a city in modeling risk at the household level. Several attributes of neighborhoods—the level of community disorganization (hypothesis 2), the presence of establishments that attract outsiders (hypothesis 3), and whether offenders are from the neighborhood (hypothesis 5)—have a significant effect on the risk of burglary and larceny even when the dangerousness of the block is held constant. This suggests that neighborhoods affect the degree of guardianship exercised, the degree to which residents are exposed and the proximity to offenders, independently of factors that may be operating at the block level.

These results are consistent with models of hierarchical target selection outlined by Taylor and Gottfredson (1986). This perspective contends that offenders choose targets by selecting smaller areas within larger areas in a sequential fashion until they ultimately choose a particular household. A particular area of the city will be chosen, for example, and then a neighborhood, and within a neighborhood, a block. The fact that attributes of neighborhoods and blocks have independent effects on the risk of property victimization at home is consistent with a selection process that considers multiple levels of geography. Because our sample was not large enough to support tests of interactions between levels of geography, we could not explicitly test the hierarchical nature of the selection process.

The Importance of Opportunity Variables

These results support the contention that opportunity variables other than proximity affect risk of victimization. Significant effects on victimization were found for occupancy (guardianship; hypothesis 10), the presence of establishments (exposure and guardianship; hypothesis 3) and community disorganization (guardianship; hypothesis 2).[19] The fact that the effects of these variables are not reduced to zero when the segment level typology is introduced, provides solid support for opportunity theory in general. The segment typology is a particularly conservative control for the dangerousness of the immediate social context. Because indicators of guardianship, exposure, and attractiveness at the unit level still have an effect on victimization when this conservative measure of proximity is used, we cannot say that opportunity is a function of social context. The behaviors of individuals that influence their exposure, guardianship, and attractiveness affect their risk of victimization.

The results provide no support for the selected environmental-design hypotheses tested. Building structure, the accessibility of the unit, and internal security measures have no effect on either type of crime (hypotheses 6, 7, and 8). When simply examining the bivariate models, multiple unit dwellings have higher rates of crime than single units. Once the demographics are introduced, however, the effect goes to zero. This suggests that it is the distribution of persons across types of housing that produces the relationship between housing structure and risk.

Taking one or more steps to increase the security of your unit, such as having locks or alarms, does not seem to affect the risk of burglary (hypothesis 9). These results must be treated with some caution, however. It may be that scaling security measures in the way we did combined effective and ineffective security measures in a way that masked the effect of a particular device or action. Also, having security devices is quite different from *using* these devices (Scarr 1973). There can also be qualitative differences in security devices, such as locks, that could explain the fact that these measures have no affect on the risk of burglary. Although all of these factors could explain the observed results, our analyses contribute to a growing literature that finds no effect of security measures on the risk of burglary. This suggests that the burden of proof must shift from demonstrating that these actions have no effect to showing empirically that they do.

Need for Separate Models for Burglary and Household Larceny

These results also provide important information on differences in the effects of criminal opportunities on the incidence of burglary and household larceny. Our findings suggest that household larceny is largely a function of exposure, whereas burglary is more a function of guardianship.

For household larceny, the presence of establishments in the neighborhood (exposure) is significant, but the level of disorganization (guardianship) is not. The extent to which neighbors on the block watch each other's homes (guardianship) does not affect risk of household larceny. Daytime occupancy (guardianship) reduces the risk of household larceny, but nighttime occupancy (guardianship) does not. All of these results support the notion that larceny is more dependent on simple exposure and less dependent on the other dimensions of opportunity such as guardianship.

Guardianship is a more important factor in determining the risk of burglary than it is for household larceny. For burglary, the level of social disorganization in the community (guardianship) affects the risk of victimization, but the presence of commercial establishments (exposure) does not. The extent to which neighbors on the block watch each other's homes (guardianship) does affect the risk of burglary but not the risk of larceny. Although occupancy during the day (guardianship) does not influence the risk of burglary, occupancy during the night (guardianship) does reduce risk.

The image that emerges from these results is that household larceny is the quintessential crime of opportunity, whereas burglary is somewhat more planned or complex. The more people who pass by household property (the greater the exposure) the greater the chance of it being stolen. Because household larceny involves theft of property outside the home, potential offenders are more likely to be exposed to potential targets during the day, when it can be plainly seen. If household members are present during the day, they can clarify ambiguities in ownership and supervise people who pass by during the course of their routine activities. Burglary is less dependent on simple exposure because the potential targets are generally concealed within a housing unit. The sheer number of persons passing by therefore does not substantially increase exposure. In addition, guardianship can be exerted by watchful neighbors because of the unambiguous nature of the crime. Unlike larceny, where ownership of goods laying about in semipublic places may be ambiguous, forcible entry is rarely ambiguous. This type of intrusion must be more covert and therefore takes place more frequently at night. Hence, the deterrent affect of night time occupancy on burglary.

LIMITATIONS AND FUTURE RESEARCH

The foregoing analysis is limited by a number of measurement problems. First, the analysis was restricted by the relatively artificial method used to operationalize different levels of analysis. The segment typology, although an improvement in many ways over previous small-area indicators, measures the "dangerousness" of the block. The effects of different attributes of the block that may influence opportunity cannot be distinguished. The segment is representative of an extremely small area that was created for sampling purposes and not analysis purposes.

A second limitation relates to the method used to perform the multilevel analysis. For multilevel analyses, samples should be drawn such that smaller ecological units are chosen from within larger units. Differences across neighborhoods within the same community and blocks within the same community could then be examined. This would insure that all factors operating at the higher level of geography would truly be held constant as the effects of factors at the lower level of aggregation are estimated. In this and most other multilevel analyses, "similar" neighborhoods are represented on the basis of certain attributes. To the extent that the characteristics introduced in the analysis capture all attributes of areas that are relevant for crime, then the lack of a true multilevel analysis is not a problem. If these characteristics do not capture all relevant variables, the results could be due to an omitted variable.

The only solution to this problem is to design a survey with a sample explicitly designed to estimate multilevel effects. This is not practical for surveys such as the NCS and BCS, which have the primary goal of generating national-level estimates. Clustering within areas, such as required for a multilevel design, reduces the overall statistical efficiency for estimating national-level crime rates. It is only through a study that is specifically designed to examine the causal mechanisms discussed above that such multilevel models could be estimated.

Other limitations of this study are due to both the small sample size and measures used on the VRS. The models employed in this analysis are very simple. The effect of one measure of an opportunity concept is assessed when sociodemographic characteristics of respondents and the segment typology are held constant. More complex models that include more indicators of opportunity concepts and interactions among indicators at different levels of aggregation would be preferable. Estimating such models could indicate that many of the effects of opportunity variables are quite different from those observed here. More complex models can only be estimated with larger samples. This could be achieved in this instance if BJS increased the size of the VRS. Alternatively, several administrations of the VRS could be combined to form a larger sample that could be used for analytical purposes.

As this article has discussed, understanding the affect of opportunity on criminal events involves a very complex set of theoretical arguments. It is only by attempting to collect information that captures this complexity, both with respect to multilevel processes and to different types of criminal events, that both the potential and the limitations of opportunity theories of crime can be realized.

NOTES

1. For purposes of this analysis, ecological context refers to the social and physical aspects of locations.

2. Several analyses of household property crime did include whether or not the residence was located in the central city. See Cohen and Cantor (1981).

3. There have been other multilevel analyses of victimization risk that include good measures of ecological context, but no behavioral measures of opportunity concepts at the person or household level. For an important study of this type see Smith and Janjoura (1989).

4. They were formed to represent "residential neighborhoods" and were defined using a combination of census block groups, enumeration districts, and police beat boundaries.

5. A number of studies exploring community crime prevention have included data on the physical design of housing units, but these studies employed very small samples and very little information on the routine activity of respondents (Skogan and Maxfield 1981; Greenberg et al. 1982; Fowler and Mangione 1981).

6. The NCS is a victimization survey used to measure the amount of crime in the United States and to understand the causes and consequences of crime from a victim's perspective. It is sponsored by the Bureau of Justice Statistics and administered by the U.S. Census Bureau. The survey is structured as a rotating panel design of housing units. Interviewers visit these units every 6 months for a total of seven visits over a 3-year period. At each visit, every person age 12 and over is interviewed.

7. The analyses presented here include urban segments as well as rural and other segments. Because rural and other segments may not conform as well to the concept of "block" as do urban segments, we conducted the analyses first including all segments, and then with rural and other segments excluded. The results do not change when the analysis is restricted to urban segments.

8. Because the VRS was administered to one panel of the NCS sample, the households included in the VRS should be representative of the larger NCS sample and the U.S. population as a whole. There should be no systematic differences, therefore, between the households included in the segment aggregation and the VRS subsample.

9. These variables were dichotomized rather than used in their more continuous form because of the need to use latent structure analysis rather than cluster analysis in creating the typology. There were two problems in using cluster analysis with the segment crime rates. First, the distribution of crime rates was very different across types of crimes. The rates for certain crimes approached a normal distribution, whereas others were highly skewed. This makes it difficult to uniformly scale crime rates in a cluster analysis. Second, given the potentially high sampling error of the segment crime rates the use of these data at an interval level was not clearly justified. Latent structure analysis does not impose any restrictions on the distribution of the variables used. In addition, making the crime rates ordinal is a more conservative approach with respect to sampling error.

10. The segments that were in the incoming rotation group at the time of the VRS (i.e., February, 1984) could not be included in the analysis because they had no historical data to use in the typology. Because the incoming rotation is a random sample of the entire NCS sample, the exclusion of the data should not introduce any bias to the sample.

11. To test whether the VRS segments conformed to the same typology found with the 1979-1983 data, a *restricted* latent structure analysis was performed. This analysis assumed the area types using the 1979-1983 data were "correct" and tested whether the VRS segments conformed to the same typology. The results of this test confirmed this assumption.

12. Telephone interviews are conducted for all units where this is acceptable at the second, fourth, and sixth visits that the interviewer makes to a sampled housing unit.

13. The measures of signs of disorder in the neighborhood and of visibility of the unit were both obtained from interviewer observation. The difference in sample Ns between the two items—7,493 versus 5,657—is due largely to missing values on the items used to construct the visibility scale and the different levels at which the variables were aggregated. The signs of disorder variable was aggregated at the segment level. The responses to this item were aggregated across households within the segment and the sum divided by the number of households responding. The segment received a score on this variable if any household in the segment responded. This seemed appropriate because the interviewer was asked to report on the area around the unit. In contrast, the visibility variable was measured at the housing-unit level. If the

360   JOURNAL OF RESEARCH IN CRIME AND DELINQUENCY

interviewer did not answer any of the items used to construct the scale, the household was deleted from the analysis.

14. It may have been more informative to treat each type of safety measure individually rather than combining them in a scale. Unfortunately this was not practical because so few housing units employed any given device. Combining these measures improved the variance, although it complicates the interpretation of results.

15. The work variable was divided according to the number of hours worked during the week: 1 = 0 hours, 2 = 1-29 hours, 3 = 30-39 hours, 4 = 40-49 hours, and 5 = 50+ hours. The school attendance variable was scored a 1 if no school was attended, a 3 if attendance was part-time, and 5 if attendance was full-time. The shopping variable was an ordinal scale ranging from 1 to 5 with the categories ranging from high to low of *every day, at least once a week, at least once a month, less often*, and *never*.

16. This was: *every day, at least once a week, at least once a month, less often*, and *never*.

17. Race of the head of household was included in the initial models tested, but was excluded from the models presented in Tables 2 through 4. This was done because this variable had no significant relationship to the risk of burglary and it was highly collinear with the segment cluster measure of the dangerousness of the residential area.

18. When only including urban segments in the analysis, the significance of the source of offenders variable drops to zero.

19. Signs of disorder in the neighborhood are interpreted here as indicators of guardianship. This follows the usage of Taylor and Gottfredson (1986, p. 393) who argue that the presence of signs of disorder indicate that residents do not feel strong attachments to the area. Given this lack of attachment, residents do not feel responsible for the maintenance of the area. They will not, therefore, intervene to fix vandalism or pick up litter. This same unwillingness to intervene extends to intervening to prevent or interrupt crime incidents.

REFERENCES

Block, R., M. Felson, and C. R. Block. 1984. "Crime Victimization and the United States Occupational Structure: Victimization Risk of the Civilian Labor Force." Paper presented at the Annual Meetings of the American Society of Criminology, Cincinnati, OH, November.

Brantingham, P. J. and P. L. Brantingham. 1981. *Environmental Criminology*. Beverly Hills, CA: Sage.

Bursik, Robert J., Jr., and Jim Webb. 1982. "Community Change and Patterns of Delinquency." *American Journal of Sociology* 88:24-42.

Cantor, David and James P. Lynch. 1988. "Empirical Test of Opportunity Theories of Victimization: Multi-level and Domain-Specific Models." Draft Final Report submitted to National Institute of Justice, Washington, DC.

Clarke, R. V. 1983. "Situational Crime Prevention: Its Theoretical Basis and Practical Scope." Pp. 225-56 in *Crime and Justice, An Annual Review of Research*, edited by M. Tonry and A. Reiss. Chicago: University of Chicago Press.

Cohen, Lawrence and David Cantor. 1981. "Residential Burglary in the United States: Life-style and Demographic Factors Associated with the Probability of Victimization." *Journal of Research in Crime and Delinquency* 18:113-27.

Cohen, Lawrence and Marcus Felson. 1979. "Social Change and Crime Rate Trends: A Routine Activity Approach." *American Sociological Review* 44:588-608.

Cohen, Lawrence, J. R. Kluegel, and Kenneth Land. 1981. "Social Inequality and Predatory Criminal Victimization: An Exposition and Test of a Formal Theory." *American Sociological Review* 46:505-24.

Collins, James J., Brenda Cox, and P. A. Langan. 1986. "Job Activities and Personal Victimization: Implications for Theory." *Social Science Research* 16:345-60.

Cornish, Derek B. and Ronald V. Clarke. 1986. *The Reasoning Criminal: Rational Choice Perspectives on Offending*. New York: Springer-Verlag.

————. 1987. "Understanding Crime Displacement: An Application of Rational Choice Theory." *Criminology* 25:4.

Fowler, F. G. and T. W. Mangione. 1981. "An Experimental Effort to Reduce Crime and Fear of Crime in an Urban Residential Neighborhood: Re-evaluation of the Hartford Neighborhood Crime Prevention Program." Draft executive summary. Cambridge: Harvard/MIT Center for Survey Research.

Gottfredson, Michael. 1984. *Victims of Crime: The Dimensions of Risk*. London: Her Majesty's Stationery Office.

Greenberg, Stephanie, William Rohe, and J. R. Williams. 1982. *Safe and Secure Neighborhoods: Physical Characteristics and Informal Territorial Control in High and Low Crime Neighborhoods*. Washington, DC: National Institute of Justice.

Hindelang, Michael, Michael Gottfredson, and James Garafalo. 1978. *Victims of Personal Crime: An Empirical Formulation For a Theory of Personal Victimization*. Cambridge, MA: Ballinger.

Hough, Michael. 1987. "Offenders' Choice of Targets: Findings from the Victims Survey." *Journal of Quantitative Criminology* 3:355-69.

Hunter, Albert. 1974. *Symbolic Communities: The Persistence and Change of Chicago's Local Communities*. Chicago: University of Chicago Press.

Jacobs, Jane. 1961. *The Life and Death of Great American Cities*. New York: Vintage.

Jeffery, C. R. 1977. *Crime Prevention Through Environmental Design*. Beverly Hills, CA: Sage.

Lynch, James P. 1987. "Routine Activities and Victimization at Work." *Journal of Quantitative Criminology* 3:283-300.

Lynch, James P. and Albert D. Biderman. 1984. "Cars, Crime and Crime Classification: What the UCR Does Not Tell Us That it Should." Paper delivered at the Annual Meetings of the American Society of Criminology, Cincinnati, OH, November.·

Maxfield, Michael. 1987. "Household Composition, Routine Activity and Victimization: A Comparative Analysis." *Journal of Quantitative Criminology* 3:301-20.

McCutcheon, A. L. 1987. *Latent Structure Analysis*. Newbury Park, CA: Sage.

McDowell, David, Colin Loftin, and Brian Wersima. 1989. "Multi-level Risk Factors for Burglary Victimization." Paper presented at the Annual Meetings of the American Society of Criminology, Reno, NV, November.

Miethe, Terance D., Mark Stafford, and J. Scott Long. 1987. "Social Differentiation in Victimization: An Application of Routine Activity/Lifestyle Theory Using Panel Data." *American Sociological Review* 52:184-94.

Newman, Oscar. 1972. *Defensible Space*. New York: Collier Books.

Sampson, R. A. 1986. "Neighborhood Family Structure and the Risk of Criminal Victimization." Pp. 25-46 in *The Social Ecology of Crime*, edited by J. Byrne and R. Sampson. New York: Springer-Verlag.

Sampson, R. A., Thomas Castellano, and John Laub. 1981. *Analysis of National Crime Survey Data to Study Serious Delinquent Behavior: Volume 5. Juvenile Delinquency Behavior and*

    Its Relation to Neighborhood Characteristics. Washington, DC: U.S. Government Printing Office.

Sampson, R. A. and J. D. Wooldredge. 1987. "Linking the Micro and Macro-level Dimensions of Lifestyle, Routine Activity and Opportunity Models of Predatory Victimization." *Journal of Quantitative Criminology* 3:371-94.

Scarr, Harry A. with J. L. Pinsky and Deborah S. Wyatt. 1973. *Patterns of Burglary.* Washington, DC: U.S. Government Printing Office.

Schuerman, Leo A. and Solomon Kobrin. 1983. "Crime and Urban Ecological Processes: Implications for Public Policy." Paper presented at the Annual Meetings of the American Society of Criminology, Denver, CO, November.

Shannon, Lyle W. with Judith L. McKim, James P. Curry, and Lawrence J. Haffner. 1988. *Criminal Career Continuity: Its Social Context.* New York: Human Sciences Press.

Skogan, Wesley and Michael Maxfield. 1981. *Coping With Crime.* Beverly Hills, CA: Sage.

Smith, D. and G. R. Janjoura. 1989. "Household Characteristics, Neighborhood Composition and Victimization Risk." *Social Forces* 68:621-40.

Sparks, Richard F., Hazel G. Genn, and David J. Dodd. 1977. *Surveying Victims: A Study of the Measurement of Criminal Victimization, Perceptions of Crime, and Attitudes to Criminal Justice.* New York: Wiley.

Stark, Rodney. 1987. "Deviant Places: A Theory of the Ecology of Crime." *Criminology* 25: 893-909.

Taub, Richard, D. Garth Taylor, and J. D. Dunham. 1984. *Paths of Neighborhood Change: Race and Crime in Urban America.* Chicago: University of Chicago Press.

Taylor, Ralph and Stephen Gottfredson. 1986. "Environmental Design, Crime and Prevention: Examination of Community Dynamics." Pp. 387-416 in *Communities and Crime,* edited by M. Tonry and A. Reiss. Chicago: University of Chicago Press.

Van Dijk, J. J. and C. Steinmetz. 1983. "Victimization Surveys: Beyond Measuring the Volume of Crime." *Victimology* 8:291-301.

[7]

THE IMPACT OF BURGLARY UPON VICTIMS

Mike Maguire (*Oxford*)*

A CONSIDERABLE body of literature has built up over the past few years emphasising the problems of the victims of sexual and violent offences and suggesting improvements in the way they are treated and compensated (see, for example, McDonald, 1976; Bryant and Cirel, 1977; Knudten *et al.*, 1977; Halpern, 1978; Holmstrom and Burgess, 1978; Miers, 1978). By contrast, victims of property crime have aroused little interest, although it is common knowledge that residential burglary, in particular, can have a serious psychological impact upon the householder. This impact has previously been described only in general terms. For example, Reppetto (1974) reported that 73 per cent. of burglary victims expressed " considerable fear " of a repeat, Waller and Okihiro (1978) that over 40 per cent. of female victims were afraid to be alone in their houses for some weeks, and Haward (1979) that 70 per cent. of victims of a selection of mainly property crimes were " very distressed ". Meanwhile, the only systematic help offered in England has come from a handful of voluntary " Victims Support Schemes", pioneered in Bristol in 1974 and backed by N.A.C.R.O. (B.V.S.S., 1975; N.A.C.R.O., 1977).[1]

The object of this paper is to provide a more detailed account of people's reactions to becoming the victim of a burglary and to consider some of the ways in which these effects might be alleviated. It is based upon interviews with 322 victims of burglary in a dwelling, carried out in the Thames Valley police force area between 1977 and 1979. The majority of these interviews took place between four and 10 weeks after the burglary was reported [2] and the victims were asked to recall the initial impact as well as the effect upon their lives during the intervening period. The interviewees were drawn from three separate police sectors, one containing a medium-sized market town and surrounding villages, one a town of 130,000 inhabitants and one a wealthy commuter area on the outskirts of London. Although representative of victims reporting burglaries in these areas,[3] they are not necessarily representative of burglary victims as a whole; for example, the third area mentioned has very few working-class residents, which affects the overall class balance of the sample. To counteract this bias,

* Research officer, Centre for Criminological Research, University of Oxford. The writer recently completed a comprehensive survey of the incidence and effects of burglary in dwellings in the Thames Valley area, 1975–79, and hopes to publish the results in book form in due course. The study was carried out by himself and a research assistant, Dr. Trevor Bennett, now a senior research officer at the Institute of Criminology, Cambridge.
    [1] The Bristol group also conducted an operational study on its first six months of operation, concluding that 7 per cent. of victims contacted (97 per cent. of whom had reported a case of theft or burglary) had suffered a " severe and long-lasting impact, affecting their life-style " and that " approximately one-third of all victims were upset to a degree which called for some help in restoring normal coping ability " (B.V.S.S., 1975).
    [2] The interviews, which lasted on average about one hour, were carried out in the victims' homes by Dr. Bennett and myself.
    [3] The response rate was 62 per cent. and there were no significant differences in terms of class, value stolen, method of entry or untidiness of search between respondents and non-respondents.

MIKE MAGUIRE

care was taken in the analysis to control for factors such as class, sex and age.

It may be of interest to look first at the manner in which people discovered that they had been burgled: 78 per cent. had been out when the burglar entered the house, 16 per cent. had been asleep in bed and the remainder had been present and awake. Only 13 (4 per cent.) came face to face with the intruder, and for the most part such confrontations were brief and non-violent, the offender either giving himself up or running away. Of those who either returned home (most commonly in the early evening) or came downstairs to discover that they had been burgled, the majority first noticed not, as one might expect, drawers turned out and property scattered about the floor but simply one or two minor changes in the appearance of the house. Open or broken windows were the most frequent first signs seen, other typical indications being ornaments dropped or knocked over, cupboard doors or drawers opened, or items moved to different places in the room. The word " ransacking " could be used sensibly in no more than 12 per cent. of cases. About 20 per cent. were in the house for some time (several days in a few cases) before they realised that articles were missing, but even among those who immediately knew that something was wrong it often took a period of ten seconds or more to associate the signs they saw with the word " burglary ". Their first instinct seems to have been to find a more " normal " explanation of what had occurred. For example:

> No. 37.   I saw everything on the floor and I thought my boys had been having a party. I was halfway up the stairs to tell them off before I did a sort of double take.

> No. 100.   I looked over where the television should be and it wasn't there. It's funny, it didn't click at all, even then. It was only when I noticed the gloves that the truth began to dawn. It was a horrible sinking feeling in my stomach.

One victim likened the feeling to being in a road accident, with an initial refusal to believe what had happened and a " sense of unreality ", followed about a minute later by " sheer panic " when the truth became clear.

Initial Impact

All victims were asked to describe in their own words their first reaction once they realised what had happened. The answers were fairly easily classifiable into six categories.

TABLE 1

What was your first reaction on discovering the burglary?

	Male	Female	All
	%	%	%
Anger/annoyance	41	19	30
Shock	9	29	19
Upset/tears/confusion	13	20	17
Surprise/disbelief	11	6	9
Fear	4	13	9
No strong reaction	21	13	17
TOTAL	100 (N=163)	100 (N=159)	100 (N=322)

THE IMPACT OF BURGLARY UPON VICTIMS

The most common reaction was one of anger or annoyance (30 per cent.); shock and general emotional upset were also relatively frequent, but only 9 per cent. said that fear was their first reaction; 17 per cent. reported feeling calm or unworried. A higher proportion of women than men reacted with shock, fear or upset, while the most frequent male response was one of anger.[4]

Of course, all these categories can include anything from mild to very severe reactions. Those who experienced shock ranged from a woman who " felt the need for a glass of brandy " to one who " shook and shook for several days " Anger ranged from indignation to blind fury and " upset " from mild depression to hysteria. Measurement of the intensity of reactions was difficult, as some victims were inclined to use exaggerated language (" petrified ", " flabbergasted ", " fuming ", etc.) to describe their feelings while others played them down in retrospect. Nevertheless, the researchers' subjective assessment was that at least 20 (6 per cent.) of the 322 victims interviewed had suffered acute distress shortly after discovering the crime. Their reactions included severe shock, trembling, panic and uncontrolled weeping. The following are examples of such cases reported in the victim's own words:

> No. 536.   I went to pieces. I just couldn't believe it. I cried so much I couldn't phone the police. I was so frightened. I cried every time someone talked to me.

> No. 825.   It was the worst shock of my life. The doctor had to give me an injection. I couldn't speak a word.

> No. 1010.   I was hysterical. I ran screaming to my neighbour and hammered on her door. Then I went icy cold and shivered for hours.

One woman said she had been found by neighbours " standing dumbstruck in the middle of the street ", and two others reported being physically sick.

The extent of the emotional impact appeared to vary considerably between different social groups. Of the above 20 victims 18 were female, 11 were working-class and eight were pensioners, all these groups being over-represented. It was also interesting that 12 were widowed, separated or divorced, although only 18 per cent. of the total sample fell into this category —a point that will be discussed later.

In addition to the 20 suffering acute distress, a further 63 victims were identified (19 per cent. of the total) upon whom the initial impact appeared to have been considerable. Female victims were again over-represented among them (although not to such a significant degree), but there was little difference by age or class. A brief selection of cases from this second category is given to illustrate the kinds of feeling experienced.

> No. 142.   I was shaken to the core. The idea of someone in my house— somehow I felt violated.

[4] There was also a class difference, although not to a statistically significant degree, working-class respondents of both sexes reporting shock, fear and upset more frequently than middle-class interviewees. " Working-class " was defined as all those households where the main provider of income was employed under Registrar-General's classes III M, IV or V, and " middle-class " those under I, II and III N. Retired and unemployed were classified according to their previous employment.

MIKE MAGUIRE

No. 144. Everything was unreal. I was in a dream. There was just this feeling that someone had been walking about in my house.

No. 650. I was really frightened—I was trembling. I thought they could have come upstairs. It never hits you till it happens to you.

No. 762. It was the most terrible feeling to think that someone's been in your house. I nearly made myself sick with shaking.

No. 861. I was very shocked at first. It's a feeling that you don't own your own house.

No. 920. When I saw the window I practically heaved up. I didn't know what to do.

No. 1597. I turned to jelly for half an hour. I was very shocked and tearful and had to have a few drinks.

No. 1717. I got the spooks. I went round looking in all the cupboards and under the beds to convince myself they weren't still in the house.

No. 1779. I am used to crime (a barrister) but it was still a bad shock, much worse than I thought it would be. I felt so unsafe.

Lasting Effects

We have seen that at least one-quarter of victims experienced some very unpleasant moments after discovering that they had been burgled. It is perhaps a matter for more concern that 65 per cent. of victims interviewed four to 10 weeks after the event said it was still having some effect upon their lives. The most common persisting effects were a general feeling of unease or insecurity and a tendency to keep thinking about the burglary.

Once the initial shock had worn off, most victims began to speculate about who had committed the offence. As less than 30 per cent. of burglaries are cleared up by the police, the majority never find the answer to the riddle and the imagination is allowed full rein. While some continued to envisage a frightening stranger (typically employing terms such as " rough ", " scruffy " or " unemployed " when asked to describe their mental picture of him), more than half came to suspect on reflection that the burglar was " somebody local " who knew them or was familiar with their habits.[5] On the whole, the latter conclusion was more likely to prolong the worry caused by the incident. Victims tended to re-interpret small events in the past— arguments with neighbours, visits to the house, " prying " questions, etc.— as related to the burglary. For example, one woman stated that she now " suspected everybody " of being the culprit. She was convinced that " he knew his way around ", having chosen one of the few times when she was not in the house to commit the offence and having quickly found some cash she had thought well hidden. She said she was " racking her brains " as to who could have done it: " You have this awful suspicion about everybody who comes near your house: the milkman, the kids, even people you have known for years." Such feelings had developed in at least three cases

[5] This was more frequently the case in housing estates or in streets close to housing areas perceived as containing " problem families ". Residents of the predominantly middle-class town we looked at were much more likely to believe that the culprit was a travelling stranger.

THE IMPACT OF BURGLARY UPON VICTIMS

into a state approaching paranoia, where the victims were convinced that somebody—they did not know who—held a grudge against them and was " watching " them. Even in less serious cases, people were inclined to search for reasons why their house had been chosen among all the possible targets in the area, and this tendency (which might be dubbed the " why me? " syndrome) seems to have been responsible for a great deal of the anxiety produced by burglaries.

Another common consequence of suspecting acquaintances—one which was named by 7 per cent. of victims as the worst effect of the burglary—was a general sense of disillusionment with humanity. An example is provided by case no. 29, a 40-year-old man living alone who lost a weeks' wages from his jacket. He said that prior to the burglary he regularly invited work-mates back for meals and social evenings and had people to stay overnight. He had always trusted people and welcomed them into his house. When he returned one evening to find his back window broken and the money taken he described his initial reaction as intense anger followed by a " complete loss of faith in people ". As he guessed, the offender was a previous visitor to the house, but even after the latter had been arrested the victim's attitude to others remained radically altered. As he put it, he had changed from an " open " to a " closed " person, and was now reluctant to have anybody in his house.

Fifteen per cent. of victims stated that they were still frightened at times as a result of the burglary. This normally took the form of fear when entering the house or certain rooms in the house or of being alone in their homes during the hours of darkness. Many of these thought that now the burglar knew the " layout " of the property he might return to steal what he had not taken originally.[6] The main physical consequences of such fear were difficulty in sleeping (8 per cent. mentioned this) and the use of tranquillisers or other drugs not previously taken (3 per cent.). In all, 6 per cent. said that their physical health had suffered as a result of the incident.

The most striking long-term psychological effect was experienced almost exclusively by women. About 12 per cent. of all females interviewed used words such as "pollution", " violation" or "a presence in the house". Many made an explicit analogy with a sexual assault, expressing revulsion at the idea of a " dirty " stranger touching their private possessions, and had felt impelled to "clean the house from top to bottom". Such effects tended to persist for several weeks and were so disturbing in two cases that the victims had decided to move house to escape them. Five others had burnt furniture or clothing touched by the burglar. The following examples show the intensity of feeling that could be aroused:

> No. 539. I shall never forget it because my privacy has been invaded. I have worked hard all my life and had my nose to the grindstone ever since and this happens. Now we can't live in peace. I have a feeling of

---

[6] In fact, only 11 of the 322 interviewed were burgled again during the period of study. We were aware of the interest by victimologists in the phenomenon of multiple victimisation (*e.g.* Sparks *et al.*, 1979, p. 231) but apart from a case where some children had stolen a neighbour's key, which they used to enter her house several times, we found no evidence of burglars deliberately returning to the same house.

MIKE MAGUIRE

" mental rape ". I feel a dislocation and disruption of private concerns. I have destroyed everything they touched. I feel so extreme about it.

No. 629.   I'll never get over the thought that a stranger had been in here while we were in bed . . . the idea that a stranger, who could be one of those horrible revolting creatures, has been mauling my things about.

No. 976.   They had gone through all my clothes. I felt a real repulsion— everything felt dirty. I wanted to move—I had nightmares, and it still comes back even now.

No. 1010.   It's the next worst thing to being bereaved; it's like being raped.

A final common effect upon victims was to change what can be called their " security behaviour ". Of those who had not been insured 43 per cent. took out a policy and 42 per cent. of those who had been under-insured increased their cover; 50 per cent. improved the physical security of their homes by fitting new locks or bolts or an alarm; 80 per cent. of those who admitted they had been careless about locking doors or shutting windows prior to the burglary said that they had become more " security-conscious " as a result (although some were already beginning to lapse). A small minority went to desperate extremes, nailing up windows, putting furniture against doors, or sleeping with makeshift weapons beside the bed. With the possible exception of insurance, most of the above activities seemed to have a greater psychological than practical purpose. Victims generally recognised that it is impossible to create a " thief-proof " house, but the very act of making it more difficult to get in gave them some sense of control. As one man put it, " I felt I was fighting back ". Others simply said they " felt better after- wards ".

In addition to describing their reactions, victims were asked what, looking back, had been the worst thing about the whole event. The question was put twice during the interview, on the second occasion asking them to choose one or more possibilities from a prepared list. Table 2 shows the results of this second exercise.

TABLE 2

What was the worst thing about the burglary?

	Selected as worst	Selected as second worst	TOTAL (*i.e.* mentioned as either first or second choice)
	%	%	%
Intrusion on privacy	41	22	63
Emotional upset	19	25	44
Loss of property	25	20	45
Disarrangement of property	4	4	8
Damage to property	3	2	5
None of these	7	27	—
TOTAL	100 (N=322)	100 (N=322)	

The outcome was that 60 per cent. selected either intrusion on their privacy

THE IMPACT OF BURGLARY UPON VICTIMS

or general emotional upset as the worst element.[7] This finding underlines the point that the emotional impact of burglary is more important to victims than financial loss. While there has been some discussion (Marcus *et al.*, 1975; Miers, 1978) of the feasibility of restitution or compensation, our study suggests that, at least where burglary is concerned, the emphasis would be placed more appropriately upon the alleviation of psychological effects.

Differential Vulnerability

It has already been pointed out that certain categories of victim (female, pensioner, separated or divorced, etc.) appear to suffer disproportionately heavy initial effects. To test relative susceptibility to longer-term effects a panel of volunteers were asked to assess each case. Ten people from a variety of backgrounds were given a copy of every victim's account of the effects the burglary had upon his or her life up to the time of interview, and were instructed to rate each one in terms of the overall impact the burglary had produced, using a scale from 1 (severe) to 5 (little or none). The answers were averaged, cases with an average of 1·5 or below being labelled " serious effects ", those with an average between 1·5 and 2·5 " fairly serious " and so on.

The groups emerged as follows:

			%
Serious	(1 to 1·5)	43	(13)
Fairly serious	(1·5 to 2·5)	71	(22)
Moderate	(2·5 to 3·5)	100	(31)
Slight or nil	(3·5 to 5)	108	(34)
		322	(100)

This exercise confirmed that, as with the initial reaction on discovering a burglary, the most serious lasting effects are largely confined to female victims. Of the 43 deemed to be worst affected 34 were women, although almost equal numbers of males and females were interviewed. For this reason, the remainder of the analysis will be concentrated upon female respondents only, looking for any significant differences between the characteristics of those women who were badly affected and those who were not.

---

[7] Of course, the low numbers who chose damage or disarrangement of property were to some extent produced by the comparatively few cases in which there was any serious damage or ransacking, and the 14 per cent. who lost no property could not select loss as the worst element. However, even allowing for these factors, victims were still more likely to select an emotional element as the worst: only 16 per cent. of those who had to pay over £15 to repair damage selected damage as the worst thing; 14 per cent. of those whose property was scattered on the floor selected disarrangement as the worst thing; and 29 per cent. of those who lost any property selected loss as the worst. Broadly similar results were obtained from the same question when there was no precoded set of choices, but they provide a little extra insight. It was striking how many victims answered with almost identical words: " *The thought that someone had been in my house* "; 22 per cent. used this phrase or a very close equivalent. The answers also showed that many of those most concerned about the loss of their property were upset by *sentimental* rather than financial value. Other replies included " disillusionment, loss of faith in people "—7 per cent., and " not knowing who had done it "—4 per cent.

MIKE MAGUIRE

The most striking finding was that no less than 21 (62 per cent.) of the 34 worst affected were separated, widowed or divorced, although only 49 (31 per cent.) of the total female population interviewed fell into this category.

TABLE 3

Effects on Female Victims by Marital Status

		Married	Single	Separated/ divorced	Widowed	TOTAL
Number of cases with	serious effects	8	5	10	11	34
	less serious effects	67	30	15	13	125
TOTAL		75	35	25	24	159

($x^2 = 19.8$ with 3 df p$>$0·001).

Other variables of victim characteristics had very little independent effect. For example, female pensioners were more seriously affected than women under 60, but much of this difference can be explained by the presence of 18 widows among the 35 pensioners.[8] Working-class women were marginally worse affected than middle-class women and women living alone worse than those living with others, but both these groups contained a higher proportion of widows and divorcees. When the figures were controlled for marital status, the differences all but disappeared. (Overall, the category of women emerging as most seriously affected was working-class widows over 60, but once one starts subdividing classifications, the numbers become too small to allow full confidence in the results.[9]) These results find some support in data collected in 1974 for a B.V.S.S. study (see note 1 earlier), where a re-analysis revealed [10] that 10 of the 12 female victims of burglary who had been most upset were separated, widowed or divorced.

Finally, it might be expected that, independent of the characteristics of the victim, the nature of the offence would make a considerable difference to its impact upon the household; for example, that night-time burglaries would create more fear than daylight offences, offences where the victim was present more than those where the house was unoccupied, " break-ins " more than " walk-ins ", and so on. However, none of these factors had any significant effect. Nor, indeed, did the type or value of the property stolen;

[8] While eight of these 18 widows suffered badly, only four of the remaining 17 older women did so. Male pensioners, too, were almost as resilient as younger male victims.
[9] Selected categories of victims interviewed, showing percentage seriously affected:

	No. in sample	Rated as seriously affected No.	%
All victims	322	43	13·4
Women	159	34	21·4
Working-class women	65	16	24·5
Women living alone	60	17	28·3
Women over 60	35	12	34·3
Divorcees	25	10	40·0
Widows	24	11	45·8
Widows living alone	18	9	50·0
Working-class widows	10	6	60·0
Working-class widows over 60	8	5	62·5

[10] Chris Holtom of Bristol University, who directed the study, kindly lent us the original data, from which we selected the 135 cases of burglary.

THE IMPACT OF BURGLARY UPON VICTIMS

people who lost nothing at all were as likely to be badly affected as those losing hundreds of pounds. The one exception was in the case of ransacking. Eight of the 18 women interviewed whose property had been seriously damaged or disarranged were among those most seriously affected.

Explanations and Implications

There is little doubt on the evidence presented here that a burglary is a significant event in the lives of a considerable proportion of victims. Almost all those interviewed had a clear memory of their reactions on discovering that their house had been entered. As many as 25 per cent. (and 40 per cent. of all female victims) were fairly seriously shocked or distressed at the time, and more than a month after the event only one-third of all victims said that they had fully recovered from the experience. Fifteen per cent. were still in some fear, about one in eight women felt " contaminated " or " violated ", and others reported worry, difficulty in sleeping, reluctance to leave the house unoccupied and a distrustful and suspicious attitude to strangers. Above all, the impression was of people struggling to recapture a lost sense of security. The irony is that the event triggering off such responses was often objectively a fairly trivial incident. Most of the victims quoted had lost very little and their houses had not been ransacked; more often than not it was still daylight when they discovered the offence and there was no sign of the offender. Many even suspected local teenagers of whom they would not be physically afraid if confronting them.

Before any remedies for the problem can be suggested, it is important to attempt to understand why it occurs. There seem to be at least three possible explanations, none of which is fully satisfactory, but which at least provide some illumination in a proportion of cases.

The first is simply that those who react badly are often people who are already experiencing a high degree of insecurity in their lives, and that *any* unexpected unpleasant experience might cause a similar reaction. This idea, although not properly testable on our evidence, might be supported by the preponderance of widows and separated and divorced women among those who suffered the worst initial impact. On the other hand, there were also a considerable number of victims to whom the above description clearly did not apply and yet who described strong symptoms of shock. Haward (1979) has also made the point that those he treated for psychiatric conditions following victimisation " were no more vulnerable to psychiatric breakdown than any other random sample of the population ".

A second possibility is that the intensity of feeling aroused is related to the importance people instinctively attach to private territory—a concept explored some time ago by psychologists such as Lorenz (1966). This is supported by the frequent mention of " violation " and disgust at " the idea of someone in my house " and by the fact that the intrusion itself is often considered more disturbing than the loss or damage. However, although many people certainly want to build a secure " nest " in which they can feel safe from outsiders, there is no evidence to show that the greater the degree of emotional investment in a home the greater the distress

MIKE MAGUIRE

will be when it is burgled,[11] nor that those who spend a great deal of their time in a house are worse affected than those who are often away from it (*e.g.* housewives compared with women in employment).

The third explanation is concerned with the public image of burglary. The word conjures up pictures of masked intruders, ransacked rooms and shadowy figures entering the bedroom while people sleep, all images perpetuated in fiction and in sensational media accounts of burglaries [12] but far from the reality of the mass of actual offences committed. Even without such influences, one has only to think back to childhood fears of " noises in the night " to understand why burglary comes high on the list of crimes people fear might happen to them.[13] It thus seems plausible to interpret the initial symptoms of shock so frequently mentioned (shivering, pallor, nausea, etc.) as a result of the combination of the unexpectedness of the event and the imagination of the victim. As previously described, many victims are temporarily unable to understand what has happened. If this state of disorientation is followed by a moment of comprehension in which a word with frightening connotations such as " burglars " suddenly leaps to mind, all sense of perspective can be lost and the victim may react to his or her preconceived image of what burglary entails rather than to the (usually less serious) reality of the situation. Many of those interviewed described their recovery from the initial impact of the burglary in terms of relief that the event had not been " as bad as it could have been ", perhaps a manifestation of the replacement of flights of imagination by a more objective manner of viewing the incident.[14]

These three explanations—which are not mutually exclusive—suggest a variety of possible strategies for reducing the adverse effects of burglary. The first points towards awareness of and action to help types of people particularly susceptible to distress. Victims Support Schemes have already found that the aged and people living alone are likely to require more support than most. Our finding that separated, divorced and widowed women are the most vulnerable groups may provide further insight and help to direct attention where it is most needed. The second implies the importance of restoring victims' sense of safety within the " territory " of the home.

[11] Although we found two specific categories of people with short-term homes—students in " digs " and service-men renting houses while stationed at a base—who were almost all unaffected by their burglaries, the numbers were too small to generalise and anyway special cultural factors may explain this. Moreover, it transpired that owner-occupiers, who might be thought to have more emotional attachment to their property than those who rent, were less seriously affected than both tenants of private landlords and council tenants. Waller and Okihiro (1978, p. 37) also found no relationship between length of residence and severity of reaction; neither did it make any difference whether or not people had put extra effort into major alterations or decoration in their home.

[12] Crime prevention literature and films could also be criticised on similar grounds. For example, the sinister silhouette used in the " Watch Out! There's a Thief About " campaign, however effective it may be in encouraging people to lock up their homes, is hardly helpful in fostering a sense of security.

[13] For example, a *New Society* survey (September 29, 1966) found that 26 per cent. of a random sample of the population " worried a great deal " about the possibility of being burgled, while only 16 per cent. worried about being physically assaulted.

[14] Sparks *et al.* (1977, p. 208) have even suggested that the actual experience of victimisation reduces fear of crime by (in most cases!) showing the victim that the reality is not as serious as the imagined event, although this finding is challenged by some Canadian research (Grenier et Manseau 1978).

THE IMPACT OF BURGLARY UPON VICTIMS

Many found it comforting to change locks or to instal new security devices, and the visit of a crime prevention officer or even simple advice from investigating officers was also helpful in this respect. A possible conclusion is that victims should be actively advised and encouraged by the police to make some changes, if only minor, in the way their homes are protected.

The third explanation merits special attention, as it can be used to justify a controversial approach to the problem which has gained some currency in the United States and Canada, but which appears from our research to contain some serious weaknesses. Waller and Okihiro, for example, have used the argument that fear of crime may often be as socially harmful as actual victimisation [15] to advocate a programme of " de-dramaticisation " of burglary, involving fewer prosecutions for minor offences, elimination of fear-producing crime prevention campaigns, and efforts to educate the public " by more frequent publicity of the peaceful nature of residential burglary ". They have also suggested that minor burglaries should be merely recorded over the telephone by civilian employees with an explanation to the public of the scarcity of police resources, so that trained policemen can concentrate upon " more serious offenders " (*ibid.* p. 105).

Unfortunately, Waller and others sometimes seem to confuse the distinction between anxiety that one might become the victim of a burglary and the feelings produced when it actually happens. Although the two are related, there are other elements involved in the latter which may not be affected by general measures to reduce fear. One which deserves special mention is reflected in the following response by McKay (1978): " I would like him [Waller] to be aware that the burglary was neither common nor dull for us. It was in fact an intrusive and psychologically violent act with long-term and enduring consequences. The impact of having our home, privacy and personal belongings violated in a distinctly impersonal fashion was, I can assure him, not dull. . . . If anything, our residual anxiety over the act was heightened by what we perceived as the *lack of reaction* by the local police. Frankly, in the aftermath of such an incident one resents being treated as mundane routine. Contact with the local force reflected less than five minutes of total conversation on the telephone with the investigating officer and with a desk officer at the station." Our results show that this represents a common feeling among victims. About one-third of the sample had some criticism of the manner in which their case had been handled by the police, by far the most frequent complaints being that the latter had displayed a " lack of interest ", had " treated us as unimportant " or had " made us feel as if we were wasting their time ".[16] There was also criticism that once the police had left, no notification was given about the progress (or lack of progress) made in the case.[17] By the same token, those who praised

[15] This is supported by studies such as those by Furstenberg, 1972; Garofalo, 1977; Hindelang *et al.*, 1978; Garofalo and Laub, 1978, which have shown a substantial level of public apprehension and a tendency to over-estimate one's chances of becoming a victim.
[16] 20 per cent. of working-class victims—who were generally more critical than middle-class victims—made remarks of this kind and 5 per cent. were extremely bitter about the way they had been treated.
[17] Only 24 per cent. had heard from the police again after the first two days. One Division had a policy of sending out " progress letters ", but this was not actually carried out in many cases.

MIKE MAGUIRE

the police often did so in terms of " the trouble they took " over the case. Significantly, their satisfaction with the police was not affected by whether or not the burglar was eventually detected.

The clear conclusion to be drawn from the answers to questions about what they wanted from the police was that victims were much less concerned with seeing an offender arrested than with receiving what they regarded as *the appropriate response to the incident*. In a state of considerable emotional upset, they had telephoned the police almost as an instinctive response,[18] with the expectation that the latter would come along and " do something " about the situation. The very routine of investigation—taking fingerprints, recording details, examining the point of entry, questioning neighbours, etc.—if coupled with a sympathetic attitude and a willingness to listen to the victim's fears, was mentioned as having a beneficial effect in helping people to come to terms with what had happened. As both the victim and the police were often well aware that there was little chance of an arrest,[19] these actions can to some extent be regarded as a kind of " ritual ", but this does not mean that they have no value. What they achieve is to " mark " the offence as an experience that others have been through in the past. As Wright (1977) puts it: " A crime is, at the least, a disturbance, at the worst, a disaster in people's lives. It is natural for people to want something to be done, just as they do when there has been an accident. This is partly out of a desire for practical action to put things back to normal, as far as possible, but partly it is because people want recognition of the offence, appropriate to its seriousness, from recording the details of a petty theft which is unlikely to be cleared up, to a full-scale murder-hunt (or, in the case of an accident or natural catastrophe, a visit by a government minister to the disaster area) . . . What offends people's instinctive sense of rightness is that the response is insufficient, rather than that it is insufficiently hurtful to the offender."

For these reasons there need not necessarily be a contradiction between encouraging a less dramatic image of burglary and at the same time taking seriously the psychological impact upon those who become victims. In other words, while it seems sensible to criticise sensational reports which increase public fear, this approach should not be taken to the extreme of making victims feel apologetic or embarrassed to report offences or to ask for attention.

Conclusions

The research outlined in this paper indicates that there are several inter-related factors to be considered if the impact of burglary upon victims is to be alleviated. In the most serious cases the reactions may be related to latent psychological problems which are triggered off by the event. Although these

---

[18] To the question " Why did you report the burglary ? ", 75 per cent. replied that it was a " normal " or " automatic " response. Under 10 per cent. initially mentioned the hope that the offender might be caught.
[19] Victims described the police estimation of the chances of arrest as " optimistic " in only 20 per cent. of cases and they themselves were even less hopeful. Moreover, American research (Greenwood, 1975; Greenberg, 1977) has shown that if there are no immediate indications at the scene of a burglary as to the identity of the perpetrator (generally a witness description or a suspected acqaintance) the chances of an arrest through detective investigation are extremely low.

THE IMPACT OF BURGLARY UPON VICTIMS

are not confined to particular groups, we have identified certain categories of people (particularly women who have been separated from their husbands by death or divorce) who appear to be especially vulnerable. A more general problem is the sense of insecurity that is fostered by the knowledge that unknown persons have entered one's house, which when fuelled by an over-active imagination can result either in suspicion and distrust of acquaintances or in fear of faceless criminals who might return to threaten life and property. Finally, there is the desire for recognition of the offence as a significant event about which " something should be done ".

Although the main objects of this paper have been to describe reactions and to raise questions, some practical conclusions may be drawn. The problem of anxiety caused by exaggeration of the threat posed by burglars can be attacked on two fronts. On the one hand it seems reasonable to attempt to reduce the general fear of crime by the kind of educative pro-gramme recommended by Waller, but on the other the effects on individual victims might be alleviated by the very opposite of another of his recom-mendations—in other words, by *more* rather than less attention to those who have actually suffered a burglary. The latter—which would also deal with the problem of the " recognition " of the offence—could be achieved by changes in police approach or by the extension of Victims Support Schemes, or ideally by both. The burden upon police time would not necessarily be greatly increased if a special effort were made to remind junior officers that what presents itself to a policeman as a trivial, routine offence, holding out little hope of an arrest, may have a vastly different meaning to a person who is experiencing victimisation for the first time. Giving simple advice on security, reassuring victims that the burglar is probably a harmless teenager unlikely to return, carrying out initial investigations in a thorough manner, and later informing people whether or not any progress has been made, although largely unproductive in " thief-catching " terms, are all valuable as aids both to victims' recovery and to police-public relations, and more emphasis could be put upon the simple yet effective technique of talking over the incident with the victim.[20] This kind of help could be augmented by Victims Support Schemes, which also offer practical help and are valuable in identifying people who may eventually need pro-fessional treatment. If these can be developed in more areas, it is important that they be taken seriously by the police and that investigating officers are encouraged to pass on to them all cases in which further help may be needed.[21]

Ultimately, of course, the question of finances and resources may decide

[20] Most of these schemes have found that one or two visits as a sympathetic listener are effective in helping people over the initial effects of burglary. Moreover, it was not uncommon for research interviews to end with the victim saying that our visit had performed a similar function. Having completed the interview we sometimes stayed to continue talking, and in the course of discussion mentioned findings that the majority of arrested burglars are teenagers, that few ever offer violence to householders, and that on average people are victimised only twice in a lifetime, all of which seemed to help people take a more realistic and balanced view of their own burglary.
[21] The Bristol scheme has established a highly successful relationship with the police, being given full access to all reports of offences. However, in other areas volunteers have had to rely on " liaison officers " for the names and addresses of people needing help and lack of enthusiasm by the police has sometimes resulted in very few referrals.

MIKE MAGUIRE

the issue; it is arguable whether or not public funds can be spared to develop support schemes and whether police administrators believe that too much time is already allocated to visits to the scenes of minor crime. Nevertheless, the damage done over the long term by the insecurity and mistrust of others that burglary fosters and by the sense of having been " short-changed " by a casual or unsympathetic response by the police seems, from the results of our study, to deserve some serious consideration.

REFERENCES

BRYANT, G. and CIREL, P. (1977). *Community Response to Rape: Exemplary Project* Washington, D.C.: L.E.A.A., U.S. Dept. of Justice.

B.V.S.S. (1975). " Summary of First Six Months Work of Bristol Victims Support Scheme ", mimeo.

FURSTENBERG, G. (1972). *Fear of Crime and its Effects on Citizen Behavior*. Washington, D.C.: Bureau of Social Science Research.

GAROFALO, J. (1977). *Public Opinion about Crime*. Washington, D.C.: U.S. Department of Justice.

GAROFALO, J. and LAUB, J. (1978). " The fear of crime: broadening our perspective ", *Victimology: An International Journal*, **3**, 242–253.

GREENBERG, B., ELLIOT, C. V., KRAFT, L. P. and PROCTER, H. S. (1977). *Felony Investigation Decision Model*. Washington, D.C.: L.E.A.A., U.S. Department of Justice.

GREENWOOD, P. W. and PETERSILIA, J. (1975). *The Criminal Investigation Process*. Vol. I. Santa Monica, California: The Rand Corporation.

GRENIER, H. et MANSEAU, H. (1979). " Les petits commercants victimes de vol a main armee en quete de justice ", *Criminologie*, *XII*, 57–65.

HALPERN, S. (1978). *Rape: Helping the Victim*. New Jersey: Medical Economics Company.

HAWARD, L. R. C. (1979). " Psychological Consequences of being the Victim of a Crime ", paper to SSRC Law and Psychology Conference, Trinity College, Oxford, September 1979.

HINDELANG, M., GOTTFREDSON, M. and GAROFALO, J. (1978). *Victims of Personal Crime*. Cambridge, Mass.: Ballinger.

HOLMSTROM, L. L. and BURGESS, A. W. (1978). *The Victim of Rape*. New York: Wiley.

KNUDTEN, R. D., MEADE, A. C., KNUDTEN, M. S. and DOERNER, W. G. (1977). *Victims and Witnesses: their experiences with crime and the criminal justice system*. Washington, D.C.: L.E.A.A., U.S. Department of Justice.

LORENZ, K. (1966). *On Aggression*. London: Methuen.

MARCUS, M., TRUDEL, R. J. and WHEATON, R. J. (1975). *Victim Compensation and Offender Restitution—A Selected Bibliography*. Washington, D.C.: L.E.A.A. U.S. Department of Justice.

McDONALD, W. F. (ed.) (1976). *Criminal Justice and the Victim*. Beverley Hills: Sage.

McKAY, B. (1978). Letter in *Liaison*, Vol. 4, No. 11, p. 4, in reply to an article " Minor Burglary," by Waller, I.

THE IMPACT OF BURGLARY UPON VICTIMS

MIERS, D. (1978). *Responses to Victimization.* Abingdon: Professional Books.

N.A.C.R.O. (1977). *Guidelines for Developing a Victims Support Scheme.* London: N.A.C.R.O.

NEWMAN, O. (1972). *Defensible Space.* New York: Macmillan.

REPPETTO, T. A. (1974). *Residential Crime.* Cambridge, Mass.: Ballinger.

SPARKS, R. F., GENN, H. and DODD, D. (1977). *Surveying Victims.* London: Wiley.

WALLER, I. and OKIHIRO, N. (1978). *Burglary: The Victim and the Public.* Toronto: University of Toronto Press.

WALLER, I. (1979). " Victimisation studies as guides to action: some cautions and suggestions." Paper presented to Third International Symposium on Victimology, Muenster, September 2–8, 1970.

WRIGHT, M. (1977). " Nobody came: criminal justice and the needs of victims," *Howard Journal, XVI,* 22–31.

[8]

THE IMPACT OF BURGLARY: A TALE OF TWO CITIES

R I MAWBY* and S WALKLATE†

* Faculty of Human Sciences, University of Plymouth, Plymouth, PL4 8AA, UK
† Department of Criminology, Keele University, Keele, Staffordshire, ST5 5BG, UK

ABSTRACT

Victims' experiences of burglary in two contrasting English cities are compared, using data from a wider cross-national survey. Perceptions of the incident are assessed in terms of financial costs and the wider impact, including the effect of the crime on children in the household, and these are considered alongside the operation of victim support in the two areas. Finally victims' reactions are compared according to concern over future victimisation and crime prevention initiatives. Overall the data suggest that while the responses of burglary victims in the two contrasting urban environments share many common features, living in a more impoverished environment with higher rates of crime influences the ways in which respondents respond to their burglary.

INTRODUCTION

In England and Wales, as in many other western industrial societies, crime is seen as a major social problem. Public perceptions of crime suggest that it rates as one of the major issues confronting citizens, while both police statistics and victim survey data indicate increasing crime rates during the 1980s and early 1990s (del Frate *et al.*, 1993; Home Office, 1994; Mayhew *et al.*, 1994). However, while much public concern may centre on violent crime, research also suggests that most citizens see burglary as particularly common, and that the impact of burglary on its victims is more severe than for most other property crime (Maguire and Corbett, 1987; Mawby and Gill, 1987; Mawby and Walklate, 1994). Most recently, a MORI poll conducted in 1994 found that for 77 per cent of respondents burglary was the main crime they feared (MORI, 1994).

Police statistics suggest an increase of over 100 per cent in burglaries during the 1980s, while the British Crime Survey (BCS) estimates are even higher (Mayhew *et al.*, 1994). While Michael (1993) has argued that for recorded crime burglary rates have increased particularly in traditionally low crime rate and less urbanised police force areas, it is still evident that burglary is concentrated in the larger cities, and within them in particular residential areas (Evans, 1989; Herbert, 1982; Mayhew *et al.*, 1993). Thus researchers on the Islington crime survey have argued that national statistics blur the dramatic problems posed by crime in the inner city (Jones *et al.*, 1986; Crawford *et al.*, 1990), while from a somewhat different perspective geographic research in the UK suggests that public perceptions of cities with better quality of life potential are closely bound to crime rates (Findlay *et al.*, 1989; Morris *et al.*, 1989; Rogerson *et al.*, 1988).

268

If burglary is then an urban problem, it is arguably a greater problem in some cities than in others. But does the fact that burglary rates vary between cities also mean that victims' experiences are equally varied? And do people in very different urban environments react to victimisation in equally different ways? Indeed, if household burglary subsumes a wider spectrum of incidents, how far does the nature of burglary itself vary?

Here we report on interviews with burglary victims in two cities that suggest a number of contrasts: Salford, a part of the Greater Manchester Police Force area and Plymouth, by far the largest city covered by the Devon and Cornwall police. While the two cities were chosen partly for their convenience, in terms of proximity, to the researchers, they were primarily selected because of their differences. Before turning to look at burglary, its impact, and victims' responses, it is appropriate therefore to begin with a brief overview of the two cities.

Plymouth, a city of some 230,000 population, is by far the largest urban area in Devon and Cornwall. A centre of tourism, its industry was traditionally centred on the dockyards, now in decline, and the city incorporates both relatively prosperous areas and deprived inner city districts (Chalkley *et al.*, 1991). Salford, while of similar size (221,000 in 1991) is markedly different in a number of respects. Established during the expansion of the woollen industry in the fourteenth century, and 'celebrated' in the paintings of Lowry and the writings of Engels (1958) and Roberts (1973), Salford rates as one of the most deprived areas of England, with low rates of owner-occupation and high levels of unemployment and single parent households (Forrest and Gordon, 1993; Monaghan *et al.*, 1994).

Salford is a division within the metropolitan Greater Manchester Police Force. Plymouth also forms a police division, although prior to 1994 the divisional boundaries included rural and small town areas to the north and east of the city. Again, there are marked differences between police force area crime rates, at least according to official statistics (Home Office, 1994), with Greater Manchester having one of the highest recorded crime rates in England and Wales, Devon and Cornwall one of the lowest. In 1993, the rate of household burglary was 1,036 for Devon and Cornwall and 2,391 for Greater Manchester, although, following Michael (1993) the rate appeared to have stabilised in the latter while still increasing in Devon and Cornwall. In both Salford *and* Plymouth, rates were above the average for the police areas as a whole.

It is also evident that within both cities crime is spatially concentrated. In Plymouth, household burglaries are concentrated to the south west of the city in a number of wards which either have high levels of social deprivation themselves or border on such areas. In Salford the household burglary rate is highest in F2 subdivision which covers part of the inner city, lowest in F3 subdivision which covers part of the new city and suburban residential area (Monaghan *et al.*, 1994). In Plymouth our study covered the whole of the city, excluding those sections of the old division falling outside the city boundary. In Salford we included the whole division except for one small part where computerisation of crime statistics created some logistical problems.

THE SURVEY

The research in Plymouth and Salford was part of a larger study contrasting the views of burglary victims in seven cities in five European countries: England, Germany, Poland, Hungary, and the Czech Republic.[1] In each city we aimed to draw samples of 400 burglaries from police records and to collate relevant information available on file. We then used this sample as the frame for a subsample of 200 victims to be interviewed: half some 6–8 weeks after the burglary, the remainder 16–18 weeks afterwards. In Plymouth each sample was drawn from 1993, of burglaries committed and recorded from the first day of February, July and November. In Salford the research began one stage later with samples drawn from July and November 1993 and February 1994. Those scheduled for interview were sent a letter from the University (of Plymouth or Salford), stressing anonymity and informing victims that the research had police approval.

Because of the complexity of an international project of this kind, our questionnaire was constructed largely of questions 'tried and tested' in earlier surveys, particularly the BCS of 1984, 1988 and 1991.[2] For the same reason, the majority of questions were accompanied by precoded answers, although we did include a number of open-ended questions and interviewers were instructed to write in verbatim comments where possible. Because of the difficulty of drawing international comparisons *vis-à-vis* social class we also avoided questions on occupation, although we did ask about employment status. We assessed social class through questions on tenure status, self perception of wealth and 'spending power' (measured by holidays abroad and ownership of cars, videos and computers). While police records and personal interviews comprised the main data collected, we also carried out semi-structured interviews with senior police officials and victim service staff. In Plymouth and Salford, in addition, we recorded victim support data on actions taken on the cases in our samples.

In Plymouth, the survey was carried out according to schedule. Four hundred cases were taken from police records and 200 interviews carried out, 100 at time period 1 and 100 at period 2. That is, 50 per cent of recorded victim households were interviewed; in 12 per cent of cases, victims refused to be interviewed; in 23 per cent of cases we were unable to contact households, either because the victim had moved or because no-one was at home on at least three occasions; and, finally, in 16 per cent of cases, no attempt at contact was made. In Salford we had rather more difficulty completing interviews. A sample of 645 records was eventually drawn but interviews were completed with only 132 victims, 71 at period 1 and 61 at period 2. Of those included in our record sample, 20 per cent were interviewed, with 29 per cent of those written to subsequently interviewed. While we have no concrete evidence to explain the difference between Plymouth and Salford, our overwhelming impression was that in Salford a significant number of refusals came from victims who were critical of the police and suspicious of a survey carried out with police approval, and that victims from poorer and more disreputable areas were under-represented among respondents.

270

In any case, the lower response rate in Salford – 29 per cent – injects a note of caution into our findings.

The data considered here thus refer to 332 interviews with burglary victims. In Plymouth 100 victims were interviewed at time 1, the first 41 days after the burglary, the last 75 days after, with a mean of 54 days; 100 more were interviewed at time 2, the first 109 days after the burglary, the last 161 days after, with a mean of 130 days. In Salford 71 victims were interviewed at time 1, ranging from 41 to 76 days afterwards with a mean of 54 days; 61 were interviewed at time 2, ranging from 98 to 146 days afterwards, with a mean of 113 days, considerably earlier than in Plymouth.

In giving overall totals we have reweighted our figures to allow for the Salford shortfall but we have used raw figures in other cross-tabulations. That said, there were some notable similarities and few marked differences between respondents in the two cities. Some of the key points of comparison have been summarised in Table 1. While similar proportions of women were interviewed in each city, the Plymouth respondents tended to be rather older, primarily because of the small proportion of those aged 60–69 among the Salford respondents. In terms of family structure, Plymouth respondents were more likely to be separated or divorced and less likely to be living in a household with other adult(s) and child(ren), and less likely to have children aged 5–15 in the household. In terms of spending power and prosperity, Plymouth respondents were slightly more likely to be owner occupiers, own a car, video, computer, or all three, and to holiday abroad. While these differences are consistent they are not great, supporting our feelings that the Salford sample was slightly skewed. Finally, considerably more Salford respondents had lived in their present area for 10 or more years.

In the following five sections, we shall compare the experiences of victims in Plymouth and Salford and consider how far the social characteristics of victims and features of the burglaries themselves influenced victims' experiences more than city of residence. First we shall describe the offences covered in the survey in more detail, and secondly the impact of the burglary in terms of both financial losses and personal perceptions. In the light of these findings we shall assess the role of victim support in the two cities and, finally, victims' responses to the crime and their perceptions of future risk.

BURGLARY

In English law, burglary is defined in the Theft Act 1968 and includes, in section 9(1), unlawful entry into a building or part of a building, followed by theft or with the intent to commit that or other specified offences. Aggravated burglary (as defined in section 10), where the offender is in possession of a firearm, explosive or other weapon, was excluded from our survey. Attempted burglary, covered by the Criminal Attempts Act 1981 was also excluded. Offences that included unlawful entry but where nothing was stolen were included, but offences where

TABLE 1
Percentage of respondents with the following characteristics

	Plymouth	Salford	Reweighted Total
Gender:			
Male	40	39.4	39.7
Female	60	60.6	60.3
Age:			
Under 40	48.2	51.3	49.8
40–49	30.7	32.8	31.8
60 or more	21.1	16.0	18.6
Lived in area:			
Under 2 years	24.0	15.1	19.6
2–9.9 years	34.0	29.6	31.8
10 years or more	41.5	55.3	48.4
Marital Status:			
Single	20	15.9	18.0
Married/Cohabiting	52	61.4	56.7
Separated/Divorced	15.5	11.4	13.5
Widowed	12.5	11.4	12.0
Household Structure:			
Single Adult	29.5	22	25.8
All Adult	42	40.2	41.1
Single Parent	6.0	6.8	6.4
Parents and Child(ren)	22.5	31.1	26.8
Tenure Type:			
Owner Occupiers	65	60.8	62.9
Renters	35	39.4	37.2
Ownership of:			
Car, video and computer	32	27.3	29.7
None	15	23.5	19.3
Holiday abroad:			
Within last 12 months	35.5	33.3	34.4
Over 12 months ago	45.0	41.6	43.3
Never	19.0	25.0	22.0

272

an attempted entry was unsuccessful were excluded. The distinction is illustrated in the following two cases from Plymouth, the second of which was excluded:

Offended used unknown instrument to force open rear ground floor window. Once inside alarm activated and exit through back door. (PL11253)

Front sash window forced using some form of instrument. The noise alerted the occupant. Window raised but no entry gained. (Data from CIS, Freetext MO).

While most European countries differ in their definition of burglary, they also generally differ from one another. Broadly speaking, the English definition is relatively wide in including unsuccessful burglaries (that is, where entry was made but nothing was stolen), where in many other countries these would be categorised as attempts, and in including incidents where entry is gained without resort to force. While in many continental countries entry through an open window or unlocked door would be classified as theft rather than burglary, in other countries so too would entry by means of a credit card to ease back a doorcatch or by deception. Having said that, as is the case nationally (Mayhew *et al.*, 1993), almost all the cases in our Plymouth and Salford samples related to entry through a door or window, although in many cases it was unclear whether or not entrance had been forced. The most distinctive aspects of the burglary were the time when the offence took place and whether household members were present.

Burglaries were least likely to occur in the morning (10 per cent), with far more in the afternoon (25 per cent) and a few where victims were unsure as between the morning and afternoon (5 per cent). About half took place in the evening (22 per cent), at night (25 per cent),, or one or the other (4 per cent). In 9 per cent of cases victims could not approximate the time of the offence. Asked directly, 39 per cent said it took place in daytime, 47 per cent at night and 4 per cent at dawn or dusk, with 11 per cent unsure. Salford burglaries were more common in the daytime (44 per cent compared with 33 per cent) and especially in the afternoons (31 per cent compared with 19 per cent). In about two thirds of burglaries the house was empty. This was more commonly the case in Salford (70 per cent) than Plymouth (63 per cent). Overall three scenarios were relatively common. In 33 per cent of cases the burglary took place in daytime when the house was empty. This was particularly the case in Salford (38 per cent); less so in Plymouth (27 per cent). In such cases victims often described arriving home to discover the burglary or being summoned home after the burglary had been witnessed by someone else, most commonly a neighbour:

While the respondent was out shopping two youths cut the telephone line and smashed the French windows at the rear of the house with a shovel from the garden. A neighbour challenged them and phoned the police. They fled after gaining entrance to only one room (SAL321).

Respondent returned from afternoon out to find door on security chain and was unable to open it. She realised someone was – or had been – in the house. The police were already in the street dealing with another burglary so she got them to go round the back to check. (SAL72).

'I was out and the young lady next door saw the back door open and called the police. When I got back the police were here.' (PL17594).

In other cases respondents sometimes did not realise until later that the burglary had taken place. For example:

'I came home about three in the afternoon. I noticed things looked a bit strange. I entered the bedroom and some drawers were open. I went into the kitchen and the back window was open.' (PL24953).

'I came home before my husband but didn't notice anything. When my husband came home he asked where the video was and we noticed we had been burgled.' (PL343134).

Secondly, in 26 per cent of cases the offence took place after dark when someone was in the house. This was slightly more common in Plymouth (29 per cent) and usually reflected burglaries during the night. In some cases respondents described being woken up and disturbing the burglar:

'I was asleep in the living room and at 5am I heard a noise in the kitchen and I thought it was my girlfriend. The living room door opened and a man poked his head around the door, saw me looking at him and then ran off.' (PL24843).

'I was upstairs in bed at about 11.30 and I heard some glass breaking. I leapt out of bed and put all the lights on and ran down the stairs and whoever it was ran off.' (PL38497).

In others, the offence was not discovered until later, usually but not always the next morning:

Respondent in bed – woken up by police officer who had found handbag stolen in burglary and who came in and woke up respondent. (PL20771).

274

'I came down in the morning. In the living room I had cupboards open and
when I went into the bathroom the window was open. I came back in here
and saw the video was gone.' (PL17574).

Thirdly, in 23 per cent of cases the burglary took place after dark when no-one
was in. These usually happened either when the respondent was out until late or,
less commonly, when the victim was away but the time of the offence was
registered by a neighbour witnessing the crime.

Additionally, some burglaries took place in the daytime when someone was at
home (7 per cent), although the victim was not always aware of the offence at the
time. For example:

'I was upstairs in the house and I heard something downstairs. I looked out
of the window and saw four men climbing out of the window and leaving
the house.' (SAL526).

'I was in the kitchen cooking on the 2nd July, and I had the French doors
open. I turned and saw someone in the living room. I said "oy" and they ran
out ... I immediately phoned the police.' (PL17210).

'My youngest son and I were watching TV in the living room and the back
door was open. My bracelet, watch, camera and dictaphone were on the side
and someone just came in and took them.' (PL35169).

A similar number occurred when the house was empty for some time and the
victim was unable to specify the time of offence (7 per cent). In fact, all those
classified in this way were from the Plymouth sample where, commonly, the
victim returned home from holiday to discover the aftermath of the crime.

As these examples indicate, in over three quarters of cases in our samples (77
per cent) no-one was aware of the crime at the time. In 12 per cent the respondent
or some other household member realised the burglary was taking place and in
12 per cent someone else, usually a neighbour, witnessed the incident. Where the
respondent was not at home we asked where he or she was. Most commonly they
were engaged in leisure pursuits (30 per cent), at work (21 per cent), away from
home for the weekend, on holiday (14 per cent) or shopping (12 per cent).
Plymouth victims were more likely to be involved in leisure activities (39 per
cent) while in Salford burglaries were relatively common when the respondent
was out shopping (19 per cent).

It is clear that the circumstances surrounding the crime varied for different
victims and that these variations were similarly reflected in the slightly different
experiences of victims from Plymouth and Salford. Equally there were differences in terms of the losses suffered by victims.

THE COST OF CRIME

In defining burglary we have noted that a 'completed' burglary does not necessarily entail theft or damage, but can amount to no more than entry with intent.
That said, 90 per cent of our respondents said that items had been stolen and 70
per cent that damage had been incurred; 96 per cent said that they had suffered a
financial loss due to theft and/or damage. Generally Salford victims were more
likely to have suffered loss, particularly damage (77 per cent compared with 62
per cent in Plymouth). However, the cost of items stolen was slightly higher in
Plymouth. Overall the estimated median value of the items stolen was £717, but
variations were marked, with 18 per cent losing £2000 or more, 7 per cent less
than £50.

We can also consider what items were stolen. Electrical goods (including
cameras) were the most common target, taken in 67 per cent of burglaries, with
jewellery (41 per cent) and cash (38 per cent) also frequently taken. Receptacles,
possibly used for carrying other items, were stolen in 22 per cent of incidents and
credit cards, saving books and the like in a further 17 per cent. Electrical items
were more likely to be taken in Salford, cash and cards in Plymouth.

In addition to the financial implications of the crime, exactly half our respondents said they had lost items of sentimental value. Those were commonly items
such as jewellery or watches that had been handed down in the family, or which
reminded the victim of a special occasion or the memory of a dead spouse or
child. However respondents also cited other items, such as videos of their children
when young, which were irreplaceable. For example:

'It was his (late husband's) wedding ring and my ring from 18th. Don't have
much but it's just things we bought one another.' (SAL134).

'My ring 'cos it was for my sixteenth birthday, and the other was a charm
ring for Valentine's Day.' (SAL136).

'The trinket box had some earrings my gran had given me.' (SAL557).

'Jewellery ... wife's engagement ring ... daughter's christening items ...
video tapes of the family growing up. ...' (SAL665).

'The biggest heartbreak for me was my handmade Omega watch especially
made for me in America 25 years ago ... it was unique.' (PL350750).

'The film inside the video camera was of the children at Christmas and past
birthdays.' (PL43134).

'My mother's engagement ring which she left to me when she died. I didn't
know how much it was worth.' (PL24880).

276

'The watch was an 18th birthday present.' (PL24885).

The wider impact of such losses is illustrated in the response of one widow when subsequently asked what her first reaction to the crime had been:

'Just burst into tears ... I cried for nearly two days, every time I thought about my wedding rings – you see I was widowed ... just couldn't believe it.' (SAL106).

Answering the same question, a Plymouth man noted:

'Anger was the main thing. The watches were the only things in the house that meant anything to me. Especially my granddad's pocket watch. That watch really meant a lot to me – it represented my family history.' (PL30959).

Losses – financial or sentimental – were often compounded by expenses caused by damage to the house. While 70 per cent of victims said that damage had been caused, 43 per cent said that it had amounted to more than £20 worth and 6 per cent estimated the cost of damage at £1,000 or more. Usually this was where patio doors and double glazing were involved. Most commonly, damage was to doors and windows during entry:

'They broke the window to get in. Well, not just broke it but the frame was damaged as well as when they took the glass out. It was a whole unit.' (SAL387).

'They broke the lock on the window and tore the curtain getting in. Other than that there wasn't any mess apart from mud from shoes.' (PL38251).

In other cases damage or mess was caused in a search for valuables:

'They ransacked the house. They even took my quilt cover off the bed ... Everything was chucked all over the place where they had been searching for stuff. All the drawers were open, all my jewellery was thrown all over the place. The place had been ransacked.' (PL34946).

Moreover, for a small minority of victims, the situation was aggravated by what was clearly wanton vandalism:

'Many things were broken and stood on. Drawers were turned out and things were deliberately smashed.' (SAL601).

'Threw everything around – smashed poles, mirrors, etc. Broke two doors to get in.' (SAL723).

'Urinated on curtains, faecal matter spread into carpet; whole house turned upside down – drawers, cupboards etc emptied and tipped on floor.' (PL112953).

For those suffering loss or damage, insurance is critical, and indeed – as our survey confirmed – insurance requirements were a prime reason for reporting the crime. Nevertheless, only 69 per cent of respondents were insured. The fact that this is higher than the 50 per cent cited in the 1992 BCS is indicative of the inclusion of both attempts and unreported burglaries in the latter (Mayhew *et al.*, 1993; p. 60). Overall, 60 per cent of victims, or 87 per cent of those who were insured, made a claim, and only 3 per cent of those claiming had their claim rejected. However, only 29 per cent of respondents said that their loss was fully covered by their insurance. In many of the remaining cases, victims were required to pay the first, say, £50.00 of their loss, while in other cases insurance companies disputed the value of goods itemised in claims. While it is important that companies ensure that they are not defrauded by victims, clearly a number of people in our samples felt aggrieved at the way they were treated. For example:

'They make you feel you are telling lies.' (PL38189, Q62).

Another said resignedly:

'This insurance thing is a bit of a nuisance ... We've got to accept it as a fact of life actually.' (PL2497).

As well as cases where the insurance claim was rejected, in others victims described the difficulties they experienced before their claim was accepted. For example:

'They are disputing the claim – the chainsaw and stuff. I went to the insurance ombudsman and now the insurance company are thinking of paying out ... We have been to the Citizen's Advice Bureau and all ... They knocked loads of money off. The video they only allowed us £100 ... .' (PL35275).

In another case, an elderly widow explained that her claim had been rejected:

'Because they didn't break in. They just walked in, so they wouldn't pay me any insurance.' (PL17210).

When later asked what was the worst thing about the incident she noted:

278

'I'm upset about the insurance too. I pay £90.00 per year for insurance and they wouldn't give me anything.' (PL17210, Q62).

In this case, with the victim's permission, we referred the case to Victim Support who eventually pressured a very reluctant company to honour the claim.

It is difficult o establish the extent of such criticisms because we did not ask any broader questions about victims' experiences with making claims. What we can say is that while for many victims financial losses are eased (but not eliminated) where they are covered by an insurance policy, for some the attitude of their company or its representative exacerbates the wider problems they face. It is to the wider impact of burglary that we now turn.

THE WIDER IMPACT

It is widely accepted that the impact of burglary is not merely financial and that

TABLE 2
Percentage of victims affected during the first few days after the crime

	Plymouth (n = 200)	Salford (n = 132)	Reweighted Total
Very much	31.0	43.9	37.5
Quite a lot	37.0	25.8	31.4
A little	24.5	28.0	26.3
Not at all	6.5	1.5	4.0
NA	1.0	0.8	0.9
Total	100	100	100

victims react in a variety of ways to different aspects of the crime. When we asked respondents how much they had been affected, personally, at the time, just over one third said they had been affected 'very much' with a further third affected 'quite a lot'. As is evident from Table 2, Salford victims appeared somewhat more affected than their counterparts from Plymouth.

What then did respondents feel when they initially learnt about the crime? We asked an open-ended question concerning their first reaction. Overall, nearly a third (31 per cent) of victims cited anger or annoyance:

'Yes, surprisingly enough I wanted to get my hands on them ... and I'm not usually a brave person at all.' (PLY34897)

'Angry that someone had invaded my private space ... .' (PL20755)

'Pretty peeved off and angry. I wanted to get hold of the bastards what done it.' (PL35049)

More commonly, people described their first feelings in terms of shock (33 per cent), fear or worry (15 per cent), upset or distress (8 per cent), shaken up or feeling sick (5 per cent), or even as crying (3 per cent).
For example:

'Shock. I couldn't talk. The inside of me was trembling – couldn't even talk proper when the policeman came.' (SAL449)

'My first reaction – I was devastated – you know. Well, then you calm down after a bit. Then there was the fear of being in on my own. You know, at night with the kids.' (SAL387)

'I was petrified. I wouldn't stay in the house.' (PL27883)

In complete contrast a small number (3 per cent) mentioned relief – that they had not been at home or that not much had been stolen or damaged – a reaction perhaps prompted by the disparity between the reality of burglary and more lurid media accounts:

'Not too distraught at the time as I was grateful I wasn't in at the time.' (PL28313)

'Well in a way I was very much aware it could be so much worse. So I was relieved there wasn't any damage.' (PL15735)

We then asked respondents if they, or anyone else in their household had suffered any emotional reactions after the crime. A large majority – 96 per cent in Plymouth and 91 per cent in Salford – answered in the affirmative. Almost all of these (91 per cent of all respondents) said that they personally had been affected. Rather less said that someone else had been affected. When asked about other adults who lived in the household 83 per cent said that they had been affected and 53 per cent of those with children at home said they had.
We then offered respondents a prompt card listing five reactions cited in the literature: anger, shock, fear, difficulty sleeping and crying/tears. As is clear from Table 3, the most common reaction among respondents was one of anger, followed by shock. Fear and sleeplessness were cited by a large minority of respondents, with about one fifth admitting to tears. While the figures for other adults in the household were generally lower, the pattern was broadly similar. However, among children fear appeared the most common reaction, followed by

280

TABLE 3
Percentage of Victims who said that they or, if applicable, other adults or children in their household had experienced the following emotional reactions

	Plymouth			Salford		
	Self (n = 200)	Other Adult (n = 129)	Child (n = 113)	Self (n = 132)	Other Adult (n = 94)	Child (n = 110)
Anger	78	61	16	77	61	8
Shock	56	46	14	56	42	18
Fear	31	24	32	41	30	30
Sleeplessness	43	27	18	30	18	10
Tears	22	16	21	21	17	22

tears and shock. It also seems from Table 3 that victims in the two cities described their feelings slightly differently. Plymouth victims were more likely to report sleeping difficulties – for themselves, other adults and children. Salford respondents in contrast were more likely to describe themselves and other adults as afraid and less likely to feel that their children had felt angry.

The question of children's reactions to burglary is an interesting one, given Victim Support's recognition that by concentrating their attention on adult householders they may have been missing one group in particular need of help. Reflecting this, some VS Schemes, the Bedfordshire county scheme being a notable example, have made a special effort to address the problems faced by children in victimised households. Our findings here suggest that while children were not, at least according to adults from their households, as likely to be affected as were the adults, they did suffer a number of effects. For example:

'I feel guilty because of my children. They are devastated and there is nothing I can do. I can't afford to replace their things ... They are still upset and staying with my mum.' (PL17419, Q62)

In other cases respondents cited concern for their children's safety as influencing their own responses, although overall those with children were only marginally more affected themselves. Nevertheless, concern for their children did shape many victims' perceptions.

'Mainly I was afraid to sleep there – in a sense more afraid for the children.' (PL21134, Q23)

'I froze. They'd been in my house. They could have touched my little girl. It's horrible.' (PL34889, Q23)

The fact that some victims were more concerned on their children's behalf than were the children themselves, reflects in part the lack of awareness among very young children. As one respondent noted:

'Not really sunk in with the children.' (SAL134, Q27)

To assess this in more detail, we compared respondents' views on the effects of the burglaries on their children according to the ages of the latter, distinguishing between those with children aged nought–five, those with children aged six–15 and those with children in both age groups. Asked whether their children had suffered any emotional reactions, 25 per cent of parents of nought–five year olds responded in the affirmative compared with 71 per cent of parents of six–15 year olds and 61 per cent of those with children in both age groups. Numbers are

TABLE 4
Percentage of victims who said that their children had experienced the following emotional reactions according to the ages of the children

	Only younger children (n = 36)	Only older children (n = 48)	Both (n = 23)
Anger	5.6	20.8	4.3
Shock	0.0	29.2	13.0
Fear	11.1	43.8	34.8
Sleeplessness	8.3	20.8	8.7
Tears	13.9	22.9	30.4

relatively small here, but as Table 4 indicates, the pattern is a clear one, with children in families where there are no younger children generally most affected and young children least affected. Indeed in the former case it appears that emotional reactions, of one sort or another, are relatively common.[3]

It is clear that most victims were affected by the incidents at the time, as were the majority of other adults in the household. Children were less affected, although where the children were old enough to understand the significance of the event their reactions were greater. What of the longer term impact of the crime?

We asked respondents two questions about differences in their feelings over time. First, we asked how their 'feelings about the crime changed over time'. While a significant minority (23 per cent) said that they had not been affected, or that the effects had worn off quickly, most said that they had 'felt bad' at some stage. Some 32 per cent said that they had been affected at the time but things

282

had improved since, while 19 per cent reported various fluctuations in their feelings. For example, some felt reasonably calm at the time but worse a few days later. Finally, 24 per cent said they had not – at the time of interview – got over the burglary. The range of responses is reflected below:

'You accept it. It's done and that's it.' (PL112152)

'I was very practical then – after the police interview I broke down.' (PL11150)

'I don't feel angry any more and have tried to convince myself it could have been worse.' (PL25037)

'It hasn't got better. I'm too scared to live here.' (PL34883)

'I barricade myself into the house at night now.' (PL34889)

'Even today I feel bad. I don't feel so violent but my daughter won't stay in the house on her own. We have even redecorated the rooms.' (PL38192)

'Can't go out much 'cos I'm paranoid – if I go out always rushing back.' (SAL211)

Both the range of responses and the fact that the incident had a devastating affect on so many victims are reflected in answers to a later question, how long it had taken for the main effects to wear off. While 35 per cent answered a 'matter of hours' or 'a few days', 32 per cent said that it had taken over a month or that the effects were still with them. Interestingly, 41 per cent of Salford respondents fell in this category compared with 26 per cent of Plymouth victims, corresponding to the distinction noted earlier in terms of those personally affected at the time. In other words, the impact of the crime appears to have been greater for Salford victims and to have lasted longer.

It might be suggested that those interviewed soon after the burglary would tend to dramatise the incident. To test this we compared the responses of those interviewed at time 1 with those interviewed some 10 weeks later. Strikingly, there were no significant differences. Respondents in our two subsamples were equally likely to describe themselves as very much affected, to feel that the effect had lasted for as long, and to describe the same emotions. In this sense then, the impact of burglary is neither one that is exaggerated at the time nor a memory that fades after three or four months.

To assess their overall feelings about the crimes, we asked our samples to describe, in their own words, 'the worst thing about the incident.' While their replies are by no means surprising, and indeed reflect the findings of earlier studies (Maguire, 1982; Maguire and Corbett, 1987), they are nonetheless worth reiterating here. Essentially they cover five issues. First, there is fear that the burglar might return, combined with a complaint that respondents had had to adjust their behaviour, with the result that the quality of their lives had worsened. For example:

'The fear of a return visit. The thought that they know what's here and will come back again ... that they will come back again and get the things we have replaced.' (PL38184)

'That I didn't hear anything at all ... It's a bit frightening because sometimes I'm here on my own ... You just don't feel safe in your own home any more.' (PL38061)

'Just worry that they're going to come back. It's always in the back of your mind when you come home, if anyone has broken in again.' (PL35100)

'Just not being able to relax and sleep at night feeling safe. That's all.' (PL20987)

'Being on your own and scared after it's happened.' (SAL221)

'You can't settle proper now ... lights have to be left on, doors bolted ... just don't feel secure in your home.' (SAL124)

Second, and related to this, was concern over why their home had been targeted, with corresponding speculation that the offender was someone who knew them:

'How did they know I was away? They also burgled my sister on the same day. How did they know we were both away?' (PL27841)

'That we were away at the time and someone came in. You wonder if it's someone you know – if someone is watching what you are doing.' (SAL79)

Third, and most commonly, was indignation that their privacy had been invaded, that their home and its contents were in some way violated or infected. For example:

'I would say the fact that someone had been in my bedroom, sat on my bed, and gone through my things. Material things can be replaced but the feeling of intrusion will never go away.' (PL38529)

'The thought of someone being through my house, looking through my things. It's a strange feeling – it affected me more than I thought it would ...' (PL12430)

284

'The fact that your private belongings have been overturned. It really is upsetting ... photos and private papers ...' (PL17636)

'Invasion of privacy. It made it better that they wore gloves ... The flesh hadn't actually touched our things.' (PL20755)

'It's an invasion of privacy – the Home's the Castle sort of thing ...' (SAL130)

'The feeling that someone's been in your house when you're not there. It's an invasion of your privacy.' (SAL74)

'You feel isolated ...' (SAL267)

Fourth, there was a feeling of injustice: that one had worked hard for one's possessions which had been taken by a burglar who, correspondingly, had not worked for them:

'The fact that I'd saved hard for the things that were stolen and they just came in and helped themselves ...' (PL24885)

'That I've worked hard for everything and they've just been able to come in and get it for nothing.' (PL112657)

Finally, some focused on the loss itself. In some cases the emphasis was on the financial loss, in others on the loss of items of sentimental value. In the latter case especially, victims sometimes blamed themselves for not being more careful. For example:

'Well I'm not insured and I haven't got any money and I was just really pissed off.' (PL35049)

'My television going. It's all the company I've got.' (SAL72)

'The video tape being taken and the memories lost.' (PL43134)

'Losing my mother's ring ... absolutely ... My mother only died in April and I'm still recovering from that ... and now I've lost the one thing she gave me. My mother wore the ring for 60 years and now it's gone and I feel it's my fault.' (PL2488)

Similar views were expressed time and time again, and indeed our interviewers frequently commented on the fact that victims of all types reiterated the same points with almost monotonous regularity. However this should not be taken to mean that all burglary victims are equally affected or indeed that they are affected in the same ways. This is well illustrated if we compare responses according to two sets of variables, the characteristics of the victims interviewed and the nature of the incident.

In the latter respect we compared reactions according to when the burglary took place and who was in the house at the time, the value of goods stolen, whether or not anything of sentimental value was stolen, whether damage was caused and whether the items stolen were covered by insurance.

Perhaps surprisingly, nighttime burglaries did not evoke more concern than those occurring in daytime. Indeed, 43 per cent of victims of daytime burglaries but only 32 per cent of victims of nighttime burglaries said they had been very much affected at the time, and 39 per cent of the former and 23 per cent of the latter said the effects had lasted at least a month. There was similarly little indication that the small number who were home alone at the time of the crime were more affected. Indeed, where the house was empty victims were more likely to say that the effects had lasted at least a month. They were also more likely to describe their reaction as one of anger, whereas those at home alone were the most likely to mention shock or fear.

The pattern was rather clearer when we considered the extent of loss or damage. Those whose financial losses were greatest, who lost items of sentimental value, incurred damage or were not insured were most likely to be affected 'very much' and to suffer for a longer period of time. It also appeared that where damage occurred or there was loss of items of sentimental value, victims more often described themselves as afraid or suffering from insomnia.

What then of variations in the impact of the burglary according to the characteristics of the victims? In fact, while age variations were negligible (and confined to Plymouth) there were marked differences according to the gender and social status of respondents. Women were more likely to describe the impact of the crime as severe and long lasting than were men, and given the over-representation of women among respondents this tends to affect the overall totals. Only 28 per cent of men, but 42 per cent of women said the crime had personally affected them 'very much', while 24 per cent of the former and 37 per cent of the latter said that the effects had lasted at least a month.

While men more often described their reaction as anger, women were more likely to say they were afraid or shocked and to admit to crying or sleeplessness. There was also a marked variation according to the social status and prosperity of victims. Most affected were those with none of the three luxury items we asked about, those who had had no recent holidays abroad, and those who perceived themselves as relatively poorly off. Similarly, as illustrated in Table 5, while feelings of anger were widespread, in other respects those in rented accommodation were most severely affected. Overall then, those who were least powerful and most vulnerable prior to the offence were most likely to be affected by it.

As a final note, it is interesting, in the light of current concern for victims of repeat victimisation (Bridgeman and Sampson, 1994; Farrell and Pease, 1993),

286

TABLE 5
Percentage of Victims who said that they had been affected in the following ways

	Owner Occupier (n = 210)	*Rented* *Accommodation* (n = 122)	*Total* (n = 332)
Personally affected 'very much'	33.3	41.0	36.1
Angry	78.1	76.2	77.4
Shocked	51.9	63.1	56.0
Afraid	30.5	41.8	34.6
Had difficulty sleeping	36.2	40.2	37.7
Cried	15.7	30.3	21.1
Affects took over a month to wear off	26.7	40.1	31.6

to consider differences according to whether victims had experienced previous burglaries over the last five years. Overall, more Salford victims (34 per cent) had suffered an earlier burglary than was the case in Plymouth (27 per cent). Controlling for this difference it appeared that repeat victims were more likely to express anger and to say that the effects had been slower to wear off. On the other hand they were less likely to have been shocked and – in Salford at least – less likely to say they had cried or had difficulty sleeping. It thus seems that while the burden of a second burglary may aggravate the difficulties of the first experience, in other ways people may be made more aware of the problems and learn to better deal with them.

SUPPORT FOR VICTIMS

Perhaps the most obvious sources of support for burglary victims are informal ones – kin, neighbours, friends or colleagues. Only one per cent of respondents said they had not talked to anyone like that about the crime, and most had talked to a wide variety of people. Overall 84 per cent said they had spoken to their families outside the immediate household, 79 per cent to friends, 72 per cent to neighbours, 64 per cent to other household members and 49 per cent to work colleagues. In general, Plymouth victims reported speaking to more people about the incident; for example 78 per cent said they talked about it to their neighbours.

A large majority (84 per cent) said they found people they talked to 'supportive or helpful' with family seen as most helpful, then friends, and least so neighbours and colleagues. For example, family help was appreciated:

'I was able to speak in more detail with my family.' (PL38049)

On the other hand, people in general – and neighbours in particular – were not all a source of support, for a variety of reasons:

'They weren't supportive or helpful. They were just nosey.' (PL112197)

'Everybody looks and says, "Thank God it wasn't me!".' (SAL679)

'Because burglary is common place today. Nobody really cares about it any more.' (PL20833)

'Just didn't want to ... didn't trust the people round there. The people out there are the sort of people who would have done your house over anyway.' (PL21134)

Victim Support has emerged in the last twenty years as an additional source of help to victims of crime. Established as a local community resource rather different from statutory agencies employing professionals, visits are generally carried out by volunteers (Mawby and Gill, 1987). And while schemes now cover a broader spectrum of crimes than in the early days, burglary remains a crime with which Victim Support is closely associated in England and Wales, if less so abroad (Mawby and Walklate, 1994). There are, however, marked differences between Victim Support schemes in different parts of England and Wales, based on resources and local preferences (Maguire and Corbett, 1987; Maguire and Wilkinson, 1993; Mawby and Gill, 1987; Russell, 1990). For example, some schemes in low crime areas may have sufficient volunteers to provide face to face contact with most referrals, while in other places, including many high crime inner city areas, small numbers of volunteers may be swamped by large numbers of referrals. Partly because of this, some schemes contact high proportions of referrals by letter or phone, or may indeed screen out victims at the first 'gate'. While Plymouth is relatively short of volunteers compared with less urban schemes in the South West, it nonetheless provides a contrast with the more urbanised Salford.

The Plymouth scheme has employed a full-time co-ordinator since 1987, a part-time deputy co-ordinator since 1990 and a part-time administrator since 1993. There are currently about 18 volunteers. Co-ordinators regularly visit the five police stations in the city and aim to collect computer printouts of all victims. Cases are then identified for contact based on co-ordinators' perceptions of the seriousness of the crime and the vulnerability of the victim. As the co-ordinator explained:

'Now we have the name of the victim, the address, the age, the type of crime and small, sort of, amount of information as to what happened. Actually it

288

is not enough. There are things that we don't know, if people are disabled or ... often if we did it would obviously prioritise our reason for going ... We go through and pick out all the burglaries, attempted burglaries or burglaries with intent. Usually we can go by age then. If it's an attempted burglary on a young person we very often won't do anything about it, if it's over 60 we will try and contact them ...'

Having made the decision to respond to a case, the co-ordinator then decides how to make contact:

'There are three ways in which we contact victims; visits, letters and telephone calls. Ideally we like to send a visitor out, but because of lack of resources, the shortage of volunteers, we can't always find people to go out ... we still try to visit all the *burglaries*. It is just that we prioritise, we try to go to the older ones first of all and then the younger ones, whatever age. The only reason we send letters to burglary victims is when we just haven't got anyone.'

While in some respects the Salford scheme operates similarly, in others it is rather different. It has a full-time co-ordinator, and about 21 volunteers. Unlike Plymouth, referrals are gained by telephone contact with the clerks in each of the four subdivisions. Whether or not those referred are visited depends on resources, although to an even greater extent than in Plymouth, the co-ordinator stressed that lack of resources, high levels of crime, and especially more serious crime, meant that burglary victims were less likely than six or seven years ago to be visited:

'When Victim Support started the work was predominantly burglary. I hardly ever see a burglary victim now – it's assault, victims of armed robbery and Jean – the deputy – deals with sexual assault and domestic violence. Volunteers do court work. The original reason for Victim Support has got lost. There is such a demand for serious crime and that's long term work and very hard. We've made a policy decision to maintain contact with burglary victims. We could leave the burglary victim outside given the volunteers we've got ... schemes are developing into two tier services.'

Our interviews with co-ordinators thus suggest that while Victim Support might not contact all burglary victims, Plymouth victims might fare rather better than those living in Salford. Responses to a series of questions on the questionnaire bore this out. Given a prompt card with a list of agencies that might have offered help, 69 per cent of Plymouth victims said they had some form of contact with Victim Support compared with only 35 per cent of Salford victims; similarly 13 per cent of the former but only 6 per cent of the latter said they in fact received help or useful advice from Victim Support.

289

The more obvious presence of Victim Support in Plymouth was also illustrated in questions on general awareness of helping agencies. Asked if they knew of any organisations that assisted victims of crime, other than the police, 73 per cent of Plymouth respondents and 52 per cent of Salford respondents spontaneously mentioned Victim Support. When those who did not were directly asked whether or not they had heard of Victim Support, 78 per cent of those remaining in Plymouth and 60 per cent in Salford answered in the affirmative. That is, in total 94 per cent of Plymouth but only 85 per cent of Salford victims said they had heard of Victim Support.

Of course, the fact that victims said that they had had some contact with Victim Support is no guarantee that this was in fact the case. Respondents may have forgotten, or confused Victim Support with some other agency. They may have rejected the offer of help. Or Victim Support may have contacted another member of their household. We therefore also analysed Victim Support files in the two cities. In Plymouth, Victim Support had no record of 26 per cent of our sample, which may be because of a failure of communication with the police or, less likely, an initial decision not to include cases as referrals. The remainder had however been contacted in some way; 23 per cent by letter, 3 per cent by phone and 58 per cent by visit, although in nearly half of these no direct contact was achieved and a personal note was left by the volunteer. By contrast, Salford Victim Support was more likely to contact victims by letter only and less likely to visit: 40 per cent were sent a letter, 2 per cent phoned and only 29 per cent visited. However, rather more of those visited were actually seen (70 per cent). The extent to which pressures in Salford lead to less visits is illustrated if we consider those aged 60 or more, the most likely to be visited in each city. in Salford only 42 per cent of these were visited and 29 per cent actually seen; in Plymouth 64 per cent were visited and 36 per cent seen.

PERSONAL SECURITY AND FUTURE RISK

As we have seen, concern over the possibility of further burglaries is a central issue for many victims. We therefore asked our respondents what security precautions they had taken and how worried they were about future crime.

First we offered respondents a show card and asked if they had any of a list of security measures at the time of the offence, even if they were not in use. Victims most commonly mentioned double locks or deadlocks (64 per cent), chains or bolts on the doors (57 per cent), and window locks (55 per cent), with dogs (15 per cent) and alarms (11 per cent) less common and window bars (1 per cent) rare. In almost all respects, Salford victims appeared better equipped with 'security hardware' at the time of the offence; for example 71 per cent had double locks or deadlocks and 70 per cent door chains or bolts.

The above list of crime prevention measures primarily relate to target hardening which people carry out on their own behalf. In other respects, people may take precautions that involve co-operating with other people and/or adapting their

290

behaviour. We later asked respondents what they had done, since moving to their present accommodation, to avoid crime or minimise its effects, listing a number of lifestyle changes and co-operative measures, as well as target hardening. It was evident that people adopted a variety of responses to the threat of crime. For example, target hardening approaches were reflected through the fitment of special locks to doors (43 per cent) and windows (40 per cent), and property marking (19 per cent); and while only 14 per cent said they had joined a neighbourhood watch (NW) scheme, 49 per cent said they had avoided leaving their home unoccupied more than was necessary. Again it seemed that Salford victims had taken more precautions than their Plymouth counterparts. For example, 24 per cent had had their property marked, 17 per cent were NW members and 36 per cent said they avoided leaving their home unoccupied unnecessarily. Moreover, 15 per cent of Salford victims compared with 8 per cent in Plymouth had a burglar alarm.

But if respondents, in Salford particularly, had been burgled despite the precautions they had taken, how did they respond after the offence? In general, replies reflected a 'more of the same' philosophy, with the most common strategies adopted since the burglary paralleling the most common responses prior to the burglary: avoiding leaving the house empty (34 per cent), informing a neighbour when out (27 per cent), and fitting special locks to doors (28 per cent) and windows (19 per cent). The one exception is a dramatic increase in burglar alarms, with 29 per cent saying they had had an alarm fitted since the burglary.

There was, moreover, a notable difference in emphasis in the reactions of Plymouth and Salford residents. After the burglary, Plymouth victims seemed more willing to invest in security hardware such as window locks and burglar alarms. For example, in Plymouth, 33 per cent had an alarm fitted compared with 25 per cent in Salford, with the result that at the time of interview 40 per cent from each sample had a burglar alarm. On the other hand, Salford victims were more likely to respond by turning to their neighbours for help or by avoiding leaving the home unoccupied. The latter point is well illustrated in answers to a later question on changes in time spent out of the house; 25 per cent in Salford but only 14 per cent in Plymouth said they now went out less often.

The overall result of these changes meant that at the time of interview Plymouth victims were at least as well protected against the risk of future offences as far as 'locks and bolts' security was concerned, but Salford victims had taken more precautions that involved behavioural changes: they were less likely to go out, more likely to ask neighbours to keep an eye on the home and more likely to be in NW Schemes.

However, there is a fundamental problem here. A greater dependence on neighbours assumes a degree of support and co-operation within the neighbourhood which may not be available. Indeed, when we subsequently asked about perceptions of the neighbourhood, Salford residents (19 per cent) were less likely than Plymouth residents (29 per cent) to describe their area as one in which people helped each other, and as is clear from Table 6 that they were also less satisfied

291

TABLE 6
Percentage of respondents who were satisfied with the area in which they lived: Plymouth and Salford

	Plymouth (n = 200)	Salford (n = 132)	Reweighted Total
Very Satisfied	31.0	15.9	23.5
Satisfied	46.0	50.0	48.0
Dissatisfied	14.5	20.5	17.5
Very dissatisfied	8.0	12.1	10.1
DK/NA	0.5	1.6	1.1

with the area. Yet they were no more likely to see themselves as moving in the future. The picture here then seems to be one of Salford victims being less willing to leave the home unoccupied and more concerned about the area they live in, but unable to move; trapped within both area and home.

This is further illustrated if we turn to consider feelings about future victimisation. We asked respondents how safe they felt 'walking alone in the area after dark' and 'alone in your own home at night'. Overall victims were more concerned about their vulnerability outside the home. In each case, as Table 7 illustrates, Salford victims expressed most concern. Similarly when we asked how worried they were about being burgled, mugged or robbed or having their home vandalised, Salford respondents rated higher on all three, but especially

TABLE 7
Percentage feeling safe when 'walking alone in the area after dark' and 'alone in your own home at night': Plymouth and Salford

	Walking Alone		In own home alone	
	Plymouth (n = 200)	Salford (n = 132)	Plymouth (n = 200)	Salford (n = 132)
Very safe	20.0	5.3	33.5	16.7
Fairly safe	31.0	32.6	38.0	51.5
Bit unsafe	24.0	28.0	19.0	24.2
Very unsafe	22.0	34.1	9.0	7.6
DK/NA	3.0	0.0	0.5	0.0

292

TABLE 8
Percentage who worry about burglary, mugging/robbery and home vandalism: Plymouth and Salford

	Burglary		Mugging/Robbery		Vandalism	
	Plymouth	Salford	Plymouth	Salford	Plymouth	Salford
Very worried	27.0	34.8	22.0	40.2	21.0	26.5
Fairly worried	44.5	41.7	22.0	25.0	34.5	38.6
Not very worried	24.5	20.5	36.5	31.1	28.5	31.1
Not at all worried	3.5	3.0	18.0	3.0	14.0	3.0
DK/NA	0.5	0.0	1.5	0.8	2.0	0.8

vis-à-vis mugging or robbery (Table 8). Indeed, feelings about area were also related to feelings of personal safety, underlining the relationship between burglary rates, area of residence and perceptions of future risk.

Other variables were also correlated with feelings about personal security. In particular, women were more concerned than men, and poorer people, as measured across a number of indices, were also particularly worried and felt less safe. For example, only 18 per cent of those rating themselves very or fairly well off said they were very worried about a further burglary, compared with 32 per cent of those rating themselves average and 38 per cent of those rating themselves poor or very poor. Interestingly, those with a burglar alarm were no less worried about crimes against the home. This may be because possession of an alarm fails to increase peace of mind. However it may instead reflect the fact that more worried people are more likely to purchase alarms, a tendency suggested by the fact that those with burglar alarms seemed more worried than other people about street crimes.

SUMMARY

In a Labour Party document, Michael (1993) dramatically suggests that a house in England and Wales is burgled every 24 seconds. He also shows that for the year ending June 1992 insurance companies paid out £712 million in claims associated with burglary. It is clear, then, that burglary is a routine feature of urban life. However, whilst it might be routine in quantity it is still a crime which is far

293

from routine for the victim. The evidence presented here from burglary victims in Plymouth and Salford clearly indicates that burglary can affect individuals in quite fundamental ways, with women and children being particularly vulnerable to its impact. It is also clear that the practices of insurance companies can on occasion exacerbate this impact, coming close to a further, though secondary, victimisation.

What is clear from this analysis is that victims' experiences as victims and their perceptions of their victimisation are clearly related to their experiences within their living environment. Recorded crime rates, and rates for burglary specifically, are higher in Salford than in Plymouth. Salford residents similarly tend to be more impoverished than their Plymouth counterparts. While our respondents differed in some respects consistent with this, we have suggested that non response bias in Salford has resulted in a minimising of differences between our two samples. Nevertheless, respondents from Salford clearly lived in an environment which was more susceptible to crime and poverty than did Plymouth victims. Their experiences of their burglaries, and the impact burglary had upon them, reflect these differences.

Feelings of dissatisfaction with one's area of residence, concern over the safety of its streets and lack of financial resources are all closely entwined with feelings about the impact of the burglary. In consequence, those living in Salford, objectively and subjectively a less adequate environment, were more affected than were Plymouth residents. For example, they were more likely to say they were 'very much' affected at the time and more concerned about future victimisation. However, given the pressures under which Victim Support operates in areas such as Salford, victims there were less likely to have been contacted by Victim Support than were their Plymouth counterparts.

Our findings may thus be interpreted on two levels. On the one hand, victims in the two quite different cities reacted in broadly similar ways to their experiences. Burglary was clearly seen as a serious, intrusive crime that affected most victims to some extent. On the other hand, Salford victims appeared to be more severely affected, and we have argued that this is understandable given the wider social environment within which the burglaries occurred. Crime does not take place in a vacuum, and reactions to crime are more readily understood in terms of the quality of life 'enjoyed' by victims. It is thus the environmental context, rather than differences between individual victims, that best explains the differences between victims' reactions in the two cities.

NOTES

1   The research team comprises Rob Mawby (Director), University of Plymouth and Sandra Walklate, University of Salford, England; Dobrockna Wojcik and Zofia Ostrihanska, Polska Akademia Navk, Warsaw, Poland; Ilona Gorgenyi, University of Miskolc, Hungary; Gerd Kirchoff, Abteilung Monchengladbach, Germany. The project was funded by the Central European University contract 7/91-92, total award $55,200. Additional travel funds were supplied by NATO: contract CRG 920530, total award 277,000 BF.

294

2   These, and many of the other questions, were taken from the 1988 British Crime Survey
     Questionnaire. In addition, questions from the 1984 and 1992 BCS were also included. We are
     grateful to Pat Mayhew for permission to use these questions. Other questions were written
     specifically for this project.
3   As Table 4 illustrates, effects were in general more pronounced where there were older children
     only than where there were both. This may be because in the former case there were more older
     children who might have been affected, or because in the latter case, 'older' children were
     relatively younger.

REFERENCES

Bridgeman, C. and Sampson, A. (1994). *Wise After the Event: Tackling Repeat Victimisation.*
     National Board for Crime Prevention; London.
Chalkley, B., Dunkerley, D. and Gripaios, P. (1991). *Plymouth: Maritime City in Transition.* David
     and Charles; Newton Abbot.
Crawford, A., Jones, T., Woodhouse, T. and Young, J. (1990). *Second islington Crime Survey.*
     Middlesex Polytechnic; London.
del Frate, A.A., Zvekic, U. and Dijk, J.J.M. can (1993). *Understanding Crime: Experiences of
     Crime and Crime Control.* UNICRI; Rome.
Engels, F. (1958). *The Condition of the Working Class in England.* Penguin; Harmondsworth.
Evans, D.J. (1989). 'Geographical analysis of residential burglary' In D.J. Evans and D.T. Herbert,
     eds:*The Geography of Crime*, pp. 86–107. Routledge; London.
Farrell, G. and Pease, K. (1993). 'Once Bitten, Twice Bitten: Repeat Victimisation and its
     Implications for Crime Prevention'. Home Office Crime Prevention Unit Paper 46. HMSO;
     London.
Findlay, A., Rogerson, R., Paddison, R. and Morris, A. (1989). Whose quality of life?. *The Planner,*
     75 (15) pp. 21–2.
Forrest, R. and Gordon, D. (1993). *People and Places: a 1991 Census Atlas of England.* School of
     Advanced Urban Studies; Bristol.
Herbert, D. (1982). *The Geography of Urban Crime.* Longman; London.
Home Office (1994). *Criminal Statistics for England and Wales, 1993.* HMSO; London.
Jones, T., MacLean, B. and Young, J. (1986). *The Islington Crime Survey.* Gower; Aldershot.
Maguire, M. (1982). *Burglary in a Dwelling.* Heinemann; London.
Maguire, M. and Corbett, C. (1987). .*The Effects of Crime and the Work of Victim Support Schemes.*
     Gower; Aldershot.
Maguire, M. and Wilkinson, C. (1993). *Contacting Victims: Victim Support and the Relative Merit
     of Letters, Telephone Calls and Visits.* HMSO; London.
Mawby, R.I. and Gill, M.L. (1987). *Crime Victims: Needs, Services and the Voluntary Sector.*
     Tavistock; London.
Mawby, R.I. and Walklate, S. (1994). *Critical Victimology.* Sage; London.
Mayhew, P., Maung, N.A. and Mirrlees-Black, C. (1993). *The 1992 British Crime Survey.* (Home
     Office Research Study 132). HMSO; London.
Mayhew, P., Mirrlees-Black, C. and Maung, N.A. (1994). *Trends in crime: findings from the 1994
     British Crime Survey.* Home Office Research and Statistics Department Research Findings 14.
     HMSO; London.
Michael, A. (1993). Safe as Houses? Burglary of Homes: an Analysis. Labour Party; London.
Monaghan, L., Taylor, I. and Walklate, S. (1994). *Crime Audit Salford 1994.* University of Salford;
     Salford.
MORI (1994). *Public Attitudes to Crime.* Research conducted for *Reader's Digest Magazine.*
Morris, A., Findlay, A., Paddison, R. and Rogerson, R. (1989). Urban quality of life and the
     North–South divide. *Town and Country Planning,* **58** (7/8) 207–10.
Roberts, R. (1973). *The Classic Slum.* Harmondsworth: Penguin.

295

Rogerson, R., Findlay, A. and Morris, A. (1988). The best city to live in. *Town and Country Planning*, **557** (10) 270–3.

Russell, J. (1990). *Home Office Funding of Victim Support Scheme – Money Well Spent?* (Home Office Research and Planning Unit, Paper 58). HMSO; London.

[9]

Residential Burglary in the Republic of Ireland: A Situational Perspective

C. NEE and M. TAYLOR

C. Nee is Graduate Student and M. Taylor is Professor of Applied Psychology, Department of Applied Psychology, University College, Cork, Ireland

Abstract: This paper describes interviews conducted with a sample of 50 convicted residential burglars imprisoned in the Republic of Ireland. The interviews were structured to establish the nature of their criminal career, the characteristics of the burglaries they committed, their occupational style and their general lifestyle. The results of the interviews are presented in terms of the decision to offend, occupational style and target selection and sentencing as a deterrent. The results confirm the importance of environmental cues in the selection of property to burgle, but attention is drawn to the probable role of multiple cues and cue salience. A behavioural interpretation of these results is proposed.

Residential burglary is an example of a largely non-violent crime for which a number of authors have discussed the importance of environmental influences. Such discussions have been termed situational analyses (Clarke 1980) and it might be argued that most U.S. and British research in this area in the last decade has adopted a fundamentally situational thrust. This approach is characterised by an emphasis on the contribution of environmental features in the aetiology of criminal behaviour. Newman in his work on 'defensible space' is perhaps the earliest author to develop this perspective (Newman 1972). Other authors, such as Scarr (1973) Repetto (1974) and Waller and Okihiro (1978), have examined this approach to the analysis of burglary within a North American context and two recent British studies have further developed it. Maguire and Bennett (1982) in their analysis of burglary focussed on a variety of residential areas primarily in the Greater London region. They identified three categories of burglar:

(i) high level – small network of careful and committed criminals, highly organised and socially exclusive;
(ii) middle range – by far the largest category, skilled but not so well socially organised, and
(iii) low-level – individuals practically indiscriminate in their social or organisational life, who engage generally in petty crime.

Maguire and Bennett assessed and attempted to verify the validity of several situational cues during target choice, including occupancy cues, security cues and vegetational cover. Their findings suggested that in terms of preventing burglary, target hardening in itself did not appear to be effective. Community-based initiatives involving imagination and empathy with the offenders' perceptions are put forward as a more realistic approach.

More recently Bennett and Wright (1984) have published an extensive empirical study greatly extending our insight into the burglars' behaviour. Their aim was to assess the validity of the assumptions on which situational crime prevention techniques are based by investigating the burglars' perspective of burglary. Situational cue validity was assessed using a variety of methods, including semi-structured interview, videotape and two photograph methods; consistency was found between the responses on each method. Bennett and Wright divide their population into three types, in terms of their decision to offend; the planner, the searcher and the opportunist. Only 7% of a sample of 117 burglars fell into the 'opportunist' offence category and reported responding 'there and then' to a set of attractive situational cues. In contrast, the majority of burglars make a series of decisions about their offence before reaching the scene of the crime, at which point a rational response is made to a variety of environmental cues associated with a particular property. The typical burglar is an active, rather than passive, respondent.

The following reports an extension of the analysis of residential burglary to a population in the Republic of Ireland, and presents in addition a *rationale* in which to locate situational analyses of burglary. More specifically, the study seeks to:

(i) evaluate the degree to which the Irish residential burglar is sensitive to the kinds of environmental cues in the immediate criminogenic environment which appear to characterise the British residential burglar, and
(ii) investigate in a more general sense features of the Irish residential burglars' occupational style.

Method and Sample

A sample of 50 convicted, residential burglars were interviewed from three penal institutions; Cork Prison, Fort Mitchell (Spike Island) and Mountjoy Prison, Dublin. Potential subjects were identified either from the general register, recommendations of prison officers and welfare officers, or recommendations from the subjects themselves.

After gaining consent to take part in the study, a structured interview was conducted with each subject. The interview schedule was designed to explore four main areas. Firstly, a brief and unobtrusive review of the subject's criminal career. Secondly, categorisation of the subject's typical burglary, using Maguire and Bennett's (1982) categories of high-level, middle-range and low-level. This was assessed by identifying typical targets, target goods, estimated value of stolen goods, and average amount received by the subject. The third and fourth areas, occupational style and general lifestyle, were examined in much greater detail, looking at temporal patterns, means of entry, mood levels, number of associates, financial habits, appreciation of prison life and appreciation of the victim. Situational cues such as architecture, occupancy and security considerations were also examined. On several occasions subjects were asked to rate the importance of variables in decision making. Interviews took approximately 50 minutes, and each interview was tape recorded and subsequently analysed. Co-operation from subjects was good.

Results and Discussion

The following summarises quite complex qualitative results. These are presented in terms of three broad inter-related areas: the decision to offend, occupational style and target selection, and the perception of sentencing as a deterrent.

The Decision to Offend

During the interview, subjects were asked to rate eight factors with respect to their degree of importance in the subject's decision to burgle. The factors related to mood level, peer group pressure, situational factors and instrumental needs. Seventy-two per cent rated the need for money as the most important factor in their decision to burgle. This is of interest given that 80% of the sample reported that they go out to burgle an average of four times per week, and 74% claimed that half the burglaries they commit are lucrative. This may be an exaggeration, but the general impression given in the interviews was that this sample of burglars went through a lot of cash. Sixty-two per cent claimed to be generally low in money when they went out to burgle. The remainder claimed they had no shortage of money, and were often more confident in their performance when this was the case; their lifestyle rather than need appeared to demand that they worked consistently. Fourteen per cent rated a combination of need for money, situational factors and challenge as equally important in their decision to offend, and 70% (whilst not putting these first) rated mood as totally unimportant. These results appear to support the view of the offender as a 'rational' agent, making decisions under a variety of prevailing circumstances and whose motivational needs appear to be not the result of a single decision but of a whole sequence of decisions, a number of which may have occurred away from the scene of the crime.

It may be useful to note the employment history of the sample. Seventy-four per cent had experience of full-time employment in their past, and 58% reported that they had been involved in crime during employment. Whilst it was not possible to explore this issue further in this study, it suggests a complex relationship might obtain between employment and the decision to offend.

Occupational Style and Target Selection

As in Maguire and Bennett (1982), 'middle-range' burglary accounted for the major part of the present sample (84%). In other respects, however, this study revealed important differences between Irish burglars and their British counterparts, notably in the areas of disposal of the proceeds of the crime, a relevant issue when considering target selection and occupational style. Though stolen property was typically easily resaleable, 58% always used a fence, 28% sometimes used one, and a further 10% were cash burglars (who didn't need a buyer). Unlike in the U.K., receivers for stolen goods appear to be readily available in Ireland, and renowned professionalism and systems of referral do not seem to be important in the middle-range burglary world to gain access (see Bennett and Wright 1984). Fences seem to be extensively used, perhaps because of the country's small population and the consequent reduction in discrete outlets for stolen goods Also, convictions for 'fencing' under Irish law are notoriously difficult, which diminishes effective legal control. Five subjects in fact worked on a commission basis for their buyers who might order, for example, two videos which the burglar would supply two days later. There are obvious implications here for both legislative and law-enforcement policies to address this problem. Of the non-middle-range burglars, 12% were categorised as high-level burglars specialising in valuable jewellery and antiques, and preferring to work by day; only one subject in this category went without the use of a buyer. The remaining 4% were low-level burglars specialising mostly in coin meters and petty cash in 'non owner-occupied' property.

Differences emerged from the data with regard to planning vs. spontaneity in burglary, and it was convenient to use Bennett and Wright's (1984) terminology to label them. Fourteen per cent were 'planners' in that they planned the burglary of a particular house over a period of time, responding primarily to wealth cues inherent in their targets and then watching patterns of mobility in the residents. If deterred, this group would prefer to go home and return on another date rather than look for another target. Notably, there was no preference for 'lack of occupancy' in the planner group, they burgled less frequently and tended to be more successful. Ten per cent of the sample were 'opportunists', in that their decision to burgle was usually spontaneous. They rated opportunity and attractiveness of targets as more important than the need for money, and were probably influenced by situational cues to the greatest extent. This group also reported enjoyment, impulse and job satisfaction as the most important factors in making them re-offend when discharged from prison.

The remaining 76% fell in the 'searcher' category. They were primarily motivated by instrumental needs and decided to offend in the first instance away from the scene of the eventual crime. Situational cues apeared to become important when they had set out to *search* for a suitable target. *Chart 1* summarises the importance of a variety of situational factors in target selection.

Of the entire sample 88% restricted themselves to 'middle class' housing areas and wealthy residential areas; the entire sub-groups of 'planners' and 'high-level' burglars fell into this category. The remaining 12% were indiscriminate in their choice of areas. The burglar enters a

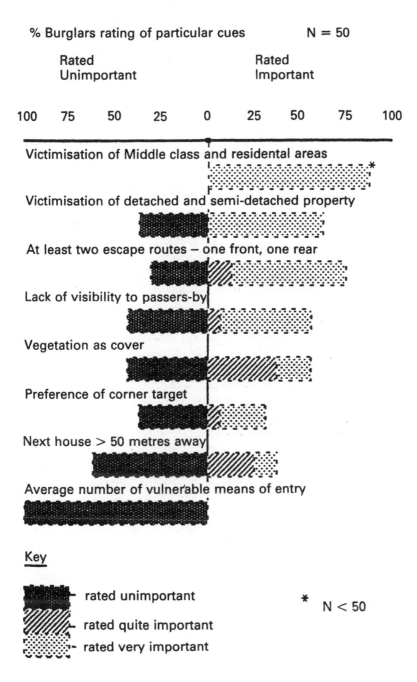

CHART 1
Bar Chart Sumarising Relative Rated Importance of Eight Situational Cues

% Burglars rating of particular cues   N = 50

Rated   Rated
Unimportant   Important

100   75   50   25   0   25   50   75   100

Victimisation of Middle class and residental areas

Victimisation of detached and semi-detached property

At least two escape routes – one front, one rear

Lack of visibility to passers-by

Vegetation as cover

Preference of corner target

Next house > 50 metres away

Average number of vulnerable means of entry

Key

— rated unimportant   * N < 50

— rated quite important

— rated very important

suitable area, some 38% alone (for reasons of lucrativity and secrecy), but more often than not (62%) with one or two associates (for reasons of physical help and surveillance).

The most important environmental factors reported in evaluating choice of target was the existence of at least two escape routes, one front and one to the rear. This suggests that rear access of any kind greatly

CHART 2

Bar Chart Summarising Relative Related Importance of Five Security Cases

% burglars rating particular security cases

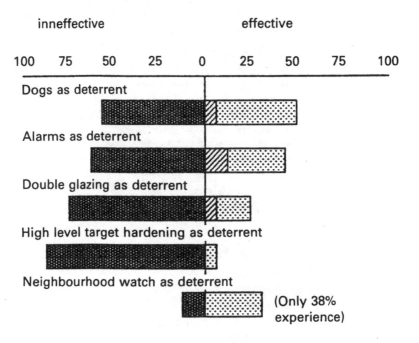

inneffective   effective

100   75   50   25   0   25   50   75   100

Dogs as deterrent

Alarms as deterrent

Double glazing as deterrent

High level target hardening as deterrent

Neighbourhood watch as deterrent

(Only 38% experience)

Key

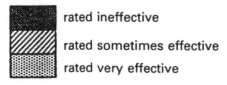

rated ineffective

rated sometimes effective

rated very effective

110

increases target vulnerability, and this preference appears to have reduced the importance of vegetational cover and lack of visibility from the front of the house in comparison with British studies, 24% and 50% respectively rating these factors as very important.

A variety of security cues were assigned some degree of effectiveness, but none were seen as total deterrents. From *Chart 2*, it can be seen that lack of effectiveness outweighs effectiveness in all cases but one. Only dogs and alarms were seen as any kind of deterrent, and these usually only conditionally. Target hardening in general, however, was seen as ineffective by 92%, as some point of entry was always left vulnerable. This lends further support to Winchester and Jackson's (1982) position on the inadequacy of target hardening as a crime prevention technique. Occupancy of a property is a factor obviously demanding the attention of burglars, but not always for obvious reasons. The literature to date, reveals a mixture of findings – some authors have found a lack of occupancy to be highly influential in target selection (for example, Maguire 1982; Scarr 1973). In contrast Waller and Okihiro (1978) found occupancy was often unimportant in their sample. Chappell (1968) found occupancy unimportant, if occupants were asleep, and Bennett and Wright (1984) also found occupancy only conditionally deterred their sample of burglars. The present finding supports the view that occupancy is a conditional deterrent. Only 52% rated lack of occupancy as very important, just over a third were conditionally deterred by occupants who weren't asleep, and 12% preferred occupation (though again asleep) because there were generally more valuables such as cash, jewellery and cheque books available if the residents were at home. Two members of the present sample confronted residents if their searches were fruitless, and one assaulted if his demands were resisted. One regional trend was apparent in this respect: 68% of the Mountjoy sample (Dublin) rated preferred lack of occupancy very highly. Despite these variations in preferences, 96% of the sample checked various occupancy cues to ascertain the presence/absence of occupants, and *Chart 3* summarises the popularity of cues used. Actually knocking on the front door was the most popular check and 22% used this method only. If this was responded to, subject would reduce suspicion by asking directions or for water for their car radiator, etc.

Finally, subjects were asked to identify the single most attractive thing about a recently successful target. Their response to the most popular features are summarised in *Chart 3*. Taking concepts relating to risk, reward and ease of entry (Bennett and Wright 1984), factors relating to risk (lack of occupancy) were mentioned most frequently in assessing target attractiveness, with potential reward second (decor and cars) and ease of entry third (open or timber windows). Interestingly, no security cues were mentioned at all.

An important note is that 86% of the sample rated five or more of the ten cues offered to them as important in target selection and 42% rated seven to nine as important. The use of these cues at the scene of the crime, therefore, appears to be unquestionable. Having selected a target, the

CHART 3
Most Attractive Feature of Recent Successful Burglary

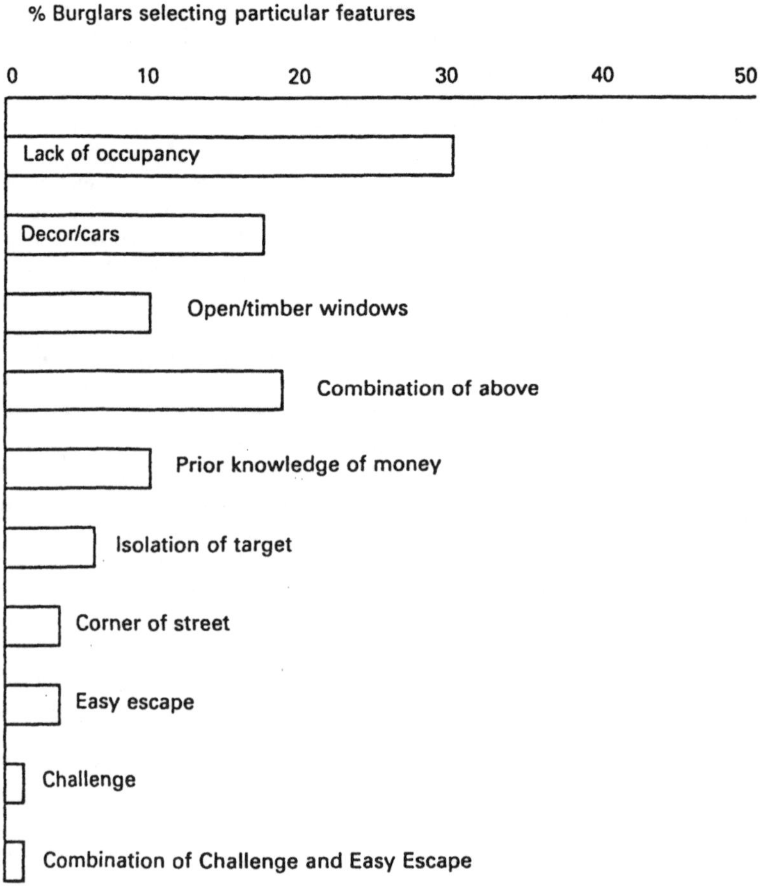

% Burglars selecting particular features

| 0 | 10 | 20 | 30 | 40 | 50 |

Lack of occupancy

Decor/cars

Open/timber windows

Combination of above

Prior knowledge of money

Isolation of target

Corner of street

Easy escape

Challenge

Combination of Challenge and Easy Escape

burglar appears to exhibit a sequence of relatively predictable behaviour; 80% break into the house through a door or window on the ground floor; vulnerable points of entry are never scarce. Entry through the rear is most popular though security is generally better here.

Between 90% and 98% of the sample reported no feelings of guilt, no hostility or desire to confront their victims and avoided damaging the house and contents during a burglary. Consideration of the victim, in fact, was virtually non-existent. These findings are similar to those reported by Bennett and Wright (1984) and Maguire and Bennett (1982), and generally dispel many of the beliefs held about behaviour during a burglary. After the burglary, 64% hide their stolen goods and contact the fence within the next day or two; 26% contact their buyer immediately, and 10% restricted themselves to cash theft. Sixty-eight per cent go home after a successful burglary (or burglaries) and the remaining celebrate.

The literature reveals wide variation in temporal trends for burglary. The Irish pattern, on the basis of this sample, seems to be as follows: 80% go out on average four times per week, and enter at least two vulnerable targets. Thirty-eight per cent prefer week days, 14% the weekend, and 48% have no preference. There is generally no preferred time of year, though 24% mentioned Christmas/Winter. Fifty per cent preferred to work by night, with a slight preference towards the early hours of the morning rather than evenings, 24% preferred the daytime, and 26% worked at anytime.

Sentencing as a Deterrent

As a society we have ambivalent views on the role of prison as a factor in crime prevention, although many professionals doubt its value. The burglars in this sample revealed interesting views on prison, and its deterrent effect, on the crimes they committed. Only 12% considered the immediate risk of apprehension at the point of target entry as very worrying, 26% were only slightly worried by the risk, and 40% did not consider it at all; indeed, 22% reported the risk added excitement and challenge to the burglary. In general, emotional responses reported to the risk of prison, and its effects, were very low. Ninety-four per cent described prison life as tolerable, and 4% described Cork prison as enjoyable. Only 12% described serving a sentence as effective in deterring their offending behaviour, 16% felt it had some effect as sentences became longer with repeated crimes, and growing responsibilities outside (such as wife and family). The rest of the sample saw committal to prison as an occupational hazard (36%), as increasing motivation to commit crime more effectively through learning skills or the desire for revenge (22%), or as only effective as a deterrent whilst 'inside' (14%).

There is little of surprise in these results. Prison has often been described as an optimum learning situation for criminal skills and the setting up of outside contacts in crime; identification with and absorption in its peculiar sub-culture may be a necessity for survival (Feldman 1979; Cohen and Taylor 1972).

Concluding Comments

There are considerable similarities between the results reported here, and those of Bennett and Wright (1984) and Maguire and Bennett (1982), in terms of target discrimination. [There are, however, a number of interesting divergences; rear access to targets, for example, in the Irish burglar appears to be more important than in the U.K. samples. Unconditional lack of occupancy as reported here appears rather more important than Bennett and Wright report, but still surprisingly low. The ambivalence towards vegetative cover is another point of departure from the U.K. studies, and mobility seems to be higher in the Irish studies (perhaps reflecting less density of population) On the other hand, whilst trends may vary, the importance of situational cues in target choice is quite clearly important in the study reported here, as in others. Our concept of the role situational cues might play in the decision to burgle is as yet far from clear. Bennett and Wright in their analysis tend to consider the importance of each cue within a vacuum. This implies a symmetry of cue salience, which is probably unrealistic. For example, if absence of burglar alarm is looked at in isolation, and rated highly attractive, it may also suggest that the presence of an alarm is equally unattractive. The picture which seems to emerge from the study reported here, is that target selection is determined by multiple cue factors, and that in reality, various combinations of cues make a house attractive to the burglar. Given this, it may well be the case that different combinations of cues will cancel out otherwise important deterrent or attractiveness factors. For example, rear access and wealth cues may make one house more vulnerable than a similar unoccupied property. In turn, lack of occupancy and isolation may cancel out the effects of a comprehensive security system. An appropriate line for further investigation would therefore appear to lie not in further survey work of the kind reported here, but in the experimental verification and manipulation of cue salience, an approach anticipated in part by Bennett and Wright.

Psychological Theory and Situational Analyses of Burglary

Though the situational perspective has gained popularity and credibility in the last decade, in terms of psychological theory it remains poorly developed. The approach lacks concrete definitions in many aspects and the reliance on operational definitions by different authors is not helpful. The notion of 'opportunity', for example, is poorly developed, as in the varying emphasis on social, individual and physical factors in the criminal situation. The perspective as it stands can be described as a pragmatic response to a set of causes and effects, and its beauty is its flexibility. However, the danger is that without a firm set of theoretical foundations to support explanation, the approach will remain endemic and patchy, and will lack coherence and real credibility. Many writers have found the innovative practicality of the approach refreshing and exciting and its potential for a more realistic and insightful appraisal of criminal activity has stimulated much crime-specific research (for example, Heal and Laycock 1986). But emphasis has been on the latter rather than on theoretical development, and it may now be time to initiate some debate on that development.

Until relatively recently, psychological thinking about crime was dominated by attempts to identify particular personal attributes of individuals that might be associated with a propensity to commit crime (see, for example, Eysenck 1970; Yochelson and Samenow 1976). These analyses have repeatedly failed to identify pathologies which do not exist in the non-offending public, and have been of little value in terms of crime control. The need for a major re-appraisal of approaches to the control of criminal behaviour was obvious.

The situational approach to crime prevention lends itself well in psychological terms to behavioural interpretations. The various cues, etc., available to the burglar might be said in behavioural terms to 'set the occasion' for the response of burglary, or in more technical terms, to act as a discriminative stimulus (Skinner 1953). A behavioural approach is a useful one to take in this context, for given that the burglar is under the control of such discriminative stimuli, recognition by the householder that his property (and its surrounds) constitutes a discriminative stimulus for the burglar offers the householder (or others interested in crime prevention) a means of effecting some control over the burglar (and thereby preventing the occurrence of burglary). He can do this by changing the discriminative stimuli which are either a part of, or evident in, his property. Conceptualising the problem in this way enables the investigator (and the householder) to draw upon an existing well-developed conceptual system for analysis and action.

In terms of the study reported here, the various cues which have been identified as exerting some influence on the burglar (target hardening, dogs, cover, etc.), when expressed in specific terms may be thought of as discriminative stimuli 'controlling' the behaviour of the burglar. If the problem is looked at in this way, this then allows the investigator to generate experimental investigations of the salience, or otherwise of particular cues and cue clusters in simulated environments, thus confirming and extending the analysis (as noted above).

Reducing the opportunities for crime through environmental manipulation may be thought to be intellectually objectionable by some schools of thought because of the behavioural standpoint from which it is derived. Behavioural approaches are often characterised as reducing freedom of choice and to 'paper-over' symptoms, without tackling the causes of the problem. In this case, the rhetoric of crime would presumably derive little comfort from the systematic assessment of criminal behaviour implied by this approach. There can be no doubt that the social context in which crime occurs is a relevant issue that merits consideration in any analysis of criminal behaviour. But the inconsistent relationships between presumed predisposing social states and actual criminal behaviour is such as to make explanations of little practical utility. Furthermore, in terms of crime prevention, even if clear relationships existed between specific causal factors and crime, (such as forms of childhood deprivation, for example), it would offer little to our capacity to control crime; would we discriminate against deprived children in some way? We often assume that causal explanations imply remedies – this may not always be the case, however, and in the case of crime, causal explanations expressed in terms of broad social parameters may offer little help to the problem of preventing crime. Development of the behavioural perspective implicit in situational analyses of crime control may usefully extend our predictive and preventative capacity, offering practical guidance to policy makers.

References

Bennett, T. and Wright, R. (1984) *Burglars on Burglary: Prevention and the Offender*, Aldershot: Gower.

Chappell, C. (1968) Unpublished thesis cited in: M. Maguire and T. H. Bennett, *Burglary in a Dwelling*, London: Heinemann.

Clarke, R. V. G. (1980) 'Situational crime prevention: theory and practice', *British Journal of Criminology*, 20, 136–47.

Cohen, S. and Taylor, L. (1972) *Psychological Survival: The Experience of Long Term Imprisonment*, Harmondsworth: Penguin.

Eysenck, H. (1970) *Crime and Personality*, London: Paladin.

Feldman, P. (1979) *Criminal Behaviour: A Psychological Analysis*, London: Wiley.

Heal, K. and Laycock, G. (Eds.) (1986) *Situational Crime Prevention: From Theory into Practice*, London: H.M.S.O.

Maguire, M. and Bennett, T. H. (1982) *Burglary in a Dwelling*, London: Heinemann.

Newman, O. (1972) *Defensible Space: Crime Prevention Through Urban Design*, New York: Macmillan.

Reppetto, T. G. (1974) *Residential Crime*, Cambridge, Ma.: Ballinger.

Scarr, H. A. (1973) *Patterns of Burglary*, Washington, D.C.: U.S. Government Printing Office.

Skinner, B. F. (1953) *Science and Human Behaviour*, New York: Free Press.

Waller, I. and Okihiro, T. (1978) *Burglary: The Victim and the Public*, Toronto: University of Toronto Press.

Winchester, S. and Jackson, H. (1982) *Residential Burglary* (Home Office Research Study No. 74), London: H.M.S.O.

Yochelson, S. and Samenow, S. E. (1976) *The Criminal Personality* (2 vols), New York: Aronson.

[10]

State differences in burglary victimisation in Australia: a research note

Timothy Phillips[a] and John Walker[b]
a La Trobe University, Bendigo
b John Walker Consulting Service, Queanbeyan

Abstract

Australian social researchers have demonstrated an ongoing interest in investigating economic, political and cultural difference between the states. The paper reports findings from an exploratory analysis of state differences in burglary victimisation in Australia. Using data from the 1993 National Crime and Safety Survey (NCSS), we investigate the extent to which some indicators of guardianship and social integration account for variation in burglary victimisation, both *within* and *across* the five Australian mainland states. More generally, we comment upon the utility of the NCSS data for research on victimisation.

Introduction

There has been an ongoing interest amongst Australian social researchers for over twenty years in economic, political and cultural differences between the states (Anderson and Western 1970; Berry 1969; Denemark and Sharman 1994; Holmes and Sharman 1977; Kelley and Bean 1988). Within this little tradition, a substantive area of investigation has been state differences in victimisation (Biles 1982, Mukherjee 1981). However, systematic research on this topic has been somewhat constrained, due to the lack of availability of appropriate data (Braithwaite and Biles 1980). Yet possibilities for further research have increased markedly over the last few years, with improved national police statistics and the results of another national crime victims survey becoming available (ABS 1994; 1993a; 1993b).

Given the availability of these data, why might further research on the matter of state differences in victimisation be important? First, for reasons of policy: crime prevention and control are basically the responsibility of state and territory governments, and any differences in rates of burglary could reflect successes or failures in policy, and hence provide valuable lessons for policy makers (Commonwealth Grants Commission 1995). Second, for reasons of analytic specificity: the issue of whether state differences are 'authentic' remains unresolved. Are these differences 'real', or do they mask victimisation patterns more amenable to explanation at the supra-state (Ellison 1991) or sub-state (Devery 1991) level? Third, for reasons of prediction: a systematic multivariate investigation of the causes of state differences in victimisation has yet to be conducted in this country.

Therefore, we decided to revisit the issue of state differences in victimisation, using data from the most recent of the national crime victims surveys, the 1993 National Crime and Safety Survey (NCSS) (ABS 1993b). Our investigation concentrated upon one of the most frequent victimisations measured by the survey: burglary. We considered the extent to which variation in burglary victimisation, both *within* and *across* the five Australian mainland states, was able to be accounted for by using data on household characteristics collected by the survey. Notwithstanding our focus upon burglary, we had a more general interest in gauging the usefulness of the survey in providing suitable data for investigating a substantive research question on state differences in victimisation.

State differences in burglary victimisation: crime statistics

Crime statistics reveal three notable regularities in burglary victimisation across the states. First, taking Australia as a whole, burglary victimisation is on the increase. Walker's (1994) analysis of police statistics and crime victims surveys over the period 1974-75 through 1990-91 demonstrated burglary to be clearly on the rise in Australia. NCSS (ABS 1993a) data indicate an 11% increase in the household burglary/attempted burglary rate over the 1983/1993 period.[1] Second, the increase in burglary victimisation has not been uniform across the Australian states. NCSS (1993a) data suggest three states experienced notable increases in burglary victimisation rates over the 1983-93 period, while two states recorded slight decreases.[2] The increase of greatest magnitude was evident in Western Australia (93%). Queensland (29%) and South Australia (27%) also experienced notable increases; New South Wales (15%) and Victoria (4%) recorded small decreases.[3] Third, and of particular interest in this context, there has been a shift from homogeneity to heterogeneity in the distribution of burglary victimisation across the Australian states. In 1983, the states broadly fitted into two categories: New South Wales and South Australia had marginally higher burglary victimisation rates than Queensland, Western Australia and Victoria. Victimisation rates across the states ranged only from a high of 6.7% per household for New South Wales, to a low of 5.6% for Victoria (ABS 1983). By 1993, the picture had changed markedly, and the Australian states were characterised by a greater level of heterogeneity in burglary victimisation rates. The states clustered into three categories. Western Australia recorded by far the highest burglary victimisation rate. Victoria and New South Wales, which had the lowest burglary victimisation rates, each recorded burglary victimisations at about half the rate of Western Australia. South Australia and Queensland were positioned between these two extremes. Burglary victimisation rates ranged from a high of 11% for Western Australia to a low of 5.4% for Victoria (ABS, 1993a). Compared to 1983, these figures suggest marked variation between the states in burglary victimisation rates in 1993.

Explaining state differences: guardianship and social integration

A range of factors has been demonstrated to predict the probability of burglary victimisation (Cohen and Cantor 1981; Cromwell et al. 1991; Miethe and McDowall 1993; Smith and Jarjoura 1989). Due to the limited scope of the 1993 NCSS survey instrument, we were constrained from developing a full range of indicators of theoretically plausible household level variables for inclusion in our model. However, we were able to develop indicators of guardianship and social integration. Both these concepts offered the possibility of providing new and interesting insights into the causes of burglary victimisation in Australia.

Guardianship is constituted in the capacity of persons or objects in a household to circumvent victimisation (Lynch and Cantor 1992; Miethe and McDowall 1993). There are two types of guardianship: the presence of persons in the household is 'primary' guardianship, while the installation of objects to prevent victimisation is 'proxy' guardianship (Garofalo and Clark 1992). Regarding primary guardianship, the logic used here is that those in full-time work or education are less likely to be at home, and aged residents are more likely to be at home, during the normal working day, which is the peak period for household burglary. Married couples, it may be argued, are more likely to be effective guardians of the home than other types of households, including single parent households and group households. In terms of proxy guardianship, the absence of security devices within a household would be expected to increase the risk of victimisation.

Households in less socially integrated neighbourhoods would be expected to have higher levels of victimisation (Durkheim 1964). These areas are frequently over-represented in terms of transient or newly arrived residents, and under-represented in the level of home ownership (Smith and Jarjoura 1989). As a consequence, residents are less likely to know others in the immediate vicinity. Therefore, people in these locales might be expected to be not only less likely to 'look out for each other', but also less likely to know who is a neighbour or 'friend' as against who is a 'stranger' (Cohen 1993).

Data, measures and methods

Data are from the most recent National Crime and Safety Survey (NCSS). This survey was conducted in mid-April 1993 by the Australian Bureau of Statistics, as a supplement to the Monthly Population Survey. Information was collected on a range of household property offences, personal offences, risk factors, reporting behaviour and neighbourhood watch membership. The survey was self-administered, with one household member aged at least 15 years of age providing information relating to the entire household. Data collection was restricted to the usual residents of private dwellings. Data were collected from 21 528 households across the five mainland states, 1004 of which were victims of burglary. Tasmania was excluded from the analysis conducted here due to the small number of victims surveyed in this state.[4] The survey response rate was 85.8% (Wong 1994). For the purposes of this analysis, weighted data were analysed. The distribution of burgled households across the five mainland states for the weighted data is presented in Table 1.

Table 1: Burglary victimisation by state: weighted data

State	Households in sample	Victims of burglary	Victimisation rate (%)
Western Australia	3233	242	7.5
Queensland	4392	228	5.2
South Australia	3160	158	5
New South Wales	5608	207	3.7
Victoria	5135	169	3.3
Australia	21528	1004	4.7

Source: ABS 1993b, Unit Record File

The dependent variable was whether the household had been a victim of a *completed* burglary in the last 12 months. Burglary victimisation was measured by a binary variable, with a code of 1 for household burgled, and 0 for household not burgled. Six independent variables were included in the analysis. Three variables were measures of primary guardianship (no person at home during the daytime; no household member aged 60 years or over; and household comprised of a married couple with or without children). One variable measured proxy guardianship (household had electronic or physical security devices). Two variables served as measures of social integration (all household members recently moved into the current address; household in rented accommodation).[5] Details of the binary coding for all variables included in the analysis are presented in Table 2.[6] Given the dichotomous character of the dependent variable, logistic regression analysis was the preferred technique for estimating the effects of guardianship and social integration upon the probability of a household being burgled.

Results

Table 3 presents the regression coefficients for five constrained logistic regression models, gauging the impact of the independent variables on the probability of being burgled, for each of the mainland states.[7] The results show that the characteristics of burgled households differ somewhat across the five mainland states. Four of the six variables generated results in the expected direction. In each of the five states, households with no member

Table 2: Coding of variables in the logistic regression model of burglary victimisation

Variable	Values	Description
Burglary victimisation	1	Victim of burglary;
	0	Non-victim of burglary;
No one home in day	1	No person stayed at home during the daytime;
	0	At least one person stayed at home during the daytime;
No aged resident	1	No household member was aged 60 years or over;
	0	At least one household member was aged 60 years or over;
New address	1	All household members have moved to the current address less than one year ago;
	0	Not all household members have moved to the current address less than one year ago;
Married couple	1	Household comprised of a married couple with or without children;
	0	All other households;
Security devices	1	Household had electronic or physical security devices;
	0	Household did not have physical or electronic security devices;
Rented accommodation	1	Household in rented accommodation;
	0	Household in non-rented accommodation.

aged 60 years or over experienced a greater probability of being burgled, compared to households with at least one member aged 60 years or over. In each state except South Australia, households comprised of a married couple (with or without children) were less likely to have been burgled, compared with all other households. In Queensland and New South Wales, households where no person stayed at home during the daytime were significantly more likely to have been burgled than households where at least one person stayed at home during the daytime. Rented accommodation proved to be at greater risk of being burgled in Queensland, compared with non-rented accommodation. However, for the other four states, there was no significant difference in burglary risk between these two types of households.

Table 3: Logistic regression co-efficients for the impact of household characteristics on the probability of burglary victimisation for five Australian states

Variable	Vic	NSW	SA	Qld	WA
No one home in day	0.24	0.34*	0.25	0.42*	0.30
No aged resident	0.70*	0.66*	0.71*	0.56*	0.42*
New address	−0.40	0.12	0.08	−0.41*	−0.68*
Married couple[a]	−0.55*	−0.80*	−0.36	−0.47*	−0.52*
Security devices	0.37	0.63*	0.18	0.68*	0.79*
Rented accommodation	0.25	0.06	0.13	0.35*	0.32

[a] With or without children
* $p < 0.05$.

The impact of household security devices and a household new address on burglary victimisation were unexpected. The counter-intuitive finding for security devices makes more sense when we consider the absence of detail in the NCSS survey pertaining to the timing of the installation of these devices. The survey fails to distinguish whether security devices were installed in a household either prior to, or consequent to, the occurrence of a burglary. Therefore, rather than the findings showing that households with electronic or physical security devices were more likely to have been burgled than households without these devices, they might more probably show that burgled households were more likely than non-burgled households to have had security devices installed. The non-predicted impact of moving to a new address on burglary victimisation calls into question the social integration explanation, as higher levels of social integration are unlikely to be associated with shorter terms of residence in a new area. Possibly, the decreased probability of victimisation associated with moving to a new address might instead be explained by the effects of life-cycle changes, such as age or household type (Hassan et al. 1996). At the very least, this interesting finding clearly needs further investigation.

We now consider the question of the explanatory utility of the household level variables in accounting for differences in the probability of burglary victimisation, as experienced by households in the five mainland states. In other words, do the six attributes of households under consideration partially account for state differences in the probability of being burgled? Or, do these household characteristics have a negligible effect? Table 4 presents regression co-efficients from two logistic regression models. The first model estimated the effects of state of household on probability of burglary victimisation. The second model extends the first by repeating the analysis, but holding constant the effects of the six household attributes already examined.

Table 4: Logistic regression co-efficients for the impact of state of household on the probability of burglary victimisation, controlling for a range of household characteristics

Variable[a]	Model 1[b]	Model 2[c]
Victoria	−0.10	−0.10
Queensland	0.40*	0.44*
South Australia	0.30*	0.31*
Western Australia	0.78*	0.89*

[a] New South Wales was the state omitted for comparison
[b] Without control variables
[c] With six control variables
* $p < 0.05$.

Referring to the first model, it is apparent that households in Western Australia, Queensland and South Australia are significantly more likely to have been burgled, compared to households in New South Wales. The model also indicated that households in Victoria did not differ significantly from those in New South Wales in the probability of being burgled. The second model introduced the six household characteristics into the equation. For these new variables to be held to partially account for state differences in burglary victimisation rates, the magnitude of the significant regression co-efficients recorded in the first model would need to show signs of having been tempered. However, the results indicate that the magnitude and direction of the effects of State of household on the probability of burglary victim-isation remain substantively unchanged. In other words, net of the effects of the six household level variables, state differences in burglary victimisation rates remain constant. Essentially, the results indicate that the six household attributes included in this study are unable to account for differences *between* the states in the probability of burglary victimisation, although they do explain some of the variation *within* states.

Discussion

The main task of this paper has been to explore the utility of a range of household level factors in accounting for variation in burglary victimisation rates across the five Australian mainland states. The analysis produced two main findings. First, guardianship was shown to be an important factor pre-dicting burglary victimisation *within* the five states. Households with no member aged 60 years or over, not comprised of a married couple, where no persons stayed at home during the day were consistently found to be more likely to be burgled than households with at least one member aged 60 years or over, comprised of a married couple, where at least one person stayed home during the daytime. This conclusion may be *profoundly* important in the light of current societal trends, including high levels of long-term un-employment and increasing trends towards home-based small business activ-ity. Since both of these trends would tend to 're-populate' the suburbs during the daytime, they would presumably result in greater levels of primary guardianship of dwellings. Strategies, such as Neighbourhood Watch, which have had somewhat ambivalent or even disappointing results in their stated aims of reducing burglaries, could be made much more effective in the future if they can harness these new trends in guardianship.

Second, while the variables included in the analysis were useful in ac-counting for some variation in *intra*-state differences in burglary victimisation, they tell us little about *inter*-state differences. The available indices of both guardianship and social integration were found to provide little explanatory insight into differences in burglary victimisation *across* the five states. Perhaps considering an extended range of theoretically important household level vari-ables (e.g., class, ethnicity), or broadening analysis to the regional or ecological levels, may provide researchers with more leverage to investigate this issue. However, neither of these possibilities is able to be systematically pursued within the NCSS data. The lack of a broader range of theoretically interesting variables characterising these data is reminiscent of the limitations of earlier crime victims surveys in Australia. Also, while ecological analysis has featured centrally in victimisation surveys internationally (Mayhew et al. 1993; Zawitz et al. 1993), the NCSS data are unable to be broken down beyond the state or metropolitan/non-metropolitan level.

98   *Timothy Phillips and John Walker*

The study of state differences in victimisation might be better approached by sampling break and enter victims, as identified by Police Records—particularly since the differences between rankings of jurisdictions, as measured by police records and as measured by the Crime Victims Survey, are marginal (ABS 1994; 1993a). These data could be used to construct explanatory variables at different levels of analysis (e.g., household, community/neighbourhood, state), provide direct access to a population of victims and give access to some data on offenders. If interstate differences in burglary victimisation *cannot* be systematically pursued within NCSS data, and if recent improvements in police databases and greater standardisation between jurisdictions are such that they can now be used for such policy-relevant analyses, this brings into serious question the whole purpose of the NCSS. In spite of many years of pleading by criminologists, it is still an extremely limited instrument compared with its equivalents in the US and the UK, and our results would suggest that its utility is marginal, even for the most frequent of the limited range of victimisations it attempts to measure.

Notes

* This research note is a substantially revised and shortened version of a conference paper included in Crime Victims Surveys in Australia, proceedings of a conference held at Griffith University 28-29 November 1994, sponsored by the Criminal Justice Commission, the Centre for Crime Policy and Public Safety, Griffith University and the Queensland Government Statistician's Office. Thanks go to David Brereton, Ross Homel, the Research and Co-ordination Division of the Criminal Justice Commission, and the Queensland Government Statistician's Office for generating tables from the 1993 NCSS Unit Record File.

1   While this paper is primarily concerned with *completed* break and enters, the figure reported here indicates the recorded increase in the victimisation rate for break and enter/attempted break and enter, as these categories were not disaggregated in the 1983 survey.

2   We posit this interpretation with caution, due to differences between the 1983 and 1993 crime victim surveys (ABS 1983, 1993a) in data collection techniques and question wording.

3   Changes in Tasmania are not reported due to an unacceptably high level of sampling error in both the 1983 and 1993 national crime victim surveys.

4   Only 73 burgled households (27 with weighted data) were available for analysis in this state.

5   Neighbourhood watch and region were excluded from the final logistic regression models. Neighbourhood watch had a negligible impact on burglary victimisation in exploratory analysis, while data on region (metropolitan/non-metropolitan) were unavailable for all five states.

6   Details of how items in the NCSS 1993 were used to construct the independent variables are available from the authors upon request.

7   Each model was constrained to include the same set of regressors, enabling comparisons to be made between the states.

References

Anderson, D. S. and J. S. Western (1970) 'State Differences in Authoritarian Attitudes' *Australian Journal of Psychology* 22: 261-264.

Australian Bureau of Statistics (1994) 'National Crime Statistics' Catalogue No. 4510.0.

Australian Bureau of Statistics (1993a) 'Crime and Safety Australia' Catalogue No. 4509.0.

Australian Bureau of Statistics (1993b) 'National Crime and Safety Survey' Unit Record Data.

Australian Bureau of Statistics (1983) 'Crime Victims Survey, Australia, 1983, Preliminary, Catalogue No. 4505.0.

Berry, J. W. (1969) 'The Stereotypes of Australian States' *Australian Journal of Psychology* 21: 227-233.

Biles, D. (1982) 'The Size of the Crime Problem in Australia' Sydney: Australian Institute of Criminology.

Braithwaite, J. and D. Biles (1980) 'Overview of Findings from the First Australian National Crime Victims Survey' *The Australian and New Zealand Journal of Criminology* 13: 41-51.

Cohen, L. E. and D. Cantor (1981) 'Residential Burglary in the United States: Life-Style and Demographic Factors Associated with the Probability of Victimization' *Journal of Research in Crime and Delinquency* 18: 113-127.

Cohen, S. (1993) 'Human Rights and Crimes of the State: The Culture of Denial' *The Australian and New Zealand Journal of Criminology* 26: 97-115.

Commonwealth Grants Commission (1995) 'Report on General Revenue Grant Relativities 1995 Update' Canberra: AGPS.

Cromwell, P. F., J. N. Olson and D. W. Avary (1991) *Breaking and Entering: An Ethnographic Analysis of Burglary* Newbury Park, California: Sage.

Denemark, D. and C. Sharman (1994) 'Political Efficacy, Involvement and Trust: Testing for Regional Political Culture in Australia' *Australian Journal of Political Science* 29: 81-102.

Devery, C. (1991) *Disadvantage and Crime in New South Wales* New South Wales Bureau of Crime Statistics and Research.

Durkheim, E. (1964) *The Division of Labour in Society* Glencoe: Free Press.

Ellison, C. G. (1991) 'An Eye for an Eye? A Note on the Southern Subculture of Violence Thesis' *Social Forces* 69: 1223-1239.

Garofalo, J. and D. Clark (1992) 'Guardianship and Residential Burglary' *Justice Quarterly* 9: 443-463.

Hassan, R., Z. Xiaowei, and S. McDonnell-Baum (1996) 'Why Families Move: A Study of Residential Mobility in Australia' *The Australian and New Zealand Journal of Sociology* 32: 72-85.

Holmes, J. and C. Sharman (1977) *The Australian Federal System* Sydney: George Allen & Unwin.

Kelley, J. and C. Bean (eds) (1988) *Australian Attitudes* Sydney: Allen & Unwin.

Lynch, J. P. and D. Cantor (1992) 'Ecological and Behavioural Influences on Property Victimization at Home: Implications for Opportunity Theory' *Journal of Research in Crime and Delinquency* 29: 335-362.

Mayhew, P., N. Aye Maung and C. Mirlees-Black (1993) *The 1992 British Crime Survey, A Home Office Research and Planning Unit Report* London: HMSO.

Miethe, T. D. and D. McDowall (1993) 'Contextual Effects in Models of Criminal Victimization' *Social Forces* 71: 741-759.

Mukherjee, S. (1981) *Crime Trends in Twentieth Century Australia* Sydney: Australian Institute of Criminology.

Smith, D. A. and G. R. Jarjoura (1989) 'Household Characteristics, Neighbourhood Composition and Victimization Risk' *Social Forces* 68: 621-640.

Walker, J. (1994) *Crime in the Third Millennium in Australia* unpublished manuscript.

100   Timothy Phillips and John Walker

Wong, B. (1994) 'Non-Response Adjustments in the 1993 National Crime and Safety Survey' in Crime Victims Surveys in Australia, proceedings of a conference held at Griffith University 28-29 November 1994.

Zawitz, M. W., P. A. Klaus, R. Bachman, L. D Bastian, M. M. DeBerry, M. R. Rand, and B. M. Taylor (1993) *Highlights from 20 Years of Surveying Crime Victims: The National Crime Victimisation Survey, 1973-92* Bureau of Justice Statistics, October.

[11]

THE TIME COURSE OF REPEAT BURGLARY VICTIMIZATION

Natalie Polvi,* Terah Looman,* Charlie Humphries,† and Ken Pease*

Research has demonstrated that the probability of repeat victimization is greater than the probability of an independent offence. The time course of elevated risk has important implications for crime prevention. For burglaries, the current received wisdom is that the characteristics of homes which make burglary more probable persist over the medium and long term. Addressing the time course question, previous research by the authors examined the change in risk of repeat burglary victimization for up to twelve months after the initial offence (Polvi et al. 1990). The study is here extended to the analysis of a four-year time period (1984 to 1987). It was found that the elevated risk of repeat burglary does not last over long time periods. Based on the present data, the risk becomes average once six months has passed and remains so subsequently. It is contended that the work should be replicated, given its surprising results. One implication of this research is that preventative action should be taken as soon as possible after a burglary.

One of the criminological legacies of the late Richard Sparks was his recognition of the importance of the phenomenon of repeat crime victimization (see Sparks 1981). In essence, the probability of being victimized a second or subsequent time is several times the rate that would be expected if offences were independent events. This seems to be true across a wide range of offence types. Sparks (1981) reviews possible reasons for this phenomenon with typical wit and lucidity. The fact is usable in crime prevention terms, since concentration of preventative effort on prior victims will be more cost-effective than concentration on a different group of similar size. This was the cornerstone of a recent, apparently successful, burglary prevention programme in Rochdale (Forrester *et al.* 1988).

Put generally, we should think in terms of a continuum of crime predictability. The more exactly a crime location can be specified in advance, the greater the opportunity for prevention or detection. At one extreme, entrapment is a seductive technique because it locates a crime precisely in place and time. At the other extreme, random distribution of crime makes the allocation of prevention and detection effort maximally difficult. The heightened probability of repeat victimization serves to move the situation towards the predictable end of the continuum. To be useful, predictability has to apply in terms of both place (target) and time. Research on multiple victimization has hitherto neglected time, tending to look at elevated risk over a standard period, typically a year, rather than at any changes in risk across time. Yet the time course of elevated risk is of crucial importance to preventative effort. Specifically, over what

* Neuropsychiatric Research Unit, Dept of Psychiatry, University of Saskatchewan and Regional Psychiatric Centre (Prairies), Correctional Service of Canada.

† Saskatoon City Police.

We wish to thank Chief Joe Penkala, Saskatoon City Police, for his co-operation and support. We also wish to thank Frank B. Garland, City Assessor, City of Saskatoon, and his associates. We thank Joanna Shapland, Gerry Rose, and Ron Templeman for helpful comments on an earlier version of this note.

NATALIE POLVI *ET AL.*

period does the elevated risk persist? When is it sensible to stop investing special effort to prevent further offending?

Analysis of burglaries in the City of Saskatoon, Saskatchewan, in 1987 showed that, in line with British data (see Forrester *et al.* 1988), the chance of a repeat burglary over the period of one year was around four times the rate to be expected if the events were independent. However, this masked a dramatic reduction within the year (Polvi *et al.* 1990). The likelihood of a repeat burglary within one month was over twelve times the expected rate, but this declined to less than twice the expected rate when burglaries six months apart were considered. Analysis of the repeat burglaries within one month showed that half of the second victimizations occurred within seven days of the first. The present note extends the analysis of Saskatoon burglary data from a single calendar year (1987) to a four-year span, 1984–7.

Burglary data were provided by the Saskatoon City Police (Records Department). The computer generated a month-by-month list of all residential burglaries in the city during 1987. For each address burgled in 1987, it listed the record of all previous burglaries from 1 January 1984 to 31 December 1986.

Because calculations involved the assumption that each burglary was associated with one dwelling, it was necessary to determine whether each address was a single unit or a multiple unit. This was accomplished with the help of the City of Saskatoon's Assessment Department.

While our 1987 data constitute a complete record of residential burglaries in that year, our 1984–6 data include only those addresses also burgled in 1987. It will be recalled that the problem was to see whether elevated risk of burglary persisted over time. Had our data comprised all burglaries in 1984, and data for subsequent years about total burglaries and repeat burglaries of these dwellings, it is obvious that we could readily calculate the persistence of risk. Limitations in data availability and resources made that impracticable. The problem is how to use retrospective data to address the issue.

For each year from 1984 to 1987 we know the total number of dwellings burgled. For 1987 alone, we know precisely which dwellings they were. We also know which of these had been burgled during the period 1984–6, and when. Intuitively, if the number of such dwellings is higher than expected, that is evidence of elevated risk of repeat victimization. We knew the number of dwellings burgled in 1987 and a specified earlier year. We knew the number of dwellings burgled in 1987 but not in the earlier year. We knew the total number of dwellings in the city in all years. We calculated the number of dwellings burgled in the earlier year but not in 1987, on the basis of the total number of dwellings in the city, the total number of burglaries in that year, and the number of dwellings burgled both in the year in question and in 1987. The only concern we were unable to resolve was whether the total number of dwellings we used in our calculations should be the number available at the end of the first or the second year of the pair, so we calculated both. They were only trivially different, and only one set (based on the number of dwellings in 1987) is presented. While the approach we took is counter-intuitive (estimating the number of dwellings burgled in 1986 which were burgled 'again' in 1984!), the series we end up with is equivalent to a prospective series.

For each pair of years (1984/1987, 1985/1987, 1986/1987) the number of dwellings burgled in neither year, in one year but not both, and in both years, was calculated and a Poisson distribution fitted. For example, 3,781 different dwellings were burgled in

TIME COURSE OF REPEAT BURGLARY VICTIMIZATION

1985 and/or 1987. In a housing stock of 70,343 dwellings, the probability of a house being burgled in neither year is 0.9460, and that of a house being burgled in both years is 0.00146, equivalent to an expected number of burgled dwellings of 103. The actual number of houses burgled in both years is 124. Thus the ratio of observed to expected is 1.21. The data are presented in Fig. 1.

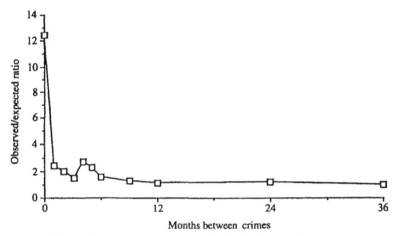

Months between crimes

FIG. 1   Ratio of observed to expected repeat burglaries, Saskatoon, by months between crimes

At the one-year point, the ratio is 1.17; at the two-year point, it is 1.21; and at the three-year point, it is 1.02. Figure 1 includes the data points in the range up to one year first published in Polvi *et al.* (1989), so as to enable the whole picture to be seen. (It is important for readers interested in the time course up to one year to read the method section of the earlier paper.) In summary, Fig. 1 reveals that the elevated risk of repeat burglary extends over only a short period, at least for burglary in Saskatoon. After around six months, it ceases to exist for all practical purposes. One would have expected a higher ratio to have persisted over a longer time, if only because houses in the worst areas would retain a higher risk of being burgled, by dint of their location in the area, rather than by reason of their prior victimization. Also, characteristics which distinguish between burgled and non-burgled dwellings (see Winchester and Jackson 1982) are likely to persist over time, thus making for a continued high risk of burglary. Certainly our study should be repeated in other cities in Canada and in other countries before its conclusions are translated into crime prevention practice. Saskatoon could be distinctive in the relative homogeneity of its housing. This could mean that, while short-term repeat victimization by the same offenders remains significant, the burglary opportunities are spread so evenly throughout the city that target selection by different burglars does not identify the same dwellings.

One feature of the data which deserves passing mention is the apparent elevation of risk four to five months after a burglary, compared with three months afterwards. The most likely explanation of this is chance fluctuation in the data; but another possibility which should be kept in mind is that this represents the period after which replacement

NATALIE POLVI *ET AL.*

of goods through insurance is virtually certain to have occurred, and thus when a repeat burglary will offer pickings as rich as on the first visit. This possibility should be tested by further research in other places.

The implications of the finding that dramatically enhanced risk of repeat burglaries persists for only a short period after the first burglary are substantial. If confirmed elsewhere, this means that special preventative measures (leafletting neighbours, advising victims, perhaps the loan of silent alarms) are realistic, since they need only endure for a month or so to have their major effect. However, they clearly need to occur very promptly, certainly no later than the day after the first offence.

Assuming that the data are not an artefact of the method used in some unsuspected way, we have to make conjectures about what is happening. Heightened probability of repeat crime victimization may be considered as occurring for three possible reasons:

1. The same offenders return, perhaps upon recognition of neglected crime opportunities, or the anticipated reinstatement of goods.
2. The first offenders tell others of the house and what it still offers. The others then burgle it.
3. Features of the house are such as to mark it out as a compellingly attractive target to all those tempted to burgle it, leading to repeat victimizations linked only by the seductiveness of the target.

The first and second alternatives are difficult to distinguish (although we regard the second as not likely to be a frequent occurrence). The proportion of re-victimizations of the third type will be high to the extent that dwellings vary in their seductiveness as targets. It is difficult to think of a city with less such variation than Saskatoon. It may be that what is shown here is the limiting case, where repeat victimization is as near exclusively of type (1) as is anywhere to be found. This makes it particularly important that the analysis should be repeated elsewhere, since the notion of area or dwelling characteristics as long-term determinants of risk of victimization stems from studies which neglect the phenomenon of repeat victimization. It is conceivable that while these characteristics determine a first victimization, it is more what is found inside which induces an offender to return.

REFERENCES

FORRESTER, D., CHATTERTON, M. R., and PEASE, K. (1988), *The Kirkholt Burglary Prevention Project, Rochdale*, Crime Prevention Paper no. 13. London: Home Office.

POLVI, N., LOOMAN, T., HUMPHRIES, C., and PEASE, K. (1990), 'Repeat Break and Enter Victimization: Time Course and Crime Prevention Opportunity', *Journal of Police Science and Administration*.

SPARKS, R. F. (1981), 'Multiple Victimisation: Evidence, Theory and Future Research', *Journal of Criminal Law and Criminology*, 72: 762–78.

WINCHESTER, S., and JACKSON, H. (1982), *Residential Burglary: The Limits of Prevention*, Home Office Research Study no. 74. London: HMSO.

[12]

BURGLARY REVICTIMIZATION

The Time Period of Heightened Risk

MATTHEW B. ROBINSON*

Research into the phenomenon of revictimization has consistently demonstrated that a very small proportion of all people and places suffer from a disproportionate amount of victimizations. Whenever victims of both personal and household crimes are likely to be victimized again, victimization is most likely to occur a very short time after the initial offences. Findings from this study confirm these ideas. Only 1.2 per cent of all residences in the jurisdiction studied suffered from 29 per cent of all burglaries reported to the police between the years 1992 and 1994. Furthermore, 25 per cent of the burglary revictimizations occurred within one week of the initial offences, while 51 per cent occurred within one month. These findings are discussed in the context of prevention of burglary revictimization.

Revictimization 'occurs when the same person or place suffers from more than one criminal incident over a specified period of time' (Ross 1994: 1). When people or places are revictimized, 'there (are) more crime than victims, so incidence is higher than prevalence, and concentration is . . . always greater than one' (Farrell and Pease 1993: 5). For example, if residential burglary revictimization was occurring in a given area, one would expect to find more burglaries reported to police than burglared residences. In other words, some targets would have been victimized by more than one burglary. Such places suffering from criminal revictimization can be thought of as 'hot spots' (Sherman *et al*. 1989). Hot spots can also exist when many one-time victims reside in a limited geographical area (Block and Block 1995: 147; Buerger *et al*. 1995; Sherman 1995: 35). For the purposes of this paper, a hot spot is a place (e.g., a residential dwelling) where criminal revictimization has occurred. This definition is consistent with the well-known hot spot research done by Sherman *et al*. (1989: 37), who analysed spatial data on 323,979 calls to the police over an estimated 115,000 addresses and intersections in Minneapolis in one year and found that 'a majority (60 per cent) of all addresses generated at least one call over the course of the year, but almost half of those addresses produced one call and no more'. Thus, many addresses produced more than one call to police. For example, all 15,901 calls to police for burglary in a year in Minneapolis came from only 11 per cent of all street addresses (hot spots). More strikingly, 50 per cent of all calls came from only 3 per cent of places.

It is now treated in the literature as common knowledge that very small segments of the population suffer from disproportionate amounts of criminal victimization, and that this phenomenon is not due to simple chance alone (Farrell 1994: 470; Polvi *et al*. 1990: 8, 1991: 411). While Sparks (1981) was one of the first in modern revictimization literature to suggest that previous crime victims were disproportionately likely to

* Department of Political Science and Criminal Justice, Appalachian State University, Boone, North Carolina.

MATTHEW B. ROBINSON

become victims again at a later time, further empirical support has been generated for the phenomenon of revictimization (Burquest *et al.* 1992; Farrell and Pease 1993; Farrell 1992, 1994; Feinberg 1980; Forrester *et al.* 1988*a*, 1988*b*; Forrester *et al.* 1990; Genn 1988; Gottfredson 1984; Hindeland *et al.* 1978; Hope 1982; Hough 1986; Johnson *et al.* 1973; Jones *et al.* 1986; Mayhew *et al.* 1993; Nelson 1980; Pease 1991, 1992; Polvi *et al.* 1990, 1991; Reiss 1980; Sampson 1991; Sampson and Phillips 1992; Shapland *et al.* 1991; Shepherd 1990; Sherman *et al.* 1989; Skogan 1990*a*, 1990*b*; Sparks 1981; Sparks *et al.* 1977; Tilley 1993; Trickett *et al.* 1992; Ziegenhagen 1976). With regard to the crime of burglary, research (Forrester *et al.* 1990; Polvi *et al.* 1990, 1991) demonstrates that revictimization is concentrated on few residences and is less likely to occur with the passage of time. Polvi *et al.* (1990, 1991) found that previously burgled dwellings in Saskatoon in 1987 were almost four times more likely than non-burglared residences to be burgled again, and 50 per cent of revictimization occurred within seven days of the initial offences. The results of the growing body of research leaves one with the sense that revictimization is a reality across all crime types, all locations, and all periods of study (Farrell *et al.* 1995: 501).

In fact, criminal revictimization may account for a large share of all criminal victimizations. If this is true, then preventing criminal revictimizations may mean preventing a large percentage of all criminal victimizations (Farrell 1994: 469; National Board for Crime Prevention 1994: 2). For example, one-half of all victimized respondents of the 1992 British Crime Survey were repeat victims. They suffered from 81 per cent of all reported crimes. Furthermore, 4 per cent of those who suffered from criminal victimizations more than once were victimized four or more times in a year, and accounted for 44 per cent of all reported crimes (Farrell and Pease 1993).

As discussed by Farrell (1994), if we can determine who it is that is most likely to be victimized by crime, particularly those who will likely suffer from more than one victimization, then we may be able to prevent criminal victimizations more efficiently. However, Farrell counsels us that 'more energy and resources' must be directed at the phenomenon of revictimization in order for this to occur. This paper is one attempt at answering the call to further revictimization research.

Why Does Revictimization Occur?

Although the purpose of this paper is to examine the time period of heightened risk for burglary revictimization, a brief review of some explanations for the phenomenon may be in order. To prevent criminal revictimization, it might be wise to understand why it happens. Sparks (1981: 772-8) was one of the first modern theorists to hypothesize about the causes of revictimization. He discussed many concepts that he believed were relevant, including victim precipitation, vulnerability, opportunity, target attractiveness, impunity and lifestyle. He wrote that a multiple victim may 'facilitate its commission—by deliberately, recklessly, or negligently placing himself at special risk . . . Anyone who fails to take reasonable precautions against crime may be said to have facilitated a crime against him'. Also, some people 'because of their attributes, usual behaviour, or their place in a social system, may be very vulnerable' to revictimization. Vulnerability factors may be related to status (e.g., sex, class), or may be ecological (e.g.,

BURGLARY REVICTIMIZATION

living in a bad neighbourhood). The likelihood of criminal revictimization is said to be highest for these groups who are most vulnerable in society (Pease 1992).

Other explanations for the phenomenon of revictimization include the routine activities approach of Cohen and Felson (1979) and the lifestyle-exposure approach of Hindelang *et al.* (1978), which emphasize the role of the lifestyle of offenders and victims and how they influence opportunities for criminal revictimization through the creation of attractive or suitable targets (Miethe *et al.* 1987). Of course, part of what determines high or low rates of revictimization are high or low rates of criminal victimization (Sherman *et al.* 1989: 43). Sparks (1981: 778) wrote that criminal victimization and revictimization may be a matter of chance alone and 'absolutely unrelated to attributes or behaviour' of the victim. However, in a study by Forrester *et al.* (1988*a*), rates of repeat burglary victimization were higher than would have normally been expected given a random distribution of burglary.

As discussed by Farrell *et al.* (1995: 386), the main question yet to be definitively answered about why criminal revictimization occurs is whether it is due to enduring characteristics about targets which make them attractive or suitable to multiple offenders (the risk heterogeneity argument), or if it is due to factors related to the initial victimization (the state-dependent argument). In support of the latter view, Polvi *et al.* (1991: 414) wrote that while characteristics of a dwelling may help determine a first offence against it, 'it is more what it found inside which induces an offender to return'. Discovering whether revictimization results from enduring characteristics of places or from knowledge learned by offenders during their initial offences, is beyond the scope of this present study. The bottom line is that revictimization can be prevented with knowledge of the time and place of its occurrence, regardless of why it occurs.

Preventing Criminal Victimization and Revictimization

Criminal victimization is more likely to occur, and in fact only possible, when three elements converge in time and space: (1) presence of motivated offenders; (2) presence of suitable targets; and (3) absence of capable guardians (Cohen and Felson 1979: 589). Crime prevention can be achieved effectively when any one of these elements is absent. Thus, if we can identify which potential targets in any given environment are most suitable for victimization, then we can design and implement crime prevention strategies to make them less suitable. This will prevent criminal victimization, or at least lessen the likelihood that a target will be victimized. For example, residences become suitable targets for burglary victimization when they are highly accessible to offenders, especially in conditions of low surveillability to neighbours and passers-by, and during periods of non-occupancy (Cromwell *et al.* 1991; Robinson 1994; Wright and Decker 1994). Theoretically, to reduce the probability of victimization, we can reduce accessibility to outsiders, increase surveillability by neighbours and passers-by, and increase periods of resident occupancy.

At the very least, crime is an event that occurs in time and space (Felson 1983). Therefore, in order to understand *and* prevent future criminal victimizations and revictimizations, we must be able to locate crime in both space and time. In the words of Polvi *et al.* (1991: 411), 'The more exactly a crime location can be specified in advance,

MATTHEW B. ROBINSON

the greater the opportunity for prevention or detection.' Of course, this holds true both for the place and the time of criminal victimization. Polvi *et al.* (1991: 411) stated it this way: 'To be useful, predictability has to apply in terms of both place (target) and time.'

Since victims suffer from multiple criminal victimizations throughout their life course, victims of yesterday are more likely than non-victims of yesterday to become victims again tomorrow (Johnson *et al.* 1973). For example, environmental characteristics which make residences more or less susceptible to criminal victimization persist for long periods of time (Polvi *et al.* 1991: 411). Perhaps the most logical way to identify tomorrow's 'where and when' of criminal victimization is to utilize past criminal data to locate yesterday's 'where and when' of criminal victimization. Given our inability to predict future criminality or victimization accurately (Farrell 1994: 511), this may be our only option. Since repeat criminal victimization is concentrated on few victims (Spelman 1995: 366), crime prevention measures should be focused upon those already victimized (Ellingworth *et al.* 1995: 365).

This paper is an attempt to identify the 'when' of one type of criminal revictimization. Specifically, the author locates the time period of heightened risk for residential burglary revictimizations relative to initial victimizations. This paper builds on previous attempts of the researcher to locate the 'where' of this type of criminal victimization and revictimization within certain neighbourhoods, on certain streets, and at certain residence types (Robinson 1994; Robinson and Robinson 1995). By continuing this research, the goal is to link the 'where' with the 'when' of burglary revictimization successfully, so that prevention of this type of phenomenon will be much more likely.

Methods

In order to determine the time period of heightened risk for burglary revictimization of residences in Tallahassee, Florida, computer-generated crime data were obtained from the Tallahassee Police Department's (TPD) 'Crime Analysis Unit'. This crime data contained addresses of residential burglaries reported to TPD, points and methods of entry, and dates and estimated times of offences. Since limited data were available, analysis could only be conducted over a three-year period. This is because only police crime data between 1992 and 1994 were stored on the police computers. Furthermore, despite the desire to examine residential burglary data for the entire city, constraints on police time and resources required limiting analysis to a smaller area. Thus, one police zone (zone 7) of TPD's jurisdiction was selected. Zone 7 was selected for several reasons. First, it contains a large proportion of residences which are representative of those who are most likely to be subjected to victimization from residential burglary—the lower class, the working class, the young, etc., meaning that burglary would be likely to exist in this area. Second, zone 7 is characterized by relatively high rates of reported crime, including burglary, which assured having a large enough sample of burglaries to work with.

Of 2,980 separate residential addresses in zone 7, a total of 848 burglaries (including completed burglaries with forcible entry and non-forcible entry, and attempts) were reported to the police between 1992 and 1994. This included 305 burglaries reported to the police in 1992, 337 burglaries in 1993 and 206 burglaries in 1994. This represents

81

BURGLARY REVICTIMIZATION

an average rate of reported burglary victimization of 94.8 burglaries per 1,000 residences in the area for the years 1992–94. This rate is much higher than the average rate of 59.9 burglaries per 1,000 residences in the United States as a whole (Bureau of Justice Statistics 1994). This comparison may underestimate the difference between the rate of burglaries for residences in zone 7 of Tallahassee, Florida (94.8/1,000 residences) and the United States as a whole (59.9/1,000 residences). The former represents only burglaries known to the police, while the latter represents crimes from the National Crime Victimization Survey (NCVS), which includes both burglaries known to the police and burglaries not known to the police.

Findings

Figure 1 displays the time period of heightened risk for burglary revictimization of residences in zone 7 of Tallahassee, Florida. Specifically, it portrays the percentage of revictimization offences which occurred within each week after initial burglary offences were reported to the police from 1992–94. As clearly indicated in Figure 1, the largest share of burglary revictimizations of residences (25 per cent) occurred within one week of the initial offences. The general pattern which emerges in Figure 1 is one which shows that as time passes, the risk of burglary revictimization generally diminishes.

Figure 2 also displays the time period of heightened risk for burglary revictimization of residences in zone 7 of Tallahassee, Florida. Specifically, it portrays the percentage of revictimization offences which occurred within each month after initial burglary offences were reported to the police. As clearly indicated in Figure 2, the majority of burglary revictimizations of residences during this time period (51 per cent) occurred within one month of the initial offences. The general pattern which emerges in Figure 2 is also one which shows that as time passes, the risk of burglary revictimization generally diminishes. In fact, after the fifth month following the initial burglary offence, the risk of burglary revictimization virtually disappears (less than 10 per cent of all reported burglary revictimizations occurred during the sixth through twelfth months after the initial reported offences).

Conclusions

This work demonstrates that there is a time period of heightened risk for burglary revictimization immediately after the initial offence. This is consistent with the conclusions of all of the previous literature regarding the time frame of heightened risk for criminal revictimization, which posits that 'the risk of revictimization is greatest in the period immediately after victimization' (Farrell 1994: 501) and that 'Revictimization is heavily skewed toward the date of the prior victimization' (Farrell 1994: 502). These findings lend further support for the notion that once a criminal victimization has occurred, it is very likely that if revictimization is going to occur, it will be more likely to happen in the short run rather than the long run.

Previous research by the author (Robinson 1994; Robinson and Robinson 1995) has also demonstrated that burglary victimization and revictimization is not highly

82

Burglary

MATTHEW B. ROBINSON

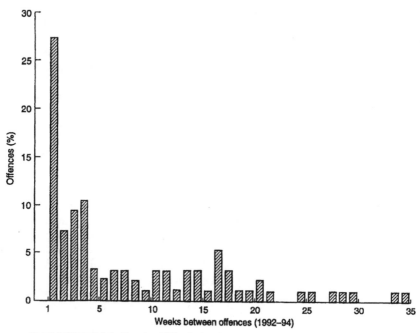

Source: Tallahassee Police Department Crime Analysis Unit

F IG . 1   Number of weeks between original offences and revictimizations

concentrated in some places, while it is in others. Some streets and some residences have been identified in this area as ones having the highest risk for burglary revictimization. Victimized and non-victimized residences have been differentiated on the basis of their environmental characteristics. For example, burgled residences were less able to be subject to surveillance to neighbours and passers-by, more accessible to offenders, and their inhabitants had more regular, predictable patterns of behaviour which left their residences unoccupied for extended period of time. Specific types of residences (e.g., student occupied apartments) had virtually no risk of burglary revictimization in this area, while others had a very high risk (e.g., working class occupied homes). As a result, between the years 1992 and 1994 in zone 7 of Tallahassee, Florida, 29 per cent of all residential burglaries were accounted for by only 1.2 per cent of all residences.

From this continuing research, the picture in regard to the place and time of burglary victimization and revictimization is somewhat clearer. Still, policy and practice are underdeveloped in the area of preventing criminal revictimization (National Board for Crime Prevention 1994: 4). Much more extensive study is needed to help locate where and when to focus preventive efforts. Regardless of whether or not such study leads to

BURGLARY REVICTIMIZATION

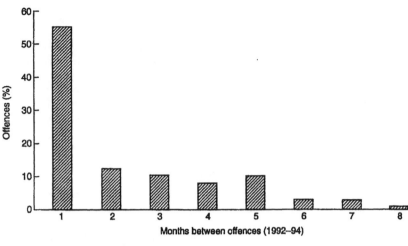

FIG. 2   Number of months between original offences and revictimization

the prevention of revictimization, at least knowing that burglary victimization and revictimization are likely to occur in certain areas and not in others, and that they are more likely to occur at some times rather than others, may improve the effectiveness of law enforcement efforts, because: 'By pointing to the most probable times and places of future offences, repeat victimization also helps identify the times and places where offenders may be found and apprehended' (National Board for Crime Prevention 1994: 2).

Policy Implications

These findings offer some very clear policy implications. In the words of Polvi *et al.* (1990: 9): 'To know that a particular person or place is prone to victimization, and when, allows temporary prevention measures to be established.' For example, given the apparent tendency for victims to be revictimized by crimes such as burglary immediately after the initial offence, preventive measures should be taken by citizens and police immediately after a crime has occurred. Thus, immediately after discovering an initial burglary, residents would be wise to expect and prepare for another. This can be achieved by altering the characteristics of the individual residence which may leave it more vulnerable to victimization. For example, bushes which obscure visibility by neighbours and passers-by of entry points could be cut back to make the residence more surveillable. Additionally, inadequate locks on entry points could be replaced with more adequate ones. Temporary or permanent alarms and lighting could be installed to ward

MATTHEW B. ROBINSON

off would-be offenders. More importantly, neighbours could be made aware of initial offences so that they will be on the look out for criminality in the immediate future. Finally, law enforcement patrols could be directed at areas where criminal victimizations have recently occurred, even if only to increase the probability of apprehending offenders who have committed the revictimizations. Preliminary evidence (Spelman 1995: 38) suggests environmental characteristics which are permanent are more important than temporary characteristics such as increased police patrols for explaining repeat victimization. Therefore, 'long-term problem solving' will be more likely to prevent its occurrence than short-term, quick-fix solutions.

References

BLOCK, R. and BLOCK, C. (1995), 'Space, Place and Crime: Hot Spot Areas and Hot Places of Liquor-Releated Crime', in J. Eck and D. Weisburd, eds., *Crime and Place*. Monsey, NY: Willow Tree Press.

BUERGER, M., COHN, E. and PETROSINO, A. (1995), 'Defining The Hot Spots of Crime: Operationalizing Theoretical Concepts For Field Research', in J. Eck and D. Weisburd, eds., *Crime and Place*. Monsey, NY: Willow Tree Press.

BUREAU OF JUSTICE STATISTICS (1994), *Sourcebook of Criminal Justice Statistics*. Washington, DC: US Government Printing Office.

BURQUEST, R., FARRELL, G. and PEASE, K. (1992), 'Lessons From School', *Policing*, 8: 148–55.

COHEN, L. and FELSON, M. (1979), 'Social Change and Crime Rate Trends: A Routine Activity Approach', *American Sociological Review*, 44: 588–608.

CROMWELL, P., OLSON, J. and AVARY, D. (1991), *Breaking and Entering: An Ethnographic Analysis of Burglary*. Newbury Park, CA: Sage.

ELLINGWORTH, D., FARRELL, G. and PEASE, K. (1995), 'A Victim is a Victim is a Victim?: Chronic Victimization in Four Sweeps of the British Crime Survey', *British Journal of Criminology*, 35/3: 360–5.

FARRELL, G. (1992). 'Multiple Victimization: Its Extent and Significance', *International Review of Victimology*, 2/2: 85–102.

—— (1994), 'Why Does Repeat Victimization Occur?', Manchester: University of Manchester, Department of Social Policy and Social Work.

FARRELL, G. and PEASE, K. (1993), *Once Bitten, Twice Bitten: Repeat Victimization and its Implications for Crime Prevention*, Police Research Group, Crime Prevention Paper 46. London: Home Office.

FARRELL, G. PHILLIPS, C. and PEASE, K. (1995), 'Like Taking Candy: Why Does Repeat Victimization Occur?', *British Journal of Criminology*, 35/3: 384–99.

FEINBERG, S. (1980), 'Statistical Modeling in the Analysis of Repeated Victimization', in S. Feinberg and A. Reiss, eds., *Indicators of Crime and Criminal Justice: Quantitative Studies*. Washington, DC: US Department of Justice, Bureau of Justice Statistics.

FELSON, M. (1983), 'Ecology of Crime', in S. Kadish, ed., *Encyclopedia of Crime and Justice*, 665–70.

FORRESTER, D., CHATTERTON, M. and PEASE, K. (1988a), 'Why it's Best to Lock the Door after the Horse has Bolted', *Police Review*, 4: 2288–9, November.

——(1988b), *The Kirkholt Burglary Prevention Project, Rochdale*, Home Office Crime Prevention Unit Paper 13. London: Home Office.

BURGLARY REVICTIMIZATION

FORRESTER, D., FRENZ, S., O'CONNELL, M. and PEASE, K. (1990), *The Kirkholt Burglary Prevention Project: Phase II*, Home Office Crime Prevention Unit Paper 23. London: Home Office.

GENN, H. (1988), 'Multiple Victimization', in M. Maguire and J. Pointing, eds., *Victims of Crime*. Milton Keynes: Open University Press.

GOTTFREDSON, M. (1984), *Victims of Crime: The Dimensions of Risk*, Home Office Research Study 81. London: HM Stationery Office.

HINDELANG, M., GOTTFREDSON, M. and GAROFALO, J. (1978), *Victims of Personal Crime: An Empirical Foundation for a Theory of Personal Victimization*. Cambridge, MA: Ballinger.

HOPE, T. (1982), 'Burglary in Schools: The Prospects for Prevention', Home Office Research and Planning Unit Paper 11. London: HM Stationery Office.

HOUGH, M. (1986), 'Victims of Violent Crime: Findings from the British Crime Survey', in E. Fattah, ed., *Crime Policy to Victim Policy: Reorienting the Justice System*. Basingstoke: Macmillan.

JOHNSON, J., KERPER, H., HAYES, D. and KILLENGER, G. (1973), *The Recidivist Victim: A Descriptive Study*, Crime Justice Monograph 4/1. Huntsville, TX: Sam Houston University, Institute of Contemporary Corrections and the Behavioral Sciences.

JONES, T., MACLEAN, B. and YOUNG, J. (1986), *The Islington Crime Survey: Crime Victimization and Policing in Inner-City London*. London: Gower.

MAYHEW, P., MAUNG, N. and MIRRLEES-BLACK, C. (1993), *The 1992 British Crime Survey*. London: HM Stationery Office.

MIETHE, T., STAFFORD, M. and LONG, J. (1987), 'Social Differentiation in Criminal Victimization: A Test of Routine Activities and Lifestyle Theories', *American Sociological Review*, 52: 184–94.

NATIONAL BOARD FOR CRIME PREVENTION (1994), *Wise After the Event: Tackling Repeat Victimisation*. London: Home Office.

NELSON, J. (1980), 'Multiple Victimization in American Cities: A Statistical Analysis of Rare Events', *American Journal of Sociology*, 85/4: 870–9 1.

PEASE K. (1991), 'The Kirkholt Project: Preventing Burglary on a British Public Housing Estate', *Security Journal*, 2: 73–7.

—— (1992), 'The Kirkholt Project: Preventing Burglary on a British Public Housing Estate', in R. Clarke, ed., *Situational Crime Prevention: Successful Case Studies*. London: Heinemann.

POLVI, N., LOOMAN, T., HUMPHRIES, C. and PEASE K. (1990), 'Repeat Break-and-Enter Victimisation: Time Course and Crime Prevention Opportunity', *Journal of Police Science and Administration*, 17/1: 8–11.

—— (1991), 'The Time Course of Repeat Burglary Victimisation', *British Journal of Criminology*, 31: 411–14.

REISS, A. (1980), 'Victim Proneness in Repeat Victimization by Type of Crime', in S. Fienberg and A. Reiss, eds., *Indicators of Crime and Criminal Justice: Quantitative Studies*. Washington, DC: US Department of Justice, Bureau of Justice Statistics.

ROBINSON, M. (1994), Environmental Characteristics of Burglaries in Private Apartment Complexes Predominantly Occupied by University Students, Zone 7, Tallahassee, Florida, 1993. Master's Thesis, School of Criminology and Criminal Justice, Florida State University.

ROBINSON, M. and ROBINSON, C. (1995), 'Once Bitten, But Not Twice Bitten: Student Apartment Burglary Cool Spots'. Paper presented to the annual meeting of the Southern Criminal Justice Association, Gatlinburg, Tennessee.

ROSS, N. (1994), unpublished paper presented to the National Board for Crime Prevention.

SAMPSON, A. (1991), *Lessons Learnt from a Victim Support Crime Prevention Project*, Home Office Crime Prevention Unit Paper 25. London: Home Office.

MATTHEW B. ROBINSON

SAMPSON, A. and PHILLIPS, C. (1992), *Multiple Victimization: Racial Attacks on an East London Estate*, Home Office Crime Prevention Unit Paper 36. London: Home Office.

SHAPLAND, J., WILES, P., JOHNSON, V. and LEEK, M. (1991), Crime at Work: The Victimization of Factories and Employees, unpublished paper. Sheffield: University of Sheffield, Faculty of Law.

SHEPHERD, J. (1990), 'Violent Crime in Bristol: An Accident and Emergency Department Perspective', *British Journal of Criminology*, 30: 289–305.

SHERMAN, L., GARTIN, P. and BUERGER, M. (1989), 'Hot Spots of Predatory Crime: Routine Activities and the Criminology of Place', *Criminology*, 27/1: 27–55.

SKOGAN, W. (1990a), 'The National Crime Survey Redesign', *Public Opinion Quarterly*, 54:256–72.

—— (1990b), 'Innovations in the Analysis of Crime Surveys'. Paper presented to the Conference on Measurement and Research Design in Criminal Justice, Griffith University, Queensland.

SPARKS, R. (1981), 'Multiple Victimization: Evidence, Theory and Future Research', *Journal of Criminal Law and Criminology*, 72: 762–78.

SPARKS, R., GENN, H. and DODD, D. (1977), *Surveying Victims*. London: Wiley.

SPELMAN, W. (1995), 'Once Bitten, Then What? Cross-Sectional and Time-Course Explanations of Repeat Victimization', *British Journal of Criminology*, 35/3: 366–83.

TILLEY, N. (1993), *The Prevention of Crime Against Small Businesses: The Safer Cities Experience*, Home Office Crime Prevention Unit Paper 45. London: Home Office.

TRICKETT, A., OSBORN, D., SEYMOUR, J. and PEASE, K. (1992), 'What is Different About High Crime Areas?', *British Journal of Criminology*, 32: 250–65.

WRIGHT, R. and DECKER, S. (1994), *Burglars on the Job: Street Life and Residential Break-Ins*. Boston, MA: Northeastern University Press.

ZIEGENHAGEN, E. (1976), 'The Recidivist Victim of Violent Crime', *Victimology*, 1: 538–50.

87

[13]

BURGLARY VICTIMIZATION, PERCEPTIONS OF CRIME RISK, AND ROUTINE ACTIVITIES: A MULTILEVEL ANALYSIS ACROSS SEATTLE NEIGHBORHOODS AND CENSUS TRACTS

PAMELA WILCOX ROUNTREE
KENNETH C. LAND

This study extends previous research on the effects of victimization in terms of fear of crime and constrained behavior by examining both micro- and macrolevel factors. In particular, we address the way in which contextual indicators of ambient risk can affect individuals' perceived risk and lifestyles through both main effects and moderating effects—where the latter cause the effects of individual-level factors on risk perception and routine activities to vary across residential communities. Results presented here suggest that increased levels of crime (as indicated by tract-level burglary rates) and disorganization (as indicated by high levels of neighborhood incivilities, for instance) have important direct positive effects on perceived crime risk, whereas neighborhood social integration decreases perceived risk. Further, tract-level crime rates have direct positive effects on protective behaviors, but community disorder, for the most part, does not lead to an increase in precautionary measures. Important moderating effects of crime and disorganization are also found. For instance, the tendency for non-Whites to perceive lower crime risk (or to feel less unsafe) than Whites is intensified in disorderly areas.

Relationships among crime victimization, fear of crime, and precautionary behavior or restricted routine activity patterns—and the effects of neighborhood or community context thereon—have been the subject of substantial research efforts by criminologists (for a recent review, see Bursik and Grasmick 1993, p. 90-111). This research indicates that victimization can

Address all correspondence to Pamela Wilcox Rountree, Department of Sociology, University of Kentucky, Lexington, Kentucky 40506. This research was supported in part by National Science Foundation Grant SBR-9310193. We would like to thank Terance D. Miethe for providing the data analyzed herein.

148   JOURNAL OF RESEARCH IN CRIME AND DELINQUENCY

increase perceived crime risk and associated fear within individuals and that this risk perception or fear can, in turn, prompt defense measures. One limitation of extant research on reactions to crime, however, is that most studies have been conducted either exclusively with individual-level data or with macro or aggregated neighborhood- or community-level data. Relatedly, the macro research that has incorporated social context has primarily emphasized the direct effects of neighborhood environment, ignoring potential moderating or conditioning effects of context. The few studies that have been conducted on the conditional influence of context focus mainly on the nonuniform effects of sociodemographic characteristics on fear across different settings (Baumer 1985; Maxfield 1984; Ortega and Myles 1987). Other important individual-level predictors of fear, such as previous victimization, have not been addressed in contextual research, and no research has modeled the conditionality or *contextuality* of relationships between individual-level risk factors and protective behavior.

In short, the extant research on the effects of victimization is limited in its attention to the possible embeddedness of individual-level explanations for fear of crime (or risk perception) and precautionary behavior within a community context. By contrast, several recent studies have addressed the ways in which neighborhood or community context both directly and indirectly affect criminal victimization (Kennedy and Forde 1990; Miethe and McDowall 1993; Rountree, Land, and Miethe 1994; Sampson and Wooldredge 1987; Smith and Jarjoura 1989). But no research to date has attempted a comprehensive micro-macro integrative analysis of the effects of victimization in terms of fear of crime and precautionary behavior, despite the fact that extant research indicates the probable importance of both types of predictors. Using hierarchical logistic and linear regression methods, this study bridges the micro-macro gap, recognizing the potential simultaneous and interactive effects of individual-level characteristics (e.g., prior victimization, lifestyle characteristics) and properties of the larger environment (e.g., characteristics pertaining to community disorganization) in explaining variation in individual-level concern about crime and precautionary behavior as outcomes of criminal victimization.

In particular, we address the question of the extent to which contextual factors affect individual-level variation in fear of crime and precautionary behavior both directly and through moderating or conditional effects, focusing on a particular dimension of fear that taps cognitive perceptions of risk. Methodological work on fear of crime by Ferraro and LaGrange (1987) suggests that often-used measures of fear are flawed in that they are actually tapping more cerebral judgments regarding risk or concern about crime rather than negative emotional responses to crime (see also Ferraro 1995). Ferraro and LaGrange argue that judgments of risk are conceptually distinct from fear of crime and that using judgments as measures for fear obscures the relationship between cognitive perceptions of risk and actual fear. Research by Warr and Stafford (1983) and LaGrange, Ferraro, and Supancic (1992) supports such a conceptual distinction because they show that risk perception, although an important predictor of fear, is not perfectly correlated with fear. Consequently, despite the fact that within the past several decades many scholars have used cognitive, judgment-based measures of safety for operationalizing the fear concept, we believe it is best to think of risk perception as a particular version or dimension of fear rather than as a comprehensive measure of fear.

EXTANT RESEARCH ON THE EFFECTS OF VICTIMIZATION

There is an extensive research literature pertaining to the effects of crime on fear. Related work has concentrated on the effects of fear on restricted activities. However, the extant work examining the elements of fear and/or restricted activity stemming from victimization has been almost exclusively either micro or macro in design.

Most of the earlier studies of fear of crime focused on the sociodemographic covariates of concern about crime, indicating that those groups thought to be more physically or socially vulnerable—such as women, the elderly, the poor, and non-Whites—tend to indeed be more fearful and oftentimes act more fearful in terms of their precautionary behavior (see, e.g., Baumer 1979; Clarke and Lewis 1982; Garofalo 1979; Stafford and Galle 1984). More recently, scholars have begun to explore interactions among the sociodemographic predictors of fear and have found age to interact significantly with both other sociodemographic variables and city- or neighborhood-level factors. For instance, Baumer (1985) found age to interact with gender and size of place such that age had a stronger positive effect on fear for men and in urban areas. Other studies have suggested that age is more strongly related (positively) to fear for Blacks (Ortega and Myles 1987) and for individuals living in low-crime neighborhoods (Maxfield 1984). Other individual-level correlates of fear beyond sociodemographic predictors have also been explored: Social-psychological variables, such as perceived risk, perceived seriousness, locus of control, and self-image have been shown to be important in explaining fear of crime specifically (van der Wurff, van Staalduinen, and Stringer 1989; Warr and Stafford 1983).

150   JOURNAL OF RESEARCH IN CRIME AND DELINQUENCY

Another popular approach has been to examine community-level indicators of fear. These macrolevel studies indicate that neighborhood-level threat can affect directly levels of fear. In their seminal work, Skogan and Maxfield (1981) tested a model in which social integration, neighborhood-level crime, and community disorder (boisterousness, drunkenness, untidiness, etc.) are thought to affect levels of fear, and they found that such structural covariates were indeed important in predicting anxiety about crime. Community cohesiveness or integration had a weak but nevertheless significant negative effect on fear, whereas crime and disorder increased fear through much stronger effects. The Skogan and Maxfield findings supported earlier work by Lewis and Maxfield (1980), which indicated that both high crime rates and incivility produced heightened concern about crime. Subsequent to these earlier community-level studies, Taylor and Hale (1986) also found strong effects on fear of perceptions of neighborhood problems, or disorder. In fact, these noncrime problems (incivilities) were stronger predictors of fear than was actual crime in their study. Lewis and Salem (1986) provided further evidence from their aggregate study across 10 neighborhoods that fear is more than simply a function of crime/victimization within an area—concern about incivility and available networks of social control (i.e., social integration, organizational strength, etc.) were also found to be of importance in understanding community levels of concern about crime. Also consistent with the Skogan and Maxfield research, Taylor, Gottfredson, and Brower (1984) found that social factors characterizing organization (e.g., strong social ties) significantly dampened fear. Finally, other structural features—such as racial composition and population size—have been found to affect aggregate levels of fear (Liska, Lawrence, and Sanchirico 1982).

In brief, general "problems of neighborhood"—which are perhaps perceived by many to be indicative or symbolic of more trouble to come (in the form of crime)—increase fear among respondents in studies that include such structural effects. These findings seem consistent with ideas regarding "broken windows" as presented by Wilson and Kelling (1982, p. 34). According to the broken windows theory, disorder and incivility within an area serve to indicate inadequate social control, and the idea is that if a community cannot control the sobriety of its members, the tranquility and tidiness of its streets, and so forth, it is inevitable that it will also be unable to control crime. The limited research done on disorder supports the proposed relationship between incivility and crime offered by the broken windows philosophy; neighborhood disorder is a significant predictor of both violent and household (burglary) victimization rates (see, e.g., Rountree, Land, and Miethe 1994). If residents perceive a positive relationship between disorder and crime—the idea that crime emerges from disorder—then fear should often accompany signs of incivility.

The findings concerning the macro main effects of neighborhood problems also support the idea originally conceived by Garofalo and Laub (1979)—that fear of crime may be more than anxiety about experiencing criminal victimization. Rather, fear of crime may represent a more general concern about problems within a community—problems that perhaps often accompany crime-ridden areas and are thus perceived in a manner similar to crime. In fact, Garofalo and Laub suggest that fear of crime may really refer to "urban unease" or concern over quality of life in the community setting. Thus, when people say that they are fearful of crime, they may not only be concerned about crime itself but also about the contextual conditions conducive to crime (also see Hartnagel 1979).

Victimization, Fear of Crime, and Routine Activities

Over the past two decades, Cohen, Felson, Land, and others have posited and refined a crime opportunity/routine activity model in which crime and victimization are understood as a function of the lifestyles or ordinary routine activities of individuals (see, e.g., Cantor and Land 1985; Cohen and Felson 1979; Cohen, Felson, and Land 1980; Cohen, Kluegel, and Land 1981; Miethe, Stafford, and Long 1987). Specifically, increases in activities that bring together motivated offenders and suitable targets (e.g., a valuable consumer product) in the absence of capable guardians (in terms of people or objects) are posited to increase risk of criminal victimization. Even though it is difficult to operationalize the crime opportunity model, many studies have appeared—with most supportive of its various implications (for a recent review, see Bursik and Grasmick 1993, pp. 60-89).

Viewing crime opportunities from a market, or supply-demand, perspective, Cook (1986, p. 6) noted that an important omission from most lifestyle or routine activity models is the explicit recognition that an "individual's exposure to risky circumstances is influenced by his concern with being victimized." Such a view is built around the assumption that individuals choose their routine activities rationally—they are neither completely socially constrained nor circumstantial phenomena. Thus individuals base their choice of activities, for example, on their risk perceptions and fear of criminal victimization. Furthermore, risk perception or fear is presumed to be rationally conceived on the part of an individual based upon such things as vulnerability, perceived seriousness, actual incidence of victimization, or neighborhood/city conditions, as the fear-of-crime literature suggests (also see Garofalo 1981, pp. 847-51, for a review of lifestyle/activity responses to fear).

Liska and colleagues have addressed certain aspects of Cook's ideas in research examining the effects of fear of crime and routine activities. In particular, Liska, Sanchirico, and Reed (1988) demonstrated a reciprocity between fear of crime and constrained behavior. They found that fear of crime constrains social behavior in the sense that fearful people engage in fewer activities outside the home or more frequently change activities because of crime. These researchers also found that constrained social activities increased fear of crime. Using both recursive and nonrecursive structural-equation macro models to explain variations across cities in the relationships among aggregated levels of fear of crime, constrained behavior, and crime, Liska and Warner (1991) suggested that the Durkheimian notion of crime's being functional to society by decreasing subsequent deviance holds albeit through a different mechanism than that proposed by functionalists. Instead of the idea that crime increases solidarity and thus decreases future crime, as Durkheim posited, Liska and Warner found that crime decreases solidarity but also decreases future crime and deviance. Crime opportunity is the key explanation offered—whereby crime has the effect of isolating individuals and restricting routine activities, and hence the opportunity for successful subsequent crime is diminished.

In short, recent research has begun to mesh traditional studies of the antecedents of fear of crime and elements of opportunity theory, focusing on the relationship between routine activities and victimization. In this way, recent progress in understanding the dynamics of fear of crime has had the effect of extending or elaborating upon routine activities or opportunity theory—routine activity patterns are no longer considered solely exogenous indicators of victimization. Rather, activities can be structured rationally by cognitive perceptions, such as the fear of crime or perceived risk, which may itself result from victimization experiences (Garofalo 1979; Skogan and Maxfield 1981).

INTEGRATING INDIVIDUAL AND CONTEXTUAL EXPLANATIONS

We seek to extend previous work on victimization, fear of crime, and routine activities by integrating micro- and macrolevel explanatory variables while focusing on a particular dimension of fear—cognitive perceptions of risk—and a particular form of routine activity—precautionary behavior. In particular, the objective is to test whether or not previous individual-level victimization experiences, along with individual-level lifestyle factors, and ambient risk, as indicated by contextual indicators of crime and disorganization, influence subsequent individual-level crime risk perception and subsequent individual-level precautionary behavior. The problem is that ambient risk can affect individuals' crime/victimization risk perception and protective behavior in two ways: through direct effects and through moderating effects—by contextualizing or conditioning the effects of individual-level factors on risk perception and restricted activities in the sense of causing these effects to vary from one context to another. Thus the uncovering of cross-level interactions in predicting risk perception and routine activities is also a major objective.

Figure 1 presents a conceptual model of these possibilities. It displays, in summary form, the embedding of an individual-level explanation of crime risk perception and routine activities within a model that incorporates contextual or neighborhood factors. At the level of the individual, previous burglary victimization has a positive influence on perceived risk, which also is affected by other individual-level explanatory (sociodemographic and routine activities) factors (positively or negatively, depending on the specific factor). An individual's previous victimization experience together with the person's risk perception and other individual-level explanatory factors then affect his or her routine activities, in particular those pertaining to safety precautions.

But, as some of the research reviewed above suggests, an individual's perceived risk and routine activities may also be affected by the ambience of the neighborhood context in which the individual resides. The box in Figure 1 identifies five of these factors, namely, the area burglary rate and indicators of neighborhood traffic (busy places), ethnic heterogeneity, neighborhood incivilities, and social integration. Direct or main effects of the contextual factors on the individual-level risk perception and routine activities variables (positive or negative, depending on the specific contextual factor) are indicated by the solid arrows in Figure 1. In addition, however, it is possible that the individual-level effects of previous victimization and other individual-level explanatory factors vary from neighborhood to neighborhood and that the contextual factors explain at least part of this variation. This possibility of moderating effects is indicated in Figure 1 by the dashed arrows from the box containing the contextual factors to the arrows connecting the individual-level part of the model. The objective of the research described below is to ascertain the extent to which the contextual factors exert direct and conditional effects on individual-level risk perception and routine activities related to precautionary behavior specifically.

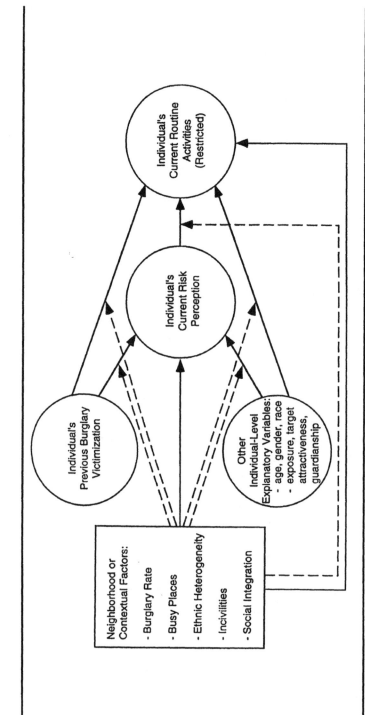

Figure 1: Effects of Individual- and Context-Level Variables on Individual-Level Risk Perception and Routine Activities

MODELS AND METHODS

This objective could be addressed in a conventional linear or logistic regression model framework wherein the contextual variables and their interactions with the individual-level explanatory variables are entered into the analysis along with the individual-level variables. Such standard statistical approaches, however, tend to ignore the implicit hierarchy involved between characteristics of individuals and of the neighborhoods or contexts in which they live.

Specifically, the independence-of-error-terms assumption on which the traditional regression approach to contextual analysis is based may not be appropriate. Such an assumption does not account for the idea that individuals clustered in the same social group often are likely to be more similar regarding certain characteristics than are individuals grouped differently. For example, individuals living in the same spatial location or neighborhood are likely to be more similar in many respects than are individuals living in different areas; therefore, independent errors cannot be assumed as they are in conventional regression models.[1] Even if interaction terms are included, the hierarchical structure of the data, with individuals nested within neighborhoods or other community contexts, is not explicitly incorporated into traditional estimation procedures.

A solution to this limitation is offered by the hierarchical linear modeling (HLM) approach, which has developed out of statistical work on Bayesian estimation of linear regression models (Lindley and Smith 1972), sociological research on contextual effects (Mason, Wong, and Entwisle 1983), and educational research on learning curves and school effects (Raudenbush, 1984; Strenio, Weisberg, and Bryk 1983; for general expositions, see Bryk and Raudenbush 1992; Goldstein 1987). The HLM approach also has been extended to logistic regression (Wong and Mason 1985); the hierarchical logistic regression model recently was applied to criminal victimization data by Rountree et al. (1994). The analyses reported below were conducted by employing HLM procedures for conventional and logistic regression (Prosser, Rasbash, and Goldstein 1991a, 1991b).[2]

Data

The data used for the analyses come mainly from a victimization survey as part of a larger Seattle, Washington, crime project. These data are supplemented with the 1989 and 1990 Seattle Police Department annual reports. The survey data were collected in 1990 on 5,302 individuals living in 300 neighborhoods (defined as pairs of blocks), and the neighborhoods are contained within larger units—100 of the 121 census tracts within Seattle. The 100 census tracts are considered a random subsample of the 114 stable census tracts within the city—those that had not changed their boundaries within the preceding three decades (Miethe and Meier 1994). The three neighborhoods within the sampled census tract each contained a street address at which a burglary had been reported in 1989; the other block in each pair bordered the block with the burglary.

Because of the clustering at the neighborhood and tract levels in combination with the fact that certain contextual data are available only at the tract level, the city block pair (neighborhood) and the census tract are contextual units of interest in this study. Approximately 18 housing units within each neighborhood and 50 housing units within each census tract were sampled using a reverse telephone directory. When compared with the 1989 NCS survey sample, the Seattle sample tends to underrepresent young adults (20-24), low-income families, and transient households and overrepresents home owners and the college educated (see Miethe and Meier 1994).[3] Also, because a simple random sample of block groups was not sampled within each tract, and instead at least one household on each block pair had experienced a burglary in the year prior to the study, the sample design also disproportionately stratifies on the basis of burglary victimization. After deleting cases with missing data, 5,090 individuals remained in the sample for the analyses reported herein.[4]

MEASURES OF SURVEY VARIABLES

The dependent variables in this study are (a) crime risk perception as a particular cognitive dimension of fear indicated by whether or not the respondent perceives his or her neighborhood to be either somewhat or very unsafe from crime at the time of the survey; and (b) restricted routine activities as indicated by the number of precautionary measures used by the respondent at the time of the survey, including locking doors, installing extra locks, installing window bars, leaving lights on (or using a light timer device), joining a crime prevention program, having neighbors watch home when away, owning a dog, owning a weapon, and installing a burglar alarm/security system.[5] As Table 1 indicates, just over 24% of respondents perceive their neighborhoods to be unsafe from crime, and respondents engage in, on average, slightly over four restrictive precautionary measures.

The independent variables in the study incorporate both micro and macro predictors of fear of crime and restricted routine activity. Individual-level variables include measures of previous victimization and the risk factors of exposure, guardianship, and target attractiveness stemming from work in the

TABLE 1: Variables, Metrics, and Descriptive Statistics[a]

Variables	Metrics	Descriptive Statistics		
		Mean	*SD*	*Range*
Dependent variables				
Perceived risk	(0 = *safe*, 1 = *unsafe*)	0.241	0.428	0-1
Safety precautions[b]	(number of precautions)	4.168	1.473	0-9
Explanatory variables				
Individual-level characteristics:				
Age	(1 = *10-19* to *7 = 70 and older*)	4.367	1.717	1-7
Gender	(0 = *female*, 1 = *male*)	0.503	0.500	0-1
Race	(0 = *White*, 1 = *non-White*)	0.150	0.358	0-1
Home unoccupied	(nights per week)	1.791	1.969	0-7
Expensive goods	(number of items owned)	2.533	1.408	0-5
Safety precautions[c]	(number of precautions)	3.837	1.509	0-9
Live alone	(0 = *no*, 1 = *yes*)	0.258	0.437	0-1
Family income	(1 = *< $10k* to 7 = *> $100k*)	3.371	1.370	1-7
Guardianship barriers	(number of barriers)	0.487	0.638	0-2
Access routes	(number of routes)	0.333	0.543	0-2
Corner residence	(0 = *no*, 1 = *yes*)	0.423	0.495	0-1
Burglary victimization	(0 = *no*, 1 = *yes*)	0.170	0.375	0-1

(continued)

TABLE 1 Continued

Variables	Metrics	Descriptive Statistics		
		Mean	SD	Range
Neighborhood-level contextual and compositional characteristics:				
Age composition	(mean age)[d]	4.367	0.656	2.40-6.0
Gender composition	(percentage male)	0.503	0.131	0.14-0.86
Average income	(mean income)[e]	3.371	0.654	1.33-5.31
Ethnic heterogeneity	(percentage non-White * percentage White)	0.090	0.079	0-0.25
Busy places	(number of places nearby)	3.441	1.340	0.82-7.19
Neighborhood incivilities	(number of indicators)	1.328	0.704	0-3.30
Social integration	(number of indicators)	3.516	0.801	1.41-5.35
Tract-level contextual and compositional characteristics				
Age composition	(mean age)[d]	4.367	0.464	3.21-5.43
Gender composition	(percentage male)	0.503	0.074	0.36-0.73
Average income	(mean income)[e]	3.367	0.514	1.85-4.72
Ethnic heterogeneity	(percentage non-White * percentage White)	0.100	0.072	0-0.25
Burglary rate	(number reported to police in 1989 and 1990/100 households)	7.463	3.903	1.81-18.52

a. The total sample size is 5,090 individuals, 300 neighborhoods, and 100 census tracts.
b. Safety precautions, when used as a dependent variable, refer to precautionary measures taken at the time the survey was administered (t).
c. Safety precautions, when used as an explanatory variable, refer to precautionary measures taken 2 years prior to the date of the survey (t-2).
d. The same response categories used in the individual-level measure for age are used here.
e. The same response categories used in the individual-level measure for income are used here.

routine activities tradition; sociodemographic indicators are also incorporated. Contextual indicators of crime and disorganization include neighborhood-level incivility, neighborhood-level population density or traffic, neighborhood ethnic heterogeneity, neighborhood social integration, and tract-level burglary rates. Compositional measures are also included at both the neighborhood and census-tract levels.

Regarding the individual-level variables first, previous burglary victimization is measured by whether or not a burglary or attempted burglary was experienced at the respondent's current home within the 2 years preceding the survey. The temporal referents of this variable are in contrast with the dependent variables, which measure perceived risk and restricted routine activities at the time of the survey. In support of the work discussed earlier integrating fear of crime studies with routine activities research, we assume that previous experience with victimization is likely to heighten perceptions of safety in the neighborhood and also increase efforts (routine activities) aimed at safeguarding against crime.

We also control for other routine activity patterns and factors associated with the ecology of crime (e.g., see Brantingham and Brantingham 1981; Felson 1994), which may affect perceptions of safety/risk and restricted routine activities in terms of precautionary behavior. Exposure, referring to how visible or accessible one is in relation to motivated offenders, is measured in several different ways. First, exposure is measured by the number of nights during the previous week that the respondent's home was left unoccupied (home unoccupied). Exposure is also measured by the number of attractive access routes there are to and from the respondent's property, including the presence of ground floor windows and the presence of an alley behind the home. Finally, exposure is measured by a third variable indicating whether or not the respondent lives in a corner residence as opposed to living in the middle of a block.

The routine activity risk factor of target attractiveness, referring to the value the target represents, is also measured by an index representing the number of expensive portable household goods within the respondent's home (expensive goods), including ownership of a portable color television, a VCR, a 35 mm camera, a home computer, and a bicycle or motorcycle. Family income is also used as a measure of target attractiveness.

Patterns of guardianship may also affect levels of risk perception and protective behaviors among respondents. One measure of guardianship is an index measuring the number of safety precautions employed by the respondent 2 years prior to the survey, including whether or not the respondent locked doors, used extra locks (i.e., deadbolts, chains, etc.), left lights on or used a light timer device, was a member of a crime prevention program, owned a

160   JOURNAL OF RESEARCH IN CRIME AND DELINQUENCY

burglar alarm, owned a dog, had neighbors watch his or her home, or owned a weapon. Measures characterizing behavior 2 years prior to the survey are used as opposed to measures characterizing safety precautions at the time of the survey (after any victimization may have taken place), which are used in the construction of a dependent variable (described above). A physical dimension of guardianship is captured by the number of guardianship barriers characterizing the respondent's home, including the presence of a tall fence or hedge obstructing the view of potential guardians and the presence of an empty house or vacant property next door. The more barriers characterizing property the less effectively others can provide guardianship. Finally, a social dimension of the guardianship risk factor is measured by whether or not the respondent lives alone. The more people with which a respondent lives, the more human guardians the individual is assumed to have. Demographic variables measuring the respondent's age, race, and gender are also included as individual-level predictors of both fear of crime and restricted routine activities.

Neighborhood-level variables measuring various indicators of social disorganization are available for the block pair level of analysis by aggregating individual responses respectively within these aggregate units. For instance, a neighborhood-level aggregate measure of community population density or traffic in terms of both residents and strangers is represented by the average number of places available for public activity, or busy places, within the neighborhood (or block pair) according to all of the respondents residing there, including the presence of schools, convenience stores, bars, fast food restaurants, office buildings, parks or playgrounds, shopping malls, hotels/motels, and bus stops. Community ethnic heterogeneity is measured by multiplying the proportion of respondents within each block pair who are White and the proportion non-White. The low socioeconomic status of a neighborhood is measured by an index averaging the number of indicators of incivilities within each block pair, including a presence of teenagers hanging out in the streets, presence of litter or garbage on the street, abandoned houses or boarded-up buildings, poor street lighting, and the appearance of vandalism (i.e., graffiti, etc.). Finally, social integration is measured by an index averaging within neighborhood block pairs the number of indicators of closeness or cohesion among community residents. The items comprising this scale include whether or not respondents recognize strangers on their block, have friends or relatives on the block, watch neighbors' property, borrow items from neighbors, have lunch or dinner with neighbors, or help neighbors with problems.

As noted earlier, the survey data are supplemented by the Seattle police data. Specifically, Part I offense rates are available by federal census tracts (these rates are unavailable for the smaller neighborhood, or block pair, units) and provide useful indicators for ambient risk among residents of given tracts. Residential burglary counts for 1989 and 1990 were combined within each tract, divided by the total number of households within the tracts (from 1990 census data), and multiplied by 100 to obtain a tract-specific, 2-year residential burglary rate for each of the 100 Seattle census tracts included in the sample, thus providing a tract-level contextual characteristic perhaps important in understanding risk perception and routine activities in addition to neighborhood-level incivility, density, heterogeneity, and integration. We assume that the more incivility-plagued, traffic-ridden, ethnically heterogeneous, noncohesive, and crime-ridden communities are more ineffective at efforts toward informal control, increasing the perceptions of crime risk among residents and increasing the likelihood of residents' engaging in precautionary measures.

In addition to the above-mentioned contextual indicators of crime and disorganization, we also include compositional measures at both the neighborhood and tract levels to control for the aggregate characteristics of the individuals residing within these units. Specifically, we control for neighborhood- and tract-level age composition (neighborhood mean age and tract-level mean age) and gender composition (neighborhood-level percent male and tract-level percent male). Compositional measures controlling for neighborhood- and tract-level income are also included. Finally, we believe race composition at the neighborhood level is adequately controlled through the ethnic heterogeneity measure described above. We include a tract-level ethnic heterogeneity measure, as well.

Model Specification and Estimation

We incorporate the individual- and contextual-level indicators described above into three-level hierarchical logistic regression models, with individuals, neighborhoods (block pairs), and census tracts being the units of interest. Given that there is little theoretical reason to separate neighborhood- and tract-level contextual effects, however, we base our decision to estimate three-level models largely on empirical grounds. First, one of our contextual variables— community-level burglary rate—is available at the census tract level only; it cannot be disaggregated to the neighborhood level. Thus incorporating the census tract level into the analysis is necessary if we wish to use this measure. Although we could create tract-level analogues of the neighborhood-level measures described above (e.g., incivilities, ethnic heterogeneity, social integration, and busy places) and estimate a two-level model with census tract as the only contextual unit, such a strategy seems inconsistent with the

162   JOURNAL OF RESEARCH IN CRIME AND DELINQUENCY

original sample design. Recall that the sample design is such that individuals are clustered within neighborhoods, and neighborhoods, in turn, are grouped within census tracts. Ignoring the neighborhood as a viable contextual unit would discount the clustering of sampled individuals at the neighborhood level and might result in dependent errors in the models—the very problem hierarchical models are designed to curb. Therefore, retaining both neighborhoods and census tracts as contextual units is, in our opinion, a methodologically sound strategy.

As conventional practice in HLM applications is to try to separate distinct effects of individual-level sociodemographic variables from compositional effects (see, e.g., Bryk and Raudenbush 1992, pp. 121-3), we include in our model specifications the compositional measures described above. In the final models reported herein, however, not all of the compositional variables are included from both levels due to high collinearity among compositional variables and between compositional variables and disorganization variables. For instance, neighborhood-level income and neighborhood incivilities are too highly correlated to be included in the same model without creating problems associated with multicollinearity. Likewise, multicollinearity problems arise when compositional equivalents across aggregate levels are included in any one model. For instance, the correlation between each of the following pairs of variables is very high: neighborhood-level gender composition and tract-level gender composition, neighborhood-level age composition and tract-level age composition, neighborhood-level income and tract-level income, and neighborhood-level heterogeneity and tract-level heterogeneity. Despite the fact that we cannot explicitly control for both tract- and neighborhood-level heterogeneity, for instance, the high correlations between these cross-level compositional equivalents provides reason to believe that when controlling for neighborhood heterogeneity, we are also providing a proxy measure for tract-level heterogeneity. Similarly, when including a measure for tract-level gender composition—to use another example—we are also adequately capturing neighborhood-level gender composition. Therefore, although we originally estimated full contextual models that included all individual-level variables, contextual disorganization measures, and compositional variables, we arrive at reduced models through the application of backward elimination procedures—which involves the deletion of insignificant or troublesome (due to collinearity) variables one at a time until a stable model is obtained. Even in the absence of multicollinearity, a model including compositional measures at both levels would be theoretically troubling, as distinctions among the effects of, say, neighborhood-level mean age and tract-level mean age would seem ambiguous at best. Thus, given that there is no theoretical basis for distinguishing neighborhood from tract-level compositional effects and given that we have no empirical evidence that compositional measures from both levels should be in the model, our reduced models are defensible.

RESULTS

Three-Level Model for Perception of Risk

The individual-level model for individual i in neighborhood j and census tract k in the hierarchical analysis of perceived risk is the following logistic regression:

$$\text{logit}(RISK_{ijk}) = \beta_{0jk} + \beta_{1jk}(AGE_{ijk}) + \beta_{2jk}(GENDER_{ijk}) + \beta_{3jk}(RACE_{ijk}) +$$

$$\beta_{4jk}(HOME\ UNOCCUPIED_{ijk}) + \beta_{5jk}(INCOME_{ijk}) +$$

$$\beta_{6jk}(GOODS_{ijk}) + \beta_{7jk}(SAFETY_{ijk}) +$$

$$\beta_{8jk}(LIVE\ ALONE_{ijk}) + \beta_{9jk}(BARRIERS_{ijk}) +$$

$$\beta_{10jk}(ACCESS_{ijk}) + \beta_{11jk}(CORNER_{ijk}) +$$

$$\beta_{12jk}(VICTIM_{ijk}) + e_{ijk}$$

(1)

where all variables represent grand-mean-centered values. Following conventional practice in multilevel hierarchical logistic regression (Patterson 1991), we include an extra binomial error term, e_{ijk}, to allow for the possibility that the variances of the individual-level sample risk probabilities are not distributed precisely as a binomial variable on the basis of the expected values of the estimated logistic regression model (substantive interpretations of this term are given later). As is conventional in hierarchical modeling methodology, all of the coefficients from the individual-level model were initially assumed to vary across Seattle neighborhoods and census tracts, corresponding to the following Level 2 and Level 3 models, respectively:

$$\beta_{qjk} = \Theta_{q0k} + u_{qjk} \text{ for } q = 0,1,\dots,12$$ (2a)

$$\Theta_{q0k} = \pi_{q00} + r_{q0k} \text{ for } q = 0,1,\dots,12$$ (2b)

Those coefficients that had variance components that did not show significant variability across Level 2 or Level 3 units (neighborhood and census tract)

164   JOURNAL OF RESEARCH IN CRIME AND DELINQUENCY

were subsequently specified as fixed (see, e.g., Bryk and Raudenbush 1992). The resulting Level 2, or between-neighborhood, model is as follows:

$$\beta_{0jk} = \Theta_{00k} + u_{0jk}$$

$$\beta_{3jk} = \Theta_{30k} + u_{3jk}$$

$$\beta_{4jk} = \Theta_{40k} + u_{4jk} \tag{3}$$

$$\beta_{12jk} = \Theta_{120k} + u_{12jk}$$

$$\beta_{qjk} = \Theta_{q0k} \text{ for } q = 1,2,5\text{-}11$$

The resulting Level 3, or between-tract, model is as follows:

$$\Theta_{00k} = \pi_{000} + r_{00k}$$

$$\Theta_{q0k} = \pi_{q00} \text{ for } q = 1\text{-}12 \tag{4}$$

As these between-neighborhood and between-tract equations imply, several coefficients exhibited significant variability across Seattle contextual units. The results shown in Table 2 come from the random coefficient model for perceived risk obtained by combining the individual-level, between-neighborhood, and between-tract models. As the chi-square statistic at the bottom of this table indicates, this model—containing individual-level predictors only, with four coefficients varying across neighborhoods and one coefficient varying across census tracts—is a significant improvement over a baseline fear-of-crime model containing only a constant term and a Level 1 extra binomial error term, with the constant allowed to vary across neighborhoods and census tracts.

The random-effects panel of Table 2 shows significant variance components for the intercept and the coefficients for the race, home unoccupied, and burglary victimization variables. The mean logit of risk perception (π_{000}), adjusted for the effects of Level 1 predictors, varies significantly across census tracts and neighborhoods.[6] In addition, the effects that race (π_{300}), home unoccupied (π_{400}), and burglary victimization (π_{1200}) have on logit(risk perception) are significantly different across neighborhood (block pair) contextual units. The Level-1 extra-binomial error term is also significant, indicating that there remains unexplained heterogeneity at the individual level in this model.[7]

The fixed-effects panel of Table 2 reveals several interesting individual-level main effects. In particular, males and non-Whites are less likely to

TABLE 2: Random Coefficient Regression Model for Logistic Regression Coefficients of Crime Risk Perception in Seattle[a]

Fixed Effect	Coefficient	SE	Exp (Coefficient)	t-ratio[b]
Mean risk, π_{000}	0.242	0.017	1.274	14.526
Age, π_{100}	−0.010	0.004	0.990	−2.726
Gender, π_{200}	−0.039	0.011	0.962	−3.491
Race, π_{300}	−0.096	0.020	0.909	−4.752
Home unoccupied, π_{400}	0.004	0.003	1.004	1.144
Family income, π_{500}	−0.013	0.005	0.987	−2.732
Expensive goods, π_{600}	0.005	0.004	1.005	1.097
Safety precautions, π_{700}	0.013	0.004	1.013	3.259
Live alone, π_{800}	−0.003	0.014	0.997	−0.192
Guardianship barriers, π_{900}	0.013	0.009	1.013	1.460
Access routes, π_{1000}	0.040	0.011	1.041	3.711
Corner residence, π_{1100}	0.017	0.014	1.017	1.191
Burglary victimization, π_{1200}	0.110	0.017	1.116	6.550

Random Effect	Variance Component	z-score	p-value
Level 3			
Mean risk, r_{00k}	0.022	5.620	< .05
Level 2			
Mean risk, u_{0jk}	0.007	4.247	< .05
Race, u_{3jk}	0.024	3.041	< .05
Home unoccupied, u_{4jk}	0.0005	2.029	< .05
Burglary victimization, u_{12jk}	0.016	2.532	< .05
Level 1			
Level 1 extra binomial error, e_{ijk}	0.141	45.729	< .05

NOTE: Model chi-square: 187.9; degrees of freedom: 15; $p < .05$; $N = 5,090$.
a. The Level 2 unit is the neighborhood; the Level 3 unit is the census tract.
b. The t-ratio calculations are based upon the complete estimates for coefficients and standard errors provided by the ML3E program rather than being based upon the rounded figures presented in columns 1 and 2.

experience the feeling of being unsafe from crime. Age is negatively related to logit(risk perception), meaning that older sampled respondents were actually less likely to feel unsafe. The findings for race and age contradict previous related research on fear, whereas the finding that females feel more unsafe in comparison with males is more consistent with the literature on fear. Other significant individual-level predictors include income, safety precautions, access routes, and burglary victimization. Specifically, by examining

166   JOURNAL OF RESEARCH IN CRIME AND DELINQUENCY

the exponentiated coefficients, it can be seen that each of these variables has the following approximate relative effects on the odds of feeling unsafe: a unit increase in income—approximately a 1.3% decrease in the odds; a unit increase in safety precautions—a 1.3% increase in the odds of feeling unsafe; a unit increase in access routes—a 4% increase; and burglary victimization— a 12% increase.[8]

NEIGHBORHOOD-LEVEL AND TRACT-LEVEL CONTEXTUAL EFFECTS ON PERCEIVED RISK

Given that several coefficients have been found to display significant variability across neighborhoods and/or census tracts, we next seek to ascertain the extent to which this variability can be accounted for by the contextual, disorganization factors defined above. Further, to be able to estimate contextual effects net of individual-level effects and to distinguish individual-level effects from compositional effects, we control for neighborhood- and tract-level compositional differences. Thus the initial contextual specifications at Levels 2 and 3 were as follows:

Level 2

$$\beta_{qjk} = \Theta_{q0k} + \Theta_{q1k}\text{MEAN AGE}_{jk} + \Theta_{q2k}\text{PERCENT MALE}_{jk} +$$

$$\Theta_{q3k}\text{MEAN INCOME}_{jk} + \Theta_{q4k}\text{ETHNIC HETEROGENEITY}_{jk} +$$

$$\Theta_{q5k}\text{BUSY PLACES}_{jk} + \Theta_{q6k}\text{INCIVILITIES}_{jk} + \tag{5}$$

$$\Theta_{07k}\text{INTEGRATION}_{jk} + U_{qjk}, \text{ for } q = 0,3,4,12$$

Level 3

$$\Theta_{00k} = \pi_{000} + \pi_{001}\text{MEAN AGE}_k + \pi_{002}\text{PERCENT MALE}_k +$$

$$\pi_{003}\text{MEAN INCOME}_k + \pi_{004}\text{ETHNIC HETEROGENEITY}_k + \tag{6}$$

$$\pi_{005}\text{BURGLARY RATE}_k + r_{00k}$$

However, as indicated earlier, our initial full contextual specifications were reduced significantly. The Level 2 and Level 3 specifications corresponding to the reduced contextual models reported herein are as follows:

Level 2

$$\beta_{0jk} = \Theta_{00k} + \Theta_{02k}\text{PERCENT MALE}_{jk} +$$

$$\Theta_{04k}\text{ETHNIC HETEROGENEITY}_{jk} +$$

$$\Theta_{06k}\text{INCIVILITIES}_{jk} + \Theta_{07k}\text{INTEGRATION}_{jk} +$$

$$\Theta_{08k}\text{HETEROGENEITY*INCIVILITIES}_{jk} + u_{0jk} \qquad (7)$$

$$\beta_{3jk} = \Theta_{30k} + \Theta_{36k}\text{INCIVILITIES}_{jk} + u_{3jk}$$

$$\beta_{4jk} = \Theta_{40k} + \Theta_{46k}\text{INCIVILITIES}_{jk} + u_{4jk}$$

$$\beta_{12jk} = \Theta_{120k} + u_{12jk}$$

$$\beta_{qjk} = \Theta_{q0k} \text{ for } q = 1,2,5\text{-}11$$

Level 3

$$\Theta_{00k} = \pi_{000} + \pi_{001}\text{MEAN AGE}_k + \pi_{003}\text{MEAN INCOME}_k +$$

$$\pi_{005}\text{BURGLARY RATE}_k + r_{00k} \qquad (8)$$

$$\pi_{q0k} = \pi_{q00} \text{ for } q = 1\text{-}12$$

The contextual variables in the above models were also grand-mean centered. These between-neighborhood and between-tract models, in combination with the individual-level perceived risk model (Equation 1), specify the variation in the adjusted mean logit of risk perception as a function of neighborhood-level gender composition (percentage male), neighborhood ethnic heterogeneity, neighborhood-level incivility, neighborhood social integration, and an interaction between incivility and heterogeneity.[9] The intercept is also specified as varying according to tract-level mean age, mean income, and burglary rate. The variability in the effects of the race and home unoccupied variables across neighborhoods is estimated as a function of neighborhood incivilities. Coefficient estimates and summary statistics for the three-level reduced contextual hierarchical logistic model for crime risk perception are presented in Table 3. As the significant chi-square statistic implies, the contextual model containing the direct and moderating effects of the neighborhood- and tract-level indicators, along with compositional

168   JOURNAL OF RESEARCH IN CRIME AND DELINQUENCY

TABLE 3: Estimated Effects of Community Characteristics on Logistic Regression Coefficients for Crime Risk Perception in Seattle[a]

Fixed Effect	Coefficient	SE	Exp (Coefficient)	t-ratio[b]
Mean risk				
Base, π_{000}	0.228	0.008	1.256	28.172
Neighborhood percentage				
male, π_{020}	0.097	0.053	1.102	1.848
Neighborhood heterogeneity, π_{040}	−0.053	0.109	0.948	−0.490
Neighborhood incivilities, π_{060}	0.139	0.014	1.149	10.236
Neighborhood integration, π_{070}	−0.032	0.011	0.969	−2.928
Incivility*heterogeneity, π_{080}	0.655	0.135	1.925	4.855
Tract-level mean age, π_{001}	0.032	0.018	1.033	1.761
Tract-level mean income, π_{003}	−0.046	0.018	0.955	−2.473
Tract-level burglary rate, π_{005}	0.013	0.002	1.013	5.631
Age, π_{100}	−0.007	0.003	0.993	−1.973
Gender, π_{200}	−0.043	0.011	0.958	−3.889
Race				
Base, π_{300}	−0.095	0.021	0.909	−4.471
Neighborhood incivilities, π_{360}	−0.089	0.028	0.915	−3.131
Home unoccupied				
Base, π_{400}	0.003	0.003	1.003	0.942
Neighborhood incivilities, π_{460}	0.013	0.004	1.013	3.031
Safety precautions, π_{700}	0.014	0.004	1.014	3.676
Access routes, π_{1000}	0.036	0.011	1.037	3.394
Burglary victimization				
Base, π_{1200}	0.102	0.017	1.107	6.092

Random Effect	Variance Component	z-score	p-value*
Level 3			
Mean risk, r_{00k}	0.001	1.431	> .05
Level 2			
Mean risk, u_{0jk}	0.004	2.667	< .05
Race, u_{3jk}	0.020	2.871	< .05
Home unoccupied, u_{4jk}	0.0003	1.663	> .05
Burglary victimization, u_{12jk}	0.017	2.626	< .05
Level 1			
Level 1 extra binomial error, e_{ijk}	0.141	45.938	< .05

NOTE: Model chi-square: 242.42; degrees of freedom: 5; *$p < .05$; $N = 5,090$.
a. The Level 2 unit is the neighborhood; the Level 3 unit is the census tract.
b. The *t*-ratio calculations are based upon the complete estimates for coefficients and standard errors provided by the ML3E program rather than being based upon the rounded figures presented in columns 1 and 2.

variables, is a significant improvement over the random coefficient model (reported in Table 2) containing only the individual-level characteristics.

The random-effects panel of Table 3 shows that many of the estimated variance components are still significant. Specifically, the variance component for the adjusted mean logit of risk perception remains significant at Level 2. However, the still-significant nature of this variance component should not overshadow the fact that, in the contextual model, the variance in the mean logit of risk perception is reduced by 43% (in comparison with its variance in Table 2). By contrast, the effects of race and burglary victimization on logit(risk perception) are still significantly variable across neighborhoods, and the variation in these effects is not reduced substantially when comparing results from Tables 2 and 3. Further, the Level 1 extra binomial error term is still significant, indicating that there is remaining heterogeneity at the individual level specifically unaccounted for in this contextual model. On the other hand, variance components for mean risk at Level 3 and for the effect of the home unoccupied variable at Level 2 are no longer statistically significant. In fact, variation in the adjusted mean logit of perceived risk across census tracts is reduced by 95% in this contextual model.

The fixed-effects panel of Table 3 reveals some interesting contextual findings. First, in terms of main (or direct) effects of context, the estimates of which are found under mean risk, neighborhood-level incivilities are positively related to feeling unsafe, as the macrolevel fear-of-crime literature suggests (especially the work of Lewis and Salem 1986; Skogan and Maxfield 1981; Taylor and Hale 1986). With each unit increase in signs of disorder in the tract, the odds of feeling unsafe increase by some 15%.

Neighborhood-level social integration, on the other hand, is negatively related to unsafe perceptions. Although neighborhood ethnic heterogeneity has an insignificant main effect on perceived risk, it is involved in a significant interaction with neighborhood incivilities, indicating that the positive effect of incivilities is stronger in heterogeneous areas. At the tract level, the residential burglary rate has a positive main effect on perceptions of neighborhood danger (from crime), whereas mean income is negatively related to risk perception. Because the individual and contextual variables are grand-mean centered and compositional differences are controlled, these Level 2 and Level 3 relationships represent contextual effects net of individual-level effects.

In terms of cross-level interactions or moderating effects of context on individual-level risk perception, neighborhood incivilities significantly condition the effects of the race and home unoccupied variables. Specifically,

170   JOURNAL OF RESEARCH IN CRIME AND DELINQUENCY

neighborhood incivility is involved in a negative interaction with race, implying that the tendency for non-Whites (in comparison with Whites) to feel less danger is most pronounced in disorderly communities; the negative effect of being non-White on feeling unsafe is very slight in the most orderly communities. Further, neighborhood incivilities condition the relationship between the home unoccupied variable and risk perception such that exposure in terms of leaving a home unoccupied has a stronger positive effect on risk perception in the most disorderly neighborhoods; this effect is much weaker in the most orderly neighborhoods. None of the contextual factors interacts significantly with burglary victimization. The other findings from the fixed-effects panel of Table 3 are consistent with those from Table 2. Male, non-White, and older respondents are less likely to feel that their neighborhood is unsafe. Safety precautions, access routes, and burglary victimization experiences, in contrast, increase perceived risk among respondents. Given that we have incorporated measures of compositional differences at both the tract and neighborhood levels, we feel confident that these individual-level effects are unbiased and not confounded with compositional effects.

A Three-Level Safety Precautions Model

The next step in this multilevel analysis of the effects of victimization is to examine the roles of individual- and contextual-level variables in the explanation of variability of individual-level safety precautions. The analysis proceeds here in the same sort of steps as before, with the only difference being that the Level 1 models are linear models now because the dependent variable is a scale rather than a dichotomy. Table 4 presents the results obtained from an initial random coefficient regression model in a HLM analysis combining individual-level, between-neighborhood, and between-tract models of precautionary behavior. The random coefficient model represents an obvious improvement over a baseline model predicting safety precautions using only an intercept (varying at Levels 2 and 3) and an error term.

In terms of significant random effects, adjusted mean precautionary measures (referring to time of the survey (t), not t-2, years) vary significantly across Seattle neighborhoods and census tracts.[10] The effects of previous safety precautions (referring to precautions taken 2 years prior to the survey date) and previous burglary victimization vary significantly across neighborhoods. So, being a victim or nonvictim influences safety precautions differently according to neighborhood context, and the effect of previous safety

TABLE 4: Random Coefficient Regression Model for Regression Coefficients of Routine Activities (Safety Precautions) in Seattle[a]

Fixed Effect	Coefficient	SE	t-ratio[b]
Mean precautions, π_{000}	4.196	0.025	165.653
Age, π_{100}	−0.009	0.008	−1.093
Gender, π_{200}	−0.037	0.025	−1.461
Race, π_{300}	−0.081	0.039	−2.111
Home unoccupied, π_{400}	−0.008	0.007	−1.193
Family income, π_{500}	0.061	0.011	5.675
Expensive goods, π_{600}	0.015	0.010	1.436
Safety precautions (t-2), π_{700}	0.698	0.011	67.730
Live alone, π_{800}	−0.119	0.032	−3.676
Guardianship barriers, π_{900}	0.027	0.020	1.364
Access routes, π_{1000}	−0.029	0.025	−1.189
Corner residence, π_{1100}	−0.012	0.030	−0.412
Burglary victimization, π_{1200}	0.382	0.042	9.134
Perceived risk, π_{1300}	0.100	0.032	3.181

Random Effect	Variance Component	z-score	p-value
Level 3			
Mean precautions, r_{00k}	0.034	4.303	< .05
Level 2			
Mean precautions, u_{0jk}	0.036	4.541	< .05
Safety precautions (t-2), u_{7jk}	0.010	3.949	< .05
Burglary victimization, u_{12jk}	0.147	3.726	< .05
Level 1			
Level 1 effect, e_{ijk}	0.749	46.419	< .05

NOTE: Model chi-square: 4,164.10; degrees of freedom: 15; $p < .05$; $N = 5,090$.
a. The Level 2 unit is the neighborhood; the Level 3 unit is the census tract.
b. The t-ratio calculations are based upon the complete estimates for coefficients and standard errors provided by the ML3E program rather than being based upon the rounded figures presented in columns 1 and 2.

precautions on current precautionary behavior varies according to neighborhood.

Regarding fixed effects, previous victimization and feelings of risk both have significant positive effects on restricted routine activities in terms of safety precautions. Precautionary measures are also affected negatively by race, implying that non-Whites (in comparison with Whites) engage in fewer precautions. Further, income is positively related to safety precautions, and living alone is negatively related to such measures. Finally, previous safety

172   JOURNAL OF RESEARCH IN CRIME AND DELINQUENCY

precautions (measures taken by respondent 2 years prior) have a large direct effect on present precautionary measures.

NEIGHBORHOOD-LEVEL AND TRACT-LEVEL CONTEXTUAL EFFECTS ON SAFETY PRECAUTIONS

Table 5 presents the findings for the reduced models resulting from the addition of the contextual effects and interactions to the hierarchical model depicted in Table 4 while also controlling for differences in composition across neighborhoods and census tracts. The contextual model is an improvement over the model with only individual-level predictors.

The random-effects panel of Table 5 indicates that the contextual variables introduced are not sufficient in reducing to insignificance the variance components associated with mean precautionary measures, previous safety precautions, and previous burglary victimization at the neighborhood level. Thus the effect of safety precautions is still variable across neighborhoods as are the effects of prior safety precautions and burglary victimization experiences on these current precautionary measures. Further, the variance component for mean precautions at Level 3 is also still significant, indicating that current precautions continue to exhibit significant variability across census tracts after taking into account tract-level crime (burglary rates). However, it should be noted that there is still a substantial reduction in the variance in adjusted mean levels of safety precautions across neighborhoods and census tracts. Specifically, the neighborhood-level variance is reduced by 36% and the tract-level variance is reduced by 62%. The reductions in variance components for safety precautions and burglary victimization, however, are not nearly as significant.

There are several contextual factors that exhibit significant main effects, net of individual-level effects. For instance, those living in more integrated, cohesive neighborhoods are much more likely to engage in safety precautions. Also, tract-level income and the tract-level residential burglary rate both increase precautionary behavior. None of the neighborhood-level contextual variables is involved in significant interactions with the individual-level variables that had varying effects across neighborhoods (previous safety precautions and burglary victimization experiences). The remaining individual-level effects in Table 5 are similar to those found in the model without contextual variables, except that age emerges as significant, having a negative effect on safety precautions, and the coefficient for race falls slightly below standard levels of significance.[11]

TABLE 5: Estimated Effects of Community Contextual Characteristics on Regression Coefficients for Routine Activities (Safety Precautions) in Seattle[a]

Fixed Effect	Coefficient	SE	t-ratio[b]
Mean precautions			
Base, π_{000}	4.180	0.019	216.805
Neighborhood mean age, π_{010}	0.055	0.029	1.897
Neighborhood heterogeneity, π_{040}	−0.103	0.241	−0.430
Neighborhood integration, π_{070}	0.196	0.025	7.803
Tract-level percentage male, π_{002}	−0.194	0.258	−0.749
Tract-level mean income, π_{003}	0.124	0.044	2.855
Tract-level burglary rate, π_{005}	0.018	0.005	3.294
Age, π_{100}	−0.024	0.008	−2.887
Race, π_{300}	−0.072	0.040	−1.815
Family income, π_{500}	0.045	0.010	4.289
Safety precautions (t-2)			
Base, π_{700}	0.687	0.011	64.256
Live alone, π_{800}	−0.115	0.031	−3.699
Burglary victimization			
Base, π_{1200}	0.387	0.041	9.350
Perceived risk, π_{1300}	0.123	0.032	3.887

Random Effect	Variance Component	z-score	p-value
Level 3			
Mean precautions, r_{00k}	0.013	2.720	< .05
Level 2			
Mean precautions, u_{0jk}	0.023	3.392	< .05
Safety precautions (t-2), u_{7jk}	0.010	3.955	< .05
Burglary victimization, u_{12jk}	0.141	3.646	< .05
Level 1			
Level 1 effect, e_{ijk}	0.747	46.552	< .05

NOTE: Model chi-square: 102.60; degrees of freedom: 0; $p < .05$; $N = 5,090$.
a. The Level 2 unit is the neighborhood; the Level 3 unit is the census tract.
b. The t-ratio calculations are based upon the complete estimates for coefficients and standard errors provided by the ML3E program rather than being based upon the rounded figures presented in columns 1 and 2.

CONCLUSION

The analyses presented here have shown that both microlevel factors and social context are of importance in understanding individual behavior. Just as victimization risk varies significantly across community context, so do the apparent effects of criminal victimization—namely, risk perception and routine activities. Further, several individual-level predictors of risk and activities vary in their effects across Seattle neighborhoods and census tracts. Thus the embeddedness of individual-level explanations for perceived risk and restricted activities or precautionary behavior within a community context is evident.

Concerning the main microlevel effects, previous victimization is a key predictor of risk perception. Supporting previous work by Cook (1986) and extant macrolevel work by Liska and Warner (1991), previous experience with crime or victimization and subsequent increases in perceived risk or feelings of being unsafe, in turn, are significant predictors of restricted routine activities in terms of safety precautions. Such findings, then, support the idea that routine activities are not only predictors of victimization but they can be structured as a result of experiences with crime.

Contextual indicators of crime and disorder at the neighborhood and tract levels are able to account for some of the variation in perceived risk, routine activities, and the effects of microlevel antecedents. In terms of direct effects of context on perceived risk, most of the findings support an explanation— that areas characterized by signs of ineffective social control will produce fear or "unease" among residents—paralleling and complementing a social disorganization theory of crime. For instance, neighborhood incivility increases feelings of danger (being unsafe)—with the strongest effects of incivility being seen in heterogeneous areas—and neighborhood-level social integration decreases perceived crime risk. Further, tract-level residential burglary rates directly increase perceptions of risk, whereas tract-level income decreases perceptions of risk. Each of these findings suggests that residents of disorganized, crime-ridden areas recognize the ambient risk associated with their local environments (stemming from the perceived relationships among social disorganization, crime, and victimization likelihoods) and react "rationally" to this risk by feeling relatively unsafe from crime.

However, the findings presented here suggest that indicators of social disorganization per se do not serve to make people more cautious. In fact, most of the neighborhood-level indicators of disorganization have insignificant effects on safety precautions. Only social integration—actually a measure of social organization—affects precautionary behavior significantly. The more integrated the neighborhood, the more cautious are residents' activities. The tract-level burglary rate, on the other hand, increases precautions. Hence signs of disorder are positively related to victimization and risk perception, and perceived risk is positively related to safety precautions, but signs of disorder, for the most part, are not related to safety precautions. The fact that the safety precautions measure used in the current study (locked doors, security system, light timer device, etc.) is most relevant to burglary victimization risk specifically is perhaps important. In particular, residents of disorganized communities are often not worried about burglary specifically, though they often perceive their neighborhood to be unsafe from crime in general (Rountree and Land forthcoming). Thus, given that the safety precautions measure used here refers largely to household protective measures and fails to tap measures aimed at guarding the person, the insignificant relationships between many of the disorganization measures and precautionary behavior are logical (see Warr 1985 for a discussion of the effect of fear on lifestyle precautions versus home security precautions).

It appears to be the ambient risk associated with burglary victimization specifically that causes such protective behaviors because only tract-level burglary rates—not signs of disorganization—relate positively to safety precautions. Further, because social integration is presumably more common in higher socioeconomic status areas—which often have higher rates of theft/burglary in comparison with other types of crime—the positive relationship between neighborhood integration and safety precautions (geared mainly toward hardening the home) is understandable: Greater property-hardening tactics are likely to be evident in areas that are much more likely to feel the effects of property crime in relation to other types of crime. Consistent with our finding and explanation of the integration-precautions relationship is the positive, significant relationship between tract-level income and precautionary behavior. Higher income areas are, like integrated areas, often more likely to experience burglary and theft in comparison with other types of criminal victimization, and residents of these areas thus seem to respond to this theft/burglary-specific ambient risk by engaging in relatively more home security measures. Not only may residents of wealthier, integrated areas fear burglary specifically more so than other neighborhoods but they also have greater resources (monetary and otherwise) for addressing this concern through optimal precautionary behavior.

Beyond main effects, one of the contextual variables included in these analyses also had moderating effects in the sense of conditioning the effects of several individual-level predictors of perceived risk through cross-level interactions. First, neighborhood incivilities are involved in a negative interaction with race in predicting perceived crime risk, suggesting that non-Whites are less concerned about safety than Whites in especially disorderly neighborhoods. The negative relationship between non-White and risk perception is much less significant in very orderly areas. Such a finding can perhaps be understood by considering patterns of racial and economic segregation in conjunction with previous research on the strong influence that novelty (unfamiliar environments) has on feelings of danger and fear (Warr

176   JOURNAL OF RESEARCH IN CRIME AND DELINQUENCY

1990). Warr's research implies that individuals tend to evaluate neighborhoods in which they fit in as safer than other neighborhoods, even when official crime rates show otherwise. Therefore, if, due to segregated residential patterns, non-Whites are more likely than Whites to feel at least some sense of familiarity in neighborhoods characterized by high levels of incivility, they are perhaps also more likely to feel at ease or relatively safe in such areas.

Neighborhood incivilities also interact with exposure (in terms of home unoccupied) in predicting perceived risk such that the main (positive) effect of exposure is stronger in, relatively speaking, disorderly communities. Both of the interactions related to the conditional effect of neighborhood incivilities emphasize the importance of structural characteristics of communities that are indicative of ambient risk contextualizing the effects of individual-level characteristics. Neighborhood factors not only play a direct role in predicting perceived risk and precautionary behavior but they also provide a context into which we can embed certain individual-level explanations. However, despite the progress made here in examining this potential embeddedness, there were other individual-level effects that varied across neighborhoods yet were unexplained by specific significant micro-macro interactions. Thus our findings suggest that a new direction in the fear-of-crime research might be further refinement of the moderating effects of ambient risk on fear of crime (or perceived risk) and routine activities as effects of victimization.

However, more theoretical work needs to be done so that cross-level interactions, such as those found here, can be better explained and interpreted. We found it virtually impossible to predict or theorize about cross-level interactions before obtaining our results because such interactions had yet to be discovered. In short, hierarchical logistic and linear modeling have allowed us to see patterns in the data not before detected. In this sense, the state of the field is such that methods exist for examining cross-level interactions, but researchers are rather hard-pressed to predict or interpret such interactions due to scant attention given to the theoretical mechanisms underlying the moderating role of social context in relationships between individual characteristics and perceived risk or restricted routine activities. Further, the discovery of cross-level interactions is sufficiently new that our results require corroboration in other studies before their stability can be presumed. The cross-level interactions discovered here need to be tested for stability through replication using different samples from different cities or regions. Consequently, even before extensive theoretical work is done in attempting to account for cross-level interactions, replication on other data—to make sure that the findings here are not unique to these data—is essential.

NOTES

1. See Hox and Kreft (1994) for a thorough discussion of the statistical limitations of traditional multilevel models. They suggest that the use of ordinary significance tests in cases involving even a small amount of covariation between the observations within groups or categories violates the "assumption of independence of residual error terms," which leads to underestimates of standard errors and overestimates of *t*-ratios and therefore can lead to "Type I errors that are much larger than the nominal alpha level" (p. 285).

2. An ideal approach to addressing the model presented in Figure 1 would be through the use of longitudinal panel data and hierarchical structural models, with the capacity to estimate reciprocal effects. However, hierarchical modeling methods for structural equation systems are only beginning to be developed (Muthen 1994). Furthermore, the data used in the present study were not generated by a panel study and do not require fully simultaneous structural equation methods. Yet, given the lagged measures available from the cross-sectional data as well as the multilevel sampling design, the use of separate hierarchical regression models for the estimation of fear of crime and restricted activities is appropriate.

3. See Miethe and McDowall (1993) or Miethe and Meier (1994) for a more thorough review of interview procedures and sample selectivity.

4. We imputed missing values on income using a group mean substitution method; those observations with missing responses for income were assigned a value equal to the mean score for their particular city-block pairs.

5. It should be noted that the perceived risk measure has a four-category ordinal response scale associated with it in the Seattle survey. However, due to the inability of the ML3E software (used for the analyses reported herein) to handle ordinal response variables in the ideal fashion (e.g., through an ordinal logit model), we decided to dichotomize the response categories to create a binary response variable that then could be estimated with the standard logistic technique available in the software. Tests were conducted to discern the best way to split the categories into a dichotomy via an ordinal logit model in which all three possible cutpoints are estimated (e.g., see Winship and Mare 1984 for review of this procedure). These results suggested that the risk measure was best split into categories of perceiving the neighborhood to be either somewhat or very unsafe versus perceiving the area to be somewhat or very safe.

6. Because grand-mean centering of the predictors was used, the intercept represents mean logit(risk perception) in group *jk*, adjusted for the effects of Level 1 predictors (see, e.g., Bryk and Raudenbush 1992, pp. 25-31).

7. The usual interpretation of this type of result is that risk probabilities are not constant across measured groups (here, neighborhoods and census tracts), so that some unmeasured source of individual-level heterogeneity must be present in perceived risk responses. Even though we cannot explain this "hidden heterogeneity," the incorporation of the variance of the e_{ijk} term into the model estimation gives the assurance that we are broadly allowing for such heterogeneity when evaluating the estimates of the fixed part of the model (Patterson 1991, p. 13).

8. As is usual in logistic regression analyses (see, e.g., Neter, Wasserman, and Kutner 1989, pp. 588-9), the exponentiated values of the estimated regression coefficients reported in the third column of the fixed effects panel of Table 2 can be interpreted (after subtracting 1.0 and multiplying by 100) as indicating the percent of change expected in the odds of experiencing the dependent variable per unit change in an explanatory variable relative to a baseline category.

9. During preliminary analyses of these data, we tested for interactions between contextual variables in predicting variance components. Such analyses indicated that there was a significant interaction between neighborhood incivility and racial heterogeneity in predicting the variation

178   JOURNAL OF RESEARCH IN CRIME AND DELINQUENCY

in the average log odds of perceived risk across neighborhoods. Thus we include this interaction term in the Level 2 equation for β_{0jk}. Because this was the only significant interaction among contextual factors found, the neighborhood-level model for β_{0jk} is the only Level 2 or Level 3 model that includes such an interaction term.

10. Again, because grand-mean centering of predictors is used in these analyses, the intercept here represents mean precautionary measures, adjusted for the effects of Level 1 predictors.

11. Again, due to the fact that we control for compositional differences, we conclude that the individual-level effects presented in this model are unbiased.

REFERENCES

Baumer, Terry L. 1979. "Research on Fear of Crime in the United States." *Victimology* 3:254-63.
———. 1985. "Testing a General Model of Fear of Crime: Data from a National Sample." *Journal of Research in Crime and Delinquency* 22:239-55.
Brantingham, Paul J. and Patricia L. Brantingham, eds. 1981. *Environmental Criminology*. Beverly Hills, CA: Sage.
Bryk, Anthony S. and Stephen W. Raudenbush. 1992. *Hierarchical Linear Models: Applications and Data Analysis Methods*. Newbury Park, CA: Sage.
Bursik, Robert J., Jr. and Harold G. Grasmick. 1993. *Neighborhoods and Crime: The Dimensions of Effective Community Control*. New York: Lexington Books.
Cantor, David and Kenneth C. Land. 1985. "Unemployment and Crime Rates in the Post-World War II United States: A Theoretical and Empirical Analysis." *American Sociological Review* 50:317-32.
Clarke, Alan H. and Margaret J. Lewis. 1982. "Fear of Crime Among the Elderly." *British Journal of Criminology* 22:49-62.
Cohen, Lawrence E. and Marcus Felson. 1979. "Social Change and Crime Rate Trends: A Routine Activities Approach." *American Sociological Review* 44:588-608.
Cohen, Lawrence E., Marcus Felson, and Kenneth C. Land. 1980. "Property Crime Rates in the United States: A Macrodynamic Analysis, 1947-77; with Ex Ante Forecasts for the Mid-1980's." *American Journal of Sociology* 86:90-118.
Cohen, Lawrence E., James R. Kluegel, and Kenneth C. Land. 1981. "Social Inequality and Predatory Criminal Victimization: An Exposition and Test of a Formal Theory." *American Sociological Review* 46:505-24.
Cook, Philip J. 1986. "The demand and supply of criminal opportunities." Pp. 1-27 in *Crime and Justice: An Annual Review of Research*, Vol. 7, edited by Michael Tonry and Norval Morris. Chicago: University of Chicago Press.
Felson, Marcus. 1994. *Crime and Everyday Life*. Thousand Oaks, CA: Thousand Oaks Press.
Ferraro, Kenneth F. 1995. *Fear of Crime: Interpreting Victimization Risk*. Albany, NY: SUNY Press.
Ferraro, Kenneth F. and Randy L. LaGrange. 1987. "The Measurement of Fear of Crime." *Sociological Inquiry* 57:70-101.
Garofalo, James. 1979. "Victimization and the Fear of Crime." *Journal of Research in Crime and Delinquency* 16:80-97.
———. 1981. "The Fear of Crime: Causes and Consequences." *The Journal of Criminal Law and Criminology* 72:839-57.
Garofalo, James and John Laub. 1979. "The Fear of Crime: Broadening Our Perspective." *Victimology* 3:242-53.

Goldstein, Harvey. 1987. *Multilevel Models in Educational and Social Research.* New York: Oxford University Press.

Hartnagel, Timothy. 1979. "The Perception and Fear of Crime: Implications for Neighborhood Cohesion, Social Activity, and Community Affect." *Social Forces* 58:176-93.

Hox, Joop J. and Itag G. Kreft. 1994. "Multilevel Analysis Methods." *Sociological Methods and Research* 22:283-99.

Kennedy, Leslie W. and David R. Forde. 1990. "Routine Activities and Crime: An Analysis of Victimization in Canada." *Criminology* 28:137-51.

LaGrange, Randy L., Kenneth Ferraro and Michael Supancic. 1992. "Perceived Risk and Fear of Crime." *Journal of Research in Crime and Delinquency* 29:311-34.

Lewis, Dan A. and Michael G. Maxfield. 1980. "Fear in the Neighborhoods: An Investigation of the Impact of Crime." *Journal of Research in Crime and Delinquency* 17:160-89.

Lewis, Dan A. and Greta Salem. 1986. *Fear of Crime: Incivility and the Production of a Social Problem.* New Brunswick, NJ: Transaction Books.

Lindley, Dennis V. and A.F.M. Smith. 1972. "Bayes Estimates for the Linear Model (with Discussion)." *Journal of the Royal Statistical Society,* Series B. 34:1-41.

Liska, Allen E., Joseph J. Lawrence, and Andrew Sanchirico. 1982. "Fear of Crime as a Social Fact." *Social Forces* 60:760-70.

Liska, Allen E., Andrew Sanchirico, and Mark D. Reed. 1988. "Fear of Crime and Constrained Behavior Specifying and Estimating a Reciprocal Effects Model." *Social Forces* 66:827-37.

Liska, Allen E. and Barbara D. Warner. 1991. "Functions of Crime: A Paradoxical Process." *American Journal of Sociology* 96:1441-63.

Mason, William W., George Y. Wong, and Barbara Entwisle. 1983. "Contextual Analysis through the Multilevel Linear Model." *Sociological Methodology* 1983-1984:72-103.

Maxfield, Michael G. 1984. "The Limits of Vulnerability in Explaining Fear of Crime: A Comparative Neighborhood Analysis." *Journal of Research in Crime and Delinquency* 21:233-50.

Miethe, Terance D. and David McDowall. 1993. "Contextual Effects in Models of Criminal Victimization." *Social Forces* 71:741-59.

Miethe, Terance D. and Robert F. Meier. 1994. *Crime and Its Social Context: Toward an Integrated Theory of Offenders, Victims, and Situations.* Albany, NY: SUNY Press.

Miethe, Terance D., Mark C. Stafford, and Scott Long. 1987. "Social Differentiation in Criminal Victimization: A Test of Routine Activities/Lifestyle Theory." *American Sociological Review* 52:184-94.

Muthen, Bengt. 1994. "Latent Variable Modeling of Longitudinal and Multilevel Data." Paper presented at the annual meeting of the American Sociological Association, Los Angeles, California, August.

Neter, John, William Wasserman, and Michael H. Kutner. 1989. *Applied Linear Regression Models.* Burr Ridge, IL: Irwin.

Ortega, Suzanne T. and Jessie L. Myles. 1987. "Race and Gender Effects on Fear of Crime: An Interactive Model with Age." *Criminology* 25:133-52.

Patterson, Lindsay. 1991. "Multilevel Logistic Regression." Pp. 5-18 in *Data Analysis with ML3,* edited by Robert Prosser, J. Rasbash, and H. Goldstein. London: Institute of Education, University of London.

Prosser, Robert, J. Rasbash, and H. Goldstein. 1991a. *ML3: Software for Three-Level Analysis.* London: Institute of Education, University of London.

————. 1991b. *Data Analysis with ML3.* London: Institute of Education: University of London.

Raudenbush, Stephen W. 1984. "Applications of a Hierarchical Linear Model in Educational Research." *Dissertation Abstracts International* 45:1713A.

180   JOURNAL OF RESEARCH IN CRIME AND DELINQUENCY

Rountree, Pamela Wilcox and Kenneth C. Land. Forthcoming. "Perceived Risk Versus Fear of Crime: Empirical Evidence of Conceptually Distinct Reactions in Survey Data." *Social Forces.*

Rountree, Pamela Wilcox, Kenneth C. Land, and Terance D. Miethe. 1994. "Macro-Micro Integration in the Study of Victimization: A Hierarchical Logistic Model Analysis across Seattle Neighborhoods." *Criminology* 32:387-414.

Sampson, Robert J. and John D. Wooldredge. 1987. "Linking the Micro- and Macro-Level Dimensions of Lifestyle-Routine Activity and Opportunity Models of Predatory Victimization." *Journal of Quantitative Criminology* 3:371-93.

Seattle Police Department. 1989. "Total Part I Offenses by Federal Census Tract of Occurrence." In *1989 Annual Report.* Seattle, WA: Author.

————. 1990. "Total Part I Offenses by Federal Census Tract of Occurrence." In *1990 Annual Report.* Seattle, WA: Author.

Skogan, Wesley G. and Michael G. Maxfield. 1981. *Coping with Crime: Individual and Neighborhood Reactions.* Beverly Hills, CA: Sage.

Smith, Douglas A. and G. Roger Jarjoura. 1989. "Household Characteristics, Neighborhood Composition and Victimization Risk." *Social Forces* 68:621-40.

Stafford, Mark C. and Omer R. Galle. 1984. "Victimization Rates, Exposure to Risk, and Fear of Crime." *Criminology* 22:173-85.

Strenio, J.L.F., H. I. Weisberg, and A. S. Bryk. 1983. "Empirical Bayes Estimation of Individual Growth Curve Parameters and Their Relationship to Covariates." *Biometrics* 39:71-86.

Taylor, Ralph B., Stephen D. Gottfredson, and Sidney Brower. 1984. "Block Crime and Fear: Defensible Space, Local Social Ties, and Territorial Functioning." *Journal of Research in Crime and Delinquency* 21:303-31.

Taylor, Ralph B. and Margaret Hale. 1986. "Testing Alternative Models of Fear of Crime." *The Journal of Criminal Law and Criminology* 77:151-89.

van der Wurff, Adri, Leendert van Staalduinen, and Peter Stringer. 1989. "Fear of Crime in Residential Environments: Testing a Social Psychological Model." *The Journal of Social Psychology* 129:141-60.

Warr, Mark. 1985. "Fear of Rape Among Urban Women." *Social Problems* 32:238-250.

————. 1990. "Dangerous Situations: Social Context and Fear of Victimization." *Social Forces* 68:891-907.

Warr, Mark and Mark Stafford. 1983. "Fear of Victimization: A Look at the Proximate Causes." *Social Forces* 61:1033-43.

Wilson, James Q. and George L. Kelling. 1982. "Broken Windows." *The Atlantic Monthly* March:29-38.

Winship, Christopher and Robert D. Mare. 1984. "Regression Models with Ordinal Variables." *American Sociological Review* 49:512-25.

Wong, George Y. and William M. Mason. 1985. "Multilevel Analysis." *Journal of the American Statistical Association* 80:513-24.

[14]

Repeat Burglary Victimisation:
Spatial and Temporal Patterns

Michael Townsley, Ross Homel and Janet Chaseling
Griffith University

To date there has been little Australian research on repeat victimisation. This is a study of repeat burglary in an area of Brisbane using police calls for service data. We demonstrate: (a) the prevalence of residential repeat victim addresses ('hot dots') is of a similar magnitude to that found in studies in the United Kingdom; (b) the time distributions of revictimisation are identical with those found in studies in the UK and elsewhere; (c) 'hot spots' (small areas with high crime density) can be identified by statistical analyses of spatial concentrations of incidents; (d) unstable hot spots tend to be temporary aggregations of hot dots, whereas stable hot spots seem to reflect more the social and physical characteristics of certain localities; and (e) the overall incidence of burglary could be reduced by at least 25 per cent if all repeat victimisation could be eliminated. There are a number of areas where concepts and techniques for repeat victim research could potentially be strengthened: (a) clarifying the connections between hot dots and hot spots, particularly through exploration of the concept of a 'near repeat address'; (b) applying survival analysis to the data on the time periods between victimisations; and (c) using moving average techniques to examine changes in the spatial distributions of burglary over time.

Burglary has been a growing problem, both in Queensland and in Australia as a whole, for the past 20 years, although police statistics and crime victim surveys indicate that the Queensland rate is close to the national average (Criminal Justice Commission, 1996). However, there are indications that the rate may have peaked, with recent marked declines in the burglary rate in Queensland (Queensland Police Service, 1998). If Australia follows the US trends, this recent decline may presage a long term and substantial decline in the incidence of burglary (Decker, 1998; Langan & Farrington, 1998). Nevertheless, as Decker points out, even in the

The authors would like to thank the Queensland Police Service (Chief Superintendent Doug Smith, South Eastern Region), the Beenleigh Police Division in particular for all their invaluable assistance in this study, the Criminal Justice Commission (particularly Dr David Brereton, Director, Research and Prevention) for access to data, use of resources, collegial support and valuable advice and, finally, the anonymous reviewers who provided valuable suggestions for improvement.

Address for correspondence: Michael Townsley, School of Criminology and Criminal Justice, Mt Gravatt Campus, Griffith University, Brisbane QLD 4111, Australia.

MICHAEL TOWNSLEY, ROSS HOMEL AND JANET CHASELING

context of unprecedented declines, burglary remains a serious problem that poses challenges for prevention.

In the past decade the concept of repeat victimisation has gripped the criminological imagination, so much so that Skogan observed that "Probably the most important criminological insight of the decade has been the discovery in a very systematic fashion of repeat multiple victimisation" (cited in National Institute of Justice, 1996, p. 3). According to the British Crime Survey, repeat victims probably account for between 60 to 80 per cent of all crime incidents, yet are a small minority of all victims, at most around 20 per cent of the victim population (Ellingworth et al., 1995; Farrell & Pease, 1993; Farrell, 1995). There is clearly considerable potential for reducing overall crime rates if repeat victimisation can be reduced or eliminated. However, perhaps surprisingly, there has been very little research in Australia on repeat victimisation.

In this paper we use the tools of spatial and temporal analysis of calls for service data in the Beenleigh police division to explore the phenomenon of repeat victimisation, with a view to developing explanatory models and devising more effective preventive strategies. In addition, we explore briefly some of the improvements in methodologies that would enhance the study of repeat victimisation.

Beenleigh is a semi-rural district about half way down the Brisbane-Gold Coast 'corridor', stretching from the South East Freeway to the coast. The population is predominantly low income with unemployment at 13 percent, compared to a state average of 9.6 per cent (ABS, 1996). Public housing for the police division comprises 19.5 per cent of housing (compared to a state average of 13 per cent) (ABS, 1996). The Beenleigh police division has the sixth highest burglary rate in Queensland (Criminal Justice Commission, 1996).

This study partly replicates the Cambridge (UK) study by Bennett and Durie (1996), where preliminary analysis identified burglary hot spots and repeat victimised addresses. Innovative aspects of the study attempted to describe hot spots and how they vary over time. Our work is based on 18 months of data from calls for service for break and enter offences in Beenleigh, and identifies both hot spots and repeat victimisation. It arises from the Beenleigh Calls for Service Project (Criminal Justice Commision, 1998), the main aim of which was to determine to what extent problem oriented policing (POP) initiatives could reduce telephone calls for service.

Research on Repeat Victimisation

Repeat victimisation, where a place or person experiences more than one criminal offence within a given period of time, has been a recognised phenomenon since the early study by Johnson et al. (1973) and the seminal publications by Sparks et al. (1977) and Hindelang et al. (1978), but it has only been in the 1990s that extensive research has been conducted. Since the early seventies, repeat victimisation has developed from a concept of purely academic interest to the point where some police services now organise their responses to specific crimes on the basis of repeat victims data (Pease, 1998).

It must be acknowledged, however, that research involving repeat victimisation is reliant on overcoming two methodological factors that limit the detection of

REPEAT BURGLARY VICTIMISATION: SPATIAL AND TEMPORAL PATTERNS

repeats: the accurate recording of addresses on police information systems (Farrell & Pease, 1993) and the sensitivity of the time window. The time window can undercount repeats by being not long enough or by not detecting repeat incidents that lie either side of the time window, also known as the 'edge effect'.

Despite these problems, there is intensified interest in the academic literature with the realisation that some areas experiencing high crime rates over long periods of time have consistently high rates of repeat victimisation (Hope, 1995; Trickett et al., 1992; 1995). The argument is that *concentration* (the mean number of victimisations per victim) rather than the *prevalence* (the percentage of the potential victims who are actually victimised in a given time period) is the main reason why the *incidence* of victimisation (total crime incidents per capita) is so high in some areas. If confirmed in subsequent research, this finding has important implications both for criminological theory and for prevention strategies.

Perhaps the main reason for the growing interest in repeat victimisation, for both academics and practitioners, is the success of the Kirkholt Burglary Prevention Project, UK (Forrester et al., 1988; 1990). This was the first project in which an attempt was made to prevent burglary events by focusing on previously burgled properties. The logic was simple and relied on two key findings from the English research of the 1980s: the best predictor of future victimisation, of a place or person, is that of prior victimisation; and a numerically small group of people suffers a large proportion of all crime through repeatedly being victimised (Pease, 1998).

Farrell and Pease (1993) show from British Crime survey data that throughout the 1980s, about 14 per cent of the population were victimised on two or more occasions in the past year, and that this group accounted for 71 per cent of all incidents. The three per cent who experienced five or more crimes suffered nearly a quarter of all the crime reported. To the extent that individual crimes, such as burglary, are not reported with 100 per cent frequency either to the police or to survey researchers, *multiple* victimisations will necessarily be even more under-reported, suggesting that even the skewness found by Farrell and Pease understates the case for *rationing* crime prevention resources by concentrating on those who have already been victimised (Chenery et al., 1997; Mukherjee et al., 1997; Pease & Laycock, 1996). They also cite data (Polvi et al., 1990; 1991) that the risk of victimisation is greatest in the period immediately after the victimisation, which has obvious implications for prevention but also cries out for theoretical explanation.

Farrell and Pease (1993) argue that the most likely explanations of repeat burglary victimisation are that some offenders return to take things they overlooked the first time, and that they tell others of the opportunities. Thus a bonus flowing from this approach to crime prevention, from the police point of view, is that prevention and detection are brought together. Maximum prevention is achieved if action is taken within 24 hours, with strategies including temporary locks and alarms, surveillance by neighbours and even in extreme cases 'lying in wait' for offenders.

In the light of these research findings the rationale for the underlying strategy of Kirkholt is apparent: the prevention of repeat victimisation (that is, the future victimisation of one-time victims) resulted in significant impacts on absolute levels of domestic burglary. Within five months, a 60 per cent drop in burglary was observed and after three years, the Kirkholt Housing Estate recorded a 75 per cent decrease in the level of burglaries with no apparent displacement, geographically or

MICHAEL TOWNSLEY, ROSS HOMEL AND JANET CHASELING

offense-wise (Farrell, 1995; Forrester et al., 1988; 1990). Measures such as security upgrading, cocoon neighbourhood watch and removal of coin operated gas meters were combined to prevent revictimisation, which did in fact fall dramatically.

Not surprisingly, this result received a great deal of attention. Replications of the Kirkholt project in the UK have been numerous (Farrell, 1995; Pease, 1998; Tilley, 1993). In addition, there have been applications of similar techniques to other offence types such as school burglary, racial attacks, domestic violence, and car theft (Farrell & Pease, 1993; Farrell, 1995; Pease, 1998). Although no other project has actually achieved the same impact on crime levels as Kirkholt, it has recently been proposed as an example of international best practice (Waller & Welsh, 1998). However, it must be remembered that transferring crime prevention projects is a risky practice. Both Tilley (1993) and Crawford and Jones (1996) explore the replication of projects and identify a number of dimensions, including social, cultural, spatial and temporal, that need to be taken into consideration before interventions can be successfully 'cut and pasted'.

Virtually all of the ground breaking research in repeat victimisation has been carried out in the UK. The evidence in favour of repeat victimisation is so compelling that the reduction of repeat victimisation is now a key performance indicator for police in that country. Police services are responsible, in their jurisdiction, for identifying and reducing repeat victimisation and evaluating the method (Pease, 1998). There have been isolated studies regarding repeat victimisation by US researchers (mainly Fienberg, 1980; Lauritsen & Quinet, 1995; Nelson, 1980; Robinson, 1998; Roundtree et al., 1994; Sparks, 1981; Spelman, 1995), but most of these have been modelling exercises of limited use to practitioners. Presently the Police Executive Research Forum (PERF) is conducting a large three city experiment in Dallas, San Diego and Baltimore to replicate the UK research.

Time Course of Revictimisation

The time course of revictimisation was first explored by Polvi et al. (1990, 1991). They showed that the risk of revictimisation was greatest immediately after the offence. The chance of experiencing a second offence within a year of the first was four times the expected rate, but a second offence within a month was roughly twelve times more likely than expected. The length of the elevated risk period has significant implications for crime prevention practices (Spelman, 1995). Indeed, one of the critical elements in the success of the Kirkholt Project was the timing of the interventions. Security upgrading and the temporary loan of alarms were carried out as soon as possible after the report by the victim, sometimes within 24 hours (Forrester et al., 1988; 1990).

The time course has been shown to fit an exponential curve (Bowers & Hirschfield, 1998; Ratcliffe & McCullagh, 1998; Spelman, 1995). Polvi et al. (1990) estimate for all repeat burglaries occurring within the same month "28 per cent of repeat burglaries occur on the same day or adjacent days" (p. 11). By the end of the first week, half of the month's repeat burglaries had occurred. This means that in one day 28 per cent occur but the following six days account for a comparatively meager 22 per cent.

Nonetheless, the modelling of the time course of revictimisation is not without its problems. Time courses show between-times of all repeats, not just the between-time of the first and second incident. This means that chronically victimised addresses are represented more than once (the between-times for first-second, second-third, third fourth, etc... victimisations). By virtue of being chronic victims, they will most likely have smaller between-times than other, less victimised addresses. So they have more frequent, shorter between-times which tends to inflate the number of shorter between-times. The only way to circumvent this problem is to do a time course analysis for the between-times of each pair of victimisations. Unfortunately, this is of limited appeal because N for each pair of victimisations will decrease with victimisations and the confidence intervals for each time course will increase to a point that is unuseable (Broadhurst & Maller, 1991a). Survival analysis techniques are the most obvious way out of this dilemma, as they take into account diminishing risk periods and incomplete data (Morgan, forthcoming).

Hot Spots and Crime Mapping

Farrell and Pease (1993) identify as a challenge for future research elaboration of the relationship between repeat offending, repeat victimisation (hot dots) and crime hot spots. The development of repeat victimisation research in the UK has run parallel to the development of research into spatial distributions of victimisation in the US. Computer mapping of crime is not widespread but most medium to large police departments automate the geocoding of criminal incidents (Rich, 1995; Mamalian, 1999). Although crime hot spots have received some attention in the academic literature, their use has been more widespread in police forces.

Spatial studies of criminal activities have consistently demonstrated that certain locations experience crime far more than others. For example, Sherman et al. (1989) showed that 3 per cent of possible locations accounted for 50 per cent of the annual crime count in Minneapolis. Many explanations for spatial concentration have been proposed but there is little theoretical consensus (Baldwin, 1979; Eck, 1998). Technological improvements, such as computer processing speed, memory, graphical capability and desktop publishing quality have improved our capacity to quantify factors but a lack of well constructed theory ultimately limits research. Technology has placed the field beyond the present reach of theory (Baldwin, 1979).

Hot spots of crime are small areas that have statistically significant high levels of crime relative to surrounding areas. STAC (Spatial and Temporal Analysis of Crime) is a computer program developed by the Illinois Criminal Justice Authority that determines the area with the highest density of incidents and uses an algorithm to calculate a hot spot boundary. STAC is one of the more widely used empirical methods of identifying hot spots. It has been used in a number of studies (eg Block & Block, 1995; Canter, 1998; Eck, 1998; Hirschfield et al., 1995; Johnson et al., 1997; Rengert, 1997).

The usefulness of hot spot analysis becomes clearer when the areas are mapped and relationships between the environment and criminal activity are explored. For example, Block (1998) studied hot spots of gang-related drug activity in order to predict gang-related violence, while Hirschfield et al. (1995) explored the relationship between social disadvantage and hot spots of crime. Block and Block (1995) examined hot spots of violence offences in relation to the location of licensed premises and Harries (1995) has analysed locations of homicide and social stress

MICHAEL TOWNSLEY, ROSS HOMEL AND JANET CHASELING

(poverty, unemployment, residential stability). All of these studies have demonstrated that hot spots are related in predictable ways to features of the social and physical environments.

One of the major criticisms of spatial studies of crime, particularly those involving hot spots, is a failure to account for temporal trends in offending (Bennett, 1996; Rengert, 1997). There is evidence, for a number of offence types, of increased offending during particular times of the day or year. For example, the frequency of assaults compared across calendar months generally follows a cycle of increased offending in the summer months (Queensland Police Service, 1998, p. 19), while Rengert (1997) showed that peak times for auto theft varied widely depending on city location. By ignoring time, hot spots become a one-off, static measure of offending, with reduced analytic specificity. Indeed, generalisations about hot spots on the basis of analyses that ignore the time dimension may be as misleading as those that ignore the effect of aggregation on relationships (the ecological fallacy).

Bennett (1996) is one of the few researchers to consider seasonal variation. He developed a method that provides a degree of stability and some protection from seasonal effects by taking eighteen months of data and partitioning the entire data set into three six-monthly blocks. The inherent stability of the patterns could be related to how well they emerged across all three time periods. The locations of the stable hot spots were used to identify the area targeted for preventive interventions (Bennett, 1996).

Australian Studies

Computer crime mapping has had some limited applications in Australia, largely restricted to in-house analyses by law enforcement agencies (Cameron, 1998). The few published studies include Criminal Justice Commission (1997), Devery (1992) and Jochelson (1997). There is a little more published research on repeat victimisation (e.g., Criminal Justice Commission, 1997; Morgan, forthcoming; Mukherjee and Carcach, 1997), with several projects in progress in Queensland (Criminal Justice Commission, 1999) and South Australia (Fisher et al., 1999). Mukherjee and Carcach analysed two Australian victimisation surveys, the National Crime and Safety Survey (1993) and the Queensland Crime Victim Survey (1995), and demonstrate that the extent of repeat victimisation is of a similar magnitude to that revealed in the British Crime Survey (for example, 2.4 per cent of property victims experience over half the incidents).

The Present Study

The research presented in this paper emerged from a joint Queensland Criminal Justice Commission (CJC) and Queensland Police Service (QPS) initiative, the *Beenleigh Calls For Service Project* (Criminal Justice Commission, 1998). Its main aim was to determine to what extent Problem Oriented Policing (POP) initiatives could reduce telephone calls for service.

There are several reasons in a study of repeat victimisation to focus on burglary:

1. Burglary is a relatively well reported offence, due to insurance companies' policy of not proceeding on a claim until the incident is reported to the police.

2. Burglary has accurate location information. The owner, the tenant or a neighbour is invariably the individual reporting the offence and it can be assumed that these individuals would be able to provide address information.

3. Burglary is a crime against property. Properties are easier to 'manage' than people for prevention purposes.

4. Burglary generates sufficient numbers of incidents. The Beenleigh Police Division has the sixth highest residential burglary rate of all police divisions in the state (Criminal Justice Commission, 1996). In Queensland burglary is second only to theft in frequency (Queensland Police Service, 1998, p. 4). Burglary calls make up nearly 14 per cent of all calls for service in the Beenleigh Police Division (Criminal Justice Commission, 1997).

Data

The source of crime data for this research was a police information system called IMS (Incident Managment System). IMS is a computerised job card database, used primarily for command and dispatch duties. Requests for service come in from three sources; the community, other police divisions and emergency services. Communication room operators enter details onto a job card that appears on a computer screen. IMS is used throughout the state at the region level, except for Brisbane metropolitan regions, which have their own more developed command and dispatch system, ESCORT (Emergency Service Communications and Operation Resource Tracking).

Every offence category is represented on IMS by a three digit code. The code is used twice on each job card; once, when the IMS operator first receives the telephone call (an *r-code* or reported code) and the second time when a police officer verifies the nature of the incident (a *v-code* or verified code).

The time frame of this research spans eighteen months, from June, 1995 to November, 1996, inclusive. All jobs in the Beenleigh Police Division with a break and enter *v-code* within the time frame were included in the study. This amounted to 1750 verified break and enter incidents.

A great deal of time was spent cleaning the IMS data. Almost without exception, the IMS address location fields were unuseable for our purposes (consistent with the universal experience of other repeat victim researchers). Two phases of data cleaning were conducted:

1. Completion of addresses. Many of the IMS records were incomplete, with street names being spelt incorrectly, missing street numbers, complete addresses missing, property or business names instead of an address. Much work was done to correct or complete erroneous or missing addresses.

2. Uniform format of addresses. Various spellings and abbreviations of road type descriptors (street, road, court, crescent, lane, etc.) severely hindered accurate location. In some instances, an incorrect descriptor was used. A uniform format was developed that could be used by mapping software and for identifying repeat addresses.

Even when these phases were complete, it was not possible for many incidents occurring on non-residential properties to distinguish individual offices, shops and warehouses (only the whole complex could be identified).

MICHAEL TOWNSLEY, ROSS HOMEL AND JANET CHASELING

The large amount of time spent on this phase to produce mappable data explains why hot spot mapping and analysis of repeat victimisation are not routinely performed by Queensland police, at least any that use IMS. Most police information systems are not designed for it; the main objective of IMS is to get patrol cars to incident locations as quickly as possible, so location information does not have to be in a standard format. Police are also reluctant to devote the required resources of a full-time research officer for over two months to make eighteen months of data for one offence suitable for this type of research.

The problems encountered with cleaning the data have resulted in a number of modifications to IMS. The incident address field has been separated into a series of linked fields (previously it was one long string field), and an address validation system that corrects spelling mistakes and formatting errors has been introduced. These modifications resulted in a fourfold increase in accuracy in later analyses (Criminal Justice Commission, 1998).

Determining Repeats

Once the dataset had been cleaned as much as possible, a set of distinct victimised addresses was compiled and a victimisation count for each address was calculated. This was performed using the AGGREGATE function in SPSS (on the appropriate address field) and the SQL format of MapInfo.

Repeat victimisation, for our purposes, is when a property has been recorded in IMS as burgled on more than one occasion during a given time period. Individual addresses in properties such as retirement villages and shopping centres are not generally identified in the IMS data. This means that the whole complex must become the unit of analysis, and that its rate of repeats will generally be higher than for individual addresses within it. Whether this lack of specificity matters depends on details of the immediate physical environment, the characteristics of the businesses or other targets, and the nature of the prevention strategies being planned.

Following general practice in the literature, the victimised addresses were split into two groups: residential and non-residential properties. More than 90 per cent of residential properties were single dwellings, but also included were caravan parks, retirement villages and home units. Within the non-residential group, schools, shopping centres, sporting clubs, service stations, bottle shops and other retail outlets featured prominently.

Repeat Victimisation Results

Addresses were separated into residential and non-residential property types. The following tables show the extent of recorded repeat victimisation for both property types.

Key points to note from Table 1 are that:

1. over 90 per cent of residential properties in Beenleigh police division did *not* record a break and enter during the study period;

2. of those residential addresses in Beenleigh police division which were burgled, most (83.7 per cent) were burgled only once during the study period;

REPEAT BURGLARY VICTIMISATION: SPATIAL AND TEMPORAL PATTERNS

TABLE 1

Repeat Break and Enter Victimisation of Residential Properties, Beenleigh, June 1995 to November 1996 (inclusive)

Times victimised	Estimated number of residential properties	per cent of residential properties	per cent of victimised addresses	Number of crimes	per cent of crimes
0	10,864	91.6	0.0	0	0.0
1	830	7.0	83.7	830	68.1
2	127	1.1	12.8	254	20.8
3	23	0.2	2.3	69	5.7
4	5	0.1	0.5	20	1.6
5 or more	7	0.1	0.7	46	3.8
Total	11,856	100.0	100.0	1,219	100.0

Sources: Data on total number of residential properties from ABS 1991 Census, Table B45, calls for service data from Beenleigh IMS
Notes: Percentages have been rounded to nearest decimal point. Due to rounding, percentages may not add to 100

3. just 0.4 per cent (35) of all residential properties in Beenleigh police division (3.5 per cent of burgled properties) accounted for 11.1 per cent of all reported residential break and enters during the study period;

4. a mere seven addresses, or 0.7 per cent of all victim address in Beenleigh police division accounted for 46 incidents (3.8 per cent of all incidents) during the study period.

The chance of a residential address being victimised one time only was 830/11,856 = 0.07. Having been a victim once, the chances of revictimisation were $(127+23+5+7)/(830+127+23+5+7) = 0.1633$, more than double the initial chance of becoming a victim. This probability is lower than in most other studies (Forrester et al., 1988; Polvi et al., 1990), which typically estimate the rates of revictimisation as at least four times the rate of initial victimsation.

The data in Table 1 show that the elimination of all recorded repeat victimisation in residential properties (i.e., a 100 per cent effective prevention program that stopped all revictimisation with no displacement) would prevent, in eighteen months, 227 break and enters, or 18.6 per cent of the total. This provides a theoretical 'ceiling' on the benefits that could be obtained by focusing on repeat residential incidents using police data (of course, in practise, the benefits of any prevention project implemented will fall short of this ceiling). However, we demonstrate below how the real ceiling could be higher.

Table 2 presents data on victimisation patterns for non-residential properties. It shows that:

1. a greater proportion of non-residential properties (23.3 per cent) in the Beenleigh police division were victimised during the study period;

2. 44.5 per cent of victimised non-residential properties in the Beenleigh police division were victimised more than once during the study period;

MICHAEL TOWNSLEY, ROSS HOMEL AND JANET CHASELING

TABLE 2

Repeat Break and Enter Victimisation for Non-Residential Properties, Beenleigh, June 1995 to November 1996 (inclusive)

Times victimised	Estimated number of non-residential properties	per cent of non-residential properties	per cent of victimised addresses	Number of crimes	per cent of crimes
0	754	76.7	0.0	0	0.0
1	127	12.9	55.5	127	23.9
2	41	4.2	17.7	82	15.4
3	26	2.6	11.4	78	14.7
4	13	1.3	5.7	52	9.8
5	12	1.2	5.2	60	11.3
6	1	0.1	0.4	6	1.1
7	0	0.0	0.0	0	0.0
8	2	0.2	0.9	16	3.0
9 or more	7	0.7	3.1	110	20.7
Total	983	100.0	100.0	531	100.0

Sources: Calls for service data from Beenleigh IMS
Notes: Percentages have been rounded to nearest decimal point. Due to rounding, percentages may not add to 100

3. seven locations (3.1 per cent of victimised premises) in the Beenleigh police division accounted for 20 per cent (110) of all burglaries committed on non-residential properties during the study period.

The chances of a non-residential property being victimised once only are 127/983 = 0.129. Having been victimised once, the chances of being burgled in the same eighteen month period were $(41+26+...+7)/(127+41+26+...+7) = 0.445$. This is almost three and a half times the rate for a single victimisation only. If all repeat victimisations in non-residential addresses identifiable through police data were eliminated through 100 per cent effective prevention with no displacement, 302 incidents, or 56.9 per cent of the total, would be eliminated. It seems, therefore, that the prevention potential is much greater with non-residential than residential break and enter.

In order to demonstrate clearly the differences between the two property types, Table 3 lists burglary distribution attributes and the corresponding values derived from Tables 1 and 2 for residential and non-residential properties.

In analysing Table 3, it must be remembered that in absolute terms residential properties suffer more burglaries than non-residential, 1,219 versus 531 incidents. However, victimised properties are nearly three times more prevalent in non-residential properties than in residential. The intensity of victimisation, concentration, is also higher for non-residential properties. Non-residential properties that have been victimised experience, on average, nearly one burglary more than victimised residential properties (although the possibility that separate shops or offices within the complex are being targeted on each occasion needs to be kept in mind). A higher prevalence and concentration for non-residential properties serve to yield more than a five times higher incidence, or burglary rate, than residential properties.

REPEAT BURGLARY VICTIMISATION: SPATIAL AND TEMPORAL PATTERNS

TABLE 3

Property Type and Burglary Distribution Attributes, Beenleigh, June 1995 to November 1996 (inclusive)

Distribution Attributes	Residential properties	Non-residential properties
Prevalence (percentage properties victimised)	8.4	23.3
Concentration (average victimisations/victim)	1.229	2.319
Incidence (# incidents/100 properties)	10.282	54.018

TABLE 4

Top 15 addresses, Beenleigh Police Division, June 1995 to November 1996 (inclusive)

Position	Nature of address	Frequency
1	School	25
2	Shopping centre	22
3	Motel	18
4	Shopping centre	16
5	Residential units	11
6	Shopping centre	11
7	School	10
8	School	10
9	School	10
10	School	10
11	Commercial	9
12	Residential	9
13	Residential	9
14	Residential	8
15	Retirement village	8

There may be several reasons why victimisation rates are higher for non-residential addresses in semi-rural areas like Beenleigh. Levels of insurance are likely to be higher amongst non-residential property owners than residential owners and therefore the former are more likely to report a burglary. The spatial distribution of non-residential properties, particularly commercial, retail and industrial properties, is fundamentally different to residential properties. They are commonly clustered together on main roads and they are far more dense than residential properties. It is also probably fair to say that non-residential properties are more lucrative targets (there is more to steal). Whether these factors apply more generally to other areas is difficult to determine, but UK research seems to indicate greater repeat burglary victimisation among businesses (Taylor, 1999).

Table 4, which shows the fifteen addresses with the highest number of burglaries, indicates that many of the most frequently victimised addresses are public facilities such as schools, shopping centres and commercial properties.

MICHAEL TOWNSLEY, ROSS HOMEL AND JANET CHASELING

Explaining the Low Rate of Repeat Victimisation for Residential Addresses

As noted above, the repeat rate (the proportion of repeat incidents that make up the overall crime count) seems low for residential properties compared to Kirkholt and other studies. In fact, there is a general sense of confusion over what the 'average' repeat rate is. This comes about because repeat rates can be calculated from three different sources: victimisation surveys, project impacts, and police data.

Victimisation surveys typically report between 60 to 80 per cent of property crime experienced by repeat victims (Ellingworth et al., 1995; Farrell & Pease, 1993; Farrell, 1995; Pease, 1998), in line with data from Australian surveys (Mukherjee & Carach, 1998). Kirkholt-like projects have reported between 20 to 30 per cent reductions in residential burglary (Chenery et al., 1995; Janice Webb Research, 1996).

Repeat rates generated from police statistics reflect reporting patterns of victims. This affects both the police officer's perception of the problem and the measures taken to prevent future incidents. The number of repeat incidents occurring, according to the criminal information system used, is an often overlooked, yet vitally important quantity. Repeat rates from police statistics in a number studies have ranged from 8 to 32 per cent in the UK (Bennett & Durie, forthcoming; Johnson et al., 1997; Ratcliffe & McCullagh, 1998) and 29 per cent in the US (Robinson, 1998). The repeat rate for Beenleigh is 18.7 per cent, comfortably within the above range. However, the fact that Beenleigh has the sixth highest residential burglary rate of Queensland police divisions coupled with Trickett et al.'s (1995) observation that high crime areas, in the UK, have high repeat victimisation may lead critics to question the usefulness of focusing on repeat victimisation in an Australian setting.

There is one other important factor when using police data that should be considered. There is no doubt that police data severely underestimate the 'real' extent of crime (Farrell & Pease, 1993; Sherman et al., 1989). An estimate of levels of police underreporting in Australia is given in Mukherjee et al. (1997). These authors show that based on survey data for residential break and enter in Queensland, 83 per cent of victims of a single break and enter incident report the incident to the police, compared with roughly 55 per cent of repeat victims. Adjusting for underreporting, if repeat victimisation were prevented absolutely, total residential burglary would fall by 24.3 per cent, an increase of 6 per cent due solely to the correction for underreporting. This increase is still quite conservative as the reporting rate for repeat victims will vary depending on the extent of victimisation (Chenery et al., 1997; Pease & Laycock, 1996). The estimate of reporting for repeat victims (55 per cent) will overstate the degree that chronically victims report.

If 'edge effects', the failure to detect repeats that span the start or finish of the time window, are also considered, the estimated maximum reduction would be even greater. However, although 25 per cent (plus) is a higher figure than 18 per cent, and more in line with the high repeat rates of other studies, one could still expect a higher proportion of repeats in such a high burglary area.

Morgan (forthcoming) suggests that another mechanism may be present that is suppressing the extent of repeat victimisation. He observed that, in a Perth suburb, several one-time victims tend to cluster around a repeat victim. He found the repeat victim addresses occurred first and the one-time victims were burgled later in the month. This suggests that some form of 'contagion' process was at work. Morgan named the surrounding one-time victims *near repeats*.

An hypothesis worth exploring is the relationship between the homogeneity of dwelling type in an area and its impact on repeat victimisation. If an offender specialises in breaking into a particular dwelling type and operates in an area predominantly consisting of the favoured dwelling type, it is plausible that the offender would not concentrate on a particular address, but would 'visit' other addresses that shared similar features. This is similar to Pease's (1998) concept of 'virtual repeats,' where criminal acts may be linked by virtue of victim (or target) similarity. Pease uses racial attacks (all x's look the same) and same model car theft as examples of virtual repeats. Near repeats differ from virtual repeats with respect to the spatial component; they are geographically close whereas virtual repeats are not necessarily so. It is this which makes the near repeat concept so attractive. Near repeats could be the theoretical construct needed to explain more fully the relationship between repeat victimisation and hot spots.

The Beenleigh area has several new housing estates. Typically, land development companies buy large amounts of land, about the size of a suburb, and offer inexpensive house-and-land packages. Prospective buyers generally have a choice of five or six designs to choose from. Several suburbs in the Beenleigh Police Division have developed this way and there are many pockets of nearly identical dwellings. In fact, there are some cul de sacs that are comprised of exactly the same model house. For these reasons, Beenleigh is considered an ideal site to test the near repeat hypothesis in the future.

Time Course of Break and Enter Victimisation

Analyses of the time course of victimisation are primarily concerned with the amount of time that passes between repeat events. However, the use of a time window, inevitable in any research study, means necessarily that the time course distribution is biased to short periods. For example, in the 18 month dataset in this study there are 17 adjacent month pairs, but only six twelve month combinations of time blocks. The larger the time between victimisations, the less likely that it will be detected.

One way this bias can be overcome is by adjusting the time course frequencies using a correction factor, a number that adjusts a score to make a measurement unbiased. The correction factor used here (the total number of time units divided by the number of time units until the end of the time window) is the simple weighting measure outlined in Anderson et al. (1995). At the start of the time window the correction factor is close to one, but as time passes the denominator decreases (as the number of time units until the end becomes smaller) which causes the correction factor to increase. The raw scores for the time course are multiplied by the correction factor to give the adjusted score. The increasing value for the correction factor is meant to compensate for the artifically low later month frequencies.

Figures 1 and 2 show the time course, both uncorrected and corrected, for repeat burglary victimisation in Beenleigh for residential and non-residential properties. Although the graphs relate to different property types they display similar characteristics and agree with every time course distribution ever published (Farrell & Pease, 1993; Farrell, 1995).

MICHAEL TOWNSLEY, ROSS HOMEL AND JANET CHASELING

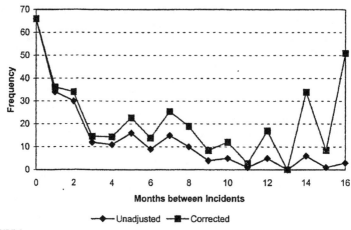

FIGURE 1

Time Course for Residential Properties Beenleigh, June 1995 to November 1996 (inclusive).

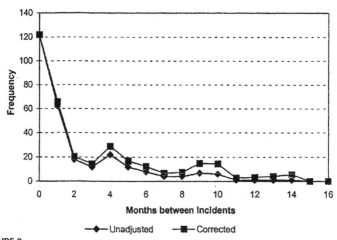

FIGURE 2

Time Course for Non-Residential Properties Beenleigh, June 1995 to November 1996 (inclusive).

Key features are:

1. Most of the repeat victimisation occurs within one to two months of the first victimisation. After that time, a large drop-off occurs and a relatively stable level is maintained for the duration of the time period. For example, across all property types, 188 addresses experienced two break and enters within the space of a month, but only 102 were revictimised in the next month. There were 54 addresses with two months between incidents.

2. For residential properties, the difference between the unadjusted and corrected frequencies becomes larger as the time between incidents increases. This is a reflection of both the mechanics of the correction factor and the erratic behaviour of the tail of the time distribution.

3. A four month 'hump', an increase in frequencies at about four months, is present for non-residential properties, and a five month hump for residential addresses. Four month humps have been observed in Canada (Polvi et al., 1990; 1991) and in the UK (Chenery et al., 1997). A US study (Robinson, 1998) reported a slight five month hump. It has been speculated that the humps reflect offenders returning for the insurance-replaced goods stolen in the earlier incident (Pease, K 1998, pers comm). Nevertheless, the humps are not statistically significantly different from the time course. The number of repeats for each hump falls within the confidence intervals at those points under an exponential regression model (Bowers et al., 1998; Johnson et al., 1997; Spelman, 1995).

More work needs to be done to understand why some properties experience long times between 'visits' and others only short ones. Perhaps with the aid of CRISP (Crime Reporting Information System for Police), an information system used by QPS to record detailed crime scene reports and case histories, a better predictive model can be developed. For example, if properties that experience short times between victimisations tend to have little taken on the initial incident and much more on the second, then that implies the first offence is used to 'scope' the dwelling and if sufficient rewards are present, then a second offence will follow quickly. On the other hand, if households that experience long between-times have a large amount stolen both times, then it would indicate offenders waiting for the replacement of stolen goods. By combining CRISP and IMS, a comprehensive and potentially powerful tool would be available for analysing the time course distribution.

Hot Spots

To observe spatial distributions of victimisation, a Geographical Information System (GIS) was used, in conjunction with an up to date digitised street map. The GIS used was MapInfo, a relatively user-friendly computer package (MapInfo, 1998).

The process of matching records from the database with specific points on a map is called geo-coding. It is not important for the purposes of this paper to outline the mechanics of geo-coding except to observe that the degree of success is directly related to the accuracy of the street map and obviously the degree of precision of the address field of the data to be mapped. Ultimately, 107 addresses, just over six per cent of the total, were not geo-coded. This occurred for two reasons: although only a few years old, the street map used in this project did not contain every address in the Police Division; and incidents outside the boundary of the Police Division sometimes appeared in the dataset, and were therefore not mapped.

Once mapped, it was observed that the incidents were concentrated in the north-west corner of the police division. A target area was selected within the Division, which was thought would capture the majority of the incidents. The area is rectangular in shape and covers over 66 square kilometres. Of the 1,643 records examined, 1,427 incidents, or 87 per cent, were contained in the target area.

MICHAEL TOWNSLEY, ROSS HOMEL AND JANET CHASELING

Just as the concept of repeat victimisation was used to illustrate numerical distributions of victimisation, hot spots were used to illustrate spatial distributions of victimisation. The standard definition for a hot spot is an area, place or address that has a high volume of crime (Block, 1995; Canter, 1998; Hirschfield et al., 1995; Sherman et al., 1989).

Bennett (1996) defined two types of hot spots, stable and unstable. Stable hot spots were those that occurred in all three time periods whereas unstable hot spots were those that occurred in at least one, but not all, time periods. Three six-month time periods were also used in the present study. The first period spans June, 1995 to November, 1995; the second includes December, 1995 to May, 1996; the third and last time period is June, 1996 to November, 1996.

The software package STAC was used to identify and locate hot spots within each of the three time periods. STAC calculates hot spots of spatially distributed data and represents the boundaries as standard deviational ellipses. For large sample, normally-distributed data, the standard deviational ellipse will include roughly 95 per cent of the incidents in the cluster. STAC relies on two parameters set by the user, the *search radius* and *the minimum number of incidents per cluster*. Combinations of parameters were tested to determine the values that would provide useful (not overly sensitive) results. The most consistent results were obtained for a search radius of 150 metres and 10 incidents per cluster (five or six hot spots were generated each time period in this manner).

The algorithm used for calculating standard deviational hot spots is a two step process. First, a grid of points is placed over the area of interest. Circles of consistent radius (equal to the *search radius*) are placed over each grid point, which are a half search radius apart. The number of incidents within each circle is tallied and the top 25 circles are kept. The program then checks for overlapping circles in the top 25 list, ie ones that 'share' incidents, and if present are grouped together, ie the union of these circles becomes a cluster. The second part of the process then starts. For each circle or cluster that has more incidents than the minimum number, the second parameter, a standard deviational ellipse is calculated. The centre of the ellipse is the arithmetic mean of the x and y co-ordinates of the incidents that comprise the cluster. STAC outputs values for 'the number of events in each cluster', 'the number of events in each ellipse', 'the area of each ellipse', 'the number of events per one million square metres' and 'the centre of the ellipse'. A more detailed description of the algorithm and equations STAC uses can be found in the STAC Users Manual (Illinois Criminal Justice Authority, 1996).

A number of hot spots were identified[1], but only three consistently appeared in all three time periods, and thus can be considered stable (see Figure 3)[2].

Hot Spot 1. The first hot spot is in an outlying suburb. This is a designed suburb, adjacent to an arterial road which is the only access route. The suburb has one main road that starts at one point on the arterial road and winds through the suburb, to finish by linking back to the arterial road. The suburb is nearly entirely residential, but includes primary and secondary schools, a train station and a small block of retail shops. The hot spot is focused on the small block of retail shops, although it does spill over to the surrounding residential properties. The shops are located on the intersection of the suburb's main road and the street linking the

REPEAT BURGLARY VICTIMISATION: SPATIAL AND TEMPORAL PATTERNS

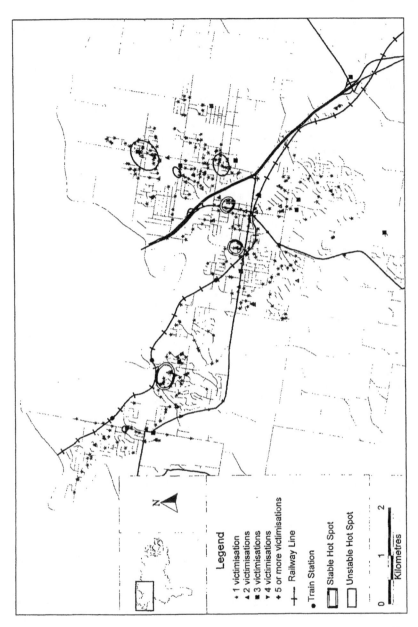

FIGURE 3
First Six Months (June to November, 1995).

MICHAEL TOWNSLEY, ROSS HOMEL AND JANET CHASELING

main road to the train station. The number of people passing through this hot spot would be substantial.

Hot Spot 2. This hot spot is centred on a major intersection of a main road and an arterial road. On one corner is a service station and adjacent to it is a complex of retail outlets. Nearby, to the north, are several large residential apartment blocks and there are numerous retail outlets scattered throughout the surrounding area. Perhaps the most interesting feature of this hot spot is the disparate land type composition. The intersection is the unofficial border of the commercial sector and the industrial sector of Beenleigh. To the east of the roundabout is the commercial sector of Beenleigh, while to the west of the intersection is the start of the industrial sector. As mentioned above, a residential area lies to the north. This hot spot experiences a large volume of traffic.

Hot Spot 3. This hot spot is centred in the Central Business District (CBD) of Beenleigh. A significant number of people visit this area by various means, a five-way main road intersection lies in the area, nearby is a train station, a major bus terminal, a secondary school, a public swimming pool, a community centre, a sports centre, several shopping centres and numerous other retail outlets. The land usage is predominantly non-residential. The properties are characterised by high levels of target hardening, particularly barbed wire, bars and grilles on doors and windows and obvious security devices, including alarms.

In general terms, all the hot spots, stable and unstable, have a high number of targets in a small area. This probably reflects the presence of paths which give immediate access to the rear of properties. In addition, many areas (paths, streets, lanes) are poorly lit and some heavily trafficked areas have street lighting on one side of the street only. Other places are characterised by large amounts of public space surrounding them. Unfortunately, this space is generally poorly maintained, being marred by litter, rusting cars, shoulder high grass and graffiti. This makes surveillance of properties difficult for place managers, security personnel, owners and tenants.

Bennett's (1996) method of accounting for seasonal variation goes a long way toward reducing the likelihood of missing seasonal cycles, but there is still a degree of the 'snapshot' problem, ie variations within the six monthly period are possible. A new mapping methodology was developed to alleviate this problem and represent spatial change smoothly, avoiding the sharp, stop-start feature of spatial patterns that may occur using methods that simply partition the time window.

Moving Average Mapping

A moving average is most often used to smooth fluctuations and to make trends clearer for a time series (Borowski & Borwein, 1989). This is achieved by taking a number of the series' previous values and averaging the scores. Similarly, the moving average mapping methodology takes a number of six monthly blocks and compares the movement of hot spots across the series. The first time period in the series uses the first six months of the dataset. The second six month time period in the series comprises months two through seven, making a five month overlap between the first time period and the second. The third time period in the series uses months three to eight, and so on until the last time period, the thirteenth, which uses months thirteen through to eighteen[3].

REPEAT BURGLARY VICTIMISATION: SPATIAL AND TEMPORAL PATTERNS

By having a five month overlap between adjacent time periods, the moving average method provides a more fluid indicator of the spatial behaviour of victimisation across time than the 'snapshot' approach. For example, at the beginning of the time frame in the Beenleigh analysis, the suburb known as Fairview, an invented name, had very high levels of burglary. Cresttown, also an invented name, had much lower levels of buglary initially. Fairview has a river bordering to the north and farmland to the south and east. To the west is Cresttown, which has a very large number of attractive targets. Figures 4 and 5 show the frequency of reported break and enter offences for each suburb, as well as the proportional split between single incidents and repeats.

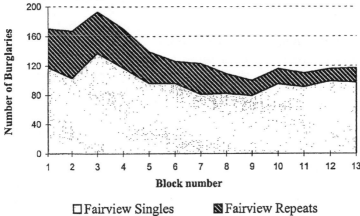

□ Fairview Singles   ▨ Fairview Repeats

FIGURE 4

The proportion of revictimisation in Fairview.

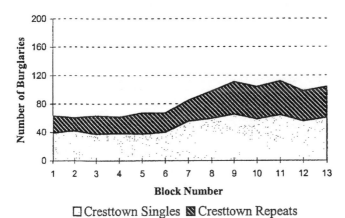

□ Cresttown Singles ▨ Cresttown Repeats

FIGURE 5

The proportion of revictimisation in Cresttown.

MICHAEL TOWNSLEY, ROSS HOMEL AND JANET CHASELING

There are two interesting features of the two graphs:

1. Fairview's contribution of repeats to the total tapers off noticeably over time, and there is a general reduction of incidents at approximately the same time as an increase in both repeats and overall incidents at Cresttown.

2. The overall decrease in Fairview is approximately 50–60 incidents (from a high of 170–180, to a low of 120) and the overall increase in Cresttown is 50–60 (from a low of 60 to a high of 110–120).

The fact that the change for the two neighbouring suburbs occurred at the same time and was of similar magnitude suggests displacement of offending from Fairview to Cresttown. It would be difficult to capture this type of phenomenon using most other mapping approaches.

Repeat Victimisation and Hot Spots

By definition, hot spots are the densest areas of criminal activity. Apart from Bennett and Durie (1996), no other researchers have looked at the composition of victimisation within hot spots, although several researchers have acknowledged that this is an important area to investigate (Farrell & Pease, 1993; Hope, 1995). It is possible that a hot spot may arise either as a result of many one or two off victimisations (high prevalence, low concentration) or as the result of relatively few chronically victimised addresses (low prevalence, high concentration — a coalescence of hot dots). Using the stable/unstable typology introduced by Bennett (1996), Table 5 shows the relationship between stability and repeat victimisation.

It is apparent that unstable hot spot areas have the highest number of high frequency repeat victim addresses (3 or more victimisations). Stable hot spots have a higher proportion of repeat victim addresses than non-hot spot areas, and the relationship is statistically significant[4]. The results for stable hot spots presented here are somewhat 'stronger' than Bennett and Durie's (1996) findings for Cambridge. For example, Bennett and Durie found that 19 per cent of all addresses burgled in their hot spot in the eighteen months were burgled more than once, but the comparable figure for stable hot spots in Beenleigh was 32 per cent.

TABLE 5

Hot Spots and Repeat Victimisation, Beenleigh, June 1995 to November 1996 (inclusive)

Number of Victimisations	Stable hot spots		Unstable hot spots		Rest	
	N	per cent	N	per cent	N	per cent
1	80	67.8	33	70.2	1,040	88.2
2	28	23.7	6	12.8	98	8.3
3	3	2.5	3	6.4	34	2.9
4+	7	5.9	5	10.6	7	0.6
Total	118	100.0	47	100.0	1,179	100.0
Area	0.4 km²		0.1 km²		62 km²	

Notes: 1. Chi-square (6) = 85.9, p = 0.000; Cramer's V = 0.18
Percentages have been rounded to the nearest decimal point. Due to rounding, percentages may not add to 100

REPEAT BURGLARY VICTIMISATION: SPATIAL AND TEMPORAL PATTERNS

The finding that some hot spots flare up because of repeat victimisation is important, and suggests that police strategies should be developed to nip 'serial break and enter' in the bud. However, it is also clear that some spots are hot because of the type of area they are, and that the whole locality, not just repeat addresses, should be the focus of attention.

Discussion

This paper has presented numerical and spatial distributions of victimisation of burglary. In the broad sense, the results agree with the findings of similar research conducted outside Australia, although there may be variations in patterns compared to the well established literature of the UK. We showed that by preventing repeat incidents, the overall burglary count could be reduced by at least 25 per cent. A number of hot spots, three of which were stable, were identified. The victimisation composition of hot spots appears to vary according to the nature of the hot spot. Unstable hot spots had a higher level of repeats than stable hot spots. The temporal distributions displayed here match very closely patterns reported elsewhere.

The problems we encountered with our data were similar to researcher's accounts from overseas (Farrell & Pease, 1993; Sherman et al., 1989). Until address validation becomes a routine feature of crime information systems, no police service will have the ability to identify hot dots or analyse them rigorously. Both hot dot and hot spot analyses are heavily reliant on the accuracy and consistency of addresses. Due to their greater experience in crime mapping, address validation has become heavily developed in the US, with several police agencies across that country reporting a 95 per cent or better hit rate in the geocoding process (Foy, 1999; Olligschlaeger, 1998).

An information system's capacity to facilitate the recognition of repeats directly affects the ability of police to deal with the problem. Actual repeat rates may be substantial, but if the rate according to the police service (i.e., generated by their information system) is significantly lower, then other, less effective techniques may become more attractive than a focus on prevention of repeats. Clearly, this sort of Type II error (a false negative) is a situation that victims, the community, police, policy makers and researchers all wish to avoid.

We recommend three extentions of existing analytical methods. The first extention involves the concept of near repeats. Although repeat burglary victimisation is a problem in Australia, there appear to be variations in patterns compared to the well established literature of the UK. The concept of near repeats has the potential to be very useful for crime analysis (offender targeting patterns, police intelligence), crime prevention (security advice tailored to specific dwelling types), town planning (distribution of similar housing types, urban development guidelines) and criminological research (added complexities of international perspectives on repeat victimisation).

Farrell and Pease (1993) identify as a challenge for future research elaboration of the relationship between repeat offending, repeat victimisation and crime hot spots. Bennett (1996) and Bennett and Durie (forthcoming) come closest to this in their Cambridge study, although Eck (forthcoming) addresses the problem in a theoretical sense. It is our contention that near repeats are important in explaining

MICHAEL TOWNSLEY, ROSS HOMEL AND JANET CHASELING

the relationship between hot spots and hot dots, although data on offender behaviour patterns and on the extent and nature of social disadvantage in the area will also be crucial (Hirschfield et al., 1995).

With the aid of CRISP, the relationship between property type homogeneity and burglary can be explored further. Aspects of the incident such as modus operandi, point of entry and amount stolen that are not recorded in IMS may prove to be critical factors to explain burglary patterns for particular dwelling types.

Our second recommendation is to use survival analysis. The major limitation of time course analysis is the inability to control for diminishing risk periods (events close to the end of the time window are not given the same chance to repeat as those at the start). Survival analysis, a quantitative method largely restricted to medical and operations research, focuses on the time until an event occurs, in this case, a repeat offence. Morgan (forthcoming) showed that substantial differences exist in burglary rates for small areas within a Perth suburb and he was one of the first to use survival analysis on repeat victimisation data (Spelman [1995] was the first).

Covariate mixture models have been used for nearly twenty years (Schimdt & Witte, 1988) to model recidivism of prison inmates and the metholodology has been well developed by Broadhurst and Maller in a series of excellent research pieces (Broadhurst & Maller, 1991a; 1991b; 1992; Broadhurst et al., 1988; see also Maller & Zhou, 1996). Modelling the time between victimisations is analogous to modelling the time between offences and seems a logical progression for those interested in time course analysis, especially since Maller and Zhou have developed tests to identify minimum follow-up periods for statistical reliability and have also addressed other conditions for effective use of survival analysis.

The advantages of applying survival analysis in this context are twofold. By fitting data to a distribution, estimates outside the time frame can be calculated; and the underlying assumptions of the particular distribution can be used to say something about the data, provided there is a good fit. Survival analysis has not been included in this analysis because an eighteen month dataset will not have sufficient observations for maximum likelihood estimation. We are currently working on a larger dataset (four and a half years) which should generate sufficient observations for this type of analysis.

We introduced moving average mapping as a method to avoid the snapshot effect that occurs whenever crime incidents are aggregated across some time period. Our third recommendation is to make greater use of this approach, because it allows the identification of seasonal and other time-related effects. A more advanced version of this concept has been developed in conjunction with animation techniques. Animated crime maps show areas 'fading in and out' depending on their temporal incidence intensity (Goldsmith & Williamson, 1998). Although maps of this type look good and impact greatly on the viewer, care must be taken not to be overly reliant on aesthetic appeal to the detriment of quality analysis. Equally this can be said for the trend toward the inclusion of interpolated surfaces in crime mapping. A number of software packages are available that build three dimensional surfaces interpolated from point data (e.g., MapInfo Professional 5.0, Surfer, Vertical Mapper). This is very useful in some areas (e.g., public release information and patrol briefings) where the exact location of a crime site may not be required, but is unlikely to replace fully point level analysis.

REPEAT BURGLARY VICTIMISATION: SPATIAL AND TEMPORAL PATTERNS

We now consider potential prevention applications, and also some future research directions.

First, the probable high level of under-reporting of repeat residential victimisation to police suggests that police should keep in touch with all households in an area known to have been broken into in the past year or so, in order both to provide support and suggest prevention strategies, but also to ascertain whether they have been victimised again but have not reported the incident(s). This would serve the dual purposes of providing a valuable public service and improving the quality of police data, hence increasing the effectiveness of police responses designed to prevent repeat burglary.

Second, and consistent with the overseas research (Farrell & Pease, 1993; Polvi et al., 1990, 1991), preventive measures need to be put in place very quickly after the 'first' burglary. This may involve such methods as 'cocoon neighbourhood watch', temporary installation of silent alarms, or intensive efforts to apprehend the offenders (Forrester et al., 1988; Criminal Justice Commission, 1997; Pease, 1998). The role of police is vital here. Our results suggest that the greatest gains are likely to be made, at least in areas like Beenleigh, by focusing on non-residential properties, especially schools and other public facilities.

Third, crime prevention through environmental design (CPTED) needs to be taken seriously as a strategy. There are large, open, public areas in many parts of the Beenleigh Police Division. Unlit tracks providing access to the rear of properties also appear to be a problem in the area. The installation of adequate lighting and the better maintenance of public areas may help repair some 'broken windows' in the more chronic areas (Kelling & Coles, 1996). At the same time, however, the amenity of the area needs to be kept in mind. Open space with trees can be a real bonus in terms of lifestyle, illustrating the familiar point that crime prevention cannot be divorced from other aspects of social policy and planning. CPTED thinking should be incorporated in an overall plan for the development of the area that gives due weight to the cost and suffering caused by repeat victimisation for burglary.

Finally, the reasons why some areas are hot, regardless of the incidence of repeat victimisation within those areas, need to be better understood. Bennett's (1996) research suggests that maybe half of all the incidents in these areas are caused by a small group of offenders who live nearby. These areas, and the offenders, could probably be characterised as 'high risk' or multiply disadvantaged (Vinson & Homel, 1975; Developmental Crime Consortium, 1999). Prevention is not just about 'designing out crime' or detecting and incapacitating repeat offenders; it is also about understanding and dealing with some of the social problems that are the primary generators of crime in hot spots and disadvantaged areas. Environmental prevention techniques and data-driven policing responses, combined with an investment in community-based prevention programs that promote prosocial developmental pathways for young people, should do much to reduce crime and related problems in areas like Beenleigh.

Endnotes

1 Both residential and non-residential incidents are included in the hot spot maps. Of the three stable hot spots, two are entirely non-residential. Future research will investigate mapping the property types separately.

MICHAEL TOWNSLEY, ROSS HOMEL AND JANET CHASELING

2   Although this is a black and white map, readers are encouraged to view the colour maps at the
     following Internet site: *http://www.gu.edu.au/school/ccj/mtmaps.html*

3   All thirteen moving average maps are viewable from the above Internet site (space restric-
     tions do not allow a full presentation here).

4   Comparing only hot spots areas, stable and unstable hot spots are not statistically significantly
     different. Given the low frequency of multiple victimisation, further analysis of this topic
     should be conducted on a larger dataset.

References

Anderson, D., Chenery, S., & Pease, K. (1995). *Biting Back: Tackling Repeat Burglary and Car
     Crime*, Crime Detection and Prevention Series Paper No 58. London: Home Office.

Australian Bureau of Statistics (1996). *Catalogue Number 2015.3 — Census of Population and
     Housing: Selected Social and Housing Characteristics for Statistical Local Areas, Queensland.*
     Canberra: ABS.

Baldwin, J. (1979). Ecological and Areal Studies in Great Britain and the United States. In N.
     Morris, & M. Tonry (eds.), *Crime and Justice: An Annual Review of Research Vol 1.* Chicago:
     University of Chicago Press.

Bennett, T. (1996). Identifying, Explaining and Targeting Burglary "Hot Spots", *European Journal
     on Criminal Policy and Research, 3*(3), 113–123.

Bennett, T. & Durie, L. (1996). Domestic Burglary Task Force: Cambridge, *Focus on Police
     Research and Development, 8* (December), 34–36.

Bennett, T. & Durie, L. (1999). *Preventing Residential Burglary in Cambridge: From Crime Audits to
     Targeted Strategies*, Crime Detection and Prevention Series Paper 108. London: Home Office.

Block, C.R. (1998). The GeoArchive: An Information Foundation for Community Policing. In
     D. Weisburd, & T. McEwen (eds.), *Crime Mapping and Crime Prevention: Crime Prevention
     Studies Vol 8.* Monsey NY: Criminal Justice Press.

Block, R.L. & Block, C.R. (1995). Space, Place and Crime: Hot Spot Areas and Hot places of
     Liquor-Related Crime. In J.E. Eck, & D. Weisburd (eds.), *Crime and Place: Crime Prevention
     Studies Vol 5.* Monsey NY: Criminal Justice Press.

Borowski, E.J. & Borwein, J.M. (1989). *Dictionary of Mathematics.* London: Collins.

Bowers, K., Hirschfield, A. & Johnson, S. (1998). Victimisation Revisited: A Case Study of Non-
     Residential Repeat Burglary on Merseyside, *British Journal of Criminology, 38*(3), 429–451.

Broadhurst, R.G. & Maller, R.A. (1991a). Estimating the Numbers of Prison Terms in Criminal
     Careers from One-Step Probabilities of Recidivism, *Journal of Quantitative Criminology, 7*(3),
     275–290.

Broadhurst, R.G. & Maller, R.A. (1991b). *Sex Offending and Recidivism*, Research Report No 3.
     University of Western Australia: Crime Research Centre.

Broadhurst, R.G. & Maller, R.A. (1992). The Recidivism of Sex offenders in the Western
     Australian Prison Population, *British Journal of Criminology, 32*(1), 54–80.

Broadhurst, R.G., Maller, R.A., Maller, M.G., & Duffecy, J. (1988). Aboriginal and Nonaboriginal
     Recidivism in Western Australia: A Failure Rate Analysis, *Journal of Research in Crime and
     Delinquency, 25*(1), 83–108.

Cameron, D. (1998). *Computer Crime Mapping and Hot Spot Analysis — Examples of their use in the
     USA, England and Australia and a review of the QPS position.* Queensland Institute of
     Technology: Unpublished Masters thesis.

Canter, P. (1998). Geographic Information Systems and Crime Analysis in Baltimore County,
     Maryland. In D. Weisburd & T. McEwen (eds.), *Crime Mapping and Crime Prevention: Crime
     Prevention Studies Vol 8.* Monsey NY: Criminal Justice Press.

Chenery, S., Holt, J., & Pease, K. (1997). *Biting Back II: Reducing Repeat Victimisation in
     Huddersfield*, Crime Detection and Prevention Series Paper 82. London: Home Office.

REPEAT BURGLARY VICTIMISATION: SPATIAL AND TEMPORAL PATTERNS

Crawford, A. & Jones, M. (1996). Kirkholt Revisited: Some Reflections on the Transferability of Crime Prevention Initiatives, *Howard Journal*, 35(1), 21–39.

Criminal Justice Commission (1996). Residential Burglary in Queensland. *Research Paper Series*, 3(1). Brisbane: Author.

Criminal Justice Commission (1997). *Hot Spots and Repeat Break and Enter Crimes: An analysis of police calls for service data*. Brisbane: Author.

Criminal Justice Commission (1998). *Beenleigh Calls for Service Project: Evaluation Report.* Brisbane: Author.

Criminal Justice Commission (1999). *Residential Break and Enter Prevention Pilot Project: Queensland component of the joint National Anti-Crime Strategy/National Crime Prevention Residential Break and Enter Pilot Project*, Report 1. Author.

Decker, S.H. (1998). What Burglars Say about Burglary: A Problem-Solving Approach. In T. O'Connor Shelley, & A. Grant (eds.), *Problem Oriented Policing: Crime Specific Problems, Critical Issues and Making POP Work*. Washington: Police Executive Research Forum.

Devery, C. (1992). *Mapping Local Government Areas: Assault and Break and Enter in Waverley*, General Report Series, Sydney: NSW Bureau of Crime Statistics and Research.

Developmental Crime Prevention Consortium (1999). *Pathways to prevention: Developmental and early intervention approaches to crime in Australia (Full Report)*. Canberra: National Crime Prevention.

Eck, J.E. (1998). What Do These Dots Mean? Mapping Theories with Data. In D. Weisburd, & T. McEwen (eds.), *Crime Mapping and Crime Prevention: Crime Prevention Studies Vol 8*. Monsey NY: Criminal Justice Press.

Eck, J.E. (forthcoming). Policing and Crime Event Concentration, *The Criminal Event Perspective: Advances in Criminological Theories*. New Brunswick, US: Transaction Publishers.

Ellingworth, D., Farrell, G., & Pease, K. (1995). A victim is a victim is a victim? Chronic victimisation in four sweeps of the British Crime Survey, *British Journal of Criminology*, 35(3), 360–365.

Farrell, G. (1995). Predicting and Preventing Revictimisation. In M. Tonry, & D.P. Farrington (eds.), *Building a Safer Society. Crime and Justice Vol 19*. Chicago: University of Chicago Press.

Farrell, G. & Pease, K. (1993). *Once Bitten, Twice Bitten: Repeat Victimisation and Its Implications for Crime Prevention*, Crime Prevention Unit Paper 46. London: Home Office.

Fienberg, S.E. (1980). Statistical Modelling in the Analysis of Repeated Victimisation. In S.E. Feindberg, & A.J. Reiss Jr (eds.), *Indicators of Crime and Criminal Justice: Quantitative Studies*. Washington: Bureau of Justice Statistics.

Fisher, J., Chorley, J., & Riches, M. (1999). *Residential Break and Enter Prevention Pilot Project: South Australian component of the joint National Anti-Crime Strategy/National Crime Prevention Residential Break and Enter Pilot Project*. Report 1. South Australian Attorney-General's Department.

Forrester, D., Chatterton, M., & Pease, K. (1988). *The Kirkholt Burglary Prevention Project, Rochdale*, Crime Prevention Unit Paper 13. London: Home Office.

Forrester, D., Frenz, S., O'Connor, M., & Pease, K. (1990). *The Kirkholt Burglary Prevention Project: Phase II*, Crime Prevention Unit Paper 23. London: Home Office.

Foy, B. (1999, February 11). Format for address field(s) — proposal for a standard, *Crimemap*, [On-Line] Available E-mail: listproc@aspensys.com [1999 February 11].

Goldsmith, V. & Williamson, D. (1998). Introduction to the Presentation of Cartographic Animations, [On Line] Available URL: http://everest.hunter.cuny.edu/~dougwill/nij_survey/introduction.html [1998 August 24].

Harries, K. (1995). The Ecology of Homicide and Assault: The Baltimore City and County, 1989–91, *Studies on Crime and Crime Prevention*, 4(1), 45–60.

Hindelang, M., Gottfredson, M.R., & Garofalo, J. (1978). *Victims of Personal Crime: An Empirical Foundation for a Theory of Personal Victimisation*. Cambridge MASS: Ballinger.

MICHAEL TOWNSLEY, ROSS HOMEL AND JANET CHASELING

Hirschfield, A., Bowers, K., & Brown, P.J.B. (1995). Exploring Relationships between Crime and Disadvantage on Merseyside: An Analysis using Crime Statistics, Census Data and Geographical Information Systems, *European Journal on Criminal Policy and Research*, 3(3), 93–112.

Hope, T. (1995). The Flux of Victimisation, *British Journal of Criminology*, 35(3), 327–342.

Illinois Criminal Justice Information Authority (1996). *Spatial and Temporal Analysis of Crime User's Manual*. Chicago: Author.

Janice Webb Research (1996). *Direct Line Homesafe: An Evaluation of the First Year*. Nottingham: Janice Webb Research.

Jochelson, R. (1997). *Crime and Place: An Analysis of Assaults and Robberies in Inner Sydney*, General Report Series. Sydney: NSW Bureau of Crime Statistics and Research.

Johnson, J.H., Kerper, H.B., Hayes, D.D., & Killenger, G.G. (1973). *The Recidivist Victim: A Descriptive Study*, Criminal Justice Monograph, 4(1). Texas: Sam Houstan University.

Johnson, S.D., Bowers, K., & Hirschfield, A. (1997). New Insights in the Spatial and Temporal Distribution of Repeat Victimisation, *British Journal of Criminology*, 37(2), 224–241.

Kelling, G. & Coles, C.M. (1996). *Fixing Broken Windows*. New York: Free Press.

Langan, P.A. & Farrington, D.P. (1998). *Crime and Justice in the United States and in England and Wales, 1981–96: Executive Summary*, US Department of Justice. Washington: Bureau of Justice Statistics.

Lauritsen, J.L. & Davis Quinet, K.F. (1995). Repeat Victimisation among adolescents and young Adults, *Journal of Quantitative Criminology*, 11, 143–166.

Maller, R.A. & Zhou, X. (1996). *Survival Analysis with Long Term Survivors*. Brisbane: Wiley.

Mamalian, C.A. & LaVigne, N.G. (1999). The Use of Computerised Crime Mapping by Law Enforcement: Survey Results, *National Institute of Justice Research Preview*. Washington: National Institute of Justice.

MapInfo Corporation (1998). *MapInfo Professional 5.0 User's Guide*, New York: Troy.

Morgan, F. (forthcoming). Repeat burglary in a Perth suburb: Indicator of short-term or long-term risk, *Crime Prevention Studies*.

Mukherjee, S. & Carcach, C. (1998). *Repeat Victimisation in Australia: Extent, Correlates and Implications for Crime Prevention*, Research and Policy Series No. 15. Canberra: Australian Institute of Criminology.

Mukherjee, S., Carcach, C., & Higgins, K. (1997). *A Statistical Profile of Crime in Australia*, Research and Policy Series No. 7. Canberra: Australian Institute of Criminology.

National Institute of Justice (1996). Measuring what Matters. Part One: Measures of Crime, Fear and Disorder, *A Report from the Policing Research Institute*. Washington: US Printing Service.

Nelson, J. (1980). Multiple Victimisation in American Cities: A Statistical Analysis of Rare Events, *American Journal of Sociology*, 85(4), 870–891.

Olligschlaeger, A.M. (1998). Artificial Neural Networks and Crime. In D. Weisburd, & T. McEwen (eds.), *Crime Mapping and Crime Prevention: Crime Prevention Studies Vol 8*. Monsey NY: Criminal Justice Press.

Pease, K. (1998). *Repeat Victimisation: Taking Stock*, Crime Detection and Prevention Series Paper 90. London: Home Office.

Pease, K. & Laycock, G. (1996). Revictimisation: Reducing the Heat on Hot Victims, *NIJ Research in Action Series*. Washington: National Institute of Justice.

Polvi, N., Looman, T., Humphries, C., & Pease, K. (1990). Repeat Break and Enter Victimisation: Time Course and Crime Prevention Opportunity, *Journal of Police Science and Administration*, 17(1), 8–11.

Polvi, N., Looman, T., Humphries, C., & Pease, K. (1991). The Time-Course of Repeat Burglary Victimisation, *British Journal of Criminology*, 31(4), 411–414.

Queensland Police Service (1998). *Statistical Review 1997–98*. Brisbane: GOPRINT.

Ratcliffe, J.H. & McCullagh, M.J. (1998). Identifying Repeat Victimisation with GIS, *British Journal of Criminology*, *38*(4), 651–662.

Rengert, G. (1997). Auto Theft in Central Philadelphia. In R. Homel (ed.), *Policing for Prevention: Reducing Crime, Public Intoxication and Injury, Crime Prevention Studies Vol 7*. Monsey NY: Criminal Justice Press.

Rich, T. (1995). The use of computerised mapping in crime control and prevention programs, *NIJ Research in Action Series*. Washington: National Institute of Justice.

Robinson, M. (1998). Burglary revictimisation: The time period of heightened risk, *British Journal of Criminology*, *38*(1), 78–87.

Roundtree, P.A., Land, K.C., & Miethe, T.D. (1994). Macro-Micro Integration in the Study of Victimisation: A Hierarchical Logistic Model Analysis Across Seattle Neighbourhoods, *Criminology*, *32*(3), 387–413.

Schimdt, P. & Witte, A.D. (1988). *Predicting Recidivism using Survival Models*. New York: Springer-Verlag.

Sherman, L., Gartin, P. & Buerger, M. (1989). Hot Spots f Predatory Crime: Routine Activities and the Criminology of Place, *Criminology*, *27*(1), 27–55.

Sparks, R. (1981). Multiple Victimisation: Evidence, Theory and Future Research, *Journal of Criminal Law and Criminology*, *72*, 762–778.

Sparks, R., Genn, H., & Dodd, D. (1977). *Surveying Victims*. London: Wiley.

Spelman, W. (1995). Once Bitten, Then What? Cross-sectional and Time-course Explanations of Repeat Victimisation, *British Journal of Criminology*, *32*(3), 366–383.

Taylor, G. (1999). Using Repeat Victimisation to Counter Commercial Burglary: The Leicester Experience, *Security Journal*, *12*(1), 41–52.

Tilley, N. (1993). *After Kirkholt: Theory, Method and Results of Replication*, Crime Prevention Unit Paper 47. London: Home Office.

Trickett, A., Ellingworth, D., Hope, T., & Pease, K. (1995). Crime Victimisation in the Eighties: Changes in Area and Regional Inequality, *British Journal of Criminology*, *35*(3), 343–359.

Trickett, A., Osborn, D., Seymour, J., & Pease, K. (1992). What is different about high crime areas?, *British Journal of Criminology*, *32*(1), 81–89.

Vinson, T. & Homel, R. (1975). Crime and disadvantage: the coincidence of medical and social problems in an Australian city, *British Journal of Criminology*, *15*(1), 21–31.

Waller, I. & Welsh, B.C. (1998). Reducing Crime by Harnessing International Best Practice, *National Institute of Justice Journal, October 1998*, 26–32.

[15]

PROPERTY CRIME VICTIMISATION: THE ROLES OF INDIVIDUAL AND AREA INFLUENCES

ALAN TRICKETT*, DENISE R. OSBORN and DAN ELLINGWORTH

Quantitative Criminology Group, Faculty of Economic and Social Studies, University of Manchester, Manchester M13 9PL

ABSTRACT

The likelihood of being a victim of property crime is modelled using the characteristics of the individual household and of the area. In addition to total property crime, we separately consider the components of burglary, theft and criminal damage. In all cases, both area and individual variables are significant predictors of victimisation risk, but the area is generally more important than the individual. We also find that an unexplained correlation remains between households within the same area. To caricature our overall results, young professionals living in detached or semi-detached houses in poor areas are particularly likely to fall victim to crime.

INTRODUCTION

Much is known about the characteristics of areas which vary in their rates of offenders and offending. Ecological factors, often expressed through the social disorganisation theory of Shaw and McKay (1942), provided the basis of such research over a long period. Recent empirical work for the UK in this tradition includes Sampson and Groves (1989) and Osborn *et al.* (1992), both of which use the British Crime Surveys (BCS) to obtain local area victimisation rates. Sampson and Groves set out to test the social disorganization theory explicitly; they use BCS information to create macro-level indicators of intervening dimensions and exogenous sources of social disorganisation, and find much support for their extended theoretical model. In Osborn *et al.* we employed census data at the area level to represent the characteristics of the resident community. Our results concerning the nature of areas prone to high property crime were in broad agreement with those of Sampson and Groves.

A contrasting strand of literature concerns the nature of individual differences associated with different victimisation experiences, often formalised in lifestyle and routine activity theories of crime. Using North American data, Kennedy and Forde (1990) and Miethe *et al.* (1987) find that lifestyle indicators are important predictors of household property crime. On the other hand, however, the results of Maxfield (1987) suggest that only household composition is important for household victimisation in the 1982 BCS.

---

* To whom correspondence is to be addressed

274

Considered separately, ecological and individual theories neglect the inter-relationship of criminogenic factors at the community and individual levels. Bottoms and Wiles (1992; p. 31) emphasise the complexity of "the natural and built environment, the political, economic, social and cultural contexts and structures of areas and the actions of individuals and corporate bodies within areas" which result in the spatial distribution of crime victimisation and its changes over time.

Farrington (1993) contends that, despite over fifty years of work, no separate neighbourhood or individual effect on offending rates has been demonstrated. "In investigating influences on offending, the major problem is that most allegedly criminogenic factors tend to coincide and tend to be inter-related. For example, adolescents living in physically deteriorated and socially disorganised neighbourhoods tend also to come from families with poor parental supervision and erratic parental discipline and tend also to have high impulsivity and low intelligence... The concentration and co-occurrence of these kinds of adversities makes it difficult to establish their independent, interactive and sequential influences conclusively, because no previous researcher has simultaneously measured all the most important individual, family and neighbourhood factors in any research project" (p. 7). That Farrington's provocative conclusion is tenable in relation to studies of offending rates may cause surprise and dismay. The fact that it is almost certainly true also in respect of victimisation may occasion less surprise, but no less dismay.

The victim has not been studied with the intensity of the offender. Determinants of offending, such as social disorganisation, are conceptually distinct from individual determinants like parental supervision. This is less true of area and individual determinants of victimisation. Yet they are distinct. It is perfectly possible for area and individual determinants of victimisation to have opposing influences. By incorporating both individual and area factors in the same modelling process, this paper attempts to clarify the contributions of these factors on property victimisation at one place and time.

Farrington (1993) concluded that longitudinal, and if possible experimental, studies should be undertaken to clarify the picture on offending rates. Certainly longitudinal studies of the victim would also be advantageous. Meanwhile, cross-sectional studies of data sources such as the major victimisation surveys do afford insights into how area and individual factors merge and interact to create contemporary victimisation risks. Studies of this kind are helpful in focusing resource and effort upon vulnerable groups, and in understanding the nature of their vulnerability.

In incorporating both area and individual household characteristics, this paper follows in the tradition of Sampson and Wooldredge (1987), Kennedy and Forde (1990) and Hale *et al.* (1994). The work is closest to that of Sampson and Wooldredge in examining victimisation through the BCS; like the other two studies, however, we use census data to measure area characteristics. As argued more fully in our earlier paper, Osborn *et al.* (1992), we prefer to use census data because that obtained from a sample, such as the BCS, is inevitably measured with error and measurement errors in explanatory variables lead to biased coefficient estimates.

We develop parallel sets of models for the probability of being a victim of any type of property crime and the probability of victimisation within each of three subsets of property crime (theft, burglary and criminal damage). Because we have available a richer set of explanatory variables than that of Sampson and Wooldredge, we are able to clarify the factors which distinguish victims from non-victims across the different subsets of property crime.

THE VICTIMISATION DATA

In order to model the probability of a household experiencing property crime, we use data in the binary "yes/no" form. Thus, our dependent variable takes the value unity when the household has suffered property crime victimisation over the relevant period and is zero when the household has not been so victimised. As discussed above, the victimisation probability is to be modelled using individual and area characteristics. The area of residence provides our area characteristics: to ensure that any victimisation takes place within this area, we restrict our attention to crime relating to the physical dwelling and its contents. Theft of milk bottles from the doorstep is excluded due to its trivial nature.

Victimisation information is extracted from responses to the Main Questionnaire of the 1984 BCS[1]. We use the 1984 BCS, rather than the later 1988 sweep, because of the closer proximity of the former to the 1981 Census. The reference period comprises the calendar year 1983 and the early part of 1984, with the precise part of 1984 included depending on the date of interview.

Households which moved during the reference period present a problem. They account for 7.6 percent of the 1984 BCS sample of households, but for 13.3 percent of victims of property crime as defined in this paper. Thus, these households experience nearly twice the overall rate of victimisation. Assuming the rate of moves is constant, equal proportions of the recall period would, on average, be spent in the new as in the former dwelling. However, as many as 72 percent of the property victimisations for this group occurred in the former dwelling.

Neither the date of moving nor information about the location of a former dwelling is available in the 1984 BCS. Consequently, it is not possible to relate pre-moving crime experience to the length of period involved or to appropriate area characteristics. Although we do not separately investigate victimisation at the former dwelling, our first category of any property crime at any residence obviously includes such experience.

Moving house may be an indicator of not yet having established local friendship networks. To use it in this context we need to ensure that the crime information relates only to the period after a move. A second category of interest is, therefore, victimisation in the present residence. In this analysis we do not weight households who have moved to reflect their effective reference period of less than a year, again because the data of the move is not available. We do, however, control for the shorter reference period by including a binary explanatory variable for length of residence of less than a year.

Our remaining three categories disaggregate property crime in the present residence into burglary, theft and criminal damage. Burglary is unauthorised entry (attempted or actual) into the dwelling and stealing, or attempting to steal, property. Theft is then other theft from inside (that is, by someone authorised to be in the dwelling) or from outside. Our final category, criminal damage, is defined as defacing or otherwise damaging inside or outside the dwelling.

MODELLING PROPERTY VICTIMISATION

Introduction

We wish to examine the roles played by the characteristics of the individual household and of the area in explaining property crime experience. In doing so, we include, as far as practical, those explanatory variables suggested as important by previous victimisation research. In particular, we use the results of Sampson and Wooldredge (1987) and Osborn *et al.* (1992), since these two studies are closely related to that undertaken here.

The micro level predictors are provided by the BCS itself, which reports characteristics relevant to the specific dwelling and its occupants. The Small Area Statistics from the 1981 Census are used to provide information about the locality at the level of the parliamentary ward.

Some explanatory variables appeared to play no role in explaining victimisation and were dropped from our models. Two decision rules were employed in deciding whether to exclude such an explanatory variable. Firstly, the variable had to fail to attain a significance level of ten percent across any of the five crime categories examined. Secondly, since we were interested in the relationship between individual and area effects, we always retained the variable at one level if it had a counterpart at the other aggregation level which was significant at ten percent. Thus, for example, we retain the individual level indicator denoting a single parent household even though it is never significant, because the area level proportion of single parent households is significant through the portmanteau vulnerability variable.

It may be noted that the BCS information includes the ACORN area type, which is defined at a relatively low level of aggregation on the basis of demographic, employment and housing characteristics. It has been used by Hough and Mayhew (1985) in examining victimisation risk. In our analysis, however, ACORN was not statistically significant, presumably because we adequately capture area information through other variables.

In Osborn *et al.* we also found regional effects, where region is defined at a high level of aggregation[2]. For the present study, our consistent finding across many models was that the North West and East Anglia are different from the remainder of England and Wales. Therefore, our models below include dummy variables for these two regions only.

Micro Level Variables

At this level, Sampson and Wooldredge (1987) use demographic characteristics, together with lifestyle and target attractiveness measures. They, however, used the 1982 BCS, and the latter type of information was not collected in 1984. Since, however, their variables did not play very important roles in predicting victimisation in the categories of burglary or theft, the loss of this information may not be serious. Nevertheless, target attractiveness may be an important concept and we adopt proxies as discussed below.

Target attractiveness involves the presence of goods desirable to the offender, which will be positively correlated with household income. Income information is sought in the BCS, but the high rate of non-response would imply a serious loss of information from its use. As a proxy we include a dichotomous variable for socio-economic group, which takes the value of unity when the head of the household is in a professional category.

The type of dwelling also proxies income. Further, it proxies guardianship, since detached and semi-detached houses are enclosed in their own ground which may afford more victimisation opportunities to the potential offender. We use four categories for the physical structure, with detached or semi-detached house being the base with which comparisons are made. The category of flats which are not self-contained captures households who may be particularly vulnerable due to the difficulty of adequately securing their properties.

Two further variables relating to housing and the house market are length of residence at the current address and tenure. Mention has already been made of moving house as a possible indicator of not yet having established local friendship networks. Here we employ a number of categories, with more than ten years at the current address being the base for comparison. The binary tenure variable is unity when the household lives in rented accommodation. Tenure and length of residence enable us to study at the micro level the influence of the housing market and residential mobility, which have been considered at more aggregate levels by Bottoms *et al.* (1992) and Sampson and Groves (1989).

For some potential offenders, particularly for crimes of criminal damage, ethnicity[3] may be a factor in target attractiveness. To investigate this, our ethnicity variable distinguishes separately Afro-Caribbean and Indian sub-continent from the base category of white plus "others".

Particular types of households which may be especially vulnerable due to lifestyle or lack of guardianship include single parent and one person households. The former is included in our models, but the latter was excluded under our decision rules. Similarly, we could find no effect for the presence of children. The

278

age of the head of the household will proxy, to some extent, both lifestyle and guardianship; this variable is included.

Area Level Variables

Previous ecological studies in the tradition of Shaw and McKay (1942) indicate a large number of variables which may be included to provide a picture of the community context and social cohesion of the area within which the household resides; see Sampson and Groves (1989), Sampson and Wooldredge (1987). We found, however, that complex relationships existed among the area level variables we were investigating, which made it very difficult to determine separate effects for some variables. We alleviated this problem by representing some aspects of the nature of areas through portmanteau variables formed from the original Census information.[4]

It has already been noted that we use the Census Small Area Statistics as the source for our area characteristics. Our data refers to the parliamentary ward within which the household resides. To facilitate comparison of effects across variables, the data on each Census variable was standardised by subtraction of its mean and division by its standard deviation.

We investigate a number of indicators for area deprivation and family disruption, including (each expressed as a percentage of all households): households with no car, having more than one person per room, living in accommodation which is not self contained, and single parent households. The final two were used in modelling area property crime in Osborn *et al.* (1992), but no role was found there for the first variable. For the present study we have summed the percentages of single parent households and households living in non self-contained accommodation (after standardisation) to form a single indicator. We refer to this indicator as vulnerability, since both variables are associated with a lack of guardianship. The percentage of households with no car is our measure of poverty. In contrast to the deprivation measures, the percentage of households in the professional classes is included as a measure of affluence. This may be important since an affluent area may attract offenders who live in other areas.

Sampson and Wooldredge (1987) and Osborn *et al.* (1992) include the area percentage of single person households, arguing that this may be associated with decreased guardianship. Both also include measures of the labour market. In this study, however, neither single person households nor employment/unemployment were significant and both have been excluded.

Areas with low residential stability may be expected to have low levels of community guardianship and hence increased victimisation risks of all types. Stability is captured here through the percentages of households in public authority housing and in privately rented accommodation, together with the percentage of households which moved during the year prior to the Census. Of these, 'private rented' and 'moved' indicate the presence of households who may change address at short notice; these two variables were also highly correlated and (after standardisation) they were summed to form our portmanteau variable transience.

The percentage of flats, used by Sampson and Wooldredge (1987) was investigated but dropped due to statistical insignificance. However, a direct measure of urbanisation, namely, people per hectare, is included. This latter variable, measuring population density, played an important role in the models of Osborn *et al.* (1992).

Additional variables are used to capture the demographic profile of the area. In particular, the percentages of adult females, elderly and youths between 16 and 24 are included. The last may capture the presence of potential young offenders, while the elderly may provide guardianship for the area. We represent the elderly by the percentage of the population over state retiring age. In common with our earlier ecological analysis (Osborn *et al.*, 1992), we could find no predictive power for the percentage of under 5 year olds; in contrast with that work, however, the variable for 5 to 15 year olds was insignificant for the models here and was dropped. Although imperfect, the Census measure of the ethnic minority percentage is included to represent the racial diversity of the area.

Methodological Issues

We have now discussed the dependent variables (in section 2) and the explanatory variables (section 3), so that the one missing ingredient is the model for combining these. Due to the dichotonomous nature of our victimisation data, linear regression is inappropriate. Therefore, we have employed logistic (or logit) regression which ensures that the estimated probability of victimisation always lies between zero and unity; see, for example, McCullagh and Neldor (1989; pp. 107–108).

Logistic regression is a type of nonlinear multiple regression used to predict the probability of household i being a victim of property crime in a specific category. We denote this victimisation probability by π_i. Although not linear for π_i, logistic regression can be considered as a linear regression which predicts the log odds ratio, namely the (natural) logarithm of the odds ratio $\pi_i/(1-\pi_i)$. Nevertheless, because it does not predict the probability by a linear function, a logit coefficient cannot be directly interpreted as the change in the probability of victimisation arising from a change in the corresponding explanatory variable.

To ease interpretation, we have chosen to present the exponential of each logit coefficient, denoted in the tables as exp(B), rather than the coefficient itself. Since the exponential is the inverse of the natural logarithm, the exponential of the log odds ratio yields the odds ratio $\pi_i/(1-\pi_i)$. Then exp(B) is the estimated multiplicative effect on the odds ratio of increasing the corresponding explanatory variable by one unit. Consider, for example, the binary explanatory variable 'renting'. An exp(B) of 1.5 for this variable would imply that a household living

280

in rented accommodation would face an estimated odds ratio fifty percent greater than a household similar in all other respects except that it was an owner-occupier. If the probability of victimisation is small, $\pi_i/(1-\pi_i)$ is approximately equal to π_i and the multiplicative effect given by exp(B) also applies approximately to the probability itself.

In all cases an exponent greater than unity implies that the variable or category considered has a positive effect on the probability of victimisation, with an exponent less than unity having the opposite implication. Readers may wish to compare our results with the earlier ones of Hale *et al.* (1994), Kennedy and Forde (1990), or Sampson and Wooldredge (1987), all of whom present the estimated logit coefficients. Since a negative logit coefficient yields an exp(B) of less than one, and a positive logit coefficient an exp(B) greater than one, the direction of effect is simple to compare.

In addition to these exponents, we show the observed significance level (denoted sig) for each variable or category. This is the (two-sided) probability of obtaining a more extreme coefficient than that estimated when the variable has no influence on victimisation. Once again, for comparison with previous studies, it may be noted that a significance level of less than .05 is effectively equivalent to a "t-ratio" greater than 2 in absolute value. For a categorical variable with more than two categories, an overall significance level is also presented: this refers to a joint test on all categories compared with the base. It should be noted that this significance level is given on the line containing the variable name, which also shows the base category in parentheses.

The models reported in the tables are estimated using variables at both the micro and region/area levels. Goodness-of-fit is measured by the conventional model chi-square statistic, which compares the estimated model to one which has no explanatory variables other than a constant.

In order to examine the explanatory power of the variables at the two different levels of aggregation, we also estimated separate logit models using only regional variables and area characteristics (thereby omitting the individual level variables) and using only individual characteristics (omitting the region/area level variables); in each case a constant was included. At the base of our tables we report the decrease in the model chi-square which results when each of these models is compared with the overall model with both individual and region/area variables. Since it happens that thirteen coefficients are used for each of individual and region/area, these enable a comparison to be made on the relative explanatory power of micro versus macro variables. The significance of the omitted variables is also tested using a chi-square distribution with 13 degrees of freedom (McCullagh and Neldor, 1989; p. 119).

RESULTS AND DISCUSSION

Introduction

As noted above, property victimisation is studied in five categories. The first two categories differ only in including or excluding victimisation in a previous residence for those who have moved within the reference period. The final three categories separately consider burglary, theft and criminal damage victimisation at the present residence.

The immediately following discussion relates to the effect of including or excluding crimes at any previous residences during the reference period. We then consider in turn the property crime victimisation of any type at the present address, while the results for the separate models of burglary, theft and criminal damage are discussed in the section following. Diagnostic tests which check the validity of the logistic regression assumptions are presented in the final section where we focus particularly on an explained area effect which we uncover.

All Residences Compared with Present Residence

Table 1 shows the results using, as the dependent variable, property crime victimisation at all reference period residences and at the present residence. The only coefficient showing substantial change is that for being at the current address for under one year. In each case this coefficient is highly statistically significant, but moving apparently increases the probability of victimisation for the former model and (self-evidently) decreases it for the latter.

A move during the recall period is associated with a higher probability of property crime victimisation when all residences are considered. Indeed, exp(B) of 1.7796 indicates that a move increases the odds ratio by an amazing 78 percent. To our knowledge, no previous study using the crime survey data has examined this effect, and it is so important here that it certainly warrants further investigation.

The relationship between moving house and victimisation is no doubt complex. Intuitively the most important factor would be that being victimised enhances or introduces a determination to move. Possible other alternatives are that a For Sale notice is a clue to burglars that a house may be unoccupied or, if occupied, may elicit less guardianship by neighbours who know that the potential victim will soon be leaving.

The exp(B) value of .55 for the category of 'under a year' implies that the odds ratio for victimisation at the present address is almost halved by a move. This is compatible with the period at the current address being, on average, half the total reference period.

Although the model chi-square statistic is highly significant for both models, a larger value is obtained when all crimes are considered. This is presumably because there are more victimisations to be explained. In both cases, more

282

TABLE 1

Logistic Regression Results for All Property Crime

Variable	All Residences		Present Residence Only	
	Exp(B)	Sig	Exp(B)	Sig
HOUSE STRUCTURE (Detached/Semi)		.0491**		.0412**
Terraced House	.8542	.0346**	.8253	.0124**
Self-Contained Flat	.9698	.8081	.9577	.7414
Not Self-Contained Flat	.6188	.0417**	.6683	.1035
HOW LONG AT PRESENT ADDRESS (Over 10 years)		.0000**		.0000**
5 to 10 years	1.1044	.2612	1.1107	.2368
2 to 5 years	1.3811	.0004**	1.3891	.0003**
1 to 2 years	1.1324	.3391	1.1111	.4230
Under 1 year	1.7796	.0000**	.5496	.0001**
HOUSE TENURE: RENTING	1.2445	.0039**	1.1695	.0458**
PROFESSIONAL SOCIO-ECONOMIC GROUP	1.4776	.0000**	1.4774	.0000**
ETHNICITY OF RESPONDENT (White and 'others')		.0346**		.0314**
Afro-Caribbean	.5976	.0459**	.5625	.0316**
Indian Sub-continent	1.3709	.1347	1.3371	.1776
SINGLE PARENT HOUSEHOLD	1.1964	.3218	1.1902	.3642
AGE OF HEAD OF HOUSEHOLD	.9855	.0000**	.9856	.0000**
REGION (Rest of England)		.0005**		.0001**
North West	1.3292	.0015**	1.3795	.0004**
East Anglia	.6325	.0294**	.6034	.0202**
AREA VARIABLES				
VULNERABILITY	1.2124	.0000**	1.2244	.0000**
TRANSIENCE	.9022	.0009**	.8994	.0009**
PEOPLE IN ETHNIC MINORITY	.9893	.8287	.9911	.8595
PEOPLE OVER STATE RETIRING AGE	.8861	.0192**	.9066	.0657*
PEOPLE PER HECTARE	1.0253	.5694	1.0241	.5990
PEOPLE AGED 16–24	1.1871	.0015**	1.1824	.0026**
ADULT FEMALES	1.1129	.0434**	1.0817	.1509
ADULTS IN PROFESSIONAL SOCIO-ECONOMIC CLASS	.9907	.8730	.9606	.5083
HOUSEHOLDS IN PUBLIC AUTHORITY HOUSING	.8913	.0305**	.8950	.0413**
HOUSEHOLDS WITH MORE THAN ONE PERSON PER ROOM	.9170	.1481	.9083	.1176
HOUSEHOLDS WITH NO CAR	1.3074	.0009**	1.3033	.0014**
Constant		.0000**		.0000**

TABLE 1 continued

	GOODNESS-OF-FIT			
Test	Statistic	Sig	Statistic	Sig
Overall Model χ^2	440.38	.0000**	393.80	.0000**
Decrease in χ^2: Individual Variables Omitted	173.64	.0000**	139.63	.0000**
Decrease in χ^2: Region and Area Variables Omitted	230.06	.0000**	232.09	.0000**

* Statistically Significant at 10% level
** Statistically Significant at 5% level

explanatory power is obtained using the region and area variables alone compared with the individual variables alone. Indeed, the model chi-square using only region/area variables is more than 60 percent that of the overall model, with this rising to almost 65 percent when victimisation at the present residence is considered. Thus, it appears that for property crime in aggregate, the place of residence is more important in determining the risk of victimisation than the characteristics of the individual household.

In the subsequent discussion we examine victimisation experience for the present residence only, using the 'under one year' category to control for the different length of reference period for households who have moved.

Victimisation at the Present Residence

The professional socio-economic group face a substantially increased risk of victimisation, in line with the proposition that such households represent attractive targets. Indeed, compared to non-professionals, being a professional increases the odds ratio by almost fifty percent. It is also the case that the base house structure category of detached or semi-detached dwellings face a greater risk than other categories, which is also in accord with their being more attractive targets. In comparison with this base, terraced houses exhibit the most significant effect, but that of non self-contained flats is the most substantial in terms of the size of effect as measured through exp(B). Indeed, exp(B) indicates that being in this last category reduces the odds ratio by about one-third compared with a detached or semi-detached dwelling. Thus, the reduction in attractiveness appears to be more important than the lack of guardianship implied by not living in self-contained accommodation.

According to Table 1, households living in rented accommodation face higher victimisation risk than those living in owned accommodation. This renting effect is, however, only just significant at the 5 percent level.

In accord with people forming friendship networks over time and, through these, guardianship being increased, we find that those living more than ten years at the current address have lower victimisation risk than others. It is interesting, however, that the highest victimisation risk appears to be faced two to five years after arrival. Indeed, this two to five year effect is here highly significant compared to ten years of residence.

The results for ethnicity indicate that the Afro-Caribbean and Indian sub-continent groups are, apparently, different from each other, but only the former face significantly different risks from whites. Indeed, contrary to the prediction that non-whites may be targets, this Afro-Caribbean group has an estimated odds ratio a little over half that of an otherwise comparable white household.

Other results which do conform to our expectations based on lifestyle and guardianship are those for single parent households and the age of head of household. Although the significance level for the former is not impressive, only two percent of the sample constitutes single parent households, so that there is relatively little information on the effect. The exp(B) for age of head of household implies that each additional year decreases the odds ratio by about one and a half percent and this is very highly significant.

The unexplained regional influences for the North West of England and East Anglia, mentioned in section 3, are evident for the present residence results in Table 1.

We turn now to the area effects captured at the parliamentary ward level. Not all the variables used here are important in Table 1: the ethnic minority, population density (people per hectare), the percentages of adult females and of adults in professional socio-economic classes together with households with more than one person per room all have insignificant effects.

On the other hand, four area variables are very powerful predictors of an individual household's victimisation risk. These are our portmanteau vulnerability and transience measures, together with the population aged 16 to 24 households with no car. Perhaps surprisingly, the first two variables have effects in opposite directions. As predicted, victimisation risk increases with the reduced guardianship and increased social disorganisation indicated by higher values of area vulnerability (single parent households and households not living in self-contained accommodation). In contrast, area transience (percentage of households who moved and in private rented accommodation) apparently reduces property crime risks, contrary to prior expectations. It is difficult to rationalise higher levels of residential mobility leading to lower victimisation risk in general. The result obtained here could be peculiar to the United Kingdom in the early 1980s, where recession hit many areas hard and there was pressure to move in order to obtain employment.

We argued in Osborn *et al*. (1992) that the population of 16 to 24 year olds may represent potential offenders, and here we again find their presence in an area increases risk. Our earlier ecological study could, however, find no role for the percentage of households with no car. In contrast to that result, this variable

285

is highly significant in Table 1, with an increase of one standard deviation in the percentage of households without a car increasing the odds ratio by almost a third. Measured in those terms, this is the strongest effect recorded in the table by any area variable and indicates the role of area poverty in property crime risk.

To characterise our results, the households facing the largest property victimisation risk are young, affluent, professional households living in rented accommodation within a deprived area of North West England. The next sub-section develops such characterisations.

Examples of Victimisation Probabilities

To indicate the impact of individual and area influences in a different way to that of Table 1, we examine here the estimated risks faced by six exemplars of households in two different types of areas in each of two regions. Detailed descriptions of these exemplars and areas are contained in the Appendix. The households are characterised mainly through the attributes of the head of the household as being young, mid-age or retired and professional or non-professional. Two areas in the North West, namely Fallowfield and Broadheath, and two areas in East Anglia, Kings Hedges and Ely Northern, are used for comparison purposes. Of these, Fallowfield and Kings Hedges are relatively central within conurbations, whereas Broadheath and Ely Northern are less urban in nature.

Table 2 gives the estimated probabilities of suffering property crime victimisation for each of these six household types within each of the four areas. Once again, the area data is from the 1981 Census. The coefficient estimates underlying Table 1 relating to the present residence have been used in calculating these probabilities.

TABLE 2

Estimated Probability of Being the Victim of Any Property Crime (Present Residence Only)

Household Type	Area			
	Fallowfield	Broadheath	Kings Hedges	Ely Northern
Young Professional	.5489	.3373	.3159	.0892
Young Non-Professional	.4418	.2495	.2318	.0601
Mid-Aged Professional	.4319	.2413	.2240	.0576
Mid-Aged Non-Professional	.3469	.1818	.1678	.0406
Retired Professional	.3355	.1744	.1608	.0390
Retired Non-Professional	.2478	.1211	.1112	.0258

286

Whatever the household type, those in the North West are more likely to suffer victimisation than their counterparts in East Anglia. Likewise, whatever the household type, those in urban areas are more prone to victimisation than their counterparts in the less urban areas. Holding the area and the head of household's age constant, the professional is substantially more vulnerable than the non-professional. Irrespective of professional status, the older the head of household then the less likely is the prospect of victimisation. All these effects follow directly from the estimated coefficients of Table 1.

Perhaps more interesting, however, is the fact that even the most vulnerable stereotype household, namely the young professional, is less at risk in Ely Northern than the least vulnerable household stereotype in any of the other three areas. Further, it appears that the retired non-professional in Ely Northern faces a victimisation probability little more than one tenth of that faced in Fallowfield. Within an area, the greatest contrast of young professional to retired non-professional in a relative sense is in Ely Northern, where the former faces more than treble the probability of the latter.

In making such comparisons it should be noted that fairly extreme area types have been selected, and this is emphasised by contrasting the North West with East Anglia. The age range of 28 (for the "young") to 66 (for the "retired") has, however, been chosen as being typical rather than extreme. Nevertheless, the relatively greater impact of the region and area compared with the individual is also compatible with their roles in terms of goodness-of-fit as reported in Table 1.

The Components of Property Crime

Having discussed the factors which influence overall property victimisation risk, here we concentrate on comparing these influences across the three categories of burglary, theft and criminal damage. Once again, we discount the coefficient for 'having lived at the current address for less than a year' because of the shorter effective reference period for households which have moved.

Looking across the three categories in Table 3, only two coefficients are significant at the five percent level across all three. Both are micro-level, and they relate to having lived at the same address between two to five years and being in a professional socio-economic group. Thus, it does appear that the three categories are genuinely different, so that it is appropriate to model them separately.

Further inspection reveals, however, that similar predictors apply for burglary and theft, which can be distinguished from criminal damage. Thus, age of head of household, area vulnerability and transience are highly important predictors for the first two categories, but not for the third. On the other hand, living in a terraced house appears to offer significant protection from criminal damage while being of Indian ethnic origin increases the risk of such damage.

At the area level, the purely demographic variables (the percentages of elderly, of 16 to 24 year olds, and of adult females) have their strongest roles in predicting criminal damage. The effect implied is compatible with young adults providing a local supply of potential offenders for criminal damage, with the presence of a higher proportion of old people, though not of women indicating increased area guardianship.

Indeed, overall, the area predictors appear to be remarkably strong for criminal damage. In addition to the demographic effects already discussed, houses in deprived areas (represented by a high percentage of households without cars) and with few professional people, but low percentages of public area housing, are especially prone to these crimes. The strength of these effects is underlined by the fact that 70 percent of the overall model chi-square can be achieved by the use of region and area variables alone.

Before leaving Table 3, we should make a few other remarks in relation to the results for burglary and theft. Being a professional household or, possibly, from the Indian sub-continent, residing in the North West of England and in an area with a high percentage of no car households appear to be important in determining the victimisation probability for burglary, but the effects of these variables are less strong for theft. On the other hand, living in rented accommodation and in East Anglia (the latter influence being downward) play stronger roles for theft. Also, the overall model chi-square values in Table 3 indicate that, in common with Sampson and Wooldredge (1987), our models explain burglary better than theft.

Another important difference between burglary and theft is the relative importance of the region and area variables. The micro variables alone yield a model chi-square 41 percent that of the overall value for burglary, but 59 percent in the case of theft. Indeed, theft is the only one of the categories studied here for which the explanatory power of the micro variables exceeds that of the macro level predictors.

Diagnostic Tests and Multilevel Modelling

Here we turn to some tests on the validity of the assumptions underlying the logistic regressions results of Tables 1 and 3.

In principle, all the statistical significance tests reported above depend on the validity of the logit specification used for modelling victimisation probabilities. This logit specification itself has many aspects and Table 4 shows test statistics and significance values[5] for tests of the assumption that the victimisation log odds ratio is a linear function of the explanatory variables, of the use of the logistic distribution and of the assumption of independence of observations. The details of the tests are discussed in Trickett *et al.* (1993).

Due to its importance below, it should be noted that the estimation and statistical testing of the conventional logistic regression model assumes that the

288

TABLE 3

Logistic Regression Results for Burglary, Theft and Criminal Damage

Variable	Burglary		Theft		Criminal Damage	
	Exp (B)	Sig	Exp (B)	Sig	Exp (B)	Sig
HOUSE STRUCTURE (Detached/Semi)		.2478		.6840		.0062**
Terraced House	.9172	.4754	.9542	.6621	.6645	.0007**
Self-Contained Flat	1.0894	.6534	.8861	.5197	.7462	.1551
Not Self-Contained Flat	.5240	.0954*	.6715	.2508	.5354	.1368
HOW LONG AT PRESENT ADDRESS (Over 10 years)		.0003**		.0001**		.0051**
5 to 10 years	1.0906	.5465	1.1903	.1610	.9984	.9909
2 to 5 years	1.5283	.0028**	1.3549	.0178**	1.4078	.0143**
1 to 2 years	1.4599	.0510*	1.0084	.9641	1.0495	.8183
Under 1 year	.6351	.0577*	.4797	.0013**	.6050	.0439**
HOUSE TENURE: RENTING	1.1568	.2408	1.3166	.0113**	1.2608	.0557*
PROFESSIONAL SOCIO-ECONOMIC GROUP	1.7840	.0000**	1.4589	.0006**	1.3247	.0214**
ETHNICITY OF RESPONDENT (White and 'others')		.1350		.3854		.0757*
Afro-Caribbean	.7353	.3947	.6263	.2241	.7111	.4060
Indian Sub-continent	1.6515	.0842*	.7653	.4637	1.8715	.0409**
SINGLE PARENT HOUSEHOLD	1.2334	.4315	.9852	.9553	1.3626	.2706
AGE OF HEAD OF HOUSEHOLD	.9833	.0000**	.9792	.0000**	.9953	.2374
REGION (Rest of England)		.0000**		.0213**		.1583
North West	1.7985	.0000**	1.2108	.1449	1.1925	.2092
East Anglia	.7986	.5451	.4490	.0208**	.6258	.1608
AREA VARIABLES						
VULNERABILITY	1.2608	.0000**	1.2935	.0000**	1.1017	.1125
TRANSIENCE	.8752	.0084**	.9085	.0344**	.9287	.1303
PEOPLE IN ETHNIC MINORITY	.9505	.4728	.9762	.7352	1.0315	.6927
PEOPLE OVER STATE RETIRING AGE	.9277	.4020	1.1398	.0725*	.6631	.0000**
PEOPLE PER HECTARE	1.1507	.0311**	.8814	.0538*	.8220	.2549
PEOPLE AGED 16–24	1.0767	.4182	1.1379	.0935*	1.2534	.0091**
ADULT FEMALES	1.0501	.5678	.9607	.5909	1.4314	.0001**
ADULTS IN PROFESSIONAL CLASS	1.1805	.0942*	.9055	.2464	.8023	.0267**
HOUSEHOLDS IN PUBLIC AUTHORITY HOUSING	.8741	.1182	.9244	.3023	.8190	.0182**
HOUSEHOLDS WITH MORE THAN ONE PERSON/ROOM	.9795	.8159	.9039	.2513	.8448	.0787*
HOUSEHOLDS WITH NO CAR	1.6476	.0002**	1.1240	.2995	1.3436	.0257**
Constant		.0000**		.0000**		.0000**

TABLE 3 continued

Test	Statistic	Sig	Statistic	Sig	Statistic	Sig
Overall Model χ^2	301.60	.0000**	176.44	.0000**	148.46	.0000**
Decrease in χ^2: Individual Variables Omitted	91.34	.0000**	92.58	.0000**	43.40	.0000**
Decrease in χ^2: Region and Area Variables Omitted	177.35	.0000**	71.87	.0000**	109.53	.0000**

* Statistically Significant at 10% level
** Statistically Significant at 5% level

TABLE 4

Diagnostics for Logistic Regression Models

Dependent Variable	Test	Statistic	P-Value
	Functional Form	0.487	.4853
Any Property Crime	Logistic Distribution	0.079	.7787
All Residences	Independence	12.77	.0004**
	Intra-ward Correlation	0.0145	
	Functional Form	0.001	.9748
Any Property Crime	Logistic Distribution	0.009	.9244
Present Residence Only	Independence	10.95	.0009**
	Intra-ward Correlation	0.0135	
	Functional Form	3.454	.0631*
Burglary	Logistic Distribution	3.347	.0673*
Present Residence	Independence	5.828	.0158**
	Intra-ward Correlation	0.0098	
	Functional Form	2.309	.1286
Theft	Logistic Distribution	2.710	.0997*
Present Residence	Independence	9.673	.0019**
	Intra-ward Correlation	0.0127	
	Functional Form	0.063	.8018
Criminal Damage	Logistic Distribution	0.033	.8580
Present Residence	Independence	4.825	.0280**
	Intra-ward Correlation	0.0089	

*Statistically significant at 10% level
** Statistically Significant at 5% level

Burglary

observations have been selected independently of each other. In the present context, a simple random sample of households in England and Wales would conform to the independence assumption. Although it is known that the BCS sampling scheme does not yield a simple random sample, the independence test is designed to detect whether the observations can be treated as if they resulted from a random sample.

For the functional form and logistic distribution checks, only burglary gives any cause for concern. Even here, however, these two test statistics are acceptable at a five percent level of significance, so that these test results are generally satisfactory.

On the other hand, each of the five models fails the independence test at any conventional significance level, and this result necessitates further consideration. This test is designed to ascertain whether, having allowed for the effects of all explanatory variables, there remains some unexplained correlation between individual households within a ward. Due to the interest in this correlation, its estimated value is shown in Table 4, in addition to the statistic which tests its significance. The results clearly show that the correlation is numerically small, but nevertheless important statistically. The sampling strategy of the BCS enables some interpretation to be placed on this outcome.

The BCS sampling scheme implies that households are selected from a geographical subset of a ward; namely, a polling district. This close clustering of respondents may result in a more homogeneous set of households than would result from a random sample from the entire ward. Thus, we may be detecting what could be called a neighbourhood effect at a level between the individual and the ward. It is plausible that community variables of the type used by Sampson and Wooldredge (1987) may be able to explain this correlation. Nevertheless, there remain statistical problems consequent upon aggregating up sample information and, in any case, they did not test whether such an unexplained intra-ward correlation was present for their models.

While Miethe (1991) was unable to establish empirically the existence of a neighbourhood effect, the results here indicate that it may exist. Whether it is due to the grouping of individual households in close proximity, to the characteristics of the neighbourhood itself in some unmeasured way, or to the interaction of the two, cannot be established at the present time. This does, however, represent a question for future research, as the implications for crime prevention are obvious.

For this study, having established the significance of the 'within ward' correlation, we estimated multilevel logit models which explicitly allow for this correlation through the use of an unobserved random component common to each household within a ward (Goldstein, 1991). Although this multilevel modelling confirmed the existence of this ward level component, the estimated coefficients for the explanatory variables and their significance levels changed only very marginally. This is compatible with the finding of Table 4 that the correlation is weak, despite its statistical significance. Therefore, to conserve space, the multilevel estimates are not reported here, but detailed results are available from the authors on request.

CONCLUSIONS AND SUGGESTIONS FOR FURTHER RESEARCH

The findings of this study emphasise that both area and individual characteristics play important roles in determining the likelihood of property crime victimisation. A number of aspects of this deserve further comment.

The first is that area and individual characteristics combine in ways which make intuitive sense but which do not operate in the same direction. For instance, the proportion of no car households in an area is associated with higher risks of property crime, particularly for burglary and criminal damage. However, target choice within an area falls heavily on professional people living in detached and semi-detached dwellings. To caricature, richer people in poorer areas suffer property crime particularly heavily. Conversely, relatively low risk is faced by poor people living in rich areas.

Secondly, where the household lives generally plays a stronger role in determining the probability of victimisation than the individual level characteristics. This supports the work of Rengert and Wasilchick (1985) and Carter and Hill (1979) which showed that offenders generally operate in areas in which they feel comfortable. Thus, it appears that target selection is determined firstly by the area characteristics and secondly by the nature of the individual household within that area.

Although the points just made about the role of individual and region/area apply broadly whatever type of property crime is considered, the strength of the relative effects of the separate variables are not the same across the categories of burglary, theft and criminal damage. In particular, in contrast to these first two categories, the demographic make-up of the area of residence dominates the risk of experiencing criminal damage. Variables, such as age of head of household, which are highly important for the other two categories appear to play no role for criminal damage. Also, theft, in contrast to the other two categories, is explained more by the individual than by the place.

The fourth aspect meriting attention is the fascinating high property victimisation risks borne by those who move. Neighbourhood effects on offending are testable by examining the change in criminality of those who move (see Osborn 1980). This has important theoretical as well as practical implications. Similarly, the possibility that those who move house take their victimisation risks with them is an important testing ground for theories about the contribution of victim lifestyles to the risks they bear. Further, if moving households do take high risks with them, there is then a tension in relation to our finding above that the area is more important than the individual in determining victimisation risk. We intend to address this issue in further research.

This study has focused on the probability of a household suffering property crime victimisation. Our earlier work, including Trickett *et al.* (1992) and Osborn

292

et al. (1992), has emphasised that multiple victimisation is crucial to area crime rates, and that its determinants may not be the same as those for the simple form of victimisation considered here. Our current work is building on the present study to see whether the roles of the individual and area are different for multiple versus simple victimisation. We also intend to pursue the role and interpretation of the unexplained intra-ward correlation detected for victimisation.

APPENDIX: HOUSEHOLD STEREOTYPES AND THEIR AREAS

A1. Household Stereotypes

The household stereotypes of Section 4.4 were based principally on the characteristics of the head of the household. The six stereotypes are defined as follows:

Young Professional:

28 years old, buying a semi-detached house and having lived there between 2 and 5 years.

Young Non-professional:

28 years old, renting a terraced house and having lived there between 2 and 5 years.

Mid-age Professional:

45 years old, buying a semi-detached house and having lived there between 5 and 10 years.

Mid-age Non-professional:

45 years old, buying a terraced house and having lived there between 5 and 10 years.

Retired Professional:

66 years old, owning a detached house and having lived there over 10 years.

Retired Non-professional:

66 years old, renting a terraced house and having lived there over 10 years.

A2. Characteristics of the Four Selected Areas

To give the background for the areas in which the stereotype households of Section 4.4 have been located for comparative purposes, the table below gives the standardised data for the area variables pertinent to each of the four areas:

	Fallowfield	Broadheath	Kings Hedges	Ely Northern
Vulnerability	1.7537	−0.6869	2.4214	−1.0477
Transience	1.0399	−1.2581	0.0700	1.3260
Ethnic minority	1.5711	−0.3617	−0.1352	−0.4484
Over state retiring age	−0.1440	−0.4543	−1.3861	0.4802
People per hectare	2.6539	−0.1665	1.2188	−1.1081
People aged 16–24	1.2389	−0.4696	1.0593	−0.7695
Adult females	0.3237	−0.2821	0.5907	−1.0096
Professional class	−1.1727	0.2153	−0.8078	1.9998
Public authority housing	0.5071	−0.8410	2.1671	−0.2168
More than 1 person per room	1.6704	−0.6139	0.0891	−0.7726
Households with no car	1.7279	−0.4639	0.1175	−0.9494

The Constant term for the present residence model of Table 1, included for readers who may wish to calculate their own probabilities, is −1.2679.

NOTES

1   The 1984 BCS selected addresses on the basis of a multi-stage stratified sample, using the electoral register as the sample frame. The method is detailed in the Technical Report (NOP Market Research Ltd., 1985). For the present purposes, it should be noted that the resulting sample of 11,030 individuals aged at least 16 was drawn from 600 parliamentary electoral wards. Although sampling ultimately was by individual, the questionnaire sought information about property crime experience for the entire household.
2   Specifically, the Registrar-General's standard classification was used. This divides England into eight areas: the South East, South West, West Midlands, East Midlands, East Anglia, North West, North, and Yorkshire and Humberside. Wales is a separate region.

294

3   Ethnicity relates to the respondent and was coded by the interviewer. Samples in the Afro-Ca-
     ribbean and Indian categories were relatively small (1.6 and 1.7 percent respectively of the
     total sample compared with 96.3 for white).
4   Where variables were combined, statistical tests were always performed to check the validity
     of the combination.
5   In each case, under the null hypothesis that the specification is correct, the test statistic is
     asymptotically distributed as chi-squared with one degree of freedom.

ACKNOWLEDGEMENTS

The support of the Economic and Social Research Council (ESRC), under award
number R000233150, is gratefully acknowledged. We would also like to thank
our colleagues in the Manchester Quantitative Criminology Group, especially
Tim Hope, Ken Pease and the late Cathie Marsh, together with Pat Mayhew of
the Home Office.

REFERENCES

Bottoms, A.E., Claytor, A.C. and Wiles, P. (1992). Housing markets and residential community
    crime careers. In *Crime, Policing and Place: Essays in Environmental Criminology* (D.J. Evans,
    N.R. Fyfe and D.T. Herbert, eds). Routledge; London.
Bottoms, A.E. and Wiles, P. (1992). Explanations of crime and place. In *Crime, Policing and Place:
    Essays in Environmental Criminology* (D.J. Evans, N.R. Fyfe and D.T. Herbert, eds). Routledge;
    London.
Carter, R.L. and Hill, K.Q. (1979). *The Criminal's Image of the City*. Pergamon; New York.
Farrington, D.P. (1993). Have any individual, family or neighbourhood influences on offending
    been demonstrated conclusively? In *Integrating Individual and Ecological Aspects of Crime*
    (D.P. Farrington, R.J. Sampson and P.-O.H. Wikstrom, eds). National Council of Crime Preven-
    tion; Stockholm; Sweden.
Goldstein, H. (1991). Nonlinear multilevel models with an application to discrete response data.
    Biometrika, **73**, 43–56.
Hale, C., Peck, P. and Salked, J. (1994). The structural determinants of fear of crime: an analysis
    using census and crime survey data from England and Wales. *International Review of Victimo-
    logy*, **3**, 211–233.
Hough, M. and Mayhew, P. (1985). *Taking Account of Crime: Key Findings from the Second British
    Crime Survey*. Home Office Research Study No. 85. Her Majesty's Stationery Office: London.
Kennedy, L.W. and Forde, D.R. (1990). Routine activities and crime: an analysis of victimisation
    in Canada. *Criminology*, **28**, 137–152.
McCullagh, P. and Neldor, J.A. (1989). *Generalized Linear Models*, second edition. Chapman and
    Hall; London.
Maxfield, M.G. (1987). Household composition, routine activity, and victimisation: a comparative
    analysis. *Journal of Quantitative Criminology*, **3**, 301–320.
Miethe, T.D. (1991). Citizen-based crime control activity and victimization risks: an examination
    of displacement and free-rider effects. *Criminology*, **29**, 419–439.
Miethe, T.D., Stafford, M. and Scott Long, J. (1987). Social differentiation in criminal victimiza-
    tion: a test of routine activities/lifestyle theory. *American Sociological Review*, **52**, 184–194.
NOP Market Research Limited (1985). *1984 British Crime Survey: Technical Report*. NOP;
    Southampton.

Osborn, D.R., Trickett, A. and Elder, R. (1992). Area characteristics and regional variates as determinants of area property crime levels. *Journal of Quantitative Criminology*, **8**, 265–285.

Osborn, S.G. (1980). Moving home, leaving London and delinquent trends. *British Journal of Criminology*, **20**, 54–61.

Rengert, G. and Wasilchick, J. (1985). *Suburban Burglary*. Charles C. Thomas; Springfield Illinois.

Sampson, R.J. and Groves, W.B. (1989). Community structure and crime: testing social-disorganisation theory. *American Journal of Sociology*, **94**, 774–802.

Sampson, R.J. and Wooldredge, J.D. (1987). Linking the micro- and macro-level dimensions of lifestyle-routine activity and opportunity models of predatory victimisation. *Journal of Quantitative Criminology*, **3**, 371–393.

Shaw, C.R. and McKay, M.D. (1942). *Juvenile Delinquency and Urban Areas*. Chicago University Press; Chicago.

Trickett, A., Osborn, D.R., Seymour, J. and Pease, K. (1992). What is different about high crime areas? *British Journal of Criminology*, **32**, 81–89.

Trickett, A., Osborn, D.R. and Ellingworth, D. (1993). Simple and repeat victimisation: the influences of individual and area characteristics. Discussion Paper ES239, Department of Econometrics and Social Statistics, University of Manchester.

[16]

Commercial Burglars in the Netherlands:
Reasoning Decision-Makers?

Dr. Eric Wiersma[1]

This paper explores the extent to which commercial burglars can be characterised as reasoning decision-makers.[2] Do they make careful calculations before and during the commission of a burglary? And, how do commercial burglars evaluate and deal with security systems? These questions will be answered by focusing on the accounts given by burglars themselves. A majority of those interviewed showed much cunning, resourcefulness and professionalism in preparing and carrying out their burglaries. Judging by their statements more than 80% of the commercial burglars in the sample can be characterised as to some degree, rational. Furthermore, most security measures appear to have no deterrent effect and interviews provide several illustrations of how commercial burglars try to overcome security systems. The measures which had the best deterrent effect seemed to be a guard inside the building or dogs around it. The paper concludes by drawing some policy implications for crime prevention and stresses that the rationality of offenders should not be underestimated.

Introduction

In my case everything is planned well, I won't take any risks.

I go inside rather professionally and before I leave I break a window to make it look like a burglary of a first offender.

These statements by two different commercial burglars indicate that burglars make some calculations before they decide to burgle a company. The extent to which offenders make rational choices in deciding to commit their crimes has received considerable attention over the past decade.[3] While most previous research on burglary has, with a few exceptions,[4] focused mainly on residential burglary, this article focuses on commercial burglary. The aim is to explore the extent to which the decision to commit a commercial burglary and the way it is carried out are the result of a process of careful calculation and deliberation. Additionally, the burglars' perceptions of security are examined in order to determine which security measures have the greatest deterrent effect in their judgement.

The idea behind the research was that an understanding of the decision-making process and of the way security measures are perceived is crucial to the prevention of commercial burglary. This point has been acknowledged in previous studies of offenders' decision-making.

International Journal of Risk, Security and Crime Prevention

For instance, Bennett and Wright state that:

> Unless a crime prevention strategy is perceived by potential offenders as a constraint on crime, it is unlikely to have a preventive effect.[5]

Similarly, another study stresses the importance of interviewing offenders pointing out that:

> because offenders are the source of the crime, it would seem absurd not to avail oneself of their versions of what they are doing and why.[6]

Therefore, this article puts the emphasis on the offenders' views by focusing on the results of 83 interviews with commercial burglars conducted during the course of research into commercial burglary in the Netherlands. However, it is perhaps helpful to begin with a discussion of the methodology.

Methodology

In all, 83 interviews with commercial burglars were conducted. Most were incarcerated and in detention centres throughout the Netherlands.[7] In order to create a relaxed atmosphere and to obtain their confidence, the interviews were semi-structured. Furthermore we were careful to ensure that the offenders were describing a situation that was typical for them. All respondents were volunteers who agreed to be interviewed after a guarantee of anonymity and confidentiality.[8]

The representativeness of such a sample cannot be conclusively determined because the parameters of the total population are unknown. However, the results show that those interviewed were fairly diverse in a number of ways. So the sample was at least not one-sided and probably provides a good insight into a range of methods, experiences and motives of burglars.[9]

The method of retrospective interviewing carries the risk that interviewees 'rationally reconstruct' their choices and methods. In other words they paint a more rosy picture of their methods than was actually the case. Cromwell et al describe this phenomenon as follows:

> Burglars interviewed in prison or those recalling crimes from the past either consciously or unconsciously may engage in rational reconstruction - an interpretation of past behaviour through which the actor recasts activities in a manner consistent with 'what should have been' rather than 'what was'. Offenders are inclined to tell not how things went, but how things should have gone.[10]

It is also possible that some respondents tried to impress the researchers by exaggerating their account.[11] But by asking in-depth questions and probing vague and inconsistent answers an attempt was made to overcome this problem.

The data drawn from the 83 interviews with offenders are presented in terms of generalised patterns. The reader should bear in mind that what is being described is a social pattern that was consistently observed. Quotations from offenders are presented as illustrations of this. The quotations are very close to verbatim and do not distort the respondent's language or intentions; the quotations have not been edited to correct grammar, except where this was necessary to make the meaning clear.

Offenders' backgrounds

The majority of the interviewed offenders were Dutch males, between twenty and thirty years old, with little or no schooling. More than half of the respondents were unemployed at the time of the burglaries. One-third characterised their youth as problematic. To use their own words:

> When I was six years old, I had to live on my own.

> I have experienced so many things ... I have led the life of a 45 year old man, but I am only 25 years old.

Apart from commercial burglary, the offenders had committed a number of other offences. The majority of the offenders had been active in crime for years, and had certainly not restricted themselves to burglary of businesses. More than half had committed residential burglaries, one-fifth had been involved in car theft and a quarter in theft from cars. Most had also committed violent, sometimes even seriously violent, crimes. For instance, about one-third had carried out a robbery and 14% had been involved in attempted murder.[12] Almost all were responsible for more than just one commercial burglary. The information on their criminal background points to the conclusion that the majority of the sample can be characterised as 'professionals' rather than as 'novices'. It is interesting to note that most seemed not to be dedicated to one type of crime. This is also noted by Walsh who recorded that 84% of the commercial burglars interviewed in the course of his research had also committed several other offences such as robbery and assaults. He concluded that:

> For this group, burglary seemed to be only a small episodic part of a life of crime in general, where perhaps things are done on the basis of a combination of occurring need and occurring opportunity, rather than a dedicated pursuit of one crime type.[13]

On this basis it is possible to conclude that a considerable number of the interviewed offenders had developed some sort of criminal career often starting with shoplifting and ending with armed robbery.

Deciding to commit a commercial burglary

In interviews respondents were asked what had motivated them to commit a commercial burglary. Half gave the need for money (instrumental reasons) as the primary motivation. One respondent explained the motivation for his burglaries as follows:

> I stopped working not because I didn't like it, but because I didn't make enough money, e.g. if you earn 6,000 guilders a month, after taxes you've only one-third left, and my friends, they did robberies and were in the drugs trade drove cars three times bigger than mine, so I said to myself, I want that too.[14]

Subsidiary motivations such as the influence of others, expressive needs, the need for drugs or alcohol, were cited by a smaller percentage of our respondents. Approximately 39% mentioned that they also committed burglaries in part for the excitement and thrill of it. As one respondent stated:

> It maybe sounds strange, but for me, burgling a company is just a thrill, it is challenging trying to get inside the company.

Over a third (36%) of the respondents stated that they 'just drifted into it', referring to the influence of others. The greatest percentage of the proceeds from burglary was spend on drugs and alcohol (50%) and on the activity the respondents described as 'leading the luxury life' or 'partying' (74%).[15] For example:

> You only live once, so we spend it on drugs, gambling, luxury, going out and partying.

> Drugs, cars, luxury clothes, just leading the fancy life.

The motivation for burglary has received considerable attention in previous studies; the findings in these seem to be quite consistent with findings reported here. Scarr found out that the need for money to buy drugs and to lead a fast and expensive life are the most important motives for burglars.[16] Similarly, Cromwell et al noted that their respondents stressed their need for money to fulfil expressive needs as the primary motivation for their criminal behaviour. According to their respondents, the greatest percentage of the proceeds from burglary went on the purchase of drugs and alcohol and on activity the informants labelled as 'partying'.[17]

The results of this study tend to confirm that the motivations of commercial burglars do not differ from those of residential burglars and as such support the conclusions of Butler.[18]

When this sample were asked why they choose a commercial premises rather than a residence a variety of reasons were offered:

> I won't steal from people who are working for their money.

> I do not break into dwellings, because I wouldn't like it either when somebody breaks into my house.

> When you're caught, you receive a more severe punishment.

> Household burglary is too risky, besides it ain't worth the risk, for just one lousy video or television set.

International Journal of Risk, Security and Crime Prevention

It was remarkable that approximately 13% of those interviewed said they used the profits of the burglary for setting up a drugs business; the money they earned from burglary was invested in buying drugs with the aim of dealing in them:

> I used the money for buying XTC-pills in Amsterdam and selling them profitably elsewhere.

Preparing for commercial burglary

The majority of our respondents usually worked methodically. In many cases an employee of the company to be burgled was the source of information (56%). This is illustrated by the following quote:

> We often received tips from employees, sometimes they even helped us by giving the working schedules of the security-guards.

Apart from inside tips, intelligence was gathered through observation of the company building (84%) and, to a lesser degree, of security personnel and the type of security measures (38%). The information commercial burglars seek is how to enter the building, whether there are burglar alarms and the location of the money or goods. For example:

> We even pretended to be applying for a job during which we looked around, finding out how to get in or what kind of loot is available.

Other information which some burglars collected beforehand concerned the question of how to get rid of the stolen goods. As one respondent noted:

> First thing you do, is look for a fence, who could buy your stuff, otherwise you're nowhere.

If these results are compared with Walsh's study on commercial burglary, it is interesting to note that half of his respondents 'relied upon advanced data collection', while the other half 'operated on the spur of the moment'.[19] The majority of respondents here seemed to be less opportunistic, judging by the preparations they made before a commercial burglary. A large majority (more than 80%) collected advance information on the company and were prepared for conducting a commercial burglary.[20]

In contrast to this professional approach, which is indicative of rationality, Cromwell et al found that the majority of their offenders operated in an opportunistic way. Given a large number of potential targets, 75% of their burglars tended to select the most vulnerable.[21] According to their own accounts, a majority of respondents in this study did not operate opportunistically but worked out ways of overcoming impediments to the commercial burglary, especially in dealing with security measures. Of course situational vulnerability played an important role but was not decisive in whether they would burgle the company or not. As will be shown later, other factors play an important role. Most of the respondents here can be characterised as professional burglars:

> the professional burglar chooses his targets on the basis of other factors than situational vulnerability and conceives ways in which he or she can overcome impediments to the burglary.[22]

It should be borne in mind that the differences between results here and those of Cromwell et al as regards the degree of rationality or professionalism shown by burglars might, apart from the difference in the type of offence, be explained by the difference in methodology. In their study residential and household burglars were not only interviewed, but they were taken to a potential crime-target in order to determine whether the rationality expressed in the interviews matched with that demonstrated at crime-scene. This additional method is known as the 'stage activity approach' and is meant to avoid the disadvantage of rationally reconstructing the past.[23] A discussion of this method is beyond the scope of this article, but it is reasonable to assume that if this approach had been used, the outcome might have been different.

Choosing the target

In choosing a target commercial burglars focus particularly on the location of the building and the goods or money they seek. Approximately 61% considered the location of the company to be a decisive factor in the decision whether to burgle the company or not. For 51% of the

International Journal of Risk, Security and Crime Prevention

offenders the type of loot was the most important determining factor; 44 % of those interviewed considered the presence of an alarm to be an influential factor in their decision to choose a target. A majority of the offenders had a preference for buildings on a business estate, or at least for the absence of residences in the vicinity of the target. As one respondent stated:

> An ideal location to break in is on a business estate, there are lots of companies, no people around, so you won't be disturbed and if you've had one company you can lay your hands on another.

A minority of the offenders mentioned that there was a subjective component which influenced their decision whether or not to attack a particular target at a particular moment. One respondent noted:

> If the feeling ain't right, I won't go in there it's like some clock inside, which says you'd better not go in. That is to say, I won't break in that evening, but I will break in the next evening, I won't let it go.

This illustrates that subjective factors do influence the decision to break in, but these are part of a rational calculation. The element of 'feeling good' leads to a displacement of the burglary, in this case a displacement of time.

Most of the respondents showed no preference as regards the type or size of building, or the type of firm. Most offenders have a clear idea of the goods they will find. Their favourite loot is money, audio visual equipment, hardware and smokers' requisites, and all goods that sell well or are asked for by customers:

> You're just delivering what the customer orders.

Most burglaries occur in the evening or at night. The majority of offenders do not have a preference for a specific season or a specific month or week. Most operated as part of a team in their own town or the surrounding area. The means of transportation used most often is a car or a van, often stolen or hired or a scrap car to reduce suspicion and to complicate possible tracing via the registration number. Sometimes the car is stolen from the burgled company itself, as is illustrated by the following quote:

> Sometimes we take a car from the company we are going to burgle because if somebody sees you they are thinking you belong to that company, so they won't get suspicious.

According to offenders, they carefully calculate the possible risks of being caught by the police while conducting a burglary; they aim to reduce this risk by making thorough preparations.

Entering the target

The methods used most often to force an entry are breaking, forcing, smashing or kicking down windows or doors. About 12% prefer the roof as a way of getting in. Where tools were used, screwdrivers or crowbars were the most common. For 43% of the interviewed offenders, from several minutes to 30 minutes was the most popular period spent in the building. Approximately 22% of the offenders said they stayed longer than 30 minutes, and some several hours (14%). This differs significantly from the results of the study by Butler, where none of the burglars spent more than 30 minutes in the building.[24] Commercial burglary is typically a group offence, 70% of the offenders interviewed operated with two or more accomplices, with whom a certain amount of planning was done beforehand to decide who was going to do what. As one respondent put it:

> We had a fixed working method; one is checking outside, the other is checking the windows and joins you when entering the building.

Sometimes the work is divided:

> Everybody had his own task, one is good at this, the other is good at that, speaking for myself, I'm rather good at breaking locks.

Generally offenders are careful about leaving clues: they wear gloves for instance, and oversized-shoes. The following quotes illustrate some ways in which offenders try to avoid leaving clues:

> We try to avoid making a mess, so they won't see that you've been there, otherwise the place is shut down. If there is no visible damage, the burglary won't be noticed so you can burgle the place again.

International Journal of Risk, Security and Crime Prevention

Sometimes we put on oversized-shoes to fool the police; if they find these footprints, it is no evidence because they won't match with our footprints.

Security measures like extra locks and bolts, compartmentalisation, roll-down shutters, warning lights, cameras, loud alarms and the presence of security personnel do not in themselves appear to deter most offenders. Extra locks and bolts are an easy barrier to overcome for more than 80% of the respondents; roll-down shutters have no deterrent effect for 59%:

Roll-down shutters do not make any sense because you can always put a screwdriver between them.

It is quite remarkable that 15% of the respondents argued that they were attracted rather than deterred by the presence of a safe in a company. A safe was considered to be a challenge. As one respondent put it:

For us it is a kick, trying to open the safe. It is like fighting a war against the brand of the safe. When the safe is opened, it proves that we've won.

Cameras were seen as a deterrent by 32% of the offenders, but the majority were not put off. As one respondent noted:

If there are cameras, you just put something over your head.

During the interviews respondents drew a distinction between the deterrent effect of silent alarms and of loud alarms. As far as loud alarms are concerned, 60% of the offenders interviewed were not deterred by their presence. Several respondents mentioned ways of dealing with loud alarms. For example:

We always deliberately activated the alarm by waving a plastic bag from the roof inside the company building. Then we hide outside the building and waited half an hour until the police came, but they of course saw nothing, so we activated the loud alarm again. We continued this until the police thought that there was something wrong with the alarm (false) and turned it off. And when they had turned off the alarm, we went inside.

We just put some foam inside the alarm, so you won't hear anything.

The presence of a silent alarm seemed to deter more burglars than loud alarms. Approximately 50% of the respondents did not burgle a company if there was a silent alarm. The other half were not deterred by a silent alarm. Some of these mentioned ways of dealing with this type of alarm. For example:

Some of these alarms are transmitted by a telephone line; if you wanna know how these lines are situated you just go to the local government for information on these lines, After that, it is just a matter of digging a hole and cutting the lines.

We just know people who work for (Dutch) Telecom; they know exactly where the different telephone lines are and which line goes to a company, so they just switch the electricity off, so they won't notice.

It should be noted that during the interviews a difference was drawn between security personnel inside the building (guards) and security personnel who just make rounds during the night. The presence of guards in a company building was a rather effective deterrent according to the judgement of the offenders: 60% indicated that 'someone inside the building' prevents them from commercial burglary:

If there's a man inside, I won't go in, it's too risky.

In contrast with this, the presence of security guards who check the company regularly at night do not appear to deter most offenders. 74% of the interviewed offenders were not impressed by the deterrent effect of these guards, which can be illustrated by the following quotes:

Security people on a business-estate do not scare me at all; they're just driving around and do not notice you.

I think this kind of security is a waste of money; these people don't know anything about security.

The presence of guard dogs is considered to be a serious deterrent by 53% of those interviewed:

You don't see them (dogs) coming and if they're after you, you'd better be going.

International Journal of Risk, Security and Crime Prevention

Although some respondents said that they could deal with the presence of dogs, most tried to avoid them. As far as this last point is concerned Cromwell et al also found that most burglars agree that dogs are an effective deterrent to burglary. They found that:

> Although many burglars have developed contingency plans to deal with dogs (petting them, feeding them or even killing them) most burglars prefer to avoid them.[25]

Walsh found out that one-third of his commercial burglars did not like guard dogs and saw them as a deterrent.[26]

According to Butler, the presence of security guards had a significant deterrent effect on the commercial burglars he interviewed,[27] although the study did not differentiate between security guards in or outside the building. The way in which a majority of offenders plan their burglaries and deal with alarms can be classified as 'professional': they try to calculate the risks of not being caught and find ways of defeating security systems.

About half of the offenders claimed that they were usually under the influence of drugs while conducting a burglary. The majority of this group - those who used drugs during a burglary - are addicted to drugs. The interesting point, however, is that some offenders use drugs, not because they are addicted, but as a means of making the burglary easier. For example:

> To feel confident during the burglary I sometimes take some drugs, an XTC-pill. With such a pill you think you can beat the world.

> It is less risky when you take a rophypnol-pill; you're less scared, because when you're scared you take more risks.

These results are quite similar to those obtained by Cromwell et al in their study on burglary. They also found that some burglars used drugs to initiate and facilitate the commission of burglaries. Like some of the respondents here, theirs referred to the need 'to be steady' or 'keep up the nerve'.[28] Getting drugs seemed to be a major preoccupation for a majority of our offenders. Wright and Decker also found this preoccupation with drugs among their respondents; they linked this with the so-called street-culture, where drug use is an important aspect of street identity.[29] The question of whether this kind of culture exists for respondents here was beyond the scope of this article.

Conclusions

The purpose of this paper is to determine whether commercial burglars can be characterised as reasoning decision-makers.[30] The results indicate that the majority of offenders make calculations during and before the actual commission of a commercial burglary. Judging by their accounts, the offenders show much cunning, resourcefulness and professionalism in preparing and carrying out burglaries.

In order to interpret the findings in a theoretical perspective the rational choice approach is chosen: it places emphasis on the interface between offender and offence and on gaining information from offenders. It attempts to obtain a subjective understanding of the situation and assumes that offenders:

> seek to benefit themselves by their criminal behaviour; that this involves the making of decisions and of choices, however rudimentary on occasion these processes might be; and that these processes exhibit a measure of rationality, albeit constrained by limits of time and ability and the availability of relevant information.[31]

The findings support the view that most commercial burglars can, to some extent, be seen as reasoning decision-makers since they make, as has been shown, several calculations and decisions before and during a commercial burglary. Additionally, they are not deterred by various security measures. It should be stressed that this rationality is limited by certain constraints and influenced by others. Most burglaries are committed by two or more persons, some offenders are influenced by drugs, others refrain from residential burglary for moral reasons. The way the profits of burglary are spent does not seem to be rational. On the basis

International Journal of Risk, Security and Crime Prevention

of the empirical results presented here, it is argued that a majority of offenders (approximately 80%) can be characterised as what Bennett and Wright called 'limited reasoning decision makers'. Like their respondents, most interviewed burglars showed some 'limited rationality', in which it is:

> not presumed that offenders weigh all the relevant factors every time an offence is contemplated, and in which other factors (moods, motives, moral judgements, perceptions of opportunity, laziness, alcohol or narcotics consumed, the effect of others and their attitude to risk) apparently unrelated to the immediate decision often take over.[32]

The findings indicate that it is better to speak of 'limited reasoning decision makers', limited in the sense that rationality must be conceived of in broad terms: even if the choices made or the decision processes themselves are not optimal ones from the point of view of an outsider, they make sense to the offender.[33] If the burglars were to be classified as either 'opportunistic' or 'professional' following Cromwell,[34] it is clear that a majority of those interviewed would be labelled as 'professional'. That is to say, if it is assumed that there is a relation between the amount of rationality and the amount of professionalism, the more preparation, calculation and planning (rationality) a burglar engages in before and during a burglary, the more the label 'professional' is appropriate.[35] Of the remaining 20%, 10% operated in a mainly opportunistic way, while 10% operated in sometimes an opportunistic way and sometimes in a more rational way. To quote a typical opportunistic commercial burglar:

> I just select a company by chance; sometimes you're lucky, sometimes you've got bad luck.

In order to ensure that the limited rationality expressed by the respondents is not a result of the methodology, it is recommended that further offender-studies should be conducted.

But, what are the consequences for crime prevention if commercial burglars have been correctly classified as (limited) 'reasoning decision makers'? This characterisation does not mean that adequate and affordable prevention is impossible. Yet, at least some of the theory behind situational crime prevention must be questioned; most commercial burglars in this study are not easily deterred by security measures. It emerged from the interviews that business security fails in terms of the technical quality of prevention measures and of the implementation of these measures. This was confirmed by the victim surveys, which were another main strand of this research: 52% of the victimised companies did not have a security policy.[36] Giving a higher priority to better measures and policy is one obvious recommendation but these need to be subjected to evaluation. In order to develop adequate prevention strategies for preventing commercial burglaries, the rationality and professionalism of offenders cannot be underestimated.

Notes

1   E.G. Wiersma is a researcher at the Research and Documentation Centre of the Dutch Ministry of Justice, Research and Documentation Centre, Dutch Ministry of Justice, PO Box 20301, 2500 EH Den Haag, The Netherlands, tel: (31) 070-370 7265; Fax: (31) 070-370 7948.

2   The views expressed in this paper do not necessarily represent the position or policies of the Dutch Ministry of Justice. Some of the results of this research have been published previously in Kruissink, M. and Wiersma, E.G. (1995) Inbraak in bedrijven, daders, aangiftes, en slachtoffers onderzocht, Arnhem, Gouda Quint, Onderzoek en beleid, nr. 142.

3   See Bennett, T. and Wright, R. (1984a) *Burglars on Burglary; Prevention and the Offender*. Hampshire: Gower; Cornish, D., and Clarke, R. (1986) *The Reasoning Criminal: Rational Choice Perspectives on Offending*. New York: Springer Verlag; Cromwell, P., Olson, J. and Avary, D. (1991) *Breaking and Entering: An Ethnographic Analysis of Burglary*. Newbury Park, CA: Sage; Wright, R. and Decker, S. (1994) *Burglars on the Job: Streetlife and Residential Break-ins*. Boston: North-eastern University Press.

International Journal of Risk, Security and Crime Prevention

4 Walsh, D. (1986a) *Heavy Business: Commercial Burglary and Robbery*. London: Routledge and Kegan Paul; Butler, G. (1994) Commercial Burglary: What Offenders Say. In Gill, M. (ed) *Crime at Work: Studies in Security and Crime Prevention*. Leicester: Perpetuity Press.

5 Bennett, T. and Wright, R. (1984b) Constraints to Burglary: The Offenders' Perspective, in Clarke, R.V. and Hope, T. (eds) *Coping with Burglary, Research Perspectives on Policy*. London: Gower, p 181.

6 Walsh, D. (1986b) Victim Selection Procedures Among Economic Criminals: The Rational Choice Perspective. In Cornish, D. and Clarke, R. (editors) *The Reasoning Criminal: Rational Choice Perspectives on Offending*. New York: Springer-Verlag, p 49.

7 Some respondents were interviewed at a police station others at their home. For more details see Kruissink and Wiersma, op cit, p 20.

8 Ibid, pp 19-21.

9 Ibid, p 43

10 Cromwell et al, op cit, p 91.

11 See also Walsh (1986b) op cit, p 49. In this article Walsh points out six methodological problems which might occur during interviewing incarcerated offenders, but despite these he states that: 'such problems would be far outweighed by the general gain accruing from letting offenders tell their own story'.

12 For more details see Kruissink and Wiersma, op cit, pp 69-76.

13 Walsh (1986a) op cit, p 48.

14 See Repetto, T. (1974) *Residential Crime*. Cambridge, MA: Ballinger. Repetto found that 'satisfaction of a perceived need' was the primary motivation of offenders.

15 Kruissink and Wiersma, op cit, p 70.

16 Scarr, H. (1973) *Patterns of Burglary*. Washington DC: Government Printing Office. See also Bennett and Wright (1984a/b) op cit; Butler, op cit; Repetto, op cit; and Rengert, G. and Wasilchick, J. (1985) *Suburban Burglary: a Time and a Place for Everything*. Springfield: Charles C. Thomas. These studies show that among their respondents the need for money seemed to be the primary motivation for the burglary.

17 Cromwell et al, op cit. See also, Cromwell, P. (1991) The Burglar's Perspective, in Roberts, A.R. (ed) *Critical Issues in Crime and Justice*. London: Sage, p 39.

18 Butler, op cit.

19 Walsh (1986a) op cit, p 45.

20 For more details see Kruissink and Wiersma, op cit, pp 46-47.

21 It should be stressed that the results might not be completely comparable since the study of Cromwell et al deals with residential burglars.

22 Cromwell, op cit, p 42.

23 Ibid, pp 35-50.

24 Butler, op cit, p 34.

25 Cromwell, op cit, p 43. See also Cromwell et al, op cit.

26 Walsh (1986a) op cit.

27 Butler, op cit, p 38.

28 Cromwell, op cit, p 44.

29 Wright and Decker, op cit, p 40.

30 'Reasoning' refers to the amount of rationality offenders show before and during the actual offence.

31 Cornish and Clarke, op cit.

32 Bennett and Wright, op cit, p 160.

33 See also Walsh (1986b) op cit, p 44-51.

34 Cromwell op cit, p 48. Cromwell defines an 'opportunistic burglar' as follows: 'The opportunistic burglar chooses targets based upon their perceived vulnerability to burglary at a given time. Given a large number of potential targets, the burglar tends to select the most vulnerable of the target pool.'

35 See also, Walsh (1986b) op cit. It should be emphasised that there is a difference between so-called 'objective rationality' and 'subjective rationality'. The latter refers to a notion of rationality as defined by the offender. Here 'high rationality' refers to the subjective meaning. See also Bennett and Wright (1984a) op cit.

36 For more details see Kruissink and Wiersma, op cit, pp 81-84.

[17]

A SNOWBALL'S CHANCE IN HELL: DOING FIELDWORK WITH ACTIVE RESIDENTIAL BURGLARS

RICHARD WRIGHT
SCOTT H. DECKER
ALLISON K. REDFERN
DIETRICH L. SMITH

Criminologists long have recognized the importance of field studies of active offenders. Nevertheless, the vast majority of them have shied away from researching criminals "in the wild" in the belief that doing so is impractical. This article, based on the authors' fieldwork with 105 currently active residential burglars, challenges that assumption. Specifically, it describes how the authors went about finding these offenders and obtaining their cooperation. Further, it considers the difficulties involved in maintaining an on-going field relationship with those who lead chaotic lives. And lastly, the article outlines the characteristics of the sample, noting important ways in which it differs from one collected through criminal justice channels.

Criminologists long have recognized the importance of field studies of active offenders. More than 2 decades ago, for example, Polsky (1969, p. 116) observed that "we can no longer afford the convenient fiction that in studying criminals in their natural habitat, we would discover nothing really important that could not be discovered from criminals behind bars." Similarly, Sutherland and Cressey (1970) noted that:

Those who have had intimate contacts with criminals "in the open" know that criminals are not "natural" in police stations, courts, and prisons, and that they

---

The research on which this article is based was funded by Grant No. 89-IJ-CX-0046 from the National Institute of Justice, Office of Justice Programs, U.S. Department of Justice. Points of view or opinions expressed in this document are those of the authors and do not necessarily represent the official position or policies of the U.S. Department of Justice. Correspondence should be sent to: Richard Wright, Department of Criminology and Criminal Justice, University of Missouri—St. Louis, St. Louis, MO 63121.

.must be studied in their everyday life outside of institutions if they are to be understood. By this is meant that the investigator must associate with them as one of them, seeing their lives and conditions as the criminals themselves see them. In this way, he can make observations which can hardly be made in any other way. Also, his observations are of unapprehended criminals, not the criminals selected by the processes of arrest and imprisonment. (p. 68)

And McCall (1978, p. 27) also cautioned that studies of incarcerated offenders are vulnerable to the charge that they are based on "unsuccessful criminals, on the supposition that successful criminals are not apprehended or at least are able to avoid incarceration." This charge, he asserts, is "the most central bogeyman in the criminologist's demonology" (also see Cromwell, Olson, and Avery 1991; Hagedorn 1990; Watters and Biernacki 1989).

Although generally granting the validity of such critiques, most criminologists have shied away from studying criminals, so to speak, in the wild. Although their reluctance to do so undoubtedly is attributable to a variety of factors (e.g., Wright and Bennett 1990), probably the most important of these is a belief that this type of research is impractical. In particular, how is one to locate active criminals and obtain their cooperation?

The entrenched notion that field-based studies of active offenders are unworkable has been challenged by Chambliss (1975) who asserts that:

> The data on organized crime and professional theft as well as other presumably difficult-to-study events are much more available than we usually think. All we really have to do is to get out of our offices and onto the street. The data are there; the problem is that too often [researchers] are not. (p. 39)

Those who have carried out field research with active criminals would no doubt regard this assertion as overly simplistic, but they probably would concur with Chambliss that it is easier to find and gain the confidence of such offenders than commonly is imagined. As Hagedorn (1990, p. 251) has stated: "Any good field researcher . . . willing to spend the long hours necessary to develop good informants can solve the problem of access."

We recently completed the fieldwork for a study of residential burglars, exploring, specifically, the factors they take into account when contemplating the commission of an offense. The study is being done on the streets of St. Louis, Missouri, a declining "rust belt" city. As part of this study, we located and interviewed 105 active offenders. We also took 70 of these offenders to the site of a recent burglary and asked them to reconstruct the crime in considerable detail. In the following pages, we will discuss how we found these offenders and obtained their cooperation. Further, we will consider the difficulties involved in maintaining an on-going field relationship with these offenders, many of whom lead chaotic lives. Lastly, we will outline the characteristics of our sample, suggesting ways in which it differs from one collected through criminal justice channels.

LOCATING THE SUBJECTS

In order to locate the active offenders for our study, we employed a "snowball" or "chain referral" sampling strategy. As described in the literature (e.g., Sudman 1976; Watters and Biernacki 1989), such a strategy begins with the recruitment of an initial subject who then is asked to recommend further participants. This process continues until a suitable sample has been "built."

The most difficult aspect of using a snowball sampling technique is locating an initial contact or two. Various ways of doing so have been suggested. McCall (1978), for instance, recommends using a "chain of referrals":

> If a researcher wants to make contact with, say, a bootlegger, he thinks of the person he knows who is closest in the social structure to bootlegging. Perhaps this person will be a police officer, a judge, a liquor store owner, a crime reporter, or a recently arrived Southern migrant. If he doesn't personally know a judge or a crime reporter, he surely knows someone (his own lawyer or a circulation clerk) who does and who would be willing to introduce him. By means of a very short chain of such referrals, the researcher can obtain an introduction to virtually any type of criminal. (p. 31)

This strategy can be effective and efficient, but can also have pitfalls. In attempting to find active offenders for our study, we avoided seeking referrals from criminal justice officials for both practical and methodological reasons. From a practical standpoint, we elected not to use contacts provided by police or probation officers, fearing that this would arouse the suspicions of offenders that the research was the cover for a "sting" operation. One of the offenders we interviewed, for example, explained that he had not agreed to participate earlier because he was worried about being set up for an arrest: "I thought about it at first because I've seen on T.V. telling how [the police] have sent letters out to people telling 'em they've won new sneakers and then arrested 'em." We also did not use referrals from law enforcement or corrections personnel to locate our subjects owing to a methodological concern that a sample obtained in this way may be highly unrepresentative of the total population of active offenders. It is likely, for instance, that such a sample would include a disproportionate number of unsuccessful criminals, that is, those who have been caught in the past (e.g., Hagedorn 1990). Further, this sample might exclude a number of successful offenders who avoid associating with colleagues known to the police. Rengert and Wasilchick (1989, p. 6) used a probationer to contact active burglars, observing that the offenders so located "were often very much like the individual who led us to them."

A commonly suggested means of making initial contact with active offenders other than through criminal justice sources involves frequenting locales favored by criminals (see Chambliss 1975; Polsky 1969; West 1980). This strategy, however, requires an extraordinary investment of time as the researcher establishes a street reputation as an "all right square" (Irwin 1972, p. 123) who can be trusted. Fortunately, we were able to short-cut that process by hiring an ex-offender (who, despite committing hundreds of serious crimes, had few arrests and no felony convictions) with high status among several groups of Black street criminals in St. Louis. This person retired from crime after being shot and paralyzed in a gangland-style execution attempt. He then attended a university and earned a bachelor's degree, but continued to live in his old neighborhood, remaining friendly, albeit superficially, with local criminals. We initially met him when he attended a colloquium in our department and disputed the speaker's characterization of street criminals.

Working through an ex-offender with continuing ties to the underworld as a means of locating active criminals has been used successfully by other criminologists (see e.g., Taylor 1985). This approach offers the advantage that such a person already has contacts and trust in the criminal subculture and can vouch for the legitimacy of the research. In order to exploit this advantage fully, however, the ex-offender selected must be someone with a solid street reputation for integrity and must have a strong commitment to accomplishing the goals of the study.

The ex-offender hired to locate subjects for our project began by approaching former criminal associates. Some of these contacts were still "hustling," that is, actively involved in various types of crimes, whereas others either had retired or remained involved only peripherally through, for example, occasional buying and selling of stolen goods. Shortly thereafter, the ex-offender contacted several street-wise law-abiding friends, including a youth worker. He explained the research to the contacts, stressing that it was confidential and that the police were not involved. He also informed them that those who took part would be paid a small sum (typically $25.00). He then asked the contacts to put him in touch with active residential burglars.

Figure 1 outlines the chain of referrals through which the offenders were located. Perhaps the best way to clarify this process involves selecting a

152

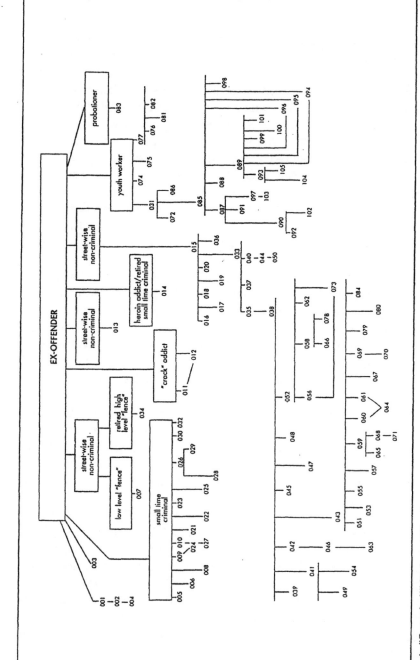

Figure 1: "Snowball" Referral Chart

subject, say 064, and identifying the referrals that led us to this person. In this case, the ex-offender working on our project contacted a street-wise, noncriminal acquaintance who put him in touch with the first active burglar in the chain, offender 015. Offender 015 referred 7 colleagues, one of whom — 033 — put us in touch with 3 more subjects, including 035, who in turn introduced us to 038, who referred 8 more participants. Among these participants was offender 043, a well-connected burglar who provided 12 further contacts, 2 of whom — 060 and 061 — convinced 064 to participate in the research. This procedure is similar to that described by Watters and Biernacki (1989, p. 426) in that "the majority of respondents were not referred directly by research staff." As a consequence, our sample was strengthened considerably. After all, we almost certainly would not have been able to find many of these individuals on our own, let alone convince them to cooperate.

Throughout the process of locating subjects, we encountered numerous difficulties and challenges. Contacts that initially appeared to be promising, for example, sometimes proved to be unproductive and had to be dropped. And, of course, even productive contact chains had a tendency to "dry up" eventually. One of the most challenging tasks we confronted involved what Biernacki and Waldorf (1981, p. 150) have termed the "verification of eligibility," that is, determining whether potential subjects actually met the criteria for inclusion in our research. In order to take part, offenders had to be both "residential burglars" and "currently active." In practice, this meant that they had to have committed a residential burglary within the past 2 weeks. This seems straightforward, but it often was difficult to apply the criteria in the field because offenders were evasive about their activities. In such cases, we frequently had to rely on other members of the sample to verify the eligibility of potential subjects.

We did not pay the contacts for helping us to find subjects and, initially, motivating them to do so proved difficult. Small favors, things like giving them a ride or buying them a pack of cigarettes, produced some cooperation, but yielded only a few introductions. Moreover, the active burglars that we did manage to find often were lackadaisical about referring associates because no financial incentive was offered. Eventually, one of the informants hit on the idea of "pimping" colleagues, that is, arranging an introduction on their behalf in exchange for a cut of the participation fee (also see Cromwell et al. 1991). This idea was adopted rapidly by other informants and the number of referrals rose accordingly. In effect, these informants became "locators" (Biernacki and Waldorf 1981), helping us to expand referral chains as well as vouching for the legitimacy of the research, and validating potential participants as active residential burglars.

The practice of pimping is consistent with the low level, underworld economy of street culture, where people are always looking for a way to get in on someone else's deal. One of our contacts put it this way: "If there's money to make out of something, I gotta figure out a way to get me some of it." Over the course of the research, numerous disputes arose between offenders and informants over the payment of referral fees. We resisted becoming involved in these disputes, reckoning that such involvement could only result in the alienation of one or both parties (e.g., Miller 1952). Instead, we made it clear that our funds were intended as interview payments and thus would be given only to interviewees.

FIELD RELATIONS

The success of our research, of course, hinged on an ability to convince potential subjects to participate. Given that many of the active burglars, especially those located early in the project, were deeply suspicious of our motives, it is reasonable to ask why the offenders were willing to take part in the research. Certainly the fact that we paid them a small sum for their time was an enticement for many, but this is not an adequate explanation. After all, criminal opportunities abound and even the inept "nickel and dime" offenders in the sample could have earned more had they spent the time engaged in illegal activity. Moreover, some of the subjects clearly were not short of cash when they agreed to participate; at the close of one interview, an offender pulled out his wallet to show us that it was stuffed with thousand dollar bills, saying:

> I just wanted to prove that I didn't do this for the money. I don't need the money. I did it to help out [the ex-offender employed on our project]. We know some of the same people and he said you were cool.

Without doubt, many in our sample agreed to participate only because the ex-offender assured them that we were trustworthy. But other factors were at work as well. Letkemann (1973, p. 44), among others, has observed that the secrecy inherent in criminal work means that offenders have few opportunities to discuss their activities with anyone besides associates—which many of them find frustrating. As one of his informants put it: "What's the point of scoring if nobody knows about it." Under the right conditions, therefore, some offenders may enjoy talking about their work with researchers.

We adopted several additional strategies to maximize the cooperation of the offenders. First, following the recommendations of experienced field researchers (e.g., Irwin 1972; McCall 1978; Walker and Lidz 1977; Wright and Bennett 1990), we made an effort to "fit in" by learning the distinctive terminology and phrasing used by the offenders. Here again, the assistance of the ex-offender proved invaluable. Prior to entering the field, he suggested ways in which questions might be asked so that the subjects would better understand them, and provided us with a working knowledge of popular street terms (e.g., "boy" for heroin, "girl" for cocaine) and pronunciations (e.g., "hair ron" for heroin). What is more, he sat in on the early interviews and critiqued them afterwards, noting areas of difficulty or contention and offering possible solutions.

A second strategy to gain the cooperation of the offenders required us to give as well as take. We expected the subjects to answer our questions frankly and, therefore, often had to reciprocate. Almost all of them had questions about how the information would be used, who would have access to it, and so on. We answered these questions honestly, lest the offenders conclude that we were being evasive. Further, we honored requests from a number of subjects for various forms of assistance. Provided that the help requested was legal and fell within the general set "of norms governing the exchange of money and other kinds of favors" (Berk and Adams 1970, p. 112) on the street, we offered it. For example, we took subjects to job interviews or work, helped some to enroll in school, and gave others advice on legal matters. We even assisted a juvenile offender who was injured while running away from the police, to arrange for emergency surgery when his parents, fearing that they would be charged for the operation, refused to give their consent.

One other way we sought to obtain and keep the offenders' confidence involved demonstrating our trustworthiness by "remaining close-mouthed in regard to potentially harmful information" (Irwin 1972, p. 125). A number of the offenders tested us by asking what a criminal associate said about a particular matter. We declined to discuss such issues, explaining that the promise of confidentiality extended to all those participating in our research.

Much has been written about the necessity for researchers to be able to withstand official coercion (see Irwin 1972; McCall 1978; Polsky 1969) and we recognized from the start the threat that intrusions from criminal justice officials could pose to our research. The threat of being confronted by police patrols seemed especially great given that we planned to visit the sites of recent successful burglaries with offenders. Therefore, prior to beginning our fieldwork, we negotiated an agreement with police authorities not to interfere in the conduct of the research, and we were not subjected to official coercion.

Although the strategies described above helped to mitigate the dangers inherent in working with active criminals (see e.g., Dunlap et al. 1990), we encountered many potentially dangerous situations over the course of the research. For example, offenders turned up for interviews carrying firearms including, on one occasion, a machine gun; we were challenged on the street by subjects who feared that they were being set up for arrest; we were caught in the middle of a fight over the payment of a $1 debt. Probably the most dangerous situation, however, arose while driving with an offender to the site of his most recent burglary. As we passed a pedestrian, the offender became agitated and demanded that we stop the car: "You want to see me kill someone? Stop the car! I'm gonna kill that motherfucker. Stop the fuckin' car!" We refused to stop and actually sped up to prevent him jumping out of the vehicle; this clearly displeased him, although he eventually calmed down. The development of such situations was largely unpredictable and thus avoiding them was difficult. Often we deferred to the ex-offender's judgment about the safety of a given set of circumstances. The most notable precaution that we took involved money; we made sure that the offenders knew that we carried little more than was necessary to pay them.

CHARACTERISTICS OF THE SAMPLE

Unless a sample of active offenders differs significantly from one obtained through criminal justice channels, the difficulties and risks associated with the street-based recruitment of research subjects could not easily be justified. Accordingly, it seems important that we establish whether such a difference exists. In doing so, we will begin by outlining the demographic characteristics of our sample. In terms of race, it nearly parallels the distribution of burglary arrests for the City of St. Louis in 1988, the most recent year for which data are available. The St. Louis Metropolitan Police Department's Annual Report (1989) reveals that 64% of burglary arrestees in that year were Black, and 36% were White. Our sample was 69% Black and 31% White. There is divergence for the gender variable, however; only 7% of all arrestees in the city were female, while 17% of our sample fell into this category. This is not surprising. The characteristics of a sample of active criminals, after all, would not be expected to mirror those of one obtained in a criminal justice setting.

Given that our research involved only currently active offenders, it is interesting to note that 21 of the subjects were on probation, parole, or serving a suspended sentence, and that a substantial number of juveniles — 27 or 26% of the total — were located for the study. The inclusion of such offenders strengthens the research considerably because approximately one third of

TABLE 1:   Contact With Criminal Justice System

	Frequency	Percent
Subject ever arrested (for any offense)?		
No	28	28
Yes	72	72
	100	
Subject ever arrested, convicted, incarcerated (for burglary)?		
No arrests	44	42
Arrest, no conviction	35	33
Arrest, conviction, no jail/prison	4	4
Arrest, conviction, jail/prison	22	21
	105	

arrested burglars are under 18 years of age (Sessions 1989). Juveniles, there-fore, need to be taken into account in any comprehensive study of burglars. These offenders, however, seldom are included in studies of burglars located through criminal justice channels because access to them is legally restricted and they often are processed differently than adult criminals and detained in separate facilities.

Prior contact with the criminal justice system is a crucial variable for this research. Table 1 sets out whether, and to what degree, those in our sample have come into official contact with that system. Of primary interest in this table is the extent to which our snowball sampling technique uncovered a sample of residential burglars unlikely to be encountered in a criminal justice setting, the site of most research on offenders.

More than one-quarter of the offenders (28%) claimed never to have been arrested. (We excluded arrests for traffic offenses, "failure to appear" and similar minor transgressions, because such offenses do not adequately dis-tinguish serious criminals from others.) Obviously, these offenders would have been excluded had we based our study on a jail or prison population. Perhaps a more relevant measure in the context of our study, however, is the experience of the offenders with the criminal justice system for the offense of burglary, because most previous studies of burglars not only have been based on incarcerated offenders, but also have used the charge of burglary as a screen to select subjects (e.g., Bennett and Wright 1984; Rengert and Wasilchick 1985). Of the 105 individuals in our sample, 44 (42%) had no arrests for burglary, and another 35 (33%) had one or more arrests, but no convictions for the offense. Thus 75% of our sample would not be included in a study of incarcerated burglars.

We turn now to an examination of the patterns of offending among our sample. In order to determine how many lifetime burglaries the offenders had committed, we asked them to estimate the number of completed burglaries in which they had taken part. We "bounded" this response by asking them (a) how old they were when they did their first burglary, (b) about significant gaps in offending (e.g., periods of incarceration), and (c) about fluctuations in offending levels. The subjects typically estimated how many lifetime burglaries they had committed in terms of a range (e.g., 50-60), then were prompted with questions about the variation in their rate of offending over the course of their burglary career. We recorded what offenders agreed was a conservative estimate of the number of lifetime burglaries. More than half of the sample (52%) admitted to 50 or more lifetime burglaries. Included in this group are 41 offenders (40% of the total) who have committed at least 100 such crimes.

The measure of lifetime burglaries, of course, does not provide an estimate of the *rate* of offending. For that, we calculated "lambda" (Blumstein and Cohen 1979) — that is, the annual number of lifetime burglaries — for each subject by using our interview data. We arrived at this figure by subtracting age at first burglary from age at time of initial interview; from this, we subtracted the number of years each offender spent "off the street" in a secure residential facility (prison, jail, secure detention, or treatment center). This gave us the denominator for the lambda measure, the number of years at risk. The number of lifetime burglaries was divided by years at risk to get lambda. Approximately two thirds of the sample (68%) averaged 10 or fewer burglaries a year over the course of their offending careers — a finding not out of line with lambda estimates for burglary derived from arrest data (Blumstein and Cohen 1979). It should be noted, however, that there was great variability in the rate of offending among our sample; 34% committed, on average, less than five burglaries a year while, at the other extreme, 7% committed more than 50 such crimes yearly. This subgroup of exceptionally high rate offenders accounted for 4,204 of the 13,179 residential burglaries (32%) reported by our subjects. This result compliments previous research based on self-reports by prison inmates that has shown great variability in individual crime rates, with a small group of very active criminals being responsible for a disproportionate number of offenses (e.g., Greenwood 1982; Petersilia, Greenwood, and Lavin 1977).

The final portion of the analysis compares offenders who have and have not ever been arrested *for anything* in terms of (a) their total lifetime burglaries, and (b) their lambda (see Table 2).

TABLE 2:   Comparisons of Sample Members by Any Previous Arrest Status

	Number	Mean	s	t*
	Total lifetime burglaries by any previous arrest			
Yes	67	120	166	
				.04
No	20	232	324	
	N = 87			
	Lifetime burglary lambdas			
Yes	67	13	21	
				.03
No	20	28	38	
	N = 87			

*Because sample selection was not random, the *t*-test results must be interpreted cautiously.

The differences for these measures are pronounced. The mean lifetime burglaries for those who have never been arrested for anything is nearly double that for those who have been arrested. The variability in the group that has not been arrested is evident in the standard deviation (s = 324). A small subsample of this group has committed very few lifetime burglaries. Those in this subsample are mostly juvenile females who have offended infrequently over a very short period of time. But for this, there would be even larger differences between the groups. The mean lambda for those who have not been arrested is twice that for their arrested counterparts. This measure also displays considerable variation, as evidenced by the high standard deviation. Nevertheless, among those who have not been arrested, there are a number of offenders whose existence often has been doubted, namely high-rate criminals who successfully have avoided apprehension altogether.

CONCLUSION

By its nature, research involving active criminals is always demanding, often difficult, and occasionally dangerous. However, it is possible and, as the quantitative information reported above suggests, some of the offenders included in such research may differ substantially from those found through criminal justice channels. It is interesting, for example, that those in our sample who had never been arrested for anything, on average, offended *more* frequently and had committed *more* lifetime burglaries than their arrested counterparts. These "successful" offenders, obviously, would not have shown up in a study of arrestees, prisoners, or probationers — a fact that calls into question the extent to which a sample obtained through official sources is representative of the total population of criminals.

Beyond this, researching active offenders is important because it provides an opportunity to observe and talk with them outside the institutional context. As Cromwell et al. (1991) have noted, it is difficult to assess the validity of accounts offered by institutionalized criminals. Simply put, a full understanding of criminal behavior requires that criminologists incorporate field studies of active offenders into their research agendas. Without such studies, both the representativeness and the validity of research based on offenders located through criminal justice channels will remain problematic.

REFERENCES

Bennett, Trevor and Richard Wright. 1984. *Burglars on Burglary: Prevention and the Offender*. Aldershot, England: Gower.
Berk, Richard and Joseph Adams. 1970. "Establishing Rapport with Deviant Groups." *Social Problems* 18:102-17.
Biernacki, Patrick and Dan Waldorf. 1981. "Snowball Sampling: Problems and Techniques of Chain Referral Sampling." *Sociological Methods & Research* 10:141-63.
Blumstein, Alfred and Jacqueline Cohen. 1979. "Estimation of Individual Crime Rates from Arrest Records." *Journal of Criminal Law and Criminology* 70:561-85.
Chambliss, William. 1975. "On the Paucity of Research on Organized Crime: A Reply to Galliher and Cain." *American Sociologist* 10:36-39.
Cromwell, Paul, James Olson, and D'Aunn Avary. 1991. *Breaking and Entering: An Ethnographic Analysis of Burglary*. Newbury Park, CA: Sage.
Dunlap, Eloise, Bruce Johnson, Harry Sanabria, Elbert Holliday, Vicki Lipsey, Maurice Barnett, William Hopkins, Ira Sobel, Doris Randolph, and Ko-Lin Chin. 1990. "Studying Crack Users and Their Criminal Careers: The Scientific and Artistic Aspects of Locating Hard-to-Reach Subjects and Interviewing Them about Sensitive Topics." *Contemporary Drug Problems* 17:121-44.
Greenwood, Peter. 1982. *Selective Incapacitation*. Santa Monica, CA: RAND.
Hagedorn, John. 1990. "Back in the Field Again: Gang Research in the Nineties." Pp. 240-59 in *Gangs in America*, edited by C. Ronald Huff. Newbury Park, CA: Sage.
Irwin, John. 1972. "Participant Observation of Criminals." Pp. 117-37 in *Research on Deviance*, edited by Jack Douglas. New York: Random House.
Letkemann, Peter. 1973. *Crime as Work*. Englewood Cliffs, NJ: Prentice-Hall.
McCall, George. 1978. *Observing the Law*. New York: Free Press.
Miller, S. M. 1952. "The Participant Observer and Over-Rapport." *American Sociological Review* 17:97-99.

Petersilia, Joan, Peter Greenwood, and Marvin Lavin. 1977. *Criminal Careers of Habitual Felons*. Santa Monica, CA: RAND.

Polsky, Ned. 1969. *Hustlers, Beats, and Others*. Garden City, NJ: Anchor.

Rengert, George and John Wasilchick. 1985. *Suburban Burglary: A Time and a Place for Everything*. Springfield, IL: Thomas.

————. 1989. *Space, Time and Crime: Ethnographic Insights into Residential Burglary*. Final report submitted to the National Institute of Justice, Office of Justice Programs, U.S. Department of Justice.

Sessions, William. 1989. *Crime in the United States—1988*. Washington, DC: U.S. Government Printing Office.

St. Louis Metropolitan Police Department. 1989. *Annual Report—1988/89*. St. Louis, MO: St. Louis Metropolitan Police Department.

Sudman, Seymour. 1976. *Applied Sampling*. New York: Academic Press.

Sutherland, Edwin and Donald Cressey. 1970. *Criminology—8th Edition*. Philadelphia, PA: Lippincott.

Taylor, Laurie. 1985. *In the Underworld*. London: Unwin.

Walker, Andrew and Charles Lidz. 1977. "Methodological Notes on the Employment of Indigenous Observers." Pp. 103-23 in *Street Ethnography*, edited by Robert Weppner. Beverly Hills, CA: Sage.

Watters, John and Patrick Biernacki. 1989. "Targeted Sampling: Options for the Study of Hidden Populations." *Social Problems* 36:416-30.

West, W. Gordon. 1980. "Access to Adolescent Deviants and Deviance." Pp. 31-44 in *Fieldwork Experience. Qualitative Approaches to Social Research*, edited by William Shaffir, Robert Stebbins, and Allan Turowitz. New York: St. Martin's.

Wright, Richard and Trevor Bennett. 1990. "Exploring the Offender's Perspective: Observing and Interviewing Criminals." Pp. 138-51 in *Measurement Issues in Criminology*, edited by Kimberly Kempf. New York: Springer-Verlag.

[18]

How Young House Burglars Choose Targets

RICHARD WRIGHT and ROBERT H. LOGIE

*Richard Wright is Associate Professor, Department of Administration
of Justice and Research Fellow, Center for Metropolitan Studies
University of Missouri, St. Louis, U.S.A.
Robert Logie is Lecturer, Department of Psychology, University
of Aberdeen*

*Abstract: This article reports the results of an empirical study designed to determine what
features of the immediate environment are important to juvenile house burglars in their selection
of targets. The study involved two main subject groups: (i) convicted juvenile burglars; and
(ii) adult householders. Subjects were presented with photographs of houses and asked whether
or not they would choose them as a burglary target on the basis of the information available.
These photographs were identical for each subject apart from a controlled factor. Data also were
gathered from participants via a checklist procedure, a short interview and a surprise recognition
test. The findings indicated that young burglars largely concurred as to the factors which
influenced their decision when choosing a target. However, their choice of factors differed in
several important respects from those which householders believed to be important to such
offenders. The implications of this work for environmental crime prevention strategies are
discussed.*

Recommendations for the prevention of residential burglary have made
increasing reference to the alteration of situational cues emitted by
potential targets and their surroundings (for example, Winchester and
Jackson 1982). These recommendations rest on specific assumptions
about what features of the environment are taken into account by house
burglars. Until recently, however, little was known about the way in
which burglars perceive physical opportunities for crime (Mayhew *et al.*
1979; Mayhew 1979).

In the absence of sound empirical knowledge, many 'situational'
prevention schemes aimed at, among other crimes, house burglary were
implemented on little more than 'informed hunches' (Waller 1979).
Although in some cases the introduction of such schemes was followed by
a reduction in burglary, it is unclear whether the schemes themselves
produced this drop (Titus 1984). A rational, cost-effective approach to the
situational prevention of residential burglary requires a thorough understanding of the way in which offenders perceive targets. It makes little
sense, particularly at a time of fiscal restraint, to alter the environment
without first determining whether (and, if so, to what extent) burglars
view these alterations as a constraint on crime.

This article reports the results of an empirical study designed to determine what features of the *immediate* environment are important to juvenile house burglars in their selection of targets.

Literature Review

A considerable amount of research has been conducted on the influence of environmental factors on crime (for example, Brantingham and Brantingham 1981). Much of this research has concerned residential burglary, though little of it has addressed the question of what features of potential targets are taken into account by house burglars. Nevertheless, there is some information that bears on this issue. For example, several studies have compared the characteristics of victimised and non-victimised dwellings. They have consistently shown that victimised houses differ from non-victimised ones in that they are less 'surveillable' (Waller and Okihiro 1978; Dietrick 1977; Winchester and Jackson 1982) and more often left unoccupied (Winchester and Jackson 1982).

A few researchers have attempted to tap more directly the factors which influence burglars by interviewing them. Their conclusions are consistent in relation to some cues, but not others. Walsh (1980), Maguire and Bennett (1982) and Waller and Okihiro (1978) all reported that burglars prefer houses they can approach and enter without being seen. Bennett and Wright (1984) noted that house burglars specifically were worried about being observed by neighbours. Another consistent finding is that burglars prefer unoccupied houses (Scarr 1973; Reppetto 1974; Waller and Okihiro 1978; Maguire and Bennett 1982; Bennett and Wright 1984; Walsh 1980).

However, there is little agreement among those who have interviewed burglars regarding the influence of security hardware on target choice. Scarr (1973), Letkemann (1973) and Rengert and Wasilchick (1985) concluded that burglars consider the type of lock fitted, whereas Maguire and Bennett (1982), Bennett and Wright (1984) and Walsh (1980) found that they usually do not take this into account.

The information gleaned from these interviews, while suggestive, does not constitute a firm foundation on which to build situational prevention schemes. The interviews were conducted in a situation far removed from that in which burglaries typically occur thereby calling into question the validity of offenders' responses.

In an attempt to approximate more closely the situation in which targets are selected, several researchers have used video-recordings, photographs or miniature models of houses (for example, Reppetto 1974; Walsh 1980). The most elaborate research of this type was conducted by Bennett and Wright (1983, 1984). They employed three different experimental methods, each designed to explore a different aspect of offenders' target selection. The first method involved showing a video-recording of houses to a sample of convicted burglars. The offenders were asked to assess each of the houses as a potential target and to decide if they would break into it if they were looking for a house to attack.

93

The second experiment involved showing photographs of various aspects of houses to a separate sample of burglars. The burglars were given a complete front view of each house and asked to select additional photographs in an order that reflected their normal method of choosing targets. Again, they were asked to give reasons for each selection and for their final decision as to whether or not the house was suitable for burglary.

These two experimental methods identified a wide range of factors which seemed to affect burglars' choice of targets. However, the experiments did not examine the independent influence of individual factors on that process. The third experiment was an exploratory study designed to investigate the feasibility of using photographs of houses to address this problem. Three photographs were taken of various aspects of five houses; a complete view of the front of the house, a close-up of the front door and a close-up of a ground floor window. Both of the close-up shots revealed details of locks, where these were fitted. Two sets of photographs were produced that were identical apart from a controlled factor. One set of photographs presented the houses in a supposedly favourable state (from a burglar's point of view), while the other set presented them unfavourably. Five factors selected on the basis of the results of the first two experiments and the recommendations of crime prevention specialists (that is, crime prevention officers attached to various British police forces), were manipulated in the study: (i) whether an alarm was visible; (ii) whether the house was surrounded by bushes (offering cover); (iii) whether there was a car in the driveway of the house itself (suggesting occupancy); (iv) whether there was a car in the driveway next door (indicating the presence of neighbours), and (v) whether the window had a security lock. Twenty convicted burglars were shown the houses in a hypothetically favourable condition (surrounded by bushes, without an alarm visible and so on), and another 20 saw them in an unfavourable condition. Each individual, however, was presented with a mixture of favourable and unfavourable targets. The offenders were asked to look at the three photographs of each house and to report whether they would choose it as a target.

Two of the five factors (whether an alarm was visible and whether the house was surrounded by bushes) had a statistically significant influence on offenders' choices. The presence of a car in the driveway of the house also seemed to have an affect on target selection, although this was not significant. The presence of a window lock or a car in the neighbour's driveway did not affect the burglars' decision making.

This work has contributed to an understanding of those situational factors that may be crucial in the prevention of residential burglary. However, the evidence is not sufficiently strong to allow more general conclusions to be drawn. The third experiment, for example, included only a small number of houses and each factor was studied individually on just one of them. So, for example, a particular house may have been disliked not because there was a car in the neighbour's driveway, but because it appeared that there was little inside worth stealing.

94

There are two further limitations to the studies carried out by Bennett and Wright. First, recent crime statistics suggest that a substantial proportion of solved residential burglaries are committed by juveniles (Webster 1986; Home Office 1984) and the results reported above are applicable only to adult offenders. Second, it is unclear whether the pattern of results obtained for burglars matches that which would be obtained for non-burglars. A comparison with a sample of non-burglars might shed some light on the extent to which those factors assumed by the general population to be important in burglary prevention reflect those which offenders actually consider when choosing a target.

With such problems in mind, the present study was designed to extend the preliminary work carried out by Bennett and Wright in a more systematic and rigorous fashion.

Method

Subjects Groups

Burglary Group

The ten individuals in the burglary group were all in a remand centre for juvenile offenders in East Anglia. They were interviewed only after we had obtained permission from the juveniles themselves, their parent or guardian, their social worker and the local social services department. This was a time-consuming and often frustrating process. We were able to approach only a small proportion of the juveniles. The remand centre was by definition a short-stay facility and there was often not sufficient time to gain the permissions required before the juvenile went to court or was released.

All bar one of the 13 juveniles approached agreed to take part in the research. In two of these cases, however, a parent or social worker refused to allow them to do so. Those taking part were all male and their ages ranged from 15 to 17 years. They were selected on the basis that they had been convicted of residential burglary on at least one occasion, although they may have been involved in and/or convicted of other offences as well. None of them reported having used alcohol or drugs immediately prior to their burglaries which, for the most part, had been committed during daylight hours. In all cases, we were careful not to give the impression that we viewed the burglars as having specialised knowledge. This was to avoid feelings of esteem associated with breaking the law.

Control Group

The ten individuals in the control group were all selected at random from a larger group of volunteers who were members of the subject panel of the Medical Research Council Applied Psychology Unit in Cambridge. Those chosen to take part in the study were all householders aged 21 to 60 years. They tended to have had at least twelve years full-time education, and many had attended a college or university. As such, the sample was not matched in any way to the burglary group. Rather, it represented, loosely

95

speaking, its 'opposition', that is, people with a personal interest in preventing these cr

Materials

Target Photographs

Black and white photographs were taken of 20 houses. Six of the houses were detached, eight were semi-detached and six were terraced. There were six photographs of a full front view of each house, and two close up shots showing details of the front door. The photographs were arranged as follows:

(i) A full view of the front of the house as it normally looked with no additional physical features.
(ii) One close up of the front door showing details of a 'latch' type lock.
(iii) A full view of the front of the house with a 'dead bolt' type lock fitted to the door.
(iv) A close up of the front door showing the 'dead bolt' lock.
(v) A full view of the front of the house with a 'Beware of the Dog' sign clearly visible.
(vi) A full view of the front of the house with a burglar alarm clearly visible.
(vii) A full view of the front of the house with a hedge or fence superimposed on the photograph.
(viii) A full view of the front of the house with a car parked in the driveway or in the road out front.

This allowed for a possible six sets of photographs constructed such that each house was shown in each of six conditions across the sets. Within one set, however, a given house was shown in one condition only. For example, house number one would be shown in set 1 as a straight house with no factors added. In set 2 it would appear with a burglar alarm, in set 3 with a 'Beware of the Dog' sign (but no burglar alarm), in set 4 with a hedge superimposed, in set 5 with a car in the driveway, and in set 6 with a 'dead bolt' lock fitted to the front door. In contrast, house two might appear in set 1 with an alarm installed, in set 2 with a 'Beware of the Dog' sign and so on.

Within any one set the five factors were represented three times; on a terraced, a semi-detached and a detached house. In addition, the 'straight' house comprised one that was terraced, one that was detached and three that were semi-detached.

Recognition Photographs

The sets of photographs for recognition were based on the target sets. Within each set, half of the photographs were identical copies of those in the corresponding target set. The remainder involved a change to the original photograph, comprising in some cases the addition of a factor to a dwelling which was originally presented as a 'straight' house. In other cases, a factor was removed from the original. Within each set of

96

photographs and for each factor, one house had that factor removed for the recognition test, while a second house had it added.

Checklist

The checklist consisted of 30 characteristics of houses. Some were chosen because they hypothetically were attractive to a burglar (for example 'newspapers stuffed in the letterbox'), others were chosen because they were thought to be unattractive (for example 'T.V. on'), and the remainder were chosen because they seemed to be neutral (for example 'a brick house'). Each item on the checklist was read out to the interviewee who was required to indicate whether (a) this factor would tend to attract a burglar, (b) this factor would tend to 'put off' a burglar, or (c) this factor would make no difference as to whether a house was chosen as a target. Two versions of the checklist were made up, with the 30 items arranged in a different random order for each.

The items to be included were categorised roughly into ten groups, and these are shown in *Table 1*.

Questionnaire

The subjects also were asked a number of questions about themselves. In the case of the burglary group this largely involved questions about their offending history. Members of the control group were asked about their own home and any home-security measures they had adopted.

Design and Procedure

The initial part of the study involved showing photographs of houses either as they normally appear, or with one of the five factors added to the photograph. Each subject was instructed to look at the photograph and indicate whether a burglar would find the house attractive or unattractive. They were asked to make their decision on the basis of the information as it was presented in the photograph, without the possibility of returning at some later time to commit the offence.

This experiment rests on an assumption that the subjects will notice the factors being presented. Of course, that may not always be the case. To address this possibility, we followed the experiment with a checklist procedure. After all 20 photographs had been shown, items from a checklist of features of houses were read out to the subjects. Thirty features were presented in a random order, and subjects were asked to indicate whether each would attract, deter or make no difference to a burglar.

These features were intended to cover those aspects of the physical environment which may be taken into account by a burglar, but which could not easily be shown in a photograph. We also included the factors examined in the photographs as a source of additional evidence.

Subjects next were asked the questions described briefly in the 'Materials' section, with the choice of questions appropriate to the subject group.

Finally, the subjects were given a surprise test of their ability to notice

97

TABLE 1

Items Contained in Checklist Arranged According to Categories of Features that are Attractive (+), Unattractive (−) or Neutral to Burglar's Decisions

1.	Car in drive	Occupancy	−
2.	Porch light on	Occupancy	−
3.	Light on in front room	Occupancy	−
4.	Car in neighbour's drive	Occupancy	−
5.	Light on in hall	Occupancy	−
6.	TV on	Occupancy	−
7.	Full milk bottles on doorstep	Occupancy	+
8.	Newspapers stuffed in mailbox	Occupancy	+
9.	Dog in house	Dog	−
10.	Locks on windows	Locks	−
11.	Dead bolt lock on door	Locks	−
12.	Latch type lock on door	Locks	−
13.	Detached house	Wealth	+
14.	Bungalow	Wealth	+
15.	Well kept garden	Wealth	+
16.	Leaded windows	Wealth	+
17.	Untidy garden	Wealth	−
18.	Terraced house	Wealth	−
19.	Unkempt paintwork	Wealth	−
20.	Open fields at back of house	Cover & access	+
21.	Large hedge in front of house	Cover & access	+
22.	Window open upstairs	Cover & access	+
23.	Sash windows	Cover & access	+
24.	Windows that open out	Cover & access	+
25.	Double glazing	Cover & access	−
26.	Neighbour's window overlooking back of garden	Cover & access	−
27.	Semi-detached house	Cover & access	−
28.	Burglar alarm	Alarm	−
29.	Brick house	Neutral	
30.	Front door painted red	Neutral	

changes in the photographs they had been shown originally. There is evidence from the experimental psychology literature that relevant information is remembered better than irrelevant information (for example, Pitchert and Anderson 1977). This procedure, therefore, helped to rule out the possibility that the burglars had been deceptive in the earlier part of the experiment.

The photographs were presented one at a time in a random order. Subjects were told that they had seen all of the houses in the initial experiment, although some had been altered. They were asked to look at each photograph carefully and to decide whether the house had been changed in any way.

Results

Target Selection

Percentage data for the different photograph conditions and three house types are shown in *Table 2*. From the table, it is clear that overall the burglars agree with the non-offenders that the presence of a dog or burglar alarm makes a house an unattractive target. There is disagreement between the groups where a 'dead bolt' lock has been fitted. The control group believed that these houses would be less attractive than the straight ones. The burglary group, however, produced virtually the same proportion of 'yes' responses regardless of whether or not a 'dead bolt' lock was fitted.

TABLE 2

Percentage of 'Attracted' Responses to Photographs of Target Houses, by Factor Studied, House Type and Subject Group

	Burglars	Controls
Straight house	58	64
Dead bolt lock	60	53
Burglar alarm	23	20
Cover	83	60
Dog	30	23
Car	3	50
Detached	60	52
Semi-detached	44	53
Terraced	32	37

There were even larger discrepancies between the groups regarding the impact of the presence of a car or 'cover'. The burglars were greatly attracted to houses with a hedge or fence, but they were put off those with a car in the drive. For the control group, cover made little difference. The presence of a car affected this group's decision to some extent, but the effect was not nearly as great as that for the burglar group. As regards type of house, there is a clear order of preference in the burglary group, with detached houses being seen as most attractive and terraced houses as least attractive. The control group viewed semi-detached and detached houses as equally attractive. However, they concurred with the burglars that terraced houses were the least prone to burglary.

Checklist

The percentage of responses to the items on the checklist are shown in *Table 3*. The data shown have been summarised by grouping the 30 items in the checklist under ten categories of factors. Some of the categories were

initially considered attractive to a burglar, some were considered
unattractive, and two were considered neutral. (The details of the
grouping were shown in *Table 1*). Some of these data were amenable to
statistical analysis by the chi-square test (χ^2). A significant χ^2 value
indicates that the two groups differed in their choice of response. Where a
χ^2 value is not shown, the relevant value was not statistically significant.

TABLE 3

*Percentage of Each Type of Response to Potentially Attractive (+), Unattractive
(–), or Neutral Factors by Subject Group*

	Burglars			Controls		
Factor Group	Attract	Put off	Doesn't Matter	Attract	Put off	Doesn't Matter
Looks Occupied (–)	7	48	45	8	80	12
Looks Unoccupied (+)	85	0	15	100	0	0
Dog (–)	0	80	20	0	100	0
Locks (–)	13	17	70	10	73	17
'Wealthy' (+)	65	15	20	48	15	37
'Not Wealthy' (–)	0	77	23	13	30	57
Cover & access (+)	76	6	18	76	8	16
No cover & access (–)	0	47	53	3	60	37
Alarm (–)	10	80	10	0	100	0
Neutral	0	0	100	0	0	100

There appears to be some agreement between the groups that the
presence of a dog makes a house a less tempting target. There is also
general agreement that an alarm is a deterrent, although some burglars
suggested that this might attract them on the grounds that it indicated
there was something inside worth stealing.

The presence of locks shows a much more dramatic difference ($\chi^2 = 68$,
$p < 0.001$) between the groups than that found in the photograph
procedure. Around 73% of the control responses reflected a belief that
locks would deter burglars, while only 17% of the burglars' responses
indicated that locks would put them off. In some cases, a lock was actually
considered by the burglars to be an attractive feature. However, this
applied to 'latch' type locks only.

More burglars than controls were attracted by signs of wealth ($\chi^2 = 7.6$,
$P < 0.05$). However, the controls greatly underestimated ($\chi^2 = 48$,
$p < 0.001$) the extent to which a 'lack of wealth' would put off the
burglars. Items like a poorly-tended yard, a terraced house or unkempt
paintwork all indicated to the burglars that the houses would have little

100

inside worth stealing. The control group recognised that these features would not make a property attractive to offenders. But they did not realise quite *how* unattractive they were to a burglar. There was broad agreement between the groups that cover and ease of access would make a house more attractive as a target. There was also general agreement that the lack of such factors would make the property a less attractive target. However, householders overestimated ($\chi^2 = 7.4$, $p < 0.05$) the extent to which burglars would be put off by such cues. Both groups indicated that the neutral items would make no difference to a burglar's decision.

Recognition Test

The percentage of correct recognitions for each factor is shown in *Table 4*. It is immediately apparent that the performance of the burglars is better than that of the controls. This difference was statistically significant as measured by a t-test ($t = 2.83$, $p < 0.01$).

TABLE 4

Percentage of Correct Recognitions for Each Factor by Subject Group

Factor	Burglars	Controls
Lock	75.0	50
Dog	72.5	55
Cover	95.0	78
Alarm	77.5	73
Car	82.5	60
Mean Performance	80.5	63.2

The tendency for some factors to be better recognised than others is especially interesting. One prediction might be that the physical size of the factor in the photograph would determine whether it was remembered or not. For example, locks and beware of dog signs are quite small and may not have been noticed, whereas cars and hedges are quite large items and should have been better recognised.

Among the controls, performance was close to chance or 'guessing' (50%) for locks and beware of dog signs. However, it was also quite low for the presence of a car. In contrast, the burglars were quite accurate in remembering whether or not any of these factors had been present in the original photograph.

The presence of cover was remembered reasonably well by both groups. A very few burglars incorrectly remembered the presence of cover and this was true for only one photograph. Thus, it may be a peculiarity of that photograph. Surprisingly, 22% of the control responses involved incorrect recognition of this factor and this was not limited to one particular house.

Putting it another way, it was possible to introduce a hedge that covered half the house or remove a wall from in front without some of the controls noticing.

Alarms were remembered slightly better by the burglars, but both groups did reasonably well for this factor.

Discussion

The results for target selection and checklist procedures are in broad agreement, suggesting that the photograph method is indeed a useful technique in this context. It also suggests that the burglars clearly noticed the relevant factors in the photographs, and that there are important distinctions between the two groups studied.

The recognition procedure further supported our confidence in the veracity of the burglars' responses. The superior recognition memory in the burglars cannot easily be explained in terms of how long each sample looked at the photographs, as this was equated in the two groups; nor can it be accounted for by educational level since this would predict that the control group would show better performance. A more likely explanation is that the burglars are revealing a measure of expertise in coding the photographs originally and thus they are more likely to notice these factors as having been changed.

One puzzling finding is the fact that the presence of locks is relatively easily remembered by the burglars despite their initial suggestion that locks would make very little difference to them in choosing a target. There are a number of possible explanations for this result. One is that our recognition memory procedure is simply not a very good measure of the importance to burglars of various factors. However, this seems unlikely as it would be difficult to explain why the burglars show much better recognition performance overall than the controls.

A second possibility is that the burglars are deliberately trying to mislead the experimenter by claiming that locks are not important, while alarms are. This is dubious since locks were shown to be unimportant to burglars in the photograph method, where they were not specifically asked about this factor, as well as in the checklist. Also, why should they give misleading answers for locks, alarms, and dogs, while providing apparently consistent responses for cover? It may be that this is a partial explanation; perhaps a minority of the burglars adopted a misleading strategy. However, this explanation is inadequate as it stands. A more likely explanation is that although burglars may not be put off or attracted to a house on the basis of door locks, they may consider them in terms of how access could be obtained. If a 'latch' type lock is present, this can be opened easily with a credit card or something similar. If a 'dead bolt' lock is fitted, then entry can be gained through a window. The lock therefore may be influential in deciding *how* to break in, but not in whether or not to do so. This, plus the possibility that our procedure draws attention to the door, is likely to result in better recognition performance.

In addition, by the time burglars are close enough to a house to see the

102

type of lock fitted, they probably have decided to break in and are fairly committed to doing so.

Conclusion

The results reported above were derived from a study involving small samples of juvenile burglars and law-abiding adult householders. As such, any generalisations based on these findings should be viewed cautiously until the research is carried out on a larger scale. Nonetheless, there are two reasons for placing confidence in the results. First, the burglars were largely consistent in their responses. The data were collected over a seven month period and the juveniles concerned were interviewed individually while in a short-stay remand hostel. It is unlikely therefore that they colluded in their responses, resulting in sample bias. Second, the factors cited by juvenile offenders as influential in their target selection mirrored the cues identified by adult burglars in other studies. Clearly, this adds a degree of confidence to the findings despite the small sample size. For example, the youngsters typically saw the presence of cover (surveillability), cars (occupancy) and dogs or alarms (occupancy 'proxies', that is, alternatives to human presence) as affecting their choice of houses. These factors have been identified as critical to older offenders as well (for example, Waller and Okihiro 1978; Bennett and Wright 1984). Similarly, the young burglars agreed with their older counterparts who, in several studies, have indicated that locks are not a major deterrent (for example Walsh 1980; Maguire and Bennett 1982; Bennett and Wright 1984).

In contrast, the householders thought that locks had an important impact on target choice. Their responses probably reflect the emphasis of past burglary prevention campaigns, many of which have focussed on the importance of security hardware. Whatever the explanation, it is clear that the homeowners were not fully attuned to the way in which these burglars actually chose houses. They overestimated the importance of some factors, while underestimating the importance of others.

Perhaps residential burglary could be reduced simply by providing householders with accurate information about the factors that influence burglars' choice of targets? Although some of these factors will remain beyond their ability to manipulate, others like signs of occupancy and the amount of cover can be controlled fairly easily.[1]

Notes

[1]*Acknowledgements*

The research on which this paper was based was funded by the Office of Research Administration, University of Missouri–St. Louis. The research was conducted while Robert H. Logie was working at the Medical Research Council (U.K.) Applied Psychology Unit in Cambridge, England. We are grateful for the additional support of the Medical Research Council and for the co-operation of the Social Services Departments involved.

References

Bennett, T. and Wright, R. (1983) 'Burglars perception of targets', *Home Office Research Bulletin, 15,* 18–20.

Bennett, T. and Wright, R. (1984) *Burglars on Burglary: Prevention and the Offender,* Aldershot: Gower.

Brantingham, P. and Brantingham, P. (1981) *Environmental Criminology,* Beverly Hills: Sage.

Dietrick,, B. (1977) 'The environment and burglary victimisation in a metropolitan suburb' (paper presented at the Annual Meeting of the American Society of Criminology, Atlanta, unpublished).

Home Office (1984) *Criminal Statistics: England and Wales 1983,* Cmnd. 9349.

Letkemann, P. (1973) *Crime as Work,* Englewood Cliffs: Prentice-Hall.

Maguire, M. and Bennett, T. (1982) *Burglary in a Dwelling,* London: Heinemann.

Mayhew, P. (1979) 'Defensible space: the current status of a crime prevention theory', *The Howard Journal, 18,* 150–9.

Mayhew, P., Clarke, R., Burrows, J., Hough, J. and Winchester, S. (1979) *Crime in Public View* (Home Office Research Study No. 49), London: H.M.S.O.

Pitchert, J. W. and Anderson, R. C. (1977) 'Taking different perspectives on a story', *Journal of Educational Psychology, 69,* 309–15.

Rengert, G. and Wasilchick, J. (1985) *Suburban Burglary: A Time and a Place for Everything,* Springfield: Thomas.

Reppetto, T. G. (1974) *Residential Crime,* Cambridge, Ma.: Ballinger.

Scarr, H. A. (1973) *Patterns of Burglary,* Washington, D.C.: U.S. Government Printing Office.

Titus, R. (1984) 'Residential burglary and the community response', in: R. Clarke and T. Hope (Eds.), *Coping with Burglary,* Boston: Kluwer-Nijhoff.

Waller, I. (1979) 'What reduces residential burglary: action and research in Seattle and Toronto' (paper presented at the Third International Symposium on Victimology, Muenster, unpublished).

Waller, I. and Okihiro, N. (1978) *Burglary: The Victim and the Public,* Toronto: University of Toronto Press.

Walsh, D. (1980) *Break-Ins: Burglary From Private Houses,* London: Constable.

Webster, W. (1986) *Crime in the United States – 1985,* Washington, D.C.: U.S. Government Printing Office.

Winchester, S. and Jackson, H. (1982) *Residential Burglary* (Home Office Research Study No. 74), London: H.M.S.O.

Part II
Policy Response

[19]

Small Business Crime: The Evaluation of a Crime Prevention Initiative

Kate J. Bowers[1]

There has been a dearth of evaluation research concerned with assessing the effectiveness of crime prevention schemes that aim to reduce levels of crime committed against businesses and non-residential properties generally. This paper describes the implementation of a scheme aimed at reducing small business crime, with a particular emphasis on burglary in the county of Merseyside. Details of the results of an evaluation of the scheme are then given. The evaluation found that contact with a Crime Prevention Officer significantly reduced levels of crime against businesses. Advice offered by such experts was more effective than the isolated installation of target-hardening measures. The paper also attempts to gather evidence regarding the means by which and the situations in which particular crime prevention measures are effective at reducing levels of crime.

Keywords: Commercial victimization; repeat burglaries; situational crime prevention; evaluation; small businesses

Introduction

An area of criminology in which research has the potential to make an impact on practice is in the evaluation of crime prevention initiatives. The current political climate has encouraged investment in evaluation studies in an attempt to increase the impact of government resources by establishing which techniques are successful at reducing crime and in which circumstances they succeed. This is the aim of an in-depth evaluation, funded by the Home Office, of a recent national burglary reduction scheme.

Much crime prevention to date, and therefore the majority of evaluations, have concentrated on residential crime, especially residential burglary. For instance, a large-scale evaluation of the Safer Cities programme has been conducted.[2] The programme was nation-wide, and the evaluation of its domestic burglary element utilized information collected from 300 different schemes. The evaluation used before-and-after surveys and local police crime statistics. Control areas were set up, so it was possible to measure the extent to which any changes in the action areas reflected changes elsewhere. The overall results were comprehensive, showing that the survey and the crime figures both identified reductions in levels of burglary. Some evidence of displacement, both to other areas and to other types of crime, was found.

A further residential burglary intervention, the 'Biting Back' initiative implemented in an area of Huddersfield, concentrated efforts on victims of repeat burglary. An in-depth evaluation of the scheme proved that it had been successful in reducing both overall levels of burglary and levels of repeat burglary against domestic dwellings over its period of operation.[3]

Crime Prevention and Community Safety: An International Journal

An area which now needs addressing is the prevention of crime against non-residential properties, such as schools, businesses or community facilities. Evidence has been found to show that levels of crime against non-residential properties are often higher than those against their residential counterparts. The Commercial Victimisation Survey, conducted by the Home Office, found that 25 per cent of a national sample of retailers and 24 per cent of manufacturers had suffered from at least one burglary in 1994.[4] This can be compared with five per cent of residential households being burgled in one year, according to the British Crime Survey.[5] A study of burglary conducted on Merseyside found similar results using police data, reporting that 23.7 per cent of non-residential properties had experienced burglary in a one-year period, in comparison with 3.3 per cent of residential properties.[6]

There are several reasons for the relative lack of initiatives focusing on the business sector, and indeed on the non-residential sector generally. First, public concern about crime tends to focus on the residential community.[7] Second, the business community often sees crime prevention as a relatively low priority in its drive towards profitability, and therefore a balance needs to be found between profit and security.[8] Lastly, it is particularly difficult to obtain reliable information on business victimization; indeed, it is a hard enough task just to determine the number of businesses in operation in an area at a particular point in time.[9]

Notwithstanding these problems, there have been some evaluations of crime prevention initiatives focusing on non-residential properties. The most comprehensive of these was Tilley and Hopkins' evaluation of the Small Business and Crime Initiative (SBCI).[10] This demonstrated that such a commercial crime initiative can achieve significant reductions in crime in a small area (the area of operation was two streets in London). However, it also concluded that:

> Further research is needed to understand better what switches businesses on to high levels of victimisation and what switches them off. [11]

The SBCI evaluation broke new ground in evaluation research. However, more needs to be done to help assess the effectiveness of business crime prevention initiatives. Specifically, more evidence is required concerning larger-scale initiatives that target a wider area than did the SBCI. As pointed out above, more information is also required concerning the method by which crime prevention initiatives are succeeding, in addition to reports of whether burglary rates have been reduced. The importance of determining the context within which and the mechanism by which crime prevention measures are successful has been highlighted as being an important issue in contemporary evaluation research.[12] These issues will be addressed by this paper, which details the results of an evaluation of an initiative, operating in the Merseyside area, aimed at the reduction of crime against small businesses throughout the County (the 'Small Business Strategy').

The second section of this paper will begin by describing the method by which businesses in the Merseyside area that were particularly vulnerable to crime were identified; this includes a description of a baseline survey of businesses in the region to establish initial levels of crime against businesses. It then describes how the most vulnerable businesses received assistance in improving their security. In particular, there is a discussion of the role of Crime Prevention Officers from Merseyside Police in providing advice to businesses. This part of the paper then goes on to examine some of the potential limitations of the system that was used to prioritize and assist these businesses, and to report lessons learnt in the course of the implementation process.

In the third section, the evaluation framework that was used to assess the effectiveness of the business crime initiative described in the second section is outlined in general terms. The fourth

Crime Prevention and Community Safety: An International Journal

section goes on to describe the results of the survey-based part of this evaluation. Methodological issues are covered concerning the administration of a follow-up evaluation survey to the businesses that had participated in the earlier baseline survey. The effect of the initiative on crime in general and on particular types of crime is reported. There is then a discussion that compares the effectiveness of different crime prevention measures taken to help secure businesses, and a preliminary exploration of the mechanism by which these measures reduce crime.

Finally, the fifth section aims to complement the survey-based evaluation with an analysis of changes in police data on recorded burglaries by comparing burglary incidence rates before, during and after the initiative was implemented within the initiative's operational area and elsewhere in the County of Merseyside.

Implementation of the Small Business Strategy

Targeting need
The Small Business Strategy (SBS) of the Safer Merseyside Partnership (SMP) was set up in order to combat the problem of excessive victimization against non-residential properties. The SBS concentrated on businesses with fewer than 25 employees, that were not part of a larger business, and that were situated in the most deprived neighbourhoods of Merseyside. These neighbourhoods (or 'Objective 1' areas) are those recognised by the EU as qualifying for grant aid, and are home to 485,000 (roughly one-third) of Merseyside's residents. The strategy also required that businesses involved in the scheme were located in residential areas. It was therefore likely that, for example, small, family-run corner-shops would be included in the scheme. Due to their size and location, the establishments meeting the strategy's criteria were likely to have fewer resources to channel into crime prevention.

Businesses meeting the criteria were identified using a Geographical Information System. In the phase of the SBS that was evaluated, a stratified sample of 1000 of these businesses (which totalled 2517) were each visited by one of a team of six interviewers, who assessed the crime risk of the property. Business owners were asked questions regarding the level of victimization they had experienced over the previous year. Specifically, questions focused on any incidents of burglary, attempted burglary, criminal damage, fraud, forgery, assault, robbery, employee theft, theft by customer, or theft from customer. Other questions assessed the adequacy of crime prevention measures that were in place in the property, and the level of concern felt by the business owner regarding crime in the area. The survey also examined any possible variation in crime risk associated with different businesses and trading activities.

Each completed survey was then scored to assess the overall vulnerability of the business. Each business was placed in one of three categories: high, medium or low risk. The scoring system gave particular weight to businesses that had experienced repeat burglary. The score also reflected the adequacy of crime prevention measures already installed at the business premises.

Those businesses that scored high or medium risk on the survey were then asked whether they would like to be visited by a Crime Prevention Officer (CPO) from Merseyside Police. The CPOs provided the business owners with advice in relation to specific crime prevention measures, and, in the case of the high-risk properties, put forward recommendations to the SMP for target-hardening measures.

The SMP provided financial assistance towards the installation of these recommended measures, using Single Regeneration Budget funding. The grant aid offered, up to a value of £1500 per property, were 50 per cent contributions towards the total cost of the measures, in order to encourage

Crime Prevention and Community Safety: An International Journal

the proprietors to match the funding and upgrade their security. The measures that were recommended included burglar alarms, CCTV systems, roller shutters, window locks, and occasionally detection devices.

Of the 1000 businesses visited, 470 surveys were completed in full. In all, 140 businesses were visited by a CPO, and a subset of these (46) also received offers of financial assistance from the SMP towards the cost of installing recommended crime prevention measures.

The role of Crime Prevention Officers

The visits made to vulnerable properties by CPOs from Merseyside Police, mentioned above, made up a critical element of the SBS intervention. This section will therefore outline the content of these visits in more detail.

CPO visits to the high- and medium-risk businesses involved detailed risk assessments of the *particular* property. Internal and external appraisals of existing security measures and of the property's layout were carried out. During this process 'weak spots' were identified, and recommendations for improvement of security measures were made on the basis of the appraisals. The CPOs had some details of current security measures in advance of the visit, through information collected during the initial survey, and this assisted in the appraisals. Further information was elicited from business owners regarding their current security practices, and advice was given on the way in which changes to routine staff activities could improve security. Advice was tailored to the *types* of crime frequently experienced by the business, which was also available to the CPO, from the survey data, in advance of the visit.

Some of the areas that were covered in the CPO visits included:

- critical assessment of the layout of premises, eg the planning of displays, position of staff, placement of security mirrors;

- practical advice on 'weak spots', eg securing rear access, using security lights, encouraging natural surveillance;

- encouraging 'thoughtful' routine activities, eg keeping money in tills to a minimum, being careful with keys, not disclosing information to a stranger, not leaving valuable items unattended;

- promoting consideration of crime prevention in future alterations, eg checking the security of new doors, windows or other alterations/extensions to the premises;

- giving advice on target-hardening measures, eg specifying which additional measures would be of most benefit and most cost-effective, giving advice on the upgrading of existing measures;

- leaving information on products and services (although recommendations on particular companies are not given), on good crime prevention practice, and on how to get further advice in the future.

An important point to emphasize is the unique nature of each visit. Many sources of information were used to ensure that the advice offered was tailor-made for the individual business owner. For instance, preparation before the visit helped to establish the type of area the business was located in, and any particular crime problems that area faced. Examining the property and its surroundings at

Crime Prevention and Community Safety: An International Journal

both the front and the rear, and asking the business owners to give their own account of what they perceived as problems and potential solutions, also assisted in identifying the most valuable type of crime prevention advice for the particular business.

Some implementation concerns

One problem facing the Small Business Strategy implementation team was the 'learnt helplessness' of the most vulnerable proprietors within the business community in relation to victimization, and their underlying belief that crime was simply a marginal cost to be endured. Many business owners seemed to put up with, or even expect, a certain level of victimization, and felt that neither the police nor any additional investment in security would have much impact in reducing their future crime risk. This is reflected in the percentage of the businesses that reported different types of crime to the police. For example, incidents of shoplifting, employee theft and fraud were reported to the police by less than a third of business owners.

Other issues raised by the implementation included the high number of empty or boarded-up properties found by the surveying team; this reflected the high turnover of small businesses in the Merseyside area. For purposes of regeneration it is important to make these properties viable for new business ventures. The SMP liaised with other agencies to address this problem.

A further issue raised was the importance of providing proprietors with support and encouragement to invest time and money in security measures; crime prevention strategies concentrating on giving grants for physical target-hardening alone are likely to have little impact on decreasing vulnerability. It is also important to provide tailor-made advice to business owners. This guidance should include encouraging a problem-orientated approach to the identification of what was making the property vulnerable, and assisting in the identification of the most cost-effective and affordable security devices, as well as examining everyday operational routines that minimize future crime risk. The need for this type of crime prevention advice was also highlighted in the Leicester SBCI study.[13]

An area for potential improvement in the implementation of the SBS was that of grant take-up. Although 46 properties were offered financial assistance, only 17 actually completed the grant application process. Two reasons were given for this low take-up: first, the forms that needed to be completed for assistance were found to be very complicated; and second, the grants were offered for limited periods, and only consisted of a contributions of up to 50 per cent, which were prohibitive conditions for some business owners. These issues were addressed in the second round of the strategy. A detailed description of the SBS implementation and the targeting procedure that was used to identify vulnerable properties is available elsewhere.[14]

Evaluation methods

In order to produce a more reliable evaluation, it was decided that a dual approach would be taken, using information from a follow-up survey and from Merseyside Police's Recorded Crime System to assess the impact of the SBS. This had the advantage that it could determine the effect of the scheme at the level of both the individual and the area.

The survey design enabled the longitudinal tracking of individual properties that either had or had not been assisted by the SBS. However, since the scheme required that specific criteria were met in order for a business to be surveyed in the first instance (ie, the baseline survey

Crime Prevention and Community Safety: An International Journal

described above), this information does not reflect changes that might have occurred in levels of victimization in the non-residential community as a whole (ie, any area-level effects of the scheme).

The area-level analysis, based on recorded crime, allowed comparisons between fluctuations in the burglary rate in the scheme's areas of operation with those occurring elsewhere. For instance, how did the burglary rate in residential parts of Objective 1 areas (the scheme areas) compare with that in non-residential parts?

In addition to studying changes in levels of crime, it is possible to assess the wider impacts of the scheme in terms of the initiative's side-effects. For example, information was collected from survey participants regarding their fear of crime and their levels of satisfaction with the police. Any positive side-effects identified, such as a decrease in the fear of crime, have implications for the identification of particularly successful and cost-effective schemes. However, it is outside the scope of the current paper to outline results connected with these issues; its primary concern is rather to focus on the direct effect of the initiative on levels of crime—and in particular on levels of burglary—and to try to gain some insight into the method by which the initiative is achieving any reduction in these levels.

An evaluation survey of small businesses

This following section describes results which have been compiled from the information collected in the evaluation phase of the SBS. The evaluation form was designed to obtain information from businesses that had responded to the baseline survey described above, and asked for information on the following:

- levels of victimization of the property since the last survey had been conducted;

- details of any up-date/installation of security measures since the last survey, and information regarding the funding of these measures;

- information concerning dealings with the SMP and other agencies;

- details of the mechanism by which any attempted burglary had failed;

- details concerning the detection of offenders when an incident of crime had occurred.

These questions, in combination with information from the baseline survey, allow the evaluator to track the progress of businesses over time and assess the effectiveness of steps taken by the SBS initiative. The last two types of question should also help to shed light on the degree to which different crime prevention and detection measures are effective in different circumstances. The surveyors visited all 470 businesses that had responded in the initial baseline phase of the SBS survey described earlier.

Response levels and reliability issues
In all, the evaluation surveyors collected information from 326 (70 per cent) of the 470 businesses that had originally responded to the baseline survey. The most common reasons why information was not collected from the remaining 144 businesses was that they had been shut down and boarded-up (42 per cent), or that, after several attempts, the manager could not be contacted (43 per cent), although, in some cases, he/she had refused to take part in the evaluation survey (15 per cent).

Crime Prevention and Community Safety: An International Journal

SBS intervention and target-hardening measures

Many of the tables below classify respondents on the basis of whether or not they were involved in the SBS intervention. Overall, 105 (32 per cent) of those surveyed in the evaluation phase had been involved in the SBS intervention. The evaluation respondents also included all 17 properties that had been assisted by the SMP with physical target-hardening.

It was important to collect information from all the businesses regarding target-hardening. It is very likely that a certain number of those that did not receive assistance from the SBS had upgraded or installed security measures at their business location since the baseline survey, by financing the measures themselves or even through assistance from elsewhere (for instance another crime prevention agency, or a landlord). Without this information, any analysis of the effectiveness of different measures would be vitiated, since it would not identify all businesses that had improved their security.

For the purposes of analysis, therefore, the evaluation survey respondents were split into four categories: those who *were* involved in the intervention[15] and *had* target-hardened their property; those who were involved in the intervention but had *not* target-hardened; those who were *not* involved in the intervention but *had* target-hardened; and those who were not in the intervention and had *not* target-hardened. Table 1 below summarizes the numbers falling into each of these categories.

Table 1. Evaluation survey respondents and crime prevention measures

Type of action	Number of cases	Percentage of cases
Target-hardening only	73	22.4
Target-hardening and intervention	63	19.3
Intervention only	42	12.9
No action	148	45.4

The table shows that a substantial proportion of the properties surveyed had target-hardened their properties within the intervention period, although they were not involved in the SBS intervention. In the tables that follow, where the impact of the SBS is being assessed, the analysis simply distinguishes between those who were and were not involved in the intervention. However, where the effectiveness of a particular type of measure is being assessed, the analysis uses information from all the properties that installed or upgraded their security system with that measure, irrespective of the way in which it was funded.

Changes in levels of crime

Tables 2a–2c overleaf compare levels of crime experienced by the businesses surveyed in the baseline and the evaluation studies. Examining Table 2a first, it is apparent that there are some overall differences in the levels of crime experienced: in all crime types, with the exception of robbery, the number of businesses suffering from the crime was lower in the evaluation study than in the baseline study. This implies that the prevalence of crimes against businesses has dropped over the period of the initiative. This is especially true in the case of burglary, attempted burglary, shoplifting, and fraud and forgery, where the overall number of businesses suffering from these crimes appears to have dropped substantially. Although this trend is encouraging, it is not so far possible to attribute these declines in prevalence to the SBS initiative.

Crime Prevention and Community Safety: An International Journal

Table 2a. Overall changes in number and percentage of businesses experiencing crime

Crime type	Baseline survey		Evaluation survey		Difference in %	% change
	%	Number	%	Number		
Burglary	18.0	58/322	11.4	37/325	-6.6	-36.7
Attempted burglary	29.1	95/321	17.1	55/322	-12.0	-41.2
Criminal damage	37.2	120/323	35.6	114/320	-1.6	-4.3
Shoplifting	43.8	141/322	35.0	112/320	-8.8	-20.1
Employee theft	4.7	15/319	2.0	6/307	-	-
Fraud and forgery	36.4	117/321	20.3	65/330	-16.1	-44.2
Robbery	5.6	18/323	6.8	22/323	+1.2	+21.4
Assault	20.7	67/323	16.5	53/322	-4.2	-20.3
Theft from customer	7.5	24/321	6.8	22/323	-0.7	-9.3

Notes:

The following conventions apply throughout Tables 2a–c and 3a–c:
% = percentage of businesses experiencing crime type.
Number = number of businesses suffering crime type as a fraction of those responding to the question.
Difference = difference in prevalence rates for baseline and evaluation: (increase (+) or decrease (-).
% change = change in crime rate as a percentage of the baseline prevalence rate.

In some tables there are insufficient cases of employee theft to conduct an analysis.

In order to begin to assess the impact of the SBS, the information given in Table 2a needs to be separated into two further tables: one that tracks the victimization of the businesses involved in the SBS intervention, and one that tracks the non-intervention group. This information is shown in Tables 2b and 2c respectively. The most striking result when comparing these two tables is that although levels of burglary decreased in both groups, there is a far more marked decrease in burglary in the SBS intervention group.

In fact, for the intervention group, the prevalence of burglary dropped from 32.4 per cent to 13.3 per cent, which is a decrease in the prevalence rate of 58.9 per cent between the two surveys. This can be compared to a drop from 11.4 per cent to 10.5 per cent in the non-intervention group, an overall decrease of only 7.9 per cent. This huge decrease in the prevalence of burglary in the intervention group was also tested for statistical significance.

Chi-squares were performed to assess whether there were any differences between the proportion of businesses that were victims and non-victims in the baseline and evaluation surveys. Results show that there are significant differences in these proportions in the intervention group, due to the decline in the number of victims. In fact, the chi-square figure reaches a significance value of $p < 0.005$. There was no significant result for burglary in the non-intervention group.

Table 2b shows that the change in levels of successful burglary was the greatest percentage decrease in the intervention group of all the crime types. This is not surprising, since the SBS initiative was targeted primarily at businesses that had experienced successful burglary. In addition, there had also been substantial decreases in other types of crime as well. This is particularly marked in the case of attempted burglary and of fraud and forgery, which saw percentage decreases of 48.9 per cent and 55.3 per cent respectively; both achieved a high level of statistical significance for the intervention group. However, when these results are compared with those for the non-intervention group, it can be seen that caution needs to be

Crime Prevention and Community Safety: An International Journal

exercised in attributing these decreases to the SBS initiative. This is because the non-intervention group also saw a large decrease in these offence types, although it is not as significant as those observed in the intervention group.

Table 2b. Changes in number and percentage of businesses experiencing crime for the intervention group

Crime type	Baseline survey		Evaluation survey		Difference in %	% change
	%	Number	%	Number		
Burglary	32.4	33/102	13.3	14/105	-19.1	-58.9
Attempted burglary	49.0	50/102	25.0	26/104	-24.0	-48.9
Criminal damage	51.5	53/103	45.6	47/103	-5.9	-11.5
Shoplifting	55.3	57/103	43.3	45/104	-12.0	-21.7
Employee theft	2.9	3/102	0.0	0/100	-	-
Fraud and forgery	46.1	47/102	20.6	21/102	-25.5	-55.3
Robbery	6.8	7/103	5.8	6/104	-1.0	-14.7
Assault	24.3	25/103	20.2	21/104	-4.1	-16.9
Theft from customer	8.7	9/103	7.8	8/103	-0.9	-10.3

Lastly, it is interesting to observe that Table 2b shows that for the intervention group there were decreases in the prevalence of all the crime types dealt with by the survey. This means that it is unlikely that there has been any crime type displacement experienced by the intervention group whereby offenders return to the same target but commit another type of crime.

Table 2c. Changes in number and percentage of businesses experiencing crime for the non-intervention group

Crime type	Baseline survey		Evaluation survey		Difference in %	% change
	%	Number	%	Number		
Burglary	11.4	25/220	10.5	23/220	-0.9	-7.9
Attempted burglary	20.5	45/219	13.3	29/218	-7.2	-35.1
Criminal damage	30.5	67/220	30.9	67/217	+0.4	+1.3
Shoplifting	38.4	84/219	31.3	67/216	-7.1	-18.5
Employee theft	5.5	12/217	2.9	6/207	-	-
Fraud and forgery	32.0	70/219	20.2	44/218	-11.8	-36.9
Robbery	5.0	11/220	7.3	16/219	+2.3	+46.0
Assault	19.1	42/220	14.7	32/218	-4.4	-23.0
Theft from customer	6.9	15/218	6.4	14/220	-0.5	-7.2

Table 2c shows the same general trend in crime, although there were increases in levels of criminal damage and robbery in the non-intervention group. When the numbers involved are examined, it can be seen that these are not trends to cause alarm, since there is only a slight increase in prevalence in each case. Table 2c therefore shows that there is no evidence of target displacement of crime. In other words, it does not appear to be the case that offenders that were targeting the intervention group businesses have started to target those in the non-intervention group. However, to be certain that target displacement has not occurred, information would be required from all other businesses not surveyed, and from residential properties, to ensure that burglars have not switched to other property types.

Crime Prevention and Community Safety: An International Journal

Table 3a. Overall changes in number and percentage of businesses experiencing repeated incidents of crime

Crime type	Baseline survey		Evaluation survey		Difference in %	% change
	%	Number	%	Number		
Burglary	54.3	31/57	33.3	12/36	-21.0	-38.7
Attempted burglary	54.4	49/90	50.0	27/54	-4.4	-8.1
Criminal damage	54.3	63/116	71.6	73/102	+17.3	+31.9
Shoplifting	75.5	83/110	75.5	74/98	0	0
Employee theft	30.8	4/13	50.0	2/4	+19.2	+62.3
Fraud and forgery	73.2	82/112	70.0	42/60	-3.2	-4.4
Robbery	5.6	1/18	45.0	9/20	+39.4	+703.6
Assault	58.3	35/60	65.2	30/46	+6.9	+11.8
Theft from customer	50.0	12/24	42.1	8/19	-7.9	-15.8

Tables 3a-3c show changes in levels of repeat incidents of crime against businesses between the baseline survey and the evaluation survey. It is important to track this, because reducing repeat victimization, especially repeat burglary, was one of the original objectives of the SBS initiative. Table 3a shows that for the whole sample there were some overall changes in levels of repeat victimization. There was a marked decrease in the number of burglary victims suffering from repeat incidents of the crime (54 per cent in the baseline survey and 33 per cent in the evaluation). Other trends show a small decrease in the number of repeat victims of attempted burglary and of fraud and forgery, and an increase in the number of victims experiencing repeat criminal damage and repeat robbery. The decrease in repeat burglary and the increase in repeat criminal damage and robbery result in significant chi-square tests.

Table 3b. Changes in number and percentage of businesses experiencing repeated incidents of crime for the intervention group

Crime type	Baseline survey		Evaluation survey		Difference in %	% change
	%	Number	%	Number		
Burglary	67.6	23/34	26.7	4/15	-40.9	-60.5
Attempted burglary	60.9	28/46	60.0	15/25	-0.9	-1.5
Criminal damage	57.1	28/49	69.2	27/39	+12.1	+21.2
Shoplifting	74.4	32/43	72.5	29/40	-1.9	-2.6
Employee theft	33.3	1/3	-	0/0	-	-
Fraud and forgery	69.8	30/43	75.0	15/20	+5.2	+7.5
Robbery	0.0	0/7	50.0	3/6	+50.0	-
Assault	66.7	14/21	68.4	13/19	+1.7	+2.6
Theft from customer	55.6	5/9	50.0	4/8	-5.6	-10.1

In Tables 3b and 3c this information is separated into data for the intervention and non-intervention groups. The most striking result seen from these tables is the decrease, for the intervention group, in the number of repeat victims of commercial burglary between the baseline survey and the evaluation. The percentage of burglary victims experiencing repeat incidents fell from 67.6 per cent to 26.7 per cent during this time. This result is statistically significant at the $p < 0.01$ level. In contrast, the number of victims of burglary experiencing repeat incidents in the non-intervention group was very similar for the baseline and evaluation surveys (37.5 per cent and 38.1 per cent respectively). In fact, the prevalence of repeat burglary amongst burglary victims was much higher in the intervention group at the baseline stage, but had become lower than the non-intervention group by the evaluation stage. It is possible to conclude that the SBS intervention had an effect on the level of repeat burglary experienced by participants.

Table 3c. Changes in number and percentage of businesses experiencing repeated incidents of crime for the non-intervention group

Crime type	Baseline survey		Evaluation survey		Difference in %	% change
	%	Number	%	Number		
Burglary	37.5	9/24	38.1	8/21	+0.6	+1.6
Attempted burglary	47.7	21/44	41.4	12/29	-6.3	-13.2
Criminal damage	52.2	35/67	73.0	46/63	+20.8	+39.8
Shoplifting	76.1	51/67	77.6	45/58	+1.5	+2.0
Employee theft	30.0	3/10	50.0	2/4	+20.0	+66.7
Fraud and forgery	75.4	52/69	67.5	27/40	-7.9	-10.5
Robbery	9.1	1/11	42.9	6/14	+33.8	+371.4
Assault	53.8	21/39	63.0	17/27	+9.2	+17.1
Theft from customer	46.7	7/15	36.4	4/11	-10.3	-22.1

Interestingly, Tables 3b and 3c also show some evidence of increasing levels of repeat victimization. Repeat robbery and repeat criminal damage rose significantly in the intervention and non-intervention groups respectively. Since these crime types are still property crime, this raises the issue of whether there has been any displacement of repeat crime to other crime types associated with the SBS implementation. However, these trends are not reflected by any overall increases in the prevalence of criminal damage or robbery from the figures in Table 2, and in the case of robbery in the intervention group, there are only small numbers to analyse in Table 3, which decreases the reliability of this result.

Changes in burglary rate by type of intervention and type of crime prevention measure
Table 4 below gives further details about burglary rates and type of intervention. As explained above, it was important to obtain information from both intervention and non-intervention businesses regarding the extent and the effect of target-hardening. As expected, given the mechanisms used to identify vulnerable businesses, prevalence rates before the initiative were highest in the intervention groups. However, prevalence rates were also higher in the baseline survey for those businesses that made their own decision to target-harden their properties than for those who had not taken any action. This implies that business owners are more likely to take crime prevention action after they have been victimized.

Table 4. Burglary rates by type of intervention

Intervention	Baseline survey		Evaluation survey		Difference in prevalence between baseline and evaluation
	Number burgled	% burgled	Number burgled	% burgled	
Target-hardening only	15/73	20.5	12/73	16.4	-5.9
Target-hardening and intervention	18/62	29.0	6/63	9.5	-19.5
Intervention only	15/40	37.5	8/42	19.0	-18.5
No action	10/147	6.8	11/147	7.5	+0.7

Crime Prevention and Community Safety: An International Journal

Table 4 shows that there was a decrease in the prevalence of burglary in *all* the groups where some action was taken, and a slight increase in the group where no action was taken. This shows that any one of the type of actions described in the table is effective in reducing levels of burglary. However, it is also apparent that the largest reductions in the prevalence of burglary occurred in the groups that were involved in the SBS intervention. This suggests that visits from the Crime Prevention Officers and liaison with the SMP had an effect over and above that produced by simply target-hardening a property. It also shows that it is important to give businesses crime prevention advice and to encourage owners to think about crime prevention, in addition to improving or installing physical target-hardening measures. It is worth noting that the group that experienced the biggest decrease in levels of burglary had both elements of the intervention: target hardening and a visit from a CPO, which indicates that a combined approach is particularly effective.

It is useful at this point to examine reasons why the CPO visits were successful at reducing burglary rates, even in the absence of target hardening. In recent years the role of Crime Prevention Officers within the Police has been changing. An interview with a CPO from Merseyside Police revealed that there has been increased pressure due to a lack of funding in the area. This meant that it was very difficult to visit more than one site of crime a day. In addition, victims that were visited within a short time frame were generally restricted to those that police records identified as repeat victims. Furthermore, victims not fitting certain criteria could only get advice from a CPO by telephone or by visiting a police station in person.

One of the most likely explanations for the success of the visits undertaken by the CPOs in helping to reduce crime against businesses is, therefore, the fact that a visit had actually been made *at all* to the vulnerable properties involved. The SBS put a formal framework on the particular sites that were to be visited, which prioritized those at risk and also brought the CPOs into contact with business that had suffered from crime but did not report many of these incidents to the police. Although there was no extra budget for the CPOs to conduct the site visits, the SBS motivated the CPOs to concentrate on the small business sector for a period of at least several months.

Results from the earlier baseline survey demonstrated that many of the vulnerable businesses involved had not had any formal, or indeed informal, crime prevention advice for a number of years, if at all. Therefore, having an unlimited amount of time with a crime prevention expert who cared about the security of the site and was available to give *specific* advice on issues such as layout, natural surveillance, staff behaviour, and cheap and effective ways of improving current security, inspired business owners to take steps to implement the recommendations given.

In essence, the proactive nature of the SBS in reaching businesses that had had little or no contact with crime prevention experts, or had limited knowledge of good crime prevention practices, was a major reason for its success. A further factor was, of course, the standard of the advice given to businesses; the CPOs working on the SBS were all experts in the field and had received training in the provision of crime prevention advice. Furthermore, as mentioned above, the advice that was given was *tailor-made* for the particular business, which was also a distinct advantage of an approach that involved individual site visits.

Table 5 examines the effect of different *types* of target-hardening measure on the prevalence of burglary. It is evident that all the measures listed in the table, with the exception of security lighting, appear to have had an effect; however, there are particularly small numbers in some of the categories, which means there are likely to be problems with the reliability of these results. In addition, the fact that there have been overall decreases in levels of burglary should be taken into account. Some measures that appear to be particularly effective in combating burglary (Table 5) are roller shutters, window locks and window protection, although these results are far from conclusive.

Table 5. Burglary rates by type of security measure

Security measure installed in intervention period	Baseline survey Number burgled	% burgled	Evaluation survey Number burgled	% burgled	Difference in prevalence between baseline and evaluation
Burglar alarm	15/58	25.9	12/60	20.0	-5.9
Roller shutters	10/32	31.3	5/33	15.1	-16.2
Window locks	6/13	46.2	1/13	7.7	-38.2
Window protection	5/14	35.7	2/14	14.3	-21.4
Reinforced doors	9/31	29.0	6/31	19.4	-9.6
CCTV	5/28	17.9	3/29	10.3	-7.6
Security lighting	0/16	0	2/17	11.8	+11.8
Security fencing	3/9	33.3	2/9	22.2	-11.1
Other measures	2/10	20.0	1/10	10.0	-10.0
Security procedures	1/5	20.0	0/5	0	-20.0

Table 6 gives some information regarding the *modus operandi* (MO) of successful burglaries before and after the SBS intervention. Again, the information should be treated with caution due to the small numbers involved, but generally it can be seen that the most common form of MO, both before and after the intervention, was where offenders had entered through the door. Also common before intervention was entry through roller doors and through windows other than a main shop window. These MOs were less common after the SBS intervention. Table 6 does not show any firm evidence of MO displacement between the baseline and evaluation surveys.

Table 6. MO of successful burglaries before and after intervention

MO of entry to premises	Total for baseline	% for baseline	Total for evaluation	% for evaluation
Door	16/56	28.6	13/33	39.4
Roller door	13/56	23.2	3/33	9.1
Main shop window	4/56	7.1	4/33	12.1
Another window	12/56	21.4	3/33	9.1
Perimeter fence	4/56	7.1	3/33	9.1
Roof	8/56	14.2	3/33	9.1

Note: The percentages in Tables 6 and 7 do not add up to 100 since more than one response might apply. The percentages are based only on those who responded to the question and do not include cases where the respondent 'did not know' or where data was missing.

The mechanism by which measures are effective for crime prevention and detection
Table 7 displays figures indicating the reason why incidents of attempted burglary had failed. This could provide information on the types of measure that are particularly effective at preventing burglary. This question was asked of those experiencing attempted burglary in the evaluation phase of the survey. The table shows that the most common reason given for burglary failure was a burglar alarm alerting the public. Although most businesses are now equipped with a burglar alarm, this result demonstrates that they are still an effective measure in deterring crime. Reinforced doors also caused burglary failure in a significant number of cases. This might be an issue to focus on in any future crime prevention initiative, since Table 6 demonstrates that entry through a door was still a common MO for successful burglary, even following the SBS initiative. Roller shutters also appeared to be an effective deterrent (Table 7). Finally,

Crime Prevention and Community Safety: An International Journal

simply being located in an area where there is a public presence can cause burglaries to fail. This ties in with the guardianship element of the routine activities theory, which states that the three elements required for a crime to occur are a motivated offender, a suitable target and a lack of capable guardianship.[16]

Table 7. Reasons for failure of attempted burglaries

Reason for failure	Number	% of Cases
Burglar alarm alerted public	10/38	26.3
Reinforced doors	8/38	21.1
Roller shutters	7/38	18.4
Disturbed by public	6/38	15.8
Burglar alarm alerted police	5/38	13.2
Other	5/38	12.5
Mortice locks	3/38	7.9
Window locks	2/38	5.3
Disturbed by security	1/38	2.6
CCTV alerted police	0/38	0

Where a crime was successfully committed, business owners in the evaluation phase were asked whether or not to their knowledge an offender was identified for the crime. The results of this are shown in Table 8. Offenders were most commonly identified for crime types such as assault, robbery and fraud. This is likely to be due to the nature of these crimes; there is some level of interaction between the offender and the business owner or member of staff in all these cases. This is less likely to be the case for crimes such as burglary and criminal damage, which are often committed in the absence of any staff.

Table 8. Incidents of crime where offenders were identified

Type of crime	Number of cases where offender was identified	% of cases where offender was identified
Assault	32/49	65.3
Robbery	9/19	47.4
Fraud	27/58	46.6
Customer theft	35/96	36.5
Burglary	7/22	31.8
Theft from customer	5/21	23.8
Criminal damage	15/88	17.0
Employee theft	-	-

Table 9 looks in more depth at the mechanism by which the offenders in Table 8 were identified. This can give us information regarding measures or procedures that are effective in the detection of particular crime types. The most common way in which an offender was detected was through identification by a member of staff, and this form of identification also led to the most convictions. Some other mechanisms of offender identification were particularly effective for certain crime types. For instance, a substantial number of shoplifters were detected using CCTV systems, which also proved to be effective in terms of convictions. CCTV also appeared to be effective in cases of robbery and assault, but less so in identifying offenders committing burglary or acts of deliberate damage. Credit card checks were effective

Crime Prevention and Community Safety: An International Journal

in the detection of fraud, and physical detection measures appeared to be useful in cases of deliberate damage. Security guards did not appear to be effective in detecting crime in the cases analyzed, although members of the public and the police assisted in some cases, especially in relation to criminal damage.

Table 9. Mechanism of offender identification

	Burglary	Deliberate damage	Shop theft	Fraud	Robbery	Assault	Theft from customer
CCTV	0	1	10 ****	1	3 *	3 *	1
Physical detection	0	2 *	N/A	N/A	0	0	N/A
Respondent/staff member	3	4	25 ***	21 ***	6 *	26 **	5
Police	1	2 *	2	1 *	1 *	1	0
Security guard	0	0	0	0	0	0	0
Member of public	1 *	3 *	0	0	0	1	0
Security alarm (eg, tagged goods)	N/A	N/A	0	N/A	N/A	N/A	N/A
Credit card check	N/A	N/A	N/A	4 *	N/A	N/A	N/A
Police alerted by alarm	N/A	N/A	N/A	N/A	0	N/A	N/A

Note: Figures in cells = number of offenders detected. * = number of convictions. For example, 10 shoplifters were detected using CCTV, and in four of these cases the offender was convicted.

Levels of crime reported to the police
Before moving on to discuss changes in Merseyside Police's recorded crime figures, it is important to establish possible levels of under-reporting. Table 10 below summarizes differences in levels of reporting of crimes to the police between the baseline and intervention surveys. Generally, there are only small differences in these levels between the surveys, with commercial burglary remaining the offence type which is most widely reported to the police. This means that commercial burglary information from police statistics is likely to provide the most accurate picture of true changes in all the types of business crime over time. Interestingly, there has been a small decrease in the number of burglaries reported to the police between the two surveys. This means that the implementation of the SBS has not provoked an increase in reporting levels in the long term, which has been found to happen with some crime prevention initiatives.

Table 10. Levels of reporting to police in baseline and evaluation surveys

Crime type	% of businesses reporting crime in baseline survey	% of businesses reporting crime in evaluation survey
Burglary	89.3	83.3
Attempted burglary	53.3	58.2
Criminal damage	44.3	37.0
Shoplifting	23.5	26.9
Employee theft	15.4	50.0
Fraud and forgery	23.2	13.1
Robbery	83.3	60.0
Assault	44.6	42.2
Theft from customer	42.9	52.4

Crime Prevention and Community Safety: An International Journal

Longitudinal information on commercial burglaries recorded by the police

In addition to direct information from crime surveys, it is also important to monitor the level of commercial burglary recorded by the police to produce the most comprehensive picture possible regarding the success of the SBS initiative. There are many issues relating to the accuracy of commercial burglary data and the production of commercial burglary rates, which are discussed in full elsewhere.[17] At this point, it will suffice to say that these issues have been taken into consideration in the following analysis, which uses 'cleaned' data.

A useful starting point is to track the total number of recorded commercial burglaries on Merseyside over the period of the intervention. Figure 1 shows that, in the three months when the baseline survey was conducted, there were 1288 commercial burglaries recorded, and that in the three months of the evaluation (depicted on the graph as 'follow-up survey') there were 1234 burglaries. This implies that overall levels of commercial burglary had fallen over this period. However, it is interesting to examine the levels of burglary recorded between these two reference points: there was a sharp rise between the beginning of the intervention period and the second quarter of 1998. After that, commercial burglary decreased steadily up to the second quarter of 1999, where it was at its lowest for the entire five-year period analyzed.

Figure 1. Number of commercial burglaries

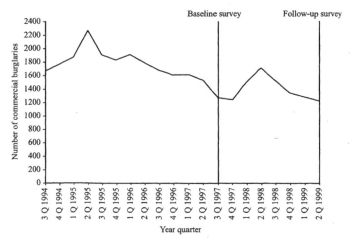

The overall decrease in levels of commercial burglary reflects findings from the survey described above. To look in more detail at the trends in the areas of operation of the scheme, the remaining figures distinguish between Objective 1 areas and other areas, and between residential and non-residential areas.

Figure 2 compares the commercial burglary rate per 1000 premises in Objective 1 areas to that elsewhere. The figure shows a differential picture for Objective 1 areas and other areas. Between the baseline survey and the evaluation, the burglary rate in Objective 1 areas rose from 36 to 40 burglaries per 1000 premises. By contrast, the burglary rate had fallen from 30 to 25 per 1000 in other areas. In a similar way to Figure 1, there was a rise in the burglary rate in both areas around the second quarter of 1998. At first sight, this slight increase in the burglary rate in Objective 1 areas brings the impact of the SBS initiative on area-level burglary rates into question. In order to assess the scheme's effectiveness in more detail, it is necessary to compare results for residential and non-residential areas.

Crime Prevention and Community Safety: An International Journal

Figure 2. Commercial burglary rates

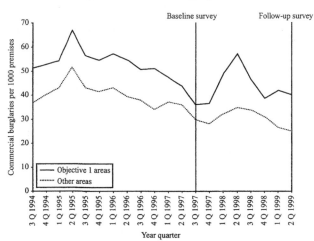

Figure 3 below shows the crime rates in non-residential parts of Objective 1 areas and other areas that are non-residential. In this case, there is a fairly noticeable increase in rates of burglary between the baseline and evaluation quarters, especially in the Objective 1 areas. In fact, the rate rose from 35 to 54 per 1000 in Objective 1 areas, and from 38 to 42 per 1000 elsewhere. Looking at the general trend in non-residential Objective 1 areas, it is apparent that the burglary rate was never as low, in the subsequent quarters of 1997, 1998 and 1999, as it had been in the baseline quarter. There was certainly no decrease in burglary rates in non-residential Objective 1 areas, or indeed in non-residential areas elsewhere since the implementation of the SBS.

Figure 3. Commercial burglary rates in non-residential areas

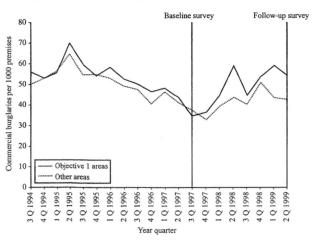

Crime Prevention and Community Safety: An International Journal

Figure 4 shows changes in the burglary rate of residential parts of Objective 1 areas and other residential areas. The SBS scheme was implemented in these residential Objective 1 areas. The figure shows that there was a dramatic decrease in the burglary rate between the baseline survey and the evaluation survey in both Objective 1 areas and in the other residential areas. In fact, burglary rates in residential parts of Objective 1 areas decreased from 38 to 23 per 1000 premises over the SBS implementation period.

Figure 4. Commercial burglary rates in residential areas

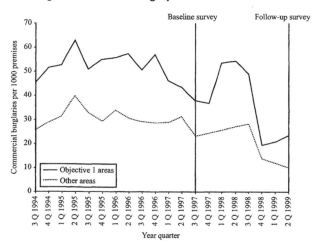

This evidence backs up the results found through the analysis of survey data above, showing that the burglary rates in the SBS operational areas decreased very noticeably after the scheme was implemented. This could indicate that the SBS had a general area-level effect, as well as an effect on the particular properties within the area that were singled out for assistance through the scheme. In other words, the fact that some properties in the area had been assisted might have discouraged offenders from committing burglary against other properties in the area, which would be a positive side-effect of the SBS scheme.

It is important to consider this drop in the burglary rate in Objective 1 parts of residential areas in relation to other residential areas. It can be seen from Figure 4 that there was a decrease in both these areas. The decrease in the burglary rate in other residential areas might be a further positive side-effect of the SBS scheme, but this seems unlikely since residential areas that are inside and those that are outside Objective 1 areas are not in general located near to each other. There may be another reason for this overall decline in levels of burglary in residential areas. For instance, it is possible that other schemes that target commercial properties in residential areas have had an effect on levels of crime. However, other known burglary schemes on Merseyside concentrate on particular areas and are thus unlikely to have an effect on residential areas as a whole throughout the region.

A further possibility in accounting for the overall reduction in levels of crime in residential areas is that there has been a sustained reduction in business owners reporting cases of burglary to the police. Once more, this is unlikely, since results from the baseline and evaluation surveys, described above, found that there was only a small variation in levels of reporting of burglary between the two surveys, although admittedly these results apply to the SBS implementation areas, and not necessarily to other residential areas.

Crime Prevention and Community Safety: An International Journal

It is useful to examine the trends in burglary rates *between* the quarters when the baseline and evaluation surveys took place. There was an initial increase in the number of recorded burglaries in the residential Objective 1 areas between the third quarter of 1997 and the second quarter of 1998. This was during the period when the SBS was implemented; all properties that were involved in the scheme had been visited by the second quarter of 1998. From then onwards, burglary rates peaked, then fell dramatically in residential Objective 1 areas. This sharp rise in recorded crime rates shortly after the baseline survey did not occur in residential areas outside Objective 1 areas. One explanation for the increase in burglary rates in the SBS areas could be that word had spread throughout the business community that the SMP were offering assistance. As a consequence, business owners were more inclined to report incidents to the police during this period, in the hope that they too would be assisted. If this increase in reporting levels is the reason for the increase in burglary rates at this time, we know that the effect was fairly short-lived, given the fact that reporting levels at the time of the baseline and evaluation surveys were very similar.

Another interesting observation is that by the fourth quarter of 1998, rates in the Objective 1 areas and other areas had converged to their closest levels within a four-and-a-half year period. This convergence is one indicator of the success of the SBS scheme, since it shows that for some time burglary rates in the scheme's operational areas were more in line with those elsewhere. In the two quarters since the convergence occurred, the burglary rate in the Objective 1 residential areas rose again very slightly, whereas the other residential areas continued to see a decline in the rate. This tendency would need to be monitored over several quarters to investigate the possibility that the SBS did have an effect on burglary rates, but only in the short term. If this proved to be the case, future crime prevention schemes should focus on ways of maintaining decreases in levels of burglary over the long term.

Conclusion

This paper has evaluated the effectiveness of the Small Business Strategy in achieving its aim of making vulnerable small businesses safer and, in particular, of reducing levels of burglary and repeat burglary against such premises. The results show that levels of burglary have been significantly reduced in the properties that were involved in the SBS intervention. The number of burglary victims that experienced repeat victimization was also substantially reduced in the intervention group. These drastic reductions were not seen in the group of properties that were not involved in the intervention.

Through examining the intervention and non-intervention groups, it was found that there was no evidence of crime displacement to other crime types, other MOs or other areas. This paper has also attempted to investigate the means by which particular methods are effective in reducing crime, although information from a larger-scale survey would be required to substantiate these results.

Recorded crime data relating to burglary from Merseyside Police backed up the findings from the survey; burglary had substantially reduced in the SBS scheme areas over the implementation period. Since the scheme did not assist all properties in the scheme area, the SBS might have had an additional effect of discouraging offenders from committing burglary against properties in the scheme area generally. However, the effect of the SBS on recorded burglary rates might be exaggerated, since a general downwards trend in crime rates was observed in other residential areas in addition to the Objective 1 residential areas in which the scheme operated.

There were also concerns that the effect of the SBS might be fairly short-term in its nature. This reflects the general dilemma, in terms of sustainability, of short-term interventions, typified by

Crime Prevention and Community Safety: An International Journal

government schemes funded through sources such as the Single Regeneration Budget. This would be an issue to examine in the future. Furthermore, non-residential areas saw a rise in levels of recorded burglary over the intervention period. Properties within these areas could be a fruitful focus for future crime prevention initiatives in the Merseyside area.

Notes

1   The author is a Research Associate in the Urban Research and Policy Evaluation Regional Research Laboratory, Department of Civic Design, University of Liverpool, P.O. Box 147, Liverpool, L69 3BX; tel: +44 (0) 151 794 3118; fax: +44 (0) 151 794 3125; email: kjb@liverpool.ac.uk. She would like to thank Alex Hirschfield, Alan Roberts, the staff at the Safer Merseyside Partnership, and the Crime Prevention Officers of Merseyside Police for their assistance with the research described in this paper.

2   Ekblom, P., Law, H. and Sutton, M. (1996) *Domestic Burglary Schemes in the Safer Cities Programme*. Research Findings No. 42, Home Office Research and Statistics Directorate. London: Home Office.

3   Chenery, S., Holt, J. and Pease, K. (1997) *Biting Back II: Reducing Repeat Victimisation in Huddersfield*. Crime Detection and Prevention Series, Paper No. 82, London: Home Office.

4   Mirrlees-Black, C. and Ross, A. (1995) *Crime Against Retail and Manufacturing Premises: Findings from the 1994 Commercial Victimisation Survey*. Home Office Research Study No. 146. London: Home Office.

5   Mayhew, P., Maung, N.A. and Mirrlees-Black, C. (1993) *The 1992 British Crime Survey*. Home Office Research Study No. 132. London: Home Office.

6   Bowers, K.J., Hirschfield, A. and Johnson, S.D. (1998) Victimisation Revisited: A Case Study of Non-Residential Repeat Burglary on Merseyside. *British Journal of Criminology*. Vol. 38, No. 3, pp 429–52.

7   Fisher, B. (1991) A Neighbourhood Business Area is Hurting: Crime, Fear of Crime and Disorders Take their Toll. *Crime and Delinquency*. Vol. 37, No. 3, pp 363–73.

8   Beck, A. and Willis, A. (1998) Sales and Security: Striking the Balance. In Gill, M. (ed.) *Crime at Work*. Vol. II: *Increasing the Risk for Offenders*. Leicester: Perpetuity Press.

9   Hollinger, R. C. (1997) Measuring Crime and Its Impact in the Business Environment. In Felson, M. and Clarke, R.V. (eds) *Business and Crime Prevention*. New York: Criminal Justice Press, pp 57–80.

10   Tilley, N.and Hopkins, M. (1998) *Business as Usual: An Evaluation of the Small Business and Crime Initiative*. Police Research Series, Paper No. 95. London: Home Office.

11   Ibid, p vii.

12   Pawson, R. and Tilley, N. (1994) What Works in Evaluation Research? *British Journal of Criminology*. Vol. 34, No. 3, pp 291–306.

13   Taylor, G. (1999) Using Repeat Victimisation to Counter Commercial Burglary: The Leicester Experience. *Security Journal*. Vol. 12, No. 1, pp 41–52.

14   Bowers, K and Hirschfield, A. (1998) High Risk, Low Risk: The Use of Data in the Identification of Potential Targets of Commercial Crime Offenders. In Gill, op cit.

15   In other words, those that were visited by a Crime Prevention Officer.

16   Cohen, L.E. and Felson, M. (1979) Social Change and Crime Rate Trends: A Routine Activity Approach. *American Sociological Review*. Vol. 44, No. 4, pp 588–608.

17   Tilley, N. (1993) *The Prevention of Crime Against Small Businesses: The Safer Cities Experience*. Police Research Group, Crime Prevention Unit Series, Paper No. 45. London: Home Office.

[20]

Critically Reviewing the Theory and Practice of Secured-by-design for Residential New-build Housing in Britain

P.M. Cozens, T. Pascoe and D. Hillier[1]

The UK government has projected a need for some 4.1 million homes by 2021 (Department of the Environment, Transport and the Regions, 1999a) and a stated policy objective of achieving 60 per cent of new-build housing on 'brownfield' sites (Department of the Environment, Transport and the Regions, 1999b). The government is clearly committed to 'designing out crime' (Department of the Environment, 1994; Crime and Disorder Act 1998), and this paper explores the secured-by-design schemes (SBD), one of the most important community safety initiatives available to planners to assist in achieving these complex aims. The rise in premises liability cases (Hanson, 1998) and the Human Rights Act 1998 illustrate the increasing importance of tackling such issues. A critical review of both the theory and practice of SBD is presented as it applies to the new-build residential environment in the British city. The implications of reviewing SBD's theoretical basis and its application are discussed.

Key Words: Secured-by-design; new-build housing; crime and community safety

Introduction

Crime and nuisance are omnipresent in modern urban society. Indeed, according to the Home Office, recorded crime has increased on average by 5.1 per cent every year since 1918, with property crime representing 91 per cent of all recorded offences in 1997 (Barclay and Tavares, 1999). However, this official measurement of crime may not be as robust as it might at first appear. Indeed, the findings of the British Crime Survey (BCS) indicate that between 1999 and 2000 crime reduced by approximately 12 per cent (Kershaw *et al*, 2001). Despite such variations in measuring it, crime is consistently reported to be one of the most important concerns, in terms of quality of life, for the general population (Social Exclusion Unit, 1998; Devon County Council, 1998; Department of the Environment, Transport and the Regions, 1999c; Rogerson, 2000).

The increasing social, economic and political importance of crime is reflected in government responses that seek to tackle both crime and its underlying causes. Such initiatives include the Crime and Disorder Act 1998 (CDA), the Police Reform Act 2002, the Crime Reduction Programme, the Social Exclusion Unit, the Urban Regeneration Programme, the New Deal, the Urban and Rural White Papers, forthcoming legislation focusing on matters such as anti-social behaviour, and the ongoing review of the government's *Planning Out Crime* circular (Department of the Environment, 1994).

In the light of the government's household projections, a policy objective of developing 60 per cent of new-build housing on brownfield and predominantly urban, inner-city locations has emerged within a broader policy framework for safer, sustainable and more liveable housing

Crime Prevention and Community Safety: An International Journal 2004, 6 (1), 13–29

(Department of the Environment, 1994; Crime and Disorder Act 1998; Department of the Environment, Transport and the Regions, 1998a; 1998b; 1999b; 1999c; 2000; Social Exclusion Unit, 1998). Significantly, there has been an increase in the number of premises liability court cases in America (Gordon and Brill, 1996; Hanson, 1998), where failure to provide 'reasonable' security and appropriately designed built environments has resulted in litigation. Gordon and Brill observe how the emerging discipline of designing out crime

> has done much to establish the reasonableness of certain crime prevention approaches and, thus, the unreasonableness of property owners who fail to take widely accepted steps. (1996:3)

Some lawyers have suggested that such ideas may soon be adopted in the UK (Infield, 2000). Indeed, in the British context Moss and Pease cite various 'designing out crime' studies and conclude:

> There are thus many circumstances in which an individual citizen, a business or a residents' group could plausibly argue that a local authority had breached section 17 [of the CDA]. (1999:16)

Furthermore, Article 1 of the Human Rights Act 1998 (HRA) concerns the right to peaceful enjoyment of possessions, while Article 8 details the right to enjoy family and home life. How such articles within the Act are interpreted in relation to crime and the fear of crime will provide interesting precedents. Indeed, Parker claims that the HRA 'has raised concerns about the future of planning becoming increasingly litigious' (2001:6).

The new-build housing debate, however, has largely focused on where such new-build developments should take place. This paper explores the issue of the design of new-build housing rather than its potential location; the possibility of evaluating the criminogenic capacity of housing design in new-build developments has already been examined (Cozens *et al*, 1999a; 1999b). As one of the major government initiatives for designing out crime, SBD is here discussed and critically reviewed, and its potential for providing residential environments which are 'safer' and less vulnerable to crime and which promote the quality of urban living is investigated.

Design and crime

One useful starting point in understanding the relationship between housing design and crime is to analyse the available crime statistics. Home Office recorded crime statistics are available for each of the 43 police force areas (Home Office, 2000), and potentially provide a consistent, if limited, database in terms of housing design at the micro level of analysis. However, access to such detailed data is restricted.

The BCS was developed in the 1980s, provides self-reported data from a sample of around 40,000 respondents concerning their experiences of crime, and attempts a more realistic assessment of the totality of crime. The BCS estimated that Home Office recorded crime statistics may only represent some 24 per cent of actual crime (Barclay and Tavares, 1999). Moreover, the remaining 76 per cent, often referred to as the 'dark figure' of crime (ie unreported and thus unrecorded crime), may well be located where, according to the official statistics, crime is low. Indeed, such statistics may systematically and routinely underestimate crime levels and create false impressions of where (and when) crime takes place. However, whilst acknowledging such shortcomings, the findings from the BCS provide an opportunity to gain some limited insights (see Table 1).

Crime Prevention and Community Safety: An International Journal 2004, 6 (1), 13–29

Table 1. The BCS: burglary by dwelling type

Dwelling type	Burglary rates per 1000 dwellings
Detached houses/bungalows	23
Semi-detached houses/bungalows	32
Terraced houses	39
Purpose-built flats/maisonettes	45

Source: adapted from Kershaw *et al*, 2001:56

Clearly, certain types of housing appear to be significantly more vulnerable to burglary. However, the varying levels of maintenance and the overall condition of each dwelling are not considered within the survey data, and the crucial influence of 'image' is also not incorporated. Another example would be houses in multiple occupancy (eg typically houses converted into flats or bedsits), which are not included in the above categories but are seen by many as one of the most vulnerable types of property. The aggregation of the survey data relating to burglary of dwellings, therefore, arguably obscures the reality that exists at both national and local levels. The BCS also provides some disaggregated data concerning burglary rates, and various aspects of housing, households and location. Indeed, as Table 2 clearly illustrates, understanding burglary is certainly considerably more complex than just analysing housing design in isolation.

Table 2. The BCS: the context of burglary

Context	Burglary rates per 1000 dwellings
Average in England and Wales	34
Flats	45
Inner-city areas	54
Council estates areas	60
Head of household unemployed	70
Head of household aged 16–24	76
Areas with high levels of physical disorder	79

Source: adapted from Kershaw *et al*, 2001:25

Crucially, the BCS is also limited by the fact that it is currently based on a sample survey and therefore is restricted in terms of its appropriateness for more locationally-specific spatial comparisons. Clearly, our understanding of housing design and crime requires more critical multi-variable analysis than that provided by using the Home Office's recorded crime statistics and BCS survey data, either in isolation or in combination.

The CDA requires every local authority and police partnership in England and Wales to prepare local strategies to address crime and the fear of crime, based on crime audits of their areas.[2] Furthermore, various reports have highlighted the need for improved urban design (Department of the Environment, Transport and the Regions, 1998a; 1998b; 1999b; 1999c; Social Exclusion Unit, 1998) to reduce migration to the countryside (Department of the Environment, Transport and the Regions, 1999b) and to create safer, more liveable cities for the increasing number of projected households in the future (Department of the Environment, Transport and the Regions, 1999a). The capacity to 'design out crime' from the built environment has therefore become a

Crime Prevention and Community Safety: An International Journal 2004, 6 (1), 13–29

recent crime prevention initiative that offers a pro-active approach to resolving the ubiquitous problem of crime and in delivering sustainable urban communities (Cozens, 2002; Knights *et al*, 2002). The government's *Planning Out Crime* circular (Department of the Environment, 1994:1) states 'crime prevention is capable of being a material consideration when planning applications are considered' and specifically recommends SBD as best practice. However, this document is currently being reviewed and updated to reflect changes in theory, practice and policy during the last decade.

SBD is theoretically underpinned by the work of Jacobs (1961), Jeffery (1971) and particularly Newman (1973) (see Steventon, 1996; Pascoe and Topping, 1998; Armitage, 1999). Newman's theory of 'defensible space' (1973) was based on research conducted in American cities, and asserts that the physical environment has the potential to create *perceived* zones of territorial influence and surveillance opportunities. The urban environment could also influence the perception of uniqueness, isolation and stigma and the citizen's sense of security in the wider environment. For Newman, 'defensible space' is:

> a surrogate term for a range of mechanisms – real and symbolic barriers, strongly defined areas of influence, and improved opportunities for surveillance – that combine to bring an environment under the control of its residents. (1973:3)

Crucially, such ideas (and SBD) rely on the assumption that the offender is involved in some form of rational decision-making process in forming a judgement to offend at a specific time or place, and that the design of the physical environment can influence this decision.

SBD: background and theory

SBD was launched in 1989 'by police forces in the South East of England to counter household burglary' (Pascoe and Topping, 1998:162). It is defined by the Association of Chief Police Officers (ACPO) as:

> a police initiative to encourage the [building] industry to adopt crime prevention measures in development design to assist in reducing the opportunity for crime and the fear of crime, creating a safer and more secure environment. (1999:1)

SBD is a broad-based initiative, applicable to new-build housing, multi-storey dwellings, sheltered accommodation, commercial buildings and refurbishments. Further developments to the scheme include 'secure stations' and 'secured car parks'. However, this paper focuses on SBD as it specifically relates to new-build urban residential developments.

The scheme is endorsed by ACPO and the Home Office Crime Reduction Unit, following consultation with the Office of the Deputy Prime Minister (ODPM). Concomitant with this initiative was the phased introduction of 'architectural liaison officers' (ALOs)[3] within the 43 police forces of England and Wales, through whom the police offer advice to housing developers (which they are not obliged to accept) concerning new-build housing projects and where modifications to existing designs are taking place. Relaunched at the Royal Institute of Chartered Surveyors (RICS) in 1999, the scheme is set out in the SBD website,[4] which presents the basic principles of SBD, discusses the concept and comments on the marketing of the scheme.

The website presents three pages of guidance on the 'development' of new housing and eight pages on aspects of the 'physical security' of the properties which should be incorporated in

Crime Prevention and Community Safety: An International Journal 2004, 6 (1), 13–29

order to meet these minimum standards. ACPO (1999) also states that 'equal weighting should be given to both the environment and physical security' (1999:2). Summarily, the guidance for 'the development' of new homes recommends:

- that roads and footpaths should be clearly defined, and should not undermine defensible space (which is not itself explicitly defined);

- that shrubs and foliage should be regularly maintained, to enhance surveillance;

- that BS5489 lighting standards should be met;

- that public/private space in communal areas should be clearly defined, secured and visible to residents;

- that dwellings should be named and numbered, to assist residents and emergency services, and that vandal-resistant locational maps should be considered;

- that public/private boundaries of dwellings should be clearly demarcated;

- that utility meters should be located outside the home; and

- that car-parking within the curtilage of dwellings should be provided or, failing that, that vehicles should be visible to residents.

The guidance for the 'physical security' of new homes recommends the use of specific standards set out by the UK Accreditation Service (UKAS) in the following areas:

- the door itself, the door frame, glazing panels, locking systems, hinges, anti-lift devices and recesses, for all front, back, side, patio and garage doors; 'enhanced security' performance standards for doors (BSI PAS 24-1, BSI PAS 23-1) and windows (BS7950) have recently been incorporated;

- communal entrances (maximum of eight households sharing), consideration of CCTV when this number is exceeded and a requirement for access control systems when four or more flats are served by a common entrance;

- security lighting designed to illuminate external doors and other vulnerable areas (eg gardens); and

- intruder alarms (standards for wire and wireless systems).

The comprehensive website generally recommends the promotion of busy movement routes through areas, but states that these should not undermine defensible space (though this is *not* defined). The website also provides information on and emphasises such matters as the creation of unobstructed views of neighbouring properties (without compromising the residents' needs for privacy) and mixed-use dwellings for generating occupation and footfall throughout the day, which can provide increased opportunities for natural surveillance, community interaction and informal environmental control. The website also provides some details on achieving symbolic barriers (rumble strips, changes of road surface, colour or texture, pillars or narrowing of carriageways) in order to give the impression that a development is private and in controlling access since 'a key element in the security of any development is to discourage casual intrusion by non-residents through the development' (quoted in Pascoe, 1999:14).

Crime Prevention and Community Safety: An International Journal 2004, 6 (1), 13–29

SBD: practice, policy and process

Since 1989, at least 35,000 homes in Britain, on 3700 estates and involving 630 separate companies, have been constructed to SBD standards (Pascoe and Topping, 1998). Indeed, Schneider and Kitchen (2001:274) estimate that this represents approximately two–three per cent of all new-build housing constructed in the period 1989–96. Three recent SBD evaluations (Armitage, 1999; Pascoe, 1999; Brown, 1999) have all reported positive results in terms of reduced levels of crime and fear of crime.

Armitage (1999) utilised Home Office recorded crime statistics and a residents' survey in studying 25 SBD estates and 25 non-SBD estates, comprising some 660 and 522 dwellings respectively. These were matched in terms of location, age, housing tenure and environmental risk factors (estates were selected which scored between 0 and 2 on Winchester and Jackson's (1982) Environmental Index of Risk). Armitage found that the SBD sample 'experienced a far lower prevalence of crime than ... the non-SBD sample' (1999:iii). Fewer residents of the SBD properties reported being the victims of crime than non-SBD residents, and they also reported feeling less unsafe at night when alone and whilst on the streets. On two refurbished estates where a 'before and after' analysis was available, reductions in crime of 66 and 50 per cent respectively were recorded. Armitage (2001) also reported that the effectiveness of SBD in reducing crime had increased significantly between 1994 and 1998.

Brown studied Home Office recorded crime statistics relating to SBD and non-SBD designs (1682 and 7491 Housing Association properties respectively) and found that the SBD properties

> suffered a burglary and vehicle crime rate of at least a third of that suffered by non-SBD properties and two thirds the rate of criminal damage. (1999:58)

Brown's study reported a 40 per cent reduction in burglary from dwellings and a 25 per cent reduction in vehicle offences for SBD properties. The findings also supported the effectiveness of both surveillance and target-hardening in reducing levels of recorded crime.

Pascoe (1999) utilised Home Office recorded crime statistics and data derived from a self-report questionnaire survey of the residents of ten different public-sector housing estates across England and Wales. His study found that residents' perceived levels of both crime and recorded crime had been reduced following modifications to SBD standards in 'before and after' comparisons with non-SBD properties. These included flats, semi-detached houses, terraced houses, maisonettes and detached houses.

Armitage (2000) reports that the additional cost of building a three-bedroom house to SBD standards varies between £90 and £1259 (depending on the developers' operating standards), and notes that the average cost of burglary to the victim is £1670. Armitage argues that 'the extra expenditure required to build or refurbish housing to SBD standards would appear to be a worthwhile investment' (2000:4). The initiative has gained sufficient political support and momentum that it is now compulsory for all new-build social housing projects in Wales to be built to SBD specifications.

At a recent seminar on 'Crime and the Environment' at New Scotland Yard (for a review see Cozens and Plimmer, 2000), it was tentatively accepted that SBD can be an effective approach, although discovering and understanding the precise reasons for this was still an ongoing research objective. At the conference, Brown (2001) highlighted a lack of understanding for the current theoretical support for SBD, namely defensible space. However, the Minister of State responsible for housing expressed disappointment at the lack of interest exhibited by the private sector in applying SBD (Michael, 1999). Indeed this is one of the most unsatisfactory aspects of SBD. In

Crime Prevention and Community Safety: An International Journal 2004, 6 (1), 13–29

2001–2 some 166,000 housing units were built by the private sector and some 16,700 by the public sector. Over 90 per cent of new houses are sold to owner-occupiers, and the proportion of new-build public-sector homes has fallen by over one third in the last five years, such that currently some 70 per cent of the UK housing stock is owner-occupied. Although no data is readily available, it is estimated that private developers currently commission less than ten per cent of SBD assessments. It is thus self-evident that the potential impact of SBD on reducing crime and incivilities is significantly constrained. Consequently, the SBD scheme is having little impact on the vast majority of British housing. An essential step is to understand how the principles and practice of designing out crime can be applied in a way which will appeal to private developers.

In policy terms, Section 17 of the CDA imposes a duty on each local authority to

> exercise its functions with due regard to ... the need to do all that it reasonably can to prevent crime and disorder in its area.

Local crime prevention strategies must therefore consider crime *and* the fear of crime. Indeed, Moss (2001) presents several examples of case law where crime was found to represent a material consideration, and the potential for fear of crime has recently been utilised in the refusal of planning permission for several developments (Seddon, 2001). The Department of the Environment explicitly recommended SBD, setting out basic principles for designing out crime and claiming the scheme provided 'guidance for developers and planning authorities on best practice' (1994:2).

In the specific process of SBD accreditation, housing developers are encouraged to liaise with their local ALO before any plans and proposals are drawn up. A formal application for accreditation is then made, requiring the completion of a detailed proforma; when the ALO is satisfied that the standards have been agreed and will be met the developer is entitled to advertise the development as 'SBD-approved'. The certificate is not awarded until after the development is complete and a detailed inspection has taken place to confirm that the standards have been met. Schneider and Kitchen reflect upon the influence of SBD and comment that the scheme 'continues to affect the quality of what gets submitted to local planning authorities and what gets built all over the country' (2001:256).

Evaluating SBD

A review of SBD research, applications and documentation has raised several issues regarding the theory, practice and usefulness of SBD, both as a crime prevention initiative and as impacting on new-build housing schemes. Crucially, a review of the three most recent and seminal evaluations of SBD (Armitage, 1999; Brown, 1999; Pascoe, 1999) shows clearly that they do not focus exclusively on housing design or on how this variable might influence the performance of SBD properties compared with similar non-SBD properties.

Armitage (1999) makes no specific reference to the design of properties or the layout of streets. It is reported that the SBD properties were less vulnerable than their 'matched' non-SBD counterparts, but the reader is not presented with any detailed statement of the housing designs. Consequently, the study demonstrates that SBD works, but without establishing why—and target-hardening, rather than design *per se*, could well be the crucial factor, or vice versa.

Brown collected data on some 9173 Housing Association properties in Gwent (South Wales), but the study did not set out to analyse crime and fear of crime in relation to the design or the street layout of the 1682 properties which met SBD standards (1999:60). Instead, it focused on the effectiveness of SBD compared with non-SBD properties, and again target-hardening improvements to the SBD properties potentially represents the dominant variable in the comparison. Crucially, however, 3.5 per cent of the SBD sample related to flats or shared

Crime Prevention and Community Safety: An International Journal 2004, 6 (1), 13–29

accommodation, compared to 10.1 per cent of the non-SBD sample. Such properties have been shown to be more vulnerable to crime (Kershaw *et al*, 2001) and may partially compromise the findings. Furthermore, the recorded burglary rates at night (ie between 6.00 pm and 6.00 am) were significantly higher than in the non-SBD properties.

Pascoe (1999) collected self-reporting survey data from residents and found that perceptions of safety were associated with the perceived privacy of the street. Although Pascoe's study analysed SBD as applied to a range of design types, the actual design/layout modifications were not explicitly discussed.

This is not a critique of these three studies; rather, it highlights the fact that although there is confidence that SBD works, both critics and proponents are still unaware as to precisely why it works. Topping and Pascoe comment that 'the biggest challenge now is to identify which parts of the scheme are having the desired effects' (2000:27). Indeed, on review, the studies demonstrate that a target-hardened property is safer and perceived to be safer than similar properties less obviously secured with target-hardening measures—but provide few insights into housing design as such.

The design vs target-hardening debate

Notwithstanding the comments made above, it has been argued that SBD concentrates too extensively on target-hardening and defensive measures and not sufficiently on the design of the space or on whether people would positively choose to reside in such developments (Rudlin and Falk, 1995:56). Furthermore, Pascoe (1993a) concluded that ALOs over-emphasised target-hardening and that this emphasis exceeded the support provided by published research evidence (Pascoe and Topping, 1998). Studies by Brown and Altman (1984) and Allat (1984) demonstrated that target-hardening had an impact on crime, but the majority of this research suggested that its role was at best neutral (Maguire, 1980; Mayhew, 1984) while at worst it might actually increase the risk of crime (Bennett and Wright, 1984). Indeed, Pascoe and Topping (1998) found more support in the literature for the second element to SBD (target-hardening is the first), ie that burglars are 'rational opportunists' and interpret learned cues from the environment in the process of making the decision to offend; this finding is also supported by Pascoe (1993b).

Crucially, within the SBD literature (Association of Chief Police Officers, 1999) and website, no explicit reference to any particular housing design is to be found. The defensible space concepts of SBD, as they currently relate to 'the development', are discretionary and subject to interpretation. Physical security and the target-hardening elements are highly explicit— details of approved manufacturers and suppliers are also provided. Although the highly complex nature of the relationship between design and crime does require such a discretionary approach, the imbalance arguably encourages emphasis on the prescriptive and narrow dimension of physical security. This disparity is certain to be increased if the ALO does not have an informed understanding of the principles of SBD as they relate to housing design and layout, and there is a further weakness where the ALO does not have confidence in the process. This confidence in turn has been weakened by criticisms from a small number of vociferous academics promoting opposing viewpoints. Such an approach is perfectly valid in the academic world but is totally alien to police culture, where the questioning of authority is routinely discouraged.

Reviewing SBD in action

In consideration of the discretionary approach to the development of new housing, and in the absence of an explicit and consistent policy preference in the guidelines for a particular type of housing design, it is noteworthy that SBD was initially dominated by the use of the cul-de-sac layout, at low

Crime Prevention and Community Safety: An International Journal 2004, 6 (1), 13–29

densities and most predominantly in suburban areas (Steventon, 1996; Schneider and Kitchen, 2001). It is argued, therefore, that initial applications of SBD lacked flexibility. The accreditation was predominantly awarded to one design configuration (cul-de-sacs) rather than applying the principles to the full range of housing designs. This trend ignored the defensible space qualities that may be innate within other designs, particularly terraced housing. Indeed, the intervisibility and enhanced surveillance provided by terraced housing has been supported by a number of researchers (Newman, 1975; Pascoe, 1993b; Steventon, 1996; Hillier and Shu, 2000a; Cozens *et al*, 2001) and by the UK government, explicitly by the DETR (Department of the Environment, Transport and the Regions, 1998a). Indeed, Pascoe (1993b) claims that streets of terraced properties arranged in grids are considered by burglars to be more secure than many cul-de-sacs.

Hillier (quoted in Fairs, 1998) is in agreement with this insight. Although defensible space was associated with the cul-de-sac (possibly as a result of Newman's application of his ideas to privatised 'enclaves' in the 1990s), Newman commented that 'the decision to make the private dwelling inward-looking has removed much of the opportunities for natural surveillance' (1973:150). He also supported both the presence of users and the existence of through movement of traffic and footfall:

> Traditional residential streets are safe because they have pedestrian and vehicular movement along them and occasionally, police patrols; and most importantly, they are supervised by residents in bordering buildings. (1975:59)

This crucial intervisibility is vital to defensible space: 'To feel continually that one is under observation by other residents ... can have a pronounced effect in securing the environment for peaceful activities' (1975:78).

Similarly, research being carried out at University College London (Hillier and Shu, 2000a; 2000b) claims that:

> on the whole, linear integrated spaces with some through movement and strong intervisibility of good numbers of entrances (highly 'constituted') are the safest spaces. (2000b:4)

This research, which analysed a range of housing designs, including cul-de-sacs, found that certain configurations were significantly more at risk from burglary. In particular, risk of crime was higher for cul-de-sacs which were linked together by pathways and experienced low pedestrian flows (Fairs, 1998). However, a study by Brantingham and Brantingham (1993) has raised a series of questions concerning crime risk and the volume of pedestrian and traffic flows along access routes.

Despite these findings, Pascoe and Topping commented that the cul-de-sac still represented 'the preferred option for most crime prevention officers' (1998:166). Steventon (1996) claims that the prevailing belief that terraced designs are in conflict with defensible space theory is the main reason for the exclusion of design layout from current SBD advice. The findings from this and other studies certainly raise doubts about SBD relying on any one design solution. Reinforcing such a perspective, Steventon notes that most ALOs receive only limited formal training—a two-week course that teaches police officers how to read site plans and submit a planning application, and introduces defensible space criteria 'set in tablets of stone' (1996:243).

This is not to argue that designs such as the cul-de-sac do not have a role to play, but this should represent one design option rather than *the* solution. For example, a cul-de-sac that appears private, has some of the houses occupied during the day, has symbolic barriers, does not promote pedestrian throughput and has back-to-back gardens promises to be one of the potential solutions to delivering successful SBD applications.

Crime Prevention and Community Safety: An International Journal 2004, 6 (1), 13–29

One DETR objective is to achieve 'better design', in safe, sustainable and liveable communities with average urban residential densities of between 30 and 50 dwellings per hectare (Department of the Environment, Transport and the Regions, 2000). It is highly debatable as to how far SBD can contribute to this aim in its present form, as it is predominantly applied at low density and in suburban settings for the public sector (Steventon, 1996).

Indeed, commenting on the flexibility of SBD, Pascoe (1992; 1993a; 1993b) recommends 'returning to the greater flexibility, shown by some of the designers, at the creation of the scheme' (quoted in Van Soomeren and Woldendorp, 1996:185). Furthermore, Topping and Pascoe (2000), in assessing the impact of the SBD scheme over its first ten years (1989–99), concluded that there had been significant developments in legislation (Department of the Environment, 1994; CDA 1998) which now make crime a material consideration in planning applications. Furthermore, there have been extensions to the scheme to include refurbishments, car parks, commercial buildings, sheltered accommodation and flats, and the Dutch have significantly adopted and adapted the scheme. However, Topping and Pascoe argue that 'the only changes to the specifications of the scheme have been the fine tuning of physical security criteria' (2000:72).

Re-inspection

Crucially, much research suggests that the maintenance and upkeep of the urban environment can reduce crime (Ross and Jang, 2000; Kraut, 1999) and deter offenders, and prove a vital component of the design-affects-crime debate (Wilson and Kelling, 1982; Ross and Mirowsky, 1999; Cozens *et al*, 2001). However, there is currently a lack of consideration within SBD for the potential physical decline of such estates over time, as a result of poor management, lack of maintenance procedures and a dearth of detailed monitoring. SBD accreditation is 'for life', and unlike the 'secure stations' and 'secured car parks' schemes there is no reassessment or re-inspection—whereas other countries which have adopted and adapted the scheme, such as Holland, seek vigorously to 'police it', with examples of certification being revoked if standards fall below a predetermined benchmark. The SBD literature acknowledges this point, claiming that: 'It is essential that a programme of management is in place to maintain the physical development and its environment' (Association of Chief Police Officers, 1999:4); however, in practice this appears not to be operationalised. This is not presented here as a negative perspective on the initiative, but rather as a positive contribution to promoting the long-term viability of SBD projects. It is argued that such initiatives could represent a 'cradle-to-grave' approach to new-build housing design, where the long-term safety, sustainability and liveability of such estates is maintained from the design stage, to a continued management phase, and finally through to demolition and redevelopment (the 'whole life scenario').

Periodic and planned liaison with ALOs and housing estate managers can assist in sustaining a physical environment which residents value and which is safe, retaining its 'positive' image throughout its useful life. A multi-agency approach incorporating those managing the urban fabric, cultural and community groups, the police and urban analysts should provide a framework that will sponsor sympathetically designed and safer spaces in which communities can be encouraged to participate in and benefit from the routine policing of the build environment.

It is suggested the SBD can be significantly strengthened by considering the long-term management of such estates. The fact that currently the initiative is 'for life' will arguably reduce the effectiveness of SBD, especially if such estates begin to become poorly maintained and exhibit signs of vandalism, decay and dereliction. Indeed, Armitage (2001) has recently shown that some approved SBD estates are already beginning to display multiple indications of physical and social decline A re-evaluation and re-accreditation system, similar to the 'secure stations' and 'secured car

Crime Prevention and Community Safety: An International Journal 2004, 6 (1), 13–29

parks' schemes, seems to be the logical way forward. Such issues of re-inspection are clearly an essential component of providing critical long-term evaluations of SBD applications. Until this takes place, evaluating the viability, impact and sustainability of SBD remains unscientific and primarily a matter of opinion.

Policy

Although there is clear government support for SBD as a policy initiative (Department of the Environment, 1994), designing out crime is advisory in policy terms, is discretionary in practice and, crucially, receives no government funding. Section 17 of the CDA states that crime prevention *can be* rather than *must be* considered as a material consideration in the decision to grant planning permission. Crucially, the decision whether to adopt an SBD scheme for new housing lies solely with the developers, and planning authorities are currently advised to consult with ALOs in assessing new developments (Department of the Environment, 1994). However, ALO advice is non-mandatory, and although planning permission for developments is increasingly being refused on crime prevention grounds, the planning applications and appeals processes are certain to be more controversial as a result of such a discretionary policy framework. Moss and Seddon note that Planning Policy Guidance Notes have generally overtaken government circulars as the main source of national policy guidance. However, they conclude that 'at present reference to the issue of community safety is limited' (2001:27). They also note an example of an evolving crime and disorder partnership in Wakefield Metropolitan District, where an ALO from West Yorkshire police has been seconded to the development control team, enhancing the community safety strategy. Crucially, Moss and Seddon also suggest that:

> it should not be assumed that all planning officers will be fully conversant with Circular 5/ 94 or the implications of s.17 of the CDA. (2001:29)

Training: ALOs, planners and housing developers

ALO training is arguably inadequate (Steventon, 1996). The dissemination of theoretical knowledge and operational experiences among existing ALOs, and more extensive training relating to the complex issues of surveillance, territoriality and 'image', and to how 'defensible space' may (or may not) be decoded, may help to strengthen the SBD award. Indeed, current training is limited to a two-week course with the option (often limited by funding and operational constraints) of further professional development by attending several university-based courses. These include the Certificated Programme in Community Safety and Crime Prevention managed by the Safe Neighbourhoods Unit at the University of the West of England, and a range of short courses provided by the Planning School at Oxford Brookes University. Furthermore, it is debatable how many ALOs are actually solely responsible for designing out crime—many are routinely employed in other positions, and thus with inevitably competing priorities. ALOs' knowledge base is often largely dependent on individual motivation, home study, and liaison with supportive planners and architects willing to share their knowledge (often itself limited) of the concepts and experiences of designing out crime. Currently, ALOs find themselves with only a restricted knowledge of operationalising the full range of principles, based upon defensible space dominated by an extensive, albeit prescriptive array of target-hardening mechanisms (windows, doors, locks and alarms).

Furthermore, although courses such as those mentioned above are being taken by a small number of planners, most planners and housing developers are likely to receive only a cursory insight into the complexities of designing out crime. Indeed, the government's Design Against Crime in

Crime Prevention and Community Safety: An International Journal 2004, 6 (1), 13–29

Education studied 36 institutions offering design courses at undergraduate and postgraduate level, and found that 'currently, environmental, disability and demographic issues are perceived as of greater relevance to design than crime' (Home Office and Department of Trade and Industry, 2000:28).

Street lighting

In the SBD studies of Brown (1999) and Pascoe (1999), street lighting was a crucial factor affecting the effectiveness of SBD after dark. Brown's (1999) study revealed that SBD properties had higher rates of recorded burglary than non-SBD properties after dark, and that there was a noticeable increase in such offences within the SBD sample. Furthermore, Pascoe (1999) reported that 22 per cent of residents of SBD-accredited properties felt that street lighting was inadequate, and the study recommends that SBD could be enhanced by concentrating on improving street lighting (and also controlling and reducing through movement, and making the streets feel more 'private'). Armitage (1999) did not provide any temporal analysis of crime rates in her study but her findings demonstrated that residents of SBD estates reported that they felt safer after dark, both in the home and on the street.

Farrington and Welsh (2002) discuss various theories which explore why improved lighting may reduce crime. Primarily, upgraded street lighting provides increased surveillance opportunities (by improving visibility and by encouraging more 'eyes on the street' in the way of increased activity). This thinking is supported by those advocating situational crime prevention, who argue that physical alterations (including lighting) can reduce opportunities and rewards for offenders whilst also increasing the risk of being seen and potentially apprehended. Additionally, improved lighting can enhance community pride and cohesion, as Farrington and Welsh argue:

> [Lighting] can act as a catalyst to stimulate crime reduction through a change in the perceptions, attitudes and behaviours of residents and potential offenders. (2002:30)

Crucially, a recent evaluation of the British street lighting standard BS5489 (Cozens *et al*, 2003), which is the statutory requirement, found that many streets do not currently meet the standards set, and that the latter may themselves require re-evaluation. Cozens *et al* (2003) reported that since levels of lighting are dictated by Home Office recorded crime statistics and road traffic and pedestrian flows, such a process is myopic, potentially creating places with low lighting levels where fear of crime may be high, while the Home Office recorded crime statistics may be low. Furthermore, many street lighting studies suggest upgrading lighting levels to meet BS5489 (indicating that they did not meet this benchmark). In the three SBD studies mentioned above (Armitage, 1999; Brown, 1999; Pascoe, 1999), improving the lighting levels to BS5489 to satisfy the SBD requirements was carried out—but lighting was nevertheless still identified as being problematic in two of them (Brown, 1999; Pascoe, 1999), highlighting the limitations associated with BS5489 and the effectiveness of SBD after dark.

Recommendations

Notwithstanding the redrafting of the government's *Planning Out Crime* circular (Department of the Environment, 1994) several recommendations are provided here to suggest how SBD could be revised and applied throughout the urban fabric.

- The collection, compilation, analysis and dissemination (and scientific interrogation wherever possible) of the full range of SBD schemes as they have been variously applied across the UK (to grid layouts incorporating terraced, semi-detached and detached designs, cul-de-sacs, flats and other applications) is required. This should explicitly include schemes which have subsequently been accepted as a 'success' as well as those considered as 'failures'.

Crime Prevention and Community Safety: An International Journal 2004, 6 (1), 13–29

- A thorough review of SBD principles and guidelines is required, to probe the following issues:

  – redressing the current imbalance between design/layout and target-hardening measures;

  – dispensing with the continuing preference (in practice) for the cul-de-sac design;

  – applying the principles of defensible space (Newman, 1973) rather than a 'generic' (and highly controversial) representation;

  – reviewing the lighting standards currently recommended, and implementing them in association with SBD;

  – establishing and clarifying which organisations are responsible for the long-term management of SBD estates, and the creation of a framework by which this can be achieved; and

  – researching precisely what makes SBD a 'success' or a 'failure'.

- A thorough review and extension of the training currently provided to ALOs, planners and housing developers in the principles of designing out crime and defensible space (Newman, 1973) is required. Furthermore, strengthening the relationships between these key players and the promotion of a synergy of ideas in the planning applications process appears necessary. Consideration could be given to the innovative approach adopted by Wakefield Metropolitan Council, of incorporating an ALO permanently onto the design control team (Moss and Seddon, 2001).

- There needs to be a move away from a policy and process framework that is currently static, advisory and discretionary, and towards its transformation into one that is robust, mandatory and dynamic.

Conclusions

This review of SBD shows that evaluations have reported that such an approach does reduce crime and the fear of crime. However, further analysis suggests that SBD could be revised and significantly improved. Currently, it lacks flexibility concerning the issue of design and initially over-emphasised one design: the cul-de-sac. This has produced a mismatch between SBD in theory and SBD in practice.

Operationally, SBD is currently short-term and episodic in character, and arguably over-relies on target-hardening measures. Although target-hardening can be effective, its long-term contribution requires systematic analysis as part of any SBD initiative. Furthermore, SBD is discretionary and without central government funding (except for social housing in Wales). Additionally, the vagaries of the planning process and market considerations combine to further limit the adoption of SBD as an initiative.

Crucially, it may be the perception of SBD as an over-prescriptive, target-hardening exercise for low-density, suburban cul-de-sacs in predominantly 'privatised' spaces that serves to discourage many house-builders and planners from considering it as a viable and worthwhile option.

Indeed, Schneider and Kitchen (2001) discuss two initiatives which sought to utilise and interpret the same defensible space principles of designing out crime in their developments. In Hulme in

Crime Prevention and Community Safety: An International Journal 2004, 6 (1), 13–29

Manchester's inner city, redevelopment was influenced by the 'New Urbanist' movement and set out to reject the SBD approach. In contrast, Salford's Crime and Disorder Reduction Strategy preferred to use SBD as one of the available tools. Crucially, Schneider and Kitchen (2001) identify permeability and levels of street activity as being variously interpreted as they relate to defensible space. 'New Urbanism' seeks to increase both the permeability of areas and street activity, and interprets defensible space and SBD as being supportive of more 'private' areas with limited permeability and a greater emphasis on residents-only activity.

However, Schneider and Kitchen observe that whilst there are distinct similarities in terms of how defensible space and designing out crime is interpreted and implemented, there also appears to be a clash of ideas particularly relating to permeability. They argue that such approaches produce

> a range of choices that people ought to have available to them in or on the edges of our city
> if urban/metropolitan living is to be encouraged. (2001:225)

Neither of these options is superior; they are simply different, and will result in the emergence of markedly different environments. Crucially, however, the police are key players in crime and disorder partnerships across the country, and their input will tend to be informed predominantly by SBD principles and how these are currently interpreted and implemented. The increase in premises' liability (Hanson, 1998) and the requirements of the HRA certainly strengthen the need for such partnerships. Crucially, the Planning Inspectorate is bound by these HRA requirements (Moss, 2001).

SBD has been shown to reduce crime and the fear of crime (Armitage, 1999; Brown, 1999; Pascoe, 1999). However, 97–98 per cent of new-build housing between 1989 and 1996 was not constructed to SBD's *minimum* standards (Schneider and Kitchen, 2001). Describing SBD, Felson (1998) suggests that much of its underlying principles are 'common sense' (quoted in Armitage, 1999:2), but the scheme itself is clearly not yet common practice.

Notes

1   Dr Paul Cozens is a Research Fellow at the School of Technology, University of Glamorgan in South Wales; email: pmcozens@yahoo.com. Dr Tim Pascoe is Associate Director and Leader of the Crime Risk Management Unit at the Building Research Establishment, Garston, Watford. Dr David Hillier is Head of Geography at the School of Technology, University of Glamorgan in South Wales.

2   Crime audits provide a potential reservoir of localised information which, if organised at a national level, would enable crime analyses to be far more detailed and focused.

3   In some police forces, ALOs are designated as 'crime prevention design advisors'.

4   See *http://www.securedbydesign.com*.

References

Allatt, P. (1984) Fear of Crime: The Effect of Improved Residential Security on a Difficult to Let Estate. *The Howard Journal*. Vol. 23, pp 170–82.

Association of Chief Police Officers (1999) *The Secured by Design Award Scheme*. London: ACPO.

Armitage, R. (1999) *An Evaluation of Secured by Design Housing Schemes Throughout the West Yorkshire Area*. Huddersfield: University of Huddersfield.

Armitage, R. (2000) *An Evaluation of Secured by Design Within West Yorkshire*. Briefing Note No. 7/00. London: Home Office.

Crime Prevention and Community Safety: An International Journal 2004, 6 (1), 13–29

Armitage, R. 2001. *Secured by Design in West Yorkshire*. Paper presented to a Conference of Architectural Liaison Officers, Blackpool, 2nd–4th May.

Barclay, G.C. and Tavares, C. (eds) (1999) *Information on the Criminal Justice System in England and Wales*. Digest No. 4. London: Home Office.

Brantingham, P.J. and Brantingham, P.L. (1993) Nodes, Paths and Edges: Considerations on the Complexity of Crime and the Physical Environment. *Journal of Environmental Psychology*. Vol. 13, pp 3–28.

Bennett, T.W. and Wright, R. (1984) *Burglars on Burglary*. Aldershot: Gower.

Brown, B. and Altman, I. (1984) Territoriality, Defensible Space and Residential Burglary: An Environmental Analysis. *Journal of Environmental Psychology*. Vol. 3, pp 203–20.

Brown, J. (1999) *An Evaluation of the Secured by Design Initiative in Gwent, South Wales*. Unpublished MSc thesis, Scarman Centre, University of Leicester.

Brown, J. (2001) *Secured by Design in Gwent*. Paper presented at a Conference of Architectural Liaison Officers, Blackpool, 2nd–4th May.

Cozens, P.M. (2002) Sustainable Urban Development and Crime Prevention Through Environmental Design for the British City, 2002: Towards an Effective Urban Environmentalism for the 21st Century. *Cities: The International Journal of Urban Policy and Planning*. Vol. 19, No. 2, pp 129–37.

Cozens, P.M., Hillier, D. and Prescott, G. (1999a) Crime and the Design of New-Build Housing. *Town and Country Planning*. Vol. 68, No. 7, pp 231–3.

Cozens, P.M., Hillier, D. and Prescott, G. (1999b) The Sustainable and the Criminogenic: The Case for New-Build Housing Projects in Britain. *Property Management*. Vol. 17, No. 3, pp 252–61.

Cozens, P.M., Hillier, D. and Prescott, G. (2001) Defensible Space: Burglars and Police Evaluate Urban Residential Design. *Security Journal*. Vol. 14, No. 4, pp 43–62.

Cozens, P.M., Neale, R.H., Whitaker, J., Hillier, D. and Graham, M. (2003) A Critical Review of Street Lighting, Crime and the Fear of Crime in the British City. *Crime Prevention and Community Safety: An International Journal*. Vol. 5, No. 2, pp 7–24.

Cozens, P.M. and Plimmer, F. (2000) Crime and its Relationship to Environment. *Property Management*. Vol. 18, No. 2, pp 89–91.

Crime and Disorder Act 1998. London: HMSO.

Department of the Environment (1994) *Planning Out Crime*. Circular No. 5/94. London: HMSO.

Department of the Environment, Transport and the Regions (1998a) *The Layout of Residential Roads and Footpaths*. Design Bulletin No. 32. London: HMSO.

Department of the Environment, Transport and the Regions (1998b) *Places, Streets and Movement: A Companion Guide to Design Bulletin 32*. London: HMSO.

Department of the Environment, Transport and the Regions (1999a) *Projection of Households in England to 2021*. London: HMSO.

Department of the Environment, Transport and the Regions (1999b) *Towards an Urban Renaissance*. Final Report, Urban Task Force. London: HMSO.

Department of the Environment, Transport and the Regions (1999c) *A Better Quality of Life: A Strategy for Sustainable Development for the United Kingdom*. London: Home Office.

Department of the Environment, Transport and the Regions (2000) *Planning Policy Guidance Note 3: Housing*. London: DETR.

Devon County Council (1998) Quality of Life Survey. At *http://www.devon.gov.uk/quality/contents.html*.

Fairs, M. (1998) End of the Road for the Cul-de-sac. *Building Design*. No. 1373, p 1.

Farrington, D.P. and Welsh, C. (2002) *Effects of Improved Street Lighting on Crime: A Systematic Review*. Research Study No. 251. London: Development and Statistics Directorate, Home Office.

Crime Prevention and Community Safety: An International Journal 2004, 6 (1), 13–29

Felson, M. (1998) *Crime and Everyday Life*. 2nd edn. Thousand Oaks, CA: Pine Forge.

Gordon, C.L. and Brill, W. (1996) *The Expanding Role of Crime Prevention Through Environmental Design in Premises Liability*. Research Brief, National Institute of Justice. Washington, DC: US Department of Justice.

Hanson, R.K. (1998) Liability on Franchise Premises: Footing the Bill for Crime. *Business Horizons*. Vol. 41, No. 4, pp 53–8. At *http://www.findarticles.com/cf_0/m1038/n4_v41/21015195/print.jhtml*.

Hillier, B. and Shu, S. (2000a) Crime and Urban Layout: The Need for Evidence. In Ballintyne, S., Pease, K. and McLaren, V. (eds) *Secure Foundations: Key Issues in Crime Prevention, Crime Reduction and Community Safety*. London: Institute of Public Policy Research.

Hillier, B. and Shu, S. (2000b) *Do Burglars Understand Defensible Space?* London: Space Syntax Laboratory, University College London. At *http://www.bartlett.ucl.ac.uk/spacesyntax/housing/BillCrimePaper/BillCrimePaper.html*.

Home Office (2000) *Criminal Statistics, England and Wales*. London: Government Statistical Service.

Home Office and Department of Trade and Industry (2000) *Design Against Crime in Education*. London: HMSO.

Human Rights Act 1998. London: HMSO.

Infield, P. (2000) Personal discussion, Suzy Lamplugh Trust seminar on 'Responding to Workplace Violence', London Voluntary Resource Centre, Holloway, October 10th.

Jacobs, J. (1961) *The Death and Life of Great American Cities*. New York: Vintage Books.

Jeffery, C.R. (1971) *Crime Prevention Through Environmental Design*. Beverly Hills, CA: Sage.

Kershaw, C., Chivite Mathews, N., Thomas, C. and Aust, R. (2001) *The 2001 British Crime Survey*. Home Office Statistical Bulletin. London: Home Office.

Knights, B., Pascoe, T. and Henchley, A. (2002) *Sustainability and Crime: Managing and Recognising the Drivers of Crime and Security*. Watford: Building Research Establishment.

Kraut, D.T. (1999) Hanging Out the No Vacancy Sign: Eliminating the Blight of Vacant Buildings from Urban Areas. *New York University Law Review*. Vol. 74, No. 4, pp 1139–77.

Maguire, M. (1980) *Burglary as Opportunity*. Home Office Research Bulletin No. 10. London: Home Office.

Mayhew, P. (1984) Target Hardening: How Much of an Answer? In Clarke, R. and Hope, T. (eds) *Coping with Burglary*. Hingham, MA: Kluwer-Nijhoff.

Michael, A. (1999) *Forty-Per Cent Cut in Burglary Proves that Partnership Helps Cut Crime*. Press release W99648-Hou, 11th October. Cardiff: National Assembly for Wales.

Moss, K. (2001) Crime Prevention v Planning: Section 17 of the Crime and Disorder Act 1998. Is it a Material Consideration? *Crime Prevention and Community Safety: An International Journal*. Vol. 3, No. 2, pp 43–8.

Moss, K. and Pease, K. (1999) Crime and Disorder Act 1998: Section 17, A Wolf in Sheep's Clothing? *Crime Prevention and Community Safety: An International Journal*. Vol. 1, No. 4, pp 15–19.

Moss, K. and Seddon, M. (2001) Crime Prevention and Planning: Searching for Common Sense in Disorder Legislation. *Crime Prevention and Community Safety: An International Journal*. Vol. 3, No. 4, pp 25–31.

Newman, O. (1973) *Defensible Space: People and Design in the Violent City*. London: Architectural Press.

Newman, O. (1975) Reactions to the 'Defensible Space' Study and Some Further Readings. *International Journal of Mental Health*. Vol. 4, No. 3, pp 48–70.

Parker, G. (2001) Planning and Rights: Some Repercussions of the Human Rights Act 1998 for the UK. *Planning Practice and Research*. Vol. 16, No. 1, pp 5–8.

Pascoe, T. (1992) *Secured By Design: A Crime Prevention Philosophy*. Unpublished Msc thesis, Cranfield Institute of Technology, Cranfield University.

Crime Prevention and Community Safety: An International Journal 2004, 6 (1), 13–29

Pascoe, T. (1993a) *Domestic Burglaries: The Police View.* BRE Information Paper No. 20/93. Watford: Building Research Establishment.

Pascoe, T. (1993b) *Domestic Burglaries: The Burglar's View.* BRE Information Paper No. 19/93. Watford: Building Research Establishment.

Pascoe, T. (1999) *Evaluation of Secured by Design in Public Sector Housing.* Final Report. Watford: Building Research Establishment.

Pascoe, T. and Topping, P. (1998) Secured by Design: Assessing the Basis of the Scheme. *International Journal of Risk, Security and Crime Prevention.* Vol. 2, No. 3, pp 161–73.

Police Reform Act 2002. London: HMSO.

Rogerson, R. (2000) *Quality of Life in Cities.* Glasgow: Department of Geography, University of Strathclyde. At *http://www.globalideasbank.org/BOV/BV-374.HTML.*

Ross, C.E. and Jang, S.J. (2000) Neighbourhood Disorder, Fear and Mistrust: The Buffering Role of Social Ties with Neighbours. *American Journal of Community Psychology.* Vol. 28, No. 4, pp 401–20.

Ross, C.E. and Mirowsky, J. (1999) Disorder and Decay: The Concept and Measurement of Perceived Neighbourhood Disorder. *Urban Affairs Review.* Vol. 34, No. 3, pp 412–32.

Rudlin, D. and Falk, N. (1995) *21st Century Homes: Building to Last.* London: Urban and Economic Development Group.

Schneider, R.H. and Kitchen, T. (2001) *Planning For Crime Prevention: A Transatlantic Perspective.* London and New York: Routledge.

Seddon, M. (2001) *Planning Out Crime.* Paper presented at a Conference of Architectural Liaison Officers, Blackpool, 2nd–4th May.

Social Exclusion Unit (1998) *Bringing Britain Together: A National Strategy for Neighbourhood Renewal.* London: HMSO.

Steventon, G. (1996) Defensible Space: A Critical Review of the Theory and Practice of a Crime Prevention Strategy. *Urban Design International.* Vol. 1, No. 3, pp 235–45.

Topping, P. and Pascoe, T. (2000) Countering Household Burglary through the Secured by Design Scheme: Does it Work? An Assessment of the Evidence, 1989–1999. *Security Journal.* Vol. 14, No. 4, pp 71–8.

Van Soomeren, P. and Woldendorp, T. (1996) Secured by Deign in the Netherlands. *Security Journal.* Vol. 7, No. 3, pp 185–95.

Wilson, J.Q. and Kelling, G.L. (1982) The Police and Neighbourhood Safety: Broken Windows. *Atlantic Monthly.* March, pp 29–38.

Winchester, S. and Jackson, H. (1982) *Residential Burglary: The Limits of Prevention.* Home Office Research Study No. 74. London: HMSO.

[21]

Crime Detection and
Prevention Series
Paper 77

Solving Residential Burglary

Timothy Coupe
Max Griffiths

Editor: Barry Webb
Home Office
Police Research Group
50 Queen Anne's Gate
London SW1H 9AT

3. How burglaries are solved: the effectiveness of police operations

Residential burglaries accounted for 16% of all recorded crime, while their investigation consumed c.7% of all police human resources in the study area (West Midlands Police Activity Analysis, 1992-94); policing burglaries cost an estimated £3 million per annum. The survey of victims revealed that the burglary caused some disturbance, either emotional or physical, to the victim's life in 92% of incidents. It also had longer term effects on a majority of victims, particularly women, with levels of worry remaining high for at least 18 months after the burglary. These effects concerned the fear of another burglary that often resulted in greater security consciousness and nervousness. Nearly 30% of victims were so concerned by what had happened, and frightened by the risk of it happening again, that they wanted to move house to a less vulnerable area and dwelling.

Few of the residential burglaries considered in the study had been solved as a result of 'primary' investigation by the start of 1995; only 5.8%[3] were recorded as detected. The bulk remained and will remain unsolved. Although a further 25-30% will probably be cleared up as secondary detections[4] by Summer 1995, it is almost certain that at least 65% of these crimes overall will never be solved and that many of the criminals responsible for them will never be brought to justice. The record for the recovery of stolen property was worse, with stolen property recovered in only 7% of the burglaries examined in the study. Therefore, a victim was unlikely to see his or her property again if the offender managed to leave the scene of the crime without being caught and this loss was unrecoverable for the 48% of burglary victims who were uninsured. The total financial cost of burglaries over the six months, in terms of stolen property and household repairs, was estimated to be approximately £6 million.

The cost of burglaries, in both financial and emotional terms, makes their effective investigation essential. The main objective of this research was, therefore, to evaluate the effectiveness and efficiency of the police activities used to solve burglaries. In order to improve the effective use of resources, the activities that have the greatest impact on solving burglary cases and recovering stolen property should be more fully employed, while ineffective activities should be scaled down or even eliminated, provided this would not seriously damage the victim's view of the force. Detection rate, time spent on investigation and victim satisfaction were used to measure effectiveness.

3 By January 1995, the number of recorded primary detections had risen to 340. This principally reflected delays in recording detections onto the police database. The profile of detection methods were little different from the survey sample of 256, although detections from forensic evidence were slightly under-represented.

4 The number of secondary detections that are obtained depends on the use of TICs and prison write offs. The number of TICs has declined over recent years due to offenders being less willing to accept crimes; in all but one sub-division prison write-offs were the main tool for obtaining secondary detections. The ratio of primary:secondary detections may alter if sub-divisions change their policy towards prison visits or offenders become less inclined to have burglaries written off.

HOW BURGLARIES ARE SOLVED: THE EFFECTIVENESS OF POLICE OPERATIONS

The burglary investigation process

The police respond to residential burglary in terms of six principal activities:

- the initial despatch of a police unit in response to the burglary alert, and investigation at the scene;

- visits by SOCOs who carry out forensic assessment at the bulk of burglary sites;

- screening by the Criminal Investigation Department (CID);

- following up evidence provided by witnesses;

- visits by CID officers to the burglary sites;

- other CID activities, including surveillance, targeting known offenders, tracing stolen property.

Detection methods

In the course of these activities, West Midlands Police used various methods to investigate and solve burglaries. They either caught the burglar 'in the act', or they collected evidence and information in order to identify the offender. Most burglaries were solved as a result of operations carried out in response to the burglary incident. A substantial minority of detections were the result of further CID activities. Only a few detections, however, were based on predicting either the offender's identity or the dwellings to be burgled. The following six methods were used:

Operations following the burglary

- The police can catch the offender in the act of committing the crime, leaving the crime scene or in a street near the victim's dwelling.

- Evidence provided by witnesses at the scene of the crime can lead to the identification of an offender. Suspect names and descriptions, vehicle descriptions, details of stolen property are the main types of data. Information can be supplied to the first officer at the scene by witnesses, and to CID during subsequent visits. Sometimes information is supplied after police visits to the scene.

- Forensic evidence or a distinctive modus operandi (MO) at the crime scene can lead to the identification of the offender, or assist in confirming his guilt.

- Carrying out surveillance of the places where burglars may sell stolen property in order to identify burglars and receivers and to block this means of disposal.

Other operations

- The use of crime pattern analysis, including the identification of repeat burglary,

HOW BURGLARIES ARE SOLVED: THE EFFECTIVENESS OF
POLICE OPERATIONS

to anticipate likely future burglary victims, and to carry out 'targeted patrolling'
or surveillance in order to catch the burglar in the act.

• Carrying out surveillance of known burglars in order to catch them in the act.

In practice, many detections are the result of the interplay of a number of factors,
rather than attributable to a single investigation method. Confirmation, for
instance, that it is the offender who has been caught in a street in the vicinity of
the victim's dwelling may be provided by identification of the stolen property he is
carrying. Similarly forensic evidence may be used to confirm identification evidence
provided by informers or by witnesses, while the identification of a suspect offender
by an officer from a description provided by a witness to the crime may prompt a
visit to the offender and the identification of stolen goods in his possession.

The principal methods and operations used in the primary detection of the
burglaries in the sample are shown in Table 1.

Table 1: Principal methods and operations used to detect burglaries		
Detection method	% of detections	Number
Offender caught at or near the scene	43	90
Questioning witnesses (victims and neighbours) at the scene	34	70
Collection of forensic evidence essential in detection	6	13
Subsequent CID investigation, based on information from local contacts (1%) and informants (4%)	5	11
Subsequent investigation (generally CID) involving surveillance (4%) and/or stop-checks (1%)	5	11
Arrested for another offence	3	7
Additional information discovered by the victim	3	6
Miscellaneous	1	1
Total detections at 30/9/94 (excl. non-response)	100	209

Various types of evidence, information and activities were used to solve the
burglaries. It is striking that the majority of primary detections (77%) were due to
either offenders being caught at or near the scene of the crime, or resulted from
investigations based on evidence from witnesses at the crime scene. As a
consequence detected burglaries were generally solved quickly. Relatively few
detections (only 10%) were principally attributable to 'proactive' policing methods
and operations.

HOW BURGLARIES ARE SOLVED: THE EFFECTIVENESS OF POLICE OPERATIONS

The purpose here is to identify the activities, operations and residential environments in which these methods of investigation were most successfully employed, and how much time and effort was expended in carrying out these activities in order to achieve detections. This information forms the basis for recommendations to adjust existing operational practices so that more cases are solved.

The burglary alert and the initial response

Most, 75%, of burglary incidents were reported to the police following their discovery by victims often on their return to the dwelling or upon waking. Others were notified by neighbours, and sometimes by victims themselves, while in progress. In response to this alert, the control room despatched a police unit to attend the burglary, with all haste if the burglar was believed to be still there. This was normally the nearest, available patrol car, but occasionally it was a local beat officer or a detective. The person reporting the incident was questioned, and victims and often neighbours were interviewed at this, or at a later stage, if they were unavailable at the time. The dwelling was checked for evidence.

In general, one or two officers were despatched to the burglaries in the study sample. After receiving a request from the control room, they took an average of 30 minutes to attend the incident, and spent 30 minutes at the burglary, talking to the victim, and often their neighbours, and assessing the burglary site for forensic and other evidence. Once the victim had called the police for help, they expected them to arrive within the hour, and preferably within half an hour. Twenty-nine percent thought the police took too long, and the longer they took to get to the victim, the more the victims expressed dissatisfaction, irrespective of whether or not the case was solved. When they took over an hour to respond, 60% of respondents thought they had waited too long. The average response time viewed as adequate was 31 minutes, indicating that the police response and the public expectation of that response are broadly in line. However, where the police were viewed as responding too slowly, there was a large discrepancy between the average, actual response time of 65 minutes and the average expected time of 17 minutes. While there might be some exaggeration on the part of dissatisfied victims, there appears to be a desire among burglary victims for a response within 30 minutes.

Officers spent more time, 53 minutes on average, and collected additional evidence at incidents which were subsequently detected. They spent an average of 29 minutes at burglaries which would remain unsolved. While at the scene of the crime, 13% of the police units had to leave to attend to another more pressing alert. Investigations shortened in this way were less likely to be detected, even though officers were just as likely to have interviewed neighbours and obtained information from them. Fewer investigations were cut short where there was an indication that available evidence would lead to detection.

7

HOW BURGLARIES ARE SOLVED: THE EFFECTIVENESS OF
POLICE OPERATIONS

Catching the offender in the act

Forty three percent of all primary detections result from the offender being caught
at or near the scene. However, the findings indicate that the incidents where
offenders were successfully caught in the act represent a minority, only 10%, of the
burglaries reported as 'in progress'[5]. Therefore, there appears to be potential to
significantly enhance primary detections by catching more burglars in the act since
90% of the burglars observed got clean away, and only 3% of these were
subsequently detected by other means. To fully exploit this potential, however,
would require sufficient officers to ensure a quick police response and, where
necessary, a search of the area.

Successfully catching offenders at or near the scene depended on:

* how quickly and in what numbers the police responded;

* the size and crime levels of the areas officers had to police;

* offender behaviour including:

    * the length of time the offender spent in the victimised dwelling;

    * the stage of the burglary when the offender was spotted;

    * the time of day that the burglary was committed;

* characteristics of the residential environment.

The likelihood of capture was, therefore, dependent on the nature of the police
response to an alert and the demands placed on the local police, but also the area's
environmental characteristics and the characteristics of the incident itself, over
which the police were unable to exercise any control (Figure 1).

Catching offenders immediately is very cost-effective, despite the extra officers that
are typically despatched. The average time spent at all detected and undetected 'in-
progress' incidents was 47 minutes. Since only 10% of them were detected, an
average of 7.6 hours was spent at the scene per detected incident compared with
17.1 hours for all other detections. An improvement in the success rate would make
caught in the act (CIA) detection even more economic.

---

5   Police control room logs were used to identify the burglaries that were coded for an immediate
    response. The immediate response burglaries where there were persons on or leaving the premises
    were identified as being reported 'in progress'. Not all the detections classified as 'caught in the act'
    are included in this sub-sample mainly due to the offender being detained before the burglary was
    reported or as a result of a police operation.

HOW BURGLARIES ARE SOLVED: THE EFFECTIVENESS OF POLICE OPERATIONS

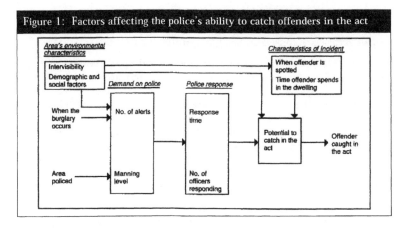

Figure 1: Factors affecting the police's ability to catch offenders in the act

Nature of the police response

A rapid response enabled burglars to be caught in the act. Where burglars escaped capture, police officers took twice as long to respond, averaging 10 minutes to arrive at the scene after receiving the alert from the control room[6], compared with only five minutes where offenders were caught. In 77% of incidents where burglars were caught, the police arrived at the scene in five minutes or less. However, a five minute response did not guarantee capture. Even with responses as quick as this, the majority of burglars, 85%, evaded capture. The arrest rate improved substantially when a quick response was combined with more than two officers attending. This resulted in 26% of offenders at 'in progress' scenes being captured. This would suggest that something like a quarter of the undetected 'in progress' burglaries or a further 1.5-2% of all burglaries could potentially be solved, as many as 115 additional detections.

Although the police response time and number of officers who attend are both important in the detection of 'in progress' burglaries, their relative importance does vary. When a burglary was reported 'in progress' and the offender was on the premises a quick response time was more important than the number of officers that attended. However, when the offender had just left the premises, the number of officers that attended became more important.

The findings across sub-divisions suggest that responses of five minutes or less are feasible, with some sub-divisions achieving much higher levels than others. Five

---

6   Therefore, all response times that are quoted exclude the time taken for the alert to be transferred via the control room to the police unit.

HOW BURGLARIES ARE SOLVED: THE EFFECTIVENESS OF
POLICE OPERATIONS

minute responses showed considerable variation, from as low as 15% to over 80%.
Responses by over two officers also varied substantially, attending over 35% of 'in
progress' incidents in three areas, and less than 10% in three others.

As a result of the variation in the speed and staffing of the police response, there
were considerable differences between sub-divisions in the percentage of burglaries
in progress that were caught in the act. In four of the sub-divisions, offenders were
caught in the act in over 24% of all the burglaries reported 'in progress', whilst, in
four others, less than 10% were caught. The most successful sub-division achieved
37%, and the least successful, 3%. The differences between sub-divisions indicate
that successfully catching burglars in the act did not simply result from police units
being advantageously located and thus able to arrive quickly at the scene. It
suggests that there is a potential to increase the numbers of 'in progress' detections
in the less successful sub-divisions so that they match the levels in others.

Rapid responses of this order should be attainable in many urban areas, especially those
with higher population densities. They may not, however, be possible in rural areas.

Area size and crime levels

In the sub-division with the lowest capture rate for 'in progress' burglaries, officers
had by far the largest area to cover, two and a half times that of the next largest
sub-division. Their average response times were the slowest and the smallest
average number of officers attended the incidents. In the sub-division with the next
lowest CIA rate, the area covered by each officer was of average size. However, this
sub-division's officers had the most crime, particularly burglary, to deal with. The
sub-division with the highest CIA rate covers an average size area, had low to
average levels of crime and burglary per officer and the fastest average response time
(5.8 minutes). However, its crime levels and staff resources were comparable to
most of the other sub-divisions, which fared less well.

It would appear that the numbers caught in the act could be raised by taking steps,
for instance by adjusting staffing procedures for burglary responses, to ensure a
quicker response to burglaries reported in progress. It is likely that, in the sub-
division where officers had a much larger area to cover and the one where crime
rates were higher, extra human resources or the redeployment of existing staff would
be needed to achieve additional detections. In rural areas and certain rural-urban
fringe areas, population distribution and other local geographical characteristics will
mean that additional patrolling would have little if any impact on detection.

Offender behaviour

The number of officers and their attendance times were more important where the
burglary alert was reported at a later stage in the burglary and when the offender
spent less time in the victim's dwelling. About half the 'in progress' burglary alerts

HOW BURGLARIES ARE SOLVED: THE EFFECTIVENESS OF
POLICE OPERATIONS

were reported as the offender was leaving the premises, and these cases had a lower CIA rate (5%) than those where the witness reported the burglar breaking in or observed him at work (19%), though it improved five-fold to 24% when more than two officers attended in less than five minutes. In general, when the offender spent less time at the burglary, the time the police took to arrive, predictably, proved more crucial in the offender's capture. The offender visited just one room in about a fifth of the burglaries reported 'in progress'. In these circumstances, when the police attended in three minutes or less, all but one offender was caught while longer response times resulted in a capture rate of only 3%.

The timing of 'in progress' burglaries also has an important bearing on both their numbers and their successful detection, partly as a result of the demands placed on police resources at different times of the day and because of the cover that darkness provides for the criminal. Slightly more burglaries than expected were reported 'in progress' at night (00:00 to 06:00) and during the weekend, possibly reflecting the higher occupancy rates at these times. In contrast, there were fewer during the mornings (06:00 to 12:00). Fewer offenders were captured when burglaries were reported in progress during the middle of the night (22:00 to 01:00) and mid-afternoon (15:00 to 17:00) (Figure 2). The mid-afternoon and night capture rates were less than one-seventh of the rest of the day's, and appear to reflect periods when many burglaries are reported. During the afternoon period, both the number of officers attending and their response times are much worse than at other times. In contrast, low capture at night reflected the improved cover and poorer visibility rather than police staffing practices and response times.

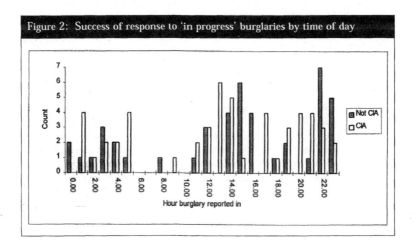

Figure 2: Success of response to 'in progress' burglaries by time of day

HOW BURGLARIES ARE SOLVED: THE EFFECTIVENESS OF
POLICE OPERATIONS

Characteristics of residential environment

The characteristics of the residential environment influenced the numbers of
burglaries reported 'in progress', and also affected their detection. The probability that
a burglar is spotted at work depended on the ease with which the dwelling's
approaches could be seen by neighbours, and by the socio-demographic profile of the
neighbourhood which determined who was likely to be at home at different times of
the day, and, therefore, likely to observe him. The ability to report an incident 'in
progress' may well be hampered by not having a telephone in the dwelling, and it is
notable that fewer burglars were reported at work where the victimised dwellings were
located in the most deprived enumeration districts. Residents of these areas may also
exhibit a reduced willingness to contact the police because of either intimidation or
higher criminal activity within the total population.

Once a burglary was reported 'in progress', the offender was more likely to be caught
in the more deprived areas where the burgled property was likely to be less secure
than its neighbours' properties and have less cover around it, probably making it
more likely that an offender was spotted. Improved responses to 'in progress' alerts
are likely to particularly benefit victims in these areas by virtually ensuring the
return of property that was commonly uninsured.

Practical implications

The findings indicate that there is a potential to augment the number of 'in
progress' detections, principally by improving attendance times and ensuring that
the police respond in sufficient numbers. Officers should aim to reach crime scenes
in five minutes or less from receiving alerts from the control room, and, where
possible, in three minutes, so that burglars leaving the crime scene can be intercepted.
At least three officers should be despatched in order to maximise the chances of
apprehending burglars who have left the crime site, but are still in the vicinity. There
are two main ways of achieving this. The first is to prioritise responses to 'in progress'
burglary alerts, whenever this is feasible, especially during the mid-afternoon period
when there is a greater opportunity to catch more burglars in the act.

The second way, if other duties permit, would be the creation of more single-crewed
units. These could provide 60% more cover, with a probable increase in operating
costs of less than 10%. Additional cover should reduce the time taken for a unit to
attend and this should increase the probability of capturing the offender, by
improving the chances of a police presence before criminals have left the victims'
dwellings or while they are still nearby. However, in most 'in progress' incidents it
would still be necessary for three officers to be despatched to the scene of the
burglary, even if they were operating as three separate single-crewed units. Single-
crewed units would be particularly valuable at the peak hours for 'in progress'

HOW BURGLARIES ARE SOLVED: THE EFFECTIVENESS OF
POLICE OPERATIONS

burglary alerts, improving police cover when there is the greatest potential for burglars to be caught in the act.

An increase in the use of single-crewed units would have to take account of all the other demands placed upon officers as well as their safety, with lone officers potentially more vulnerable. While attending residential burglaries, there is a 45% chance that a single officer might be faced with more than one offender, though a second officer would be expected to arrive within minutes. Although a multiple officer unit can more easily co-ordinate their response at the scene of 'in progress' alerts, particularly in terms of the deployment of officers in the nearby streets, the evidence available indicates single-crewed units charged a similar number of offenders to multiple response units.

Given the advantages of interviewing neighbours, it is necessary to balance the benefits of single crewed units against the additional time needed to cover tasks where the presence of two or more officers would be helpful. Besides arriving at the scene more quickly, the benefits are that fewer interviews would be curtailed by other more urgent calls, officers would be unoccupied less often at the scene and extra officers could be more fruitfully engaged elsewhere. On the other hand, single officers would need more time to interview neighbours and comfort victims. There would be little change if two single-crewed units were always despatched to burglary incidents.

The behaviour of teams on arrival at the scene is likely to be critical when every minute counts, and unfortunately there is little measured information on this, especially when the burglar has left the premises. In order to determine the best way of dealing with burglaries reported 'in progress', it would be necessary to examine the success of the strategies employed by officers at the scenes of different burglaries.

Summary

A tenth of all burglaries were reported as they were taking place, but the police caught only a tenth of these offenders in the act, often in the better resourced sub-divisions. Most of those who escaped were not subsequently caught, but even when they were, this increased the police effort per case, and stolen property was generally not recovered. Many more burglars could be caught at or near the scene by despatching officers more quickly and in greater numbers. Given the dearth of evidence collected in the bulk of burglaries, this offers the greatest potential to improve detection, and enhance the victim's regard for the police, especially if more uninsured property is recovered.

The findings indicate that the number of burglaries solved and the amount of property returned could be increased by about a third. Catching more burglars in the act would require either more resources or some redeployment of personnel, particularly during the afternoons on weekdays when many of the least successful responses to 'in progress'

HOW BURGLARIES ARE SOLVED: THE EFFECTIVENESS OF
POLICE OPERATIONS

burglaries were made. The use of single-crewed units should be especially considered at
these times. Home Office funded research is currently being carried out with the
assistance of the West Midlands Force into the influence of staffing strengths and
dispositions on the successful detection of 'in progress' burglaries.

Questioning the victim

The first officer/s attending questioned 94% of burglary victims. Some useful
information was provided by 18% of victims. Although their evidence was the key
factor in solving under 1% of the cases, this represents 19% of all primary
detections. The different types of evidence obtained from victims, and their role in
the investigations, are shown in Table 2. Where victims were not questioned, it was
because they could not be contacted when the burglary was discovered, for instance
if they were on holiday.

Table 2: Evidence provided by the victim			
Type of evidence[7]	Total number of burglaries where this evidence was provided	% of cases that were detected	% of cases where witness evidence was the most important factor in the detection
Definite suspect	120	22	20
Suspect vehicle	35	11	11
Possible suspect	378	5	2.6
Further intelligence	378	1	0.5

On average, officers spent 26 minutes at the burgled dwelling, talking to the victim
and assessing the burglary site. This constituted a total of 2350 hours of police time,
and represented 58.7 hours of effort per burglary detected primarily through
evidence provided by the victim, excluding travel time to and from the scene.
However, police visits to the scene have an important bearing on how victims view
the service provided by the police.

The victims' satisfaction with the service provided by the police partly depended on
the length of time spent at the scene and the attending officer's manner. While
23% of respondents were dissatisfied when the police spent 20 minutes or less at the

---

7 The categories that were used to define the types of evidence were determined with police assistance.
   Further intelligence generally covered evidence that was not likely to be very significant in any
   investigations, for example very vague suspect descriptions.

HOW BURGLARIES ARE SOLVED: THE EFFECTIVENESS OF
POLICE OPERATIONS

scene, this fell to 8% when they stayed over twenty minutes, and to 2% when they were there for over 30 minutes. Increasing the level of service to at least 20 minutes for all burglary visits over the study period would have needed an extra 80 to 100 officer hours. This might be contemplated where there would be some other benefit, possibly a more detailed recording of MO or a fuller assessment of the site's potential for forensic evidence.

Since visits to the dwelling have an important bearing on victim satisfaction, as well as providing the witness evidence from the victim that will be critical for the success of a fifth of the burglary cases that are solved, this time can be regarded as a reasonable use of the police's resources. The initial visit to the dwelling, in addition, provides the opportunity to question neighbours, whose vigilance can supply the officers with good suspect or vehicle details that result in the subsequent solution of the case. It should be noted that approximately 15% of the detections from witnesses' evidence are failed 'in progress' burglaries, a quarter of which may be solved by the above recommendations concerning the response to 'in progress' burglary alerts.

Questioning the victim's neighbours

The first officer/s attending the burglary questioned the victim's neighbours in 52% of all burglaries. An average of two households were questioned. Although this had no effect on the victim's regard for the police, 22% of the cases where neighbours were contacted provided useful information, and 5% led to a detection. Information from neighbours was the main factor in the detection of 14% of the burglaries that were solved.

The quality of evidence

The amount and type of information gathered is shown in Table 3. Although officers spent an average of 8 minutes questioning neighbours, where useful information was obtained this rose to an average of 13 minutes. The better the quality of information collected, the longer it took. Details of a definite suspect, a suspect vehicle or a possible suspect took 20 minutes to collect, but were more likely to lead to cases being solved. In the cases where both neighbour and victim provided information, about 1.6% of all burglaries, there was a particularly high chance of a successful detection. While, in general, only 5% of cases where there was evidence from witnesses at the scene were solved, 17% of those where there was evidence from both the victim and a neighbour were successfully detected. This is because when both the victim and neighbour/s provided information it was generally of better quality than when only one or other of them gave any evidence.

HOW BURGLARIES ARE SOLVED: THE EFFECTIVENESS OF
POLICE OPERATIONS

Table 3: Evidence provided by neighbours			
Type of evidence	Total number of burglaries where this evidence was provided	% of cases that were detected	% of cases where witness evidence was the most important factor in the detection
Definite suspect	61	22.9	19.7
Suspect vehicle	118	7.6	6.8
Possible suspect	244	4.1	3.7
Further intelligence	237	1.3	0.4

Cost of questioning neighbours

Although the success rate of interviewing neighbours is low, it is comparatively
cost-effective, since it does not normally involve a special journey to the crime
scene. Only a little additional time is needed to question neighbours, an average of
8 minutes per case, where a single officer attends the scene, and no extra time when
there are two or more officers. In general, no additional travel time was incurred.
Since 45% of the units responding to burglaries where neighbours were questioned
were single-crewed, the cost of interviewing neighbours was 180 hours, or an
average of 6 hours per detection obtained through evidence from neighbours. Any
recommendation to increase the proportion of single officer patrols might tend to
be at the cost of the extra time needed to question neighbours, unless two such
patrols or double-crewed patrols were despatched to the non-emergency incidents.
However, even if all patrols were single-crewed, interviewing neighbours would still
be comparatively cost-effective: for this study, it would have been an average of 13.3
hours per primary detection. This might be expected to rise if more burglars
reported while committing the offence are caught in the act, since it was victims'
neighbours who raised the alert in a majority of these cases.

Should more neighbours be interviewed?

Since police visits were made to almost all reported burglaries, there may be a
potential to economically boost detections by questioning neighbours in the cases
where this did not occur, particularly where the circumstances of the burglary
match others where evidence from neighbours has proved most useful. There will be
little potential for improved detection if the reason for not interviewing neighbours
was because no one was at home, or because they would have been prevented from
seeing anything by darkness or the layout of the houses, their gardens and other
open spaces. If, on the other hand, neighbours were not contacted because fewer

HOW BURGLARIES ARE SOLVED: THE EFFECTIVENESS OF POLICE OPERATIONS

officers responded to the burglary alert, or because the initial visit to the burglary scene was cut short by more pressing calls for assistance, then there may be some scope for improved detection.

In fact, neither the numbers of officers attending the burglary scene, nor the shortening of investigations to attend other incidents, affected whether or not neighbours were questioned, or the amount of useful information obtained from them. Although single officer patrols tended to question fewer neighbouring households at each incident they dealt with than multiple officer units, this had no effect on the amount or quality of information collected. These findings suggest no potential detections were missed because of the way burglary responses were crewed. They may also indicate that single-crewed patrols may be as effective as multiple officer patrols in dealing with burglary incidents.

However, many neighbours estimated to be at home when the burglaries occurred were not contacted, especially during the mornings (6am to mid-day), when only 28% were interviewed, and at night, when 13% were seen. In contrast, rather more, 45%, were contacted during the evenings (6pm to midnight), while even during the afternoons (mid-day to 6pm), when contact peaked at 74%, there were still many who were available but were not seen. This might suggest that officers missed an opportunity to gather incriminating evidence. Nevertheless, since only 13% of the neighbours questioned during the mornings provided useful information, it seems unlikely that much would be gained by extending questioning to more neighbours at this time.

In contrast the small number of neighbours questioned during the night (midnight to 6 a.m.) provided useful information in 40% of cases. Nevertheless, questioning the 87% not contacted at night is unlikely to be worthwhile since contact only took place at this hour because neighbours were perceived or known to be awake, and may well have discovered the burglary. As a result it is not recommended that officers should rouse neighbours during the 'small hours'! In general, contacting more neighbours in the busy afternoon period is likely to prove the most beneficial time. If it is assumed that half the people not questioned at times other than midnight to 6am were available for questioning, then an additional 11 detections might result if they were contacted.

Summary

Interviewing neighbours was a cost effective activity that led to the solution of an important number of cases. Although the gains from questioning more neighbours would be modest, in view of the small additional effort required, it is, nevertheless, sensible for officers to do this wherever possible, particularly in the afternoon period.

HOW BURGLARIES ARE SOLVED: THE EFFECTIVENESS OF
POLICE OPERATIONS

Visits by SOCOs

SOCOs attended the burglary site as soon as possible to collect forensic evidence.
This was generally on the day the burglary was reported. If any forensic evidence
was found, the local CID were notified and the evidence was tested. If a fingerprint
was found, it was run through the computer to identify if a match with a known
print existed.

SOCOs visited the site of about 90% of all the burglaries that were committed.
However, forensic evidence was found and tested in only 9% (470) of the c.5200
burglaries that were visited and it proved useful in under 1%[8]. Although it was the
main factor in 6% of the cases that were solved, in an additional 11% it was used as
supporting evidence.

Three quarters of the forensic evidence found was fingerprints and the rest consisted
of blood, footprints and fibres. Owing to the heavy workloads, there was a delay of
between one and three months in testing fingerprint evidence. Blood was found at
1-2% of the burglary sites that were visited. This suggests that the survey area would
provide c.130 samples per annum from burglaries for the DNA library. Since
burglars commit multiple offences, these may offer the potential for as many as 5-
10% of cases to be solved.

Evaluation of SOCO visits

The burglary victims estimated that, on average, SOCOs spent 20 minutes at each
burglary. Excluding access and testing time, 1730 hours were used to obtain 12
detections, representing 144 hours per detection.

Although forensic evidence plays a significant role in investigation and detection,
evidence was found in only a small number of burglaries that were visited. If the
number of burglaries visited could be reduced whilst maintaining the useful
evidence that is found, large savings could be made. A reduction in the number of
burglary sites visited could help to eliminate the delays in forensic testing. This
would lead to the earlier detention of offenders, and to the prevention of the extra
burglaries they might commit.

There is no evidence to show that dispensing with many SOCO visits would lower
the victim's regard for the service provided by the police[9]. Indeed, it actually
damaged this regard in the small proportion of cases where victims regarded the
SOCOs' visits as too short or their manner unsatisfactory. Five percent of the

---

8   It is possible that the number of burglaries where forensic evidence was found is an underestimate,
    because the figures were provided by detectives who may not have detailed forensic evidence in all
    the burglaries where it was found and tested.

9   This finding should be treated with caution because only a small number of victims were not visited.

HOW BURGLARIES ARE SOLVED: THE EFFECTIVENESS OF
POLICE OPERATIONS

victims considered that the SOCO's visit was too short, viewing officers as either incompetent, discourteous or unsympathetic and these people tended to be less satisfied with the overall service provided by the police.

Limiting SOCO visiting

All available crime scene information has been tested, but, other than for aggravated burglaries and 'caught in the act' cases, no reliable predictor of useful forensic evidence was found. While there may be evidence at some burglary sites which more detailed forensic examination might uncover, there could be substantial savings if first officers at the scene could be more selective rather than, as at present, routinely requesting a SOCO visit. Situations where officers specialise in burglary, such as the West Yorkshire "Crime Car" initiative, can result in greater selectivity in requesting SOCO visits (see Audit Commission, 1993 and Taylor & Hirst, 1995), though there is little precise information concerning the impact of reducing SOCO visits in this way on the collection of forensic evidence and detection rates. Recent work has examined police use of forensic science generally (eg Tilley & Ford, 1996; McCulloch, 1996) and ACPO/FSS have produced guidelines for good practice. Further useful work in this area could be carried out to identify predictors that could be reliably used to exclude the unpromising sites and enable SOCOs to focus on those more likely to provide valuable evidence.

CID Screening

If the offender was not caught in the act or shortly afterwards, responsibility for the investigation was generally transferred to the CID or to the burglary squad, in the case of the sub-divisions that had one. The CID's principal duties were to screen burglary cases and follow up witness evidence, make additional visits to the crime scene and conduct any further investigations and operations. The effectiveness of screening procedures, and therefore, the use of evidence provided by witnesses, are considered in section four.

Visits by CID to the crime scene

CID officers visited the scene of 36% of all burglaries and collected useful information from witnesses in 16% of these (or 6% of all burglaries). However, in all but 2.4% of these visits, the information obtained did not improve on that collected by the first officer at the scene, though when there was new information, it always resulted in a detection. The bulk of the visits to the scene made by the CID appear to be duplicated effort.

For the 'average' burglary, one or two detectives visited the burglary sites two weeks after the incident, and spent 22 minutes there. Excluding access time, which, given the fact that the visits were generally not by telephone appointment, is likely to be

HOW BURGLARIES ARE SOLVED: THE EFFECTIVENESS OF
POLICE OPERATIONS

greater per visit than for the response to the initial burglary alert, 1050 officer hours
were used to obtain 8 detections, representing 131 hours per detection. This appears
less cost-effective than other police activities.

Though the CID visit evoked a negative reaction from a minority of victims (6% of
those visited) who thought the visit was too brief, in general, CID visits had little
or no effect on the victim's perception of the service offered by the police.

Since CID visits had little impact on either detection rates or victim satisfaction, it
would seem that savings could be made by reducing the number of visits to the
scene. It would, however, be desirable to achieve this while retaining the subset
where new information was collected and resulted in cases being solved. Since 5 of
these 8 detections arose from victims' own additional investigations, it would seem
that, at most, there would be a risk of losing only three detections if the number of
CID visits to the scene were substantially reduced. Additional savings might also
result if these visits could be made by appointment, where appropriate, or, where
the victim does not have a phone, if visits are made at a time when victims are
likely to be at home, such as Sunday morning.

Further CID activities

Further CID activities consisted of the use of surveillance, informants, stop-checks,
and admissions made by suspects during questioning when arrested for another
offence. Other activities, including checking for stolen property and the
investigation of possible offenders, were used infrequently, and any analysis of these
would be anecdotal. Some additional detections were based on investigations
carried out by the victims themselves.

Together, these additional CID activities accounted for almost 12% of the primary
detected cases and, in general, achieved a high rate of successful detection,
averaging 23%. This includes the questioning of suspects which was aimed at
solving other crimes besides burglary, and, perhaps, partly because of this, had a
poorer success rate. When these are excluded, the detection rate was 29% for the
other activities.

Use of surveillance

Surveillance operations were employed to investigate 0.6% of burglaries, and this
resulted in a quarter of them being solved (9 burglaries). On average, six hours were
spent on each operation, indicating officers were not undertaking prolonged or
widespread surveillance. Surveillance was usually based on good evidence
accumulated from a variety of sources, such as witnesses, local contacts and police
intelligence, and because of this, longer was spent on the complete investigation
where surveillance was used: an average of 32 hours, compared with 3 hours for a

HOW BURGLARIES ARE SOLVED: THE EFFECTIVENESS OF
POLICE OPERATIONS

'standard' investigation. However, a surveillance operation was no more likely to take place if a CID officer had visited the scene.

Their high detection rate indicates that the right people had been targeted. Used as an additional method of solving a case where there was evidence pointing to a suspect, but none of it was conclusive, they provide a cost-effective means of detection. Their unequal application across the sub-divisions suggests that there may be scope for a modest extension of their use.

Use of informants

Information was provided by registered informants on 7 burglaries, all of which were solved. In five of these cases, the information led to the offender being found with stolen property or admitting the offence. In one of the other cases, the offender was caught in the act, and in the other, the informant's information complemented a suspect description to produce a detection.

Local contacts, e.g. social services, were questioned in 0.6% of burglaries, and were the main factor in the detection of 6% of these (2 burglaries), and contributed to the detection of a further 12% (4 burglaries) of these cases. Therefore, 18% of cases where information was provided proved fruitful.

Use of stop-checks

Stop-checks of suspects or suspect vehicles were carried out during the course of 0.4% of burglary investigations. They were successful in 30% (7) of these incidents, as a result of suspects being stopped shortly before or after burglaries had been reported, and often because of a description provided by a witness at the scene.

Victims' investigations

In 3% (6 cases) of detected burglaries, the principal reason for success was the provision of extra information by witnesses, often the victims themselves, after the initial visit from the police. In four cases, the victim supplied the suspect's name, which they had uncovered from a variety of sources, and in another the victim recovered the stolen property, and indicated the offender to the police. This is assuredly the most cost-effective detection method from the police's viewpoint! It characterised poorer residential areas, younger offenders, and victim's property which was not covered by insurance or had high sentimental value.

Suspect admissions

Suspects were questioned in 1% of burglary cases, after having been arrested for other offences, and this resulted in 10% of these incidents (7 burglaries) being solved. When suspects admitted the offence, it was normally because there was good evidence, such as stolen property, linking them to the burglary. Where the

HOW BURGLARIES ARE SOLVED: THE EFFECTIVENESS OF
POLICE OPERATIONS

questioning of suspects was unsuccessful, they had been questioned about the
burglary on the basis of weaker, more circumstantial evidence.

Summary

These further activities undertaken by the CID accounted for an important
minority of detections. In view of their cost-effectiveness, a modest and selective
increase in their use would help in solving more cases.

Victims' satisfaction with police operations

It is reasonable for victims to expect a good quality service from the police, and this
has been recently endorsed by the introduction of a Victim's Charter. The way
contact with victims is handled also affects their regard for the police, and is likely
to condition their future response in neighbourhoods where officers may need
assistance with other crimes as well as burglary. The victims of all crimes
collectively represent a substantial subset of the general public, and as a 'high
volume crime', burglary incidents, therefore, offer an opportunity to the police to
influence the public's perception of them. Handled well, they can enhance their
image. It is, therefore, in the interests of the force to make the most of their contact
with victims and their neighbours, since care taken over the relationship between
police and victim will benefit both parties.

Although the way the police handled burglaries was generally quite well regarded,
there appears to be some scope for improvement. While 53% of victims were
satisfied with the service provided, 29% considered it as adequate, and 18%
expressed dissatisfaction. Satisfaction increased where the police solved the crime,
and when stolen property was returned, most notably when it had not been insured.
Predictably, early success affects victims' perceptions, with 70% of victims whose
burglaries were primary detected being satisfied with the service provided. It is to be
expected, therefore, that any improvement in detection rates that results from
implementing the recommendations based on the analysis of police operations will
improve the public standing of officers. In fact, 40% of those who were dissatisfied
reported they would have been satisfied if the offender had been caught.
Subsequent clearing up of burglaries through secondary detection may well also
have an impact, though its assessment was beyond the scope of the current research.

Where investigations were unsuccessful, there was considerable variation in victims'
opinions, with 30% of the victims of unsolved burglaries satisfied with the outcome,
30% regarding the outcome as 'adequate', but 40% of respondents wanting to
change the way the police carried out the investigation of their case. The features
that both impressed and displeased indicate how the force should address the issue
of improving regard for their work.

HOW BURGLARIES ARE SOLVED: THE EFFECTIVENESS OF
POLICE OPERATIONS

It has already been stated that victim satisfaction depended upon the response time to the burglary alert, the attending officer's manner and the time spent by the officer at the scene, but it was independent of visits to the scene by SOCOs or detectives. It was also found that victims who received extra contact from the police were more satisfied with the service provided, no matter what the outcome of the investigation. This contact was generally made by telephone (46%), a police visit (22%), or a letter (27%), but the way victims were contacted made no difference to levels of satisfaction in either detected or undetected burglaries. While these contacts particularly concerned people whose burglaries were solved, police officers made further contact with 61% of all victims. It seems that satisfaction with the way the police handled burglaries could be improved quite cost-effectively by notifying every victim of the outcome or progress of their case, either by letter or by telephone. Since older people were better disposed towards the force and were happier with the service provided by the police, any comparison of victim satisfaction in different police areas should take account of demographic variation.

Summary

Victims were generally satisfied with the service provided by the police. Victims were predictably pleased when the offender was caught or property recovered. They were less happy when there was a slower response to the burglary alert, and when the first officer attending seemed rude or uninterested or spent too little time with them. While additional visits did not appear to affect victims, they were often dissatisfied when there was no information on the progress or outcome of their case.

[22]

Home Office Research Study 164

Safer cities and domestic burglary

by

Paul Ekblom,
Ho Law
and Mike Sutton
with assistance from Paul Crisp
and Richard Wiggins

A Research and Statistics Directorate Report

Home Office
Research and
Statistics
Directorate

London: Home Office

Summary

Phase 1 of the Safer Cities Programme set up just over 500 schemes to prevent domestic burglary. Most upgraded physical security, though some mounted community-oriented initiatives as well. The schemes usually centred on local neighbourhoods or estates. The results of a major evaluation of nearly 300 of the schemes are reported here.

Key points

- Overall, the schemes reduced burglary and were cost-effective. Simply implementing action in a police beat reduced local risks by nearly 10 per cent.

- Physical security measures against burglary seemed to work independently. But community-oriented activities (e.g., to increase awareness and promote crime prevention) needed reinforcement with action against other types of crime, or against crime in general. Taken as a whole, the burglary schemes worked better in this wider context.

- The overall cost of each burglary prevented was about £300 in very high-crime areas. It was about £900 when risks were at the lower end of the scale. The average financial cost of a burglary to the state and the victim was about £1,100. Grossed up, a very approximate estimate for the total benefit from Safer Cities burglary action was 56,000 burglaries prevented at a saving of about £31 million – not far short of the cost of the entire Programme.

- Reduction in burglary risk was greater where there was more intense burglary action but to achieve these bigger falls cost disproportionately more. 'Marginal cost' estimates per extra prevented burglary ranged from about £1,100 in the highest risk areas to about £3,300 in the lower-risk ones. In monetary terms extra expenditure was justified only in high risk areas but there are other considerations (see below).

Safer cities and domestic burglary

- Low-intensity action seemed to displace some burglaries to nearby areas, and to cause burglars to switch to other property crime within the actual scheme area. But when action was of moderate intensity or more, neither problem occurred. In fact, adjacent areas also benefitted from some reduction in burglary, and other crime decreased in scheme areas.

- Although only a few people were aware of preventive action in their area, if they were aware, and the action was intensive, they worried less about burglary. If they were aware but it was low level action, they were actually more worried than before.

- People's perceptions of their area's quality improved only where action was most intensive.

The Safer Cities Programme

Phase 1 of Safer Cities started in 1988 and ended in Autumn 1995. It aimed to reduce crime and fear of crime, and to create safer environments for economic and community life to flourish. Safer Cities was part of the Government's wider plan, Action for Cities, set up to deal with the multiple problems of some larger urban areas.

Safer Cities was locally based and took a 'partnership' or multi-agency approach. In each of 20 cities or boroughs, the Home Office funded a project co-ordinator and a small team recruited locally from various professional backgrounds. Each team was guided by steering committees representing local government, the police, probation, voluntary bodies and commerce.

The projects tackled a range of crime problems – e.g., domestic and commercial burglary, domestic violence, vehicle crime, shop theft, disorder, and sometimes fear of crime. Some projects focused on the city as a whole (e.g., publicity campaigns and multi-agency co-ordination of strategies). But most schemes were local and focused on vulnerable people, particular institutions or localities.

A variety of local organisations were invited to bid for funds from Safer Cities grants (up to £250,000 annually per city). Some 3,600 schemes were started, using £30 million, of Safer Cities money in direct and administrative costs. Just over 500 schemes focused on domestic burglary – spending £4.4 million in Safer Cities grants.

A problem solving approach

All Safer Cities action was meant to take a rational, problem-solving approach:

- analysing crime and other data to identify local crime patterns and set objectives

- adopting tailor-made preventive measures, drawing on a range of methods

- evaluating what was done and making changes as necessary.

Safer Cities action against burglary

This evaluation centred on domestic burglary – an aspect of Safer Cities where the impact on crime could be more readily measured. Domestic burglary was often targeted by co-ordinators, preventive practice is relatively well-developed, and burglary schemes tend to have localised effects. Just under 300 of the total 500 burglary schemes were underway or completed by Summer 1992. This evaluation focuses on these schemes which consisted of:

- target-hardening (e.g., door, window and fencing improvements; entry systems; alarms; and security lighting) – used in three in four schemes

- community-oriented action (e.g., supplying 'tool libraries' to help DIY security installation, fostering Neighbourhood Watch and property marking, employing workers to raise burglary awareness among householders and local agencies) – used in nearly one in ten schemes

- other activities e.g., the distribution of leaflets and small house-to-house surveys.

The amount spent per scheme ranged from a few pounds for leaflets to over £100,000 for major target-hardening. The number of households covered

Safer cities and domestic burglary

ranged from a single block to a whole district. The average number of households covered was 5,200. About one in three schemes had 'levered-in' funds from other sources as well as Safer Cities money (although this was not consistently recorded). More Safer Cities money itself was spent in the schemes with levered-in funds – so Safer Cities funds were not simply being used to substitute for other sources.

How much money was spent in 300 schemes

All 300 schemes (average)
Safer Cities money per scheme £8,700
No. of households covered   5,200

Two-thirds schemes with no levered funds
Safer Cities money   £7,300

One-third schemes with levered-in funds
Safer Cities money   £11,300
Levered-in funds   £17,800

The evaluation approach

Some individual Safer Cities burglary schemes have been evaluated (Tilley and Webb, 1994). But an assessment of the cost-effectiveness of the schemes as a whole provides the best picture of what a large-scale prevention programme can do. Outcome was measured in two ways:

• before-and-after surveys – 7,500 household interviews were carried out in over 400 high-crime neighbourhoods in 11 Safer Cities and eight comparison cities. The 'before' surveys took place in late-1990, the 'after' ones in late-1992. Although it was not known at the start of the evaluation where action would be initiated, in the event, the surveyed areas covered a sufficient number of schemes – 96 of the 300 set up

• local police crime statistics covering the period 1987 – 1992. They encompassed 700 police beats in 14 Safer Cities, and included coverage of 240 burglary schemes. There were also city-level statistics in nine comparison cities.

The two sources were complementary. The police figures covered a wider area, and a longer period. The surveys provided information about householders' experience of crime whether or not reported to the police, and their perceptions about crime.

The average effects of burglary action in small areas were studied by looking for changes in risk in:

• Safer Cities areas where nothing was done

• Safer Cities areas with burglary schemes of varying 'intensity' (see box below)

• a set of comparison cities.

Scheme intensity

A universal measure of action input was needed to estimate the effects of a variety of burglary schemes spending different amounts in different ways and covering areas of different sizes. When action took place in an area its 'intensity' was measured by dividing the total amount spent by the total number of households in the area. It was not possible to say which individual households had been the focus of action. Adjustments were also made for how long action had been in place. If more than one scheme covered an area their intensities were combined. Population data from the 1991 Census and scheme data from the Safer Cities Management Information System were also used. Linking all this data needed purpose-built computer software in a Geographic Information System.

Intensive schemes were either costly ones, or more modest ones concentrated on a small area. Including levered funds, the intensity of action in the surveyed areas ranged from 1p to £113 per household. The mean was £16 – relatively few areas exceeded this by much. The range in the police beats was similar, but because the areas were larger, and therefore not always fully covered by schemes, the average was lower, at £4.

The survey results

There was good evidence from the surveys that Safer Cities schemes reduced the risk of burglary in the areas they covered. Table S.1 shows how risks changed across the different types of area. The risks here are the proportion of households burgled once or more in the past year – a 'prevalence' measure.

Safer cities and domestic burglary

Table S.1
Changes in burglary risk according to the household surveys

	Safer Cities					Comparison Cities
	No action	*Low intensity*	*Medium intensity*	*High intensity*	*All action areas*	
Percentage of households burgled once or more in last year						
Before	8.9	10.3	12.7	13.4	11.6	12.0
After	10.2	9.3	9.9	7.6	9.1	12.4
Percentage change (Before to After)						
	+15	-10	-22	-43	-21	+3

Between 1990 and 1992, burglary risks in the comparison cities rose by three per cent, In Safer Cities areas where there was no burglary action, risks showed a bigger increase, of 15 per cent. But where there was action, risks fell: by 10 per cent in low-action areas (under £1 of Safer Cities funds per household), 22 per cent in medium-action areas (£1 – £13), and by 43 per cent in high-action areas (over £13). The overall fall was 21 per cent.

The actual changes in burglary in different types of area are shown in Table S.1 but statistical modelling is a more accurate way of assessing the effect of Safer Cities. This takes other factors into account which may coincidentally influence crime levels, and thus bias the result. An advanced statistical technique – multi-level modelling – analysed the effect of background trends in crime and demographic differences across areas and between survey respondents. Figure S.1 compares the level of risk in the action areas observed in the 'after' surveys with the risk that would have been expected had the Safer Cities action not been set up but area characteristics and background trends in crime stayed the same. All areas with action (including levered funds for completeness) had a large drop in risk compared to expectations. Risks were 24 per cent less than expected in the 'after' survey in low-action areas, 33 per cent in medium-action areas and 37 per cent in high-action areas.

Figure S.1
Expected and observed risks of burglary from the survey figures

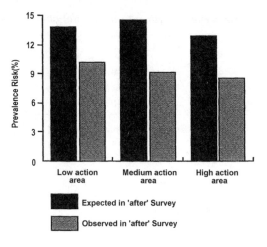

The results from police figures

Police figures gave the same picture as the surveys. Thus, again taking account of area differences and background trends (in particular a widespread drop in crime in about 1987–90 which then reversed), a Safer Cities 'effect' was once more observed. Risks continued broadly as expected until 1990, the year in which action began. Then, in 1991, all police beats in action areas had a reduction in risk. In 1992, risks in high action areas continued to decline. Risks in medium action areas increased a little, but were still below expected. In low action areas risks rose slightly above what was expected, suggesting that where action is insufficiently intensive its effect is short-lived.

The overall picture

Both the survey and police figures showed that the schemes' impact had two distinct components:

• setting up any action substantially reduced burglary risks in the area. Risks fell by nearly 10 per cent in police beats, and by more in the surveyed neighbourhoods, although that estimate can be calculated in different ways, with different results. (Smaller territories of measurement and different samples of schemes could explain the higher estimate in the surveys, although in any case margins of error were large.)

Safer cities and domestic burglary

- the more intense the burglary action, the greater the additional drop in risk. This extra marginal reduction was estimated to be 0.5%–1.0% for each extra £1 of action per household in the action area.

Cost-effectiveness

The value of Safer Cities can be assessed by comparing burglary costs with the cost of prevention. The average burglary costs the state and the victim in financial loss (measured in urban areas) about £1,100. This is based on all burglaries, including those not recorded by the police and does not allow for any psychological cost. Burglary prevention costs were estimated from the statistical models but, as with any cost-effectiveness calculations, assumptions had to be made. A critical one was how long a 'Safer Cities effect' would last – estimated at two years.

The estimates from the recorded crime figures are on the lower curve in Figure S.2. (The survey ones are very similar.) The level of risk for which costs of prevented burglaries are shown are the annual number of burglary incidents per 100 households. This is an incidence risk rather than the prevalence one earlier, to take account of the fact that some households are burgled more than once in a year. The fact that more burglaries happen than are recorded by the police is also allowed for in the costing.

Figure S.2
Cost effectiveness estimates: results from police figures

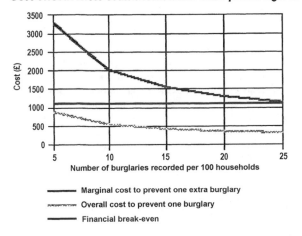

Number of burglaries recorded per 100 households

— Marginal cost to prevent one extra burglary

⋯⋯ Overall cost to prevent one burglary

— Financial break-even

As might be expected, it was cheaper to prevent a burglary in areas with higher burglary risk. Thus, the amount spent from both Safer Cities and other funds was about £300 per prevented burglary at the highest end of the risk scale (25 burglaries per 100 homes in a year). It was about £900 at the lower end (five burglaries – roughly equivalent to the national average). Grossing up to an estimated total spend on local domestic burglary schemes of £6.6 million (including levered funds) produces a very rough estimate of 56,000 burglaries prevented by the Safer Cities Programme, and a resultant saving to victims and state of £31 million. This is of the same order as the entire cost of the Programme.

The overall cost figures show that, at levels of risk typical of cities, preventive action is worth implementing. Once it is agreed to take action in an area, consideration must be given to whether it is worth spending more to try and achieve a greater reduction in burglaries. This will involve estimating what are known as 'marginal' costs. One would expect marginal costs to be higher than overall costs because they discount what is achieved simply by a scheme being in place. This proved to be the case.

The marginal cost of preventing a burglary additional to those prevented by the schemes, as they typically operated, can be estimated with the statistical models. This marginal cost (the upper curve on Figure S.2) would range from about £3,300 in lower-risk conditions to £1,100 in higher-risk ones. The preventive cost in higher-risk areas, then, matches what a burglary costs state and victim financially. The implication is that more intense schemes only offer good value for money in higher-risk areas. But taking into account psychological costs would broaden the range where value was achieved.

Displacement

Reducing burglaries in a scheme area sometimes led to burglaries being displaced to adjacent areas. Where this occurred, the overall positive effect of Safer Cities was diminished, as well as its cost-effectiveness. However, this displacement did not always happen. Rather, where burglary action was of moderate or higher intensity (estimated at over £4 per household), the preventive effect reached beyond the area covered by the scheme – so-called 'diffusion of benefit'. But even with the sophisticated methods employed, it was not possible to estimate how the savings in the target areas and some of the adjacent areas balanced against the losses from displacement in others.

Displacement to different forms of offending – 'crime switch' – was also assessed. The results indicated that when burglary action was low intensity, some switch to other property offences did occur. But when action was of moderate or higher intensity (over £5 per household), there seemed to be a reduction in the risk of other property crimes too.

An extra benefit of burglary action in an area was the protection it appeared to afford against 'inward' displacement from neighbouring burglary schemes. It also protected against 'crime switch' to burglary when Safer Cities action had been taken against other crime types.

Worry about burglary

The before and after surveys asked householders how worried they were about burglary. They were also asked if they were aware of any crime prevention initiatives in their area. After the Safer Cities action, people generally showed no increase in awareness that action against crime had been taken in their area but those interviewed would not necessarily be in a household which had been targetted. Also, awareness of action is generally low with any preventive initiative. The exception was in high-intensity areas, which showed a marked increase in awareness.

Those individuals who were aware of action worried less about burglary where the action was intensive. However, where action was of a low level, those who were aware of action were actually more worried than before. This may be because they were alerted to a burglary problem, but did not see it being tackled effectively. A similar finding was that people's views about the quality of their area only improved where action was greatest.

The value of a comprehensive approach

Two or more Safer Cities schemes were often combined in a locality. Of the burglary action areas covered by the surveys, a third had target-hardening schemes alone; a third had other (usually community-oriented) burglary action alone, and a third had combined action. Most of the burglary action areas also had Safer Cities action targetted on other crimes or crime in general (a factor incorporated in the costs). Disentangling the combinations which worked best against burglary was difficult. The survey data provided some indications.

Target-hardening reduced burglary under all conditions. Purely community-oriented burglary action only worked in tandem with action against other crimes. The best combination was when all elements were present. When burglary action was considered as a whole, the support of action against other crimes seemed more generally important. Like other studies, then, this evaluation suggests a comprehensive approach is best, although target-hardening could work alone.

The lessons for policy and practice

This evaluation bears on several key questions about burglary prevention programmes such as those in Safer Cities. The findings are relevant to both central policy and local practice, particularly in regard to action through co-ordinated local initiatives in a partnership context.

Is co-ordinated local action against domestic burglary worthwhile?

Action of the type taken in Safer Cities (Phase 1) was cost-effective in the areas, with the higher burglary risks typical of cities, where burglary schemes were targetted. As mentioned earlier, there was some evidence that this cost-effectiveness was reduced in places because burglars shifted their attention elsewhere. But there were also signs, at least when action was intensive, that burglars avoided a wider area than that in which the action occurred. This increased cost-effectiveness. Whether these losses and gains cancel each other out cannot be assessed with any precision.

A further caveat is that no evidence is available of the cost-effectiveness of other ways of arranging local preventive action, or of wider alternatives such as police patrolling. Careful evaluations of these alternatives are needed.

How did the action work?

The fact that the mere presence of burglary action seems to reduce burglary risk, suggests that 'area' processes are operating rather than those which act to defend individual homes. Offenders, alert to any action in an area, find it unattractive to operate there. Supporting evidence for this comes from two sources:

- the existence of crime displacement to adjacent areas

- the 'protective' influence of existing burglary action in an area against inward displacement from adjacent action, and against 'crime switch' to burglary.

Diffusion of benefit (in areas with more intense action) suggests that offenders are being guided by illusory risks of being caught beyond the boundaries of schemes. But in general, the kind of impact measured may be shorter- rather than longer-term.

Where is it best to target action?

By and large, targetting areas with moderate to high rates of burglary, typical of cities, promises the best returns. The main difficulty in achieving such targetting in future programmes is the lack of readily accessible local crime data. (Obtaining the data, both to supply co-ordinators with local 'crime profiles' of their cities and to support this evaluation, was extremely slow and labour intensive.) Geographic Information Systems would help and, if operated to a common standard, would facilitate local and national evaluations of crime prevention initiatives.

What amount of action is needed?

Generally, the more the better, but it is not entirely straightforward. More intensive schemes seem to:

•   stop displacement of burglaries to other areas

•   have a beneficial spillover effect to other areas

•   prevent switching to other forms of property offending.

They may also give economies of scale in implementation and have a more durable effect.

However, less intense action also had an impact. So in future programmes reducing scheme intensity (by cutting the spend per scheme, or increasing the area each scheme covered) would allow a greater coverage of areas and/or households. But here the impact would be narrower. There seems to be an important threshold of action beneath which, even if burglary is reduced, people's views of their area do not improve, they remain unaware of what is being done, and they continue to worry about burglary. The best estimate of this threshold is a spend of roughly £20 per household in an area. At this intensity, displacement should also be much less of a problem, since it appeared to be countered at about the £4 level upwards.

What sort of action to take?

A comprehensive strategy which combines action against burglary with action against crime in general is most appropriate. It would appear that 'community-oriented' action against burglary should not be introduced alone. In addition, it seems more effective to bring schemes together across adjacent areas. This decreases the chance of burglary being deflected elsewhere, since it is known that burglars tend to be unwilling to travel greater distances.

Well-publicised action is likely to be more effective. This should reassure householders, and send a stronger deterrent message to offenders. But action of the appropriate kind and intensity obviously needs to be taken, not just announced. Finally, publicity should also be handled carefully, to avoid raising unrealistic expectations and causing possible resentment that some households are losing out to others.

[23]

Helping the Victims

Martyn J. Gay, Christopher Holton and M. S. Thomas

Introduction

In order to protect society, the main emphasis of the British penal system has traditionally been upon the detection of crime and the punishment of the offender. Recently, a more enlightened attitude has been adopted by such organisations as the National Association for the Care and Resettlement of Offenders (NACRO), which aim to support the offender in an effort to prevent recidivism. Very little attention, however, has been paid by either voluntary or statutory bodies to assess the needs of the victims of crime. The main role of the victim at law has been as a source of evidence to secure a conviction against the offender, and the Criminal Injuries Compensation Board only provides recompense in cases of actual physical injury, a small minority of victims. In this setting, the Bristol Victims Support Scheme was concerned with the initial twofold aim of identifying the unmet needs of the victims, and at the same time, to research the subject.[1]

Method

The Bristol Victims Support Scheme (BVSS) is a local project, set up under the auspices of NACRO, in the early 1970's. In 1972, a Management Committee was formed, including a Barrister, a Police Inspector, a Senior Probation Officer, a Consultant Psychiatrist, and a Senior Official from the Social Services. It was constituted as a sub-committee of NACRO, and was financed by a £1,500 loan from them in 1973. This enabled the project to commence on 1st January, 1974.[2]

The area chosen was a section of South Bristol with a population of approximately 150,000 people. This was administratively convenient as it coincided with:

1. a complete Police division
2. Social Services area
3. a sector of Bristol Health District (Teaching).

It also represents a cross-section of urban society—an old established residential area both publicly and privately owned, and two densely populated housing estates. The victims visited also represented a range of social classes comparable with the distribution in the population at large.

Our theory was that any crime, however trivial, might have a devastating effect on its victim. We aimed to visit every victim of

Burglary

crime in the designated area, to assess their needs and to offer assistance where possible. Each case was also fully documented for research purposes.

Every morning the project administrator contacted the police, and obtained details of all those against whom an offence had been committed in the previous 24-hour period (name, address, and briefly, the nature of the crime). The administrator then allocated the victims between the team of trained volunteers. The volunteers were ordinary members of the public coming from all walks of life. Initially, there were eight volunteers including students, housewives, a vicar and a tax inspector, but later, because of the volume of work, others were enlisted and trained.

These volunteers each provided two referees and were interviewed by the Management Committee. Before the scheme commenced, they were given an intensive course of lectures on the following topics:

> Need assessment
> Crisis intervention
> Community resources
> Welfare rights
> Legal procedures
> Police involvement

To monitor their progress and help with their difficulties, the volunteers attended fortnightly case-work sessions, supervised by the Senior Probation Officer. The volunteers aimed to provide advice on insurance, information regarding the Criminal Injuries Compensation Board, guidance on legal matters, assistance in claiming any applicable State Benefits or referral to the appropriate helping agencies. However, the primary aim was the provision of an emotional outlet for those unable to cope with their distress in a crisis.

With this preparatory training the scheme commenced as planned on 1st January, 1974.

Results

Between 1st January, 1974, and 30th June, 1974, a total of 926 victims were notified to the scheme (roughly twice the expected figure). Of these, 446 victims were visited, and in 315 cases contact was successfully made. In view of the demand, after the first month victims of theft from cars were not approached personally but contacted by letter and offered help in this way.

The results of the 315 cases were analysed in order to predict the more vulnerable categories of person. It is notable that crimes of violence represent a small proportion of the offences (2 per cent), which is in concordance with the national figures. This 2 per cent is not included in our results, as the numbers were sufficiently small to be investigated individually.

The degree of emotional disturbance was assessed by the volunteers and categorised into two groups, for the purpose of statistical analysis:

(a) Maximum disturbance, very severe upset, and moderate disturbance (102).
(b) Slight or undetectable degree of upset (213).

These findings were correlated with other factors:

(i) Sex
(ii) Age
(iii) Social class
(iv) Absolute financial value of loss
(v) Relative financial impact of loss. (£5 might be a devastating loss to an old-age pensioner, but no more than a source of annoyance to a business man)
(vi) Attitude to offender
(vii) Social isolation (living as single)
(viii) Previously a victim, repeated experience
(ix) Attitude to the offer of help

The figures obtained were analysed statistically, and the chisquare test applied.

(i) Disturbance Correlated with Sex of Victim

Disturbance		Male	Female	
Maximum	102	49	53	$\chi^2 = 6.476$
Slight	213	136	77	$p \leqq 0.05$

It is significant that a higher percentage of severe disturbance was found in women than in men.

(ii) Disturbance Correlated with Age of Victim

Disturbance		Child Adolescent Young Adult	Middle Age	Old-age	
Maximum	100	54	26	22	$\chi^2 = 3.941$
Slight	202	127	46	29	$p \leqq 1/5$
	%	29	36	43	

These figures were not highly significant, but there was a slight tendency to a higher degree of disturbance in the older age groups.

(iii) Social Class
No detectable difference in response.

(iv) Disturbance Correlated to Absolute Loss

Disturbance		£10	£10–50	£50+	
Maximum	102	32	49	21	$\chi^2 = 15.177$
Slight	213	115	75	23	$p \leq 0.001$

(v) Disturbance Correlated to Relative Loss

Disturbance		Small	Large	
Maximum	102	62	40	$\chi^2 = 19.453$
Slight	213	72	141	$p \leq 0.001$

These figures show a very significant relationship between relative and absolute degrees of financial loss. These figures hold good, even if the degree of insurance cover is taken into account.

(vi) Disturbance Correlated to Attitude to Offender

Disturbance		Hostile and Sympathetic	Other	
Maximum	102	75	27	$\chi^2 = 29.867$
Slight	213	85	128	$p \leq 0.001$

Those with the strongest feelings towards the offender, whether sympathetic or hostile, were those who showed the greatest degree of emotional disturbance.

If a further comparison is made between those who are hostile and those who are sympathetic, there is some indication that those who are hostile are those who are more likely to be disturbed.

(vii) Disturbance Correlated to Social Isolation

Disturbance		Single	Not Alone	
Maximum	102	30	72	$\chi^2 = 8.872$
Slight	213	31	182	$p \leq 0.01$

Fifty per cent of victims living alone are likely to be disturbed. Of those who are not alone, only 28 per cent disturbed.

(viii) Disturbance Correlated to Previous Victim Status

Disturbance		Previous Victims	Non-Previous Victims	
Maximum	102	28	74	$\chi^2 = 3.288$
Slight	213	38	175	$p \leq 0.005$

There is a slight tendency for those who have previously been a victim of crime to be more disturbed, but this is only a trend.

(ix) Attitude to Help

The figures are not statistically significant. It is interesting, however, that the volunteers received only five hostile responses to offers of help.

Conclusions

In this paper we have presented the more significant results from the questionnaires of the pilot study.

A need has been demonstrated, unmet by existing services, which themselves are overloaded. In view of the results, it would be possible to devise a service, restricting visits to those groups most likely to be vulnerable:

1. Women rather than men.
2. In the older age groups.
3. Living alone.
4. Suffering the experience for a second time.
5. Experiencing moderate to severe financial loss.
6. Experiencing clear feelings towards the offender.

For financial reasons, the scheme was terminated in October 1974, but reinstituted in a modified form in March 1975 for a further limited period with a loan of £1,000 from Bristol Round Table. The future after that will again be in doubt, and begs the question which body, if any, will take responsibility for this valuable scheme. Such bodies might be the Home Office, the Police, the Probation Service, Social Services, or the Psychiatric Services, but this has yet to be decided.

APPENDIX

Case 1

A lady aged 82 years had her home burgled and the contents of her gas meter taken. She was extremely distressed. She had been used to visiting her local community centre frequently, but since the crime refused to leave her home. The volunteer visited several times over a short period and talked with her at length. He also applied on her behalf to the Department of Health and Social Security (DHSS) for an exceptional needs grant, to cover her loss. In addition, this volunteer contacted the local street warden scheme to ensure that someone from the local community was aware of her situation. He continued to visit and obtained bolts which he fixed to her windows himself to help restore her confidence in the house's security.

Case 2

An elderly gentleman who lives with his deaf sister suffered a "walk-in" theft while his sister was sitting in another room. £40 was taken— the victim's entire savings. This was intended to purchase a suit to attend a wedding. The volunteer wrote to the DHSS on behalf of the victim, who is illiterate, and obtained a grant to cover the cost of a new suit so that he was able to attend the wedding.

Case 3

A man of 20 had his motorcycle stolen and was deeply upset, having bought it only four days ago. Having seen the volunteer, he realised that he could claim on the insurance, and was assisted by the volunteer in doing this.

RESEARCH SCHEDULE PART I

1. Series No. ....
2. Date Notified to Programme.
   ....
3. Action instigated ....
4. Name ....
5. Address ....
   ....
   ....
6. Male/Female ....   Child/Adolescent/Young Adult/
7. Age ....   Middle Age/Pensioner
8. Official Description of
   Offences:
   ....
9. Nature of offence against
   victim: 1, 2, 3, 4, 5, 6, 7, 8, 9, 10, 11
10. Help required ....   None/Financial/Emotional/
                                          Practical/Other
11. Help offered .... None/Financial/Emotional/
                                          Practical/Other
12. Other Agency already
    involved? .... Yes/No
13. Other Agency referred to ......   Yes/No
14. Agency—Statutory ....   GP/Social Services/Hospital/
                                          Probation/DHSS/Other
15. Agency—Voluntary ....   Community Centre/Youth
                                          Service/Other
    Effect upon victim:
16.   —Physical 1/2/3/4/5
17.   —Emotional 1/2/3/4/5
18.   —Financial 1/2/3/4/5
19.   —Other 1/2/3/4/5
20. Effect upon other members of
    family ....   Yes/No
21. If *Yes*, type of effect .... Physical/Emotional/Financial/
                                          Other
22. Assessment of financial loss ...   Immediate
                                          Subsequent
23. Whether victim of previous
    offence .... Yes/No
24. If *Yes*, in last .... Year/5 years/6-10 years/10 years
                                          or more
25. Type of previous offence ......   Police classification
26. Insurance cover ....   Complete/partial/nil
    Rating of the Effects of Help
27. Attitude towards offer of help   1/2/3/4/0
28. Effective use of help offered ...   1/2/3/4/0 (Rater's assessment)
29. Effectiveness of help ....   1/2/3/4/0 (Client's assessment)
    b. Effect on family 1/2/3/4/0
    c. Number of contacts ....
    d. Attitude to offender ....

Helping the Victims   269

PART II

Family Network

30. Civil Status	Single/Married/Legally separated/ Divorced/Widowed/Don't Know
31. Current Marital/Family Status	Child/Adolescent with family/ Living with spouse/Living as single/Cohabiting: hetero./homo. Don't know
32. Social Class	I, II, III, IV, V. Don't know
33. Exact Occupation	(if old age pensioner, last occupation)
34. Father's Occupation	(if young person)
35. Children in family	(Number)
36. Whether children involved in offence	Yes/No
37. Kinship Rating (BOTT)	1, 2, 3, 4
b. Unrelated help	

PART III

38. Was offender apprehended? ...	Yes/No
39. Was offender charged?	Yes/No
40. Was offender convicted?	Yes/No

REFERENCES

1. Holton, C.: *Circumstances of Victims,* Synopsis of Howard League Lecture, Nov. 1974.

2. Naylor, Judith M. M.: Personal Communication. The Needs of the Victims of Crime against the Individual in South Bristol.

Acknowledgements: Alan Heywood, Sr. Clinical Psychologist, Glenside Hospital, Bristol; BVSS (Bristol Victims Support Scheme) Volunteers.

Dr. Martyn J. Gay
Dept. of Mental Health, Bristol Royal Hospital for Sick Children, St. Michael's Hill, BS2 8BJ, England.
C. Holton
Dept. of Extramural Studies, Bristol University, Bristol, England.
Dr. M. S. Thomas
Dept. of Mental Health, Bristol Royal Hospital for Sick Children, St. Michael's Hill, Bristol, BS2 8BJ, England.

[24]

POLICE RESPONSE TO CRIME: THE PERCEPTIONS OF VICTIMS FROM TWO POLISH CITIES

R. I. MAWBY[a], Z. OSTRIHANSKA[b] and D. WOJCIK[b]

[a]*Department of Social Policy and Social Work,
University of Plymouth, England*
[b]*Instytut Nauk Prawnych, Polskiej Akademii Nauk,
Warszawa, Poland*

(Received 3 March 1996; in final form 1 December 1996)

While police structures and functions have changed dramatically in post-communist societies, as yet little research has been carried out to either evaluate these changes or monitor victims' perceptions of the 'new' police. Here we report on an exploratory study that monitors the experiences of 398 burglary victims in Poland, and compare the findings with those from England. While Polish victims perceived the police as having changed in a number of ways, and were especially positive about the improved 'victim-proneness' of the police, they were generally far more critical of the police than were their English counterparts. This to some extent reflects differences in police procedures and to this extent is amienable to change, but our tentative conclusion is that criticism of the police is more a reflection of the rising crime rate and public feelings that if crime is out of control then the police are to blame. If our view is correct then it would appear that public evaluation of the police will be unlikely to improve until fear of crime is reduced, which raises further issues as far as operational policing is concerned.

KEY WORDS: Policework; burglary; Poland; victims; evaluation; post-communist consumers

INTRODUCTION

In recent years there has been a blossoming of articles and books addressing policing in different societies and policing issues in an international context (Bayley 1994; Mawby 1997). However while considerable attention has been devoted to analyses of communist or

236   R. I. MAWBY *et al.*

socialist societies, much of this focus has been on the USSR (or the new Russia), China and Cuba (see for example Mawby 1990), with little available on Eastern Bloc countries. Moreover, the emphasis has been on general discussions or analyses of secondary data rather than original research. The current article aims to reset the balance by reporting on a recent research project in Poland.

The dearth of material on Central and Eastern European policing systems is particularly regrettable since in these societies policing has been subject to dramatic changes over the past hundred years. The period up until the Second World War saw the gradual emergence of 'modern' police forces, which in countries occupied by the Germans then became subsumed under the Nazi war apparatus. In the period following, under Soviet domination the police were reorganised. Finally, the move towards democratic government has seen an emphasis upon reconstitution of the police. The relationship between form of government and policing style, and indeed the narrower question of how easy it is to transform the police, became key questions of interest both in their local contexts and in wider debates on the role of the police in society. At the same time, increasing crime rates and an escalation in fear of crime (Del Frate *et al.* 1993) raise questions concerning public security and the relationship between citizens' perceptions of the crime problem and their evaluations of police and policing.

THE POLICE IN POLAND

While there is little written on the Polish police prior to the 1940s there is no reason to suppose that it differed much from the continental model of policing described for Hungary by Rudas (1977), where a centralised, paramilitary police emphasised the maintenance of public order while accepting responsibility for a variety of administrative tasks. During the Second World War the role of the police under Nazi occupation heightened public disapproval and shortly after liberation it was replaced by locally based civic militia (Dzialuk 1994). However by October 1944 these had been replaced by a centralised, paramilitary civic militia under the Head of Public Security. In 1945 the Internal Security Corps (KBW) was formed and in 1946 a volunteer force, the

Volunteer Reserve of the Civic Militia, was established. Both of these organisations came under the control of the Communist Party (Dzialuk 1994).

A number of changes were made during the next 40 or so years, but essentially the Polish police maintained a Soviet-style organisation, with their functions clearly geared towards social and political control. The civic militia was organised centrally and incorporated the powerful mobile public order police, the ZOMO. The secret police, the KBW, and the border police were largely autonomous and operated as powerful agencies. There is little evidence of the police being accountable to the public, and where citizens were involved, for example in the police reserve, it is clear that this strengthened the role of the party in police policy-making rather than enhancing public accountability.

The fact that the police were closely identified with the communist regime was further underlined by the role of the police in maintaining that regime in the face of public protest in the 1980s (Jasinski 1995). Moreover the protests inspired by the Solidarity Movement meant that the police, previously feared and – in public at least – obeyed, became the object of widespread criticism and condemnation. Not surprisingly then, the formation of the new government in 1989 was followed almost immediately by a series of significant changes to the police in terms of personnel, structure and functions (Dzialuk 1994; Fogel 1994, 16–27; General Police Headquarters 1994).

Before the end of the year ZOMO had been replaced by 22 provincial crime prevention units, the 'political and educational service' of the militia had been closed and the volunteer reserve dissolved. Then in 1990 a new Police Act provided the basis for the creation of a new police force to replace the civic militia. The numbers of 'security service officers' was reduced to a tenth of the former secret police and both these and the uniformed police were subject to rigorous verification procedures to weed out former party activists. Further measures were taken to divorce the police from the political machine, and in addition a police union was formed, Poland joined Interpol, and police ranks were demilitarised. Attempts at decentralisation and enhanced local accountability have been made, for example through enabling towns to appoint additional town guards and by requiring local police chiefs to hold weekly open sessions at which they may be required to justify their policies and practices to local people. An emphasis on crime prevention and the introduction of community initiatives such as neighbourhood watch are also indicative of change (Mikusinski 1995).

In other respects, though, changes have been inevitably slow. For example the police retain a number of administrative responsibilities and lack of funds mean that proposals to change their uniforms and so distance them from the former military image have been delayed. Moreover while there has been a degree of decentralisation, with considerable local autonomy at *voivodship* (county) and territorial levels, the police is still a national organisation.

It is also important to consider how far the public *perceive* the police to have changed. Here the indications are more pessimistic. For example the second international crime survey (ICS) (Del Frate *et al.* 1993) suggests that the public have low levels of confidence in their police. Only 31% of victims reported crime to the police, and of these only 16% said they were satisfied with police response. And only 27% of respondents said they thought the police did a good job in controlling crime in their locality. A similar disenchantment is described among victims of burglary. Only 54% of burglaries described in the ICS were reported, victims giving as their main reasons for not reporting the fact that the police could (44%) or would (17%) do nothing (Siemaszko 1993). Ostrihanska and Wojcik (1993) also describe burglary victims in Warsaw as having little confidence in the ability of the police.

One element here is the link between evaluations of the police and perceptions of the crime problem. Certainly the recorded crime rate rose steeply at the end of the 1980s (Gruszezynska and Marczewski 1995), although since then there has been a decrease in the rate of burglary (Jasinski and Siemaszko 1995, 84–85). The political, social and economic climate in Poland, moreover, appears conducive to rising crime. For example dramatic social change has undermined traditional values, economic changes have increased inequality, scarcities have encouraged the growth of a black market, and firearms are more readily available for purchase. On the other hand some of the increase may be more perceived than real. Victims may now be more willing to report crimes to the police, police under-recording practices may be less common and media presentation of crime has intensified (Siemaszko

1995a, 1995b; Szumski 1993). What is, however, abundantly clear is that the public perceive there to be a crime problem (Del Frate *et al.* 1993; Jasinski 1995; Szumski 1993; Wojcik *et al.* 1997) and it is not unlikely that the changes that have taken place in recent years, including changes in policing, may be seen as contributing to this problem.

THE CURRENT RESEARCH

The research described here is part of a larger survey of victims' perceptions of crime in six cities in four countries. [1] While interviews were conducted with key personnel and police records were analysed, the research centred on interviews with up to 200 victims of household burglary in each city. Samples were drawn from police files, using a definition of burglary similar to that deployed in the ICS. We targeted one specific offence type in order to ensure that in comparing victims' reactions in different cities we were, to a large extent, comparing like with like, and chose burglary because it is an offence commonly reported to the police (Del Frate *et al.* 1993) and one that is known to affect victims considerably (Maguire and Corbett 1987; Mawby and Walklate 1994). The questionnaire included about 100 questions, many of which had been tried and tested in various versions of the British Crime Survey (BCS) [2]: these covered, among other things, offence details, the impact of the crime on victims, contact with helping agencies, details of contacts with the police and evaluation of the police.

In Poland our research was conducted in two cities, Warsaw and Lublin. Warsaw, with a population of over one and a half million,

---

[1] The research team comprises Rob Mawby (Director), University of Plymouth and Sandra Walklate, University of Salford, England; Dobrockna Wojcik and Zofia Ostrihanska, Polska Akademia Navk, Warsaw, Poland; Ilona Gorgenyi, University of Miskolc, Hungary; Gerd Kirchoff, Abteilung Monchengladbach, Germany. The Project was funded by the Central European University: contract 7/91–92, total award $ 55,200. Additional travel funds were supplied by NATO: contract CRG 920530, total award 277,000 BF.

[2] Many were taken from the 1988 British Crime Survey Questionnaire. In addition, questions from the 1984 and 1992 BCS were also included, and we are grateful to Pat Mayhew for permission to use these questions. Other questions were written specifically for this project.

has been the capital since the beginning of the seventeenth century. Almost destroyed in the Second World War, its centre was imaginatively rebuilt in the postwar period, contrasting markedly with the dour flats that characterised the postwar homes building programme. Lublin is also dominated by postwar high-rise developments, but there the similarity ends. With a population of some 330,000, it lies to the south east of Warsaw. An important industrial centre, albeit currently with a high unemployment rate, its strategic location made it an important trade and cultural centre in the past, and it found brief fame at the end of the Second World War when it was the seat of the (nonsocialist) new government. It is the principal city in the county of Lubelskie, and the seat of the county police headquarters.

Bartnicki (1989, 139), noting that 'Regional variations in crime in Poland are very significant', confirms the findings of studies in other countries that 'the problem of crime is greatest in highly urbanised and industrialised areas', particularly Warsaw, characterised by high rates for both burglaries and robberies. More recently, an increase in organised crime and an escalation in violence in Warsaw have been alleged (Brzezinski 1995).

The crime rate in Lublin is, according to official statistics, lower, especially for burglary (Bartnicki 1989), and the Head of the County police certainly saw the situation as different from that in Warsaw (to which he was, incidentally, transferred shortly after our interview). Nevertheless he saw the high unemployment rate and the influence of Russian and Ukrainian migrants as contributing to the crime rate, and felt that public concern was aggravated by sensational newspaper reporting.

In each of the two cities samples were drawn from police records over a twelve month period from 1993 to 1994. Overall 198 interviews were conducted in Warsaw, 200 in Lublin. While here we shall concentrate on the data for Poland, we shall put it in perspective by comparing responses with those from the two English cities in our survey, namely Plymouth and Salford. In Plymouth 200 interviews were conducted in 1993; in Salford, where we experienced some difficulty completing our quota, 132 interviews were conducted for crimes over a twelve month period between 1993 and 1994. To aid comparison we have here reweighted our samples to produce equal numbers in each city. Additionally, since women were slightly over-represented among respondents and since gender is related to both perceptions of crime and views of the police, we have reweighted such that each subsample contains equal numbers of men and women.

Some of the key findings from our research are described in the following three sections. First we describe the characteristics of burglary victims interviewed in the survey. Then we consider the service provided by the police and victims' evaluations of that service. Finally we discuss victims' more general views of the police.

THE SAMPLES

Combining Warsaw and Lublin 41% of respondents were aged under 40, 48% were 40–59 and 12% aged 60 or more. Warsaw victims were slightly older than those from Lublin. Overall though, it was clear that respondents were more likely to be aged 40–59 than those from England, where 50% were aged under 40 and 19% 60 or more. The differences here are clearly related to family structure. Given that housing is in short supply in Poland, there is a tendency for relatives to live together in one household: thus single generation households are less common, and this applies to both adult children and the elderly (Turner *et al.* 1992). Consequently we also found that respondents were more likely to be married (74% compared with 58%), less likely to be single (8% compared with 19%) and less likely to be widowed (7% compared with 12%).

This was also reflected in terms of family structure. In Poland respondents came predominantly from households comprising either two or more adults but no children (54%) or adults and children (39%).[3] The 'luxury' of living alone was experienced by only 7% of respondents compared with 27% in England. While households containing children were relatively common (39%), these children were also notably older than those from our English sample.

It comes as no surprise to find that residential status of respondents from Poland were also distinctive. About half were owner-occupiers, which, while lower than in England is considerably more than would have been found a decade ago (Muziol-Weclawowicz 1992), and 90%

---

[3] Children were defined as those aged under 16.

Table 1 Comparision of Wealth/Status of victims from the four cities (reweighted data).

	Plymouth	Salford	Warsaw	Lublin	Total
Percentage who:					
were owner occupiers	67	62	50	51	58
owners of three luxuries	32	27	17	12	22
had holidayed abroad within two years	49	45	21	17	33
Rated themselves poor	17	10	25	37	22

lived in flats, a marked contrast with Plymouth (16%) and Salford (11%). Respondents were also likely to have lived in their current area for some considerable time, again reflecting the Polish housing market. Thus 66% of Warsaw victim and 55% from Lublin had lived there for at least ten years.

Owner occupation is of course one indication of wealth or status. We included three others, relating to the ownership of three 'luxuries' (car, video and computer), holidays abroad and self-rating of wealth. Intra and international comparisons of answers to these three questions revealed two patterns. First, in general Polish victims were poorer than English victims. Second, from the four cities Plymouth respondents tended to be the most prosperous, Lublin respondents the least so. These differences are illustrated in Table 1. One other feature of lifestyle is perhaps worth noting here, namely earlier experiences of burglary. We asked victims whether they had been the victims of a burglary previously within a five year period. In this respect clearly English victims were disadvantaged. Only 12% of Warsaw and 18% of Lublin respondents were revictimised, compared with 26% from Plymouth and 34% from Salford.

VICTIM/POLICE INTERACTIONS

Here we shall consider firstly the involvement victims had with the police over the current burglary, and then their perceptions of police response. While most of the data are derived from interviews with victims, we have also incorporated where appropriate details from our discussions with the police. Where differences emerged between Warsaw and Lublin these have been noted.

By definition all crimes in our survey were reported to the police, and only 6% of victims expressed any doubts about contacting the police. This is particularly notable, given that only 37% of victims were insured,[4] meaning that for most people one of the more common reasons for reporting crime did not apply. While most victims of earlier burglaries said they had reported these, the proportions who did not (12%) is higher than in England (1%), suggesting that there may have been a change in recent years. Most victims contacted the police by phone. However 17% visited the police station in person, considerably higher than for our English samples (4%). In Poland, as in England, the police almost always visited the scene of the crime, although they were not necessarily very quick at doing so; in 16% of crimes they arrived within 20 minutes of the offence being reported, whilst in 33% of cases they took at least 80 minutes. This was especially the case in Warsaw, where 44% of victims said the police took at least 80 minutes, and in general reflects a lack of police resources. Thus a number of victims said that the police explained they could not come sooner, either because no car was available or, in Lublin, because they had run out of petrol. As one respondent sarcastically noted:

'They took 30 minutes. They told me they were late because they had no petrol in the car. I didn't ask them about how they take their daughter to the kindergarden every day. I am sure they don't use their own petrol'. {LUB014}

Senior management in the two cities described responses to burglary rather differently. In Warsaw public requests are logged by the police and a team of officers, some in uniform, some in plainclothes visit the site together, at the same time gathering forensic evidence. The normal period for investigation is 30 days after which the police file a closure statement with the prosecutor's office. Victims *should* be informed if the crime is detected. The police also regularly hold exhibitions of allegedly stolen goods so that victims can identify their property and help clear up other crimes from a detected burglar. In Lublin it is normal for uniformed officers only to attend the scene of crime; technical services are provided only if, in the views of the police, the seriousness of the crime warrants it. In both cities the police sometimes

---

[4] In England the comparable figure was 70%. More details of victims' concerns and the impact of the current offence are contained in Wojcik *et al.* (1997).

remove locks (that have been forced) and store them as evidence of MO, although the police admitted this was rarely effective.

Victims' accounts differed from these in a number of respects. For example, almost three quarters of victims said they had had contact with a plainclothes officer, and about two thirds with a technician, but less than half mentioned uniformed officers. On the other hand, Lublin victims were more likely to have contact with uniformed police and Warsaw respondents with technicians. The former were also more likely to say that the burglary had been cleared up: 12% compared with 3% in Warsaw. The equivalent figure was 5% in England.

The quantitative material, however, disguises the true extent of the interaction between police and victims. If the victim is not present when the police are called, the police will often remove the locks, search for fingerprints and then seal the property. The returning victim then has to contact the police to open up the property and do something immediately about making it secure. In most cases, moreover, victims and their households will be required to attend the police station to have their fingerprints taken so that they can be eliminated, or to get an insurance claim form. This rather laborious process is illustrated in the following quotes:

'Two armed uniformed policemen. They left after about three minutes and called the investigation team. We waited for them for about twelve hours – not allowed to touch anything. Four or five plainclothes people arrived, all behaving very bureaucratically. They took fingerprints. This took about five hours. Later my husband had to go to the police station twice'. {WAR218}

'Two uniformed policemen arrived. When they saw that it was a burglary they called the police station. Then the investigation officers came. They wrote the report, took the locks for an examination. They stayed in the house till 5.00 a.m.'. {WAR203}

'We arrived at the police station about 2.00 a.m. and my husband asked if we could get into our flat and sleep there – it was sealed by the police. On the Sunday morning, a plainclothes policeman came and then two others arrived and took the fingerprints (mine also), and took photographs. Then I was summoned to the police station and talked to some plainclothes policemen. Next we got the information about the discontinuance of proceedings'. {WAR409}

'There were stamps on the seals saying where to go. I went with my neighbour to the police station and they told me they would be two hours because they were very busy... Two policemen arrived and then other technicians. Later I was at the police station to get a certificate, because it is necessary to get insurance'. {WAR221}

POLICING CRIME IN POLAND 245

'A policewoman came – in plain clothes. She wrote the report, and two policemen in uniform. Afterwards a technician came – he took photos examined the finger-marks, took the locks. Next day I gave them additional information on the stolen objects'. {LUB123}

'Two policemen and an expert who examined our locks. They took the locks and the keys for examination. They looked for fingerprints but found none. We were called to the police station to give our fingerprints. They were nice...' {LUB015}

Despite the last comment, the overall impression here was that victims felt the police, far from being meticulous, were being over-bureaucratic and tending to make a drama out of a crisis. In the light of the negative impressions of the Polish police given in earlier research, it is therefore apt to consider how victims felt the police had responded to their crime.

We have already noted the length of time the police took to arrive, and 35% felt the police had responded too slowly. For example:

'I thought they would arrive straight away – search the area and eventually check. I was naive'. {WAR517}

'Twelve hours! My husband phoned them at 9.00 p.m., they came at 9.00 a.m. It was because they had so much to do they told us'. {WAR327}

As one victim noted, even though there was no chance of catching the burglar:

'It didn't matter, but psychologically it was important for us. It meant that they are not interested in us'. {LUB031}

Victims were even less positive about the extent to which the police had kept them adequately informed. Only 14% said they had been kept very or fairly well informed, with 79% saying they were either 'not very well' or 'not at all well' informed, and no less than 69% felt the police should have kept them better informed. Almost as many (58%) said that the police had not put enough effort into their case. It comes as no surprise then to find that 63% professed themselves either fairly or very dissatisfied with the way the police handled the case. Asked to select their main criticisms from a prompt card, only 4% said the police were impolite and 7% said the police made mistakes. In all other cases over 10% of victims found fault with the police: because

246   R. I. MAWBY *et al.*

their property was not recovered, the crime was undetected, there was
no feedback, the police did not do enough, were not interested or too
slow. This level of criticism is illustrated in the following quotes:

'Why should they interview and upset me without any results?'. {LUB023}

'Police isn't interested at all'. {LB024}

'Very indifferent attitude to the case... Slack approach by the police. Lack of any
interest in the case'. {LUB027}

'They are not interested in victims. They told us they would come to take our
fingerprints but they didn't'. {LUB031}

'What counts are the results, not the methods. There were no results'. {WAR531}

'They have done nothing'. {WAR533}

'The private shop pays the police. They are very quick to come whenever they are called
by the shopkeeper. But they are too late when they are needed by the ordinary people'.
{WAR305}

'It is ridiculous, a waste of time. They do nothing'. {WAR025}

'They didn't want to write the report because the flat wasn't insured! They told me that
it will only make their statistics worse, they will not find the offenders'. {WAR332}

'Complete lack of interest'. {WAR019}

'The police didn't make an effort to find the burglars and recover the stolen goods. I
am sure the police did not make an attempt'. {WAR504}

These findings have been summarised in Tables 2 and 3 where we have
also included the reweighted figures for England. Two points are
worth emphasising here. First, in general Polish victims were more
critical of police response than were English victims, with Plymouth
victims in general being most positive in their evaluations of police
performance, Lublin victims least so. This is well illustrated if we
combine the four key questions on police performance (speed, effort,
information, overall satisfaction) and scale respondents from 0–4,
where 0 signifies no criticism of the police and 4 criticisms on all four
items. Mean scores were 1.18 in Plymouth, 1.53 in Salford, 2.47 in
Warsaw and 2.61 in Lublin. Second, though, as Table 3 illustrates, it
is notable that with the exception of criticisms over lack of feedback

POLICING CRIME IN POLAND 247

Table 2 Percentage of victims in the four cities (reweighted samples) who felt:

	Plymouth	Salford	Warsaw	Lublin	Total
Police were not quick enough	25	26	37	33	30
Police kept them very/fairly well informed	29	15	7	20	18
Police should have kept them better informed	40	52	65	73	57
Police did not put in enough effort	28	37	54	62	45
Very or fairly satisfied overall	77	61	19	23	45

Table 3 Percentage of all victims who were dissatisfied with the police for the following reasons (reweighted data).

	Plymouth	Salford	Warsaw	Lublin	Total
Didn't do enough	10	23	17	26	19
Impolite	3	1	5	3	3
Slow	7	10	11	11	10
Made mistakes	0	0	6	8	4
Property not recovered	2	15	42	55	30
Crime undetected	4	16	44	52	29
No feedback	11	21	44	48	32
Not interested	8	21	22	17	17

the two major areas of concern in Poland related to the low clear up rate: the police failed to detect the crime or recover the stolen property. While this may to some extent reflect the lack of insurance among Polish victims, clearly the Polish police were being criticised for a performance that was, objectively, no worse and possibly better than that of their English equivalents!

WIDER VIEWS ON THE POLICE

Given this level of criticism of how the police dealt with their burglary, what did victims think about the police in general? Most said their view had not been altered, for example that the police were no better than expected:

'My attitude towards the police was never positive and it wasn't changed'. {LUB005}

While not surprisingly only 6% said their views had changed for the better, 23% said they had changed for the worse. As one respondent put it, when asked what occupations she most admired:

'The policeman – till the burglary. Not now'. {WAR216}

Relatively few respondents said they knew any police officers well enough to speak to by name. Only a quarter answered in the affirmative, and no one said they knew a local officer this well.

It is, of course, common place in Western societies to report widespread citizen – and victim – dissatisfaction with levels of policing. In Poland most victims adopted similar viewpoints. No less than 94% said that there were too few police in their area, with 39% saying that there were fewer than before. In each case these figures were significantly *higher* than in England, but the comments made by victims were depressingly familiar:

'I haven't ever seen a policeman here. They are not here!'. {WAR330}

'(I)n the cars but not in the streets'. {WAR319}

'There are enough policemen in the station but not in the streets'. {WAR22}

'I haven't seen a single policeman in my street for ten years'. {LUB10}

'They can't be seen in the streets but there is a lot of them at the police station'. {LUB6025}

Victims were also more likely to feel that they had too little say in how their area was policed: 87% compared with 58% in England. The overwhelming picture then is of victims who felt impotent in the face of rising crime and who expressed little confidence in the police:

'Ordinary people have no influence'. {WAR531}

'Police do not respond when people tell them about hooligan gangs'. {WAR12}

'We fight to have a police station here but with no results'. {LUB101}

There is, however, one exception to this negative portrayal, namely what we might term the 'victim-proneness' of the police. For example we asked respondents if they felt that the way the police dealt with victims of crime had improved in recent years. While the majority said there had been no change, 26% said there had been improvements, with only 6% saying the police had got worse. In comparison, in England while slightly more said the police had improved, almost as many said things had deteriorated! This is illustrated if we compare the ratio of improved/deteriorated. This was most positive in Warsaw (7.13 : 1), then Lublin (2.26 : 1), then Plymouth (1.48 : 1), and lowest in Salford (0.96 : 1). From victims' verbatim comments it is evident that much of the criticism in England reflects victims' concerns that the police no longer have sufficient resources to provide an adequate service to victims. That is, it is not a criticism of the police themselves. Nevertheless, the fact that in Poland, where victims were even more critical of the inadequacy of police resources, they were more likely to see a change for the better is encouraging. The following comments illustrated the point:

'They are more tolerant and gentle'. {WAR023}

'They are more kind. They don't consider themselves superior now'. {LUB627}

However for one victim, this change in attitude did not disguise a lack of effectiveness:

'They are kind, but helpless'. {LUB018}

We also tapped respondents' views on police 'victim-proneness' by asking them how sympathetically they felt the police responded to the victims of burglary, disasters such as fire or flood, and rape or sexual assault. Responses, summarised in Table 4, illustrate that while respondents in Poland – and indeed elsewhere – were uncertain about

Table 4 Percentage of respondents who felt that the police were sympathetic towards victims.

	Burglary		*Disaster*		*Rape/Sex Offences*	
	Warsaw	*Lublin*	*Warsaw*	*Lublin*	*Warsaw*	*Lublin*
Very sympathetic	20	13	38	56	22	38
Fairly sympathetic	65	69	28	15	30	17
Not very sympathetic	9	11	3	4	14	11
Didn't know	6	7	31	24	34	33

expressing an opinion for incidents where they had no direct experience, they overwhelmingly considered the police sympathetic. Moreover differences in the responses of Polish and English victims were slight and to a large extent reflected the greater likelihood of the former to say that they did not know. Polish victims were indeed considerably more positive in their responses than were German victims (Mawby and Kirchhoff 1996).

Nevertheless, just as Polish victims were more critical of the way the police handled their case, so they were, with this exception, more generally negative in their views of the police. This is well illustrated if we consider responses to a question on which three, from a list of twelve occupations, respondents most admired. While in England 26% of victims chose the police, in Poland only 9% did so. And while in England the police ranked fourth behind nurses, doctors and fire officers, in Warsaw they ranked sixth and in Lublin ninth, generally being outranked by doctors, teachers, scientists, nurses, fire officers, journalists and lawyers. It seems then that while victims see the police as more sympathetic in their approach to victims than in the past, in other respects their views of the police in general, like their evaluations of police response to their burglary, are negative compared with English victims.

DISCUSSION

A number of recent changes have been made in attempts to transform the police from that of an agency of social and political control into an institution that is more responsive to the public. The fact that victims perceived the police to be more 'victim-prone' in their approach is indicative of the fact that there has been some success in modifying public images of the police. However in other respects respondents were relatively critical of the police, presenting a rather pessimistic set of findings for those committed to police reforms.

On one level public reaction may be understood as a rational response to police inadequacies. For example, the police are inadequately funded, response times were longer than in England and police procedures do appear particularly cumbersome, placing considerable burdens on the public. However victims' evaluations are not solely explicable in terms of police performance. While Polish victims were very critical of the police regarding lack of feedback they were also very critical of the police for not catching their offenders or returning their property, where the Polish police were no worse, and possibly slightly better, than their English counterparts. That is, in a situation where the police in both countries were 'unable to deliver' English victims accepted this as not the fault of the police, Polish victims did not.

But if Polish victims are more critical of the police regardless of what the police actually do, this is clearly not because they associate the police of today with the police of yesterday. Respondents gave no indication of this. In contrast, Polish victims were more likely than those in the other countries in our survey to express concern about crime and to perceive the problem as worsening (Mawby 1995; Wojcik *et al.* 1997) and those who were most concerned about crime and safety were most likely to criticise the police. Combined with the more qualitative material from our surveys, this suggests that while in the early phase of post-communist Poland the public may have been concerned to change the police from an agency of repression to a service institution, five years later, with crime seen as on the increase, the 'new' police were targeted as at least partly responsible. A more open government, with greater public awareness of crime, may thus under-mine attempts to create a more open police. Certainly some of our respondents seemed to hanker for the old days when the more repressive police at least appeared to be able to keep crime under control!

While these conclusions are tentative they do caution us about the reform process. Where public concern is grounded in reality we can present fairly straightforward recommendations: for example to im-prove police response times and rethink the policy of removing locks from entrance doors. However where the relationship between police-work and public evaluation of policing is more tenuous it is more difficult to suggest changes in policy. Ultimately though it is crucial that 'softer' policing is not blamed for the apparent increase in crime. It would indeed by ironic if a more open society was itself the precipitor of a return to a more repressive form of policing.

References

Bartnicki, S.P. (1989) "Crime in Poland: trends, regional patterns and neighbourhood awareness", pp. 135–60 in D.T. Evans and D.T. Herbert (Eds.) *The Geography of Crime*. London: Routledge.

252   R. I. MAWBY *et al.*

Bayley, D.H. (1994) *Policing for the Future.* New York: Oxford University Press.

Brzezinski, M. (1995) "Crime concerto engulfs Warsaw", *Guardian*, 21 March.

Dzialuk, I.R. (1994) "National Police Profile, Poland", appendix V pp. 102–115 in D. Fogel *Policing in Central and Eastern Europe.* Helsinki: HEUNI.

Fogel, D. (1994) Policing *in Central and Eastern Europe.* Helsinki: HEUNI.

Frate, A.A. del, Zvekic, U. and Dijk, J.J.M. van (1993) *Understanding Crime: Experiences of Crime and Crime Control.* Rome: UNICRI.

General Police Headquarters (1994) "National Police Profile, Poland", appendix IV pp. 91–101 in D. Fogel *op cit.*

Gruszezynska, B. and Marczewski, M. (1995) "Recorded crime and penal policy", pp. 11–19 in J. Jasinski and A. Siemaszko (Eds.) *Crime Control in Poland.* Warsaw: Oficyna Naukowa.

Jasinski, J. (1995) "Crime Control in Poland: an overview", pp. 6–10 in Jasinski and Siemaszko (Eds.) *op cit.*

Jasinski, J. and Siemaszko, A. (Eds.) (1995) *Crime Control in Poland.* Warsaw: Oficyna Naukowa.

Maguire, M. and Corbett, C. (1987) *The Effects of Crime and the Work of Victim Support Schemes.* Aldershot: Gower.

Mawby, R.I. (1990) *Comparative Policing Issues: The British and American Experience in International Perspective.* London: Routledge.

Mawby, R.I. (1995) *Crime Victims: Needs and Services in Four European Countries: Final Report.* (CEU). Plymouth: University of Plymouth.

Mawby, R.I. (Ed.) (1997) *Comparative Policing: Issues for the Twenty First Century.* London: UCL Press.

Mawby, R.I. and Walklate, S. (1994) *Critical Victimology.* London: Sage.

Mawby, R.I. and Kirchoff, G. (1996) "Coping with crime: a comparison of victims' experiences in England and Germany", pp. 55–70 in P. Davies, P. Francis and V. Jupp (Eds.) *Understanding Victimisation: Themes and Perspectives.* Newcastle: University of Northumbria Press.

Mikusinski, W. (1995) "City and violent crime", pp. 68–72 in Jasinski and Siemaszko (Eds.) *op cit.*

Muziol-Weclawowicz, A. (1992) "The housing market in Warsaw according to the mediators of the estate agencies", pp. 207–17 in B. Turner, J. Hegedüs and I. Tosics (Eds.) *The Reform of Housing in Eastern Europe and the Soviet Union.* London: Routledge.

Ostrihanska, Z. and Wojcik, D. (1993) "Burglaries as seen by the victims", *International Review of Victimology*, **2**(3), 217–26.

Rudas, G. (1977) "The changing role, responsibilities and activities of the police in a developed society", *International Review of Criminal Policy*, **33**, 11–16.

Siemaszko, A. (1993) "Poland", pp. 631–7 in del Frate *et al.* (Eds.) *op cit.*

Siemaszko, A. (1995a) "Unreported crime", pp. 20–27 in Jasinski and Siemaszko (Eds.) *op cit.*

Siemaszko, A. (1995b) "The media and crime", pp. 77–82 in Jasinski and Siemaszko (Eds.) *op cit.*

Szumski, J. (1993) "Fear of crime, social rigorism and mass media in Poland", *International Review of Victimology*, **2**(3), 209–215.

Turner, B., Hegedüs, J. and Tosics, I. (1992) *The Reform of Housing in Eastern Europe and the Soviet Union.* London: Routledge.

Wojcik, D., Walklate, S., Ostrihanska, I., Mawby, R.I. and Gorgenyi, I. (1997) "Security and crime prevention at home: a comparison of victims' response to burglary in England, Poland and Hungary", *International Journal of Risk, Security and Crime Prevention*, **2**(1), 237–247.

[25]

House Burglars and Victims

D. Nation and J. Arnott

After local research had shown that house burglary attracted the highest rate of custodial sentences, Plymouth probation officers David Nation and John Arnott developed a group programme designed to offer a credible non-custodial option and to change offending behaviour through encounters with victims and prisoners, plus reparation and crime prevention tasks. They evaluate their first four completed programmes.

Whilst there is a great deal of experience and information available about groupwork that dealt with more general 'offending behaviour', very little work has been done specifically with house burglars.

However, we were very impressed by the work of two projects, one in Bristol run by Jonathan Hopkinson and Rick Wall of Avon Probation Service for a year or so, and one by Dr Gilles Launay[1], psychologist at Rochester Youth Custody Centre, for several years. Both these projects included victims in the group sessions. The victims were involved because it had been found that they alone were able to convey to the burglars an awareness of the misery caused by house burglary.

Over the next year a great deal of work was put into the design of a programme and, aided by a psychologist, a script was prepared which was so detailed that when we began the first group of burglars and victims, we were able to do so with a good deal of confidence — an essential ingredient! Necessary liaison work was entered into with other agencies and an evaluating system designed. By February 1990 the whole programme was ready to roll. The first group started in March 1990 and, by December, four groups had been completed.

Rationale

Most burglars tend to be immature in outlook. Associated with that immaturity is a self-centredness which allows them very little access to or awareness of the feelings of others. This immaturity insulates burglars from the distress they cause. This insulation can also be contrived and burglars who are more mature will admit to deliberately shutting off any thoughts about their victims as vulnerable, ordinary people. Focussed exposure to the emotional upset of victims can strip away the insulation. The burglars need to get to know the victims as people and, once that has happened, they

Even more mature burglars will admit to deliberately shutting off thoughts of their victims as vulnerable, ordinary people.

become vulnerable to the emotions of the victims. The burglars can then see the sort of distress their offending has caused, and all their usual excuses become less effective.

We were encouraged to learn that experience elsewhere indicated that an additional advantage in victim-offender meetings is that they are often of considerable benefits to the victims. Fear and anger are common emotions for victims to suffer and those emotions can become quite disabling, sometimes seriously so. Meeting offenders has given great relief to victims by helping them deal with those emotions. In addition, the meetings destroy

frightening stereotypes and reassure victims, many of whom are keen to help burglars move away from offending.

We decided also to try to influence burglars by including a visit to nearby Dartmoor Prison. Having learned in the meetings with victims how their burgling has affected others, the burglars would learn how their offending can affect them and their future. The prisoners, because of their personal experience, have a unique contribution to make in the challenging of burglars' attitudes.

Finally, a reparation content is included in the scheme. This would:

- Expose the burglars once again to people who are anxious about the possibility of being burgled.
- Require them to carry out work related to their offending, as part of their punishment.
- Show the wider community ex-burglars doing something positive.
- Appeal to sentencers in much the same way as does Community Service.

The Programme

There are ten sessions at which attendance is required as a specified activity (Section 4A) within a probation order. The first four require the probationers to explore with victims the effect that burglary has had upon them all. The fifth session is held in prison. Here three of four selected long-term prisoners whose offending has included house burglary, challenge the probationers' attitude and behaviour. In addition the probationers get either an introduction to or a reminder of what it is like to serve a long sentence in an adult prison. The next four sessions require the probationers to fix locks, safety chains and other security devices in the homes of vulnerable people, usually single parents, the elderly or disabled, who could not normally afford such protection. The fittings are provided at no cost to the occupant.

64

The programme ends with a review session in which the victims are not involved. The purpose of this is to hear what the probationers have felt about the experience, reinforce the themes of the programme and deal with any outstanding business.

Liaison

The diverse nature of the scheme means it is dependent upon the organisers working in partnership with several other agencies. Liaison is therefore crucial and extremely time consuming. Effort must be made initially to convince other agencies of the viability and sound basis of the scheme. Once support is forthcoming and the scheme is underway, each agency must be kept up to date with the progress of the scheme, its success or otherwise, and regular meetings should take place to ensure that any difficulties occurring along the way are promptly resolved.

The agencies involved are:

- Victims Support Scheme (VSS) who refer victims.
- The Police, whose Crime Prevention Officer surveys the properties to which locks are to be fitted.
- The local Housing Department which provides most of the fittings free of charge where they own the property.
- Community Associations who identify residents eligible for the reparation work.
- The Prison Governor and staff, without whose support the session in the prison obviously could not take place.

Referrals

The scheme places us in the unusual position of working directly with members of the public, namely the victims. Because of this, all burglars referred by report writers are interviewed by one of the officers running the group. We would decline any burglars

who we felt would be unable to cope with the frank exchanges which go on in the meetings without distressing victims. However, we find that the majority of house burglars have been acceptable. The VSS co-ordinator was greatly involved in interviewing victim referrals and observing the sessions for the first two groups. Working together in this way enabled us to agree upon an approach and procedure for the future. VSS are thus reassured that the particular needs of victims are fully considered.

We decline any burglars who seem unable to cope with frank exchanges without distressing victims.

Feedback

We give a firm undertaking to sentencers that we will report back to them on the progress of each probationer going through the group. So a system has been devised which ensures that this is done. For those probationers who are able quickly to complete the course, one report is sent at the end of it. For others whose progress is delayed, interim reports are sent. Another important element is regular feedback to supervising officers on attendance and performance.

Evaluation

Data must be available which can provide a reliable indication of changes in attitude and behaviour brought about by the group. We check that attendance of the group has improved the understanding and awareness of each side for the other. In addition, the questionnaires completed by participants are designed to establish:

- Changes in the levels of anxiety and fear recorded by the victims.
- Changes in the victims' views about sentencing for house burglars.
- Changes in attitudes of both victims and probationers towards the concept of reparation and mediation.

65

- How helpful and interesting all participants have found the group.
- What suggestions participants might have for improving the sessions.

We follow quite closely the methods used by Gilles Launay in Rochester to monitor attitude changes.

It is useful to identify the re-offending of probationers going through the scheme. Probation records can be used in most cases to monitor re-offending over a 2 year period, since most orders are of the length. In other cases, the assistance of the police is required to confirm offending.

Promoting the Group

The first task is to persuade report writers that they should consider recommending the scheme in appropriate cases. The second is to convince sentencers that in such cases, they could sensibly and confidently use the scheme to reduce house burglaries.

As soon as all arrangements with other agencies had been finalised, we circulated colleagues with information about the scheme and details of the referral procedure. We also arranged to attend team meetings occasionally to

Sentencers felt that breach procedures would not be sufficiently strict and that the public would regard it as a 'let off'.

answer questions and encourage referrals. Colleagues writing reports on house burglars know from Devon's Risk of Custody Scale that these offenders almost always are at risk of custody. They were willing to consider these offenders for the scheme once they were assured that sentencers were lilkely to accept this as an alternative to custody. That we undertook to try to attend court to speak to recommendations, was an added attraction. There has been an adequate flow of referrals throughout.

Presentations were made to the Probation Liaison Committee. Sentencers' main concerns were predictable and understandable. They were concerned that breach procedures would not be sufficiently strict and that the public would regard the disposal as a 'let-off' for the offender. We had built in an extremely strict breach procedure and the support of so many agencies helped reassure sentencers on the second point.

We have always felt that it was our duty also to promote the group amongst the general public. We cannot simply assume that they are aware how demanding the programme is for offenders and how much more is likely it is to prevent re-offending than prison sentences. So we take every opportunity to broadcast our work and why we believe that it presents a better long-term means of protecting the public. We also keep the public informed of re-offending rates and results of attendance for both victims and burglars.

However, it is sensible not to allow coverage to occur in a haphazard way. We agreed a media strategy and ensured that when our work was exposed to public gaze, we were ready and able to deal with it. The idea that two parties in conflict, whom the criminal justice system does its best to keep apart, are brought face-to-face, arouses considerable interest. We found that both local and national media have been interested in the group and provided a good deal of coverage. Victims and probationers have often been willing to take part in the publicity effort but we always ensure that confidentiality is maintained, unless we have their signed authority.

Resources

There are major resource implications in running this group. It is generally accepted that groupwork is effective but does not save time over individual work. The point we would emphasise

66

is that running this programme is even more demanding of staff resources than most groups. The planning, organisation, preparation, review and evaluation of the sessions are time consuming but, so far as this group is concerned, there are significant other resource implications. These are: liaison with other agencies; managment of the reparation work; feedback to sentencers; dealing with non-attendance and implementing breach procedures immediately where appropriate; and monitoring attitude changes and re-offending. We estimate approximately seventy officer hours per group are involved, with additional help from PSA workers who supervise the reparation sessions.

Results

After 4 groups the questionnaires completed before and after the meetings indicate that victims:

- found the meetings worthwhile and interesting,
- felt relaxed enough in the sessions to speak openly,
- feel less 'angry' and 'worried' after the meetings.

The burglars:

- found the sessions 'interesting', indicating a rare degree of interest and involvement,
- felt that attendance of the Group has increased their awareness of the effects of house burglary upon victims,
- afterwards felt that victims view them less negatively, thus increasing their self-esteem.

Although it is still early days, the reoffending record of the burglars is encouraging too. The average probationer is 22 with 5 previous convictions. One year into the scheme, with an average period since sentence of 9 months, 44% have reoffended. Only one probationer has house burgled again, indicating a reoffending rate of 6%.

Latest official figures show reoffending rates after custodial sentences of 62% for the 17-20 age group *(Prison Statistics, 1989)* within 2 years. Phillpotts and Lancucki[2] found that 87% of those in that age group with at least 5 precons reoffended within 6 years.

Observing the impact made on the probationers by the group discussion makes us extremely confident that the experience is bringing about worthwhile change. Lack of contact between the offender and the victim after the offence is a development of modern civilisation, perhaps exacerbated by urbanisation. Work done with juveniles and imaginative initiatives in mediation launched in many parts of this country in recent years, has informed and encouraged our work. If our early optimism is justified, we would hope that the approach we have taken can offer the courts an effective response to house burglary and, in due course, other serious crimes.

References

1. Gilles Launay 'Bringing Victims and Offenders Together: A comparison of Two Models' *Howard Journal,* Vol 24, No 3, August 1985.
2. G. Phillpotts and L. Lancucki *Previous Convictions, Sentence and Reconvinction* (HORU Study No.53) Home Office, 1979.

Note

A Practitioner's Manual is being published by Devon Probation Service, giving full details of how this scheme was planned and implemented, a script for the victim burglar meetings, information about the monitoring and evaluation systems being used, and audio and video tapes of live discussion. Available from: Devon Probation Service Headquarters, Second Floor, Queen's House, Little Queen Strèet, xeter EX4 3LJ price £75.

67

[26]

PRIVATE COPS ON THE BLOCK: A REVIEW OF THE ROLE OF PRIVATE SECURITY IN RESIDENTIAL COMMUNITIES

LESLEY NOAKS

*Cardiff School of Social Sciences, Cardiff University,
50 Park Place, Cardiff, CF1 3AT*

(Received 15 May 1998; in final form 26 August 1999)

This paper considers developments with regard to privatisation of security services in the British residential sector. While a reduction in state dominance of security has been apparent for some time in the commercial sector, such trends are a more recent development in residential areas. The paper reviews the context in which such developments are taking place, drawing on empirical research in a community with private security patrols. It is argued that significant changes are taking place in the relative inputs of public and private policing to community law and order, with significant transformations in some residents' experience of policing. Drawing on evidence from the empirical research, a range of related issues are discussed, including, regulation and the nature of the relationship between public and private policing.

KEY WORDS: Private policing; residential communities; security; commodification; surveillance

INTRODUCTION

Private security companies operating in commercial and business sectors have made considerable inroads into the state's dominance of protective services (Johnston, 1992; Jones and Newburn, 1998). The extension of privatised services into residential communities is, however, a much more recent and emerging trend. While the United Kingdom does not yet match Davis' (1990) image of Californian communities which 'isolate themselves behind walls guarded by gun-toting private police and state-of-the-art electronic surveillance', the public attitudes and thinking which underpin a growing demand for fortress style security are increasingly evident. Provision of protection for person and property is increasingly 'fragmented and commodified' (Loader, 1997), effecting a radical departure from the traditionally state-dominated status of policing and law enforcement (Sheptycki, 1997). Loader (*ibid*) refers to the involvement of a 'plethora' of agencies in the 'patchwork' of provision, including 'public, commercial and voluntary' groups. Ericson and Haggerty (1997) refer to the contemporary 'quilt' of security provision, acknowledging input from both private and public groups. This paper is concerned with the role of private policing and draws on empirical research in a residential area (pseudonym, Merryside) where patrols are provided by a commercial company to households which elect to subscribe to the scheme. While such developments have attracted significant media interest and police concern as 'the most visible encroachment of private security into the traditional domain of the public police' (Jones and Newburn, 1998: 59), previous research has not considered the impact of such provision on communities and their residents. This gap is particularly apparent with regard to empirical studies on the dynamics of private provision, how it actually works on the ground, and especially in how it is perceived by subscribers and non-subscribers. This paper addresses these issues and seeks to fulfil Johnston's (1992: 220) call for greater attention to the perspective of the consumer in provision of policing services.

The aims of the paper are to consider the role and functions of the private police and to explore how these are defined and evaluated by both subscribers and non-subscribers to the private policing scheme. The paper will begin with a review of Britain's trend toward privatisation of criminal justice services, including the re-emergence of private policing, with a particular focus on developments at a community level. An account of the study's methodology and the nature of the research area will be provided. Data from the empirical research will be discussed, concluding with a review of issues emanating from developments with regard to privatisation, including questions of accountability and regulation and possible models of provision in the private sector. Attention will be given to the inter-relationship between private and public policing and the consequences of that for individual residents' constructions of the crime problem and law enforcement in their community. Finally the discussion will deal with the 'public good' aspects of policing and the potential for community polarisation as a result of such developments.

THE TREND TOWARD PRIVATISATION OF CRIMINAL JUSTICE SERVICES

A hallmark of the 1980s Thatcher government in Britain was a shift from public to private service provision, a trend that included criminal justice organisations. Major reviews of the functions of policing in the early 1990s (Audit Commission, 1990; Sheehy Report, 1993) contributed to a general scepticism that the police could single handedly deal with what was perceived to be a growing crime problem. Despite some expressions of serious concern about the ethics of allowing private commercial interests to impinge on matters of criminal justice (see, for example, Rutherford, 1990) the drive toward privatisation has become increasingly evident, especially in the key areas of prisons and policing.

The coming together of on the one hand, governmental enthusiasm for the privatisation of criminal justice services and on the other a 'climate of fear' (Stanko, 1990) fuelling demand for enhanced personal safety, revealed a major marketing opportunity which commercial companies in some areas were eager to exploit. Identifiable high levels of anxiety in relation to crime (Hough, 1996) provide an important backdrop to the increasing trend toward commodification of security. Crime control has increasingly become a cultural phenomenon (Garland, 1996) embedded in the daily routine of individual citizens. Crime has become an increasingly salient feature of individual's lives and responses to it have become rooted in institutional practice. Private guards, and a range of other security products, represent a shift toward responding to personal security as a commodity to be bought in the market place.

THE RE-EMERGENCE OF PRIVATE POLICING: AN EVOLUTIONARY PROCESS

The shift from a substantial reliance on public policing as a means of maintaining community law and order to some resort to private services has been a gradual process rather than an abrupt separation. The discourse

146   L. NOAKS

of policing in the 1970s began to call for police/ public partnerships to tackle community crime problems. Various self policing strategies began to emerge in calls for what Johnston has termed 'responsible citizenship.' In particular the government and police forces in the U.K. gave enthusiastic support to the establishment of a network of neighbourhood watch schemes wherein residents would actively participate as the eyes and ears of the police on the streets. Official support has been ongoing for such schemes despite, at best, equivocal evaluations of their effectiveness (Bennett, 1990) and at the current level of resourcing senior police managers continue to believe that some form of active public support is a necessity to effective police functioning. The discourse continues to be one of participatory policing, with continuing calls for policing strategies that maximise 'citizen contact'. Nogala (1996) has suggested we need more mixed markets with regard to policing and less of an exclusive reliance on the public police as the sole enforcers of law and order. My research provides an example of a community where the 'top up' policing is provided by a commercial group who have sought to market their security functions. Input from such groups has impacted on the policing experience of residents who have bought into the scheme and, to a lesser extent, of 'free-riders', with 'knock on' affects from the actions of their neighbours. A question needing to be addressed is how this commercial relationship between residents and private guards converts into a relationship between public and private police. Whereas, historically, the police have had the potential for a direct relationship with all citizens, in neighbourhoods where private police are operating this will commonly be transposed into a tripartite 'alliance' incorporating privatised services. New patterns of policing require a fundamental review of the relationships between public and private police and residents in areas with commercial patrols. The question needs to be asked as to whether there is the potential for public and private police to work in partnership and for alliances to be formed to enhance policing and surveillance of communities.

METHODOLOGY

The research on which this article is based has been ongoing since June 1996 and has included frequent contact with private guards, public police and community residents. The first stage of the project was an ethnographic study of the commercial company providing residential patrols. The ethnography has involved shadowing of guards in carrying out their duties and at a management level attention to the evolution of the company. Alongside this, interviews were undertaken with senior police personnel to gauge the strategic policy responses to the emergence of private police in the force area. One year into the project a community survey was undertaken with samples of subscribing customers and of residents who had elected not to join the scheme. An interview schedule, combining closed and open questions, was used in the collection of survey data. The questionnaire explored, in particular, residents' attitudes to their community, their perceptions of the local crime problem (including experiences of victimisation and fear of crime) and the role of public and private police. Two hundred and fifty face to face interviews were completed, of which 44% (111) were with subscribers to the commercial scheme.

The community under study has operated with input from private guards for the past eight years. The locality serviced by the private security firm consists of a mixture of public and private housing, mostly built since the early 1980s, on the outer perimeter of a large city in Southern Britain. The estate constitutes a large and expanding development with over 4,000 homes and a population approaching 12,000. The layout of the neighbourhood is such that the two types of accommodation are clearly physically demarcated with the private developments built around the perimeter of the social housing. Although there is only the width of a road between the public and private parts of the estate, this main thoroughfare provides a clear boundary separating the two elements. Until the summer of 1997, the private guards worked exclusively in the private sector but at the request of some residents they have since begun to offer their services in the public housing. At the time of writing the security company has a director (who has managed the company for the past five years) and five security guards. Foot and vehicle patrols are provided between 11pm and 6am and an on call service is available to subscribers at other times. At the outset of the research some 600 households were members of the scheme, with active canvassing for new members being undertaken by the company. Residents contribute a weekly charge of £2 per week with pensioners charged £1.

148   L. NOAKS

RESEARCH FINDINGS

Public Perceptions of the Role of the Private Police

In exploring how community members saw the role of private guards, a number of the survey questions asked about perceptions of their most important functions and residents reasons for joining the scheme. In asking these questions, the focus was on how the public prioritised the potential roles of the private police in their communities. I was interested in whether subscribers' motivation for joining was to enhance crime prevention and/or investigation, or whether they were seeking a more general input not solely restricted to crime. Johnston (1992: 204) highlights the ways in which expansion of the private security sector requires attention to the relationship between privatisation and social control. He argues that Cohen was mistaken in the early 1980s in arguing that the private sector could never infringe state dominated public policing. While there is some debate regarding levels of invasion (Shearing and Stenning, 1983; Jones and Newburn, 1998), there is consensus that, initially in commercial fields, and more recently in residential zones, the private sector has adopted a role in the maintenance of social order. In the same way that Shearing and Stenning (1983) addressed displacement of sovereignty in commercial worlds, this work seeks to explore any equivalent transfer of role and functions in the residential sphere.

Survey results showed that the crime prevention role was a priority for subscribers, in particular an enhanced physical presence from private guards on the streets. This is borne out by the fact that 74% of subscribers saw the presence on the streets provided by private security as the most important thing that they did in the locality. This compared with 11% who referred to their role in community activities, such as checking on youth in public places or strangers, 10% who mentioned the on call service and quick response rates and only 2% who referred to private guards catching offenders. When asked what private security had to offer in the area, subscribers most commonly referred to regular patrols (23%) and a deterrent to crime (23%). Such provision was linked by subscribers to their personal sense of security, with 45% stating that their reason for joining the scheme was to gain peace of mind and enhanced feelings of safety. Others referred to improved surveillance (23%), levels of crime in the area (20%), greater levels of availability

PRIVATE COPS ON THE BLOCK 149

than the police (11%), recent victimisation (7%) and good response times (1%). This preventative image coincides with how the director of the company sees the service offered:

I see what we offer as preventative not arrest based. Two arrests in a year is all that could be expected but what we offer is high profile security.

In interviews subscribers welcomed regular contact with guards and stressed their importance as a source of local knowledge:

They are a good source of local information. Private security guards are around the area and talk to people.

It can be argued that private schemes, particularly small scale organisations, are well placed to offer local surveillance and knowledge. In the case of this private scheme, the director is a resident in the area and is well known and recognisable to many of his service users. The company is run in a participatory style with provision of regular newsletters and guards making house to house calls, on a weekly basis, to collect payments. Customers are actively encouraged to share their concerns about any suspect activities in the neighbourhood and to keep the company informed as to when they are away from home. Researcher shadowing of the guards as they go about these duties suggests that they have a role and level of knowledge regarding the locality and residents that parallels, or even exceeds, that traditionally provided by community police officers. This is supported by the survey findings with one subscriber commenting:

They are nice men, you can get to know them. They alert you to potential problems. The fact sheet with what is going on is particularly important as I work full-time and have limited contacts in the area.

For these subscribers, the value of the scheme was directly linked to the manner in which it bolstered their sense of security in enhancing their knowledge of the area. Such knowledge and a responsive mode were valued attributes and derive from the fact that subscribers felt they could approach their private services with 'trivial' crime problems that they would not present to what they perceive to be an over-stretched police service. One subscriber commented:

150   L. NOAKS

They are on call so if you see anything day or night you can call them. They stop people who are acting suspiciously. I reported someone to them a couple of weeks ago, acting suspiciously. They took the description and went after him. I have confidence in them.

This evidence would suggest that subscribers to private schemes experience a greater sense of direct influence and 'ownership' with regard to their local crime situation, which serves to counter the perceived non-responsive mode of the police:

If you are worried at night the police take a long time but security are near so can be there quickly.
They came around after a garden theft, they asked questions about the incident. At least they showed an interest, unlike the police.

These responses to the role of the private police suggest that they are compared favourably with the public police, with a range of measures used to judge their performance. These vary from speed of response, to being a listening ear for residents' complaints and a source of local knowledge, through to a public order and social control role. What is evident is that some residents conceived of the role as broad ranging, extending beyond a concern solely with crime and over-lapping substantially with the role of the public police.

Satisfaction Levels

Surveys addressing attitudes to policing suggest that dissatisfaction is commonly linked to low levels of surveillance by the police (British Crime Survey, 1994). There is a consistent demand for more policing 'on the ground' and a physical presence in local communities provided by foot rather than vehicle patrols. The expansion of commercial companies in this sphere is evidence of their success in exploiting perceived gaps in public provision. Johnston (1992) suggests that all too often the criminal justice system, including the police, is experienced as 'bureaucratic, insensitive, unresponsive and inefficient' and it is possible that the potentially more user friendly privatised policing services are in an advantageous position to capitalise on this. My evidence regarding satisfaction levels with the private security services suggests that in this locality, the hands-on 'high profile' service is positively received. 92% of subscribers to the service were either satisfied or very satisfied with the job that private security was doing in the neighbourhood. The most common reason cited for satisfaction was a lack of trouble in the area. Four-fifths (80%) had no concerns about how the company was operated, although a minority expressed concern regarding the behaviour and character of the guards and a failure of the company to fulfil initial promises. When asked, 'do you believe that the presence of private security has any impact on how people behave in this area?', 14% felt they had no impact, 78% that they acted as a deterrent and only one person thought their presence could be provocative. A majority, 76%, thought levels of crime in the area had decreased as a result of the presence of private security. Subscribers attributed a significant effect to private security despite the fact that only night time patrols were provided and the service operated at low levels of active intervention with regard to potential 'suspects'. In the non-subscriber sample, 12% of respondents had been approached by a guard in the previous nine months (in many cases this involved canvassing to join the scheme), and 3% considered that the approach had been unjustified, with one describing the behaviour of the guard as aggressive. One in four (25%) of non-subscribers were dissatisfied with the role played by private security; 35% were satisfied; and a majority, 40%, had no view. Those who were positive most commonly cited the regular presence of guards as the reason for satisfaction and those that were negative said that they did a poor job. A majority, 68%, of non-subscribers said that nothing bothered them about how the company operated, while 10% were either suspicious of the character of the guards or felt they could be overly zealous. In terms of impact on how people behaved in the area, 47% felt they acted as a deterrent, 4% that their presence could be provocative and 40% that they had no impact. 43% thought levels of crime in their area had decreased as a result of the presence of private security. While satisfaction levels are at a lower level for non-subscribers to the scheme, there is no evidence of a ground swell movement of dissatisfaction that might undermine the role that such groups play in the community. Similarly, while some subscribers expressed resentment of the 'free-rider' effect experienced by some of their non-contributing neighbours, this was not a majority view. When asked 'What is your view of residents who have not joined the scheme?', 42% of subscribers felt this was a question of personal choice; 29% felt it was unfair and resented free-loading; 9% felt they were stupid not to take up the option; and 9% expressed a wish that more would join in order to facilitate expansion of the company. Again, however, the level of animosity expressed against non-subscribers did not pose a threat to the continuing viability of the commercial group.

Loader (1997: 152) has suggested that patrols offered by groups other than the police may prove insufficient to meet public demand for greater protection, lacking the 'symbolic aura' provided by the public police. My research suggests that many subscribers and non subscribers do ascribe a positive effect to the commercial group and perceive such a service to have had a direct positive impact on anxiety regarding crime:

You feel safer because you know they are around and you feel they are on your side.

The company unquestionably recognised the commercial value of providing a visible presence, reflected in the wearing of uniforms, identifiable vehicles and the use of strong arc lights shone at properties at night. During vehicle patrols the guards would make a point of stopping the vehicle and shining the spotlight at certain properties saying that some residents requested this as '*the sense of a security presence was important to them*'. It is however oversimplistic to think that the physical presence of private security guards will necessarily dispel all residents' fears and increase a sense of personal security. For a minority of residents, the high visibility profile of uniformed guards increased their personal assessments of crime risks in their locality. The use of arc lights at night caused them to feel that there was something out there that they needed to be protected against. Despite the constant clamour in public surveys for increased street patrols by the public police, some residents admitted that they interpret the lack of a police presence on the streets as a positive signal that in reality there was little crime in their area about which the police needed to be concerned. For this group, introducing private patrols into the district directly undermined this construction of their local crime problem.

Despite this, evidence from my research would suggest that the public police have cause to be concerned about comparative satisfaction levels when their performance is measured against that of the private police. Approximately a third (35%) of respondents said that they were either dissatisfied or very dissatisfied with the role of public police in the area. While, 42% were either satisfied or very satisfied, with the remainder having no view. The most common reason cited for satisfaction was that the police were doing the best they could 'against the odds'. Those expressing dissatisfaction were most likely to refer to the lack of a police presence in the area, with more than half stating that as the reason for their negative response. This helps explain the enhanced levels of satisfaction with private policing, from subscribers and others, with the preventative surveillance ethos of the commercial group responding directly to the public priority for a police presence. The findings support Jones and Newburn's (1998: 246) proposal that the public police, faced with a 'wide functional remit', will find it increasingly difficult to compete in provision of targeted patrols for residential communities. However, despite a perception on the part of residents that private security provided the major surveillance role, there continued to be demands for them to provide more in the way of patrols. A half of subscribers wanted patrols in the early evening and 13% favoured 24 hour patrols. Private security was also criticised for an over reliance on vehicle patrols and insufficient coverage on foot:

The van drives up, turns around and goes off again, that isn't going to do much.
There are insufficient patrols, they don't check out the area, they never leave their cars.

Such criticisms are familiar to public police patrols and goes some way to supporting Loader's (1997) suggestion that public demand for surveillance is in danger of being insatiable.

Relationships between Public and Private Police

Jones and Newburn (1998) review the nature of connections between 'public' and 'private' policing bodies and suggest that relations can be co-operative, competitive or one of co-existence. My research reveals a reluctance on the part of the public police formally to acknowledge the role and possible contribution of private officers. In part this derives from, and is justified by, the lack of formal regulation of private schemes. Fully aware of the dubious image of some schemes, the police are wary of affiliating themselves with potentially mismanaged or even corrupt groups. In Merryside, minimal levels of communication between the two groups fed into acrimonious situations, with each policing body complaining about the actions of the other. The divisional superintendent described relations with the commercial group as 'distant', commenting that there was 'suspicion on both sides'. The private police complain that the police fail to acknowledge their contribution to maintaining law and order in the community and ignore their input. The company director feels that it is often 'a question of personalities':

> Some officers love us and recognise that we can be a good source of information and backup.

On the other hand, he has had cause to complain regarding the failure of the police to respond to 999 calls for backup. The most recent incident related to a gang of youths stoning a company vehicle and the guards. The police claimed never to have received the call. At the same time, police managers complain that the guards:

> have a tendency to come in all guns blazing. They are trying to justify their role. We suspect that they listen in on police messages and they can be very disruptive to police operations.

There is an apparent unwillingness on the part of the police to acknowledge any role for private groups and a situation of stand-off in relation to active co-operation. No formal channels of communication exist and what contacts occur do so in the climate of complaint described above. While Wakefield (1997) raises questions about the nature of possible partnerships in the public-private dichotomy, my research identifies the public police as rejecting any possible collaboration with private groups operating in their sector. This was evidenced in local responses to the Crime and Disorder Act (1998), with the commercial company excluded from strategic plans to promote community safety.

Despite evident support in this community for private security, or at least the role they are seen to fulfil, there was evidence that a majority of residents did not favour their replacing public police but looked for them to work in partnership as a value added service. This was linked to residents' attitudes to the powers held by private security guards, with 8% of respondents of the view that the powers of private security guards should be decreased, 45% favouring no change and 26% wanting to see their powers increased. One in five respondents failed to respond to this question, typically because of a lack of knowledge on the current status of private guards. Many saw an increase in powers as inappropriately raising the status of commercial guards:

I would not want to increase their powers, in doing that we would be paying for a second police force.
If you increase their powers they are tending to take over the job of the police and we don't want that.
Keep their powers the same. They do take the job off the police but it is right that they should have to pass things on to the police.

While the public welcome the input from private security, they are clear that there need to be parameters and boundaries limiting the role of the guards. Both subscribers and non-subscribers favour partnership and a co-operative working together, which as suggested above, does not happen in practice in this locality.

Despite a resistance by many of the residents to the principle of private guards usurping the role of the public police, evidently many subscribers see the private guards as their first point of contact when suspicious events or disturbances occur in their locality or home. Much information that would traditionally have been passed to the police is now more likely to be routed to the private company:

They offer instant accessibility, they are always there, I would ring private security before the police.
They provide instant response and action and they are quicker than the police, so I don't bother with the police.

A failure to address this situation will mean that the police are increasingly likely to receive partial accounts of their local crime scenario, with implications for police effectiveness and subsequent public satisfaction. This diversion of information toward the commercial group, in a climate of lack of communication between the public and private bodies, will contribute to an increasing marginalisation of the role of the police in the lives of a substantial number of residents. Such developments detract from the role of the police as 'knowledge brokers' (Ericson and Haggerty, 1997) and prevent them acting effectively as 'co-ordinators' of local knowledge of risk. Ericson and Haggerty (*ibid*: 73) have also suggested that a community policing input is important in underpinning and providing legitimation for police enforcement roles. In this community, where the police are perceived by many to provide a minimal community presence, their role is in danger of being further undermined by the presence of commercial services. As suggested above, it is feasible that a community role can be appropriately subsumed within the role of commercial groups. However, what is needed is greater acknowledgement and debate regarding the changes occurring in the experiences of residents and communities where private guards are making a substantial contribution to the maintenance of community law and order.

ISSUES FOR THE FUTURE

With police resources becoming increasingly stretched in relation to workload, it seems an opportune time for the government to have requested the Chief Constable of Surrey to explore the possibilities of privatisation of some of the current functions of public policing (*Guardian*, 17 July 1998). This research as a piece of work concerned with the dynamics of private provision has served to highlight some of the key questions that such a review will need to consider. These will include the relative effectiveness of large and small scale organisations in providing private security; questions of accountability and regulation; potential for change in the working relationships between the public and private police; rationalisation of financing systems and possible disparity of experiences for residents in a shift to private models of provision.

This case study of an area where private guards make a core contribution reveals significant transformations in residents' experience of policing. A proportion of them are choosing to share crime concerns with private rather than public police and relying on the private guards as their source of security. In Merryside this in part reflects the local status of the company and its small scale. Such a situation would perhaps be more difficult to achieve if the security service was provided by a more bureaucratic large scale commercial group.

An increased use of private police would also require a willingness to rethink the relationship between public and private policing, with a number of key issues demanding attention. If the police are to enter into partnership with commercial bodies then they will require a greater degree of regulation of private organisations than is currently the case. While acknowledging the government's commitment to a licensing system for the contract guarding industry, official sanctioning of the expansion of private patrols into residential areas will require a level of accountability beyond the current regulatory concern solely with the deployment of guard dogs (George and Watson, 1992). One criticism of private provision has been that commercial protection services have traditionally been associated with enforced compliance and the notion of the protection racket (Tilley, 1985). Such a perspective and concern that local knowledge will not be used benignly is reinforced by the current absence of regulation regarding the activities of private commercial groups:

You don't know who they are and how trustworthy they are (non-subscriber).
I was initially concerned about their reputation, it felt like protection money, but their subsequent reputation has not borne this out (subscriber).

The recent White Paper (HMSO, 1999) sets out the government's intentions regarding regulation, with proposals for the establishment of a Private Security Industry Authority. It is proposed that such a body would take responsibility for licensing individual staff, although there are no proposals for statutory regulation of individual companies, via minimum standards or other procedures. While a voluntary company scheme is recommended, this is not intended to be binding on all organisations or a condition for future operation. In the light of public concern about the unregulated status of the industry, government commitment to addressing the matter would appear to be timely, and a necessary prerequisite to any further expansion of the industry. However, it remains questionable whether the current proposals go far enough to secure enhanced confidence in the private security industry.

Acknowledgement of such schemes will also formally reduce police dominance on issues of law and order at a time when surveys of public satisfaction with the police are showing some slippage in public support (Skogan, 1996). Consequently, the police are likely to feel particularly threatened by private competitors with the potential to offer a more focused and apparently efficient service. This situation is further complicated by the provisions of the Police and Magistrates Courts Act 1994, which further enhance the potential for the public police to contract out their services for private hire, potentially situating themselves in direct competition with groups in the private sector (Wakefield, 1997). Such contexts help explain why private companies operating in this area are encountering a degree of official resistance, particularly from senior police managers, and an unwillingness to openly acknowledge their potential to make a contribution. While the police cannot be said to have been actively resistant, their response to the work undertaken by profit-making schemes is generally negative. Recent press reports of police reaction to private patrols in the Bristol area are that:

The patrols are fighting a battle not just against the criminals but against the scepticism of many police. Senior officers believe the company's existence exacerbates fear of crime, on which its profits depend. (*The Times*, 11 October 1997)

In my research area any formalisation of the relationship with the private group would be premised on a partial and uneven service, with enhanced security limited to those with an ability to pay, and with a majority of residents excluded from an enhanced service. Responding to a new and emerging market, commercial operators, many of which are small scale, are assessing viability and establishing their businesses based on residents' willingness to support the scheme financially. No coherent planning underpins the manner in which private schemes are emerging, and the pattern of coverage is uneven and totally at the whim of commercial enterprise and public willingness to pay. Other commentators have expressed disquiet about the trend toward privatisation as detrimental to 'democratising security' as a social good (Loader, 1997: 152) and as compounding inequity in experiences of policing with 'dualistic policing: private policing for the rich, coupled with "a poor police policing the poor"' (Johnston, 1996b: 66). Other models, however, exist in the UK of local councils purchasing a security service to supplement public policing and passing on the financial cost to all residents (Johnston, 1996, *The Times*, October 1997) and direct provision by local councils, such as Wirral and Sedgefield (Jones and Newburn, 1998). These may be important strategies to address the elitism and potential for social exclusion encased in selective commercial models. However, evidence emerging from this study is, that for some residents, policing can be provided by the commercial sector while retaining a community profile and that commercialisation need not be diametrically opposed to community cohesion:

They make the community stronger by connecting people. It makes a difference, the area is better since private security started operating.

Whatever particular model is adopted we are at a critical juncture in the U.K. in the relative balance between public and private policing.

The coverage provided by private groups is expanding in both commercial and residential sectors. The 'security quilt' is undergoing change in how it is constructed. The emerging trend in the U.K. with regard to increasing privatisation of policing follows an international pattern, with some Western industrialised countries at a more advanced stage in relative contributions of public and private groups to law and order maintenance (Shearing, 1992). If, however, the creeping establishment of privatised neighbourhood patrols in the U.K. does represent a major realignment of the relative contributions of public and private policing to the maintenance of social order, then a blinkered refusal to acknowledge that change is occurring is likely to be a dangerous strategy. By failing to recognise that groups are emerging on their patch, the police are opting out of important debates that need to take place on the relationships between public and private police. It is timely to address the question as to whether the public police might find that collaboration has a positive potential. Are the private guards, for example, a good source of local intelligence that the current disposition of non co-operation is failing to exploit, or are the police correctly rejecting private policing as a long term threat to their industry? Acknowledgement that private guards are being employed by residents and that the trend is an increasing one would allow some of these critical questions to be addressed.

With an acknowledgement that the U.K. is at a cross-roads in the relative inputs of private and public police to community protection and safety, the issues of regulation and accountability of private police officers cannot be ignored. It might be argued that British policing is in the process of coming full circle with communities seeking to re-introduce the historical model of local watches. The new police of early nineteenth century Britain developed as a direct consequence of the perceived inadequacies of the system of parish constables and watchmen (Emsley, 1997). As we draw to the end of the twentieth century professional police forces in the U.K. need to address the re-emergence of private local forces seeking actively to supplement their role in promoting community safety.

160   L. NOAKS

References

Audit Commission (1990) *Effective Policing: Performance Review in Police Forces.* London: HMSO.

Bennett, T. (1990) *Evaluating Neighbourhood Watch.* Aldershot: Gower.

Davis, M. (1990) *City of Quartz.* Verso.

Emsley, C. (1997) 'The History of Crime Control and Crime Control Institutions' in Reiner, R., Morgan, R. and Maguire, E. (eds.) *The Oxford Handbook of Criminology,* 2nd edition, OUP.

Ericson and Haggerty (1997) *Policing the Risk Society.* Oxford: Clarendon Press.

Garland, D. (1996) 'The Limits of the Sovereign State', *British Journal of Criminology,* **34**(4), pp. 445–71.

George, B. and Watson, T. (1992) 'Regulation of the Private Security Industry', *Public Money and Management,* **12**(1), pp. 55–57.

The Guardian 17 July 1998.

Home Office (1999) *The Government's Proposals for the Regulation of the Private Security Industry in England and Wales.* Cm 4254. London: The Stationery Office.

Hough, M. (1996) *Anxiety about Crime: findings from the 1994 British Crime Survey.* London: Home Office.

Johnston, L. (1992) *The Rebirth of Private Policing.* Routledge.

Johnston, L. (1996a) 'What Is Vigilantism?' *British Journal of Criminology,* **36**(2).

Johnston, L. (1996b) 'Policing diversity: the impact of the public-private complex in policing' in Leishman, F., Loveday, B. and Savage, S.P. (eds.) *Core Issues in Policing.* Longman: London.

Jones, T. and Newburn, T (1998) *Private Security and Public Policing.* Oxford: Clarendon Press.

Loader, I. (1997) 'Thinking Normatively About Private Security', *Journal of Law and Society,* **24**(3), September 1997.

Mayhew, P. and White, P. (1997) *The 1996 International Crime Victimisation Survey.* London: HMSO.

Mirrlees-Black, C., Mayhew, P. and Percy, A. (1996) *The 1996 British Crime Survey.* London: HMSO.

Nogala, D. (1996) How Policing Gets Privatised: Patterns of the New Security Economy. Unpublished conference paper, Crime and Social Order in Europe conference, September 1996.

Reiner, R. (1997) 'Policing and the Police' in Maguire, E., Morgan, R. and Reiner, R. (eds.) *The Oxford Handbook of Criminology.* Oxford: Oxford University Press.

Rutherford, A. (1990) 'Prison Privatisation in Britain' in D. C. McDonald (ed.) *Private Prisons and the Public Interest.* New Brunswick, NJ: Rutgers University Press.

Shapland, J. and Vagg, J. (1988) *Policing by the Public.* London: Routledge.

Shearing, C. D. and Stenning, P. C. (1983) 'Private Security-implications for social control', *Social Problems,* **30**(5).

Shearing, C. D. (1992) 'The relation between public and private policing' in Tonry, M. and Wilson, N. (eds.) *Modern Policing.* Chicago: University of Chicago Press.

Sheehy Report (1993) *Report of the Enquiry into Police Responsibilities and Rewards,* Cm 2280 1, 11. London: HMSO.

Sheptycki, J. (1997) 'Insecurity, Risk Suppression and Segregation', *Theoretical Criminology,* **1**(3), August 1997.

Skogan, W. (1996) 'Public Opinion and the Police' in Saulsbury W., J. Mott and T. Newburn (eds.) *Themes in Contemporary Policing*. London: Police Foundation/Policy Studies Institute.

Stanko, E. (1990) *Everyday Violence*. London: Unwin Hyman.

Tilley, C. (1985) State Making as Organised Crime in '*Bringing the State Back In*'.

The Times 11 October 1997.

Wakefield, A. (1997) 'Who Guards the Guards? Investigating an Unregulated Industry', unpublished conference paper. American Society of Criminology Meeting, November 1997.

[27]

The Kirkholt Project: Preventing Burglary on a British Public Housing Estate

Ken Pease

Department of Social Policy, University of Manchester,
Manchester, UK

A program of residential burglary prevention is described. It targeted prior victims, since the probability of repeat victimization is dramatically higher than that of first victimization. A package of measures, including the removal of the most obvious source of cash, target hardening, and "cocoon" Neighborhood Watch, achieved a reduction of burglary to 25% of its preimplementation level within 3 years. The attractions of the prevention of repeat victimization as a general strategy of crime prevention·are described.

Keywords: Burglary; prevention; victimization; Neighborhood Watch; utilities

Introduction

Kirkholt is an area of public housing near Rochdale, a town 10 miles north of Manchester, in northern England. It comprises some 2280 dwellings. In 1985, about one dwelling in four was burglarized. This was many times the national figure. Hough and Mayhew (1985) identified housing types associated with high, medium, and low levels of burglary. Kirkholt housing was of a type with a medium rate of burglary nationally. Despite this, the rate of recorded burglaries on Kirkholt was *double* the figure for recorded and unrecorded burglaries in housing types at *high* risk.

The Kirkholt Project is reported in two papers produced by the Home Office Crime Prevention Unit (Forrester *et al.*, 1988, 1990). The purpose of this paper is to give a personal overview of the project and its significance. The author jointly directed the evaluation of the project throughout its existence. The project had major inputs from local police, probation services, and victim support services. Systematic information was gathered from interviews with domestic burglary victims, their neighbors, and known burglars. The way in which the Kirkholt initiative grew out of the data is detailed in Forrester *et al.* (1988) and will not be repeated here.

It was found that (in 1986) the chance of a second or subsequent burglary was over four times as high as the chance of a first burglary; that is, a burglary flags the high probability of another burglary. Reference to the 1984 British Crime Survey showed this pattern to be national and is consistent with the pioneering work of Sparks (1981). Subsequent research in Canada (Polvi *et al.*, 1990) showed the same pattern and suggested that the period of greatest risk of repeat victimization is within 6 weeks of the first. To put the position as it applied to Kirkholt in 1986 more concretely, nearly half of those burglarized in December 1986 had been attacked at least once before during 1986.

The Elements of Phase I of the Kirkholt Project

The central strategy was the prevention of repeat victimization. Elements of the initiative are summarized below.

Perhaps the most obvious factor in the burglary profile of Kirkholt was the taking of money from electricity and gas prepayment meters. These meters are a payment method whereby money is deposited in exchange for fuel dispensed. Deposited money is kept in a fuel meter in the home and emptied by the utility company once every month or 3 months. Forty-nine percent of burglaries on the estate involved the loss of meter cash [see Hill (1986) for a fuller account of the problem nationally]. In Kirkholt, utility boards agreed to the replacement of meters after a burglary, with the agreement of the householder.

Overwhelmingly, Kirkholt burglars entered a dwelling by the first route that was attempted. A security uprating of the homes of burglary victims was put in hand, together with postcoding of valuables. The primary requirement of the upgrading was that it did not consist of token locks and bolts, but, instead, dealt with the real points of vulnerability as evident in the entry methods described by burglars and their victims. The security rating was based on crime prevention officer advice in the light of our information and communicated through the local police officer. Alongside this uprating, a system of monitoring burglary techniques on the estate was set in place so that security advice could be based on changing burglary practice. The key agency in uprating security was the town's Housing Department, which agreed to disburse already agreed funds in the way suggested by the project.

The most publicized element of the Kirkholt scheme, initiated in 1987, has been cocoon Neighborhood Watch. By this device, the residents of the six or so houses or flats contiguous with a victimized dwelling were asked to look out and report on anything suspicious around the burglarized home to prevent repeat victimization. If they agreed to cooperate (as most did), they too were provided with security uprating. This kind of Watch scheme is triggered by a specific event and has a specific focus. These "cocoons" were intended to serve as nuclei of more conventional forms of organization and, in fact, developed into Neighborhood Watch schemes, which seem to be better rooted than many programs described elsewhere.

Community support was an element of phase 1 of the scheme. Project workers visited the homes of burglary victims on the estate, offering support and putting victims in touch with the appropriate agencies. In due course, project workers took over establishing cocoons, and they themselves carried out security surveys and the associated postcoding of valuables. Workers also put in place a continual monitoring of relevant burglary techniques.

In brief, the rate of burglary on Kirkholt fell to 40% of its 1986 level within 5 months of the start of the program. Repeat victimizations fell to zero over the same period and did not exceed two in any month thereafter. There was very little suggestion that crimes had been displaced from Kirkholt to bordering areas. The time period of the first evaluation was very short and was acknowledged to be so. In the foreword to the first report, phase II was described as follows: "Further action is now under way in Kirkholt building on the initial success, but this time aiming to reduce the motivation for crime. With the aid of Home Office development funds, the probation service, the police, and university researchers are seeking to tackle the linked problems of alcohol and drug abuse, debt, and unemployment. A further report describing this second phase, and an evaluation, will be prepared in due course" (foreword to Forrester *et al.*, 1988, p. iii). In what follows, I will describe the transition of the project from its first to its second phase.

Phase II

The aims of the project were described in the application for development funds by the Greater Manchester Probation Service as being to

a. Maintain the target hardening/support to victims initiative.

b. Secure community ownership of the project.
c. Seek additional offender/community initiatives.

Alongside phase II elements, phase I remains in place in most relevant particulars. The Local Authority Housing budget of £75,000 set aside to improve the security hardware of victimized dwellings over 3 years has run out. The procedure has now been integrated into the normal Housing Department budget, so that burglary victims throughout Rochdale receive a priority response instead of being routinely added to the repair list, as happened prior to 1987.

Elements of phase II include a school-based crime prevention program, provision for offenders from the Kirkholt area to attend groups to address their problems, a cheap savings and loan scheme for Kirkholt residents, better informed probation officers, and better-served courts in consequence.

The change in the burglary rate on Kirkholt is presented as *Table 1*. The table shows a month-by-month scrutiny of burglaries from dwellings. To facilitate comparisons by individual month, the information is separated into four 12-month periods. The first is March 1986 to February 1987 (the preimplementation year); the second is March 1987 to February 1988 (the first year of implementation); the third is March 1988 to February 1989; and the last March 1989 to February 1990. *Table 2* presents a comparison be-

Table 1. Number of Burglaries from Dwellings in Kirkholt: Pre- and Postprevention Intervention

	Year (March to February)			
Month	1986/7 (Pre)	1987/8 (Post 1)	1988/9 (Post 2)	1989/90 (Post 3)
March	54	42	14	18
April	61	30	21	10
May	52	17	15	9
June	28	10	5	8
July	40	10	7	2
August	39	16	13	14
September	42	22	29	18
October	27	16	9	9
November	36	14	9	12
December	23	16	18	18
January	64	10	17	6
February	60	20	10	8
Total for year	526	223	167	132
Average/month	44	19	14	11
% fall on previous year		58%	25%	21%
% fall on 2 year's previous			68%	41%
% fall on 3 year's previous				75%

Table 2. Comparison of Household Burglaries in Kirkholt with Remainder of Police Subdivision

	Kirkholt		Remainder of Police Subdivision	
Year	No. Burglaries	% Change on 1986	No. Burglaries	% Change on 1986
1986	512	—	2843	—
1987	317	−38	2880	+1
1988	170	−67	2311	−19
1989	145	−72	2160	−24

tween Kirkholt and the remainder of the police sub-division of which it is part. (For reasons of procedure that need not be considered here, it is regretted that these comparisons are for calendar years, not periods as calculated for *Table 1*. Thus, data in *Tables 1* and *2* are not exactly comparable, although their close similarity is evident.) Comparisons with Rochdale more generally yield a similar picture. Provisional cost-benefit analysis (see Forrester *et al.*, 1990) suggest the project is well "in the black."

The Kirkholt initiative has now relinquished its "demonstration project" status. The community now "owns" the program, and the Kirkholt Community Crime Prevention Group, comprising residents of the estate, now operate it. A second probation officer helps to translate the continuing data into application. For instance, newcomers to the estate are now dispropor-tionately likely to become burglary victims, and this is leading to consideration of the modified reintroduc-tion of cocoons for these people. Further, old people are highly victimized during the traditional holiday period of early September; action is being formulated to combat this at the time of writing.

Just Another Crime Prevention Project?

As was stressed in the first published report of the Kirkholt Project (Forrester *et al.*, 1988), our choice was to prevent burglary by any means at hand. The disadvantage of this was and still is that the contri-bution of the various elements of the program were not distinguishable. We are aware of many limitations in both the conduct and the evaluation of the project, but we still believe that the Kirkholt experience does have some novel aspects that may be worthy of emulation.

The cornerstone of the Kirkholt Project was a rec-ognition of the relationship between repeat victimi-zation and crime prevention. To acknowledge that victimization predicts further victimization is to ac-knowledge that victim support and crime prevention are two sides of the same coin. Some of the advantages of the prevention of repeat victimization are as follows:

- Attention to dwellings or people already victimized has a higher "hit-rate" of those likely to be victim-ized in the future.
- Preventing repeat victimization protects the most vulnerable social groups, without having to identify those groups as such, which can be socially divisive. Having been victimized already probably repre-sents the least contentious basis for a claim to be given crime prevention attention.

- Repeat victimization is highest, both absolutely and proportionately, in the most crime-ridden areas (Trickett *et al.*, submitted), which are also the areas that suffer the most serious crime (Pease, 1988). The prevention of repeat victimization is thus com-mensurately more important the greater an area's crime problem is.
- The rate of victimization offers a realistic sched-uling for crime prevention activity. Preventing re-peat victimization is a way of "drip-feeding" crime prevention.
- Even from the unrealistic view that crime is only displaced, avoiding repeat victimization at least shares the agony around (see Barr and Pease, 1990).

Most centrally, the strategy set out above creates a symbiotic relationship between victim support and ef-ficient crime prevention, to their mutual benefit. In establishing the project, biological similes like sym-biosis and cocooning constantly came to mind. In the first project report, the program was described as being more like horticulture than like engineering. Growth, osmosis, and suffusion were notions that repeatedly suggested themselves. This is important in suggesting that the protection of highly vulnerable places or peo-ple brings with it some process whereby the less vul-nerable are also protected.

I have described the process whereby repeat vic-timization is addressed as "drip-feeding" crime pre-vention. Perhaps the drip-feeding metaphor should be elaborated a little to illustrate the point. The con-sistent "drip" response to victimization effort gener-ates an effect that suffused throughout Kirkholt. This brought to mind the drip-feed that suffuses naturally throughout a body. More sudden or large-scale in-tervention could not be absorbed. In responding to victimization with crime prevention effort, a natural place is dictated for that effort. Unlike projects that seek, for example, to uprate security or give publicity to saturate an area, response to victimization is paced and focused. In practical terms, a smaller staff is re-quired to drip-feed, rather than to bludgeon crime prevention activity.

The emphasis on repeat victimization that under-pins the Kirkholt Project has emerged in our thinking as an important strategy of crime prevention gener-ally. Whatever the particular and undoubted defects of the Kirkholt Project itself, we hope that this per-spective is incorporated into other projects in the fu-ture. It is also to be hoped that the combination of agencies and interests in the program in the common pursuit of burglary prevention will also be found elsewhere.

References

Barr, R., and Pease, K. (1990). Crime placement, displacement and deflection. In M. Tonry & N. Morris (Eds.), *Crime and justice: A review of research* (Vol 12). Chicago: University of Chicago Press.

Forrester, D., Chatterton, M., and Pease, K. (1988). *The Kirkholt Burglary Prevention Project, Rochdale.* Crime Prevention Unit Paper 13. London: Home Office.

Forrester, D., Frenz, S., and O'Connell, M. (1990). *The Kirkholt Burglary Prevention Project: Phase II.* Crime Prevention Unit Paper XX. London: Home Office.

Hill, N. (1986). *Prepayment coin meters: A target for burglary.* Crime Prevention Unit Paper 6. London: Home Office.

Hough, M., and Mayhew, P. (1985). *Taking account of crime: Key findings from the 1984 British Crime Survey.* Home Office Research Study No. 85. London: HMSO.

Pease, K. (1988). *Judgements of crime seriousness: Evidence from the 1984 British Crime Survey.* Research and Planning Unit Paper 44, London: Home Office.

Polvi, N., Looman, T., Humphries, C., and Pease, K. (1990). Repeat break-and-enter victimisations: Time course and crime prevention opportunity. *Journal of Police Science and Administration, 17,* 8–11.

Sparks, R. F. (1981). Multiple victimization: Evidence, theory and future research. *Journal of Criminal Law and Criminology, 72,* 762–778.

Trickett, A., Osborn, D., Seymour, J., and Pease, K. How are high crime rate areas different? *British Journal of Criminology,* in press.

[28]

The Theory and Research Behind Neighborhood Watch: Is It a Sound Fear and Crime Reduction Strategy?

DENNIS P. ROSENBAUM

This article takes a critical look at the theory and research behind the highly touted community crime prevention strategy known as Neighborhood Watch. While correlational studies of neighborhoods and citizen participation are numerous, there is a paucity of rigorous experimental evaluations that test the proposed "Implant Hypothesis," that is, that collective citizen participation (and the social processes it allegedly activates) can be implanted in neighborhoods where it does not currently exist. However, there are both theoretical and empirical reasons to challenge some of the basic assumptions underlying the Neighborhood Watch approach to reducing crime, reducing fear of crime, and restoring a sense of community. The hypothesis that Watch programs increase fear of crime and may have other effects is examined. The implications of this assessment for theory development and public policy are explored.

We are entering the heyday of community crime prevention. Never before has the notion of citizen involvement in crime prevention received such widespread support from law enforcement, the media, the general public, the federal government, and even the academic community. While endorsements continue to expand at a rapid pace, the question remains whether collective citizen action is an effective strategy for controlling crime, reducing fear of crime, and building a sense of community. This article takes a critical look at one of the most popular forms of community crime prevention—Neighborhood Watch (also known as Block Watch, Apartment Watch, and so on). The empirical support for this crime prevention strategy is reviewed, but at the core of

DENNIS P. ROSENBAUM: Visiting Associate Professor in the Department of Criminal Justice, University of Illinois at Chicago.

104   CRIME & DELINQUENCY / JANUARY 1986

this article is a theoretical critique of the current thinking about how and why this approach is expected to produce the hypothesized outcomes.

NEIGHBORHOOD WATCH: THE COMMUNITY SOLUTION

We have witnessed a sizeable evolution and expansion in the definition of "community crime prevention" over the past fifteen years (cf. Bickman et al., 1976; Lavrakas, 1985; McPherson and Silloway, 1980; Rosenbaum, 1986; Yin, 1979). Everything from youth recreation programs to architectural redesign is now subsumed under the title of "community crime prevention." However, at the heart of community crime prevention in the United States is a set of related programs that Feins (1983) refers to as the "Big Three"—Block Watch, Operation ID (engraving property), and home security surveys. Block Watch is justifiably considered one of the "Big Three" because of its widespread utilization by law enforcement (Cunningham and Taylor, 1985) and community organizations (Feins, 1983), because of the strong public support it has received in opinion polls (Gallup, 1982), because of national policy that has specifically encouraged this type of program through the Community Anticrime Program and the Urban Crime Prevention Program (see DuBow and Emmons, 1981; Roehl and Cook, 1984), and, finally, because of the numerous claims of success in reducing crime (Lurigio and Rosenbaum, 1986).

Essentially, *Neighborhood* or *Block Watch* involves citizens coming together in relatively small groups (usually block clubs) to share information about local crime problems, exchange crime prevention tips, and make plans for engaging in surveillance ("watching") of the neighborhood and crime-reporting activities. The first block meetings are often arranged by crime prevention officers from the police department or "community organizers" employed by local community organizations. Block group meetings involve presentations regarding the opportunity to participate in property marking (engraving) and home security survey programs offered by the police, as well as to set up a phone "chain" or "tree" for surveillance and support. The meetings frequently involve less formal discussions of feelings and perceptions among participants regarding the local crime problem and what can be done about it.

Why Neighborhood Watch is currently so appealing to law enforcement and policymakers is less relevant here than the theory-based reasons for its implicit and explicit endorsement among criminal justice scholars. At the heart of this support is a recognition that many neighborhood residents are fearful and isolated because of crime. Citizens often respond to crime by restricting their behavior and installing numerous security devices to protect their property (Lavrakas, Skogan, Hertz, Salem, and Lewis, 1980). In discussing this "retreat behind locks, bars, alarms, and guards," the National Advisory Commission on Criminal Justice Standards and Goals (1973) noted that "although these prophylactic measures may be steps in self-protection, they can lead to a lessening of the bonds of mutual assistance and neighborliness" (p. 46). Indeed, in the context of discussions about "neighborhood decline" (cf. Taub, Taylor, and Dunham, 1982), there is talk about a declining sense of community or a reduction in social cohesion. One of the main explanations for high levels of crime, incivility, and fear of crime in certain neighborhoods is the erosion of informal social control processes that are believed responsible for maintaining order (Jacobs, 1961; Greenberg, Rohe, and Williams, 1985; Wilson and Kelling, 1982).

Neighborhood Watch has been recommended as a feasible and attractive solution to these crime-related neighborhood conditions. This crime prevention strategy has been conceptualized as a collective, "public-minded" strategy as opposed to the individual-focused, "private-minded" responses to crime that are typical of most citizens (cf. Schneider and Schneider, 1978). More important, Watch programs are consistent with the two primary theoretical models behind community crime prevention today, namely, informal social control and opportunity reduction. Jane Jacobs (1961) articulated the basic principle behind the informal social control model as it pertains to crime control:

> The first thing to understand is that public peace . . . is not kept primarily by the police, necessary as police are. It is kept primarily by an intricate, almost unconscious network of voluntary controls and standards among the people themselves, and enforced by the people themselves" [p. 31-32].

Recently, researchers have sought greater theoretical precision in making the connection between informal social control processes and community crime prevention programs such as Neighborhood Watch. Specifically, the hope for Watch programs is that they will produce the social contact and social interaction necessary to strengthen informal social control bonds and thus enhance community social cohesion (Dubow and Emmons, 1981; Greenberg et al., 1985; Rosenbaum, Lewis, and Grant, 1985; Silloway and McPherson, 1985; Yin, 1979). Perhaps the biggest hope for the watch model, as articulated by these theorists, is that it will reduce fear of crime via this collective process. Residents would be stripped of their reasons for social isolation and distrust after developing friendship patterns with neighbors and working jointly toward reducing the common problem of crime.

The opportunity reduction model as applied to Neighborhood Watch is actually a derivative of earlier theorizing about how changes in physical design characteristics will reduce criminal opportunities (Jacobs, 1961). At the core of what became known as "crime prevention through environmental design" (Jeffrey, 1971) and "defensible space" theory (Newman, 1972) is Jane Jacobs's (1961) argument that there must be natural surveillance ("eyes on the street") to reduce the opportunities for crime. Neighborhood Watch, one could argue, was historically built on research showing an inverse relationship between surveillance opportunities and crime rates (e.g. Newman, 1972; Reppetto, 1974). Through social (rather than physical) means Watches seek to encourage *intentional* surveillance rather than merely create *natural* surveillance opportunities. Thus, Neighborhood Watch holds the promise of increasing collective surveillance of the neighborhood, where residents become the "eyes and ears" of the police and report any suspicious or criminal activity in the area. This type of territorial "neighboring" is expected to reduce the opportunity for criminal activity by letting would-be criminals know that the risk of detection and apprehension has increased. Also, to the extent that block meetings stimulate residents to take individual measures to protect themselves or their property, (although unrelated to the hypothesized surveillance effect) then the opportunities to engage in personal and property offenses in these particular neighborhoods should diminish. This opportunity reduction model suggests that fear of crime will decrease as residents perceive a decrease in their risk of victimization.

Empirical Support and Its Limitations

Two primary types of empirical information have been used to support the concept of Neighborhood Watch—(a) neighborhood studies on citizen participation and reactions to crime and (b) evaluations of crime prevention programs. The reactions-to-crime research has provided the basis for most scholarly endorsements of the concept, as it provides considerable support for the informal social control model (see Greenberg et al., 1985, for a thorough review). For example, research has shown that fear of crime is lower in neighborhoods where residents feel more responsibility and control over what happens in the area (Greenberg, Rohe, and Williams, 1982; Skogan and Maxfield, 1981), where the number of incivilities or disorders, such as litter and teenagers hanging out, is low (Skogan & Maxfield, 1981; Taub, Taylor, and Dunham, 1981), and where neighbors are perceived as available to provide assistance when needed (Sundeen and Mathieu, 1976). Thus fear of crime appears to be influenced by the perceived level of social order in the neighborhood, leading Greenberg and her colleagues to recommend that communities "develop programs that familiarize local residents with each other and with the neighborhood to help encourage intervention and to reduce fear" (Greenberg et al., 1985, p. 17). While the enhancement of informal social control in neighborhoods characterized by disorder is a seemingly desirable objective, our ability to accomplish this remains very questionable, as this article will address in more detail later.

Another aspect of the reaction-to-crime literature that has been interpreted as supportive of watch-type programs is the research focused on citizen participation in local community organizations—groups that often serve as vehicles for Neighborhood Watch programs. For example, studies have shown that "participators" in local voluntary organizations exhibit higher levels of informal social interaction in the neighborhood than "nonparticipators" (Kasarda and Janowitz, 1974; Hunter, 1974). The assumption that more social interaction will reduce the level of crime or fear of crime in the community will be examined later.

Unfortunately, there are many problems with the implication that research on reactions to crime provides useful information about the possible benefit of watch-type programs. There is only enough space here to articulate the most fundamental problem—that of internal validity. This body of research is based, almost exclusively, on cross-sectional data that do not easily allow causal inferences. Hence, we have little confidence that the characteristics and behaviors that distinguish participants from nonparticipants are attributable to the Neighborhood Watch program (or the act of participation) rather than preexisting

Burglary

CRIME & DELINQUENCY / JANUARY 1986

differences between the two groups. Self-selection is one of the biggest threats to the validity of nonexperimental evaluation research in many fields, and it is no less of a problem in this case. Research has been quite clear about *who* participates in community activities and *where* these individuals live, and thus serves to document this self-selection process. Studies have consistently shown that participation in voluntary organizations is largely a middle-class phenomenon, that is, participants tend to be in the middle-income range, married with children, homeowners, and well educated (Lavrakas et al., 1980; Skogan and Maxfield, 1981; Wandersman, Jakubs, and Giamartino, 1981). Futhermore, these individuals tend to live in neighborhoods characterized by a shared set of norms regarding public behavior. In their reanalysis of survey data from three cities and 60 neighborhoods, Greenberg et al. (1982) found that collective crime prevention programs like Neighborhood Watch were more prevalent in neighborhoods with racial and economic homogeneity.

A number of studies indicate that these homogeneous, typically middle-class areas are generally characterized by much stronger informal social controls. That is, residents feel more control over their environment (e.g., more willing to intervene), feel more responsible for crime prevention (i.e., less reliant on police), and generally feel more positive about, and similar to, their neighbors than residents of typical lower-class neighborhoods. (Boggs, 1971; Greenberg et al., 1982; Hackler, Ho, and Urquhart-Ross, 1974; Taub et al., 1982; Taylor, Gottfredson, and Brower, 1981).

All of these empirical observations leave unanswered the fundamental question of whether the *introduction* of a community crime prevention program (and Neighborhood Watch in particular) can make a difference in the perceptions, attitudes, and behaviors of local residents. The important question here is whether informal social control (and other processes supposedly activated by watch-type programs) can be *implanted* in neighborhoods where they have not naturally developed. Let us refer to this as the *Implant Hypothesis* and begin to explore the empirical support for this proposition. What evidence can be amassed to show that crime, fear of crime, and related neighborhood responses have declined as a direct result of Neighborhood Watch-type interventions?

TESTING THE IMPLANT HYPOTHESIS

Titus (1983) reviewed nearly two dozen evaluations of burglary prevention programs (which is the central focus of most watch programs) and found that participating individuals were less victimized and/or target areas had lower burglary rates than their comparison groups. However, showing participator-nonparticipator differences, again, is not quasi-experimental because participator characteristics are confounded with intervention effects. Unfortunately, most "evaluations" of Neighborhood Watch are not very useful for testing the Implant Hypothesis. At our request, Leonard Sipes (using documents at the National Criminal Justice Reference Service) identified 111 programs that claim "success" with Neighborhood Watch by reporting reductions in crime and occasionally reductions in fear of crime and other outcomes (Lurigio and Rosenbaum, 1986). While many writers in the mass media and elsewhere have been quick to conclude that these success stories are truly indicative of the power of watch-type programs, these conclusions are not based on hard evidence. For example, 92% of the projects collected data using the one-group pretest-posttest design— a very weak research design that is subject to many threats to validity (see Campbell and Stanley, 1966; Cook and Campbell, 1979). Oftentimes, only police crime statistics were examined in the target area. The low quality of evaluation research in this field has been recognized by several researchers (Greenberg et al., 1985; Lurigio and Rosenbaum, 1986; Skogan, 1979; Yin, 1979). To summarize these concerns, the program evaluations are "characterized by weak designs, an under-use of statistical significance test, a poor conceptualization and definition of treatments, the absence of a valid and reliable measurement of program implementation and outcomes, and a consistent failure to address competing explanations for observed effects" (Lurigio and Rosenbaum, 1986, p. 20).

If the large majority of evaluations in the field are seriously flawed, what evidence can be amassed to test the Implant Hypothesis? While strong community crime prevention evaluations have been conducted in Hartford, Connecticut (Fowler and Mangione, 1982) and Portland, Oregon (Schneider, 1975) neither of these interventions was limited to Neighborhood Watch. In my judgment, only two evaluations to date can be viewed as reasonably strong tests of the Neighborhood Watch model—the well-known Seattle evaluation (Cirel et al., 1977; Lindsay and McGillis, 1986), and our recently completed Chicago evaluation (Rosenbaum et al., 1985, 1986). Briefly, the Seattle evaluation yielded generally positive results, showing a reduction in residential burglary in the target areas relative to the control areas. In contrast to the Seattle evaluation, the Chicago evaluation found generally negative results, showing increases in a variety of social problem areas, including fear of crime. Because the Chicago evaluation is, to my knowledge, the first quasi-experimental test of the full range of hypotheses derived from both the informal social control and opporunity reduction models, a brief description of this research is provided.

The Chicago Evaluation. The Ford Foundation funded Northwestern to conduct a rigorous process and impact evaluation of community crime prevention programs being planned in Chicago neighborhoods (See Lewis, Grant, and Rosenbaum, 1985; Rosenbaum et al., 1985). The intervention was an attempt by experienced volunteers from local community organizations to organize residents of selected neighborhoods using door-to-door canvassing, block meetings, and neighborhood meetings, with emphasis on the Block Watch model. A quasi-experimental research design was employed for the impact evaluation, namely, the "Untreated Control Group Design with Pretest and Posttest" (cf. Cook and Campbell, 1979). A one year lag was scheduled between the pretest (n = 3357) and posttest (n = 2824), from February, 1983, to February, 1984, and extensive telephone surveys were conducted with residents in both panel samples and independent random samples. Control groups included three carefully selected untreated neighborhoods in Chicago for *each* of the four target neighborhoods, and a city-wide random sample.

Seven primary hypotheses were tested that capture the current theorizing about the impact of such programs (Rosenbaum et al., 1985). Specifically, Neighborhood Watch was expected to (a) stimulate residents' awareness of and participation in crime prevention meetings, (b) enhance feelings of efficacy and personal responsibility for preventive action, (c) produce a number of behavioral changes related to preventing victimization and informally regulating social behavior, (d) enhance social cohesion in the neighborhood, (e) reduce crime and various types of disorders, (f) reduce fear of crime and related perceptions of crime, and (g) improve citizens' general perceptions of the neighborhood and attachment to the community as a place to live. Multi-item scales were carefully constructed to measure each of these variable domains.

The results of the Chicago evaluation indicate that although residents' awareness of the program and levels of participation increased significantly (indicating *some* success with program implementation), there was a consistent lack of support for the main hypotheses stated above. That is, the large majority of comparisons revealed no significant differential change over time between the treated and untreated areas. Furthermore, the majority of the significant findings ran *counter to* the main hypotheses. Specifically, the three neighborhoods with the strongest evidence of program implementation showed significant *increases* in a number of problem areas, including increases in fear of crime, perceptions of the crime problem, vicarious victimization, concern about the future of the neighborhood, and the likelihood of moving out. Additional analyses were conducted to rule out rival hypotheses. A series of block-level analyses (in one area with treated and untreated blocks) suggested that the unexpected declines on important outcome measures were most likely the result of neighborhood-level activities (e.g., neighborhoodwide meetings). Stated differently, the block meetings produced almost no effects across twenty-one separate outcome measures.

The basic question we are left with is—what went wrong? Is Chicago just another case of "implementation failure" or is there the more devastating possibility of "theory failure"? Given a very serious effort by experienced organizers to implement the Neighborhood Watch program in one neighborhood, there is some rationale for pointing the finger at the theoretical model guiding these actions. While the Chicago evaluation should not be viewed as the "final word" on the effectiveness of Neighborhood Watch, these data should encourage us to take a closer look at the theoretical underpinnings of this popular strategy.

What Is "Theory Failure"?

There is some confusion (or difference of opinion) about what constitutes a failure of *implementation* versus a failure of *theory*. Conceptually, there is little ambiguity. Implementation failure occurs when the program is not implemented as planned or is not implemented at all. Without setting in motion the "causal process" that is expected to produce the desired outcomes, the underlying theory cannot be tested (cf. Suchman, 1969; Weiss, 1972). Theory failure occurs when the program activates the supposed "causal process," but this process does not produce the desired effects. However, when conducting evaluations in this field, researchers point to different data elements as signals of theory failure. For example, some evaluators have suggested that the theory underlying Neighborhood Watch cannot be fully tested unless it can be shown that territorial surveillance has been enhanced (Yin, 1985). Others have emphasized that the theory is being tested immediately by whether or not citizens choose to attend block meetings when given the opportunity (Silloway and McPherson, 1985). Thus, one might ask— where does implementation failure stop and program failure begin? If researchers begin to think in terms of developing an implementation theory, as well as an impact theory, then a broader view of theory failure is possible, with the opportunity to disconfirm relationships (hypotheses) at many different points in the supposed causal process. Some of these possibilities are outlined below.

CHALLENGING THEORETICAL ASSUMPTIONS

The attraction of Neighborhood Watch rests on a number of key assumptions about neighborhood processes and social behavior. While several of these assumptions are theory-based, others are simply popular beliefs accepted by the general public as statements of fact. In any event, these assumptions (which are rarely challenged) need to be explicitly stated and critically examined. Only the more problematical assertions are discussed below.

- *Assumption 1*: Neighborhood Watch can be easily implemented on a large scale to provide citizens with an opportunity for participation in crime prevention activities

National surveys reveal that 82% of the American public would "like to have a crime-watch program in the neighborhood" and 81% report being interested in joining (Gallup, 1982), but only 5% actually belong to a "local crime watch group" (Gallup, 1981). Does this gap between intentions and actual behavior suggest that citizens are "all talk," or that they have tried a watch group and don't like it, or that they have never been invited to participate?

One could make the argument that this low level of citizen involvement is partially attributable to a lack of opportunity to participate. Given that local community organizations do not have the resources or the single-issue focus needed to make Neighborhood Watch their mainstay, police have emerged as the main "providers of opportunity" in recent years. However, anecdotal evidence and local surveys indicate that the level of investment in crime prevention activities among law enforcement agencies remains very minimal despite all the talk about this being their top priority. For example, in the state of Pennsylvania a rare survey of "municipal crime prevention practitioners" revealed that the average law enforcement agency devotes only 2% of its total person time to crime prevention activities (Pennsylvania Commission on Crime and Delinquency, 1984). The Commission report concludes that "although there is an abundance of crime prevention activities in many local municipalities, those with planned, targeted programs involving Neighborhood Watch on an organized basis are not common" (p. 11).

There is little reason to think that these findings do not apply to other cities and states across the country. Certainly a few cities such as Detroit and San Diego have taken Neighborhood Watch very seriously and have "organized" literally thousands of residential blocks (Feins, 1983), but these appear to be the exceptions. Regardless of this activity, the bigger problem is that law enforcement agencies seem to count their successes in terms of quantity, rather than quality. The words of the Pennsylvania Commission were carefully chosen—Watches that are "planned," "targeted," and "organized" are rare. Police will frequently set up, or be invited to attend a Block Watch meeting, but efforts to plan the contents or maintenance of these activities beyond the first meeting is quite unusual from my experience. These observations are consistent with the preliminary findings of the National Assessment of Neighborhood Watch that indicate that watch programs are not as "systematic" or "coordinated" as the popular definition suggests (Garofalo and McLeod, 1985).

If citizens have not been given a "real" opportunity to participate in a "systematic" watch program, then what would it take to provide this opportunity? How many door-to-door contacts and "flyers" are needed to stimulate participation? How many meetings are needed? How many people must attend, and must a block captain be elected? Although practitioners have often suggested that a block is not successfully

114   **CRIME & DELINQUENCY / JANUARY 1986**

"organized" unless you hold at least two meetings and involve 50% of the households per block (Silloway and McPherson, 1985), neither prior research nor theory provide any clues regarding the amount or "dosage" of community organizing that is needed to make the program appealing to local residents or produce the desired effects.

The lack of opportunity for most citizens can be remedied, but "good" community organizing requires a substantial commitment of time and energy. Nevertheless, we have seen that when adequate resources are conscientiously employed, both governmental agencies (Lindsay and McGillis, 1986; Silloway and McPherson, 1985) and community organizations (Lewis, Grant, and Rosenbaum, 1985) can provide citizens with a "reasonable" *opportunity* for involvement in Neighborhood Watch. However, this does not imply that participation will be forthcoming or that participation will produce the desired effects, as discussed below.

- *Assumption 2*: If given the opportunity to participate in Neighborhood Watch, most citizens would find the program appealing and would become involved regardless of social, demographic, or neighborhood characteristics.

There is a widespread belief that Neighborhood Watch can be successfully implemented anywhere and anytime if only the effort is made. This important belief is the cornerstone of the "shotgun" crime prevention policies adopted by many local governments, but it conflicts strongly with research findings regarding the natural distribution of citizen participation and informal social control.

As noted earlier, research suggests that collective participation is largely a middle-class phenomenon that emerges in more stable neighborhoods, and watch-type programs are no exception. A recent national survey of 530 Neighborhood Watch programs revealed that residents living in the areas served by these programs are predominately white, have middle or upper incomes, are single-family home owners, and have lived in their current location for at least five years (Garofalo and McLeod, 1985). In addition, there is a long line of scholarly work on urban neighborhoods that suggests that informal social control is less likely to develop in low income, and culturally heterogeneous neighborhoods (see Greenberg et al., 1985, for a review).

Thus the notion that programs like Neighborhood Watch will be adopted in *any* neighborhood is based on a number of assumptions that are inconsistent with prior research. Greenberg et al. (1985) have articulated some of the relevant assumptions:

> A basic assumption of crime prevention programs with a neighborhood orientation is that their success depends on collective citizen involvement. It is assumed that neighborhood residents already know one another or would like to get to know one another; are willing to cooperate with each other in such activities as watching each others' houses and intervening in crimes; and, most importantly, have shared norms for appropriate public behavior. Many of the activities of community crime prevention programs depend upon mutual trust and a willingness to take responsibility for each other's safety [p. 19].

The problem, as research suggests, is that neighborhoods that need the most help (i.e. have the most serious crime problems) will be the least receptive to such programs because these residential areas are characterized by suspicion, distrust, hostility, and a lack of shared norms regarding appropriate public behavior.

While these studies of urban neighborhoods and citizen participation suggest some limitations on program applicability, they do not directly test the Implant Hypothesis stated earlier because of the self-selection problem. That is, we do not know whether nonparticipating neighborhoods or blocks can be motivated to get involved in watch-type programs regardless of their characteristics. This brings us to the much smaller (but more relevant) body of research that entails quasi-experimental evaluations of Neighborhood Watch interventions. For example, the Chicago program mentioned earlier was carried out in four middle-class neighborhoods, and although participation in block and neighborhood crime prevention meetings increased significantly after one year (relative to control neighborhoods), the absolute increase was from 12% to 16% of the households, leaving 84% of the households as nonparticipants. However, in several neighborhoods, community groups invested a minimal effort toward organizing blocks, and thus the opportunity to participate was minimal.

The Minneapolis Test. Perhaps the strongest test of the hypothesis that citizens *will* participate in Block Watch *if* given the opportunity is currently underway in Minneapolis, where the municipal-based Minneapolis Community Crime Prevention Program is conducting a special project in cooperation with the Minneapolis Police Department and the

116   **CRIME & DELINQUENCY / JANUARY 1986**

Police Foundation. What is noteworthy about the Minneapolis project is the wide variety of neighborhoods that were exposed to this intervention, and the intensity of this systematic effort to organize Block Watch in each area. The preliminary results are now available and strongly disconfirm the Implant Hypothesis (DuBow, McPherson, and Silloway, 1985; Silloway and McPherson, 1985). The findings show that even after a substantial organizing effort (averaging 2 ᶾ hours per block), the level of citizen participation was quite low. While residents on 85% of the target blocks were invited to attend at least one block meeting, only one-fifth of the households responded affirmatively. On the average, fewer than nine people per block attended the meetings.

Perhaps the most important finding in Minneapolis is that different levels of success were experienced when seeking to organize different types of neighborhoods. Organizers tried significantly *harder* (i.e., arranged more meetings, made more contacts) in neighborhoods with lower socioeconomic status and less homogeneity, but experienced *less* success in terms of citizen attendance. Thus organizers did not give up on blocks that were initially difficult to organize, but the extra effort did not pay off.

These findings are consistent with the results of Henig's (1984) assessment of the Washington, D.C. Neighborhood Watch program. This post-hoc evaluation found that participation was more likely to occur and be sustained on blocks that were "undergoing gentrification" and included fewer kids, fewer elderly, fewer minorities, and more home owners.

In sum, there is now some evidence to suggest that Neighborhood Watch is not a suitable strategy for certain neighborhoods or blocks. If this strategy does not stimulate substantial levels of participation, even after serious attempts by trained community organizers, then the theoretical underpinnings of the approach need to be modified. Silloway and McPherson (1985), in discussing the Minneapolis findings, conclude that the assumption of "*voluntary* participation" underlying the Block Watch model is "highly problematical."

- *Assumption 3*: If and when citizens get together at Block Watch meetings, the assumption is made that this interaction and discussion will produce a number of immediate effects. These effects include reaching a consensus about problem definition, reducing fear of crime, increasing group cohesion, and increasing participation in both individual and collective crime prevention actions after the meeting.

The social interaction that takes place at Block Watch meetings is poorly documented, yet we entertain wonderful ideas about how these meetings are highly constructive—how they alleviate the fears of local residents and set in motion an organized plan of action for fighting neighborhood crime. Field work in this area suggests that citizens use these meetings informally to discuss the local crime problem, to learn about individual and home protection measures, and to set up a "phone tree" of block residents to share information about suspicious activities observed in the area (Lewis et al., 1985; McPherson and Silloway, 1980). With the exception of meetings that are well organized by crime prevention officers or community organizers, there is usually an open agenda for residents to exchange thoughts and concerns, and take the meeting in whatever direction is suitable to their immediate needs.

Problem Definition. The first problematical assumption is that local residents will agree as to the nature of the crime problem and then agree that Block Watch is the best way to respond. Only recently have researchers begun to recognize and discuss the extent to which residents in multicultural, multi-ethnic neighborhoods hold conflicting views about the causes, nature, and appropriate responses to the local crime problem (Bennett and Lavrakas, 1985; Podolefsky, 1984). For example, residents who define the problem in terms of local poverty, drug abuse, or unemployment would be less inclined to support a watch-type program than residents who feel that the problem is attributable to the presence of suspicious strangers in their neighborhood. The former would rather invest their time and energy in programs that address the "root causes" of crime, (what Podolefsky and DuBow, 1981, call the "social problems" approach), while the latter are more interested in preventing victimization (what Lewis and Salem, 1981, call the "victimization perspective"). Also, identifying "strangers" in heterogeneous neighborhoods can be extremely difficult. These processes help to explain why particular neighborhoods, such as the Mission District in San Francisco, have rejected the victimization prevention approach (Podolefsky, 1984).

Fear Reduction. One of the most critical (and troublesome) assumptions of the Neighborhood Watch model is that this strategy is a promising mechanism for reducing fear of crime in urban communities. The opportunity reduction model suggests that fear is the result of exposure to crime, and therefore fear can be directly reduced by lowering residents' actual risk of victimization. The social-control model suggests that fear is the result of a perceived decline in informal social control, and therefore fear can be indirectly reduced by somehow restoring a sense of social organization and cohesion in the community.

Neither of these models provides a clear basis for predicting that the meeting *itself* will directly reduce fear of crime. However, such an outcome has been assumed (cf. Feins, 1983; DuBow and Emmons, 1981; Rosenbaum et al., 1985). The idea behind this hypothesis is that social interaction at these meetings provides concerned citizens with social support and reassurance that something can be done, both collectively and individually, to affect the local crime problem. Indeed, a basic derivation of social comparison theory (Festinger, 1954) is that people affiliate with similar others to reduce anxiety (cf. Schachter, 1964). Moreover, in many cases, the meetings provide participants with a plan of action (i.e., watching out for suspicious activity and improving personal and household security) that seems efficacious, and thus might be expected to alleviate fear of crime.

This line of thinking sounds so plausible that researchers have been reluctant to posit the alternative hypothesis that such meetings are a mechanism for *heightening* fear of crime, as well as reducing feelings of efficacy and social cohesion. Nevertheless, there is research that could be interpreted as supportive of this alternative hypothesis.

As Table 1 indicates, our Chicago evaluation found that, contrary to expectation, fear of personal crime *increased* significantly in three of the four target neighborhoods (relative to control groups). My best interpretation of these effects is that they were due to neighborhoodwide meetings for which organizers sometimes exploited the "worsening crime problem" as a tactic to achieve a higher turnout. In other quasi-experimental work, the exemplary Seattle program, although showing a reduction in burglary, was also associated with a marginally significant increase in fear of crime (see Cirel et al., 1977, p. 68).

Research on the personal correlates of participation in community crime prevention is not inconsistent with this less favorable hypothesis. In their review of the literature, DuBow, McCabe, and Kaplan (1979) conclude that "participants of all types generally have higher fear levels" (p. 31), and that collective participation is associated with both fear and perceived risk of victimization. A look at more recent literature on crime prevention suggests that the results are mixed. Participation in collective crime prevention activities has been found to be associated with a higher perceived risk of victimization in one study (Yaden,

TABLE 1: Mean Changes in Fear of Personal Crime
as a Function of Community Organizing

Analytic Comparison	Adjusted Pretest Means[1]	Adjusted Pretest Means[1]	Change	F Value of Intervention Beta[2]
Target Neighborhood A	2.14	2.23	+.09	
vs. Control neighborhood A	1.85	1.89	+.04	6.48**
vs. Citywide sample	2.31	2.30	−.01	.08
Target Neighborhood B	2.43	2.52	+.09	
vs. Control neighborhood B	2.10	2.07	−.03	6.84**
vs. Citywide sample	2.33	2.32	−.01	3.59^M
Target Neighborhood C	2.41	2.81	+.40	
vs. Control neighborhood C	2.38	2.07	−.31	15.92***
vs. Citywide sample	2.33	2.32	−.01	12.79***
Target Neighborhood D	2.25	2.57	+.32	
vs. Control neighborhood D	2.05	2.59	+.54	.42
vs. Citywide sample	2.30	2.56	+.26	.08

1. A two-item scale was constructed to measure fear of personal crime. (Interitem correlations ranged from .50 to .74 across neighborhoods; scale range = 1-4, with higher scores indicating higher fear.) Mean scores are adjusted for all covariates in the regression equation, except the pretest.
2. Hierarchical regression analyses were performed to test the hypothesis of differential change between the target and control groups over time. Using panel data, the effect of the pretest and 7 key covariates were controlled before testing the contribution of the intervention variable (1 = target area; 0 = control area). The F value indicates the significance test on the standardized regression coefficient (Beta) associated with the intervention variable.
*$p < .05$; **$p < .01$; ***$p < .001$; m. $p < .10$.

Folkstand, and Glazer, 1973), but a lower fear of crime in another (Skogan and Maxfield, 1981). Several studies suggest that fear and participation are unrelated (Lavrakas et al., 1980; Podolefsky and DuBow, 1981; Rohe and Greenberg, 1982). Again, these correlational studies do not solve the direction-of-causality problem, but they at least suggest that participation is not a clear path to fear reduction as the anxiety-reduction hypothesis would suggest.

Why might we expect that fear of victimization would *increase* as a result of participation in watch-type meetings? A plausible explanation is that fear is exacerbated when attendees exchange information about local crime (Greenberg et al., 1985; Rosenbaum et al., 1985; Skogan and Maxfield, 1981). Our field work suggests that participants often use this opportunity to describe their direct and indirect victimization experiences and express their personal concern about the neighborhood crime problem (Lewis et al., 1985). In fact, Block Watch organizers in

120   **CRIME & DELINQUENCY / JANUARY 1986**

Seattle and Chicago are trained to encourage a discussion of victim-ization. The *Citizen's Guide to Organizing a Block Watch* (Seattle Police Department, n.d.) suggests that the organizer begin the meeting with a discussion of local crime statistics and then "ask if anyone present has been a victim of crime recently" (p.6). In Chicago, "people are encouraged to talk about recent victimization experiences" (Citizen Information Service of Illinois, 1982, p. 12). As the Seattle guide explicitly states, "the purpose of this information is to let people know there is crime in their neighborhood and anyone can be a victim" (p. 6).

With this type of discussion, more criminal activity is brought to the group's attention, as well as the fears of individual group members. Consistent with this explanation for possible increases in fear, Greenberg et al. (1982), in a study of six Atlanta neighborhoods, discovered that worry about crime increased as more information was exchanged with neighbors. Similarly, Pennell's (1978) analysis of data in three cities revealed that participation in neighborhood groups was associated with a greater knowledge of and concern about crime.

Informal discussions of victimization experiences can be as important as actual crime rates for shaping residents' fears and perceptions. The Reactions to Crime Project (Skogan et al., 1982) in three American cities found that "vicarious" or indirect victimization (i.e., knowing someone who has been a victim of crime recently) was an important predictor of higher fear levels.

In addition to one's knowledge of local crime and exposure to expressions of fear, another factor that may contribute to feelings of vulnerability are the discussions of home security measures that are a commonplace at watch-type meetings. Whether it happens via informal discussions or a formal security check, residents can be made to feel that their home is quite vulnerable to burglary or home invasion. Using a randomized experimental design in Evanston, Illinois, Rosenbaum (1983) found that burglary victims who were given a home security survey by an experienced crime prevention officer were significantly more fearful of revictimization, felt less control over their chances of revictimization, were more upset and angry about the incident, and reported less emotional and psychological recovery than victims who did not receive a home security survey. Hence, we cannot assume that well-intended efforts to share information about crime prevention will have unconditional positive effects. Although we have previously advocated programmatic attempts to increase public *concern* and knowledge about crime without simultaneously increasing public *fear*

(Lavrakas, Rosenbaum, and Kaminiski, 1983), this separation of effects may not be easy to accomplish.

Other Group Dynamics Effects. When individuals participate in a group process without strong leadership and without structure, the group dynamics can be such that significant changes in feelings and attitudes are possible, for better or worse. Along with fear reduction, watch-type meetings are expected to enhance residents' sense of efficacy and control over their local neighborhood, as reflected in the "empowerment" objectives of community organizers (cf. Emmons, 1979; Rosenbaum et al., 1985). Again, the opposite prediction seems equally plausible given the nature of these meetings. One could argue that these small group discussions serve as a "consciousness raising" experience whereby participants leave feeling *more* (rather than less) helpless in the face of uncontrollable political and social forces. For example, citizens may discover that residential transition is beyond control, or that the police have not been responsive to their pressures, or that criminal victimization is not always prevented by precautionary measures and may strike anyone at any time.

A long history of social psychological research on group dynamics gives us some insight into the functions and decision-making processes of small groups. Festinger's (1954) classic social comparison theory suggests that people participate in group activities not merely to accomplish group tasks, but to evaluate (and validate) their own feelings, opinions, and abilities against those of other group members. This process opens the door for interpersonal influence, and indeed, there is a significant body of research that indicates that small group discussions—when not constrained by structure or authority—will produce a more extreme group consensus than would be expected by averaging the initial positions of the individual group members (Kogan and Wallach, 1964). In fact, the direction of the extremization is predictable from the group's *initial* inclinations, leading researchers to label this process "collective polarization" (Doise, 1969; Moscovici and Doise, 1974; Moscovici and Zavalloni, 1969). Given that "residential transition" has been known to emerge as a topic of discussion at Neighborhood Watch meetings (Lewis et al., 1985) there is the possibility that social interaction at watch meetings will exacerbate racial prejudice. Indeed, Myers and Bishop (1970) have demonstrated that groups made up of racist individuals have become even more racist after having the opportunity for discussion.

Related to this work, the literature on small-group processes also reminds us that the internal benefits of efforts to strengthen group identification (e.g., enhanced cohesiveness) can have costs for the "out-group." Extensive social-psychological research has documented inter-group discrimination in favor of one's own group (see Brewer, 1979, for a review), Moreover, the consequences of group identification—for example, hostility, prejudice, and competitiveness toward the out group—will often occur with the mere presence of an identifiable out group and do not require a high degree of interaction, competition , or interdependence (Tajfel, 1969, 1970). In the case of watch groups, the presence of criminals, active youths, or minorities in the area can be viewed as a threat. For neighborhoods that are divided into racial, ethnic, or age groups, the crime issue may become an expression of conflict between these groups. For example, efforts to "watch" for "suspicious strangers" may become synonymous with watching for blacks or Hispanics. In this context, crime prevention programs may support one side or the other and thus intensify intergroup conflict (DuBow and Emmons, 1981; Kidder, 1978). As one would expect, to the extent that subgroups develop or preexist, the cohesiveness of the larger group will be undermined (Festinger, Schacter, and Back, 1950). Again, the widely held assumption that nothing harmful or unexpected could possibly result from community crime prevention meetings, regardless of meeting content or who participates, should not be given uncondi-tional acceptance.

Postmeeting Behavioral Effects. Finally, we must confront the important empirical question of whether watch-type programs actually produce the types of residential behavior that the social control and opportunity reduction models posit as the causal preconditions for reducing fear, incivility, and crime. Specifically, will citizens begin to interact more frequently, engage in territorial surveillance, and practice a variety of victimization prevention behaviors? Several studies have found that citizens who elect to participate in crime prevention programs are more likely than nonparticipants to engage in various crime prevention behaviors that, in turn, *may* reduce their chances of victimization (Lavrakas et al., 1980; Pennell, 1978; Schneider and Schneider, 1978). However, in the Chicago evaluation—which avoided much of the self-selection bias inherent in these participation studies—we found that neighborhoods (and blocks) exposed to the watch program generally did not differ from unexposed neighborhoods (and blocks) in terms of residents' levels of social interaction on the street, neighborhood surveillance (i.e., watching each other's home while away), home protection behaviors, self-protection behaviors, or intervention behaviors. Thus while target-area residents participated in crime prevention meetings at significantly higher levels than members of the control group, they did not allow these meetings to influence their behavior in any measurable way. Clearly, these data suggest theory failure, but more research is needed to substantiate further this conclusion.

- *Assumption 4*: Neighborhood Watch organizers (both police and community volunteers) invest in this strategy with the belief that such activities, once initiated, will be sustained.

Even if watch programs could be successfully implemented, they would still face a serious problem, namely how to maintain themselves. Researchers have documented the decline in participation and discontinuation of watches that frequently occurs with the passage of time (Garofalo and McLeod, 1985; Lindsay and McGillis, 1986; McPherson and Silloway, 1980). Block groups become inactive for a variety of reasons, and the importance of maintenance activities has been emphasized repeatedly by experts in the field. One of the main problems is the single-issue focus of many watches. Once the crime problem appears to have dissipated, the reason for the group's existence has also been removed.

This observation has led researchers to conclude that *multi-issue* community organizations are the best vehicle for sustaining citizen involvement in crime prevention activities (Lavrakas et al., 1980; Podolefsky and DuBow, 1981). However, there is also the problem of expecting too much of voluntary community groups. Programmatic efforts to provide external funding under the assumption that recipients will strictly adhere to a preplanned community crime prevention program have not been terribly successful (e.g., Lewis et al., 1985). Community groups simply have too many other agendas, as well as a shortage of resources and expertise. Thus regardless of anyone's laudable interest in strengthening community self-regulation, there should be little doubt that local government (and its many resources) play a critical role in starting and sustaining community-based programs, as well as maintaining public order. As Yin (1986) notes in his synthesis of eleven major community crime prevention evaluations, the programs that had the strongest positive effects on crime and fear were those where "citizens and police either collaborated directly or were both involved in the intervention." Heinzelman (1983) has emphasized the need for a "comprehensive" approach and has argued that "co-operative police involvement is essential (p. 2)."

> • *Assumption 5:* A final and very fundamental assumption underlying Neighborhood Watch is that the collective citizen actions implied by this strategy, if set in motion, would reduce the level of criminal activity and disorder in the neighborhood, thereby setting the stage for a reduction in fear of crime and other neighborhood improvements.

For the moment, let us put aside the alleged shortcomings of Neighborhood Watch that have been delineated up to this point, and assume that this strategy could be successfully implemented as specified by theory. The question then becomes—would Block Watch be an effective means of controlling crime and incivility? Even under these optimal conditions, there are still some reasons to question the efficaciousness of this approach.

One problem is that the Neighborhood Watch concept, as explained by the informal social control or opportunity reduction models, does not give sufficient attention to the factors that limit our ability as residents to regulate the behavior of either "good" or "bad" members of the community. First, the social-control model suggests that watch programs will restore a sense of community (through increased social interaction), and this will, in turn, pressure criminally inclined individuals and families to abide by the norms of the community. However, we should not forget that social control is a *group* process, and the many principles of group behavior that have been uncovered in 40 years of controlled research still apply. Theories of group process do not posit mechanisms by which a group can exercise control over "nonmembers." Social-control processes probably have little influence over strangers or criminals who feel no pressure to conform. In fact, the very same problem applies to "good" citizens as well, who are not members of the "group." If they do not view themselves as belonging to the Block Watch group, neighborhood organization, or even the larger "community," then group members have little leverage to regulate or change the social perceptions and behaviors of these outsiders. Proper police deployment may be the key to behavior control, but this factor is not considered in models of informal social influence.

A crucial question that emerges from this discussion is—who belongs to the target "group"? Who makes up the social unit of analysis that should be affected by the intervention? Is it everyone on the block, everyone living in certain apartment buildings, the entire neighborhood, or some other social unit? Perhaps the hypothesized effects of watch-type programs are limited to those individuals who actively participate in the group meetings, contrary to the widely held assumption that such programs can alter the pattern of informal social control at the neighborhood level. This is both a theoretical and an empirical issue that needs considerably more attention in future research.

Implicit in this discussion is another critical question, namely, what "dosage" of the "treatment" would be sufficient to modify the community's social-control mechanisms, and thus reduce crime and incivility? What scope, duration, and intensity of effort is needed to alter these social patterns? As noted earlier, the typical levels of participation in watch programs are hardly sufficient to produce occasional surveillance, let alone permanently change residents' day-to-day interactions. Social norms and control processes do not develop as a result of a few people attending one or two Block Watch meetings over the course of a year. Again, we are looking at the credibility of the Implant Hypothesis, and find it wanting. DuBow and Emmons (1981) summarize the point nicely: "The descriptions of informal social control that are found in the literature . . . illuminate processes that are the outgrowth of unplanned social forces at work over a long period of time" (p. 177).

Behavioral Mechanisms. Certainly we can envision potentially efficacious ways of enhancing informal social control, such as parental efforts to monitor and collectively regulate the behavior of children and young adolescents in the neighborhood. However, we must remind ourselves that Neighborhood Watch is not a complex strategy for shaping social behavior, but rather a simple program designed to encourage people to watch for suspicious behavior (especially residential burglary) and call the police if necessary. Adding to this the emphasis on household security measures, watch programs are best described as a strategy for preventing property victimization rather than enhancing informal social control.

Nevertheless, the main hypothesized consequences of Neighborhood Watch that are relevant to informal social control are (a) more social interaction, (b) more surveillance, and (c) more bystander intervention. The role of each of these citizen behaviors in controlling neighborhood crime remains very uncertain. If watch programs could stimulate more social interaction among neighbors, and if this effect could be documented, there is still a need to show that this change in behavior will, either directly or indirectly, reduce crime and/or acts of incivility. While the bystander intervention literature provides some empirical basis for thinking that people who interact or know one another are more likely to help one another in time of need (Bickman and Rosenbaum, 1977; Latane and Darley, 1970), the relationship to crime reduction or fear reduction has not been established (Greenberg et al., 1985).

Surveillance and bystander intervention are also problematical behaviors. The field studies involving staged crimes suggest that bystanders have difficulty (a) noticing the incident (b) interpreting the suspicious behavior as a crime and (c) actually intervening to provide help (Latane and Darley, 1970). Will collective watch programs contribute to or help alleviate such problems? Furthermore, what percentage of local crime can local residents witness? Clearly, most residents are not home during the day when most residential crime occurs, and if they did attempt to "watch" out their windows, many buildings are not designed to allow adequate surveillance of the area. After reviewing research on "the surveillance effect," Mayhew et al. (1979) conclude that "the chances of witnesses behaving in ways which will have consequences for [the offender] are often small" (p. 2). Even so, one might ask what "dosage" of surveillance is needed to deter or apprehend criminals, assuming that we could motivate citizens to be vigilant? This is another empirical question that cannot be answered at the present time.

The opportunity reduction model, besides placing a high premium on surveillance, also suggests that "target hardening" measures (i.e., efforts to make access to dwelling units more difficult), such as those commonly discussed at watch meetings, will reduce the opportunity of criminal activity in the neighborhood. The limitations of target hardening for controlling crime have been discussed elsewhere (e.g., Clark and Hope, 1984) and will not be reviewed here. However, I want to emphasize that this strategy is limited almost exclusively to property crime and does not address the violent street crime that is primarily responsible for residents' level of fear (cf. Baumer, 1978). Moreover, when a strategy is employed that seeks to protect individual households from victimization (and thus change the behavior of potential victims rather than offenders), there is always the possibility for displacement to occur, that is, a *change* in criminal activity (not the *prevention* of criminal activity) as a result of preventive efforts. As Gabor (1981) notes, "offenders may relocate the site of their activities; they may select different targets within the original site; they might alter the tactics used or the time of their violations; or they may even engage in different forms of criminality" (p. 391). Unfortunately, we know very little about the nature and extent of displacement effects, but this problem could be very critical to a strategy such as Neighborhood Watch that is forced to settle for low levels of participation scattered across individual households, blocks, and neighborhoods (cf. Reppetto, 1974). If one block, for example, is well organized and simply displaces criminal activity to the adjacent block, then the "collective benefit" for the community is questionable.

CONCLUSIONS

While Neighborhood Watch is an attractive concept, this article has raised a number of questions about the theoretical and empirical foundation of this approach to community crime prevention and fear reduction. Going beyond the correlational neighborhood research, we find a paucity of good quasi-experimental evaluations that directly test the central Implant Hypothesis, that is, that citizen participation, and eventually informal social control mechanisms, can be "implanted" in neighborhoods where they do not currently exist. Implementation difficulties are suggested by the fact that organizers—including law enforcement—have yet to give most citizens an opportunity to participate in an organized Neighborhood Watch. Theory failure is suggested by the current absence of support for some basic assumptions regarding this strategy of crime control. Specifically, there is some evidence to suggest that (a) if given the opportunity to participate, residents in the majority of high-crime neighborhoods would not participate, and (b) when citizens do participate, the social interaction that occurs at meetings may lead to increases (rather than decreases) in fear of crime, racial prejudice, and other crime-related perceptions or feelings. More important, there is little evidence that these block/neighborhood meetings *cause* local residents to engage in neighborhood surveillance, social interaction, and bystander intervention—behaviors that are posited as the central mechanisms for strengthening informal social controls and reducing the opportunities for crime. Finally, there is little evidence that Block Watches (as typically implemented) are self-sustaining.

A number of key issues regarding theory development are raised by this analysis. In particular, I have suggested that current theorizing in this area has been defective by either inadequately or falsely specifying (a) the dosage or amount of intervention that is also needed to produce the desired effects, (b) the content of the intervention that is needed, and (c) the conditions under which the hypothesized effects will occur. In a nutshell, this field needs more precise theories of both implementation and impact to estimate better the effects of such programs.

Clearly, more precise and controlled research is also needed to test the Implant Hypothesis under a variety of conditions, including differences in neighborhood and individual characteristics, as well as differences in the content of the intervention. Substantially more work is needed on the effects of crime prevention meetings on participants and on the perceptions and behavior of potential offenders. Theoretical statements must be more precise about the unit of analysis—what social unit is attempting the influence and what social unit is the target of influence? The size and composition of the social unit will greatly determine the limitations on predicted effects.

Meanwhile, in terms of current policy and practice, this analysis suggests that watch-type programs have been oversold, and the popular "shotgun" approaches to implementation should be replaced with more thoughtful and cautious planning. Specifically, there is a need to recognize that Neighborhood Watch cannot be easily implemented and sustained in all types of neighborhoods. One policy issue is whether to *try harder* to implement Neighborhood Watch in high-crime areas where obtaining citizen participation is the most difficult (cf. Greenberg et al., 1985) *or* take a more skeptical view that this type of program may be *inappropriate* for such neighborhoods (cf. Silloway and McPherson, 1985; Dubow et al., 1985). In any event, organizers should recognize that a single strategy such as "watching" is unlikely, by itself, to curtail a deeply rooted crime problem, and that multiple approaches will be necessary.

This analysis also suggests that planners should not assume that watch programs are "wired" to produce only prosocial effects and that untoward effects are impossible. Contrary to prior theoretical statements about fear reduction, there are both theoretical and empirical reasons to be concerned that residential meetings, left to themselves, may heighten residents' fears and prejudices, and may serve as a decisive force in multiethnic communities. Thus, if the strategy is pursued, the responsibility of organizers reaches beyond simply organizing an initial meeting, to encouraging discussion of the "right" subject matter in the "right" way.

However, the goal of fear reduction that has moved to the forefront of national policy on community crime prevention may need to be reexamined. Fear reduction may not be possible or even desirable given the objective of increasing citizen crime prevention behaviors. While large increases in fear of crime would be dysfunctional, models used to predict preventive health behaviors suggest that moderate increases in perceived vulnerability may be necessary to induce behavior change directed at minimizing the risk of victimization (cf. Rosenstock, 1966). Fear arousal is unlikely to be destructive if it can be channeled into action that is perceived to be efficacious.

Finally, program maintenance cannot be put aside as a "low priority." Law enforcement should not be applauded for starting programs, unless we genuinely believe that posting watch signs on the block is sufficient by itself to deter criminal behavior.

This article should not be taken as a condemnation of Neighborhood Watch, but rather as a call for social scientists, policymakers, and practitioners to think more critically about strategies that rely on citizen participation in meetings to increase informal social control and reduce criminal opportunities. By no means does this analysis suggest that we abandon the hard-fought goal of achieving higher levels of citizen participation in crime prevention, for this is clearly preferable to our current overreliance on law enforcement. Yet without a critical assessment of current theorizing and practice in this field, we cannot develop policies that are grounded solidly in principles of human behavior, and therefore, cannot implement programs that are likely to be effective.

REFERENCES

Baumer, T. L. 1978. "Research of Fear of Crime in the United States." *Victimology* 3:254-264.

Bennett, S. F. and P. J. Lavrakas. 1985. "How Neighborhoods Groups Decide What to do About Crime." Paper presented at the annual meeting of the American Society of Criminology, San Diego.

Bickman, L., P. J. Lavrakas, S. K. Green, N. North-Walker, J. Edwards, S. Vorkowski, S. S. DuBow, and J. Wuerth. 1976. "Citizen Crime Reporting Projects." National

Evaluation Program, Phase I Summary Report. Washington, DC: Department of Justice.

Bickman, L. and D. P. Rosenbaum. 1977. "Crime Reporting as a Function of Bystander Encouragement, Surveillance, and Credibility." *Journal of Personality and Social Psychology* 35:577-586.

Boggs, S. 1971. "Formal and Informal Crime Control: An Exploratory Study of Urban, Suburban and Rural Orientation." *Sociological Quarterly* 12:319-327.

Brewer, M. B. 1979. "In-Group Bias in the Minimal Intergroup Situation: A Cognitive-Motivational Analysis." *Psychological Bulletin* 86:307-324.

Campbell, D. T. and J. L. Stanley. 1966. *Experimental and Quasi-Experimental Designs for Research*. Chicago: Rand McNally.

Cirel, P., P. Evans, D. McGillis, and D. Whitcomb. 1977. *Community Crime Prevention Program in Seattle: An Exemplary Project*. Washington DC: Department of Justice, National Institute of Justice.

Citizen Information Service of Illinois. 1982. "Community-Directed Crime Prevention: An Alternative That Works." Final Report to the National Institute of Justice. Chicago: Citizen Information Service of Illinois.

Clark, R. and T. Hope, eds. 1984. *Coping with Burglary: Research Perspectives on Policy*. Boston: Kluwer-Nijhoff.

Conklin, J. E. 1975. *The Impact of Crime*. New York: Macmillan.

Cook, T. D. and D. T. Campbell. 1979. *Quasi-Experimentation: Design and Analysis Issues for Field Settings*. Chicago: Rand McNally.

Cunningham, W. C. and T. H. Taylor. 1985. "Private Security and Police in America." Report for the National Institute of Justice. McLean, VA: Hallcrest Systems.

DuBow, F. and D. Emmons. 1981. "The Community Hypothesis," in *Reactions to Crime*, edited by D. Lewis. Beverly Hills, CA: Sage.

DuBow, F., E. McCabe, and G. Kaplan. 1979. *Reactions to Crime: A Critical Review of the Literature*. Washington, DC: Department of Justice, National Institute of Justice.

DuBow, F., M. McPherson, and G. Silloway. 1985. "Organizing for the State: Neighborhood Watch as a Strategy of Community Crime Prevention." Paper presented at the annual meeting of the American Society of Criminology, San Diego.

Durkheim, E. 1933. *The Division of Labor in Society*, translated by G. Simpson. Glencoe, IL: Free Press.

Doise, W. 1969. "Intergroup Relations and Polarization of Individual and Collective Judgments." *Journal of Personality and Social Psychology* 12:136-143.

Emmons, D. 1979. *Neighborhood Activities and Community Organizations: A Critical Review of the Literature*. Evanston, IL: Northwestern University, Center for Urban Affairs and Policy Research.

Feins, J. D. 1983. *Partnerships For Neighborhood Crime Prevention*. Washington, DC: Department of Justice, National Institute of Justice.

Festinger, L. 1954. "Motivations leading to social behavior," Pp. 191-219 in *Nebraska Symposium on Motivation*, edited by M. R. Jones. Lincoln: University of Nebraska Press.

———S. Schacter, and K. Back. 1950. *Social Pressures in Informal Groups*. Stanford: Stanford University Press.

Fowler, F. J., Jr. and T. W. Mangione. 1982. *Neighborhood Crime, Fear and Social Control: A Second Look at the Hartford Program.* Washington, DC: Department of Justice, National Institute of Justice.

Gabor, T. 1981. "The Crime Displacement Hypothesis: An Empirical Examination. *Crime & Delinquency* (July):391-404.

Gallup, G. H. 1981. *The Gallup Report #187.* Princeton, NJ: Gallup Poll p. 12, 13.

———1982. *The Galup Report #200.* Princeton, NJ: Gallup Poll p. 22, 23.

Greenberg, S. W., W. M. Rohe, and J. R. Williams. 1982. *Safe and Secure Neighborhoods: Physical Characteristics and Informal Territorial Control in High and Low Crime Neighborhoods.* Washington, DC: Department of Justice, National Institute of Justice.

Greenberg, S. W., W. M. Rohe, and J. R. Williams. 1985. *Informal Citizen Action and Crime Prevention at the Neighborhood Level.* Washington, DC: Government Printing Office.

Hackler, J. C., K. Y. Ho, and C. Urquhart-Ross. 1974. "The willingness to Intervene: Differing Community Characteristics." *Social Problems* 21:328-344.

Heinzelman, F. 1983. "Crime Prevention from a Community Perspective." In *Community Crime Prevention.* Washington, DC: CRG Press.

Henig, J. R. 1984. *Citizens Against Crime: An Assessment of the Neighborhood Watch Program in Washington D. C.* Washington, DC: Center for Washington Area Studies, George Washington University.

Hunter, A. 1974. *Symbolic Communities.* Chicago: The University of Chicago Press.

Jacobs, J. 1961. *The Death and Life of Great American Cities.* New York: Vintage.

Jeffrey, C. R. 1971. *Crime Prevention Through Environmental Design.* Beverly Hills, CA: Sage.

Kasarda, J. D. and M. Janowitz. 1974. "Community Attachment in Mass Society." *American Sociological Review* 39:328-339.

Kidder, R. L. 1978. *Community Crime Prevention: The Two Faces of Delegalization.* Philadelphia: Temple University, Department of Sociology.

Kogan, N. and M. A. Wallach. 1964. *Risk Taking: A Study of Cognition and Personality.* New York: Holt, Rinehart.

Latane, B. and J. Darley. 1970. *The Unresponsive Bystander: Why Doesn't He Help?* New York: Appleton-Century-Crofts.

Lavrakas, P. J. 1985. "Citizen Self-Help and Neighborhood Crime Prevention Policy." In *American Violence and Public Policy,* edited by L. A. Curtis. New Haven: Yale University Press.

———and Herz, E. J. 1982. "Citizen participation and neighborhood crime prevention." *Criminology* 20:479-498.

Lavrakas, P. J., and Lewis, D. A. 1980. "The conceptualization and measurement of citizens' crime prevention behaviors." *Journal of Research in Crime and Delinquency* (July):254-272.

Lavrakas, P. J., J. Normoyle, W. G. Skogan, E. J. Hertz, C. Salem, and D. A. Lewis. 1980. Factors related to Citizen Involvement in Personal, Household, and Neighborhood Anti-Crime Measures. Final Report. National Institute of Justice. Evanston, IL: Northwestern University, Center for Urban Affairs and Policy Research.

Lavrakas, P. J., D. P. Rosenbaum, and F. Kaminski. 1983. "Transmitting information about crime and crime prevention: The Evanston Newsletter Quasi-Experiment." *Journal of Police Science and Administration* 2:463-473.

Lewis, D. A. and G. Salem. 1981. "Community Crime Prevention: An Analysis of a Developing Perspective." *Crime & Delinquency* (July) :405-421.

132   **CRIME & DELINQUENCY / JANUARY 1986**

Lewis, D. A., J. A. Grant, and D. P. Rosenbaum. 1985. "The Social Construction of
    Reform: Crime Prevention and Community Organizations." Final Report Vol. 2 to
    the Ford Foundation. Evanston, IL: Northwestern University, Center for Urban
    Affairs and Policy Research.

Lindsay, B. and D. McGillis. 1986. "Citywide Community Crime Prevention: An
    Assessment of the Seattle Program." *In Community Crime Prevention: Does it Work?*
    edited by D. P. Rosenbaum. Beverly Hills, CA: Sage.

Lurigio, A. J., and D. P. Rosenbaum. 1986. "Evaluation Research in Community Crime
    Prevention: A Critical Look at the Field." In *Community Crime Prevention: Does it
    Work?* edited by D. P. Rosenbaum. Beverly Hills, CA: Sage.

Mayhew, P., R.V.G. Clarke, J. N. Burrows, J. M. Hough, and S.W.E. Winchester. 1979
    "Crime in Public View." Home Office Research Study No. 49. London: Her Majesty's
    Stationery Office.

McPherson, M., and G. Silloway. 1980. *Program Models: Planning Community Crime
    Prevention Programs.* Minneapolis: Minnesota Crime Prevention Center.

Moscovici, S. and W. Doise. 1974. "Decision Makings in Groups." In *Social Psychology:
    Classic and Contemporary Integrations,* edited by C. Nemeth. Chicago: Rand
    McNally.

Moscovici, S., and M. Zavalloni. 1969. "The Group as a Polarizer of Attitudes." *Journal
    of Personality and Social Psychology* 12:125-135.

Myers, D. G. and G. D. Bishop. 1970. "Discussion Effects on Racial Attitudes." *Science*
    169:778-779.

National Advisory Commission on Criminal Justice Standards and Goals. 1973. *A
    National Strategy to Reduce Crime.* Washington, DC: Government Printing Office.

Newman, O. 1972. *Defensible Space: Crime Prevention Through Urban Design.* New
    York: Macmillan.

Pennell, F. E. 1978. "Collective vs. Private Strategies for Coping with Crime." *Journal of
    Voluntary Action Research* 7:59-74.

Pennsylvania Commission on Crime and Delinquency. 1984. "Crime Prevention Activities
    in Pennsylvania: A Survey of Municipal Crime Prevention Practitioners." Prepared
    by Bureau of Crime Prevention, Training, and Technical Assistance.

Podolefsky, A. 1984. "Rejecting Crime Prevention Programs: The Dynamics of Program
    Implementation in High Need Communities." Paper presented at the meeting of the
    Academy of Criminal Justice Sciences, Chicago, March.

Podolefsky, A. and F. DuBow. 1981. *Strategies for Community Crime Prevention:
    Collective Responses to Crime in Urban America.* Springfield, IL: Charles C Thomas.

Reppetto, T. A. 1974. *Residential Crime.* Cambridge, MA: Ballinger.

Roehl, J. A. and R. F. Cook. 1984. *Evaluation of the Urban Crime Prevention Program.*
    Washington, DC: Department of Justice, National Institute of Justice.

Rohe, W. and S. Greenberg. 1982. *Participation in Community Crime Prevention
    Programs.* Chapel Hill, NC: University of North Carolina, Department of City and
    Regional Planning.

Rosenbaum, D. P. 1983. "Scaring People into Crime Prevention: The Results of a
    Randomized Experiment." A paper presented at the 91st annual convention of the
    American Psychological Association, Anaheim, California, August.

Rosenbaum, D. P. ed. 1986. *Community Crime Prevention: Does it Work?* Beverly Hills,
    CA: Sage.

Rosenbaum, D. P., D. A. Lewis, and J. A. Grant. 1985. "The Impact of Community Crime

Prevention Programs in Chicago: Can Neighborhood Organizations Make a Difference?" Final Report Vol. 1 to the Ford Foundation. Evanston, IL: Northwestern University, Center for Urban Affairs and Policy Research.

————1986. "Neighborhood-Based Crime Prevention: Assessing the Efficacy of Community Organizing in Chicago." In *Community Crime Prevention: Does It Work?* edited by D. P. Rosenbaum. Beverly Hills, CA: Sage.

Rosenstock, I. 1966. "Why People use Health Services." *Milbank Memorial Ford Quarterly* 44:94-127.

Schneider, A. L. 1975. *Evaluation of the Portland Neighborhood-Based Anti-Burglary Program,* Eugene, OR: Institute of Policy Analysis.

————1986. "Neighborhood-Based Anti-Burglary Strategies: An Analysis of Public and Private Benefits from the Portland Program." In *Community Crime Prevention: Does it Work?* edited by D. P. Rosenbaum. Beverly Hills, CA: Sage.

Schneider, A. L. and P. R. Schneider. 1978. *Private and Public-Minded Citizen Responses to a Neighborhood-Based Crime Prevention Strategy.* Eugene, OR: Institute for Policy Analysis.

Schneider, S. 1964. "The Interaction of Cognitive and Physiological Determinants of Emotional State." Pp. 49-80 in *Advances in Experimental Social Psychology*, Vol. 7, edited by L. Berkowitz. New York: Academic Press.

Seattle Police Department. n.d. *Citizen's Guide to Organizing a Block Watch.* Seattle, WA: City of Seattle.

Silloway, G. and M. McPherson. 1985. "The limits to citizen participation in a government-sponsored community crime prevention program." Presented at annual meeting of the American Society of Criminology, San Diego.

Skogan, W. G. 1979. "Community Crime Prevention Programs—Measurement Issues in Evaluation." In *How Well Does it Work.* Washington, DC: Government Printing Office.

————and M. G. Maxfield. 1981. *Coping with Crime.* Beverly Hills, CA: Sage.

Skogan, W. G., D. A. Lewis, A. Podolefsky, F. DuBow, M. T. Gordon, A. Hunter, M. G. Maxfield, and G. Salem. 1982. *Reactions to Crime Project: Executive Summary.* Washington, DC: Department of Justice, National Institute of Justice.

Stein, A. 1976. "Conflict and Cohesion: A Review of the Literature." *Journal of Conflict Resolution* 20:143-172.

Suchman, E. A. 1969. "Evaluating Educational Programs: A Symposium." *Urban Review* 3, 4.

Sundeen, R. A. and J. T. Mathieu. 1976. "The Fear of Crime and its Consequences Among Elderly in Three Urban Areas." *Gerontologist* 16:211-219.

Tajfel, H. 1969. "Cognitive Aspects of Prejudice." *Journal of Social Issues* 25:79-97.

————1970. "Experiments in Intergroup Discrimination." *Scientific American* 223: 96-102.

Taub, R. P., D. G. Taylor, and J. D. Dunham. 1981. *Crime, Fear of Crime, and the Deterioration of Urban Neighborhoods.* Chicago: National Opinion Research Center.

————1982. "Safe and Secure Neighborhoods: Territoriality, Solidarity, and the Reduction of Crime." Final Report, National Institute of Justice. Chicago: National Opinion Research Center.

Taylor, R. B., S. Gottfredson, and S. Brower. 1981. "Informal Control in the Urban Residential Environment. Final Report." National Institute of Justice. Baltimore: Johns Hopkins University.

Titus, R. M. 1983. "Residential Burglary and the Community Response." Paper presented at the Home Office Workshop on Residential Burglary, Cambridge, England, July.

Wandersman, A., Jakubs, J. F. and G. A. Giamartino. 1981. "Participation in Block Organizations." *Journal of Community Action* 1:40-47.

Wandersman, A., J. F. Jakubs, and G. A. Giamartino. 1981. "Participation in Block Organizations." *Journal of Community Action* 1:40-47.

Wandersman, A., P. Florin, D. Chavis, R. Rich, and J. Prestby. 1985. "Getting Together and Getting Things Done." *Psychology Today* (November):65-71.

Weiss, C. 1972. *Evaluation Research.* Englewood Cliffs, NJ: Prentice-Hall.

Wilson, J. Q. and G. L. Kelling. 1982. "The Police and Neighborhood Safety: Broken Windows." *Atlantic Monthly* 127:29-38.

Yaden, D., S. Folkstand, and P. Glazer. 1973. *The Impact of Crime in Selected Neighborhoods: A Study of Public Attitudes in Four Portland Census Tracts.* Portland, OR: Campaign Information Counselors.

Yin, R. K. 1979. "What is Citizen Crime Prevention?" In *How Well Does It Work?* Washington, DC: Government Printing Office.

———1985. "Personal communication." September.

———1986. "Community Crime Prevention: A Synthesis of Eleven Evaluations." In *Community Crime Prevention: Does it Work?* edited by D. P. Rosenbaum. Beverly Hills, CA: Sage.

Name Index